P9-EML-824

AGRICULTURAL COLONIZATION IN INDIA SINCE INDEPENDENCE

The Institute gratefully acknowledges the comments and suggestions of the following who read the manuscript on behalf of the Research Committee: Professor C. A. Fisher, Professor Michael Lipton, and Professor Maurice Zinkin.

Agricultural Colonization in India Since Independence

B. H. FARMER

Published for
THE ROYAL INSTITUTE OF
INTERNATIONAL AFFAIRS
by
OXFORD UNIVERSITY PRESS
London New York Delhi
1974

Oxford University Press, Ely House, London W.1

GLASGOW NEW YORK TORONTO MELBOURNE WELLINGTON
CAPE TOWN IBADAN NAIROBI DAR ES SALAAM LUSAKA ADDIS ABABA
DELHI BOMBAY CALCUTTA MADRAS KARACHI LAHORE DACCA
KUALA LUMPUR SINGAPORE HONG KONG TOKYO

ISBN 0 19 218301 X

Printed in Great Britain
by Ebenezer Baylis & Son Limited
The Trinity Press, Worcester, and London

CONTENTS

page

Preface ix

1 INTRODUCTION 1

2 HISTORICAL BACKGROUND 5
The Pre-British Period 5
The British Period 10
The Concept of Culturable Waste 29

3 AREAS OF COLONIZATION: 1 36
The Dry Lands of Rajasthan and Western Haryana 36
The Tarai of Uttar Pradesh and Bihar 42
Greater Malnad: the Hill Areas of Malnad, Wynad, the Nilgiris, and the High Ranges of Kerala 45

4 AREAS OF COLONIZATION: 2 52
Dandakaranya 52
Assam 56
Smaller Pockets of Colonization 59
Other Land Potentially Available 64

5 NATURE AND SCALE OF COLONIZATION 67
Area Colonized and Number of Settlers: to 1963 67
Area Colonized and Number of Settlers: Later Figures 72
Comparisons with Neighbouring Countries 73
Other Forms of Assault on the Waste 75
Magnitude of the Assault on the Waste 79

6 THE BENEFICIARIES 87
Dominance of the Welfare Motive in Colonization Policy 94
Selection within the Social Welfare Categories 101
Role of the Centre, the States, and Other Bodies 107
Phases of Colonization: The Five Year Plans 111

7 NATURAL DIFFICULTIES CONFRONTING COLONIZATION 118
Aridity and Associated Hazards 119
Rainfall Variability 122
Hydrological Problems 126
Soil Problems 131
Wild Life 133

		page
8	SURVEYING NATURAL RESOURCES AND PLANNING THEIR USE	135
	Organizations Responsible for Mapping	135
	Data-providing Organizations	138
	Soil and Land Capability Surveys in Colonization Areas	144
	Surveys of Wastelands	146
	Broader Issues of Land-Use Policy	149
9	PROBLEMS OF LAND-USE TECHNOLOGY	153
	Clearing and Reclamation of Land	153
	Techniques and Problems of Irrigation and Drainage	157
	Agricultural Techniques: the Situation in 1963	164
	Agricultural Techniques: More Recent Developments	174
	Animal Husbandry and Pasture	178
	Soil Conservation	180
10	DOMESTIC ECONOMY OF THE COLONIST	182
	Income from Agricultural Land	182
	Income from Sources other than Agricultural Land	189
	Employment and Utilization of Agricultural Labour	192
	Non-Agricultural Colonists in the Economy of Agricultural Colonies	195
	Transport	197
	Marketing	200
	Credit and Indebtedness	204
	Assistance	206
11	INDUCED AGRICULTURAL CHANGE IN COLONIZATION SCHEMES	211
	Agricultural Extension	211
	Community Development and Colonization	214
	Special Provision for Agricultural Extension	216
	The Social Factor in Agricultural Change	221
	Conclusion	225
12	LAND TENURE IN COLONIZATION SCHEMES	227
	Classes of Land Tenure	227
	Size of Holdings and the 'Economic Unit'	236
	Charges to Colonists for Land and Water	242
	Tenure-by-Stages	245
	Procrastination, Confusion, and Frustration	246
	Colonists' Breaches of Conditions of Tenure Officially Imposed	247
	Co-operative Tenures in Colonization Schemes	252

page

13 SOME SOCIAL ISSUES 261
Social Cohesion and Community Action 261
Religion and Caste as Divisive Forces 264
Relations with Older Occupants 268
The Problems of Tribal Peoples 274

14 THE FUTURE OF AGRICULTURAL COLONIZATION 278
The Marginality of Land 278
Colonization, Food Supply, and Foreign Exchange 289
Colonization *versus* Intensification 291
Broader Considerations: Employment, Redistribution of Incomes, and Rehabilitation 295

Appendix
Colonies Visited by the Author 299

Glossary 303

Abbreviations for Standard References 307

Notes 311

Index of Authors and Authorities 355

Subject Index 361

TABLES

page

5.I Areas brought into Cultivation as a Result of Agricultural Colonization, 1947–63, with Later Figures for Main Areas 68

5.II Colonists Settled, 1947–63, according to Reason for Grant of Land 70

5.III Land Use, 1947–8 to 1968–9, according to Official Sources 81

5.IV Rough Estimates of Changes in Net Sown Area and 'Agriculturally Utilized Area', 1947–63 83

9.I Irrigation in Colonization Schemes, 1947–63, Visited by the Author 158–60

9.II Estimated Yields in Certain Colonization Schemes, 1963 168–9

10.I Estimated Income of Colonists from Agricultural Land in Certain Schemes, 1963 183

10.II Income from Agricultural Land of Sample Settlers, 1965–6 184

10.III Annual Income from Wages of Sample Settlers, 1965–6 191

14.I Estimates of Cost to Government in Certain Colonization Schemes 281

14.II Expenditure in Selected Colonies for Landless Labourers 283

MAPS

1 Location of Colonization Schemes 37

2 The Rajasthan Canal Project 39

3 The Naini Tal Tarai 43

4 Dandakaranya 53

Preface

THIS book could not have been written without many kinds of help from many individuals and institutions. First, I must thank the University of Cambridge and my college, St John's, for granting me periods of leave of absence in which to undertake fieldwork in India and also to complete the typescript free from teaching duties and administrative cares. In this, as in numerous other ways, my college has provided me with a perfect environment: I cannot sufficiently express my gratitude to it. And a far less venerable institution, the Centre of South Asian Studies in the University of Cambridge, has given me a great deal of valuable intellectual stimulus and practical help.

Some of those who have commented on drafts of part of this work are—or until recently were—associated with the Centre: notably Dr Clive J. Dewey, Professor Sir Joseph Hutchinson, Dr T. N. Pandey, and Professor E. T. Stokes. Others who have given me the benefit of their advice have been Professor G. Étienne, Professor A. T. A. Learmonth, Dr P. Legris, Professor Morris D. Morris, Shri Saran Singh, Professor C. T. Smith, the late Dr Doreen Warriner, and Dr A. Young; and the readers appointed by Chatham House. Dr R. S. McGregor helped by translating passages from Hindi. To all of these scholars I am most grateful. However, although I have given effect to their comments and criticisms whenever possible, I alone am responsible for the final text.

Financial assistance in connection with my fieldwork was given by the University of Cambridge; by the Leverhulme Trustees; and by the Royal Institute of International Affairs, which also made a grant towards the cost of typing the final manuscript and of preparing the maps. The Managers of the Smuts Memorial Fund in the University of Cambridge provided funds to enable me to employ a research assistant for a while on my return to Cambridge from my original fieldwork in 1963. I wish to thank all these bodies for their help.

The ladies who in fact acted as research assistants, and to whom I am very grateful for help (particularly with bibliographical problems and with the extraction of material in connection with the inquiries whose results are summarized in chapters 3 and 4) were successively Dr T. S. Adkins, Mrs M. C. Papps, Mrs R. B. L. Tristram, and Miss S. J. P. Esdaile (who also typed parts of the original draft of the book). Those who typed the rest of the draft, and completed the final typescript most expeditiously, were Miss M. Dearlove, Mrs S. J.

George, and Mrs D. P. Sherwood; they have all earned my thanks, as have Mr M. Ampleford and Mr C. Wright, who drew the maps. Mrs V. Samarasinghe and Mrs M. Lawes provided very useful help with the Index.

Neither the fieldwork in 1963, 1968, and 1971–2 on which this book is based, nor the many follow-up inquiries could have been completed without the help of a great many people in India or in the service of the government of India. In India, too, I received much hospitality and friendly companionship. It is impossible to mention by name all those who rendered invaluable assistance in these ways: and it is almost invidious to single out a few names to be recalled here. But I must express my thanks in print to the High Commissioner for India in London, and to his staff; to Shri L. J. Johnson, Shri K. N. Johry, Shri A. J. Kidwai, Shri I. P. Mathur, Shri K. P. S. Menon, Dr N. P. Patil, Shri C. C. Patro, Shri S. R. Phanse, Shri Saran Singh, and Shri B. B. Vohra; also to the Surveyor-General of India for permission to reproduce the maps.

To these gentlemen, and to others in India who may read this book, I would like to address a special paragraph. India has perhaps suffered too much unsolicited criticism from uninvited academics. I have no desire to add to the volume of such criticism. Yet if I had been merely descriptive, still more if I had praised where I did not believe praise was due, I should not have been true to my vocation. I have tried to understand what is happening in Indian colonization schemes, and, where I thought critical comment warranted, I have tried to make it, but helpfully and constructively, I hope, and not in any spirit of arrogance or dogmatism. All that I hope to achieve is further discussion amongst those responsible in India. In the same spirit, and because surprisingly little seems to be known in India of colonization elsewhere, I have tried to draw comparisons with agricultural colonies in other countries, particularly in Ceylon, where I have worked a great deal.

A word must be said on three matters to all readers of this book: first, Indian place-names. I have whenever possible, and when the context does not require otherwise, used the spelling to be found on contemporary maps of the Survey of India. Where there is a new form of a name more familiar in another form, I have given the latter in parentheses when the name first appears in the text: for example, River Krishna (Kistna). But, as is well known, the release of large-scale maps of the Survey has been severely restricted for security reasons. The names of some of the colonies studied were therefore never seen on maps (in some cases they were never seen in writing at all): if, therefore, any of them are misrepresented, the author apologizes. For reasons also connected with the same restrictions, the maps illustrating this book are neither as numerous nor as detailed as I would have wished.

Secondly, there is the problem of changing names for political units. The general rule in this book is to use the present name, except where the context requires otherwise, or in quotation. Thus 'India' means the present Republic, except, for example, in references to the India of British days. 'Pakistan' means the country as it has been since the secession of Bangladesh: that is, the former West Pakistan. 'Tamil Nadu' is used for the area now known by that name, but not for the former Madras Presidency, nor for the state that existed from independence to the partition that gave Andhra Pradesh its separate existence. 'Haryana' is similarly used for the area now so known. 'East Bengal' is, however, used for the area that is now Bangladesh for most references concerning the period before secession: to stick closely to the rule enunciated at the beginning of this paragraph would seem to imply, for example, that refugees had fled from Bangladesh, whereas in fact the establishment of that country has stanched the flow of refugees from the former East Pakistan. Ceylon, under its new constitution, adopted the ancient name of Sri Lanka on 22 May 1972. It has, however, been thought better to retain the anglicized name throughout the book, since by the time these words appear in print Sri Lanka is hardly likely to have become so familiar as Bangladesh.

Thirdly, given the adoption of metric units in India and the transition to their use in Britain, it has seemed sensible to use those units whenever possible—even though the original figures may have come to me in acres, or in one of the many kinds of *bighas*, or in Madras measures.

I wish to say how grateful I am to the authorities and staff at Chatham House for bearing patiently the long delay between the original fieldwork in 1963 and the completion of the typescript. I had optimistically hoped to complete the book by the end of 1965. But quite apart from the fact that Cambridge is a busy place and that books always take longer to write than authors expect, I took on first the directorship of the infant Centre of South Asian Studies and then, from June 1967 to June 1971, the presidency of my college. However, as I shall suggest in chapter 1, delay has had its advantages. Of the Chatham House staff, I am particularly grateful to Miss Rena Fenteman for editing the typescript so effectively.

Finally, I thank my wife and family for bearing with the absences from home necessitated by the research for this book.

B.H.F.

St John's College
Cambridge
7 June 1972

1

Introduction

IN THIS book the term 'agricultural colonization' means the establishment of people on wasteland by government organizations for agricultural purposes and in groups large enough to require completely new villages. This definition excludes such other means of opening up wasteland as the privately organized extension of cultivation, on whatever scale; and its government-organized extension by such means as State Farms or Plantations, or the expansion of existing villages. By 'colony' I mean the area subject to agricultural colonization as just defined, and by 'colonist' the settler in such a colony.

The process of colonization studied here is very similar in broad outline to that of British days in the well-known Punjab Canal Colonies, and to that still followed in Ceylon.[1]

Agricultural colonization is constitutionally a state subject in India, though inter-state migration is a Union subject.

In practice, it is not always easy to determine whether a particular project or scheme comes within the chosen definition. For example, in 1963 some 11,000 hectares under the irrigable command of the Chambal Left Bank channel in Rajasthan had been brought under the scope of the Rajasthan Colonization Act, a direct heir to the Colonization Acts of British days in the Punjab. At first sight this land was thus an agricultural colony. But it was excluded from consideration because the cultivators subject to the Act were either encroachers already on the land whose position had been regularized, or purchasers of allotments at government auctions whose operations, though for agricultural purposes and on land recently waste, did *not* involve new villages. Again, the government of Andhra Pradesh kindly arranged for the author to visit its 'colonization scheme' round Eluru Lake, in a hollow between the Krishna (Kistna) and Godavari deltas; but this, though of great interest for various reasons, did not involve either wasteland or new settlements, and was thus excluded. Other cases are more difficult, for there is no clear-cut line between colonization and the expansion of existing villages: rather is there a continuous spectrum, and some decisions on points of definition were therefore necessarily a little arbitrary.

If it is asked why the definition matters, the answer is that agricultural colonization involving both wasteland and new settlements presents a particular complex of inter-related problems—from the reclamation of land to the need for special measures of assistance to colonists settled away from their original villages—and thus, in the words of R. J. H. Chambers, forms 'a coherent and intelligible field of study'.[2] However, he also mentions the problem of where to place schemes of uncertain or marginal status;[3] and uses 'settlement' where this book uses 'colonization' ('settlement' would be ambiguous in an Indian context, where it means the settling of the land revenue due on each parcel of land).

There appears to be no other work which deals comprehensively with the agricultural colonization of wasteland in independent India. The Programme Evaluation Organisation of the Planning Commission undertook in 1968 a very useful study of a sample of colonization schemes in a number of states, but was exclusively concerned with those involving the resettlement of agricultural labourers.[4] In a more recent book V. V. Giri tried to revive interest in colonization as a means of dealing with India's chronic problems of unemployment and under-employment.[5] His approach is neo-Gandhian and visionary, and, unlike that of the Programme Evaluation Organisation, makes no attempt to be empirical.

The fieldwork for this book began in the period June to December 1963, when studies were made in New Delhi and in state capitals; but for a high proportion of the time it was carried out in the colonization schemes themselves. It had been the author's original intention to write his book on the basis of this fieldwork alone; but, as the Preface has explained, the work became subject to heavy delay. In December 1968, however, he was able to undertake further work in New Delhi, and also in Assam (which he could not visit in 1963). In December 1971 and January 1972 he conducted final discussions on policies in New Delhi, and revisited, for further and final fieldwork, the major areas of colonization: that is, those in the Tarai of Uttar Pradesh, in Rajasthan, and in Dandakaranya (defined at the beginning of chapter 4). He was also able to revisit a few smaller schemes at the same time.

In fact, the delay in writing this book had a fortunate aspect, for the work in Assam makes the geographical coverage more complete than it would otherwise have been. Of more importance, perhaps, is the fact that the fieldwork in 1971–2 has enabled me to say more about the very large, if not grandiose Rajasthan Canal Project, which was in its very early stages in 1963; and to indicate some of the crucial changes that have come about with the adaptation of colonists to their new environment in Dandakaranya and with the impact of the so-called 'green revolution' there, in Rajasthan and the Tarai, and elsewhere.

A study based on field inquiry by a single person for a total of no more than nine months in India has obvious limitations, for all the helpfulness of officials and colonists everywhere; and in spite of the useful material handed to one in almost every colony, and of the occasional references to colonization in the Press and in other printed sources. The questions that a study of this sort seeks to ask can be answered with reasonable accuracy only after careful inquiry and observation in the colonies themselves, and for this time was all too short. This study, it must be made clear right from the outset, does not pretend to be more than a reconnaissance. It is hoped that it will raise many questions for future and more detailed research.

Moreover, the author could visit only a sample, and a highly non-random sample at that, of small schemes; and a rather more random sample of the villages within large schemes. For India is a big country, and its big schemes are very big. The Rajasthan Canal Project alone would, in a few years' time, warrant a detailed study by an inter-disciplinary team able to spend at least a year in the field.

That the author is by training a geographer is probably evident throughout the study: for example, in his concern for land quality and quantity. Chapters 3 and 4, too, ask a question which may be of more interest to geographers (and perhaps to historians) than to economists and others; though that is not to say that they are irrelevant to such economic issues as that of the marginality of waste-land (taken up in the final chapter). It is hoped, indeed, that the book will interest a wide range of readers concerned with the study of India and its economic, social and political affairs, both historically and functionally. For the subject of agricultural colonization, relatively small in itself, yet cuts across a whole range of other themes of much greater moment: to take a few examples at random, the ideology and land policy of the Congress before and after independence; alternative strategies of agricultural development; and the relationship between rural poverty, government policy, and agrarian unrest.

But it is also hoped that this book will be of interest and of practical utility to those responsible for the planning and execution of projects for agricultural colonization and for similar purposes, in India and elsewhere. The book examines past and present policy with what it is hoped is a helpfully critical eye: not with any dogmatic intention, but in order to try to stimulate discussion, further examination, and reassessment.

This is not a work through which there runs a strong central argument; by the same token it is not polemic. Rather does it explore a number of themes, all relating to the basis, or origin, or functioning of schemes for agricultural colonization, and all bearing, in one way or another, on the questions about the possible future for colonization which are asked in the concluding chapter. It follows that the book could have been arranged in a number of ways. Had its author been a historian, or an economist, or a sociologist, or a practising administrator of development, he would presumably have ordered it differently; but might well have included fewer themes. The specialist in any field is asked to tolerate on the one hand what to him may seem irrelevant, and on the other an obviously inexpert handling of his own bailiwick.

In fact this present chapter is followed by a historical introduction, no mere concession to historians or to historicism, but, as one sees it, a necessary introduction to the study of the wastelands of India as the new rulers inherited them from the British in 1947; in particular, it introduces the important but misleading concept of 'culturable waste' as the Raj developed it. Chapters 3 and 4 go on from this starting-point to ask how it was that independent India, already so patently overcrowded, inherited areas of sufficient size and sparseness of population to be the scenes of agricultural colonization; they also act as a geographical introduction to the book as a whole by sketching the natural characteristics of each colonization area. Chapter 5 then introduces the reader to colonization itself by discussing its scale and scope in independent India and comparing it in these respects with other means of opening up wasteland for agriculture. Chapter 6 examines the categories of person who have supplied the colonists, and relates them to historical and ideological circumstance. In chapter 7 there is an analysis of the principal natural difficulties and hazards which have faced the colonists; following on from this theme, chapter 8 surveys the organizations which are available to forecast these difficulties and hazards and to indicate the natural resources of colonization areas, and examines the way in which these organizations have functioned in practice. Chapter 9 is concerned with the agricultural technology of the colonists, chapter 10 with the result in economic terms, and chapter 11 with the organizations whose function is to improve both technology and domestic economy in the colonies. Chapter 12 takes up important issues of land tenure and related matters as they affect colonization, and chapter 13 touches on a number of social problems evident in the colonies. The final chapter then tries, against the background of the book as a whole, to explore the criteria against which the future of agricultural colonization in India should be judged.

2

Historical Background

IT IS not the purpose of this chapter to trace in detail the long history of the occupation of wasteland in India for agricultural purposes. The sources do not exist, at least for the greater part of pre-British times; and the author lays no claim to competence as a historian. Rather is it the intention here to indicate briefly, and mainly from secondary sources, the themes in the occupance of wasteland in pre-British times which appear to be relevant to the study of agricultural colonization in contemporary India; and, from similar sources, to describe the principal characteristics of wasteland policy and of colonization in the British period, in which may be found the roots of some of the practices that have survived into independent India.

Perhaps the most important theme is that developed in the concluding section; namely, the concept of 'culturable waste' as it arose in British times, and, often misunderstood, affected thinking on the amount of waste allegedly available for cultivation by colonization or by other means. This theme, together with consideration of the criteria which determine what land is cultivable, is central to the purposes of this book; and will not have been exhausted by the time the final chapter is reached.

The Pre-British Period

Discussion of the historical background to agricultural colonization in India will, so far as the pre-British period is concerned, be confined to three themes:

(1) The survival of forest and other wasteland throughout the pre-British period and the associated pattern of discontinuous settlement;

(2) The alternate advance and retreat of the frontier between settlement and waste almost throughout Indian history (agricultural colonization playing some part in the advances);

(3) The practices and laws concerning the occupation for agricultural purposes of land previously waste.

There must, of course, have been a time when the whole of India was covered with forest or other uncultivated land. It is impossible to trace in any detail or with any degree of accuracy the stages by which the wastelands were cleared for cultivation; but it is evident from literary sources that a great deal of forest survived in all parts of India, including the plains, throughout ancient times,[1] and, for that matter, into the period (A.D. 399–414) when the Chinese traveller Fa-hsien recorded great empty tracts, 'desolate and barren', in Kapilavastu, the kingdom in which the Buddha had been born.[2] W. H. Moreland has shown that, in the comparatively recent period of Akbar (1556–1605), there was much more forest than survived at the time when he was writing (1920):[3] for instance, the Tarai forests of what are now Uttar Pradesh and Bihar came as far south as a line joining Bareilly, Gorakhpur and Muzaffarpur, while there was also forest in the Allahabad–Jaunpur area. Though the upper Gangetic Plain seems to have been heavily cultivated, it still contained jungles and hunting-grounds, and the proportion of the land under cultivation fell away very rapidly to the east into Bihar (where only one-fifth of the area tilled in 1920 was under the plough). To the west, Rajasthan was very sparsely peopled, it and other arid and semi-arid regions suffering from the lack of a consistent irrigation policy.[4]

Indeed, throughout the pre-British period, and also in early British times, one of the principal traits in the human geography of India was one that is today characteristic not of South Asia but of the peninsulas and islands of Southeast Asia—the contrast between nuclei of population, almost of all of them major agricultural areas on alluvial plains, and empty areas of forest or desert or hill.[5] And, as Ashin Das Gupta has pointed out, ancient trade was carried on 'between isolated pockets of population, hemmed in by tropical forests and the desert',[6] though in medieval times the coastline at any rate seems to have become more evenly populated so that 'relatively larger areas were drawn into trade'.

Some of the negative areas survived to be colonized or otherwise peopled in British times; some even survived to become the scene of colonization in independent India (see chapters 3 and 4 below). But the existence of areas available for these phases of colonization cannot be understood without reference to another phenomenon of the pre-British period—the tendency for settlement now to ebb, now to flow, even in the nuclear regions of the plains.[7] As Irfan Habib has said:

> The cultivated expanse of the Great Plains, the valleys and hill-slopes of India has been created in the course of a stubborn struggle against Nature, which the Indian peasant has carried on for thousands of years. Forest and waste have retreated, recovered and again retreated, in endless cycles, before his hoe and plough. Every period in Indian history has had, therefore, its 'forest line' and desert frontier, besides its political and military boundaries.[8]

Let us examine the re-advance of the waste over previously cleared and cultivated land. A Chinese traveller Hsuan-tsang who visited India two centuries later than Fa-hsien, recorded desolation in parts of the plains that were under close settlement in his predecessor's time;[9] Kalinga, on the east coast, was also thinly inhabited though formerly populous.[10] In the anarchy of A.D. 650–950, Magadha (in the plains around modern Patna) had declined and 'the jungle extended from the Himalayas to the neighbourhood of Thanesar'.[11] Later, Muhammad Tughlak (1325–51) was able to give instructions for the extension of cultivation in the 'River Country' because waste-land had been left by depopulation and dispersal of the peasantry after 'administrative blunders'.[12] Under Aurangzeb, in the second half of the seventeenth century, land was going out of cultivation because of excessive pressure exerted by the revenue administration;[13] while, a few decades before the inception of British rule in what is now Uttar Pradesh, fiscal abuses grew and land was abandoned.[14] These happenings were, moreover, not confined to the north and to Kalinga. In the eighteenth century the population of Kanara declined and towns were abandoned as a result of corruption, excessive revenue assessments, forcible movement of people, and general disorder under Haidar and Tipu, some of whose activities, indeed, are in part responsible for the existence of wastelands still available for colonization.[15] At about the same time land in the Punjab had relapsed into waste and was available for Sikh colonization.[16]

One must not give the impression that the retreat of cultivation was invariably the result of human folly, through war or through administrative action. Pestilence and famine also played their part, as in more recent times in Malwa and elsewhere. W. H. Moreland, in a classic account,[17] shows how parts of Rajasthan were 'wholly depopulated' by famine in 1647; in 1659–60 many districts lay entirely waste because of a failure of the rains (combined, it is true, with the effects of war and of the movements of armies); in 1630–1 the country round Masulipatam, in the Krishna (Kistna) delta, was 'almost ruinated'; while one of the worst recorded famines was in 1630–2 when 'Gujarat, "garden of the world", was turned into a wilderness'. Deserted villages have in fact at almost all periods been commonplace in many parts of the Indian countryside.[18]

No doubt the reoccupation of abandoned or devastated land was often a gradual, piecemeal, and spontaneous process, taking here a long time, there a short time, according to the nature and extent of the initial devastation; but there were cases of organized colonization that are of interest. Sometimes these took the form of enforced migrations, as when Ashoka deported 150,000 people from Kalinga to clear forests and to cultivate virgin lands.[19] Historians have concluded that the Mauryans, more generally, founded new settlements by drafting surplus Sudras from overcrowded areas, providing cattle, seed and other forms of assistance, and allowing remission of land revenue, as in much more recent colonization schemes;[20] and that they also organized large tracts for cultivation as 'State Farms' (though this may be to read recent agrarian phenomena into ancient history). Again, there is the case of the fourteenth-century colonization ordered by Muhammad Tughlak, to which reference has just been made, which turned out to be a fiasco for reasons all too familiar in modern times—much of the wasteland was unfit for cultivation, and the funds invested produced 'no visible effect'.[21] The encouragement of colonization, or at any rate of the occupance of the waste, was by no means confined to the north: Harihara, who ruled in the southern medieval empire of Vijayanagar, not only allowed easy terms to cultivators who cleared wasteland but also offered positive rewards.[22] A moderate revenue assessment was particularly useful in encouraging the clearing and preparation of rocky and uneven land in such regions as Kanara.[23]

Many of the Mughals, too, encouraged active occupation of wasteland; and charged half or less than half of the standard revenue during the first year of its cultivation.[24] Akbar was particularly concerned with the extension of cultivation;[25] and it has been suggested that his *karoris* were a prototype of the colonization officers of British times.[26] More recent work indicates that, although they were 'reputed to be charged especially with the task of extending cultivation', they had much wider administrative functions.[27] In any case, they do not appear to have been particularly successful as colonizers.

Later, in the Sikh period in the Punjab, Diwan Sawan Mal, governor of Multan, was active in colonizing reclaimed lands.[28]

There is a general tendency today to recognize that Indian systems of land tenure in pre-British days were more complex, and more subject to variation in both time and space, than they were thought to be by such early British writers as Sir Henry Maine;[29] and it seems likely that some 'peculiar tenures' noted by British administrators were specially designed for, or at any rate operative in, the pioneer fringe, notably in East Bengal and Wynad.[30]

This leads the discussion on to our third topic: namely, the practices and laws governing the tenure of waste for agricultural purposes in pre-British India. Here there is a great deal of obscurity, particularly over the question of the 'ownership' or 'proprietorship' of wasteland. B. H. Baden-Powell, the great authority on agrarian affairs who wrote towards the end of the nineteenth century, believed that, as time went on, rulers in India laid increasing claim to waste and to the 'ownership' of all land,[31] though in communally held villages waste as well as cultivated land was, he says, claimed by the community.[32] Most European travellers in Mughal India thought the ruler to be the proprietor of all land.[33] Certainly much of the difficulty here arises from efforts to extend British concepts of 'ownership' and 'proprietorship' to Indian conditions, partly through genuine misunderstanding, partly also through an effort, conscious or unconscious, to justify the claim to state ownership of waste made by the British rulers of India. Moreover, the situation, like systems of land tenure more generally, varied both in space and time: U. N. Ghoshal has, for instance, adduced evidence to show that in Bengal waste was held by the state in ancient times 'in absolute ownership', and that it sold plots in perpetuity.[34] (There has, of course, been a similar argument over the 'ownership' of waste in ancient and medieval Ceylon.)[35]

Whatever the truth on these questions, there seems no doubt that, in addition to granting the revenue of a village, many rulers in pre-British India also granted the right of using waste for cultivation, such a grant being readily given because of a desire to enhance land revenue.[36] Village headmen, moreover, could in many cases authorize the breaking of fresh waste. Examples have already been given of active colonization undertaken in pursuit of these policies, and of the encouragement of colonization by concessionary rates of land revenue. According to the *Arthasastra* the king had the right to evict from newly colonized lands those who neglected to cultivate them.[37]

For, if a tender concern for the revenue was a dominant motive with rulers and their agents and *zamindars*, a robust right to grow crops on the land that he had cleared has been strongly asserted by the cultivator throughout Indian history. The Laws of Manu have it, in fact, that 'land belongs to him who cut away the wood or who cleared and tilled it'.[38] Muslim law, too, endorsed the words of the Prophet: 'Whoever gives life to dead land, it is his';[39] though there seems to have been some difference of opinion as to whether such *mise en valeur* required the sanction of the state.

Certainly the modern state, as will be seen, tends to require official sanction if waste is to be used: this is true both of the British period and later. Action on the time-honoured principle endorsed both by Hindu and Muslim law is then seen as illegal encroachment, a fruitful source of friction and trouble, and that not only in India.

The British Period

General Characteristics of Assault on the Waste

As British rule was extended over India, great tracts of wasteland were encountered in many regions. In Bengal, for instance, it appears that between one-third and one-half of the total area was uncultivated at the inception of British rule.[40] Early in the nineteenth century much formerly irrigated land lay waste near Bangalore, because of the recent wars between Tipu Sultan and the British; it was estimated that some two-fifths of the cultivators had been driven from their homes.[41] Again, Khandesh in the 1820s contained the dilapidated remains of more than a hundred dams formerly used for irrigation: the country lay desolate and impoverished by wars and incursions of Bhils.[42] Assam was very sparsely peopled when British rule began there in 1826, and had been devastated by war for many years: there were many deserted villages.[43] A large part of Gorakhpur District (UP) was forested at the British conquest.[44] These examples could be multiplied many times over to show that, when British rule came to many localities, rural settlement had been recently in retreat, so that many formerly well-peopled regions carried but a sparse population. In addition, of course, there were the great tracts of desert and of central Indian forest that had never contained more than a few nomadic herdsmen or tribal cultivators.

The British period in India was, taken overall, one of unprecedented growth in population and in the cultivated area. But it would be wrong to draw the inference that the disappearance of the waste in favour of cultivation went on smoothly and continuously throughout the period. There were times, especially in the earlier years of the Raj, when there set in that ancient Indian phenomenon, a retreat of cultivation and a concomitant advance of the waste. As a consequence of famine during a number of years between 1770 and 1789, for instance, much land in Bengal became what Lord Cornwallis called 'a jungle inhabited only by wild beasts'.[45] In Birbhum District, west of the Hooghly, about a quarter of the villages disappeared and formerly well-tilled land became 'a sequestered and impassable jungle'.[46] Again, early British revenue settlements in Gurgaon District are said to have led to the abandonment of land along the Yamuna (Jumna) south of Delhi and its reversion to malarial marshland;[47] while certain nineteenth-century settlements in Bombay also led to land going out of cultivation.[48] S. S. Padhye has shown that the desertion of villages in Vidarbha (Maharashtra) continued into the nineteenth century for reasons that extend from attack by robbers to floods and famines.[49] Further, chapters 3 and 4 will show that the possibility of at least interstitial colonization in some regions of independent India arises to some extent because of the recession of cultivation during British times (for example, in the Malwa plateau).

Nor were population growth and an increase in the cultivated area causally connected in a direct way. Differing revenue systems ensured that the effect varied from area to area.[50] Thus in part of the United Provinces (now Uttar Pradesh)—in which wasteland was included in 'estates' on which revenue was paid, and not retained by the government—heavy revenue demands were met by extending cultivation into the waste. Dharma Kumar has concluded, on the other hand, that in Madras population increased greatly during the first half of the nineteenth century, but that 'as a whole there was no significant extension of cultivation':[51] for in *ryotwari* areas waste was not included in holdings, so that the solution adopted in the United Provinces was not open to *ryots*, who also lacked capital for reasons that included high revenue demands.

But, with the notable exception of certain of the areas of post-independence colonization to be examined in the next two chapters, there came, at a different date in different regions, a critical point in time beyond which rural settlement advanced strongly into the waste, no longer to relapse into major phases of retreat. In an age of predominantly static agricultural technology, the upward movement in the cultivated acreage contributed most of the increase in the all-India output, as George Blyn has shown for the period 1891–1947 in a recent notable and careful study which survived the manifold frustrations of working with Indian agricultural statistics.[52] In the more densely peopled regions, especially the age-old nuclear areas of the Plains, deserted lands were rapidly reoccupied and much of the available waste taken into cultivation; concomitantly, there came a time when landlords were no longer forced, as they had earlier been, to hunt for tenants for their unused acres—rather did tenants compete for the landlords' fields. This critical threshold was crossed in the 1870s in the area that was to become the United Provinces, and, apparently, rather earlier in Bengal.[53] In the former case by 1901 'the wasteland available was hardly enough for *abadi* and pasturage, and extension of cultivation into wasteland was regarded as undesirable'.[54] During the last half century or so of British rule there was, in fact, but little increase in the provincial cultivated area, which 'fluctuated around 35 million acres [14 million hectares], within a margin of plus or minus five per cent'.[55]

These processes were not confined, however, to the plains. Large areas of waste were taken up in the Bombay Deccan between 1840 and 1870; and, by 1870, 'very little good waste was left'.[56]

In almost all the provinces of British India the assault on the waste was mainly a matter of innumerable small, piecemeal advances: here a cultivator or a landlord took into cultivation a piece of wasteland already within his boundary, there an individual or a village community was assigned 'government waste' under the Waste Lands Rules. In some of the Native States the nature of princely rule was one of several disincentives to colonization and rural settlement, as on the Malwa Plateau. But in others the advance of cultivation into the waste went on, as in the reclamation of the *kayal* (lagoon-bed) lands of Kuttanad, in Travancore (now part of Kerala).[57]

Plantations

In a few areas there was also, of course, the opening-up of land for European-owned plantations. Mid-nineteenth century hopes for large-scale 'colonization' by Englishmen and other Europeans over wide tracts of India were, not surprisingly, disappointed.[58] The contemporary writer W. Nassau Lees, in a chapter headed 'Of the Millions of Acres of Culturable Land that now lie Waste in India', was at pains to dispel the myth that there were vast tracts available for such colonization—a myth that, in its more general form, will be discussed in the final section of the present chapter.[59] Lees laid more stress on the alleged disastrous effects of climate on Europeans than would now be generally thought appropriate. But the main grounds of his refutation were not so much the poor quality of the 'culturable waste' in general (though he recognized its poverty in Bombay) but the fact that the government of India felt bound to recognize the claims to waste on the part of Indian individuals and communities: he evidently supported the government's attitude in this matter, and sought to defend it against the charge that it threw obstacles in the way of European settlement. He pointed out, too, that very few European grantees were successful, and singled out for mention the failure of a Mr Cooke who had been ruined by trying to reclaim land in Gorakhpur District in the northeast of what is now Uttar Pradesh. Between 1830 and 1872, 153,922 hectares of land in that District (some in the swampy Tarai) were issued to Europeans, originally on fee simple grants but later on leases; by 1872 only 78,677 hectares were cultivated, it having become more profitable to work the timber than to reclaim the land.[60] (The so-called 'indigo planters' of the Gangetic Plains relied on peasant producers rather than on their own plantations.)[61]

It may be of some interest that Lees recorded, on the basis of official figures, that little or no land was available for colonization in the Bombay or Madras Presidencies because of the recognition of claims to the waste, while elsewhere the following areas were said to be at the disposal of the government:[62]

Punjab	Over 7½ million acres (3 million hectares)
Gorakhpur Dt	189,108 acres (76,923 hectares)
Benares Dt	'Some 600 sq. miles [1,600 sq. kilometres] of rolling hills'
Sind	2,028 sq. miles (5,408 sq. kilometres)
Jabalpur Dt	25,180 sq. miles (67,140 sq. kilometres)
Khasi & Jaintia Hills (Assam)	453,000 acres (183,000 hectares)
Assam (4 out of 7 Dts)	4,469,533 acres (1,808,757 hectares)
Dehra Dun (Himalaya)	141,652 acres (57,325 hectares)
Darjeeling (Himalaya)	250,000 acres (100,000 hectares)
Kumaon, Garhwal, etc.	No returns
Sundarbans	809,648 acres (327,653 hectares)
Cachar	200,000 acres (80,000 hectares) (plus 'thousands of square miles of forest')
Chittagong	'Space enough to accommodate any number of European settlers'.

In the event, however, that special form of colonization, European settlement, had little impact on wasteland except in a very few regions indeed. There were, to a very limited extent, land grants to Europeans in the Sundarbans, the belt of forested swamp at the seaward edge of the Ganga (Ganges)-Brahmaputra delta.[63] A few Europeans later settled down to grow apples in the Kulu Valley, in the Himalayas; a very few took land under the Punjab canals. But their only really significant impact on the waste was in the tea-growing areas of Assam and adjacent areas, and in the tea- and coffee-growing areas of south India.

Assam had many of the characteristics of an under-populated Southeast Asian country rather than of a part of the densely peopled Indian Plain. Certainly when taken by the British from the Burmese in 1826, it was largely in forest, and Lees writes of it just before his time (the early 1860s) as being covered by 'impenetrable jungle and rank vegetation', subject to 'deadly and noxious miasma and malaria generated thereby', and 'always looked on as a penal settlement of Bengal'.[64]

From the 1850s onwards, and especially after recovery from a period of over-extension and collapse in the 1860s, there was a great expansion of tea plantations under European (and later Indian) ownership, mainly on the higher terraces and detrital cones at the meeting-place of plains and hills, or on the lowest slopes of the hills themselves:[65] this applied not only to the northern flank of the Assam Valley towards the Himalayas and the southern flank towards the Naga Hills, but also to the meeting-place of the Shillong Plateau and the Surma Valley (partly in East Bengal, and therefore now in Bangladesh). By 1902, 468,730 hectares in Assam (nearly a quarter of the settled area—that is, the area on which land revenue was levied) were held by planters, though only about a third of this area was actually planted in tea.[66] Tea plantations had by this time also spread over former jungles and forests, with a singularly unwholesome reputation for malaria and blackwater fever, in the Duars of Bihar, Bengal and northwest Assam (Indian companies were prominent in this movement);[67] in the Himalayan foothills of Darjeeling and the Tarai jungles to the south of them;[68] and to a less extent in Tripura and the Chittagong hills.[69] It is perhaps not so well known that, after initial government stimulus and experiment, tea was planted in the Himalayas to the west of Nepal, in Kumaon and Garhwal and also around Simla and Dehra Dun.[70] By 1863 there were 37 European and 78 Indian tea-gardens in these areas, relying mainly on the Central Asian market since distance from the sea made competition with Assam for the British market almost out of the question: when changing conditions removed the Asian outlet the gardens themselves declined.

Since Assam and the adjacent areas were sparsely populated when tea-planting began, it was necessary to bring in a labour force, which came especially from Bihar (largely from among the tribal population of Chota Nagpur), from the Central Provinces, and from Madras; and many labourers who had come to the end of their spell on the estates stayed to cultivate their own holdings in the Assam Valley.[71] In the twentieth century a 'vast horde' of land-hungry peasants from Bengal has swarmed into the Valley and occupied previously unsettled waste.[72] Indeed, it is broadly true to say that immigration and colonization in the nineteenth century were associated with tea, but in the twentieth century with the occupation of wasteland for peasant agriculture.[73]

The other great area of nineteenth-century colonization by means of the establishment of plantations was in the hills of south India, especially in Coorg, Wynad, the Nilgiri Hills, and the High Ranges of Kerala—all parts of the region to be described as 'Greater Malnad' in chapter 3 below. Here coffee was originally the dominant crop: the first large-scale plantations were made about 1830 in the Bababudangiri hills, just north of Coorg, and in Wynad to the south of that state;[74] planting in the Nilgiris apparently started in 1838.[75] It was, however, in the 1850s and especially in the 1860s that coffee plantations spread most rapidly through the formerly jungle-covered hills. Almost all of the pioneer Wynad and Nilgiri planters were British individuals; as in Ceylon, it was in a later phase that company-owned estates became the rule. Cinchona was a popular crop in Nilgiri plantations in the 1860s, as is shown in an interesting map drawn at the time by Clements Robert Markham.[76] The large-scale planting of tea followed the decline of coffee and cinchona in the

Nilgiris and in Wynad in the 1890s, but involved some land previously in forest.[77] Tea and, later, rubber plantations were also established in the jungle-covered High Ranges of what is now Kerala (then Travancore); while in the Anaimalai, where coffee-planting had started in 1863, the Madras government made Reserved Forest available for tea-planting in 1896.[78] All these plantations (except those of Coorg, where Indian entrepreneurs were prominent from the outset) were, as in Assam, mainly dependent on British capital and management, and immigrant Indian labour—here mainly Tamil and Malayalam, though in early days local tribal peoples were also employed (and some were dispossessed of their land by the plantations).[79] As in Assam, there was a massive immigration from the plains (so that the Nilgiris District grew in population from an estimated 4,353 in 1821 to 311,729 in 1951) and, again as in Assam, colonization-by-plantations meant an influx not only of estate labourers but also of cultivators who cleared the waste and set up villages and agricultural holdings of their own.[80]

In the earliest days of tea-planting in Assam, in the 1830s, the government (that is, the East India Company) actually conducted experiments and made plantations.[81] But after the rule of the Company came to an end in 1858, the government and its agencies played a permissive rather than an active part in the establishment of the plantations that did so much, both in northeast India and in the hills of the south, to carry cultivation and population into previously almost deserted regions (but yet left substantial areas for post-independence colonization). It made land available on generally favourable terms—though rarely were they favourable enough to satisfy the planters. But, apart from colonization proper, to which discussion will shortly turn, direct government participation in the cultivation of the waste, or even its active encouragement, was a rare phenomenon in the British period.

The Grow More Food Campaign

The Grow More Food Campaign is one notable exception to this generalization. This was conducted during the Second World War and received a fillip from the government of India after the Bengal famine of 1943 (though the campaign did not find its genesis in the famine, as has been stated by S. Thirumalai, for in the previous year, 1942–3, the central government made a grant of Rs. 1,883,721 to the provinces in connection with it).[82] There were various aspects of the campaign: for example, the encouragement of a switch to foodcrops from other crops, and the provision of irrigation and of technical information. But the reclamation of wasteland was also stimulated, and this is the campaign's relevance here.

In some provinces such reclamation did not move, before independence, much past the survey and planning stage. In Bihar, for example, a Waste Land Reclamation Bill was passed, and a decision made to reclaim about 280,000 hectares for co-operative colonization.[83] Little more seems to have been achieved before independence; but colonization on reclaimed land is, to a rather limited extent, a characteristic of contemporary Bihar, as later references to that state will show. In Bengal (then, of course, unpartitioned) it was proposed in 1945 to conduct a survey in order to ascertain the acreage of 'culturable fallow and wasteland' lying uncultivated (there being no normal statistics of 'culturable waste' in this permanently settled province) and subsequently to bring 'the maximum possible area of such land under the plough'.[84]

Other provinces were able to report accomplishment, not merely intention, before independence. In UP it was claimed that the campaign had brought 57,000 additional hectares into cultivation by 1946, and the opinion was expressed that 'any withdrawal from the conscripted areas should be guarded against when in future the market has been stabilized'.[85] An attitude to marginal land implicit in this statement will have to be discussed at a much later stage (see below, pp. 291–2). The claim for the campaign in Bombay was for 66,000 hectares.[86] In Orissa it was reported that 258,130 hectares were reclaimed between 1943–4 and 1946–7; though it was admitted that agricultural statistics were unreliable.[87] Madras took up land for departmental and tribal cultivation in the Araku Valley, in the Eastern Ghats inland from Vishakhapatnam (Vizagapatam), now in Andhra Pradesh.[88] A larger-scale accomplishment was to bring under cultivation, with a subsidy of Rs.10 per acre, over 60,000 acres (24,300 hectares) of land under the Mettur Project on the River Kaveri (Cauvery). Just before independence a major colonization scheme was planned for the Araku Valley, but was subsequently abandoned; while the Wynad colonization scheme was planned in 1945 but received its first colonists, a batch of ex-servicemen, only in 1948, after independence. Further reclamation was undertaken in Chittoor District; and in South Kanara District permission was given for *kumri* (shifting) cultivation in part of the wastelands of seventy-four villages for a period of four years, or for the duration of the war, whichever proved to be longer.[89] Assam went further, and in 1943 encouraged not only indigenous settlement in submontane areas of Kamrup and Darrang Districts but also immigration, especially into surplus grazing reserves.[90]

Some of the princely states also took part in the campaign. Thus Hyderabad gave culturable waste for cultivation at concessionary terms, brought the plough to uncultivated parts of irrigable commands, and planned to reclaim 10,000 hectares of virgin land annually by means of tractors.[91] Cochin started government fruit and vegetable farms in the High Ranges.[92]

It is impossible to come to any reliable conclusion on the total extent of wasteland brought into cultivation as a result of the Grow More Food Campaign. Indeed, contemporary reports cast doubt on the statistics claimed by the authorities concerned: certain surveys reported an overestimation by 55 per cent of areas reclaimed.[93] But, locally at any rate, a marked impact was made on the waste; and in the campaign one can find the roots of a number of post-independence colonization schemes (for example, that in Wynad)—indeed, the general impetus was carried forward into independence.

The campaign has been criticized, notably by the foresters, for its effect on forests and on soil conservation.[94] In particular, it is claimed that as a result of the campaign slopes as steep as 45 degrees were cultivated in the Nilgiri Hills without protective measures. As in some parts of contemporary India, land-use planning was hasty and ill-considered.

Colonization

Given the subject of this book, by far the most relevant aspect of government-planned reclamation of Indian wasteland in British times was that for which the term 'colonization' was, in fact, invented, and for which it is still used in India: namely, the officially sponsored establishment of new agricultural villages on wasteland. Much of this colonization was on the grand scale, certainly on a far grander scale than that accomplished as a part of the Grow More Food Campaign or that now being undertaken in independent India (with the noteworthy exception of the schemes in the Rajasthan Desert, the Tarai, and Dandakaranya).

That is not to say, however, that agricultural colonization was not here and there and from time to time undertaken on a much smaller scale, both by the governments in the provinces of British India and by some of the princely states. A few examples must suffice. In Assam, the government was faced in the period 1920–4 with the problem of massive immigration of Bengali settlers, largely Muslims from Mymensingh District, and of their impact on Assamese villages.[95] Immigrants were given annual leases in selected areas away from these villages under what was described as a 'colonization scheme', though it lacked some of the detailed features of major schemes.

Gwalior state in the 1920s and 1930s opened up 23,625 hectares of land in order to attract what it was hoped would be 'progressive cultivators', 1,516 Gujaratis from Baroda and 3,455 Marathas from the Deccan.[96]

Other and smaller colonization schemes were, like the special colonization schemes for Harijans and tribal peoples in contemporary India, designed to rehabilitate backward groups in society. In this category falls the agricultural settlement for 'criminal tribes' (Baurias, Moghias or Baoris, Sansis and others) set up by Gwalior state at Mircabad, near Mungaoli, now in Guna District of Madhya Pradesh.[97] This was first established in 1899, a few years after the Government of India had issued a manual on the treatment of the Moghias, by measures which included the issue of lands for cultivation and whose provisions were introduced into Gwalior. The colony has since its foundation suffered a number of vicissitudes; but it still exists and it has in fact been extended since independence by the addition of the twenty-five families of the Vimukti Jati ('Liberated People') Colony.

Further colonies were established in British days for other special purposes, and have played their part in the disappearance of the waste. Thus in 1925 landless Karens from Burma were brought into North Andaman with the intention that they should establish 'forest villages' and provide labour for the Forest Department.[98] The colony suffered from malaria, many of the settlers dying. The survivors became merchants or cultivators, not forest labourers.

Not all small colonization schemes were established directly by governments. Thus in the United Provinces (though with financial and technical assistance from the government) the Arya Samaj[99] set up Aryanagar, an agricultural colony seven miles from Lucknow for members of the 'criminal tribes'. In 1939 the colony, which had previously relied on cottage industries and employment in the city as well as on farming, was reorganized as a co-operative cultivation society, thus foreshadowing similar societies in the colonies of independent India.

Colonization schemes for graduates or other relatively highly educated persons are still to be encountered in contemporary India: they, too, had progenitors in earlier times. Thus the Annamalai University in Madras set up in 1932 a scheme under which graduates and those with a School Leaving Certificate were assigned land if they expressed willingness to cultivate it and to make agriculture their profession.[100] Once again, the land was farmed co-operatively.

Private enterprise was also responsible for the Gosaba scheme for reclaiming three islands in the Sundarbans, organized, so one's source has it, by 'one Scotch, Sir Hamilton'.[101]

Finally, towards the end of the Second World War, a great deal of official thought was given to the rehabilitation and resettlement of ex-servicemen by means that included the establishment of colonization schemes.[102] However, as in the Wynad Scheme already mentioned it fell almost entirely to independent India to put into effect the schemes mooted before independence; but the pressing needs of refugees, quite unforeseen when postwar rehabilitation was being considered, changed the complexion of the postwar schemes out of all recognition.

These diverse colonization schemes, together with others on the same scale, for all their intrinsic interest and for all their foreshadowing of later colonization, are but small fry compared with the classic achievement of the British administration in the Punjab, where colonization was indeed on the grand scale. For the Punjab Canal Colonies eventually covered 2·2 million hectares of land, almost all of which had been previously waste or subject only to nomadic pastoralism or occasional catch-cropping.[103] Nothing on the same vast scale has so far been achieved in independent India, though colonization under the Rajasthan Canal and in the Dandakaranya Project may eventually do so (the Rajasthan Canal is planned ultimately to irrigate 1·9 million hectares of 'culturable command').[104] It was, of course, the construction of great irrigation channels that enabled the colonists to bring the previously arid or at any rate semi-arid *doabs*[105] of the Punjab under the plough. These canals were constructed to use the waters of the 'five rivers' that give the Punjab its name—the Jhelum, Chenab, Ravi, Beas, and Sutlej; they did not, except in a very minor way, irrigate land beyond the borders of the Punjab in the then princely states of Rajputana (thus, as will be seen, such land is still available for colonization by independent India). Again, although the Indus itself was used to irrigate a large area in Sind, it was not so used farther north, in the Sind Sagar Doab between the Indus and the Jhelum. Several schemes were prepared in British times for the irrigation and colonization of this Doab, but it was not until 1939 that work on one of them was started, only to be suspended for the duration of the war, so that it fell to Pakistan to complete the project and to colonize the Doab on lines very reminiscent of the older Punjab Canal Colonies—though with much more attention to land preparation in advance of colonization and with refugees as the principal category of colonist.[106]

The purist may, of course, argue that the area covered by the Punjab Canal Colonies[107] now lies entirely in Pakistan, so that discussion of them should have no place in a book on colonization in India. The reply must be that they formed the greatest achievement in colonization in the period under review in this historical chapter, in an India as yet undivided; and that they were in various ways the model and the inspiration for schemes of colonization, past and present, in the present territory of the Indian Republic. In the past, for example, the Annamalai University scheme for graduates, to which reference has already been made, was inspired by a scheme near Lyallpur; while the Act[108] governing colonization under the present Rajasthan Canal is closely modelled on the corresponding Act from the (British) Punjab,[109] as is a great deal of the administrative and other procedure. The Rajasthan authorities are, in fact, faced with a situation very similar in some respects to that which faced the British in the Punjab once canal irrigation was developed. For there is land in abundance, and, as in the Punjab in British days, the need is for organized colonization, the attraction and selection of cultivators who have, of necessity, to be grouped in new villages.[110]

Something, then, must be said of the Punjab Canal Colonies. But the reference can be fairly brief. For, although there seems to be no comprehensive and up-to-date assessment of the Colonies as they have fared since the disruption, migrations, and horror attendant on partition, there are several readily accessible accounts, albeit differing in emphasis, which between them admirably describe the evolution of the Colonies during the British period. Notable amongst these are, in chronological order of first publication, the writings of H. Calvert, Sir Malcolm Darling, P. W. Paustian, H. K. Trevaskis, Kazi Ahmed, and A. A. Michel.[111] Moreover, a number of points about the Canal Colonies can best be covered by bringing them into comparison with recent colonization at the relevant point in succeeding chapters.

Like their Mughal predecessors, the British made their earliest attempts at irrigation in the Punjab on the already populated and cultivated areas: on the construction, for example, of the Upper Bari Doab Canal, in the populous Lahore and Amritsar Districts. In the 1880s, however, canal construction reached much more arid and desolate country, with large areas of waste that could not possibly be brought under the plough without organized colonization. So there were founded (1886–8) the first two canal colonies, Sohag-Para (dependent on inundation canals from the Sutlej, and situated just east of Montgomery) and Sidhnai (in Multan District).[112] These two colonies, covering respectively 35,000 and 94,000 hectares, were small compared with the great Punjab schemes of later years, but large relative to many colonies in independent India. Sidhnai Colony ran into a number of problems that were to recur: the hostility of local nomadic peoples, desertions of colonists because of that hostility and the general inhospitability of the area, and the lack of a perennial water supply and of communications. It took sturdy pioneers from Amritsar District to set it on its feet.

The next Colony to be founded was on a much more ambitious scale, and depended on the harnessing of the Chenab by means of the Lower Chenab Canal, whose construction is described by Darling as 'the turning point in the economic history of the Punjab'.[113] The canal enabled the colonization of about a million hectares, most of which had been in the desolate *bar*—that is, the broad stretch of country well above and away from the rivers on either side (here the Chenab and the Ravi): arid, waste, scrub-covered, with few signs of life apart from the nomads and their herds.[114] Colonization was even more a necessity than in the two small pioneer colonies. Leaning on experience at Sidhnai and Sohag-Para, it started in 1892. In the early days colonists endured great hardship, especially from hostile nomads, inaccessibility, and cholera. By 1895, however, good crops were being taken, and there was a new eagerness to settle in the colony, an eagerness that was shared even by some of the nomads. Here, too, the town of Lyallpur was founded. Soon afterwards, in the years 1897–1904, the Chunian Colony (34,200 hectares) was set up in the Upper Bari Doab to receive settlers from the overcrowded Lahore District: this seems to have been the first attempt to relieve localized agrarian pressures.[115] A much larger project, dating from the same period (but not completed until 1921), was the Lower Jhelum Colony, started in 1902, dependent on the Lower Jhelum Canal, and eventually covering 200,000 hectares in the Jech Doab, between the Jhelum and Chenab.[116]

A further wave of colonization hinged on the Triple Canal Project (1905–17), an extremely bold feat of engineering designed primarily to irrigate the lowermost part of the Bari Doab, in Montgomery District.[117] Surplus water from the Jhelum was thus led by a new canal, the Upper Jhelum Canal, into the Chenab, from which river a further canal, the Upper Chenab Canal, led across the Rechna Doab and on over the Ravi, behind a new barrage, to form the Lower Bari Doab canal. Three colonies were strung along this great Triple Canal system: the Upper Jhelum Colony (12,600 hectares) of 1916–21, the Upper Chenab Colony in Gujranwala and Shekhupura Districts (32,000 hectares) of 1915–19; and the Lower Bari Doab Colony in Montgomery and Multan Districts (525,000 hectares) of 1912–22. The bold transfer of water from one river to another, the first attempt at the execution of a basin-wide plan, finds something of a parallel today in the works being undertaken as an outcome of the Indus Waters Agreement, one of the factors making possible the Rajasthan Canal and hence the enormous programme of colonization under it.

The last great Colony was Nili Bar, dependent on the lower Sutlej, and laying, as Darling put it, 'the long green ribbon of yet another colony . . . in the glittering wastes along the southern boundary of Montgomery and Multan [Districts]'.[118] This was begun in 1921.

Thus was the arid Punjab transformed by the creation of four great Colonies (Lower Chenab, or Lyallpur; Lower Jhelum; Lower Bari Doab; and Nili Bar) and five smaller ones (Sidhnai, Sohag-Para, Chunian, Upper Chenab, and Upper Jhelum). The general effect of canal construction and associated colonization was a great increase in production and in population (thus in Lyallpur District between 1891 and 1951 the population rose from 60,306 to 1,814,000 and its density from 6 to 230 per square kilometre).[119] The particular local effect of colonization varied considerably, however, from colony to colony and from tract to tract within the larger colonies, depending not only on conditions of soil, climate, and irrigation but also on such factors as government motives, categories of colonist, and conditions of land tenure.

In the early colonies the government had, according to Darling, two main aims in view: the relief of pressure in the congested Districts of the Central Punjab, and the creation of model villages, 'superior in comfort and civilization to anything which had previously existed in the Punjab'.[120] Some authorities (including N. Gerald Barrier) would also stress a desire to increase the revenue;[121] while in a recent review of motives in canal construction and colonization Michel has stressed the enthusiasm of young administrators and engineers, encouraged by the opportunities afforded by the rivers and plains of the Punjab, and the consequent urge 'to do something for irrigation';[122] and the fear of famine, which, especially after the severe famine of 1878, led the Government of India to look more favourably on irrigation projects in the hope that they would produce a grain surplus. Later, there was more interest in the production of cash crops like sugar-cane and cotton.

Given the concern for the overcrowded Districts and the fear of famine, together with the prevalent notion of a peasantry as a stabilizing force, it is not surprising that most of the settlers in the early colonies were 'peasant proprietors'—who, for example, held about 80 per cent of the land in the Lower Chenab (Lyallpur) Colony. Most of them came from the agricultural communities and castes of the 'old' Punjab. However, with the object, *inter alia*, of providing 'natural leaders' for the Colonies, land grants were also made to 'yeomen', 'larger peasant proprietors' who, 'by their wealth, energy or ability, had raised themselves above their fellows without ceasing to belong to the agricultural community', and to landlords.[123] Such grants were larger than those made to peasants, the yeomen receiving not less than 100 acres (40·5 hectares) and the landlord usually twice or thrice that amount. As in the case of 'middle-class colonization' in Ceylon, these classes of colonist were not conspicuously successful, either as cultivators or as the 'leaders' envisaged by the administration.[124] Their selection may be seen as resting on a misconception about the functioning of rural society, and also on a desire to placate landed interests. Grants were also made to urban capitalists (who, like landlords, tended to become absentees). Later, the idea of including colonists 'of a class above the ordinary peasant' was dropped. No 'yeomen' were selected after 1901, and the Colonies Committee reported in 1907 that 'the colonies would probably do better to rely for their future leaders among the agricultural community on men raised from the peasant class'.[125]

Provision was also made in the Punjab Colonies for the local nomadic inhabitants, whose grazing grounds had become the scene of colonization, and who so frequently attacked the early Colonies. Darling speaks with pride of the conversion of the Jangli 'from a lawless nomad into an industrious agriculturist' but admits that 'reclamation' had its difficulties and that agricultural standards amongst the Janglis lagged far behind.[126] Chapter 13 will show that in areas of colonization modern India also has its problems with tribal inhabitants whom it is desired to 'reclaim'. In both British and independent India, an attempt was also made in the Punjab Canal Colonies to provide land for other depressed classes and for criminal tribes and castes.[127]

During the Boer War the Government of India became concerned about certain needs of the army, and in the new Colonies of succeeding years, particularly those hinging on the Triple Canal Project, special grants were made for a number of military purposes:[128] for example, for horse- and camel-breeding and for ex-servicemen. In Shahpur (Lower Jhelum Colony) over 80,000 hectares were given out on horse-breeding grants. Of these military categories, only colonies for ex-servicemen find a parallel in independent India.

Land in Colonies was later given out for special agricultural purposes, 'for the growth of selected seed, for the breeding of special strains of cattle, for the supply of cantonments with milk or butter, for plantations and experiments in fruit farming, and even for the introduction of steam ploughs', to quote Darling's list;[129] or, as Trevaskis puts it with more acidity, for the 'fads of the moment'.[130]

It is implicit in what has been said already that the wastelands that formed the site for the Canal Colonies were taken to be completely at the disposal of the government, which further assumed that it could attach whatever conditions it pleased to the occupation of 'government' or 'crown' waste. Similar assumptions were, of course, made in other territories of the British empire, notably in Ceylon.[131]

In Bengal, it is true, an estate was originally allowed, on settlement with the revenue authorities, to include the waste that adjoined its cultivated portion, while in the United Provinces waste was usually divided between the village-estates.[132] But as time went on the Bengal government began to assert the rights over waste that it had always claimed in theory, and to separate as 'government waste' land, especially forests, that did not belong to any estate, notably in Assam (then part of Bengal) and in the Sundarbans and Tarai, while in Oudh excess wastelands became first government waste and then state forest. In the *ryotwari* provinces (particularly Madras and Bombay) the revenue settlement was with individuals, and involved separate assessment of each field and plot, so that, except for the allocation of village grazing grounds, there was no question of allocating surplus waste to 'estates' or to whole villages, as in Bengal and the UP respectively.[133] All waste remained government property and was available for issue by the local Revenue Officer to allow for village expansion. In the Central Provinces and the Punjab, where on original settlement there was an abundance of waste, a liberal allowance was made to each village: this usually amounted to 200 per cent of the cultivated area. But this still left a vast expanse of government waste. In the Central Provinces, most of this was declared Government Forest and reserved under the Forest Act of 1865. Areas were eventually given up for cultivation or for village purposes: but this was usually on a piecemeal basis, and great areas of forest were left (for example, in Chanda District) to be colonized by independent India.

In the Punjab, conditions were very different: indeed, their uniqueness provided the tenurial basis, as the potentially fertile alluvial plains of the five rivers provided the geographical basis and the evolution of advanced methods of irrigation the technical basis, for the Punjab Canal Colonies. As in the Central Provinces, about 200 per cent of the cultivated area was added to each village on settlement as its share of the waste; as in the Central Provinces, again, forest and grazing lands were demarcated from the government waste not allocated to villages.[134] But the forest was poor stuff compared with the jungles of central India: a stunted growth of thorns suitable only for fuel. And when all conceivable demands for *rakh*, or fuel reserves, were met there was still waste in plenty to be used for colonization.

The systems of tenure by which colonists held land in the Punjab Canal Colonies were of considerable complexity and, in particular, varied with locality and over time.[135] In the two early colonies, colonists were allowed to purchase proprietary rights for a sum that was little more than nominal, and were then free to sell their holding.

But the Punjab government was already concerned in the 1890s with the loss of land by agriculturists to landlords and townsmen, partly through sale, partly through foreclosures on mortgages; and in the Lower Chenab and subsequent colonies, while continuing to grant proprietary rights to yeomen and capitalists (indeed, land destined for the latter was often put up to auction) it only gave non-transferable occupancy rights to peasants, who thus became nothing more than Crown tenants, holding their land for so long as they paid their revenue and fulfilled the conditions specified in their grant. These conditions included residence on the land, the maintenance of a clean compound, satisfactory sanitary arrangements, and the cutting of wood from specified areas. Colonization Officers and their subordinates were thus apt to inspect allotments and house-compounds with the same sort of paternalism that characterized Ceylon colonization under the Land Development Ordinance of that country.[136]

Occupancy rights could, however, be subdivided amongst the heirs on the death of the original colonist, and the authorities became alarmed in the 1880s at the ensuing fragmentation. Moreover, there was a constant (and not surprising) tendency to evade the conditions of the grants, in response to which the colonization staff evolved a system of informal and extra-legal fines. More stringent conditions (including provision for fines) were included in grants after 1902, and the Punjab government began to prepare amendments to the Government Tenants (Punjab) Act, No. 3, of 1893 which would introduce stricter and retroactive conditions into existing grants, forbid transfer of property by will, legalize fines, and enforce strict primogeniture in an attempt to prevent fragmentation; one is again reminded of the similar attempt made under the Land Development Ordinance in the Ceylon colonization schemes.[137] The introduction of a Bill to amend the Act in these senses was the signal for widespread agitation and disturbance in the Punjab, which were exacerbated by dissatisfaction with increased irrigation charges and with the corruption that went on under the cloak of paternalism.

After much discussion, involving Calcutta and London as well as Lahore, a special Colonies Committee reported in 1908.[138] It declared that colonization was but a temporary stage and that colonists could not ultimately be subject to restrictions unknown to citizens at large. In particular, proprietary rights should be granted, for a number of reasons: first, the immemorial custom that he who reclaims the waste has 'proprietary rights'; secondly, because the colonists wished to have such rights for a variety of reasons—sentiment, the need to have security for credit, and in relation to marriage custom; thirdly, as a stimulus to development; fourthly, because the power of alienation and mobility in land implicit in proprietary rights were essential to the future development of the colonies (restricted alienation would, the Committee thought, lead to extreme subdivision and to the absence of rewards for energy or of stimulus to effort, and also tend to retain undesirables on the land). It was for very similar reasons that the Ceylon Land Commission of 1955–8 wished to see an end to the restrictive and paternalistic tenure under the Land Development Ordinance.[139]

The Colonization of Government Lands (Punjab) Act, No. 5 of 1912 accepted the Committee's arguments and created a system of tenure for the colonies under which a colonist, if he satisfied the requisite conditions, moved through three stages. In Stage I he was a tenant-at-will for not less than five years, paying an annual rent; was required to build a house and reside in the colony; and was forbidden to alienate without consent or to leave the land to more than one successor. In Stage II, which again lasted for not less than five years, he continued to pay an annual rent and could still not alienate without consent, but was secure in his tenure for himself and his heirs (without restriction as to their number or nature). He could move on to the third stage by paying the purchase price (in a lump sum or in instalments, and calculated on the unimproved value of the land); repaying any government loans; and satisfying conditions on house and field channel construction, and on the cultivation of a given percentage of the land being cultivated. The 1912 Act also abolished the residence requirement for yeomen. In the Lower Jhelum (Shahpur) Colony, it may be noted, horse-breeding grants had already been tied down to a system of primogeniture which was entirely foreign to the Punjab.

Colonization in the former province of Sind is less well documented than that in the Punjab, and started (with settlement from 1901 onwards under the Jamrao Canal, fed from the Eastern Nara River),[140] later than in the Punjab. It involved a certain amount of inter-provincial migration, especially of Punjabi small-holders and of cultivators from Rajputana and Cutch. Much greater emphasis was placed on yeoman and capitalist grants than in the Punjab; but in terms of tenure and other arrangements the precedent of the Canal Colonies was in general closely followed.

Tenure of Wasteland: Further Examples

Barrier, in the paper just quoted, is mainly interested in land tenure in the Punjab Canal Colonies because its history illustrates the way in which even a paternalistic imperial government could yield to popular pressure, and, under internal and external forces, modify its policies. The emphasis for the purpose of the present study is different. In addition to its intrinsic interest, land tenure in the Canal Colonies is seen as a potent influence on agrarian policy elsewhere in India; moreover, it illustrates an important point. This is that wasteland policy suffered a sea change during the British period. Before British times, whatever the nature in any given place and at any given time of the ruler's claim to wasteland, the use of the waste seems to have been a matter of slowly evolving and largely unrecorded traditions. But the British, as well as asserting the general right of the state to the ownership of the waste (which Trevaskis called 'a foreign doctrine'),[141] also codified their policies and practices on the issue of state wastelands for cultivation in a vast outpouring of acts, rules and orders. This process of codification, far from introducing simplicity, was a principal injector of complication into the Indian agrarian scene. New variations between one region and another were brought about—for example, by differences in the treatment of waste as between *ryotwari* areas and areas of permanent settlement. Codification, moreover, tended to freeze relationships and thus to store up complication for the future, because adaptation to new needs became more difficult.[142] Policy, however, tended to shift over relatively short periods of time for other complicating reasons. Sometimes, as in the case of the Punjab Canal Colonies just described, this was mainly because of changes in personalities and in the balance of influence between provincial governments, the Government of India, and the India Office in London; at other times, for all the alleged pragmatism of the British, it was due to changes in the climate of ideas. Thus Trevaskis ascribes the policy in the Punjab—of handing over large areas of waste to village communities—to the dominance, by the time in question, of *laissez-faire* ideas, under the influence of which the authorities were all too glad to hand over waste to any community that could assert a reasonable claim to it.[143] More recently E. T. Stokes has demonstrated the influence of utilitarian ideas, in particular the doctrine of rent, on land policy.[144] Yet another cause of complication was a result of a British tendency to misunderstand Indian agrarian institutions and thus to apply methods of control and administration which necessarily distorted what had gone before. The misunderstanding often arose because false parallels with conditions in England were read into Indian circumstances, as in the classic argument as to whether land revenue was a tax or a rent (when, in fact, it was neither, as W. Nassau Lees percipiently realized).[145]

What has already been said in the discussion of the Punjab Canal Colonies has illustrated the codifying, complicating role of the British in those aspects of land policy concerned with wasteland and colonization. But a few other examples may not come amiss. Quite early in Bengal the easy assumption that waste could be lost from view in the estates of *zamindars* ran into difficulties in the pioneer fringe of the Sundarbans, where by 1819 wastelands were being temporarily cultivated by encroachment from 'regular estates' farther inland.[146] Waste Lands Rules to put an end to irregular occupation were first issued in 1825, and the 'uninhabited tracts' of the Sundarbans were declared state property by Regulation III of 1828; but control was not very effective until 1853, when 99-year leases were introduced, to be superseded ten years later by provision for purchase ('redeemed grants'). But in 1879 the policy of proprietary settlements was abandoned in favour of leases. In 1905 a system of *ryotwari* settlement was introduced, with a special Colonization Officer to guide settlement. 'Better class cultivators' who could hire labourers were given larger allotments, and even *bhadralok* were not excluded provided they were willing to undergo agricultural training and to work like ordinary cultivators.

A similar story of shifting policy and complicating practice is discernible in the case of the government wastelands alienated under a variety of tenures for tea cultivation in Bengal and Assam.[147] Thus early leasehold grants were made under the 1838 Bengal Rules: grants were not to be below 40 hectares and not above 4,000 hectares; a quarter of the area was to be cultivated within 5 years; one-quarter of the land would be granted free of revenue in perpetuity; and full revenue was not to be levied on the remainder for 45 years. In 1854 a different system of leasehold grants under what came to be known as the 'Old Assam Rules' was instituted. The minimum grant was to be of 200 hectares (later reduced); a quarter remained exempt from revenue in perpetuity, but a low revenue was to be charged on all of the land for 99 years. There were also more complex conditions on the proportion to be cleared during successive periods. The 'New Assam Rules' were introduced in 1862, and envisaged the disposal of wastelands in perpetuity on fee simple grants. Such grants were not to exceed 1,200 hectares, and would be auctioned. On sale there would be no future revenue demand. In 1876 yet another set of rules was instituted, and comprehensive Assam Land Revenue regulations were framed. (Most of the nineteenth-century grants have now lapsed and the lands concerned are assessed on a periodic lease.) W. Nassau Lees gives an interesting contemporary account of the pressures from tea interests for sale in fee simple and of the favourable reaction to those pressures of the government of India and of Canning at home.[148]

British policy in Bengal and Assam has been attacked because, at the height of its *laissez-faire* stage, it retained insufficient control of wasteland and encouraged speculation and the tea-planting mania of the early 1860s.[149] It has been claimed that in the former United Provinces, too, at about the same time, the British 'gave away' forest land in the southern plateaux to speculators for a nominal royalty; while in Bundelkhand only inaccessible forests unfit for cultivation were declared reserved or protected.[150]

The Concept of Culturable Waste

The British claim to wasteland and the changing conditions under which wasteland was made available for cultivation form an essential part of the background to colonization in British times. The government of independent India has inherited its share of the wasteland not occupied in British times, and has applied British notions of state ownership and control to waste in former princely states; and forms of tenure initiated in British times have been replicated in post-independence colonies.

One further facet of British land administration must still be singled out for special treatment, because of its central importance to this study and because of the misconceptions and false conclusions that it has engendered. This is the concept of *culturable waste*.

For many years the government of India has published statistics of the area of the country classified as 'culturable waste'; and has also published a breakdown by states (formerly by provinces) and districts where statistical coverage was available.[151] The area under culturable waste was given provisionally as 16,612,000 hectares for 1967–8 and provisionally as 16,489,000 hectares for 1968–9.[152] There have been many warnings against taking culturable waste figures at their face value. Thus the Royal Commission on Agriculture in India (the Linlithgow Commission) remarked that a great deal of the culturable waste 'could in no conceivable circumstances be brought under tillage'.[153] Another and particularly cogent warning was given by O. H. K. Spate who said, '90 million acres [the figure quoted when he was writing and equivalent to about 36·4 million hectares] still haunt the literature, and many writers have paid no heed to these authoritative warnings, nor indeed to the witness of their own eyes.'[154] M. D. Chaturvedi, again, attacked the whole concept of culturable waste on the grounds that 'the very association of ideas leads one to assume possibilities of the extension of cultivation, where none exists. . . . The term "culturable waste", applied to lands which might be tilled but have never been known to be tilled despite the pressure of population and improved irrigation facilities, is even more misleading.'[155] A number of writers concerned with the wartime Grow More Food Campaign were also under no illusions. An editorial in *Indian Farming* drew attention to food shortages and population growth but concluded that the needed relief could not come from culturable wastes because not only were these negligible in relation to the size of the problem but also 'in a condition which precluded any possibility of profitable agriculture, at least without long-range development'.[156] Again, a writer on the campaign in Assam quoted the then current agricultural statistics but concluded that careful analysis would show that the area of land which could be brought under cultivation was not so large as the figures purported to indicate.[157]

Yet, for all these warnings, and perhaps even because some of them were issued from official sources, there have been repeated statements that take the culturable waste figures at their face value or assert that vast areas of land want for nothing but tillers. One school of thought, indeed, has it that the notion that India is overpopulated is an imperialist myth and supports this view by reference to the large areas of culturable waste.[158] Moonis Raza went so far as to claim that 'about one-third of the cultivable land has yet to be brought under the plough'.[159] (Culturable waste accounted for no more than 8·1 per cent of the 'reporting area' (that for which data are available) in 1950–1, when Moonis Raza was writing, or for 5·6 per cent (provisional figure) in 1964–5; but the percentages are raised to 27·3 per cent and 18·5 per cent respectively by the inclusion of other categories of uncultivated land and of fallows.)[160]

A similar tendency to take culturable waste (or total waste) figures at their face value, though without reference to the supposed 'imperialist myth', is also often encountered. Thus the Population Sub-Committee of the National Planning Committee reported just before independence that 'a considerable amount of waste land is available in the country; and . . . should be taken into cultivation so as to aid substantially our available food supply,—and that, too, within a short space of time' and continued, 'If the total culturable waste . . . were brought under the plough, the area under cultivation would be increased by more than 60 per cent; and the food supply may be expected to be increased, if not in the same proportion, in a very respectable proportion, say by 50 per cent of the present supply.'[161] (The figures quoted include Burma in British India, and this, of course, considerably inflates the percentages.) The sub-committee does, however, in a subsequent chapter state: 'But now [with the extension of cultivation] the chances of expansion of population have been exhausted, at least in the major provinces, hills, sand-dunes and uncultivable wastes now thwarting extension'; while the area of forests was held already to be too small; though in Burma, Assam, Rajputana, the Central Provinces, and Madras extension of cultivation was possible—in fact, it was estimated (though clearly without any survey whatsoever) that overall three-quarters of the hitherto uncultivated land could be sown 'under unremitting population pressures'.

The rest of this book will show that much misplaced optimism lies behind this Report and its recommendations for organized colonization involving inter-provincial migration. But, though events since independence have shown how little land in India, relatively speaking, can be colonized under current conditions, statements are still made from time to time that clearly imply reliance on the wasteland statistics.[162] Kingsley Davis appears to take both the statistics and the statements of the Population Sub-Committee (just quoted) at their face value in his well-known study of population in India and Pakistan.[163] The same is true of the German economist, Theodor Bergmann; and of P. T. Bauer, who in fact has it that 'a large part of the land surface of India at present uncultivated could certainly be made cultivable (especially but not only that part described officially as "cultivable [*sic*] waste") with capital expenditure on land or communications'.[164] Again, B. R. Davidson, in a study of the limitations on settlement in the Australian North, quotes Indian culturable waste statistics quite uncritically.[165] Finally, two Soviet authors, R. P. Gurvic and A. L. Batalov, refer to the 'enormous resources' of the Indian wastelands.[166]

One needs to have only a superficial knowledge of the Indian countryside to realize that the warnings on the agricultural statistics are all too evidently borne out in the field: a large proportion of 'culturable waste' is very poor land indeed, naturally infertile and often further impoverished by over-grazing and soil erosion. It is clear that many of those who have taken the figures so uncritically can have but little first-hand knowledge of India. On what, then, are figures for culturable waste based and what concepts and definitions lie behind them?

In order to answer this question it is necessary to go back to the first British revenue settlements. These, of course, took place at different times in different parts of the *Raj*; and varied in method and upshot as between *zamindari*, *ryotwari*, and *mahalwari* (village estate) areas.[167] But, generally speaking, the object of the exercise was to determine the area of cultivated land of various qualities which was to bear assessment for revenue, and to fix the assessment for each parcel. In the process, certain land was excluded from assessment (for example, the area covered by houses, ponds, and tanks). As for wasteland, some was allocated to individual or village estates, already noted, and some was retained by the government. The waste was then divided between 'culturable' and 'unculturable', as for example in the settlement of Saugor District, Central Provinces, in 1868:

51,813 acres [20,968 hectares] of land have been declared waste, and at the disposal of the Government under waste land rules. Of this, 8,430 acres [34,115 hectares] are culturable, and 43,383 acres [17,556 hectares] hill and jungle and useless except for the production of forest trees, grazing cattle and firewood.[168]

It is evident, however, that here and elsewhere no sort of scientific survey of wasteland potential was made: the division between 'culturable' and 'unculturable' was rough and ready, and tended to err on the side of optimism, classifying as 'unculturable' only land that was bare rock, or on a near-vertical slope, or otherwise 'hill and jungle and useless . . .'.

In fact, the category 'culturable waste' stands revealed from the Settlement Reports as a residual category defined purely on revenue officers' criteria: a residual category, because (with the 'unculturable waste') it was, generally speaking, what was left after the area in other categories had been defined—the cultivated land, the fallows, the forest reserves (by definition *not* 'at the disposal of the Government under the waste land rules'), the land excluded because it was, for example, built on; and a category defined purely on revenue officers' criteria because, as has just been said, there was no scientific survey on the basis of which 'culturability' could be assessed.

Thus did figures for 'culturable waste' first become available. For any given area, they tended to be revised over the years, partly because of the march of cultivation, partly because of the shifting (on an equally unscientific basis) of the shadowy boundary between culturable and unculturable land—as when, in Benares District in 1887, 'The decrease in barren, etc. land is met by a corresponding increase in culturable waste and cultivation. In 1840–41 the waste land groves, etc. were not numbered and much culturable land was entered in the records as barren.'[169] On the other hand, there was a sudden jump in the culturable waste figures in the UP in 1927 because of the inclusion for the first time of fallows of more than six years.[170] It was the duty of the *patwari* (village accountant or registrar) in northern parts of British India, and of corresponding officers elsewhere, to submit statistical returns showing the area under culturable waste, and hence to enable official statistics to be kept up to date. But the starting-point of the *patwari* was the last revenue settlement, so that his efforts, even if conscientious, did not and could not improve conceptually on the definitions and criteria there employed. Some princely states used a statistical system similar to that in British India, others were able to supply little or no relevant data. In 1949–50 an attempt was made to apply a standard statistical system to the whole country; the system of 'classification of area' was revised, but without affecting the criteria for 'culturable waste'.[171] Ex-princely states were gradually brought into the system (hence the gradual increase in the 'reporting area' which, while giving wider coverage, makes it difficult to determine all-India trends: see below, pp. 79–86).

Inspection of statistics for culturable waste in some Districts that were formerly remote and backward princely states shows, as in the case of Bastar (Madhya Pradesh), wild fluctuations, and in others (for example, Kalahandi District of Orissa) an almost unbelievably constant acreage for culturable waste (one or other of these suspicious features may also be discerned in Districts that were never princely states). Again, a survey of Dewas District (also once princely territory) in 1958–9 showed that, out of 120,021 hectares of culturable waste recorded in the Returns of Agricultural Statistics, only 59,843 hectares (just under 50 per cent) were actually lying waste, 73·8 per cent of them in occupied holdings: the rest had gone into cultivation unrecorded.[172]

In sum, official statistics of culturable waste are, for all the efforts to keep them up to date, unreliable, at least in some areas, even if one accepts their conceptual base. And figures for culturable waste, residual and unscientifically defined category that it is, give no guide to the amount of land that might be brought into cultivation at any given time under specified conditions.

Various attempts have been made from time to time to estimate what proportion of the culturable waste of India, or of some part of it is in fact available for cultivation under specified conditions, or, indeed, otherwise. One such estimate (that overall three-quarters of hitherto uncultivated land could be sown 'under unremitting population pressures') was made by the Population Sub-Committee of the National Planning Committee and has already been quoted. Baljit Singh and Shridhar Misra estimated that only 5 per cent of the culturable waste in Uttar Pradesh was actually cultivable, but did not specify their criteria.[173] S. Thirumalai stated that only 6·1 million out of 39·8 million hectares recorded as 'other uncultivated land' (that is, culturable waste *plus* permanent pastures and grazing grounds, and miscellaneous tree crops and groves not included in the net sown area) are reported as cultivable.[174] Sir T. Vijayaraghavacharya attempted no quantitative assessment but concluded that the land remaining for cultivation 'is, generally speaking, land on the margin of fertility or land which is potentially fertile, but which can be reclaimed from "culturable waste" only at an expense which is beyond the means of the ordinary individual of the middle classes'.[175] (It is not clear why he chose these classes.)

As will be shown in chapter 8, an apparently more consistent attempt was made by the centrally appointed Uppal Committee in the early 1960s to locate, state by state, large blocks of wasteland available for reclamation and for the resettlement of landless labourers, by colonization or otherwise. But it cannot be said that the committee's work did very much either to provide accurate information on the proportion of culturable waste that might, on given conditions, be cultivated; or to support the assertion that 2·2 million hectares is available for cultivation and reclamation.[176] The government of Assam, moreover, saw fit to provide its own survey of its Plains Districts, on broadly similar lines, yet in a setting and with methods of operation which make it unsound to attempt to compare its results with those published by the Uppal Committee.[177] The Assam survey did, however, reach very cautious conclusions that deserve to be applied more widely in India:

It is found that according to the actual conditions on the spot as revealed by the Survey, the Culturable Waste Land in the State is not so large as it is generally thought to be. Large areas were classified as Culturable Waste Land at the time of settlement or since long past and were so classed year after year in records irrespective of whether they are cultivable and are lying waste or not. The Survey has revealed that a great part of this area is either uncultivable and barren or is already being put to some useful exploitation.[178]

But it must be admitted that the circumstances in which the Assam government both conducted a separate survey and endorsed conservative conclusions were not such as to assist the attainment of objectivity. For the government has been, in recent years, understandably at pains to stress its inability to settle more refugees from East Bengal, and this in turn reflects general Assamese nervousness in the face of the massive immigration already referred to in this chapter (see also chapter 4 below).

No attempt will be made here to estimate the currently useful proportion of the culturable wastes or other uncultivated lands of India—on my own argument such a task is impossible, at least in the absence of the sort of surveys of natural resources that will be advocated in chapter 8. Rather shall I conclude with an attempt to refine the concepts involved. The point to be made, and indeed strongly emphasized, is that there is no absolute figure for the area of a country that may be brought from the waste into cultivation. There is only a relative figure, relative, that is, to the technology to be applied and the acceptable minimum return on the factors of production to be employed in the enterprise; and the two are related. (This is, of course, why specified conditions were mentioned in the preceding paragraph.) Clearly if irrigation is available in an area and paddy-growing agronomy contemplated, there will be a different answer to the question 'What is cultivable?' from that when dry cultivation of millets is alone involved. And land-hungry peasants in many parts of India are willing through sheer necessity to contemplate a return from the cultivation of wasteland that would fail to attract cultivators more fortunately placed. Again, if irrigation and colonization by a government agency is envisaged, there is, or ought to be, a calculation of estimated returns in relation to costs, and the result of the calculation will determine whether the scheme is economically viable and therefore, in a very real sense, whether the land involved is held to be 'culturable'.

It follows, too, that one cannot accept V. V. Giri's dictum that 'the motto should be to utilize every inch of available land anywhere'.[179]

This book will proceed, not by attempting the impossible task of defining the areas within which colonization ought to be possible under specified conditions, but by examining areas in which it has actually been attempted in India since independence; and to these areas attention must now turn.

3

Areas of Colonization: 1

GIVEN the population growth and the increase in the cultivated area during the British period, and given the proper scepticism about the surviving culturable waste expressed in the last chapter, it might well be imagined that few if any areas remain for independent India to colonize with its overflowing peasantry. Some authors have, indeed, made what may be called 'the equilibrium assumption'—that rural population has everywhere settled down to a density appropriate to local land resources so that, to quote O. H. K. Spate, 'with populations everywhere congested . . . and land-hungry, any land cultivable without prohibitive outlay would have been taken up long ago'.[1]

Yet agricultural colonization has in fact been undertaken in a number of areas since independence. The present chapter and its successor are designed to introduce the reader to these areas, and to explore the reasons why they have remained sparsely peopled until very recent times indeed (a problem that will be of particular interest to geographers and historians).

The areas in question (see Map 1) are:

(1) The dry lands of Rajasthan and western Haryana;
(2) The Tarai of Uttar Pradesh and Bihar;
(3) Greater Malnad: the hill areas of Malnad, Wynad, the Nilgiris, and the High Ranges of Kerala;
(4) Dandakaranya;
(5) Assam;
(6) A number of smaller pockets, notably those in the Chambal valley, the Malwa plateau, and other small regions;
(7) Regions in which land may be made available for colonization by the intensification of existing cultivation: for example, the Raichur Doab.

Of these, areas (1)–(3) will be dealt with in the present chapter.

The Dry Lands of Rajasthan and Western Haryana

The most obvious characteristic of this area is its dryness. Mean

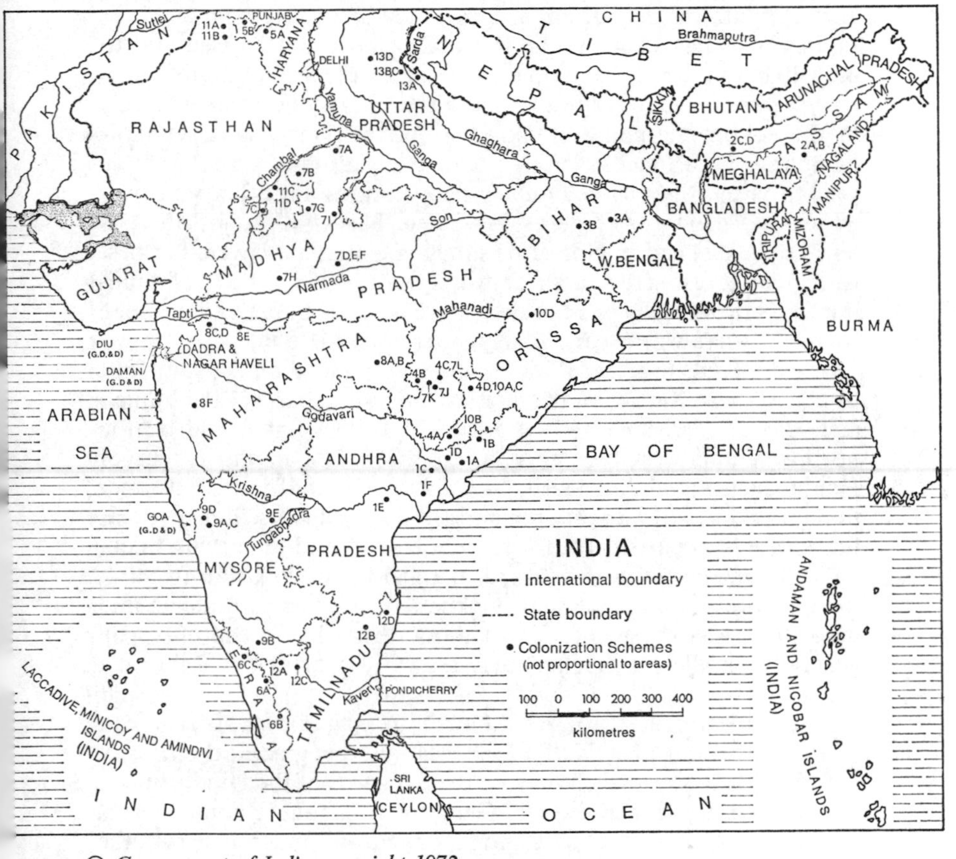

Source: Based upon Survey of India map, with the permission of the Surveyor-General of India

Map 1 India south of about 30° North latitude, showing the location of Colonization Schemes

Notes: (a) The numbers refer to the Colonization Schemes listed in the Appendix. No attempt is made to indicate the actual area covered by each scheme.

(b) The boundary of Meghalaya shown on this map is as interpreted from the North-Eastern Areas (Reorganisation) Act, 1971, but has yet to be verified.

(c) The territorial waters of India extend into the sea to a distance of twelve nautical miles measured from the appropriate base line.

annual rainfall is only 33 cm at Sirsa, in western Haryana, and falls rapidly to under 25 cm as the Rasjasthan border is crossed and to only 10 cm in western Jaisalmer. The mean figures are doubly misleading, however: for rainfall is both seasonal (concentrated largely in the southwest monsoon months) and extremely undependable (coming in occasional storms, with great variation in incidence from year to year). Moreover, summer temperatures are often well over 38 °C. and may go as high as 51 °C., so that what rainfall there is tends to be ineffective. Not surprisingly, the region is covered at best with poor thorn scrub, and, at worst, with shifting belts of sand-dunes; part of it may be regarded as true desert. Famines have been frequent (there was a particularly severe one in 1896–7).[2]

The dry lands here under discussion are bounded on the southeast by the Aravalli Range, on the northeast by those parts of the Punjab and Haryana irrigated and colonized in British times, and on the northwest and west by Pakistan. In the north, in the region of Hanumangarh and Anupgarh, the underlying landform is a former floodplain built of variable but mostly fine-grained sediments; this floodplain is in part covered with windblown sand of varying thickness. As one goes southwestward, parallel to the Pakistan frontier, the sands increase in area and thickness to produce 'a uniform and desolate waste of sand'.[3] Throughout these lands contours run generally parallel to that frontier, as will (or may) the Rajasthan Canal.

Most of Marusthali, to give the plain its *nom de pays*, is riverless. In the north, however, is that historical and geographical curiosity the 'river' Ghaggar, which may be the Sarasvati of the Hindu epics.[4] Formerly water flowed in the Ghaggar to about Hanumangarh, and then only in wet years, leaving a dry bed meandering across the desert towards the Sutlej; but of recent years the Ghaggar has regularly flooded down to and beyond Suratgarh, to the great embarrassment of the Central Mechanized Farm there. Over most of Marusthali the presence of underground water does not compensate for the absence of rivers: almost everywhere the water-table is at great depth (especially west of Bikaner, where, moreover, the water is brackish).

Soils are generally low in fertility. Where the old floodplain lies at the surface and texture is fine at or below the surface they tend to be alkaline or saline, particularly in the region of Anupgarh; and the sands let water through and tend to move with the wind. The high sand-dunes of the Jaisalmer area are, of course, difficult to reclaim and even more mobile.[5]

Most of the rural population have traditionally depended on pastoralism (some of it nomadic) and on hazardous rainfed cultivation.

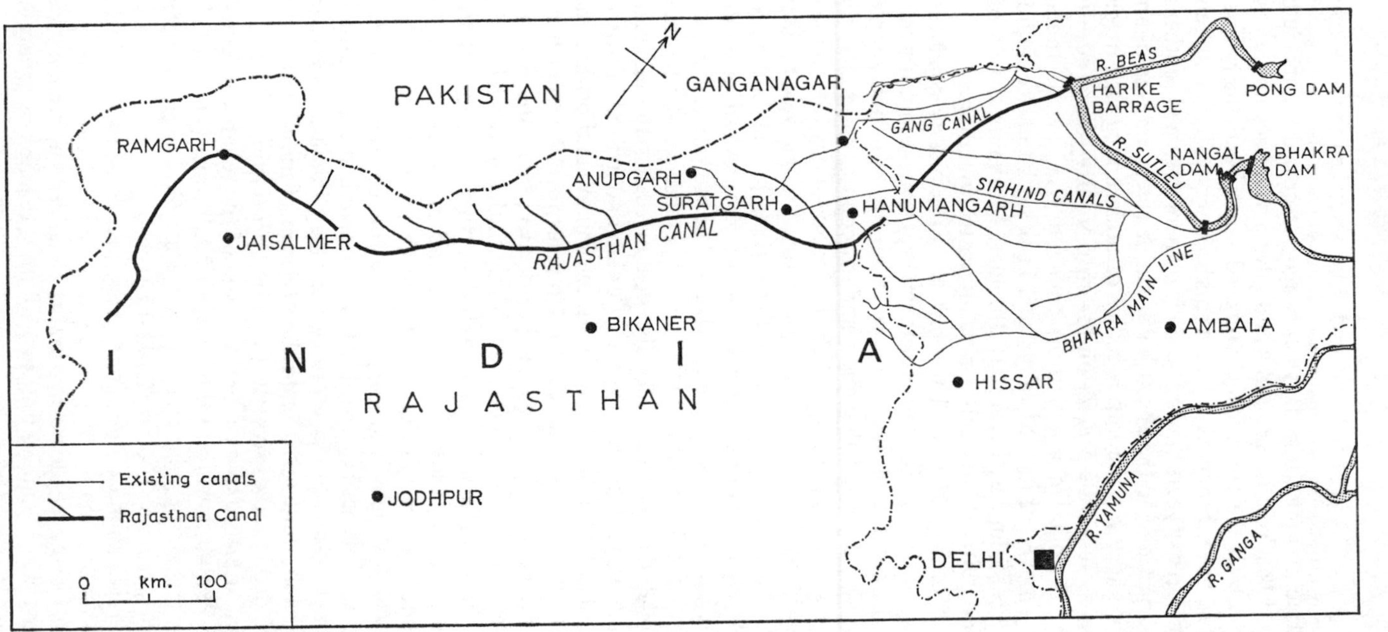

Source: Based upon Survey of India map, with the permission of the Surveyor-General of India

Map 2 The Rajasthan Canal Project

K. D. Erskine, writing some sixty years ago, described the whole of Bikaner as 'a vast pasture ground'[6] and gave a vivid account of the method by which the cultivators ploughed and sowed their sandy fields, only to have them covered with sand blown by the high desert winds,[7] while in dry years cattle and their owners streamed southeast in search of pasture.[8] In the absence of reliable rivers, or even of any rivers at all, and given the impossibility of undertaking well irrigation, there was very little protection for crops in dry years and, not surprisingly, densities of population remained very low by Indian standards—an average in 1951 of about 25 per sq. kilometre, falling below 1 per sq. kilometre in western Bikaner. Moreover, over most of the period 1901–31 the region actually lost population.[9]

The plains of Rajasthan and western Haryana clearly constitute a region of considerable difficulty for their rural population. It would be easy to dismiss the problem as one of aridity pure and simple. But there is also the point that the standard counter to aridity, the practice of irrigation, was denied to the region, or at any rate to most of it, during British times. Here and there small tanks were built to store rainwater, but these could exert but little influence on the arid landscape. Wells were for the most part out of the question, given the depth of the water-table and the brackishness of the water, except in such places as the floodplain of the Luni. The absence of perennial rivers precluded the construction by the local princely states of canals of the sort that were spreading over the Punjab and in Sind in British times. True, Bikaner, in association with the Punjab authorities, dug inundation canals from the unreliable Ghaggar in 1897[10] and there were similar canals north of the Punjab border; later, the Bikaner (or Gang) canal was constructed to bring Sutlej water from the Ferozepore headworks into the extreme northern portion of the state. Sometimes, too, water from the Sirhind and Western Jumna canals benefited Hissar District of the Punjab (now Haryana), but the supply was unreliable not only because the District lay at the tail end of distributaries but also because the canals passed through princely states outside the control of the Punjab irrigation authorities.[11] But, quite apart from the problem of unreliability, the area commanded in these ways was but a tiny proportion of the vast, dry plain that stretched away from the edge of the reliably irrigated areas of the Punjab down into the wastes of Jaisalmer (though it is worth noting that the population of Bikaner state did double between 1921 and 1941, from 660,000 to 1,293,000).

The Indian Irrigation Commission merely advocated local storage, for they saw no solution to the problem of providing reliable irrigation on a large scale outside northernmost Bikaner,[12] by reason, not only of scanty water supply, but also of the existence of separate princely states, whose interests were liable to conflict, and of *jagirdars* (that is, those to whom the rulers had assigned land on certain conditions and who could not be forced to conform to the requirements of an irrigation system). W. Burns, forty years later, saw little scope for supplementing rainfall by irrigation in Rajasthan, and advocated dry farming.[13]

New developments since the coming of independence may transform a belt of country running parallel to the Pakistan frontier from Hissar District to Jaisalmer, or even farther. These developments spring from the construction of the long-mooted Bhakra–Nangal and Harike barrages and Pong dam, and from the conclusion of the Indus Waters Agreement with Pakistan, under which India is to have ultimately almost exclusive use of the water of the Sutlej, Beas, and Ravi.[14] The Bhakra and Nangal dams control the Sutlej where it leaves the mountains: some of the water thus stored is taken by a new canal to a large area of Hissar District of Haryana and of what is now the Ganganagar District of Rajasthan (formerly the northernmost part of Bikaner state). The Rajasthan Canal, only part of which has so far been constructed, is a much more ambitious if not grandiose project, intended to irrigate a 'culturable commanded' area of 1·9 million hectares.[15] It takes off from the Harike Barrage at the confluence of the Sutlej and the Beas, but will rely mainly on the latter (to be harnessed after 1974 by the Pong dam upstream of Harike) since the Sutlej is already almost fully committed by the Bhakra–Nangal and other works. Ravi water also contributes to the Beas above Harike through the Ravi–Beas Link Canal, built 1952–4. Further links and reservoirs may later be constructed. The Rajasthan Canal, crossing the Bhakra Main Line by a spectacular siphon, was originally planned to run for 650 km or so roughly along the contour to the region of Jaisalmer, where irrigation and colonization may be difficult because of high and extensive dunes. (Pakistan is constructing massive works to take Indus and Jhelum water to tracts originally irrigated by canals deriving from the Sutlej, Beas, and Ravi.)

These projects are of course facilitated (so far as India is concerned) by the disappearance of the princely states and of *jagirs* and by the end of friction between states over the use of water; and also by the institution of central planning machinery for major projects. Construction and colonization have, however, been hampered by shortage of financial resources and by other difficulties (notably the war of November–December 1971). By December 1971, however, the feeder canal from Harike and 130 km of the canal proper (in Rajasthan) had been completed, and work was in progress on a further 65 km. It was expected that Stage I would be complete by October 1973. Stage II *may* be completed by 1978; but there are those in the Government of India who question the economic wisdom of completing it—as, indeed, does the author, for reasons that will become clear in the course of this book. Colonization under the Canal, which will be fully discussed in later chapters, made slow progress until 1968, when the programme was accelerated. By 1970–1, 167,000 hectares were under irrigation for *kharif* cropping: perennial irrigation awaits the completion of the Pong dam.

The Tarai of Uttar Pradesh and Bihar

'Tarai' is the name given to the flat belt of country running along the foot of the southernmost range of the Himalayan system, roughly from the gorge of the Ganges at Hardwar in Uttar Pradesh to the northeast corner of Bihar;[16] it passes into the very similar country known as the Duars in northern Bengal and Assam.[17] Part of the Tarai lies in Nepal,[18] and is therefore excluded from this study; while, since the author has studied the Tarai in the field only in the Naini Tal, Pilibhit, and Lakhimpur-Kheri Districts of Uttar Pradesh, attention will be given mainly to those areas, with but a distant nod in the direction of northeastern Uttar Pradesh (Basti and Gorakhpur Districts) and Bihar.

The Tarai today is a narrow belt, seldom, in the author's experience, as wide as the 60 km quoted by Legris.[19] Into it there descend from the hills innumerable streams, large and small, which first throw down the larger particles in their load (boulders, stones, and gravel) to form the belt of highly pervious ground known as Bhabar. Where the Bhabar meets the plains springs break out, and these, together with water from the streams themselves, serve to make parts of the Tarai a swamp under natural conditions,[20] with the help of such additional factors as continuing earth movements, and possibly the tendency of ancient irrigation works to cut across natural stream-lines and thus further to disorganize the drainage. Under natural conditions the Tarai was an area of tiger-infested jungle, here consisting of tall grasses with scattered trees, there of thicker forest dominated by *sal* (*Shorea robusta*).[21] When the jungle is cleared, swampiness is less in evidence, especially in the dry winter months, when the water-table lies at a depth of 1–3 metres; but during the monsoon it rises to within a metre of the surface, and flooding is a serious menace to colonization. Here, then, is a natural environment that contrasts strongly with that of the plains of Rajasthan.

Moreover, the average rainfall is much higher here: 115–27 cm in the Naini Tal Tarai (with a marked July maximum, but a little winter rain), increasing gradually as one moves eastward until the 250 cm mark is reached and passed in the Duars. Temperatures in

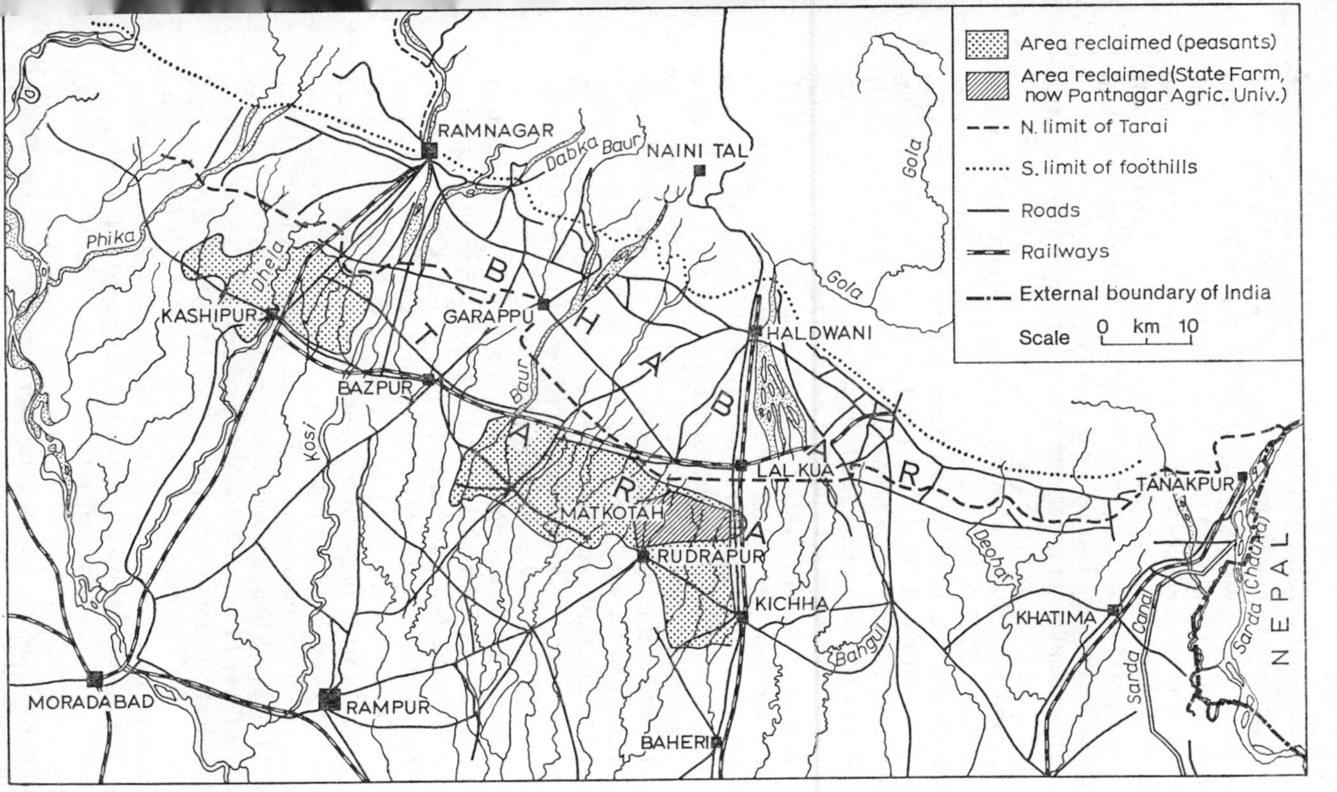

Source: Based upon Survey of India map, with the permission of the Surveyor-General of India

Map 3 The Naini Tal Tarai

the west are much as in Rajasthan, with a cool winter; but the eastern Tarai has a less continental climate. The whole Tarai, not surprisingly, is floored by recent alluvium. Most of this is of a loamy nature, but there is considerable textural variation, both in plan (from sandier soil on slight ridges and near rivers to loams and clay loams in depressions and on gentle slopes) and in profile (for shallow surface soils are underlain by sand and gravel, the disposition of lenses of permeable and impermeable strata being such that artesian wells are locally feasible).[22] Soils are naturally fertile: well stocked with calcium, potassium, and organic matter but poor in phosphates (but see below, p. 132).

Undoubtedly the Tarai has retreated before the hand of man: M. H. Rahman has claimed that it formerly stretched south as far as the middle Gogra.[23] As will be shown, settlement has apparently now advanced, now retreated; and the question must be posed why enough of it has remained to provide a basis for colonization in the last two decades. Undoubtedly much of the reason lies in the incidence of malaria. The Tarai and Duars are shown on S. R. Christophers' and J. A. Sinton's *Malaria Map of India* as a striking belt of hyperendemicity;[24] blackwater fever was apt to occur as a result of especially virulent malaria;[25] while R. S. Srivastava and A. K. Chakrabarti found *Anopheles fluviatilis*, adapted to swampy conditions, to be the sole vector.[26] Death rates were high: 45·3 per thousand in the Kashipur area, 90·5 per cent of the deaths being attributed to 'fever'.[27] Tarai tracts farther east, for example those in Gorakhpur District, had a similarly bad record.

As in the case of the Ceylon Dry Zone (parts of which were in fact called 'the Tarai of Ceylon') the Tarai does not seem always to have suffered under the dead hand of malaria: it is 'full of ancient ruins, fine old mango groves, sculptures and wells: the remains of thriving cities'.[28] Civilization seems to have flourished there (at least in Gorakhpur District) in the fourth century A.D., but to have been in decline in the seventh; and population to have been much denser in the seventeenth and possibly the eighteenth centuries than in British times.[29] It may be that, as Jules Sion suggested, political insecurity led to the decay of irrigation works, which in turn led to stagnant waters and the irruption of malaria;[30] or irrigation channels may have cut natural drainage lines and produced malarial marsh; but, whatever the cause of the decline of civilizations in the Tarai, it cannot be gainsaid that malaria was a prime reason for the failure of settlement to re-establish itself in British times. Remission of land revenue failed to attract more than a few permanent cultivators;[31] irrigation works lapsed; and in some inter-censal periods population actually declined.[32]

Until the post-independence era of active colonization, the people who managed to survive the hazards of life in the Tarai were largely tribal, and included cultivating peoples like the Tharus and Bhuksas, who seem to have developed a highish degree of immunity to malaria; the Bhuksas are described by D. Clyde as skilled cultivators.[33] There were also a fluctuating number of immigrant plainsmen, while hillmen came down for the winter months to pasture their cattle. The grazing in the Naini Tal Tarai was so plentiful that it provided relief for adjacent Districts.[34]

The Tarai was thus another region of difficulty, though for very different reasons from those prevailing in Marusthali. 'The life in this tract, like that of the rest of the Tarai as a whole, is one of continual struggle for existence against depredation of wild animals, rank and vigorous vegetation, enervating climate, bad drinking water and malaria with resulting high general and infantile mortality and low birth rate,' wrote one pair of authors about the Sarda area.[35] Another author, writing as recently as 1946, concluded that 'Oppressive moist heat, intense frosts, incidence of wild animals and malaria render human habitation impossible in this tract [the UP Tarai] which must, for a long time to come, remain the exclusive domain for animals and cattle';[36] and he went on to say that the need for anti-malarial measures, drainage schemes, and mechanized farming rendered this an area for the capitalist, not for the 'tenant of modest means'.

Yet, as will be seen, peasant colonization has in fact been accomplished—the revolutionary factor here, as in the Ceylon Dry Zone, having been the use of DDT spraying against the malarial mosquito.[37] The extent to which the physical difficulties of the Tarai have been overcome will be discussed in succeeding chapters. It is sufficient to say here that, between independence and 1972, over 50,000 hectares of the UP Tarai have been colonized for agriculture.[38] Work has now ceased there. Further inroads on the Tarai jungles have been made in Bihar, notably in Purnea District.

Greater Malnad: the Hill Areas of Malnad, Wynad, the Nilgiris, and the High Ranges of Kerala

On a journey from east to west across Mysore one travels, for the most part, across the great open plateaux of the Maidan, drained mainly by the Krishna (Kistna) and the Kaveri (Cauvery) and their tributaries. In westernmost Mysore lie the precipitous scarps and steeply plunging valleys of the Western Ghats. But between the Maidan and the scarps, in a belt in which the headwaters of the Krishna and the Kaveri are under attack from predatory streams that plunge down the face of the Ghats, there lies a belt some 30 to 80 kilometres wide, Malnad, the 'hill country'.[39] Malnad is a distinctive region of rounded, tumbled, and mainly forested hills, intersected by winding, sometimes swampy valleys, which contrasts strongly both with the open Maidan to the east and with the wild Ghats to the west. The northern Malnad lies mainly at 500–600 metres; but south of about 13° North the ground rises, in Coorg, to over 1,800 metres. South of Coorg similar, but generally lower hill country is to be found in the Wynad of Kerala, behind Kozhikode (Calicut), and in places around the slopes of the great mass of the Nilgiri Hills (whose elevation and steep bounding slopes lift them, however, into a different physiographic category).[40]

Farther south again, beyond the great gap of Palghat, analogous, though rather more accidented country occupies the lower part of the High Ranges on the Kerala–Madras border: though here the steep scarp is to the *east* (as where the Cardamom Hills drop to the plains of Madurai District); and the more gently sloping land of 'Malnad' type lies in the upper catchments of *westward*-flowing rivers like the Periyar.[41] For the purposes of this book, and for want of a better *nom de pays*, these hill areas collectively will be called 'Greater Malnad'.

Greater Malnad, thus defined, stretches altogether over 10° of latitude, and there are considerable variations in climate from one end to the other: in particular, the length of the dry season diminishes southward. But all the hills in question have in common a heavy and reliable or fairly reliable rainfall, the annual average varying from 250 cm or over in the west to 100 cm or under in the east. July is generally the wettest month. Throughout these hilly lands, temperature is to a varying extent mitigated by the effects of altitude. The heavy rains give rise to a natural vegetation cover of moist deciduous, or even evergreen forest in the west which passes into dry deciduous forest in the east, with montane forest at higher altitudes:[42] but human intervention has intruded cultivation, *Lantana* scrub, and grassland into the forest.

It is not easy to generalize about the soils of Greater Malnad with any precision; perhaps they are best described as ferralitic or ferruginous, with many of the failings (in terms of leached nutrient and low organic content) of soils of those categories.[43] The author's own observations suggest that soils vary considerably, notably in texture from sandy and stony loam to red-brown or chocolate clay loam—probably in response to parent material and slope.[44] In some places there is a notable catena effect, valley-bottom soils being markedly darker and heavier. Soils in the wetter areas (for example, Wynad) are acid. There is also much variation in depth of soil.

Greater Malnad shows up on a land-use map as a belt with a relatively low proportion of land in cultivation and a relatively high proportion in forest;[45] and, on a population map, as a discontinuous belt of sparse population[46]—sparse, that is, by Indian standards. The discontinuities arise from such pockets of higher density as those in southern Malnad and Coorg (where there are coffee plantations) and in such tea-planting areas as the Nilgiris, parts of Wynad, and the High Ranges of Kerala.

In the belts of sparser population there are, broadly speaking, two groups of peoples. First, there are tribal peoples: Naikda in Malnad;[47] Yerava, Kurumba, Kuliya, and others in Coorg;[48] Kurumba, Irula, and Mudugars in Wynad and the lower Nilgiris;[49] Mannan and Muthuvan in the High Ranges of Kerala.[50] Most of these tribes are cultivators, and amongst them the practice of shifting cultivation was formerly more widespread than at present.[51] Tribes differ greatly *inter se* in terms of crop patterns and agricultural standards:[52] many tribesmen now find employment as labourers on tea and coffee estates and elsewhere. Some have become involved in colonization schemes.

In the second place, there are plains (or plateau) cultivators who have penetrated, and are increasingly penetrating, the jungle fastnesses of Greater Malnad. In Malnad proper, Kannada-speakers (the majority group in Mysore) form a scattered population growing paddy and *ragi* in the north (where only just over 2½ per cent of the land surface is cultivated), paddy and spices in central Malnad (where the figure is nearly 15 per cent), and paddy with cardamoms and coffee in the south and in Coorg (17–30 per cent cultivated).[53] In the Kerala hills north of Palghat there is a long history of spontaneous settlement by plainsmen (mainly rice and spice cultivators)[54] while in some places, notably the Attapaddy Valley, 'jemmies' (a corruption of '*jamindar*', or '*zamindar*'), originally feudal chiefs owing allegiance to the Zamorin of Calicut, established control over tribal villages, which paid produce in return for protection. The British seem to have misconceived the position and given the jemmies 'ownership' of large forest tracts.[55] ('Private' forests in Kerala were nationalized on 10 May 1971; 'cultivable' portions were to be distributed among the landless.)[56] There is also very considerable recent and spontaneous colonization in parts of the High Ranges south of the Palghat Gap, notably in the region of the Periyar Reservoir; rubber-planting has climbed the lower slopes in the same region, and large acreages of high forest have been under-brushed so that cardamoms may be grown under the trees. Manganese mining has also brought settlement to some parts of Malnad. Quite apart, then, from the government-organized colonization shortly to be noted, these hills have for some time been a region of pioneer colonization, whether by coffee and tea planters[57] or by pioneer peasants and labourers. Characteristics of the pioneer fringe are very evident: notably a low degree of urbanization, and the poor development of communications[58] outside the plantation areas or tracts recently opened up (for example, by the improvement of roads to the Goa frontier).

Is there, then, a simple explanation for the fact that Greater Malnad has preserved uncultivated but cultivable land into the era of India's independence? Is such land merely residual, land that has not so far been encroached upon by the age-long process by which the peasant of the plains (latterly aided and abetted by the European planter) has spread his cultivation higher and higher, ever farther into the jungle-clad hills, sweeping before him, or absorbing, the forest-dwelling tribal peoples? A number of writers appear to have come to this conclusion. Thus Jacques Dupuis, perhaps following Vidal de la Blache, claims:

'Depuis des millénaires, les Indiens du Sud cultivent les plaines. Jusqu'au XIXème siècle, ils ne tentèrent point d'exploiter les massifs verdoyants qu'elles environnent. Seuls firent exception les groupes fugitifs qui, pour échapper aux invasions musulmanes, gagnèrent les massifs occidentaux ou orientaux . . . Les Indiens des plaines avaient leur système économique et leur genre de vie, non adaptés aux conditions de la montagne . . . C'est pourquoi il faut attendre l'initiation des Anglais pour assister à une véritable colonisation des montagnes du Sud.'[59]

But the answer does not seem to be so simple. Deshpande gives figures that show, for a number of *talukas* in northern Malnad, how population declined in the period 1901–21 (in Haliyal and Yellapur *talukas* consistently from 1901–41).[60] Other authors, notably L. S. Bhat and S. Silva, have claimed that, although Malnad proper has had a complicated history, it was prosperous until the middle of the eighteenth century and was a rich rice-growing area in the time of the Vijayanagar empire;[61] the evidence of inscriptions (from the time of Ashoka) and of abandoned channels and terraces, is quoted.[62] Silva goes so far as to claim that Malnad was the richest tract in the kingdom of Haidar Ali. Similar evidence for 'an abundant population' in the past has been cited in respect of the High Ranges of Kerala and their foothills.[63]

Much research on the settlement of Greater Malnad remains to be done. But it is possible to hazard a guess that, as in the Tarai, it ebbed and flowed; and that the period of vigorous British impact in the nineteenth century was a time when indigenous settlement was at a low ebb. A number of specific factors, apart from the general conditions of remoteness and forest cover, seem then to have been operative. In the first place, it is quite clear that hyperendemic malaria then lay like a pall over the whole of Greater Malnad, excepting only the higher parts of the Nilgiris and the High Ranges, and that it remained until the coming of modern methods of control.[64] The vector was *Anopheles fluviatilis*, whose larvae flourish in the innumerable small streams of these hill areas, though in larger streams there may be sufficient larvae-eating fish to control their numbers.[65] It is also quite clear that malaria had a great deal to do with high rates of mortality and with low rates of population increase, and, equally, that it was especially apt to attack immigrants from less malarial regions. Some malariologists and others have gone further, and claimed that malaria was responsible for actual depopulation: thus Jaswant Singh and C. D. Kariapa wrote of Coorg in 1949: 'Of late years the state of malaria in Coorg reached an alarming pitch, so much so that the economic conditions of Coorg were rapidly deteriorating. Village after village was being deserted. Coffee plantations were not fully functioning for lack of labour.'[66]

Possibly, then, malaria became more potent as time went on; possibly it did not exist at all in earlier times, as has already been suggested for the Tarai. It is tempting, indeed, to state as a hypothesis that the irruption of malaria, again as in the Tarai, had something to do with a breakdown in orderly government.

Secondly, Greater Malnad has had its share of commotion and this has had, from time to time and from place to place, a depressing and even depopulating effect. Thus of northern Malnad J. M. Campbell wrote, 'It was almost literally true that owing to the conduct of the Sonda chief and of Maratha freebooters there was little to govern except trees and wild beasts,' and quotes Thomas Munro as saying that in 1799 most of the land was 'destitute' and the population reduced by a third.[67] Again, Tipu Sultan, when he annexed Coorg in 1785, sent 'about 85,000 souls' to his capital at Srirangapatnam (Seringapatam).[68] True, he sent people from Mysore to replace them; but by the time the Vira Raja of Coorg had, through alliance with the British, regained his territory 'the repeated devastations of which it had been the theatre, left it little better than a vast wild'.[69] The Vira Raja had himself devastated wide areas east of his state; and Buchanan found much depopulated land there.[70] Wynad, too, was the scene of much fighting and tended to be a refuge for armies on the run, and, after the cession to Britain, of rebels.[71] Tipu also practised a scorched earth policy in Malnad in order to deny pepper and spices to the British.[72]

Tipu and his like did not only cause devastation by waging war, however. There is ample evidence that burdensome and excessive systems of taxation led to the abandonment of holdings in these difficult hill areas, where, in earlier times, assessments had been modest in view of the difficulty of clearing waste and of countering erosion.[73]

During British times, as has been seen, land in some of the hill areas tended to be brought—or to come back—into cultivation; nevertheless, there were three factors tending, locally at any rate, in the opposite direction. First, land that had been planted in coffee or some other commercial crop might be abandoned: thus unprofitability forced the closure of a number of coffee gardens in northern Malnad by 1890,[74] while leaf disease ruined a number of coffee estates in Wynad, whose landscape certainly carries the insignia of abandonment.[75] Again, the British revenue settlement of Wynad, according to Logan, broke up the pre-existing system of serfdom, the former serfs choosing to work on the new coffee estates, so that their masters' lands went partly out of cultivation.[76] Finally, the frequent complaint in hill areas—that the British, in creating forest reservations, encroached on cultivable land—is also heard here, notably in northern Malnad.[77]

The story of the movement of the pioneer fringe of agricultural settlement into Greater Malnad is thus not merely that of a single, simple advance. Even if one goes back no farther than the middle of the eighteenth century, there has been considerable oscillation of the frontier, with periods of retreat because of such factors as malaria, insecurity, punitive action, the revenue system, and the failure of crops. Some of these factors rely in turn on the position of the area on the forested flank of the great zones of movement and conflict within southern peninsular India.

Now, with malaria thoroughly controlled by DDT spraying,[78] it is possible not only for individuals to continue the march of spontaneous settlement into the areas left empty or under-cultivated by the forces just discussed, but also for government agencies to plan state-assisted colonization. Thus the Mysore government has formed a Malnad Development Board. Investigations have been made, also in Malnad, of land likely to be available, on account of relative gentleness of slope, for the extension of paddy cultivation.[79] A number of small colonization schemes, some run on a co-operative basis, have been established in northern Malnad. Further colonization schemes there are contemplated. Tibetan refugees are settled at Bylakuppe, west of Mysore City and very near the former frontier of Coorg. In Kerala the considerable Wynad colonization scheme covers well over 12,000 hectares; another in the High Ranges covers about 1,200 hectares; while in the Attapaddy Valley, behind Kozhikode (Calicut), land has been opened up for tribal peoples and others. There was also a very interesting little colony, mainly of Badagas, at Thengumarahada, in the valley of the Moyar river at the foot of the

Nilgiris. The Tamil Nadu government is opening up tea and cocoa plantations and colonization schemes in the Nilgiris and in the hills of Kanyakumari (Cape Comorin) and the adjacent area for Indians returning from Ceylon and Burma.[80]

4

Areas of Colonization: 2

Dandakaranya[1]

THE name 'Dandakaranya' is nowadays given to what is perhaps the most fascinating of all the regions examined in this and the preceding chapter—the region of forested plateaux and scarps lying behind the Eastern Ghats and between the rivers Godavari and Mahanadi (Map 3). The name is derived from a supposed identification with the Dandaka forest of the *Ramayana*.[2] A large part of Dandakaranya as here defined is covered by the area of operation of the Dandakaranya Development Authority (which comprises Bastar District of Madhya Pradesh, and Koraput and Kalahandi Districts of Orissa); but for the purpose of this book Dandakaranya will be taken to include also the very similar and well-forested country in the Chanda District of Maharashtra and in the Adilabad District of Andhra Pradesh (except where the context makes it clear that only the Authority's area is concerned).[3]

Thus defined, Dandakaranya covers a vast area some 400 km from east to west and over 300 from north to south. Bastar District alone is the size of Switzerland. The plateau is the dominant landform: relatively small areas at about 900 m poised high behind the Eastern Ghats, or at 750–900 m around Koraput town; the much larger area, 190 km from north to south and 80–130 km from east to west, of the great Jeypore–Bastar Plateau; the considerable Kalahandi Plateau, east of the last-named, at about 240–300 m, and, away in the north of Dandakaranya, the Kanker–Paralkote Plateau (270–410 m) and the Chhattisgarh Plateau (or plain) at about the same height; to the southwest lies the Malkangiri Plateau (W. V. Grigson's 'Great Southern Plain'),[4] draining away to the Godavari. The higher plateaux in this great series drop by prominent, beautiful, and often spectacular scarps to their lower neighbours: frequently the scarps are fretted and ravined by stream action, most notably on the highly dissected western edge of the Jeypore–Bastar Plateau (where there lies the wild, tumbled country known, north of the River Indravati, as the Abujhmar Hills, and, south of that river, as the Bailadila Ridge, which has rich resources

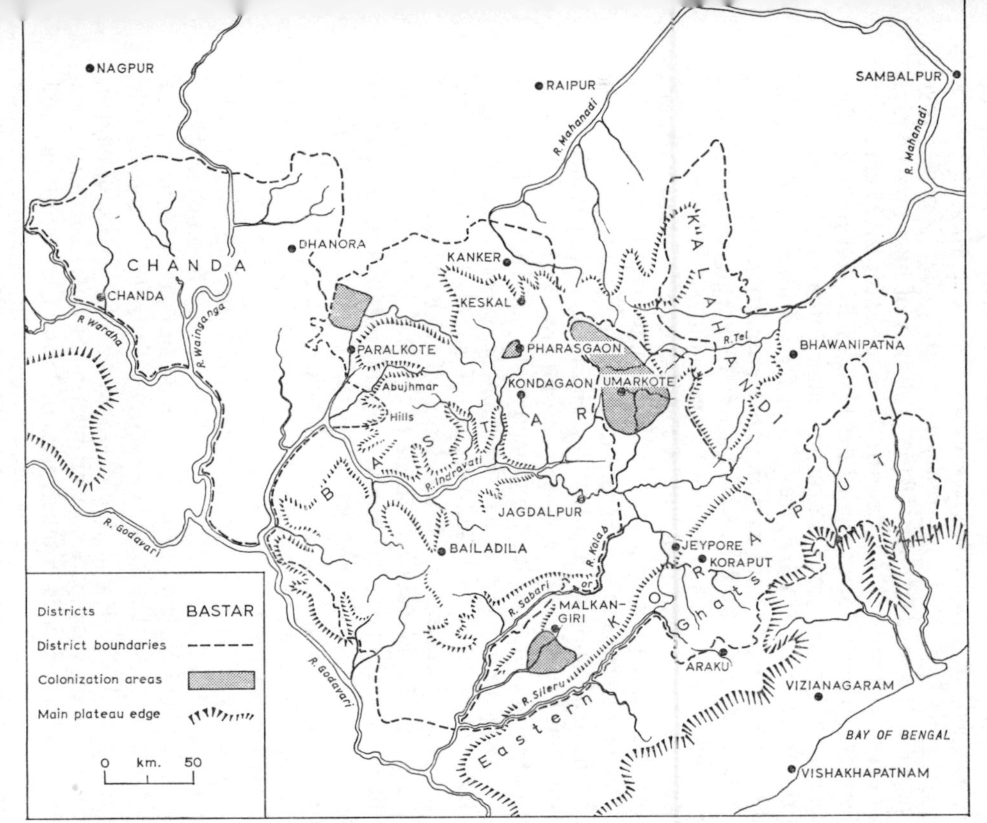

Source: Based upon Survey of India map, with the permission of the Surveyor-General of India

Map 4 Dandakaranya

of iron ore).[5] Plateaux and scarps alike are developed in crystalline rocks, largely in the gneissic complex but also in rocks of the Dharwar and Cuddapah systems.

The whole of Dandakaranya lies within the Tropics, and, in spite of altitude, temperatures never drop sufficiently to hamper cultivation (Jagdalpur, 565 m: January mean 18·9 °C.; May mean—the highest—31 °C.). On the mean annual rainfall map Dandakaranya appears as the southern part of the proboscis of high precipitation that extends westward from Bengal: the figure exceeds 125 cm everywhere except in the lower part of the Malkangiri Plateau, and often exceeds 175 cm. Hence, it is usually claimed, the dominance of *sal* forest, contrasting with drier formations farther west. But the region suffers an extreme form of monsoonal concentration of rainfall, and, as will be shown in chapter 6, the danger of inadequate rainfall at the beginning and end of the southwest monsoon.

Soils on the rolling plateaux of Dandakaranya follow catenary principles, being noticeably heavier in the valley bottoms and sandier on the intervening swells. The sandier soils are shallow, porous, and unretentive of moisture; and low in plant nutrients (especially phosphates and organic matter, less so in nitrogen and potash). Most soils are deficient in at least one main nutrient. The relatively low humus content in soil that has 'been under forest growth for centuries' is ascribed to the tribal practice of 'setting fire to the undergrowth which prevents the accumulation of dried leaves and decayed vegetation'.[6] In the Paralkote Zone of the Dandakaranya Development Authority, however, surface layers retain a thin layer of organic matter, and soils generally are deeper, and sometimes loamier, than elsewhere. Good red clay loams appear in the Umarkote Zone and in Chanda District; and black soils in places in the Malkangiri Zone.

Soil survey of Dandakaranya, though proceeding in praiseworthy fashion (see below, pp. 132–3, 144), is naturally incomplete. However, one thing is clear: although Dandakaranya's soils are varied (and include some that have to be rejected for colonization, usually on grounds of shallowness, but also because of impeded drainage), they are for the most part no whit inferior to soils that have been cultivated for centuries in other parts of India. Clearly it is not soil quality that has left so many wide stretches of the region covered by the forest on whose 'interminable' nature nineteenth-century authors were apt to comment.[7]

For even today much of the plateau land of Dandakaranya, as well as the steep scarps, is forested, largely with moist tropical deciduous species, *sal* being dominant (though in the lower, hotter, and drier Malkangiri Plateau a drier forest with teak takes over). Much of the forest is either reserved or protected: over half of the area of Bastar District is so designated. A great deal of the forest lies on comparatively gentle slopes, so that its general retention on conservational grounds is hard to justify.

Dandakaranya shows up on a population map, not surprisingly, as an area of relatively sparse population. Its peoples are in fact predominantly tribal, and consist mainly of various groups of Gonds:[8] many of these tribal peoples were, and are, cultivators, but shifting cultivation among them is declining, except in such difficult areas as the Abujhmar Hills.[9] Apart from those in Chanda District (which was part of the Central Provinces) and in Adilabad District (which was part of Hyderabad state) they were ruled, until accession to the Indian Union, by princely rulers whose origins are obscure: some of them may have been 'Rajput pilgrims on their way back as pilgrims from Puri, others aboriginal chiefs'.[10] The history of Bastar has been particularly turbulent; and some years ago the life of the former Maharaja ended in tragedy.[11]

What factors made Dandakaranya a forest-covered tribal fastness, the home of some of the strangest 'states' in the old Indian Empire, and with, apparently, land to spare for a massive programme of colonization by independent India? Much history hereabouts remains obscure. But it seems clear that, apart from penetration by pilgrims and adventurers of the sort just mentioned, and apart from a few known raids (e.g. by Muslims in 1610)[12] Dandakaranya remained on the whole remote and aloof from the main currents of Indian history (though some of its rulers did owe allegiance to the Mughals, and, later, to the Bhonslas of that Maratha frontier post, Nagpur).[13] The whole of the belt of jungle-clad hills that runs from the mouths of the Narmada (Narbada) and Tapti east to Chota Nagpur and Dandakaranya has, of course, tended to be a frontier zone, containing the plains civilizations that ebbed and flowed to the north of it.[14] When this defensive line of the Deccan proper was turned, it was usually either by means of the east coast plain, or down through the plateaux of Maharashtra,[15] which are not unlike Dandakaranya in relief, but are distinguished by their lower rainfall and sparser and more easily cleared vegetation, and by their black cotton soils, long cultivated, and thickly strewn with villages on which a marching army could live. Dandakaranya remained densely forested, thinly peopled, obviously to be avoided given the existence of the east coast and inland Maharashtran routes.

Even when plainsmen eventually encroached into the ancient Gond kingdom of Chanda,[16] the major bounding scarps, which probably presented themselves as jungle-covered and tiger-infested mountains, protected Dandakaranya's inner keep, the higher plateaux of Bastar, from being overwhelmed. Similarly, as Oriya settlement penetrated the middle Mahanadi Basin and the Khondmals, it fell short of the higher plateaux of Kalahandi.[17] There was *some* nineteenth-century immigration: of coastal people into the Jeypore Zamindari after a famine in 1876;[18] of Gonds from Chhattisgarh to Kondagaon, on the Jeypore–Bastar Plateau;[19] of plainsmen into Bastar, partly as a result of efforts by Political Agents to 'modernize' the state, which provoked an uprising in 1876;[20] and of other plainsmen into Kalahandi (whose Khond tribesmen rose in 1882 and massacred the incomers).[21] But the effect of movements such as these on the spread of cultivation was not great. Quite apart from physiography and the hostility of the tribal people, there were other factors tending to discourage the settlement of those who scaled the bounding slopes. One of these was the absence, till recent times, of roads or other communications within Dandakaranya.[22] But far more serious was malaria. The upper plateaux, in particular, long had a terrible reputation for hyperendemic malaria and for blackwater fever; and, although local tribal peoples enjoyed a measure of immunity, immigrants had no such protection.[23] Perhaps it is mainly to malaria, combined with the forbidding steepness of the main Eastern Ghats scarp, that one may attribute the otherwise astonishing fact that throughout Indian history peoples and conquerors moved along the east coast route, so near to Dandakaranya, without having more than the slightest apparent effect on its history or its people.

So it is that these widespread plateaux of Dandakaranya have preserved readily cultivable land for the modern era of government-sponsored colonization. There are a number of small, co-operative colonies in the Chanda District of Maharashtra (where also the Dina irrigation project may open up 12,000 hectares of waste and forest land).[24] The government of Andhra Pradesh had by January 1972 settled 1,000 Bengali refugees in ten villages near Khagaznagar, in Adilabad District; as many more settlers were to come. But the most considerable efforts have been those of the Dandakaranya Development Authority, operating on land made available by the state governments of Madhya Pradesh and Orissa, to settle refugees (Bengalis and Santals) from East Pakistan (now Bangladesh). Twenty-five per cent of the land cleared has, however, been made available to the states for the settlement of local tribal people. By the end of 1971, 54,508 hectares had been reclaimed and 16,061 refugees and 3,038 tribal peoples had been settled.

Assam

Chapter 2 has shown that nineteenth-century Assam (like, it may be argued, such areas as Dandakaranya and the Ceylon Dry Zone at the present time)[25] displayed the geographical characteristics of an under-peopled Southeast Asian country, rather than those of an over-peopled part of the Indian subcontinent. In spite of the massive spread of tea plantations and of Bengali settlement in the nineteenth century and in the first half of the twentieth century, Spate found it possible in 1957 to write of Assam as presenting 'the phenomenon . . . of an underdeveloped or even underpopulated monsoon country. Nowhere in India does the term "culturable waste" approach nearer to reality.'[26] The scale of the agricultural colonization accomplished in the plains of Assam since independence in fact warrants their inclusion in the present chapter as an area of major colonization.[27]

Broadly two kinds of land have been used for colonization here: remaining areas of wasteland, in forest or otherwise; and areas of former Assamese village settlement which had become liable to deep flooding and had therefore been evacuated. The first category of land is exemplified by the Kaki Scheme, in Nowgong District, where over 5,250 hectares have been colonized by agriculturists since 1951. This colony has been developed on flat or gently sloping land between the Kapili and Jamuna rivers, which flow north to the Brahmaputra through the wide hollow between the Mikir, Rengma, North Cachar, and Jaintia Hills. The area is shown on Survey of India maps[28] as under grass, with patches of forests which become more frequent southeastwards towards the Darapathar refugee colony. This was opened in 1968, and there would appear to be potential for future development, though slopes steepen as the hills are approached. Eighteen colonies, covering nearly 4,500 hectares in Cachar District, and the Saithsila Project in Kamrup District (1,050 hectares), are similarly on relict wasteland.

An example of the second category of land lies in the Barpeta Subdivision of Kamrup District. Here Baghbar colony, for refugees from what is now Bangladesh, was established in 1950, and covers about 2,800 hectares; while Gobindpur and Theka colonies, also for refugees, were established in nearby areas in 1965, and by December 1968 had covered about 600 hectares. Before the severe earthquake of 1897, which *inter alia* destroyed Shillong, most of the Barpeta–Baghbar area was covered by closely spaced Assamese villages, as is attested by contemporary maps.[29] More recent maps show not only that such major tributaries of the Brahmaputra as the Beki and Manas have been subject to drastic changes of course (though these are likely to take place in any case, without the intervention of earthquakes) but also that most of the Assamese villages have disappeared, to be replaced by low-lying wasteland or grazing reserves, with many very large *bils* (depressions filled with water during the southwest monsoon flood season).[30] The 1897 earthquake does indeed appear to have changed the level of the land hereabouts;[31] and rendered the formerly cultivated area liable to floods of such ferocity and depth that customary Assamese technology proved quite unable to maintain cultivation. Bengali cultivators, especially those from Bangladesh, are on the other hand used to a semi-aquatic existence.[32] There was a certain amount of encroachment by Bengali Muslims before independence. More recently the colonization schemes just mentioned have been established, though not without difficulty, partly because of flooding (see below, p. 128), partly for reasons of maladministration (see below, p. 247). It may be that other areas in the lands along the Brahmaputra were evacuated after the 1897 earthquake, and that these also could be recolonized—using Bengali, rather than Assamese land-use technology. Certainly there is a small colony for refugees in Goalpara District, though T. F. Rasmussen suggests that the reason for the availability of land there is that early Bengali settlers preferred the *ryotwari* tenure prevalent in the rest of the Assam plains to the *zamindari* tenure imposed on the District by the British.[33]

Rasmussen further writes, in a more general context: 'Even a casual visitor looking at the landscape will notice the large areas of uncultivated land in the Assam Valley . . . There are reasons for thinking that there is still room for a higher density of rural population.'[34] The author certainly gained the same impression during a necessarily hurried journey in Assam; and so, by implication, did Spate, as will be remembered from the quotation earlier in this section. Yet the government of Assam has been at pains to stress that large areas recorded as culturable waste are not available for cultivation, because of encroachment or physical unsuitability. According to the results of its own 'Technical Committee',[35] there was in 1963–5 a total of 126,178 hectares of culturable waste in blocks of 15 *bighas* (2 hectares) and over, made up thus:

	Hectares
Area under encroachment	27,144
Area not suitable for cultivation	49,175
Area available for immediate settlement	12,188
Area that may be available after reclamation by manual labour	14,247
Area that may be available after reclamation by mechanized process	23,424

The culturable waste in blocks of 100 *bighas* (13·4 hectares) and over amounted to 95,399 hectares according to this Committee, but to 136,036 hectares according to an earlier Committee of 1959–60.[36] Further, the state government claimed that, although 11·34 per cent of the total area of the state was forest reserve, the percentage should be raised to 40 per cent to fulfil national forest policy; and that, although land has been taken from grazing reserves for cultivation, this process 'cannot go on indefinitely'.[37] During the war, it may be noted, the government had appointed a Special Officer to see whether dereservation of grazing grounds and disforestation were possible; while Rasmussen concluded that 'With improved forest cultivation the State's need for forest products may be satisfied with a smaller area of forest land' and that 'If the hill areas can be utilized in planned forest production, the area of reserved forests in the plains might be reduced thus providing more land for agriculture.'[38]

The question of the availability of land for colonization by refugees has become a matter of political controversy. The state government claimed in December 1968 that it had agreed to take 12,000 families (of whom 10,700 had already been settled) and could, for lack of land, take no more. The Union government accordingly agreed at that time to settle refugees remaining in camps in Assam in other parts of India, especially in Dandakaranya. But this policy was challenged in the Lok Sabha by Dhireswar Kalita, a Communist member from Assam, who, *inter alia*, sought information on the possibility of settling refugees in the North East Frontier Agency; and by Bengali refugees themselves, who in January 1969 demanded resettlement in Assam, rather than in Dandakaranya, and also an independent inquiry into the availability of land in the state. In October 1969 a sub-committee from the Union Ministry of Rehabilitation was trying to persuade the government of Assam to find more land for refugees, 12,000 of whom were then in camps in the state.[39] In 1971 Assam had to cope with the arrival of yet more refugees after the tragic happenings in Bangladesh; and its defensiveness about its land became all the more understandable. The establishment of an independent Bangladesh has halted the flow for the time being at any rate.

Clearly no answer can be given here to the question of the availability of land for future colonization in Assam (but see below, pp. 148–9). The issue is clouded by social and political considerations connected with the relation between Assamese and Bengali in Assam, itself a consequence of massive migrations which have given the Assamese, though they are in a majority (57·1 per cent in 1961)[40] some of the complexes of minorities. In this respect they behave like the Sinhalese in a similar situation in Ceylon.[41]

Smaller Pockets of Colonization

In addition to the five regions already discussed there are several smaller areas in which colonization has taken place, or may take place in future.

The Chambal Valley

The River Chambal rises in the Malwa Plateau not far from Indore and flows first north across the Plateau, then across scarplands of Vindhyan sandstones, and finally northeast to join the Yamuna (Jumna) below Agra.[42] The Malwa Plateau will be dealt with later: but first there must be mentioned two regions of small-scale colonization: the ravine-lands of the Chambal below Kota, and the belts in the Middle Chambal that have become irrigable as a result of the construction of dams in the Vindhyan scarplands.

The spectacular ravine-lands of the lower Chambal, like those of the Yamuna, have often been described: 'immense pandemonia of ravines . . . not visible till we began to descend into them some two or three miles from the bed of the river', wrote Sir W. H. Sleeman;[43] 'a labyrinth of rugged ravines and green valleys covered with acacia jungle', wrote W. Crooke.[44] The ravines, which cover some 4,800 sq. km, are in fact cut in the terraces of older alluvium originally laid down by the river system when it was flowing at a higher level. Two natural circumstances have much to do with their formation. First, this is a relatively dry area (annual rainfall about 65 cm) but with a tendency to receive heavy storms in the southwest monsoon. Secondly, the alluvium, a sandy or clayey loam, contains layers of *kankar* (limestone concretions) which hold up percolating water, and so increase run-off.

It may well be that, although the Chambal ravines are still growing at the expense of the alluvial terraces, erosion began long ago. Irfan Habib quotes references to the ravine-lands and to their infestation by rebels in Mughal times.[45] Dacoits still haunt the ravines; and their control is one motive for reclamation.

Reclamation of ravines is certainly no new thing. It is an indigenous solution long adopted;[46] proposals for government action go back nearly a hundred years;[47] and, in 1963, the author studied efforts to reclaim ravines near Morena, and to settle local villagers and ex-servicemen. Not much of this work is strictly colonization since it largely takes place from established villages. Undoubtedly there is *physical* scope for this process, which involves the construction of terraces, bunds, and drainage systems; whether it is economically worthwhile is another matter (see below, p. 155), as is the theory that dacoity may thereby be controlled. It may be that, if to check erosion is the prime necessity, controlled grazing is sufficient; perhaps it is all that is worth doing. However, an aerial survey of these and other ravine-lands, and their reclamation within fifteen years, has been recommended;[48] and in June, 1971 the Madhya Pradesh government was pressing the central government for a survey of 8,000 hectares with a view to the settlement of refugees from what was then East Pakistan.[49]

A quite different category of land is, or may become, available for colonization in the middle Chambal valley below Kota, land which is benefiting from the Chambal Multi-purpose Project. This involves a great reservoir, Gandhisagar, held up by a dam in the Vindhyan sandstone scarplands, a barrage at Kota, and a right-bank and a left-bank canal taking off thence;[50] and a further dam at Ranapratapsagar, between Gandhisagar and Kota. The Project is administered jointly by the two beneficiary states, Madhya Pradesh and Rajasthan. The land to receive irrigation under the two canals will, for the most part, be that already under rainfed cultivation, much of it precariously (mean annual rainfall about 65–75 cm). But there are areas of wasteland to be brought under irrigated cultivation as the canal system is extended. Most of the land concerned, in both Rajasthan and Madhya Pradesh, was alluvial. In Rajasthan soils were deep over 95 per cent of the command area, but they were highly impermeable, and the drainage of 65 per cent of the area was moderate (that over the rest being low).[51] Drainage works were therefore recommended (for the consequences of ignoring this advice, see below, p. 163). In the Sheopur District of Madhya Pradesh some 1,200 hectares had already in 1963 been allotted to local people and to a few outsiders (e.g. Punjabis): this falls under the right-bank channel. On the left bank, in the Kota and adjacent Districts of Rajasthan, 'colonization' was started in 1960. But up to 1963 there had been no colonization as the word is understood in this book; though there may be such colonization in future.[52]

The problem has also arisen of resettling cultivators who have lost their land under the Chambal reservoirs: Gandhisagar, for example, submerged over 28,000 hectares of cultivated land.[53] Some displaced cultivators took cash compensation, but about 2,400 hectares of cleared jungle land (mainly in pockets on Vindhyan sandstone or basalt) was allotted to others.

It may now be asked why land is still available for the extension of cultivation in this middle Chambal area—particularly in apparently fertile alluvium. A clue is given by the statement in a 1931 Census Report that the Plains Division (the Division including the Chambal right-bank belt) was the only part of the then state of Gwalior which had 'not regained its mean density of 1901',[54] and by an indication in the previous Report that there had been severe droughts hereabouts in 1911–12, 1913–14, 1915–16, and 1918–19 ('an exceptionally bad year').[55] Kota, similarly, did not regain its 1891 population until 1941;[56] and, like other parts of Rajasthan, suffered severe famine, followed by virulent malaria, in 1899–1900. There was considerable emigration, and Kota and Tonk lost respectively 24 and 28 per cent of their population between 1891 and 1901.[57] It seems likely, then, that recurrent drought and famine, in the absence of irrigation, tended to depress population levels, or even to cause a decline, and hence to leave cultivable land uncultivated, at least from time to time. There were further factors. This region, a marchland on the southern border of Rajput territory, had a long history of unsettled conditions in the eighteenth and nineteenth centuries.[58] J. W. D. Johnstone reported many disused irrigation works in Sheopur and adjacent areas.[59] Communications were, moreover, very poor, as study of Survey of India maps of 1873, 1914, and 1930 will show. And, finally, there were the consequences of the fragmentation of the area between a number of princely states, to which contemporary observers attributed a part at least of the failure of the area to attract new settlement;[60] and it certainly prevented any co-ordinated use of the waters of the Chambal, which alone could have ensured the stability of local agriculture.[61]

The Malwa Plateau

This consists essentially of the area drained by the upper Chambal and its tributaries, such as the Parbati and Kali Sindh.[62] It is underlain, for the most part, by basalts, which weather in gently sloping and low-lying sites to water-retentive black cotton soils.[63] To the south the plateau ends abruptly in the steep, forested scarp overlooking the Narmada (Narbada) valley—the home of Bhil tribesmen.[64]

Several writers during the British period drew attention to the relatively low population density of the Plateau, given the fertility of its soils. Thus C. E. Luard noted that 'ample room for the extension of cultivation exists; but it is impossible to hope for any great increase in this direction unless the population rises considerably, especially in Malwa, where, owing to the very sparse population, the finest soil is lying fallow'.[65] Bhopal, too, showed a low density, '10 persons per square mile [4 per square km] less than that found on the rest of the plateau area'.[66] In 1847 there were 842 deserted villages in the Ninar area of Indore state.[67]

The reasons for these conditions seem to have been, as in the central Chambal region, a combination of drought, famine, poverty of access (in some places, at any rate), and the consequences not only of princely rule but of partition between a number of states. Famine, however, on the whole had less effect in Malwa proper, with its slightly higher rainfall and better soils;[68] though Bhopal suffered a drop in population from 952,486 in 1891 to 665,961 in 1901, as a result of the famines of 1896–7 and 1899–1900.[69] Malwa proper was not altogether exempt from famine, for it lost many people as a result of the famine of 1899–1900.[70] Jules Sion singled out the consequences of the existence of 'miniscular and ill-governed principalities';[71] while Sir W. H. Sleeman blamed the extortionate nature of the revenue system for keeping the population of villages to the minimum necessary to cultivate their land,[72] and an earlier official thought that 'the offer of liberal terms for bringing waste land into cultivation' would have beneficial results.[73]

In the last fifty years there has been a very considerable, though by no means consistent, increase in population on the Malwa Plateau. But enough uncultivated waste remained for there to be a number of pre- and post-independence colonization schemes, either on the plateau proper or in pockets of basalt-based black soil amongst the Vindhyan sandstones of parts of Bhopal: for example, pre-independence colonies in Gwalior state; recent tribal colonies at several places in Guna District and elsewhere; and an interesting scheme, on the 3,585 hectare site of the former Central Mechanized Farm of Intikheri, near Bhopal, which contains Punjabi and Sindi refugees and colonists from Kerala as well as local people. In 1950 the Government of India set up a Malwa Development Board, *inter alia* to reclaim wastelands: 60,000 hectares of culturable waste were allotted to cultivators in its first year of operation.[74]

Other Small Regions

There is a number of smaller regions in India in which colonization has taken place to such a minor extent that no more than a paragraph can be here devoted to each.

First, there is a region in the extreme northeast of the plateau country of peninsular India in which two types of colonization have taken place since independence. In the upper valleys of the Damodar and its tributaries, people displaced by the construction of reservoirs associated with the Damodar Valley project[75] have been resettled (the author saw such colonization in the area of the Tilaiya Reservoir); while in the so-called Rajmahal Hills—really a plateau—in the Santal Parganas deeply gullied and eroded land has been reclaimed and recolonized, meeting in the process formidable tenurial frustrations (see below, p. 247). This reclamation continues a process at which the Santals themselves are adept.[76] Sir J. Houlton ascribes the initial erosion of the deep, red soils of the plateau to shifting cultivation practised by hill peoples, and to failure to establish forest reserves early enough.[77]

Secondly, at the other, far western end of the great central belt of hill country, there lies Khandesh, on the southern flank of the River Tapti. This is an area of dissected, dry, Deccan Trap country, with a mean annual rainfall of about 50 cm—subject, however, to marked variability (only 20 cm fell in 1962). Some of the people hereabouts are Bhils,[78] perhaps forced into Khandesh from their homeland in the Satpura Hills by Rajput and Muslim conquerors.[79] Nineteenth-century reports speak of the existence of wasteland in Khandesh and of want of labour:[80] perhaps for reasons of periodic drought and famine, as in the Chambal valley, and because the area was long a passage-way for armies. There were certainly severe famines in 1896–7, 1899–1900, and 1900–1 (when the death rate rose to 38·13 per thousand).[81] Since then, there has been a general tendency for population to rise more or less continuously; but there are colonization schemes (on a co-operative basis and involving some Bhils) in what is now Jalgaon District.

Thirdly, there are pockets of post-independence colonization in the Eastern Ghats of Andhra Pradesh. There is no belt here corresponding to Greater Malnad; and the Ghats are fragmentary compared with the massive wall of their Western counterpart, at least south of the great eastern rampart of Dandakaranya. Rather are there small, isolated valleys, forested, or previously cultivated and then lost to cultivation, available here and there for reclamation: as at Piduguralla in Guntur District, where a colony of 200 hectares or so has been developed by ex-servicemen; or at Jeelugumilli in West Godavari District and Aminabad in East Godavari District (mainly for tribal peoples). Many of these pockets were formerly heavily malarial.

Even the east coast deltas have their unused patches, as at Kalidindi, in the Krishna delta. A land reclamation project, said to involve a target of 4,000 hectares, has also been reported from Sukinda in the Cuttack District of Orissa;[82] and there are not inconsiderable areas available for colonization, or at any rate for reclamation, under the command of the Hirakud dam in the same state.[83]

Finally, colonization is either in progress, or has been projected, in outlying islands such as the Andamans, Nicobars, and Laccadives,[84] many of which were, and in some cases still are, highly malarial.[85]

Other Land Potentially Available

Such, then, are the regions in which, for varying combinations of reasons, land has been still available for colonization in post-independence India: hitherto unirrigated deserts, malarious forests (some formerly more densely settled); remote jungle areas, far from the historic routeways of Indian history; even areas still bearing faintly the scars inflicted during periods of harrowing and depopulation two centuries or more ago.

There remains one further type of region for potential colonization: that in which cultivation takes place in large holdings (by Indian standards) and is very extensive in nature. Intensification of agriculture (for example, under irrigation) would therefore in theory at any rate make it possible to concentrate existing cultivators on a smaller area without loss of production, and so enable new cultivators to colonize the area thus released. One such region lies in the Raichur Doab, between the Krishna (Kistna) and Tungabhadra rivers in Mysore state, and now, as the channel system is extended, falling in part under the command of the great Tungabhadra project.[86]

As Spate says, this Doab 'was the marchland between the Muslim Deccani Sultanates and Hindu Vijayanagar, which city occupied a forward position on the Tungabhadra'[87] very near, in fact, to the present dam. The Doab lies athwart the great route down the western Deccan plateaux to which several references have already been made in this chapter. Partly, no doubt, for reasons of defence, given the marchland character of the region, partly for reasons of water supply, traditional settlements tend to be concentrated in large villages with one flank on a river (the Krishna, or the Tungabhadra, or one of their tributaries). Wells out in the open Doab under its mainly dark soils, give brackish or saline water; while, traditionally, there were difficulties in irrigating many parts of the Doab by means of channels from the major rivers because, in many tracts, the rivers (particularly the Tungabhadra) lie between deep banks[88] (though the Vijayanagar kings built a number of channels, some still in use).[89] The Doab is thus characterized by wide, open steppe-like landscapes, of part of which A. Butterworth said 'the scenery is particularly morose, a black desolation when the crops are off the ground'.[90] There is a low general density of population for reasons that include not only the factors already mentioned but also malaria, famine, and poverty of communications.[91] The Tungabhadra Project has, in fact, been hampered by labour shortages.[92]

Away from the villages, cultivation takes place on large holdings on a singularly unintensive basis.[93] Already, one can see a spontaneous process by which immigrants, largely Telugus from the east coast deltas, are moving in and buying up land in advance of the arrival of irrigation, often to sell it again at a handsome profit once it has been converted into paddy land. There is thus scope for government action of a sort that has been practised in the Thal colonization area of Pakistan, in the Gezira, in Jordan, and in the Badajoz Plain

(Spain), where the authorities buy or lease land that is being cultivated unintensively, or not at all, and reissue it as part of a programme of colonization.[94] So far, however, this possibility seems not to have been realized, colonization in the Tungabhadra area being confined to the resettlement on wasteland of cultivators whose holdings have been submerged under the reservoir and of a number of immigrants who came in as labourers on the project.

Similar possibilities may well exist in other parts of India, notably in the extensively (rather than intensively) cultivated parts of Maharashtra, Madhya Pradesh,[95] and Assam; and, notably, in the area commanded by the Nagarjunasagar dam in Andhra Pradesh and Hirakud dam in Orissa (where there may be as much as 8,000 hectares of waste, or at any rate under-cultivated land in private hands, some of which—rather as in the Raichur Doab—is being sold to and developed by Telugus.[96] There is also some government waste: see pp. 76–7 below).

5

Nature and Scale of Colonization

THE last two chapters have indicated the main areas in India in which agricultural colonization, as defined in this book, has been in progress since independence. The present chapter is designed to indicate the general nature and scope of this colonization by outlining:

(1) The area colonized and the number of settlers involved, so far as these can be ascertained (and, as will be seen, there are formidable difficulties here), and in comparison with colonization in neighbouring countries;
(2) The scale of colonization as compared with that of other forms of assault on the waste.

Area Colonized and Number of Settlers: to 1963

To those lacking familiarity with under-developed countries in general and with India in particular it may seem a simple matter to obtain and to tabulate data on the area that has been brought into cultivation in Indian colonization schemes since independence, and on the number of settlers involved. But to those who are more aware, at the grass roots, of the problems involved, it will come as no surprise to learn that Tables 5.I and 5.II have been constructed only with much travail, and that the reader must be warned very firmly indeed that no high degree of reliance can be placed on them.

It will be noticed that the two Tables show, first, data for colonization schemes actually visited by the author in 1963 and studied by him on the spot. The figures here were, for the most part, collected in the field, or at district or state headquarters: and the author must express his gratitude to all the officials who so willingly provided data, often in highly convenient form. But where, as sometimes happened, two sets of data were provided for the same colonization scheme or area, or where it was possible to check figures obtained in the field with those held or provided in a state capital or in New Delhi, inconsistencies not infrequently revealed themselves; and it is not easy to reconcile these by subsequent correspondence, which may indeed merely serve to widen the area of confusion.

One source of confusion and error lies in misunderstood definitions. 'Colonization' has been clearly enough defined in the introduction to this book; and every effort was made to ensure that figures collected were for colonization schemes thus defined. But it became clear on a number of occasions in the field that what local officials viewed as colonies were essentially village expansion schemes, involving no brand-new settlements; or schemes involving land already cultivated rather than reclamation from the waste. Thus one cannot everywhere be sure that the figures tabulated, even for schemes visited in the field, faithfully reflect the correct definition of colonization. Again, Table 5.I attempts to show the area actually

TABLE 5.I

Areas brought into Cultivation as a Result of Agricultural Colonization, 1947–63, with Later Figures for Main Areas

	1963			*Later Data*	
	Colonization Schemes visited by Author		*Estimated Total for State or Authority (see text) (hectares)*		
State or Authority	*No. of Schemes or Note*	*Area under Cultivation (hectares)*		*Year*	*Area under Cultivation (Major Schemes) (hectares)*
Andaman Is	—	—	7,175	—	—
Andhra Pradesh	6	1,436	7,100	—	—
Assam	—	—	14,223	1968	19,080
Bihar	2	779	3,800	—	—
Dandakaranya Development Authority	A	31,069	31,069	1971	41,700
Gujarat	—	—	Nil	—	—
Haryana	B	800	800	—	—
Jammu & Kashmir	—	—	Nil	—	—
Kerala	3	9,727	12,067	—	—
Madhya Pradesh	9	8,120	40,500	—	—
Maharashtra	6	466	2,200	—	—
Mysore	5	5,441	10,900	—	—
Orissa	4	4,000	6,100	—	—
Punjab	—	—	Nil	—	—
Rajasthan	C	154,275	156,275	1971	310,203
Tamil Nadu	4	1,210	8,769	—	—
Uttar Pradesh	4	27,473	43,655	—	—
West Bengal	—	—	Nil	—	—
		244,796	344,633		

A Total for the Authority.
B Assumptions, see text.
C Total for Bhakra and Rajasthan Canal Colonies as supplied by Colonization Commissioner, Bikaner; State total (1963) includes also estimated area elsewhere (principally oustee colonies, Chambal Valley).

Sources and assumptions: see text.

brought under cultivation as a result of the process of colonization up to 1963, *excluding* land cleared but not cultivated, or allotted for colonization and not even cleared, or cleared but used for houses, roads, reservations, and the like. But again one cannot guarantee that the tabulated areas were indeed all under cultivation in 1963; the figure may, to an unknown but probably not high degree, be an over-estimate. Finally, as will become clear in the course of this chapter, the multiplicity of agencies involved in agricultural colonization means that no one authority holds comprehensive information.

Table 5.II attempts to show for 1963 the number of colonists (that is, the number of actual persons to whom land was allotted or, in the case of joint or collective farming societies, the number of members). It does *not* show the total agricultural population of the schemes concerned (an approximation to which may be obtained by applying a factor of five, or perhaps more in some cases, to the figures tabulated); nor does it show the non-agricultural population attracted to some at least of the colonization areas. Here again, there are sources of error in misunderstood definition. A further source of trouble is provided by non-cultivating or inactive members of joint or collective farming societies; while in Haryana (as it now is) it was not easy to disentangle the colonization of waste from a far more frequent occurrence—the recolonization by Hindus and Sikhs, formerly resident in Pakistan, of land previously occupied by Muslims who had moved to Pakistan after partition.

Fortunately, there is reason to believe that the figures possess a high degree of reliability in the case of the large areas of colonization, Dandakaranya and Rajasthan, for each of these comes under one authority (the Dandakaranya Development Authority, and the Colonization Commissioner, Bikaner respectively) which kindly provided complete figures. The same happily applies also to medium-sized projects such as those in Kerala, the Uttar Pradesh Tarai, and Assam.

Finally, it will be noticed that the categories in Table 5.II are by no means mutually exclusive (compare, for example, 'unspecified landless', 'Harijans', 'Harijans and tribals', and 'tribals'): here, again, the fault lies in the data as collected. More will be said about these categories in chapter 6.

Turning to the assumed grand totals shown in Tables 5.I and 5.II, one is in general on more difficult ground. Wherever possible, officials in state capitals were asked for details of all colonization schemes since independence, in terms of areas brought into cultivation and colonists settled (by categories). Only those in Madhya Pradesh, Rajasthan, Tamil Nadu, and Uttar Pradesh (and, of course, in the

TABLE 5.II

Colonists Settled, 1947–63, according to Reason for Grant of Land

State or Authority	*Colonization Schemes Visited by the Author* — *Number of Colonists*: No. of Schemes	Unspecified Landless	Harijans	Tribals	Harijans and Tribals	Old Temporary Cultivation Lesses	Ex-servicemen	'Educated Unemployed'	'Political Sufferers'	Refugees	Immigrants from afar (not refugees)	Ex-jagirdars	Compensation	Other Locals	Land by Auction	Others	*Total*	*Estimated Total No. of Colonists (see text)*
Andaman Is	—	—	—	—	—	—	—	—	—	—	—	—	—	—	—	—	—	3,036
Andhra Pradesh	6	—	13	97	—	—	337	—	—	—	—	—	—	—	—	—	447	2,200
Assam	—	—	—	—	—	—	—	—	—	—	—	—	—	—	—	—	—	10,896
Bihar	2	112	—	—	—	—	—	—	—	—	—	—	1,001	—	—	—	1,113	5,500
Dandakaranya Development Authority	A	—	—	1,200	—	—	—	—	—	6,369	—	—	—	—	—	—	7,569	7,569
Gujarat	—	—	—	—	—	—	—	—	—	—	—	—	—	—	—	—	—	Nil
Haryana	B	—	—	—	—	—	—	—	—	—	—	—	200	—	—	—	200	200
Jammu & Kashmir	—	—	—	—	—	—	—	—	—	—	—	—	—	—	—	—	—	Nil
Kerala	3	1,532	—	25	209	—	1,998	—	1	—	—	—	—	807	—	—	4,572	6,200
Madhya Pradesh	9	542	—	131	269	—	22	—	—	50	128	—	1,400	—	—	—	2,542	12,500
Maharashtra	6	50	—	10	—	24	—	—	—	—	—	—	—	—	—	6	90	450
Mysore	4	50	39	33	—	—	—	—	—	500	—	—	2,277	—	—	—	2,899	5,390
Orissa	4	—	—	140	—	—	—	—	—	—	—	—	1,050	—	—	—	1,190	1,750
Rajasthan	C	4,304	—	20	—	11,056	91	—	4	—	—	1,841	—	—	4,995	64	22,375	22,375
Tamil Nadu	4	—	156	141	—	—	—	—	—	—	—	—	138	—	—	—	435	4,672
Uttar Pradesh	4	1,526	—	—	—	—	194	123	709	2,975	—	—	550	—	—	4	6,081	10,362
West Bengal	—	—	—	—	—	—	—	—	—	—	—	—	—	—	—	—	—	Nil
Total		8,116	208	1,797	478	11,080	2,642	123	714	9,894	128	1,841	6,616	807	4,995	74	49,513	93,000
		21,679 = 44%					3,479 = 7%			=20%	—	=4%	=13%	5,876 = 12%				

A Total for Authority.
B Assumption, see text.
C Total for Bhakra and Rajasthan Canal Colonies, as given by Colonization Commissioner, Bikaner.
For certain later figures, see text.
Sources and assumptions: see text.

Dandakaranya Development Authority) responded fully—though a partial statement (on tribal colonies) emerged from Orissa, and a very useful document from Assam. Further attempts were made through extremely helpful officials in the Department of Agriculture and in the Planning Commission in New Delhi. Apparently complete data were obtained for the Andaman Islands and for Kerala, together with figures for a number of other states (though these were not without the inconsistencies already mentioned: one state, for example, returned a smaller total number of colonists for its whole territory than those in the sample of schemes within it that had been visited by the author). And, once again, shifting definitions were to the fore. Additionally, one encountered problems of communication between centre and states in what is, after all, a very large federal structure; and there were confusing consequences of the reorganizations of state boundaries that have taken place in India since independence.

It might therefore appear that the author (and for that matter the central authorities engaged in a similar quest) is in the sad position of a statistician who has a sample, of a highly non-random nature, but does not know what proportion it is of the total population. In point of fact the situation is not quite so desperate, as will become clear if I explain the assumptions on which the estimated totals in Tables 5.I and 5.II have been arrived at. These are:

(1) That the total figures supplied by the relevant authorities for the Andamans, Assam, Dandakaranya, Kerala, Tamil Nadu, Rajasthan (but see Note C to Table 5.I), and Uttar Pradesh can be accepted (with minor adjustments to reconcile one or two inconsistencies), since the evidence is that there were here no major problems of definition, boundary change, or other important sources of confusion. It will be clear that these states include the major areas of colonization described in chapters 3 and 4; moreover for a high proportion of schemes in all of these (except, unfortunately, for the Andamans and Assam) there were data collected by the author in the field in 1963.

(2) That there were no colonies in Gujarat,[1] or in (present) Punjab, or in Jammu and Kashmir (which appeared to be the case), and also, to all intents and purposes, in West Bengal (the state government reported to the central government 'colonization and resettlement on waste lands' in certain areas, notably in Jalpaiguri District, but it seems unlikely that any significant area in this overcrowded state was, or is being colonized);

(3) That one cannot (unfortunately) improve on the estimate of 800 hectares and 200 colonists for Haryana;

(4) That in the cases of Andhra Pradesh, Bihar, Madhya Pradesh,

Maharashtra, Mysore (*less* the Tungabhadra Valley Project), and Orissa (*less* the Hirakud scheme) a very rough state total may be obtained by multiplying by five the area and the number of colonists in the schemes visited by the author; for there is evidence that in some states at any rate he worked in about a fifth of the small colonies; and in all cases (apart from the specific schemes mentioned for Mysore and Orissa) all that is at issue is a number of tiny colonies, completely overshadowed by those in other states (as the Table indeed makes clear). In the case of Orissa the number of 'oustees' settled under Hirakud must be added, from figures obtained on the spot. In the case of Mysore, there is some difficulty in assessing how many oustees were settled in colonies on land that was previously waste, as distinct from cultivated land acquired for their benefit. On the Tungabhadra Left Bank (in Raichur District, formerly in Hyderabad) discussions in the field led to the conclusion that some 1,137 families had been settled on wasteland amounting to 2,030 hectares. The author was not able to visit the Right Bank (in Bellary District, formerly in Madras) but he estimates that about the same number of families (say 1,140) were settled on about the same amount of land (say 2,000 hectares), to judge by the need in terms of families dispossessed and the accredited statement that 1,650 hectares were disafforested and added to other wasteland to accommodate them.[2]

This working for 1963 has been set out in some detail to exemplify the problems of collecting and interpreting Indian data.

One may, therefore, in the absence of firmer figures, come very tentatively to the conclusion that by the end of 1963 the efforts of independent India to achieve the agricultural colonization of wasteland had secured the cultivation of about 345,000 hectares of previously waste, or at any rate uncultivated and unreclaimed, land, and provided new villages for about 93,000 agricultural colonists or, if one includes their families, 500,000 people. But the possibility of considerable error in these conclusions will be recognized.

Area Colonized and Number of Settlers: Later Figures

Further work in India in 1968 yielded more recent data for Assam, thanks to the helpfulness of the authorities concerned: the area colonized had risen by December 1968 to an estimated total of 19,000 hectares and the number of colonists to 18,400.

Fieldwork in 1971–2 brought later data for Dandakaranya and Rajasthan (Bhakra and Rajasthan Canal areas) and also a line on the state of colonization in the Uttar Pradesh Tarai (where expansion had by then come to an end) and in Andhra Pradesh and Tamil Nadu.

In Dandakaranya the area reclaimed had grown by November 1971 to 54,508 hectares, the number of colonists to 19,099 (16,061 displaced persons and 3,038 tribals) and the area under cultivation to 41,700 hectares. Development had been fairly steady since 1963.

In Rajasthan, on the other hand, colonization under the Rajasthan Canal had got into its stride only after much delay. By September 1966, when there were 26,691 colonists cultivating 137,966 hectares under Bhakra, there were only 1,977 colonists on 23,451 hectares under the Rajasthan Canal. As was the case with Pakistan's Thal Project,[3] colonization under the Rajasthan Canal had in fact fallen seriously behind schedule. Assuming five persons in each colonist family, colonist population had increased only by some 2,000 between 1963 and 1966, compared with an increase of 22,000 required by the original Plan.[4] After 1968, however, colonization was accelerated. By 31 December 1971 Bhakra had only grown to 27,274 colonists, cultivating 138,327 hectares; but under the Rajasthan Canal there were by then 25,842 colonists and 171,877 cultivated hectares. The scale of operations in Rajasthan is now clearly much greater than that anywhere else in India.

Making reasonable but not very secure assumptions about recent colonization in areas other than Assam, Dandakaranya and Rajasthan, it is possible to estimate very roughly that from independence to December 1971 about 600,000 hectares (or $1\frac{1}{2}$ million acres) had been brought into cultivation as a result of agricultural colonization, and that this involved about 160,000 colonists or, altogether, 800,000 people.

Comparisons with Neighbouring Countries

It may be of interest briefly to compare the magnitude of post-independence agricultural colonization in India with the achievements of nearby countries in the same field.[5] Colonization schemes in Ceylon up to 31 December 1966 involved a total of 68,525 colonists settled on 128,823 hectares of land (that is, the number of colonists was under one-half and the area cultivated about one-fifth, of the corresponding figures for post-independence India).[6] The absolute scale of colonization in Ceylon was therefore—not surprisingly—a good deal smaller than that in India; though relative to the size of Ceylon, of course, the opposite is true—and, by the same token, colonization has played a much bigger part in politics, in planning, in food supply, and in other ways in Ceylon.

Pakistan's major post-independence colonization scheme, that in the Thal, between the Indus and the Jhelum–Chenab, was expected to involve 44,000 peasants on 83,682 hectares:[7] this one project, then, represents about one-quarter of the magnitude of post-independence colonization in India (in terms of colonists) and, again, plays relatively a much larger part in the national scheme of things. Of about the same order of absolute magnitude is the 'transmigration' of some 200,000 colonists (say 40,000 families) from Java to the Lampoeng and Atjeh areas of Sumatra between independence and 1963.[8] More recently 6,000–7,000 families have been resettled per annum in Indonesia.[9]

Turning to Malaysia, it may not be realized that the resettlement of squatters during the Emergency, completed by 1953, involved no fewer than 541,458 people (77,846 families), equivalent, as C. A. Fisher has pointed out, to nearly 10 per cent of the then Federation's total population;[10] or to approximately the same number of people (though to fewer families) as the whole programme of agricultural colonization in India from independence to the end of 1963. But, since each squatter family in Malaya was given only three acres (1·2 hectares) to cultivate, only about 90,650 hectares were brought into cultivation, or under one-third of the estimated addition to India's cultivated area through agricultural colonization between 1947 and 1963.

It may, of course, be argued that the resettlement of the squatters was an emergency operation different in aims and scope from Indian agricultural colonization, apart from certain special cases (see below, p. 275); and that the more recent activities of the Malaysian Federal Land Development Authority are more comparable to those in India that form the subject of this book.[11] Between 1956 and 1964 the Authority had initiated sixty-one colonization projects designed to benefit over 20,000 peasant families. This represents one-eighth of the Indian achievement over a period three times as long (1947–1971). The eventual area under cultivation in the sixty-one FLDA schemes will be over 100,000 hectares, of which, by 1964, 32,433 hectares had been planted in rubber and 3,602 hectares in oil palm. Three thousand seven hundred families a year are now being settled. These Malaysian colonies, with their emphasis on commercial tree crops, have few equivalents in India, except in Kerala (Wynad and High Ranges), and this fact should be borne in mind when one makes comparisons.

The influx into South Vietnam after the Geneva Agreement of 21 July 1954 of about a million refugees, 70 per cent of whom were peasants, was the occasion for a massive programme of colonization.[12] Between 1957 and 1962, 137,700 settlers were established in the southern Mekong delta, 70,000 in the High Plateau, and a few others on the eastern border plains. The 'agrovilles' set up in South Vietnam between 1959 and 1962, and subsequently abandoned in favour of 'strategic hamlets', bear some resemblance to the Malayan squatter resettlement projects, since they involved the regrouping into large settlements in the face of guerilla activity of a previously scattered rural population.[13] But they involved agricultural colonization only marginally, since the peasants retained their own farms and were merely given a small parcel of public land in the agroville (0·5 hectares in Tan Luoc) on which they were supposed to erect a house, dig a fishpond, and grow fruit.

Colonization in India is a relatively sporadic process. The Dry Zone of Ceylon, the great undeveloped jungles of Pahang and eastern Malaya generally, and even the Thal of Pakistan, constitute undeveloped regions which form a relatively high proportion of the national territory. India lacks such regions although the area that may be available for colonization in Rajasthan and Dandakaranya, or even the area actually colonized in the Tarai and in Greater Malnad, are large in absolute terms or compared to the size of the Ceylon Dry Zone or of Pahang.

Other Forms of Assault on the Waste

It will help to place agricultural colonization in perspective if something is now said of other means by which the Indian waste is currently under attack by agriculturists, even though the treatment cannot be quantitatively conclusive.

There are, in the first place, in several parts of the country, examples of recent spontaneous colonization, involving new settlements but not government sponsorship or organization: notably in the foothills of the Western Ghats in Kerala, and near the Periyar Reservoir in the same state. Signs of such settlement are written large on the landscape: stumps and dying jungle trees in the fields, new huts and houses far from existing villages, pioneer crops like manioc (i.e. cassava, *Manihot utilissima*) in situations in which other crops are usually grown, and will later be grown. Some of the settlers here may well be illicit encroachers on government waste or on tribal land[14] (the problems of encroachment will be discussed further in chapter 6). Other settlers have moved into private wasteland, as in Kozhikode District of Kerala,[15] which has received an influx of people from what were formerly Travancore and Cochin. Again, occupance of wasteland by unorganized colonization continues in Assam, though apparently at a diminishing rate.[16]

The large-scale reclamation of previously uncultivated land is sometimes associated with Vinoba Bhave's Bhoodan movement[17] (though, as is well known, this mainly involves the redistribution of land already in cultivation). Thus near Nilambur, at the foot of the western scarp of the Nilgiri Hills in the Kozhikode District of Kerala, local *jemmies* (*zamindars*) gave 400 hectares of teak forest as Bhoodan and a hundred colonists came in to clear the teak (which they sold) and to cultivate. The government provided loans and gave other assistance. Again, in the Santal Parganas of Bihar, at Mohanpur, private waste was given to the local Bhoodan organization, and reclaimed free of charge by the government Directorate of Reclamation; the government also provided finance with the aid of which the local Bhoodan Committee subsidized house construction by the allottees.[18] The soil in this scheme was very poor indeed, consisting mainly of quartz gravel and ironstone concretions. More fortunate were the 350 Sikh families (refugees from Lyallpur) at the Sardapuri Bhoodan Colony in the Tarai of Pilibhit District in Uttar Pradesh, who were cultivating 1,660 hectares of mainly good alluvium given by *zamindars*: the jungle here had been cleared by the colonists, who were organized in Joint Farming Societies and were reaping good harvests of rice, wheat, maize, and other crops. Loans had been provided, in this case from the Mahatma Gandhi Nidhi (Memorial Fund) at Varanasi (Benares).

In addition to colonization and aid to the Bhoodan movement (which may sometimes involve colonization of a sort), government departments in India take part in a variety of other ways in the *mise en valeur* of wasteland. Thus in Andhra Pradesh the Forest Department has plantations of coffee and of cashew-nut, the former grown for shade under surviving forest trees, and there were plans in 1963 for a total of 4,000 hectares of coffee in such places as Anantagiri, on the forested scarp that rises behind Vishakapatnam (Vizagapatam). In Kerala the Department of Agriculture had an active programme of rubber planting, with a target of over 40,000 acres, all on previously forested land;[19] up to 1963 2,749 hectares had been planted in government plantations and a further 2,550 hectares in 3½-acre (1·42-hectare) allotments, on which landless labourers and the 'educated unemployed' were settled. Further, 3,000 hectares of cardamoms were to be planted, under forest cover in Reserved Forests, mostly in 10–25-acre (4–10-hectare) allotments; while cashew-nut was being planted on wastelands in many parts of the state, notably 500 hectares on a state plantation in Cannanore District (fortunately cashew will grow on poor soils, including eroded terraces of indurated laterite).[20] In Tamil Nadu there is a scheme to plant 4,000 hectares in cashew in Ramanathapuram District.

In Orissa, again, at Gambharipalli in the area commanded by the Hirakud irrigation scheme, a 360-hectare Government Farm has been established on wasteland, formerly much gullied and eroded, which at the time of the author's visit in October 1963 was being reclaimed, mainly in order to supply planting material (mostly fruit trees) for cultivators in the Hirakud scheme. The farm was to be extended to a total of 800 hectares by taking in a further 160 hectares of government and 280 hectares of private waste, and was to be planted in 120 hectares of fruit and 320 hectares of paddy, largely though not entirely for seed. Near by, at Chakuli and Parmanpur, were respectively a 40-acre (16-hectare) farm, developed by Japanese cultivators with Japanese aid, to demonstrate improved methods of paddy cultivation, and a 60-acre (24-hectare) Government Farm for seed multiplication: both were on land formerly waste. There were proposals in Tamil Nadu (formerly Madras) in 1970 to establish a Plantation Development Corporation to settle repatriated estate labourers from Ceylon (some land had already been cleared): while the Andaman Development Corporation proposed to establish plantations on which repatriates from Burma and Ceylon and refugees from East Bengal might be settled.[21]

Another type of government enterprise, a number of examples of which have involved the extension of cultivation on to previously wasteland, is the State Farm, broadly on the Soviet model. One of the most notable of these was formerly to be seen in the Naini Tal Tarai, where, in addition to the conventional peasant colonization already mentioned, some 6,500 hectares were cleared and reclaimed and run as a State Farm, using mechanized cultivation in its fields. This Farm has now been handed over to a new Agricultural University[22] for purposes of research and demonstration and also as an endowment not unlike that of American land-grant colleges. The former Central Mechanized Farm at Jammu has, for similar reasons, been handed over to the state government of Jammu and Kashmir;[23] while that at Intikheri, near Bhopal, which was mainly cleared from the waste, is now the scene of colonization by colonists from Kerala and elsewhere.

There remains, however, the Central Mechanized Farm at Suratgarh, in Rajasthan, which covers some 12,000 hectares, of which 9,451 hectares were government waste.[24] The popular name for the farm is 'The Russian Farm', for it was set up, with Russian machinery, after the visit of Mr Bulganin and Mr Khrushchev to India in 1955 (when they visited the Tarai State Farm). There can be little doubt that the Russian leaders envisaged the project as a demonstration of the merits of large-scale, mechanized State Farms *à la Russe*.

A committee which reported in 1961 examined a number of possible sites for further Central Mechanized Farms (notably one which would involve the acquisition of a large area of privately owned land in the Raichur Doab) but made one recommendation only—the establishment of a further farm of about 12,000 hectares contiguous to the Suratgarh Farm and eventually under the command of the Rajasthan Canal.[25] This would involve nearly 5,700 hectares of waste-land, most of the rest of its area being under temporary cultivation leases. There was also a proposal in December 1966 to set up a lift-irrigated Central Mechanized Seed Farm of 4,000 hectares on the periphery of the Hirakud reservoir, and further farms in Mysore and Kerala.

This book will not attempt an exhaustive discussion of these large-scale, state-operated mechanized farms; though one or two aspects of them will be brought into the discussion at a later stage (for example, defects in physical planning in chapter 7). For the moment, they should merely be noted as one further contribution to the assault on the waste, accounting together, perhaps, for the addition to the cultivated area since independence of some 40,000 hectares (including State and Central Mechanized Farms and such enterprises as the Departmental plantations in Kerala and Andhra Pradesh, but excluding coffee or other plantations under forest trees, and the former Intikheri Central Mechanized Farm, since the area of this, now converted to a colonization scheme, is included in the total in Table 5.I). It may well be, then, that these large-scale undertakings, in spite of their more spectacular nature and of the publicity they have thereby tended to attract, have had only about a fifteenth of the impact on the waste that has been made since independence by the more conventional colonization schemes summarized in Table 5.I. It is not possible to quote figures for additional employment created by these undertakings; but, given the highly mechanized nature of many of them, it is clearly to be doubted whether they have created as many jobs per hectare as the colonization schemes.

Finally, at the other end of the scale from these large-scale enterprises, there comes the process which may be called 'village expansion', since it involves an assault on the waste based on existing village nuclei. There have been, in post-independence India, at least three strands in this process (which, it should be stressed, the author does not claim to have studied exhaustively or in the field). In the first place, there is the piecemeal, spontaneous, illicit encroachment on the waste, whose extent was so strikingly thrown up by a Pilot Survey in Dewas District, on the Malwa Plateau in the State of Madhya Pradesh, where it was found that about half the land recorded in the agricultural statistics as 'culturable waste' was in fact being cultivated. It was observed that 'large areas classified as culturable waste-land at the time of settlement or since long past, continue to be so classed year after year in the *patwari*'s records irrespective of whether they are cultivable and are lying waste or not'.[26] Some implications of this survey have already been mentioned, and others will be discussed in chapter 8; but clearly one implication is that spontaneous, creeping, and unrecorded occupance of wasteland, whether technically encroachment or not, is, if the Dewas figures are at all representative, a phenomenon very much to be reckoned with in considering the total strength of the current assault on the waste in India. Chapter 4 has, further, revealed that Telugu settlers are moving into such regions as the Raichur Doab and the area under the command of the Hirakud reservoir, and there achieving a spontaneous infilling of interstices in the pattern of cultivated land.

Secondly, there is the legal, or at any rate legalized encroachment on the waste in, around, and between villages which is constantly in progress; and which continues in independent India, under local wasteland rules administered by the revenue authorities, a process of increasing the cultivated area so characteristic of many parts of British India.

Thirdly, there has been the more purposeful and planned assault on similarly disposed parcels of waste. True, the First Five Year Plan (1951–6) and its successor (1956–61) made but a slow start in this direction, though, locally, notably in the former Madhya Bharat and Vindhya Pradesh, the authorities erred in the other direction and initiated 'a reckless drive . . . to give out the *pattas* for every bit of land that is lying fallow',[27] whether suitable for agriculture or not. But the Third Five Year Plan (1961–6) gave more impetus to the process, primarily as part of a programme for improving the condition of agricultural labour: more will be said about this programme, and its continuation into the Fourth Five Year Plan period (1969–74) in the next chapter. All that needs to be pointed out here is that vigorous action has been taken in some states; and that not all of this was village expansion, for certain colonization schemes were undertaken by state governments with central assistance as part of the programme for the resettlement of landless labourers.

Magnitude of the Assault on the Waste

Is there any way of assessing the overall magnitude of the assault on the Indian waste since independence, and then of estimating the share in that assault of colonization as defined in this book? It might at first sight appear that the answer to the first part of this question lies in the *Indian Agricultural Statistics*, which are published annually (though usually several years in arrears: thus the latest issues available at the time of writing are for 1965–6 in the case of India as a whole and the several states, and for 1958–9 in the case of Districts).[28] In particular, there are the figures for 'Net Sown Area', defined as 'the net area sown with crops and orchards, areas sown more than once being counted only once'.[29] Clearly these figures, if known with accuracy and completeness for a period of years, give a measure of change in the cultivated area—and hence, it might be thought, of the magnitude of the clearing of the waste. But there is a number of difficulties. Thus the Net Sown Area does not include all land used for agriculture in the broadest sense of the term: that is, land used not only for field cultivation but also for fallows, for pastoral activities, for the growing of tree-crops, and so on. In terms of the Indian land-use classification, one must, to obtain the total area used in these ways, add to the Net Sown Area (1) Total Fallows, made up of 'Current Fallows' and of 'Other Fallow Lands' which 'were taken up for cultivation but are temporarily out of cultivation for a period of not less than one year and not more than five years'; and (2) 'Other Uncultivated Land', which includes permanent pastures and other grazing grounds and 'miscellaneous tree crops and groves not included in the net area sown', for example, 'lands under casuarina trees [widely used as a source of fuel in Tamil Nadu], thatching grass, bamboo bushes . . . for fuel'. The final column of Table 5.III in fact includes all of these categories as well as the Net Sown Area, and has hence been headed 'Agriculturally Utilized Area', for want of a better term. It is, of course, an inflated measure of the area under agriculture in the broadest sense in which that term would be understood in, say, Western Europe, as anyone would readily testify who has ever seen an Indian village pasture-ground which is really a piece of degraded jungle; in fact, it is specifically defined to include 'grazing lands within forest areas', though how many such are caught in the statistical net is another matter. Again, Rajasthan had in 1962–3 over 8 million hectares of land in the category included in column (d) in the Table; and much of this must have been desert or semi-desert pasture.

However, to use figures for what is here called the 'Agriculturally Utilized Area' has, in the present context, certain advantages (leaving on one side, for the moment, the question of the accuracy of the underlying data). For an increase in this area is clearly a measure of the total assault on the wasteland of India, since such an increase can only be at the expense of Culturable Waste, or of Forests, or of Land not Available for Cultivation (the apparent contradiction in the inclusion of the last category will occasion no surprise): that is, it can only be at the expense of wasteland broadly defined. Moreover, to use this measure avoids a difficulty which surrounds the use of the Net Sown Area: namely, that it is very difficult to determine

(thousands of hectares)

Year	Net Sown Area (a)	Uncultivated Land: Total Fallow (b)	Culturable Waste (c)	Other (d)	Not Available for Cultivation (e)	Forests (f)	Total (g)	'Agriculturally Utilized Area' (h)
1947–48	99,354	24,654	5,471	31,940	41,013	35,845	238,277	185,948
1948–49	98,733	25,603	4,406	33,384	40,716	35,121	237,963	157,720
1949–50	114,616	23,791	6,447	40,211	48,982	40,832	274,879	178,618
1950–51	118,746	28,124	22,943	26,503	47,517	40,482	284,135	173,373
1951–52	119,400	28,962	23,929	16,473	501,73	48,889	287,826	164,835
1952–53	123,443	26,354	23,680	16,391	49,741	51,154	290,763	166,188
1953–54	126,808	24,734	22,899	16,680	49,663	51,080	291,864	168,222
1954–55	127,842	24,934	22,805	16,883	48,656	50,716	291,836	169,659
1955–56	129,156	24,127	21,537	17,358	48,396	51,343	291,917	170,641
1956–57	130,495	23,670	21,846	17,700	47,025	51,703	292,439	171,865
1957–58	128,629	25,671	21,136	18,764	46,976	52,527	293,703	173,064
1958–59	131,297	24,059	20,601	18,806	46,438	52,646	293,847	174,162
1959–60	132,429	23,374	19,922	19,198	47,246	55,265	297,434	175,001
1960–61	133,199	22,819	19,212	18,425	50,751	54,052	298,458	174,443
1961–62	135,352	21,655	18,641	18,614	50,471	54,542	299,275	175,621
1962–63	136,341	21,227	17,911	18,666	50,360	60,843	305,348	176,234
1963–64	136,438	21,286	17,659	18,993	50,236	60,995	305,607	176,717
1964–65	137,916	20,300	17,362	19,027	50,172	61,170	305,947	177,243
1965–66	136,149	22,440	17,180	19,040	50,247	60,278	305,334	177,629
1966–67 (provisional)	137,047	22,639	17,101	18,195	48,293	62,335	305,610	177,881
1967–68 (provisional)	139,702	20,833	16,612	17,949	48,087	62,323	305,506	178,484
1968–69 (provisional)	137,611	23,082	16,489	17,817	48,139	62,673	305,811	178,510

(d) Defined as 'Permanent pastures and other grazing lands' and 'Miscellaneous tree crops, and groves not included in the sown area'. (g) The total reporting area. (h) Author's term, see text; (h) = (a) + (b) + (d).

Source: Indian Agricultural Statistics and *Indian Agriculture in Brief* (for each year, latest available issue in which that year appears). Data converted from acres where necessary.

what part of an increase in the Net Sown Area is at the expense of wasteland, and what (by a process which is a form of intensification) is at the expense of fallow and other categories of 'Agriculturally Utilized Land'.

On the face of it, Table 5.III records an increase of some 38·3 million hectares in the Net Sown Area between 1947 and 1969, and an increase of 22·6 million hectares over the same period in the Agriculturally Utilized Area. The Table also shows a fairly consistent decline in Total Fallow (1951–2 to 1964–5) and Culturable Waste (1951–2 to 1968–9); an overall increase in Forests; and less consistent trends in other categories. But it is not proposed to draw further conclusions from Table 5.III, or to use it as a yardstick against which to measure the contribution of agricultural colonization in the reclamation of the waste. For to attempt so to use the all-India figures of the Table runs into difficulties for a number of reasons.

(1) There is the severe problem of the non-comparability of data as between different years in the series. It will be noticed that the total reporting area rose fairly continuously after independence, as more and more former princely states and other lands were brought within the Indian statistical framework;[30] though it became nearly stable after 1962–3.

(2) There is also the problem of the inaccuracy and unreliability of data from individual states which lie concealed in the apparently consistent trends in the means of the all-India figures. There are several reasons for unreliability. Thus it has already been seen that, if the result of the Dewas Pilot Survey is anything to go by, a good deal of land actually under cultivation may still be recorded as Culturable Waste. It is clear, too, that states have often failed to submit up-to-date statistics to the central authorities. Figures for Orissa first printed in 1954–5 were still being repeated in 1959–60. Data from Assam first reported in 1953–4 were still being repeated in 1957–8. Assam is, indeed, a particularly difficult state on other grounds. As Rasmussen has emphasized, 'the statistics published by the Ministry of Agriculture . . . are estimates—if not guesses—made by the Deputy Commissioners of the districts', there being no 'village papers' kept by *patwaris.*[31] And, as was suggested earlier, the figures for the availability of waste in Assam are clouded by social and political considerations.

(3) Problems also arise from periodical and sporadic reclassification of land. Thus Assam (a culprit once again) increased the area under 'forests', principally at the expense of 'other uncultivated land', it would seem.

(4) Finally, India in general, and certain regions of it in particular,

are all too subject to lean years, in which the Net Sown Area tends to contract and fallow to increase. It is therefore dangerous (the more so the smaller the area) to compare areas for single years at the beginning and end of a given period. It is safer to take the mean for two or more years, or, if the basic data and the nature of the inquiry justify it, to employ moving means.[32]

TABLE 5.IV

Rough Estimates of Changes in Net Sown Area and 'Agriculturally Utilized Area' 1947–63

(millions of hectares)

State	*Estimated Increase in Net Sown Area (adjusted)*	*Estimated Increase in 'Agriculturally Utilized Area' (adjusted)*
Andhra Pradesh	0·9	1·3
Assam*	0·3	0·3
Bihar	1·2	0·4†
Bombay (Gujarat plus Maharashtra)	1·7	1·8
Jammu and Kashmir* (from 1949–50)	0·0	0·3
Kerala (from 1952–3)	0·2	0·1
Madhya Pradesh	1·9	2·8
Mysore	0·2	0·2
Orissa	0·2	0·3
Punjab and Haryana	1·1	0·1
Rajasthan (from 1951–2)	4·0	4·1
Tamil Nadu	0·8	0·0
Uttar Pradesh	1·3	0·6
West Bengal	0·2	0·2
TOTAL	14·0	12·5

* A state whose statistics are particularly suspect or difficult for the required purposes.

† For reasons given in the text, the increase is in Net Sown Area *plus* Total Fallows.

Definitiosn, method of compilation, and reservations: see text.

Table 5.IV is an attempt, in which, in the nature of things, no great confidence can be placed, to overcome some of these difficulties in respect of the states of the Indian Union. The omission of Union Territories cannot seriously affect the outcome. Nothing can be done about inaccuracy and unreliability of data, except to label a particularly delinquent state with an asterisk, or to make occasional *ad hoc* adjustments such as the substitution of a figure for an earlier or subsequent year for that for a year in which the published data are particularly suspect. But some effort has been made to overcome problems of non-comparability of data, of reclassification, and of lean years for the period 1947–8 to 1962–3. The Table has not been taken beyond 1962–3 into the period up to 1965–6 for which data by states are available. For those years were indeed lean years during which there was widespread failure of rains and, in consequence, a marked abnormality in the agricultural statistics. Table 5.III suggests, in fact, that the Net Sown Area failed to maintain its upward trend and even fell back between 1964–5 and 1965–6. The latter year, further, saw an increase in Fallows and in Land Not Available for Cultivation.

Agricultural statistics for the several states were used in compiling Table 5.IV because state figures tend more readily to reveal what is generalized and concealed in all-India data: namely, the years in which in a given state there were marked changes in the reporting area, or in the area under any one kind of land use, of such an order as to force the conclusion that reclassification had been undertaken (whether or not the sources carried a note to that effect). State figures also enable one to keep an eye open for lean years. District data would, of course, have carried the analysis a stage further, given the availability both of sufficient time and of data for recent years: both were lacking.

It will also be noted that it was not found possible to use the base year (1947–8) for all states. The increases are, however, given as though they referred to the whole period 1947–8 to 1962–3. Here is an obvious weakness at the outset, but probably not a very serious one, given the relatively slow rate of change in the earlier years of independence.

The method used, both for Net Sown Area and for Agriculturally Utilized Area, was as follows.

(1) The agricultural statistics for each state, having been tabulated for the whole period in question, were studied in order to discover major breaks in series, either for the reporting area, or for one or more categories of land use. For most states there was fortunately only one such break; for some, none. In the case of states in whose series there was only one break, means were calculated for the first two and the last two years in the period before the break, and thus the mean rate of change per annum over the period. The same rate was then applied to the mean for the two years *after* the break, in order to arrive at an estimate of the figure that would have applied to Year 1 had the full reporting area, or the classification in force after the break, then obtained. The difference between this estimate

for Year 1 and the mean for the years 1961–2 and 1962–3 then gave an adjusted change in area over the whole period from the base year to 1962–3. The answer was entered in Table 5.IV in millions of hectares to no more than one place of decimals in order to emphasize once again the roughness of the estimation.

(2) Where there was more than one break in a series, the calculation was done by stages: first (as above) to obtain the base area in Year 1, given the rate of change in the period before the first break and the relevant areas after it; then to obtain a rate of change from the revised base area to that before the second break, and so a second revision of the base area; and so on, if necessary, for the third and any subsequent breaks in the series.

(3) A number of difficulties arose in applying this method: for example, where lean years distorted the calculations in spite of the use of means for two years; or where fewer than three years elapsed between base year and the year of a break, or between two breaks, so that the rate of change could not be computed from two pairs of two-year means. These were dealt with by estimating on what seemed the most suitable basis in the circumstances.

(4) From 1950–1 until 1955–6 the Forest area for Bihar was increasing almost continuously, apparently at the expense of 'Other Uncultivated Land'; while from 1947–8 until 1949–50 Culturable Waste was included in the latter category. The consequent difficulties were avoided by basing the estimate of the increase in Bihar's Agriculturally Utilized Area on Net Sown Area and Current Fallows only.

One limitation of this method, which reduces its already tenuous reliability still further, arises from the fact that some breaks in state series for the reporting area are the result of changes in state boundaries: for example, in the boundaries of the former state of Madras with the creation of Andhra Pradesh. To use the method outlined above implies that the new state and the old state are uniform in agrarian composition. But, short of elaborate District-by-District calculations, there seems no other ready and practicable solution. And, presumably, errors created by this difficulty cancel out at the all-India level (which is what matters for present purposes).

To comment briefly on Table 5.IV. The estimated and adjusted increase in the Net Sown Area (1947–8 to 1962–3) amounts only to 14·0 million hectares, compared with the increase of 37·0 million hectares suggested by an uncritical reading of Table 5.III. The increase in the Agriculturally Utilized Area shrinks from 20·2 million hectares from a similar reading of Table 5.III to 12·5 million hectares in Table 5.IV.

It is interesting that the estimated increase in the Net Sown Area is greater than that in the Agriculturally Utilized Area in the relatively crowded states of Bihar, Kerala, Punjab-Haryana, Tamil Nadu, and Uttar Pradesh, whereas the reverse is the case in the pioneer-fringe states (if they may be so called) of Madhya Pradesh, Orissa, and Rajasthan (whose absolute figures for both kinds of increase are far and away higher than those for any other state). There is a certain comforting logic in this, for it is what one would expect: crowded states naturally tend to expand their Net Sown Area at the expense of other components in the Agriculturally Utilized Area to a greater extent than less crowded states, which still have wasteland on which to expand.

As for the question that headed this section, what answer can now be given? The estimated 345,000 hectares of land gained from the waste by colonization between 1947 and 1963 is a relatively small part of the total effort, on any reading of the figures; perhaps 2·5 per cent of the estimated increase in the Net Sown Area over the same period, and 2·7 per cent of the estimated increase in the Agriculturally Utilized Area. The latter increase is probably the more meaningful measure, for both it and colonization (except for the odd colony, like Gobindpur and Theka in Assam, which occupy the site of a former grazing reserve) are concerned with land won from the waste; whereas, as has been seen, the increase in the Net Sown Area is partly at the expense of other categories within the Agriculturally Utilized Area. The impact of colonization on the waste of India as a whole is, however, by no means negligible. The area won between independence and 1963 is rather more than the whole of the estimated increase in the Net Sown Area of either Kerala, or Mysore, or Orissa in the same period; or, alternatively, of the same order as the increase in the same period of the Agriculturally Utilized Area of Orissa. Comparisons have already been made with the scale of colonization in other countries.

In the absence of suitable data it is impossible to bring Table 5.IV up to date. But, given the developments under the Rajasthan Canal and in Dandakaranya in recent years, it may well be that the area colonized between 1963 and 1971 is a higher proportion of the increase both in the Net Sown Area and in the Agriculturally Utilized Area during the same period than it was in the period 1947–63. If colonization in these two major areas continues, the proportion may also move upwards; though the relationship of colonization to other means of reclaiming wasteland may be affected if resources available in the forthcoming Fifth Plan period are sufficient to make possible a determined assault on the interstitial wastelands of India.

6

The Beneficiaries

THIS chapter will first direct attention back to Table 5.II and consider the broad categories which since independence have benefited from schemes of agricultural colonization in India; and go on to examine the way in which discussions and policies have favoured certain categories, particularly those which will be grouped together as 'the local poor'. It will then examine the extent to which similar considerations have influenced the choice of individual colonists within the predominant categories.

The chapter will go on to outline the part that the central government and the states have played in carrying out policies intended to benefit particular groups; and to review the phases (particularly in terms of the successive Five Year Plans) into which this official activity has fallen.

In Table 5.II the total figures for certain states and areas (notably Dandakaranya and Rajasthan) are transferred without change from the columns indicating colonies visited by the author to the column showing assumed grand totals (1947–63), while figures for other states and areas are adjusted upwards (see pp. 71–2 above). Now, certain categories (notably refugees, in Dandakaranya, and 'old temporary cultivation lessees' and purchasers of land by auction, in Rajasthan) are more heavily represented in the colonies visited than in India as a whole. The percentages at the foot of the Table must therefore be accepted with caution if an all-India picture for the period 1947–63 is desired.

It will be seen that refugees made up 20 per cent of the total in visited colonies in 1963 (though, for the reason just given, the all-India figure is bound to be rather less).[1] The refugees concerned comprise Bengalis and Punjabis in Tarai (which received many of its refugee colonists relatively soon after partition and the ensuing vast and tragic movement of peoples); Bengalis (mainly Namasudras, a Harijan caste) and Santals from East Bengal in Dandakaranya, where they began to be settled only after 1960 (many had spent long years in refugee camps in West Bengal, but some represented later waves of immigration into India corresponding to periods of nervousness and tension in what was then East Pakistan; Punjabis and Sindis at

Intikheri, in Madhya Pradesh); and, interestingly, Tibetans in a very un-Tibetan environment on the Coorg border in Mysore at Bylakuppe. There are also East Bengal refugees in colonies in Assam (visited in 1968). As for Bengalis in unvisited colonies, some have been sent to the Bihar Tarai, the Andaman Islands, and elsewhere; while others were sent to the highly unfamiliar environment of the Kota area of Rajasthan (but many deserted). Bahawalpuri and Kashmiri refugees have been settled in what was formerly Bhopal state;[2] and Tibetans in two further colonies, one in Mysore, one in Orissa. It was reported in June 1970 that refugees forming part of a renewed movement from East Bengal were to be settled not only in Dandakaranya and Tarai but also in Chanda District of Maharashtra, in Madhya Pradesh, and in the Raichur Doab;[3] while in May 1971 the Madhya Pradesh government appeared willing to settle refugees from the same region in reclaimed Chambal ravine-land (see above p. 61).[4] Refugees have also been settled in Adilabad District of Andhra Pradesh.

The number of refugee colonists in Dandakaranya grew from 6,369 in 1963 to 16,061 in 1971. Given this fact, and developments elsewhere, it may well be that refugees formed a higher proportion of the total number of colonists settled over the period 1947–71 than they did over the period 1947–63. But, with the flow of refugees now halted and even reversed, the proportion should in future decline.

Since most refugees have, throughout, been agriculturists, there was no other constructive solution for the vast majority of them but to try to put them on the land; and since land left by Muslims fleeing to Pakistan was inadequate for all the immigrant Punjabis and Sindis and was in any case (being in semi-arid Haryana) unsuitable for Santals and Bengalis, it may clearly be argued that colonization by refugees was often a matter of necessity and not one of choosing between one category of beneficiary and another.

The Government of India has also very little option over resettlement, in agricultural colonization schemes or otherwise, of a category of colonists which does not appear in Table 5.II (because the need to provide for it has arisen since 1963). As is well known, substantial populations of people of Indian origin or descent were built up during the colonial period in such countries as Burma and Ceylon; and the newly independent governments of those countries wish to repatriate at least a part of these populations, with or without the agreement of the Indian government. Some of the colonization schemes of the future may well contain repatriates, then; indeed, they may be settled in Dandakaranya if the establishment of Bangladesh does indeed stanch the flow of refugees thence. Proposals for plantations to absorb repatriates have already been mentioned.

A further category over whose inclusion in colonization schemes the government has had but little choice is that shown in the Table under the heading 'Compensation': this makes up as much as 9 per cent of the total in the visited colonies and perhaps about the same proportion of the assumed all-India total (1963). This category covers those resettled because their former lands were submerged in the construction of a reservoir, or for some similar reason. Clearly, in common justice, at least an option on new land has to be extended to the oustee (as the dispossessed cultivator is commonly called). In most cases studied the oustee was in fact given the option of an allotment (sometimes subject to a ceiling in the interests of 'land reform'), or of a cash payment, or of some combination of the two; sometimes, as in the case of the Bhakra works, there was a sliding scale weighted in favour of the small cultivator.[5] In some areas a high proportion chose a cash settlement.

The compensation of oustees is, of course, common practice in colonization schemes the world over. In Ceylon, for example, 6 per cent of colonists at 31 December 1953 fell into the compensation category.[6] Oustees were also prominent in such widely separated projects as the Volta scheme in Ghana (where no fewer than 91 per cent chose cash compensation), and the World Food Program settlement projects in Surinam and at Wadi Halfa in the Sudan.[7]

It should also be mentioned at this point that in Assam those who lose their land for a very different reason—its erosion by floods and laterally eroding rivers—are eligible for compensation by the allotment of new lands. There appear, however, to be no such cases in the colonization schemes studied. Official policy is that cultivators 'who have been rendered landless due to flood, erosion, requisition or acquisition will get preference over other landless persons'.[8]

There remain a number of categories of colonist in respect of which the hands of the authorities have not been so markedly forced by circumstances, so that the working of ideologies and of political considerations is easier to demonstrate. The first of these categories, 'Ex-*jagirdars*', stands apart and reflects curious circumstances in Rajasthan, to which the category is confined so far as Table 5.II is concerned, though Gujarat (not visited by the author) has also settled ex-*jagirdars* turned landless labourers.[9] The *jagirdars* were persons who, in the days of the princely states, were not only granted the revenue of the whole or part of a village (or of groups of villages) for services to the ruler, but also exercised local governmental and judicial sway. They held 62 per cent of the land in Rajasthan.[10] Their inclusion as a category of colonist under the Bhakra and Rajasthan

Canals may be seen as compensation for the loss of their powers (for *jagirdaris* are now abolished); but it probably also reflects a lingering respect for the old feudal order in Rajasthan; and, further, the fact that Rajasthan has copied many of the aspects of former British colonization policy in the Punjab, where privileges were accorded to 'yeoman farmers'.[11] By December 1971, when allotments to ex-*jagirdars* were nearly complete, a total of 1,981 had then been settled.

In selling land in colonization schemes by auction Rajasthan was once again *sui generis*, and practised a method of selecting colonists that is clearly poles removed from selection in terms of greatest need. Land has been auctioned under Bhakra to a total of 10,884 persons and under the Rajasthan Canal to 186. Here there is the interplay of a number of motives: the closely followed precedent of the Punjab Canal Colonies of British days;[12] the existence under the Rajasthan Canal of a tract of land of a magnitude denied to almost all other states, especially to those with vast populations of the needy; the local political situation; and the necessity for revenue (the financing of the Rajasthan Canal has been a perpetual problem: the Government of India has made only loans, not grants). Sales by auction were, however, suspended in March 1970 because of political objections, but sales at a reserved price have continued. And when, in November 1967, Rajasthan proposed to allot ravined land along the Chambal and its tributaries to applicants irrespective of their state or origin (as has already been mentioned in another connection), the basis was to be 'first come, first served'.[13]

The Thal Development Authority in Pakistan, faced with physical, demographic, financial, and agrarian conditions not unlike those in Rajasthan, relied on the auction ring for the disposal of part of its land;[14] while lower down the Indus, under similar conditions, 20 per cent of the land under the Gudu Barrage was to be sold in 240-acre lots to help meet the cost of the project.[15]

The Government of India and the states, including Rajasthan, have since independence demonstrated a great deal of common ground in their choice of categories to benefit from colonization schemes—when, that is, necessity had not denied them a choice (and assuming that it was mainly political and financial necessity that respectively forced Rajasthan to allot to ex-*jagirdars* and to sell by auction). What may for the moment be called 'the welfare motive' has in these circumstances tended to be dominant, or apparently so. The authorities, in other words, have sought so to allot land in colonization schemes as to benefit groups in local society who, it was thought, deserved it because of their neediness or backwardness, or to reward their services to the community, or for both reasons—rather than, for example, in order to increase production or to stimulate economic development. (This is not to say that elements of political calculation have not been intertwined with the welfare motive.)

Thus about 7 per cent of the colonists in the visited colonies (and probably a not dissimilar proportion in India as a whole in 1963) were made up of the 'deserving' categories of ex-servicemen, 'educated unemployed' and 'political sufferers'. The first of these classes, mainly to be found in immediately post-independence colonies like Piduguralla and Kalidindi in Andhra Pradesh, Wynad in Kerala and the older parts of the Uttar Pradesh Tarai scheme, needs little further comment: ex-servicemen found favour in the old Punjab Canal Colonies, were included (not very successfully) in some Ceylon Dry Zone schemes,[16] and are prominent in Pakistan's Thal.[17] The 'educated unemployed' are, of course, part of India's vast army of people with degrees or other educational qualifications who can find no jobs that they consider appropriate to their status—and, often, no jobs at all. A few of these people have been settled in the UP Tarai. (Ceylon has done proportionately far more for this category by way of allotments in colonization schemes, not with unqualified success.)[18] The 'political sufferers', now advancing in years and delightful company, are people who were imprisoned in the days of the Raj for their part in the independence movement: they were mainly to be found in the older parts of the UP Tarai colonies. In the cases of all three of these classes, clearly, there was no compulsion on the government to allot them land in colonization schemes: but they were all felt, particularly in the early days of independence, to have some claim on the state.

The 'welfare motive' is even more in evidence in the case of most of the remaining groups in Table 5.II, especially those in the categories (not mutually exclusive, it will be remembered) Harijans, tribals, Harijans and tribals, 'old temporary cultivation lessees', or unspecified landless.[19] 'Old temporary cultivation lessees' are those who held land in Rajasthan on a provisional basis at the time of the settlements of 1946–50, or were residents of Rajasthan before 1 April 1955 and occupied land on a provisional basis before 15 October 1955. It may safely be presumed that these relatively insecure tenants were not among the wealthy inhabitants of their old villages. With the Harijans, tribals and landless of other parts of India they fall into a class which may, for broad classificatory purposes, be called the 'local poor', making up 44 per cent of the total number of colonists in the colonies visited in 1963, and probably a higher proportion, around 50 per cent, nationally (for they are well represented in those states to whose total for visited colonies a factor of five has been applied in arriving at an assumed grand total). The classes, in varying proportions, are well scattered through most of the states. The category 'local poor' is not represented in the area of the Dandakaranya Development Authority, with its concentration on refugees, apart from 156 tribals settled by the Authority; though 25 per cent of the land cleared and reclaimed is handed back to the states (Madhya Pradesh and Orissa) so that it may be allotted to the local tribal people.

By December 1971 no fewer than 34,767 'old temporary cultivation lessees' had been allotted land in colonies in Rajasthan. By May 1972 such lessees occupied 47,406 hectares of land; while landless persons who had lived in one and the same Rajasthan village since 1 April 1965, or who had lived in a village within the Rajasthan Canal Project area, occupied a further 24,447 hectares (it is not possible to say precisely how many colonists are involved). Given these figures, and continued emphasis on the local poor almost all over India (apart from areas of refugee colonization), it is probable that well over half of the colonists given land in India since independence have fallen into this general category. If the establishment of Bangladesh brings a halt to the flow of refugees, the category seems likely to assume an even more dominant position for as long as colonization can be continued—and unless policies change drastically. Indeed, 400,000 hectares under the Rajasthan Canal are destined for allotment to members of the Scheduled Castes (Harijans).

The general issue of the allotment of land to tribal people and consideration of consequential problems (and indeed, the question of the definition of 'tribal', which is not as simple as it seems) will have to be left for later discussion, especially in chapter 13.

Ceylon, too, has tended to allot most of the places in its colonization schemes to those who are, ostensibly at any rate, 'landless peasants', some attention being paid to selection from districts where agrarian pressures are particularly high, though concern for strictly local peasants has also been very marked.[20] No one would pretend, however, that the supporting ideology in Ceylon has run closely parallel to that in India. Elsewhere in South and Southeast Asia concern for the poor and the landless has again been an important reason for the selection of colonists.[21]

The dominance (given a chance) of the welfare motive does not mean that it has always and everywhere been equally strong or uniformly operative in independent India. As a recent report has put it:

> The relative emphasis on settlement of different categories of person changed from time to time. Thus at one time greater importance was given to rehabilitate displaced persons or goldsmiths, at another time it was to recognise the services of those who suffered and sacrificed in the struggle for freedom or to express the gratitude for the part played by our armed forces during Chinese invasion and Indo-Pakistan war. However,

all along there has been the constant theme to ameliorate the economic backwardness to which the mass of landless agricultural labourers were condemned.[22]

Moreover, priorities have varied from state to state. Thus Assam, as has been seen, gives higher priority to 'oustees' and to victims of erosion than to the normal landless class. Political sufferers are preferred to Harijans and tribal people in Uttar Pradesh and Madhya Pradesh, but Gujarat reverses the preference.[23] However, as the quotation just made rightly has it, concern for landless agricultural labourers (many of whom are, of course, Harijans) is a constant theme.

One phenomenon that is at least in part a consequence of this concern for the local poor and the locally deserving is that a very small number of colonists, apart from refugees, have crossed state frontiers: only 128 in the colonies visited (all of whom were colonists from Kerala living, not very happily away from paddy-fields and coconut palms, on the site of the old Bhopal Central Mechanized Farm at Intikheri). This relative immobility of all but refugees no doubt also partly reflects the Hindu prejudices about migration that have often been commented upon;[24] and further, the fact that, as will shortly be seen, most colonization is primarily a responsibility of state governments. It follows that overcrowded states like Tamil Nadu and Andhra Pradesh, necessarily with but little colonization within their boundaries, have to look to other solutions of their problems. One of these, adopted by individuals rather than by the government, is the spontaneous movement of Telugus from Andhra to areas like the Raichur Doab and the middle Mahanadi, under the Hirakud dam. There have, however, been discussions about the possibility of bringing immigrants other than refugees into Dandakaranya (though up to 1971 these discussions were always overtaken by the need to provide for yet another wave of fleeing people from East Bengal). Rajasthan at one time proposed to take Gujaratis, Punjabis, and possibly people from Kerala into areas colonized under the Rajasthan Canal, and colonists irrespective of state of origin into ravine land along the Chambal and its tributaries. But so far as the Canal command at any rate is concerned, the fact that Rajasthan has had to finance so much from its own exiguous resources has made it politically impossible for it to settle anyone but its own people; while land in the Chambal ravine area has gone to local private investors.

V. V. Giri saw a colony composed of men from different states, faiths, and backgrounds, as a means of national integration.[25] But, quite apart from problems of land availability and finance, the development of linguistic nationalism in India may well make state governments chary of accepting colonists from a language group other than that of the majority of their electorate, refugees and repatriates apart (though perhaps not so for all time).

Dominance of the Welfare Motive in Colonization Policy

It is now proposed to look more closely at what has so far been rather loosely termed 'the welfare motive' in colonization. Three categories of beneficiaries (ex-servicemen, the educated unemployed, and political sufferers) can be fairly quickly dismissed. The ex-servicemen represent a thread of continuity between British welfare policies and those of independent India; for, as has been seen, such men were well represented in the Punjab Canal Colonies (though an Indian nationalist might well assert that the patriotic defenders of independent India were very different from the servants of the British Raj). The so-called 'educated unemployed' are a new category, whose recognition may be seen as a response not only to the welfare motive but also to political calculation: for the government of Uttar Pradesh (in whose colonies they are represented), has no doubt recognized, in common with governments in Ceylon and elsewhere in South and Southeast Asia, the danger inherent in the existence of an intelligent, educated, articulate, and politically active minority who are either unemployed, or occupied in work that falls far short of their expectations. Whether or not colonization, in Uttar Pradesh or elsewhere, or even land policy in a wider sense, can do more than touch the fringes of the problem is another matter. As for the political sufferers, these too are necessarily entirely a post-independence 'welfare' category.

It is clear that none of these three categories was chosen for colonization because it possessed agricultural aptitude or knowledge (nor, to anticipate a later section, have individuals within these categories been so chosen). Here is an instance of the possible conflict between what may be desirable in terms of the welfare motive and what may be desirable in terms of the maximization of productivity. Indeed, one may go further, and say that some at any rate of the sophisticated ex-servicemen colonists of Kerala (who can be exactly matched in Ceylon) are much less proficient at cultivation than at evading their responsibilities to the authorities (especially by failing to repay loans, where they display all the familiar skills of the old soldier and the barrack-room lawyer). This is not to say, however, that no member of these three categories is a productive cultivator. Some of the political sufferers in the Tarai are obtaining good yields with the help of fertilizers and improved techniques, each successfully organizing his small labour force (say of 20 men during *kharif*), and financing his farm from his own resources. Such cultivators may be reckoned among the new, progressive 'capitalist' farmers of India.[26] Productive and progressive cultivators were also not lacking among the ex-servicemen of the Wynad colony (Kerala) and could display some notable coffee gardens.

The conflict between the welfare motive and productivity is sharper in the case of the broad category, the 'local poor'. The heavy concentration on the local poor in most parts of India since independence has alreay been remarked on. It may in fact be said that, where (outside Rajasthan) there was no imperative need to deal with refugees or oustees, colonization policy has been primarily a matter of concern for landlessness, poverty, and need. This concern demands deep respect, and has, to the author's certain personal knowledge, strongly motivated many admirable public servants and political figures whose sincerity cannot be in doubt. But this is no reason for avoiding some examination of the issues involved.

Official concern for the local poor did not start with independence. Examples have already been given in chapter 2 of colonization schemes which were designed for, or at any rate included, members of backward castes or groups whom it was desired to rehabilitate: for example, 'criminal tribes' in Gwalior state and in the government-aided Arya Samaj colony near Lucknow. The Triple Canals Project in the Punjab made specific provision for 'depressed classes' as well as for former nomadic tribes and for cultivators from congested districts.[27] Concern for poverty and the consequences of agrarian congestion was therefore clearly felt not only by social welfare organizations like the Arya Samaj but also by governments in British provinces and at least some (though by no means all) princely states.

Although the authorities aided the Arya Samaj colony just mentioned, social reform movements like the Samaj were in fact bound in a web of complex and shifting relationships not only with religious but also with political movements of a nationalist flavour.[28] This seems to have been true generally of bodies concerned with the uplift of 'untouchable' and tribal communities in the first decade of the twentieth century, when, according to C. H. Heimsath, 'the political nationalist movement was evolving a strategy of mass appeal . . . under the auspices of the extremists', and concurrently showing a new concern for the common man.[29]

The intertwining of altruism and of political calculation has thus a long history. But that intertwining took on an altogether different degree of complexity when Gandhi acquired dominance over the Indian National Congress after 1920, and 'social reform became part of the political programme for national advancement'.[30]

Gandhi's concern for the untouchable castes is well known. It was he who called them 'Harijans', which may be translated as 'people of God', and conducted a long campaign against untouchability and its consequences; and in most parts of India the poorest of the local poor are Harijans.[31] Gandhi also had a strong interest in the status of cultivators in general, holding amongst other things that the earth should belong to them, rather than to the landlords; but advocating co-operative farming.[32] In all these matters, no doubt, idealism and political calculation were inextricably mixed. Certainly Gandhi's social welfare campaigns gave him a firm hold on the rural people and enabled him to lead them into the civil disobedience movement; in particular, they gave him a valuable weapon in his struggles with Dr Ambedkar for the leadership of the untouchables.[33]

Two further points are relevant to the present study. The first is that Gandhi, like many Indians after him, seems to have seen no contradiction between a policy of 'land for the tiller' and a massive increase in food supplies, provided that cultivators were 'energetic, resourceful and self-reliant'. 'There is plenty of fertile land, enough water and no dearth of manpower,' he asserted. 'Why should there be food shortage under such circumstances?'[34] The second is that, although concern for backward communities existed before Gandhi, it was his influence that was strongly felt in post-independence agrarian policy, not least in policy towards agricultural colonization in general and the choice of favoured categories as colonists in particular: partly through the preference shown to Harijans (and for that matter to tribal peoples); partly because it was Gandhi more than anyone else who made the rural poor, whether Harijan or landless labourer, a political force to be reckoned with.

Gandhi was, of course, 'both orthodox and reformist';[35] and his reformism, it has been said, was that of a Westernized liberal with a radical, revolutionary, and egalitarian outlook.[36] A Westernized, or at any rate a non-Indian outlook was even more characteristic of the group of urban, socialist intellectuals led by Jawaharlal Nehru, who were strongly impressed by Marxist ideas and by the Russian example, especially, in the present context, in relation to co-operative and collective farming.[37] The influence of this group within the Indian National Congress is evident in the *Report of a Sub-Committee of the National Planning Committee on Land Policy, Agricultural Labour and Insurance*.[38] This Sub-Committee was appointed in 1938 and reported in 1948 to the National Planning Committee, of which Nehru was Chairman. From the title and period of activity of the Sub-Committee one might reasonably expect to find in it the mainspring of agrarian policies (including those of colonization) in the early years of independence. But the *Report* is in fact mainly concerned with proposals for co-operative and collective farming, on wasteland as well as on land already in cultivation, whose effect on colonization will be dealt with in chapter 12. A number of other matters relevant to the subject of this book are touched on (for example, there is one of the classic misunderstandings on the amount of culturable waste, said to cover 140 million acres and to need only capital and labour for development, given a prior solution of the 'ownership problem' in terms of making all such waste the 'property of the community').[39] All that is in fact said in the body of the *Report* about priorities in the allocation of wasteland is that need is emphasized as a basic criterion: every adult citizen of the New India is to have access to cultivable land unless provided with alternative work.[40] This is, however, important enough as a reflection of ideology, not untinged by political calculation; and, for that matter, of the town-based lack of realism which, with much confused thinking, permeates the whole *Report*. Professor N. G. Ranga, however, in a contribution on a 'Scheme for the Protection of Agricultural Labour', though mainly concerned with guaranteed wages and the like, did stress the passion of labourers for land of their own and advocated the allocation of all unoccupied land, all land 'made cultivable by modern scientific methods', and all disafforested land, to landless agricultural labourers (but for co-operative cultivation, it is interesting to observe, in view of Ranga's later connection with the Swatantra Party and vigorous opposition to collectivization or anything approaching it);[41] while Radhakamal Mukherjee drew attention to statistics seeming to show that the ratio between the number of agricultural labourers and the number of 'ordinary cultivators' increased from 29·1 per cent to 40·7 per cent between 1921 and 1931 (but he did not specifically advocate colonization as a remedy for the condition of agricultural labour, though he did envisage inter-provincial migration).[42]

Finally, the Sub-Committee, like Gandhi, did not see the possible conflict between the dominance of welfare, given everyone's 'right' to land, and self-sufficiency within a decade in foodstuffs and in industrial raw materials, the declared aim of the agrarian reforms it proposed.[43] (Nor, for that matter, did Nehru, writing many years later: for, giving signs of yet another socio-political motive, he advocated land reform because without it he saw no possibility of amelioration in the productivity of agriculture; but saw its principal goal as the breaching of 'the ancient class structure of a society which is stagnant'.)[44]

In fairness it must be said that the Population Sub-Committee of the National Planning Committee was a great deal more realistic than the Land Policy Sub-Committee whose work has just been reviewed. Although the Population Sub-Committee quoted culturable waste figures, it recognized, as has been mentioned, that opportunities for the expansion of cultivation were limited.[45] But, as part of the planned food policy which it advocated in order to deal with pressure of population, it recommended the reclamation of wasteland through rural settlement departments. It also recommended the organization of migration from densely peopled areas;[46] it commented that provincial autonomy had led to 'provincial feeling' against colonization, but sought to minimize such 'social friction' by so planning colonies as to avoid lands near existing villages or in the possession of tribal peoples. The National Planning Committee accepted its Sub-Committee's recommendations, and thought that planned inter-provincial migration should be encouraged in order to establish zones of agricultural colonization in newly reclaimed areas.[47] (Apart from the movement of refugees, very little such migration has, of course, actually taken place.) The Population Sub-Committee's Report is, however, chiefly notable here for its unambiguous emphasis on food supply, rather than on the welfare of particular groups, as the aim of agricultural colonization.

It would take too long to review all the discussions in the years before independence which influenced the choice of beneficiaries of agricultural colonization after 1947. By no means all of these discussions took place in the committees of the Indian National Congress. Some influential contributions to the discussion came from private individuals, or from officials writing in a private capacity. One of the most noteworthy writers in the latter class was Tarlok Singh, whose *Poverty and Social Change* was published in 1945.[48] As Myrdal has rightly said, 'its philosophy and practical recommendations . . . have had considerable influence on the policy of the Congress Party and the government'[49] (not least because Tarlok Singh became a prominent and indefatigable member of the Planning Commission). It is true that the book makes no specific recommendations on colonization, in spite of its author's experience in the Indian Civil Service in the Punjab. It does, however, draw attention not only to rural poverty in general but also to the special plight of landless agricultural labourers, and no doubt had its influence on policies under which priority was given to this depressed class in colonization schemes;[50] and it does, in its general theme, powerfully reinforce the argument that, far from production and social welfare being antithetic, they are complementary. Myrdal has shown how deeply this argument has affected official economic thinking in India;[51] and it has certainly affected policy towards agricultural colonization, not always with results that have either enhanced welfare or fostered production. More recently V. V. Giri, President of India, has restated the welfare case for labour-absorptive colonization schemes in neo-Gandhian terms, and in the context of the pressing need for employment (compare below, p. 297);[52] while it has become a truism in the India of 1972 that land reform (including 'land for the landless') is necessary not only in the interests of social justice but also to contain potential agrarian unrest.

It is also relevant to remind the reader at this point that the constitution of India reflects some at least of the social welfare motives that have been mentioned in the last few pages. Thus Article 46 has it that:

> The State shall promote with special care the educational and economic interests of the weaker sections of the people, and, in particular, of the Scheduled Castes and the Scheduled Tribes, and shall protect them from social injustice and all forms of exploitation.

Under Article 338 there is a Special Officer for the Scheduled Castes and Scheduled Tribes, appointed by the President, whose duty it is to investigate and to report on all matters relating to the constitutional safeguards provided for these Castes and Tribes. ('Scheduled Castes' are defined so as to include Harijans; and 'Scheduled Tribes' so as to include most, though not quite all, of those whom this book for the moment is loosely calling 'tribal peoples': but see p. 274 below.)[53]

Inquiries conducted in India since independence also illustrate the 'welfare motive' as it is now emerging, in its considerable complexity and in its bearing on colonization, from the discussion. For example, a Commission reported on the condition of 'backward classes' in 1956;[54] and, in particular, on that of the castes and tribes once known as 'criminal tribes' (under the Criminal Tribes Act of 1897), then as 'ex-criminal tribes', but whom the Commission wished to have called by the term 'denotified communities'.[55] It will be remembered that Gwalior state set up a colonization scheme for these people. The Commission, showing the lamentable optimism of many of its predecessors over land availability, and equating landlessness with backwardness, wished the land revenue rules to be amended so that land would be issued 'to all [*sic*] the landless *pro rata* and the excess to those with uneconomic holdings'. State governments were to 'create incentives' for migration from villages in which there was insufficient land to places where land was available. How hard dies the myth that there is abundant readily cultivable land in India!

By any reckoning, however, Daniel Thorner must surely be right in asserting that 'agricultural workers form the most disadvantaged economic group in India today';[56] and therefore that group among which the 'welfare motive' has found the most ample scope. Two inquiries have supplied facts and statistics on which policy and action might be based. The first Agricultural Labour Enquiry was started in 1949, and produced in 1955 a massive set of tables on the number, distribution, and condition of agricultural labourers.[57] The second Enquiry was conducted in 1956–7, and reported in 1960.[58] Both Enquiries drew attention to the huge size of the agricultural labour force and to its general poverty and backwardness. But differences in definition and methodological problems have created difficulties (especially in making comparisons between the two surveys) which have in turn led to acute controversy.[59] Rather outside this controversy lie attempts, like those of J. E. Schwartzberg, to produce analyses of the regional distribution of agricultural labour.[60] *If* these were based on accurate and uniform data, and *if* they covered a wide enough range of parameters adequately to define the condition of the agricultural labour-force, then one would have in effect maps of the needs to be met by the application of the 'welfare motive' in colonization schemes and elsewhere.

A year after the publication of the second Enquiry, the Planning Commission's Panel on Land Reforms set up a committee under the chairmanship of R. K. Patil to report on the settlement of landless agricultural workers.[61] It drew attention to the general backwardness of these workers and to conclusions drawn from the Enquiries that there was little evidence of any trend towards improvement in their condition. In considering means of settling labourers on the land, and in the absence of data on any land made available by the imposition of ceilings on land holdings, it concentrated on culturable waste and on the surveys of wastelands then in progress. From the present point of view, its most important conclusions were that the practice of auctioning wasteland should be discontinued; and that the allotment of land should be made in the following order of priority: first, 'to ejected tenants (i.e. tenants who were ejected on grounds of resumption of land by the land holders for personal cultivation', following land reform) and oustees; and, second, to landless agricultural workers. Moreover, within each category members of Scheduled Castes and Tribes should have preference. In 'low pressure areas', 'small farmers' could also be considered after the needs of the priority classes had been met. The Patil Committee reflects the full working of the 'social welfare' motive, and had a powerful influence on land policy (including agricultural colonization).

The Commissioner for Scheduled Castes and Scheduled Tribes, appointed under Article 338 of the constitution, has also from time to time commented on the landlessness of his charges and on the implementation of land policies, of colonization and otherwise, designed to benefit them. Thus in 1963–4 he reported complaints from Madhya Pradesh that subordinate staff were not scrupulously observing the priorities in the state land code, and that ex-servicemen and goldsmiths were getting higher priority than the 'backward classes'.[62] Others, too, have drawn attention to the poverty of tribal peoples and to their exploitation by plainsmen, and suggested colonization as a remedy.[63]

From time to time, however, voices, albeit less insistent ones, have been raised in favour of augmented food production as the prime aim of wasteland policy. Thus the Uppal Committee, reporting on the wastelands of Madras, maintained that 'resettlement work [by implication, for the benefit of landless labourers] is not the be-all and the end-all of our labours'; and that its main purpose was 'to locate lands which can be . . . brought under the plough for increasing the food resources of the country'.[64]

Selection within the Social Welfare Categories

In the Punjab Canal Colonies of British days, very strong emphasis indeed was placed on the selection of 'industrious and skilful cultivators', to quote the specification for colonists in the Lower Bari Doab Colony.[65] Trevaskis explains how colonists from the 'congested districts' were chosen personally by British revenue officers, who were careful to weed out dotards, loafers, those who were physically or mentally unfit, and boys put forward merely to get extra land for their families; and to choose only from members of 'agricultural tribes' who were hereditary landowners or occupation tenants (though with holdings of inadequate size).[66] Again, Darling quotes an interesting account of the methods by which these ends were achieved by one British settlement officer, J. A. Grant, who sought to eliminate the unsuitable until he was left with 'a band of men all connected by common descent, all physically fit to take up a new life in a new country under considerable difficulties, all hard up for land, but with sufficient resources to start them'.[67]

In a nutshell, then, it was the policy in the Punjab Canal Colonies, while still having an eye to neediness, to subordinate it to ability, so far as this could be judged in the selection of individual peasant colonists. It might be expected that independent India would have reversed the emphasis, and subordinated ability to need, given the strength of the admittedly complex 'welfare motive'; and that need would, further, be measured by means of such yardsticks as landlessness and size of family (as has manifestly been the practice in Ceylon).[68] It might be expected, too, that the primacy of need would be evident in the choice of individuals within the numerous group that has here been called 'the local poor'.

In point of fact, however, and rather to his surprise, these expectations were by no means fully realized during the author's field studies. In the first place, in a fair number of colonies intended for various categories of the 'local poor', the question of the selection of individuals did not arise because the supply of would-be colonists was no greater than, and sometimes less than, the number of places available.[69] This was especially true of tribal colonies: for example, of the Araku Valley and of Jeelugumilli in Andhra Pradesh; of Kotia Pani and Kansal Banjara in western Madhya Pradesh; and of the tribal colonization schemes in the Dandakaranya area of the same state and of Orissa. But it was also true of the several small colonies in the Malnad region of Mysore and, apparently, of the co-operative Jayashree colony at Bhamer in Dhulia District of Maharashtra, where 'all those who formed the co-operative' got land (though it could be argued, in the light of what will be said in chapter 12, that to insist on co-operative cultivation is in itself to introduce the eye of a needle between the landless labourer and the land).

The lack of sufficient supply of would-be colonists is by no means confined to the 'local poor'. Refugees from camps in Bengal, and even more in Assam, have not shown any great eagerness to settle in Dandakaranya; indeed, there were riots in Assam in December 1968, fomented by refugees who wished to remain there. There are many cases, too, of oustees unwilling to leave their ancestral lands: in some cases they insisted on staying until the rising waters of a new reservoir literally threatened them with drowning. It is also surprising, given the supposed pressure on land in India, that a relatively high proportion of oustees prefer compensation in cash rather than in land. Thus only 11 per cent of the landowners affected by the Hirakud Reservoir in 1954–5 chose land (although it was reclaimed by the government); and only 650 out of 4,602 affected by the Maithon Reservoir in the Damodar Valley.[70]

The absence of a strong desire to obtain and to hold land in a colonization scheme is also at first sight suggested by the high rates of desertion which may be quoted: 37 out of 62 original colonists in the Aminabad Colony of East Godavari District, Andhra Pradesh; 519 out of 1,917 ex-servicemen in Wynad Colony, Kerala; 126 out of 149 in Maraiyoor Colony in the High Ranges of the same state; 162 out of 203 from the settlement for Kerala colonists at Intikheri, in Madhya Pradesh; about 100 out of 500 Tibetans at Bylakuppe, in Mysore; and smaller proportions from, for example, the refugee colonies in Dandakaranya,[71] from the Pabal tribal colony in Poona District, Maharashtra, and in the colonies in the Uttar Pradesh Tarai. There were also a number of desertions from Kaki

Colony, Assam, when settlers found they would have to reclaim their land. But hasty conclusions must not be drawn from such figures as these. In many of the colonies cited there were special circumstances. Thus the Kerala colonists in Intikeri were notoriously fish out of water; even more so were the Tibetans in Bylakuppe. The Pabal deserters, and no doubt some of those in Uttar Pradesh and elsewhere, were attracted by alternative urban employment. In some colonies settlers were repelled by adverse natural conditions: for example, aridity untempered by irrigation at Maraiyoor. In other cases still, desertion could not be construed as a measure of lack of pressure on land because it co-existed with severe local encroachment.

Encroachment was, in fact, seen to be a considerable problem in a number of colonization areas during the author's fieldwork (though, not surprisingly, it was usually absent or of only minor significance in remote tribal areas; and of no great moment, at least in and around colonies in Andhra Pradesh, the Malwa region of Madhya Pradesh, Tamil Nadu, Maharashtra, Mysore, and Haryana). It was particularly noted in the Damodar Valley in Bihar and in the Chambal Valley in both Madhya Pradesh and Rajasthan: in the latter state, pre-1955 encroachers had been settled on 4,119 hectares of land. There were said to be some 400 encroachers, some Communist-inspired, in 1963 in the area of the Kheri Colony in Uttar Pradesh; while encroachment on forest land, again said to be similarly inspired, was a great problem in 1968 around the Kaki Colony in Assam.[72] There was much encroachment by 1972 in the Malkangiri Zone of Dandakaranya. But nowhere was the problem more acute than in the Wynad and High Ranges of Kerala, where in 1963 large areas of land, including Reserve Forest, were under encroachment. This is not of course a surprising state of affairs given the notorious land hunger in Kerala, and given the widespread spontaneous colonization there, in the time-honoured Indian pattern, which has already been discussed.[73]

Wynad is an example of an area where a high level of desertion by ex-servicemen colonists coexists with a high level of encroachment, suggesting that desertion is not necessarily a measure of low pressure on land (though it also suggests that alternative employment was available to the deserters). The Wynad experience leads to the conclusion that, if one object of colonization is to select cultivators who will remain on the land they are allotted, then a high proportion of Wynad colonists, especially among ex-servicemen, were ill-selected.

Where the supply of would-be colonists was large enough, in relation to the supply of land, to make selection necessary, by what methods was it in fact exercised? And what criteria were applied? In some cases the first question arises, but not the second. Thus under the Rajasthan Canal, for lack of an agreed solution, colonists within categories are chosen by the simple device of a lottery; while at Sardapur Bhoodan Colony in the Uttar Pradesh Tarai it was merely a matter of 'first come, first served'; and, under the Bhakra Canal in Haryana, 'all who applied in time' were 'selected'. In other cases, the method of selection could not readily be discovered: this applied to the Intikheri colony for people from Kerala and to the admirable colony at Thengumarahada in Tamil Nadu. In yet other cases, selection seems to have been irregular: this was certainly so in the Kaki colony in Assam. Here, it was the intention to give priority in the allotment of land to 'political sufferers, followed by flood-affected families and landless agriculturists'.[74] Selection was made by a Revenue Officer, from amongst persons in these categories who applied for land in the colony. The Programme Evaluation Organisation's study disclosed, however, that 'lawyers, Government servants, professional men and others' outside the stated categories were in fact selected, many of them actually being absentees.[75] Field study confirmed that there had indeed been serious irregularities. One colonist interviewed admitted to being a Nowgong businessman by origin, though he hastily added that he had been a poor one, and the son of a cultivator: what he did not admit was that he in fact held two plots, and was actively engaged in trading as well as cultivating—and he was probably a moneylender as well. (He was, however, one of the most progressive cultivators encountered in Kaki, sowing improved strains and using fertilizers, and thus illustrates one of the dilemmas of contemporary agrarian India—that the most progressive and productive farmers are often not only those least entitled to land on welfare grounds, but also those who have obtained resources, including land, improperly.)

Kaki was by no means the only colony visited by the author where landlessness was officially a prime criterion in the allocation of land to individuals (officially in Kaki, of course, after political sufferers and flood-affected families had been catered for). For example, preference was given to landless agricultural labourers in the Aminabad, Araku Valley, and Kannaram colonies in Andhra Pradesh; Jamunia in Bihar (where landless members of the Scheduled Castes were preferred); the High Ranges and Wynad colonies of Kerala (apart from areas reserved for ex-servicemen); Moranam and Velakapuram in Tamil Nadu (colonists in the latter all being Harijans); the Amalner co-operative colonies in Maharashtra; and the Kheri, Pilibhit, and Sardapur colonies in the Uttar Pradesh Tarai. This is, of course, a long list (though it naturally excludes those major colonization areas where the preoccupation has been with refugees); and also the Rajasthan Canal colonies, where the preoccupation has been rather with insecure tenants than with the totally landless—though, as has been seen, the latter were by no means totally neglected.

Landlessness was variously defined: in Wynad, for example, it meant possession of less than 5 acres (2 hectares) of dry land or 1½ acres (0·6 hectares) of wet; in Gujarat, of less than 2 acres (0·8 hectares), flexibly interpreted; in Tamil Nadu, 5 acres dry and 2 acres wet; and maxima which varied locally in Bihar and Madhya Pradesh.[76]

Although, apart from specific provision for craftsmen and the like, all selected landless individuals were supposed to be agriculturalists, very little effort indeed has been made in post-independence India to select cultivators of proven agricultural ability:[77] the Moranam colony, where applicants were submitted to a test by Agricultural Extension Officers, was a noteworthy exception. Now, even if one accepts that priority, or some measure of priority would be given to the 'local poor' as a category, there is little justification, where the supply of applicants of virtually equal neediness is large, for failure to select those likely to make the best and most productive cultivators. It may be urged by the sociologist that study of established colonies shows little or no correlation between such success and any parameters measurable by him in advance;[78] but the settlement officers in the old Punjab knew better. J. A. Grant, whose work has already been mentioned, would first weed out the physically unfit, then examine hands in order to discover 'the real workers among the community'.[79] And Gandhi, after all, wanted cultivators who were 'energetic, resourceful and self-reliant'.

Moreover, selection procedure has in many cases been highly unsystematic, whatever the criteria officially applied. Indeed, the Programme Evaluation Organisation study asserts, with reference to the small colonies of Guna District, Madhya Pradesh, that 'there was no procedure involved in selection of settlers'.[80] Again, even though it was intended to establish a selection committee in Pilibhit colony in Uttar Pradesh, it was for some time unable to operate because of uncertainty as to whether land was to be allotted for individual or for joint cultivation.[81] A selection committee consisting entirely of officials was, however, constituted in connection with the Attur colonization project in Tamil Nadu.[82] No doubt largely because of the rarity of adequate selection machinery at the time that it was reporting, the Patil Committee of 1961 recommended a standard procedure, to follow surveys of wastelands (see below, pp.

147–9).[83] Lists of available lands were to be posted in villages containing eligible potential applicants, and applications were to be sent to the *sarpanch* (*panchayat* president) where *panchayati raj* was in operation, otherwise to a 'prescribed authority'.[84] In either case the applications, with observations, would be sent on to the Block Development Officer, or to the *Tehsildar*, as the case might be. The officer in question would then visit the villages in order to select colonists at an open meeting (that is, he would hold the equivalent of the land *kachcheri* as known in Ceylon).[85] He would publish a draft list of successful candidates, in accordance with the established priorities, invite objections, and in due course publish a final list. It is quite clear, however, that this procedure, designed to ensure public participation and to provide safeguards against malpractices, has by and large been honoured only in the breach. A Madras report of 1964 proposed to cut out the *sarpanch* (on the grounds that he would find it difficult to keep records, might delay applications, and in any case was superfluous in this context; other reasons perhaps remained unstated);[86] but it retained the important principle that the *Tehsildar* or other officer should select at an open meeting (which also, of course, would make it easier to choose *à la* Grant those who looked like good cultivators, if only authorities were wise enough to try to choose such); and it proposed final selection by a committee of official and non-official members.

In case the section now about to be concluded leaves any impression that India is peculiar in the attention it gives to the neediness of the individuals to be selected as colonists, or in the improprieties that are apt to creep into the process, a few words about practice in one or two other countries may not be out of place here. In writing on Ceylon some years ago, the author drew attention to 'the tendency to select [from the landless] a man with a large family because they increase his *need* rather than because of their effect on his *ability*'; and to the fact that 'insufficient attention is paid to those qualities . . . which make for a good cultivator'.[87] It was also clear that village Headmen sometimes recommended undesirables in order to be rid of them, and others not genuinely landless. (Since 1968, however, Ceylon has introduced a new procedure for selection, based on a points system which gives maximum weightage to a young, married, landless, credit-worthy person with two or three children only, experienced in agriculture, showing evidence of familiarity with improved practices and related skills, and holding a Practical Farm School Certificate.)[88]

Again, D. Christodoulou, writing on the land settlement operations of the Egyptian General Desert Development Organization, showed that while knowledge of agriculture and a 'good record' were among the criteria for the selection of individual colonists, so were landlessness and the possession of a large family.[89]

Finally, in Malaysia's Federal Land Development Authority schemes in 1965, applicants were chosen by means of a points system. Only a maximum of five points was given for agricultural experience, compared with maxima of ten for age (35–6 years being the preferred optimum), ten for family size exceeding five children, and five for ownership of land amounting to less than one acre.[90] In one scheme (Ayer Lanas), the consequence was that 58 per cent of the colonists were without any form of agricultural experience.

Role of the Centre, the States, and Other Bodies

Discussion may now usefully turn to the part that the central government, the states, and other bodies have played in post-independence India in carrying out policies designed to benefit the categories and individuals that have formed the subject of earlier sections; and to the organization developed to deal with agricultural colonization.

When working in Ceylon some years ago, the author found the organization of peasant colonization to be of elegant and readily comprehensible simplicity:[91] a single Department in Colombo, that of the Land Commissioner, was responsible, under the Minister of Agriculture and Lands, for deciding that a piece of land should be colonized, for the general supervision of alienation to colonists, and, through Colonization Officers, for what may be termed the 'after-care' of colonists; though the Land Commissioner, between selection of land and its alienation, handed it over to the Director of Land Development for clearing, reclamation, house construction and similar work, and though the Irrigation and other Departments also had important roles to play. The only exception at the time was in the area of authority of the Gal Oya Development Board, which there assumed the responsibility of the Land Commissioner and of the other officials concerned. A similar simplicity characterizes the organization of the Federal Land Development Authority in Malaysia.

The situation in India is very different and is, in fact, of considerable complexity. This is only to be expected in a vast country with a federal structure; but there are other reasons, notably that no one authority or department at the centre is responsible for colonization, and that in different states similar work is very differently organized.

From its establishment in September 1947 until in 1962 it merged (as the Department of Rehabilitation) in the Ministry of Works,

Housing and Supply, there was at the centre a Ministry of Rehabilitation charged with the duty of dealing with the problem of the 9 million or so refugees who migrated from Pakistan after partition.[92] Much of the work of the Ministry, including the placing of refugees in colonization schemes, was accomplished in association with other ministries of the Government of India and with state governments (a not altogether satisfactory arrangement, for states have differed in the assiduity and efficiency with which they have handled refugee colonists). The Dandakaranya project has, however, always been the particular concern of the Ministry—which issued the preliminary report[93] on it (although suggestions for the use of the region for refugee resettlement came originally, it seems, from Shri S. V. Ramamurthy, then an adviser to the Planning Commission) and which the government of India placed in 'administrative charge' of the scheme. It was, further, given the task of making arrangements whereby the state governments concerned (those of Madhya Pradesh and Orissa) should delegate relevant powers to the central government, under whose direction should function a Dandakaranya Development Authority, consisting, in addition to DDA officials, of representatives of the state and central governments.

The Dandakaranya Development Authority was thus a device, strongly reminiscent of the Gal Oya Development Board in Ceylon[94] and in turn of the Tennessee Valley Authority, for undertaking unified development on a regional (and in this case on an inter-state) basis and in the face of problems that might well have been too much for the normal state departmental machinery. The Authority set up a number of departments (engineering, irrigation, reclamation, resettlement, land, agriculture, animal husbandry and veterinary science, forest, finance, medical, education, and transport; the work of the Resettlement Department was later handled by its headquarters and by zonal administrators); and, to all intents and purposes, replaces the state governments for these purposes on the land it holds within its statutory area of authority (the Bastar District of Madhya Pradesh and the Koraput and Kalahandi Districts of Orissa—perhaps for geographical reasons that will be clear from chapter 3 it should also have included the Chanda District of Maharashtra and possibly also certain contiguous areas of Andhra Pradesh). Its powers and functions are, however, subject to a number of limitations: for example, its Forest Department does not conserve forests, but is merely concerned with the felling and extraction of useful timber in advance of reclamation; while the land to be reclaimed is merely handed over for that purpose by the state governments, rather than being vested in the Authority; so that it will eventually be for the states to issue *pattas* to colonists when the reclaimed and cultivated land is eventually handed back to them, at a date yet to be determined. This arrangement has the disadvantage that the Authority (unlike the Gal Oya Board) cannot simply decide to clear a given block within its area of authority, but has to wait for an often dilatory state government to hand it over: this has not infrequently caused delay, and has been a great handicap to rational forward planning.

The author, in studying the work of the Gal Oya Development Board some years ago, came to the conclusion that, given the circumstances in the region concerned, there was much to be said for the replacement of the normal departmental machinery by a specially constituted authority: notably because of the advantages of unified regional planning; because of the possibility of achieving a greater flexibility and initiative in planning than is normally within the reach of a bureaucracy; and because of the *esprit de corps* and sense of participation in a great undertaking that can, with the right leadership, be engendered.[95] This conclusion is not shaken by his association with an inquiry which found that, in many respects, the Gal Oya Project was economically unsuccessful.[96] Similar advantages apply to the establishment of a separate authority for the Dandakaranya project, though it has not been easy to establish the right conditions for success, for reasons that include difficulties in the higher échelons of management; friction between Bengalis and non-Bengalis, and between Oriyas and non-Oriyas in the administration (many Oriyas have a sensitivity, especially in face of the often more sophisticated Bengali, that bears the stamp of a minority complex); and political complications not unconnected with the intricacies of Bengal politics—for Bengali politicians are aware of the possibility of exploiting refugee discontent.

It is to be hoped, in fact, that if the flow of refugees has indeed ceased, and if Dandakaranya is then able to take colonists other than refugees and local tribal people, the Authority will be empowered to move into this field too.[97] It is, however, like the Damodar Valley Corporation, vulnerable to pressure from politicians for whom state boundaries and rights are more important than the principles of integrated regional development.[98]

No special comment is necessary on the national organizations that deal with the colonization of most of the other categories of colonists: this is almost entirely a matter for the states, though, as might be expected, the Ministry of Defence in New Delhi takes an interest in colonization for and by ex-servicemen. The centre has, however, been very active on behalf of the 'local poor', particularly of landless agricultural labourers (many of whom, of course, are Harijans) and to some extent of tribal peoples. Not all of this activity has been concerned with colonization: indeed, much of it has led rather to the utilization of small patches of waste (that is, to 'village expansion'). But the centre has been very much involved in the conduct of inquiries, notably the two inquiries into the state of agricultural labour already mentioned (see above, p. 100). The problems of agricultural labour (and of 'backward classes' generally) have also been the concern of the Planning Commission and of the central Ministry of Food and Agriculture, but this concern will be more conveniently covered in the next section, when the several Five Year Plans are reviewed.

In a number of states a special department or other body is responsible for colonization, more or less as in the Punjab Canal Colonies in British days. Thus in Rajasthan (where, as has been seen, colonization is quite closely modelled on British practice) the Rajasthan Canal Board has a Colonization Department under a special Colonization Commissioner. The Department is responsible, *inter alia*, for surveying existing rights in land, for land acquisition, for auctioning land and for settling and providing assistance to colonists. Punjab still has a Colonization Department at Chandigarh, but it is nowadays merely a branch of the Revenue Office concerned with the acquisition and auctioning of land for shops, factories and the like.

Madhya Pradesh has a Colonization Officer located, not in Bhopal, the state capital, but in Gwalior. This Officer, who has assistants at various strategic points, was in particular responsible for the drive to reclaim wasteland that became so evident during the second half of the Third Plan period. Tribal colonization schemes, of which there are many in the remoter areas of the state, are largely the responsibility of the Tribal Welfare Department, while the resettlement of oustees in major projects like Gandhisagar calls for the services of a specially appointed Rehabilitation Officer. Uttar Pradesh formerly had a special Colonization Department when work in the Tarai was at its height and while the State Farm was in operation, but its functions passed to the Development Commissioner for the state.

In Kerala, colonization is a task of the revenue administration; but a special Administrative Officer for the Wynad Scheme was in 1963 stationed on the spot, at Ambalavayal, while for the High Ranges colonies there was an Assistant Collector at Devicolam. The small tribal colonies in the Attapaddy Valley were cared for by the local Block Development Officer (that is, an officer whose main task is community development). In Bihar, too, it was a revenue officer, the Sub-Divisional Officer at Deogarh, who was in general charge of colonization in the Santal Parganas, though he necessarily had to work closely with officers of the state land reclamation organization (whose tractors and other equipment were engaged in preparing gulley-eroded land for colonization): at a new colonization site, Sikander, there was, further, a special colonization officer.

In Andhra Pradesh such colonization schemes as Kannaram were organized by the Revenue Department (which was also responsible for reclamation in all schemes), but the Social Welfare Department established tribal colonies and the Co-operative Department took over if colonies began as, or became, joint or collective farms. This state thus well exemplifies complications caused (not least to the research worker) by a multiplicity of agencies, which were found still to be involved in 1972.

In those states visited by the author in which there were only a few small colonies, and those on a co-operative or joint farming basis, colonization was the responsibility of the Co-operative Department, Deputy Registrars for Districts being those most clearly concerned. This arrangement applied in Tamil Nadu, Maharashtra, and Mysore.

Enough will now have been said of the general administrative arrangements for colonization to indicate that in India (unlike Ceylon or Malaysia), colonization is not seen as a single activity, but as one activity of each of a number of agencies engaged mainly in social welfare and rather less often in economic development: this is highly significant.

Phases of Colonization: The Five Year Plans

But the most important involvement of the centre with the states in the work of agricultural colonization, and the involvement most closely linked to the 'local poor' and to the 'welfare motive', is best explained in terms of the provisions of the successive centrally generated Five Year Plans for the settlement of landless agricultural labourers. But Five Year Plans have also not forgotten the food production motive: the Third Plan, for example, includes 'land reclamation' in its chapter on 'Agricultural Production', while keeping 'resettlement' firmly in a welfare context in the chapter on 'Land Reform'.[99] (There will be those who see confusion of motive here.) And, of course, there was the period before the inauguration of the First Plan when much colonization was necessarily already in train.

In the period from 15 August 1947 until the initiation about four years later of the First Five Year Plan, colonization was in fact mainly a matter of dealing with refugees, who poured into India (just as many Muslims left) following partition; of settling ex-servicemen; and, less directly, of the dying phases of the wartime Grow More

Food Campaign. Colonization for refugees was organized in such regions as the Uttar Pradesh Tarai (in Naini Tal District, where wartime discussion had envisaged settlement by ex-servicemen),[100] and in the Punjab. Ex-servicemen were settled in such places as Wynad, the Kalidindi, and Piduguralla colonies in what is now Andhra Pradesh (then Madras) and, to the tune of 194 colonists, in the Naini Tal Tarai. The Grow More Food Campaign had by this time moved out of its wartime phase (1943–7) and was associated with the optimistic proposals of the Food Grains Policy Committee to produce 10 million additional tons (10,160,000 tonnes) of foodgrains annually, 30 per cent of this total, by the reclamation of 4 million hectares of land, using tractors for reclamation and cultivation. After 1949 and a study by Sir John (later Lord) Boyd Orr there were even more optimistic emergency plans to make India self-sufficient in foodstuffs by March 1952.[101] In the event, what mechanized attack there was on the waste came from the Central Tractor Organization (CTO), set up originally in 1946. While largely concerned with weed-infested land (especially that infested by *Kans* grass in Madhya Pradesh, Uttar Pradesh, and elsewhere) this Organization contributed to colonization by, for example, helping to clear jungle in the Naini Tal Tarai, and on the Bhopal Central Mechanized Farm (later to be the site of the Intikheri colonies). By 1951, when the activities of the CTO had merged with those envisaged in the First Five Year Plan, 1·89 million hectares had been reclaimed.[102]

Tribal colonies, largely designed to settle shifting cultivators,[103] were started before 1951 in Orissa, in Bihar, in what is now Andhra Pradesh and elsewhere, and from this period also dates the very interesting and encouraging colony at Thengumarahada in the Moyar Valley on the edge of the Nilgiri Hills in Tamil Nadu, set up on their own initiative by local people. From the pre-Plan period, too, date some of the small co-operative colonies in Mysore (a foreshadowing of activity under the First Five Year Plan).

The First Five Year Plan (1951–56) had it that 'in the settlement of all newly reclaimed land, after allowing for such areas as may be required for State farms, preference should be given to co-operatives consisting of landless workers';[104] and made a provision of Rs.1·5 crores for their resettlement by and in the states. It was in fact in the First Plan period that a number of small co-operative colonies were established, for example, at Pabal in Poona District of what is now Maharashtra, at Moranam in Tamil Nadu and in the Sardapuri Bhoodan Colony in the Pilibhit Tarai. But greater numbers of colonists were settled in the Naini Tal Tarai (where co-operative farming was either no more than a façade, or it soon broke down, see p. 258 below; and where, in any case, the beneficiaries were largely refugees and ex-servicemen, as earlier, with 'political sufferers' and others); in Wynad (ex-servicemen and others); and in the Damodar Valley (oustees). Work also began under the Bhakra Canal in Rajasthan. The Central Tractor Organization continued to reclaim land, part of which was to be used for colonization, as in the Tarai; though some of the land it reclaimed is said to have lapsed into disuse.[105]

The Second Plan (1956–61) had a special chapter on 'Agricultural Workers'[106] in which the Planning Commission, working on the figures provided by the first Agricultural Labour Enquiry, made further provision for the same purpose, though the emphasis here was on the resettlement of labourers on land made available by the imposition of ceilings. In August 1960 the Planning Commission's Panel on Land Reform set up a Committee under Shri R. K. Patil on the Settlement of Landless Agricultural Workers; as a parallel move the Ministry of Food and Agriculture set up a Waste Lands Survey and Reclamation Committee with the task of surveying the land classed in the *Agricultural Statistics* as 'other uncultivated land excluding current fallows' and 'fallow lands other than current fallows'; locating areas where large blocks of land were available for reclamation and resettlement; suggesting measures for reclamation and 'terms and conditions upon which settlement should be made'; and, finally, considering the economic aspects involved.[107] (State governments were at the same time encouraged to survey wastelands available for cultivation in smaller blocks suitable for 'village expansion'.) The Planning Commission's Committee on Natural Resources, further, approved in December 1961 a study on waterlogged, saline, and alkali lands.[108]

In the states, the Second Plan period is notable for the beginning, on quite a large scale, of active colonization where little or nothing had earlier been accomplished. Madhya Pradesh (welded out of a former scatter of smaller units in 1956) is particularly notable in this connection: during the Second Plan it not only organized the Intikheri colonies on the site of the former Bhopal Central Mechanized Farm, but established a number of other colonies—for example, on reclaimed Chambal ravineland, in widely scattered areas for tribal peoples, and in the Gandhisagar area of the upper Chambal for oustees. Maharashtra, Mysore, and Madras (now Tamil Nadu) set up a few small co-operative colonies for the local landless as required by the Plan; but, again, greater numbers were settled under individual tenure in Kerala (Wynad and High Ranges), the Uttar Pradesh Tarai (Pilibhit and Kheri Districts) and in Rajasthan (now not only under the Bhakra Canals, for a beginning had been made under the Rajasthan Canal). The beneficiaries may be deduced from Table 5.II. There were also more ambitious plans for tribal colonies in Andhra Pradesh and other states.[109] In 1958 work began in Dandakaranya (at Pharasgaon).

It will be clear that, at the time of the gestation and initiation of the Third Five Year Plan (1961–66), there was a great deal of activity at the centre on the wastelands front. The methods adopted and the conclusions drawn in the various surveys of wastelands then conceived will have to be subjected to critical scrutiny in chapter 8, but meanwhile the manner of the engagement of the Planning Commission, the Ministry of Food and Agriculture, and other central bodies should be noted. A guess may also be hazarded that more attention was being directed to wastelands at this time because of the manifest failure of land reform legislation (especially the prescription of 'ceilings' on holdings) to make any very significant contribution to the resettlement of agricultural labourers on land previously cultivated in large holdings; perhaps also because of disappointment with the practical results of the Bhoodan movement.

The Third Plan itself was more forthcoming and specific than its predecessors in its references to the resettlement for agricultural labourers. True, its chapter on 'Agricultural Production' touched on the work of the Waste Lands Survey and Reclamation Committee, but only postulated, in a very general way, the reclamation of the large blocks the Committee located;[110] while the chapter on 'Agricultural Labour' still clung to the notion that surplus lands would become available as the result of the imposition of ceilings. But the same chapter mentioned the sum of Rs.8 crores[111] set aside by the centre (Ministry of Food and Agriculture) to aid state resettlement schemes for landless labourers on the 1·6 million hectares of land expected to be available as a result of the wasteland surveys (in small blocks for village expansion as well as in larger blocks for colonization, of course).[112] The Central Advisory Committee on Agricultural Labour which, the Plan went on, had recently been set up by the Planning Commission visualized the settlement of 700,000 families of landless labourers. There were also separate state resettlement schemes for further labourers.

The role of the centre had thus emerged by 1961 as the initiation of inquiries, and the stimulation of the states to undertake their own inquiries; the setting of targets and identification of areas of activity by the Planning Commission; and the co-ordination and encouragement of state activity by the Ministry of Food and Agriculture, notably by giving financial assistance. The reaction of the state governments to the surveys, targets, stimuli, and financial inducements emanating from the centre raises a question that cannot be discussed at any length here—namely, the general problem of planning in a large, ponderous federal structure under parliamentary democracy: all that can be said is that it became very clear to the author in India in 1963 that the system worked as well as it did largely because the Congress governments in the states were imbued broadly with the same ideology as the centre, and were linked through the same party machine. Until 1966, indeed, the main motives and headings in the national Plans found fairly faithful reflection in state Plans: thus the Madhya Pradesh Third Five Year Plan, 1961–6, had a section on the colonization and settlement of agricultural labourers which envisaged further surveys of wastelands and the settlement of 400 families in 'model villages' and of 650 families in 'groups and colonies', and went on 'in almost all the settlements an attempt will be made to prevail upon the settlers to do farming on co-operative basis' (contrast, however, in this connection, pp. 234–5 below).[113] The corresponding document for Rajasthan does not include comparable provision for agricultural labour.[114] But it does, of course, contain provision for the Rajasthan Canal Scheme, under which, as has been seen, allotment was eventually made to the landless on a very large scale indeed.

In terms of actual accomplishment in the states in the Third Plan period, there was some quickening of the tempo after the drive for the *mise en valeur* of wastelands. Dandakaranya came into full play in all of its three main zones; work in Wynad, in the Pilibhit and Kheri Tarai, and under the Rajasthan Canal continued—and in no case was co-operative colonization a marked feature of the activity. But there was little to report from the crowded states of Tamil Nadu and Maharashtra. And there was but little in Mysore, apart from the settlement of the Tibetan refugees at Bylakuppe. The border war with China quickened general interest in colonization for ex-servicemen.

The original Draft Outline for the Fourth Plan (1966–71)[115] never became the basis for a final Plan, still less for action; but, taking the Draft Outline for what it is worth, it is clear that it proposed to continue virtually unchanged the broad policies of relevance to this study. Emphasis was still placed on the settlement of landless agricultural labourers, and it was claimed that some 4 million hectares of culturable waste had been distributed to this class over the preceding fifteen years.[116] An outlay of Rs.45 crores on land reclamation and another Rs.10 crores 'for subsidy and loans to new settlers on waste lands and surplus lands' was proposed, presumably in addition to any provision that might be made in state Plans. 'This programme ought to play an important role in favour of the weakest layers of our agrarian structure and should be pursued with vigour.' All this, it should be noted, was included in the chapter on land reform. As in earlier Plans, land reclamation was taken up again in the chapter 'Agriculture and Allied Sectors'.[117] The target for reclamation during the Fourth Plan was fixed at a million hectares. Mention was made of the surveys of wastelands in both larger and smaller blocks (see above, p. 113), and it was again emphasized that it was families of landless labourers who would be settled on these lands. 'The cost of resettlement', it was added, 'would be shared equally between the Centre and the States.'

The original Draft Outline for a Fourth Plan was abortive, as is well known, because of change in the political situation consequent on the coming into office of non-Congress governments in a number of states. This in turn initiated a period of great difficulty in centre-state relations, and affected the composition and functioning of the Planning Commission. In effect, there was a 'holiday from planning' in India for three years or so after the end of the Third Plan period in 1965, during which time there was no central Plan in operation. So far as colonization for agricultural labourers was concerned, work was confined during those three years to what had already been initiated in the states, and was strictly limited; central government assistance was restricted to the costs of reclamation, and of the provision of cattle, seed and so on for settlers, and was also very limited.[118] Moreover, on the recommendation of the National Development Council there were to be no more centrally sponsored projects, once the Fourth Plan came into force, in fields which were constitutionally state subjects. Clearly, then, there was to be an end, for the time-being at any rate, to centrally sponsored schemes for the resettlement of agricultural labour.

A new Draft for a Fourth Plan (1969–74) appeared in 1969 and the Plan itself in the following year.[119] The problem of landless agricultural labour received its mention. But, although it was asserted that surveys suggest 2·2 million hectares of waste to be available (of which one million would be reclaimed in the Fourth Plan period),[120] attention was drawn to the limitations on a solution of the problem by the distribution of land.[121] 'Where State Governments are in possession of cultivable wastelands, or have come into possession of surplus lands, it is proposed to concentrate efforts on systematic redistribution and resettlement of lands.'[122] But it was also recognized that, with the 'virtual exhaustion of uncommitted land resources', there must be other solutions than resettlement to the problem of landless agricultural labour: 'for the large class of sub-marginal farmers, agricultural labour and landless labour the remedy lies in the provision of supplementary occupations and other employment opportunities.'[123]

Lack of financial resources has also retarded, during the Fourth

Plan period, the rehabilitation of agricultural labourers by means of the reclamation of wasteland, whether by colonization or otherwise. Priority has generally been given to land already cultivated, especially that well served with infrastructure.

However, at a conference of Chief Ministers held in September 1970 participants were at pains to stress what their states had done to distribute government waste, the Prime Minister having strongly emphasized the general importance of land reform in a context in which, as she saw it, there were increasing threats of agrarian unrest. Thus Assam, it was said, had mounted a 'crash programme' to distribute land to landless families, opening up unwooded reserved forests for the purpose. Madhya Pradesh claimed to have distributed 1·2 million hectares of waste since independence, and under a revised policy to be issuing land in blocks of not less than 20 hectares not to individuals but only to co-operatives of tribals, Harijans, and agricultural labourers (compare below, pp. 234–5). Mysore had distributed 70,000 hectares and held a further 440,000 hectares yet to be allotted: 50 per cent of the land was reserved for Scheduled Castes and Tribes. Rajasthan claimed a distribution since the First Plan period of 1·8 million hectares of culturable waste, in addition to land in the Canal areas, 70,000 hectares of it to members of the Scheduled Castes during the Gandhi centenary year. Most states, however, once again emphasized that the allocation of a few acres of 'inferior waste' was no solution to agrarian problems.

The view was, nevertheless, met in New Delhi in December 1971 that the Fifth Plan (presumably to run from 1974 to 1979) might command greater financial resources than its predecessor and see the beginning of a more heavily capitalized attack on such categories of 'inferior waste' as inter-village land heavily overgrazed by cattle. If such an attack is mounted the landless and otherwise underprivileged are bound, in the present climate of political opinion, to be the main beneficiaries. But whether it would be justified is another matter; and the rest of this book, with its close contemplation of existing colonization schemes, should throw, it is hoped, some light on the question.

7

Natural Difficulties Confronting Colonization

CHAPTERS 3 and 4 have sketched broadly the environmental characteristics of each of the major areas of agricultural colonization to be found in post-independence India. It is not intended here to labour the points made in those chapters, but rather to select a number of environmental factors that are of real importance to some or all of the recent colonies—such factors as aridity, rainfall variability, water resources, soil, and the depredations of wild life; and to examine the ways in which these factors add to the difficulties of the colonists or the authorities (while indicating, where relevant, instances in which environmental influences are more beneficent). All this will serve as a background to the discussion in later chapters of technical, economic, and social problems of colonization—indeed, more than a background, for many of these environmental factors are not passive, but all too active, and play a considerable part in such questions as the choice and impact of technology (to be raised in chapter 8), and the marginality of land and costs and benefits (to be discussed in chapter 14).

Some of these factors (notably aridity in the absence of possibilities for irrigation) will be recognized as being among those that, sometimes singly, more usually in combination, have protected the regions of recent colonization from agrarian pressures in the past. Others have sprung into prominence only with the removal or recession of the protecting circumstances (whether princely rule, or poverty of access, or some other factor). For the mere suppression of these protecting factors does not remove all difficulties, or diminish the pioneer achievement of the colonists, or render negligible the costs of overcoming remaining obstacles to colonization; any more than, despite an easy belief to the contrary among the Ceylonese, the conquest of malaria has transformed the Dry Zone of Ceylon into a Promised Land to be entered into and possessed without thought, trouble, or effort.[1]

Aridity and Associated Hazards

It may be thought that, since colonization in such arid and semi-arid tracts as those of Rajasthan and western Haryana has been contemplated only because irrigation water is available from the Bhakra and Rajasthan Canals, then there can be no problem of aridity, which, in this view, vanishes before the advancing canal waters. But, quite apart from such concomitants of aridity as strong, desiccating winds, dust-storms, moving sand-dunes and alkaline soils, some of the colonists in tracts under the Bhakra and Rajasthan Canals were suffering in 1963 from sheer shortage of water, both for their crops and for domestic purposes: while much the same was true of a large part of the Central Mechanized Farm at Suratgarh. One must allow some discount for the perpetual tendency of the farmer to complain. One must also recognize that some of the problems were almost certainly transitory; for the Bhakra Canal at the time was well short of its ultimate rate of flow because the Bhakra-Nangal reservoirs were not to attain full supply level for a further year or two, and because percolation loss from channels was still high; and the Rajasthan Canal was in a very early stage of development. However, the difficulties of some of the colonists and of the Suratgarh Farm are an indication of the impact of crude aridity, in the absence of sufficient irrigation; and a warning of the fate in store for the new colonies, and, for that matter, of the whole vast programme planned under the Rajasthan Canal if for any reason irrigation water proves inadequate. This might come about on a wide scale through over-committing water resources, or through unexpectedly high losses of water because of evaporation or percolation, or more locally through faulty levelling of distributaries or of fields themselves.

The Tohana Division under the Bhakra Main Line in the Hissar District of Haryana is a naturally arid region with a mean annual rainfall of only some 33 cm, formerly largely covered by government or private waste, but since independence partly colonized by oustees from the Bhakra-Nangal reservoirs and by local people. Though some holdings appeared well watered, at least in terms of the plan to irrigate 62 per cent of the command area annually,[2] others had a relatively small proportion of irrigated land, or in a few cases apparently none at all, and the cultivators had been in real difficulty during the *kharif* of 1963. In Haidarawala village one cultivator was unable to irrigate more than half his holding because the land had not been levelled. In Gajuwala village only 100 out of 194 hectares under command could in fact be irrigated; some holdings (notably a very small one of 0·6 hectares worked by three brothers, all Bhakra oustees) had no water at all, and had grown no crops in the 1963 *kharif*. In Gajuwala there were other problems too, notably the consequences of the fact that saline or alkaline land had been allotted, but without the extra water needed to leach out the soil.

Over the state border in Rajasthan, under the same canal, some colonists had occupied their land in advance of channel construction, but were, by 1963, receiving adequate water supplies; others were still complaining of shortage. The Suratgarh Farm, at the extreme tail end of the Bhakra Main Line, was, at the time of the author's visit in 1963, receiving water for only about four months in the year (except for some 1,200 hectares under irrigation from a distributary of the older Gang Canal).[3] The situation seemed more acute than in the Tohana Division just mentioned, and yields were being badly affected.

It must also be recognized that the dangers and difficulties associated with aridity are bound to increase in intensity as the Rajasthan Canal is extended southwestward into areas of even lower mean annual rainfall (only 18 cm at Jaisalmer): this applies alike to the costs of dune reclamation; to the consequences of inadequate water supply for cultivation, for cattle, and for domestic purposes; and to evaporation losses from channels and fields. Already, south of Hanumangarh, the Rajasthan Canal has reached dune-covered country, with wide tracts uncultivated and virtually uninhabited: most dunes are vegetated, but it is noticeable that those on which an attempt at cultivation is made become more mobile. A map seen at the Central Arid Zone Research Institute at Jodhpur indicates that the Rajasthan Canal command area is likely to include that part of the desert most dominated by dunes: over 40 per cent of the surface area throughout, and as much as 80 per cent in some parts. The alignment of the canal is, of course, largely predetermined by the contours, apart from areas to be fed by lift irrigation along the Suratgarh–Bikaner railway. But the penetration of such a dune-infested area cannot but involve many and costly difficulties in the future: these may well include higher initial costs of construction and land development, loss of water by percolation, soil problems, dust storms, and infilling of channels and ruination of fields by blown sand (made all the more mobile by cultivation). Clearly, too, the greatest care will have to be exercised with conservational measures.

In view of the difficulties of the desert environment the work of the Central Arid Zone Research at Jodhpur is to be warmly welcomed,[4] though its work has been criticized as too academic. A Desert Development Authority was formed in 1967 to improve the economy of arid areas. It was wound up in 1969, to be superseded by a Board at Union level.

The hazards associated with aridity and its inadequate control are, of course, at their worst in the desert or near-desert areas of Rajasthan and western Haryana. But they are also to be found in other regions of actual or potential colonization. Pierre Gourou has drawn attention to the 'axis of aridity', with mean annual rainfall under 75 cm, linking the Rajasthan Desert with the burning sands of Ramanathapuram (Ramnad) in Tamil Nadu, and running down the length of the peninsula through Malwa and what used to be called the 'Bombay Deccan' (now in Maharashtra and Mysore).[5] The axis, he rightly stressed, is no desert, but introduces elements of aridity and some of the associated hazards into a long and wide belt of the Deccan; it is, moreover, associated with drier types of natural vegetation than those found to east and west, notably thorn forest.[6]

Most of this axial belt is, in spite of the recurring threat of drought and of disastrous famine, densely peopled, with but little scope for more than grudging, interstitial cultivation of the waste. But, as has been seen, scope for colonization exists in Malwa, partly at any rate because of depopulation following famine; and colonies like those on the Chambal, or Intikheri near Bhopal, or again the co-operative colony at Pabal in Poona District, suffer, in the absence of reliable irrigation, some at least of the difficulties of cultivation and of water supply to be encountered in extreme form in the more truly arid lands of Haryana and Rajasthan. One of the reasons for the unhappiness of the Kerala colonists at Intikheri was the inadequacy and unreliability of the irrigation water, whose supply was, for some extraordinary reason, accomplished by pumping water from the Chamarsal River (one of the two pumps was out of action during the author's visit). Fortunately over much of this area the underlying rock is Deccan Trap, whose joints harbour water and nurture wells which may supply at least domestic water.

Farther south, but still on the axis of aridity, lies the open, steppe-like country of the Raichur Doab, with its potential for future colonization by reallocation of land and its actual spontaneous settlement by Telugu cultivators and land speculators. This also is a region of drought and famine, and it suffers from many of the problems of at least sub-aridity:[7] much will depend on the reliability of the irrigation now being provided. Already, unfortunately, there are indications that all may not go well: black cotton soils are notoriously difficult to irrigate, and it has been reported that 'some of the distributaries in Black Cotton soil did not work properly'.[8] Water-logging is already a problem on heavily irrigated lands under the Tungabhadra scheme, and salinity may well occur in future, particularly in view of the very low relief of the Doab,[9] unless improved drainage can be contrived.

Even in Assam, lack of rain can be a problem in the Kaki colony, which lies in a rain-shadow area receiving an average of only 100–25 cm, and much less in dry years like 1953, 1955, and 1956.

Rainfall Variability

There is no clear-cut line between aridity as a hazard to the colonist and the effects on him and his economy of rainfall variability: arid and sub-arid regions, notoriously those on Gourou's 'axis', are liable to drought; and when severe shortage of rainfall hits a normally well-watered area some at any rate of the insignia of aridity are reproduced. Further, there is hardly any area of post-independence colonization, except Wynad and similar high-rainfall areas in Kerala, that is not subject to rainfall deficiency likely to cause loss or even disaster to the colonist; and many were the complaints on this score to be heard in widely scattered colonies, from Bhamer in Dhulia District of Maharashtra (admittedly on the 'axis'), where over a six-year period annual rainfall had varied from 20 to 65 cm, to the Tibetan colony at Bylakuppe in Mysore (mean annual rainfall about 90 cm), where poor rains had caused a failure of the tobacco crop, or to Arwatagi, in Malnad, where the rains were normally 'assured' but where in 1963 they had been late, or to the High Ranges of Kerala (mean annual rainfall over 125 cm) where in 1963 the rains were described as 'poor'. All of these, and many other cases that could be quoted, are of course instances of the quite notorious fickleness of the monsoon and of the accompanying rainfall:[10] a fickleness which is all the harder to bear given the extreme seasonality of precipitation, for one of the favourite tricks of the monsoon is to come late and thus prolong the dry season; or to leave too soon and thus bring unexpectedly early drought. Seasonality itself one just has to take for granted in all but a few favoured regions, notably those in which irrigation is truly perennial. All this does not, of course, imply that either variability or seasonality are exclusively Indian phenomena: the Ceylon Dry Zone also suffers from the consequences of both;[11] and the same applies to many other tropical lands, notably to East Africa.[12]

One of the most striking instances of rainfall variability as it affects Indian colonization schemes, an example, as it happens, of the prolongation or early onset in some years of seasonal drought, was encountered where it might be least expected—in a region of relatively high rainfall: namely, Dandakaranya. Here, with a mean annual rainfall almost everywhere over 125 cm and in some stations over 175 cm, there is an extreme seasonality of rainfall: more than 80 per cent of the annual total, on an average, falls in the months from June to September, inclusive. The figure is as high as 91 per cent at Dhanora in Chanda District. In Dandakaranya there is a strong tendency for the southwest monsoon to arrive late and to leave early, hence for rainfall to be inadequate for unirrigated paddy cultivation at the beginning and end of the monsoon: at the beginning this may put at hazard paddy in the seedling or early transplanting stage, at the end rainfall may be insufficient to fill the ear just before harvest. Given figures for critical amounts of rainfall for 105- to 120-day paddy, the author made the following estimates of the probability of rainfall exceeding the critical amounts.[13]

Half-month	*Estimated Critical Rainfall for Rainfed Paddy (cm)*	*Probability of Rainfall Exceeding the Estimated Critical Rainfall*		
		Malkangiri %	*Kondagaon* %	*Dhanora* %
1–15 June	5	32	24	22
16–30 June	10	53	82	59
1–15 July	15	56	60	81
16–31 July	20	62	35	70
1–15 Sept.	12	68	44	54
16–30 Sept.	10	75	49	23
1–15 Oct.	10	13	11	10

Too much stress must not be placed on these results, largely because the underlying data cover too short a period. But they serve to give point to the statement that rainfall in sufficient quantities for rainfed paddy is unreliable in its incidence at the beginning and end of the monsoon. Yet the tribal peoples of Dandakaranya practise but little irrigation[14] and contrive to grow rainfed paddy, perhaps wholly or partly because they use valley-bottom sites to which water drains, and in which soils are heavier and more retentive of moisture. In Chanda District, however, small irrigation tanks are such a traditional feature of the landscape that the upper Wainganga valley has been called the 'lake country'.[15] However, rainfall there is lower and the rainy period shorter than farther east.

It will be noted that the Table makes no estimates for the month of August; this was on the assumption that rain then, at the height of the monsoon, could be taken to be adequate for rainfed paddy, an assumption that appeared to be justified by the rainfall data. But in 1965 not only was paddy transplantation delayed by scanty June and July rainfall, but August rainfall at Paralkote was only 7·04 cm, so that paddy (and other crops) were adversely affected; rainfall was also scanty, though a little higher, in other parts of the Dandakaranya project, and most of the settlers had lost hope of harvesting even 25 per cent of their paddy crop.[16]

Now the fields of the colonists in Dandakaranya are, for the most part, located on slopes and gently rolling plateau-tops, rather than in valley bottoms, since these tend to be occupied by the paddy fields of tribal people. It follows that colonists' paddy does not benefit from the process of drainage to valley bottoms which, it has just been postulated, may explain why the tribal peoples' paddy survives. The question therefore arises whether irrigation ought to be provided to ensure a crop to the colonists; and whether, given the probability of adequate rainfall and the other factors in the case, such provision would be justified.

The Dandakaranya Development Authority in fact possesses an Irrigation Department; and it is the Department's policy that each village of resettled refugees (though not of local tribal people) should have a village tank. But these tanks are a far cry from what would be understood by 'village tanks' in the Dry Zone of Ceylon or in Tamil Nadu, where the traditional tank is very much the pivot of the settlement pattern and of the agricultural system.[17] The tank is located in a strategic site, in a minor valley with an adequate catchment, and the village is sited beside it, where the water-table is high and so feeds both domestic wells and introduced trees like the coconut; channels are led from the tank to the paddy-fields in the valley bottom beneath the tank. (Unfortunately the ecological principles behind the system have been lost sight of in many of Ceylon's colonization schemes.)[18] The Dandakaranya village tanks are usually located in a hollow, but not always the most suitable one in the locality; nor the one calculated to yield the most reliable flow of water. In any case they are designed primarily, as would be the tank in the Bengal villages from which the colonists hail, for what may be described as general village purposes—drinking water for villagers and cattle, retting for jute (in Dandakaranya replaced by *mesta*), bathing, and fishing. No channels lead to the fields, but some water reaches some fields by seepage, or by spilling during the monsoon, and may save a crop there during a critical period, or even make possible a *rabi* crop. Tanks with this function are known in Dandakaranya as 'headwater tanks'. Unfortunately many of them were constructed after house lots and fields had been laid out; thus they could cause waterlogging in house lots (as in the Malkangiri village MV.2, colonized by Santals), provide ready water for some house lots but not others, and dispense their favours between paddy-fields very unevenly. There can be no doubt that the Bengali settler needs a tank so that he can at least begin to simulate in the high plateaux of Dandakaranya the semi-aquatic environment of his distant deltaic homeland; but, quite apart from the question of irrigation, a much more satisfactory solution would have been achieved if the planners had first selected a suitable catchment, then planned the tank, and only then laid out house and paddy lots.

But a more radical solution may well be thought desirable, given the estimates for rainfall probability at critical times as stated above: a solution which would more closely imitate the closely spaced village tanks of Ceylon or of Tamil Nadu—or, for that matter, of regions nearer to Dandakaranya in Andhra Pradesh, in Chanda District of Maharashtra, or in Chhattisgarh.[19]

By January 1972 the Authority had in fact gone a little way towards the provision of such tanks, or substitutes for them, for thirty-two minor irrigation works had been completed and five more were under construction.[20] That near the zonal administrative centre at Pakhanjore, in the Paralkote Zone, had very obviously made it possible to grow plantains and other garden crops, notwithstanding the marked seasonal drought. But the main effort had gone into the provision of a small number of major works. Thus the Bhaskal Dam in the Umarkote Zone had been completed in 1965 and irrigates 4,450 hectares; and the Paralkote Dam, when work is completed, will command 12,100 hectares. Both of these were planned after the establishment of the surrounding colonies, with the result that some villages and lots will be irrigated, others not. In the Bhaskal command it so happens that about 90 per cent of the irrigated area is made up of tribal allotments, whose cultivators have barely tapped the water available; whereas in the remaining lands, settled with refugees, irrigation resources are fully utilized. It might well have been a more equitable, more productive, and less costly solution to plan from the outset in terms of a large number of smaller works.

More ambitious projects are planned in the lower and hotter Malkangiri Zone. The Authority's Satiguda Dam, on which work has been started after some delay, will irrigate 15,200 hectares, while the Balimela Dam, under construction by the Orissa state government, will irrigate more than 10,000 hectares. Further, a weir at Surlikand on the Poteru River will divert water from the tail race of a hydro-electric project and, it is said, provide water for a further 57,000 hectares. Part of the benefit here will go to existing villages, largely tribal; but, if all that is planned can be brought into successful operation, it is clear that problems of drought for present and future colonists in the Malkangiri Zone will be largely solved. This Zone, in fact, has the largest potential of any in Dandakaranya, given the present pattern of development. It was learnt in January 1972 that the Orissa government is willing to release a further 16,000 hectares here to the Dandakaranya Development Authority: most of this should eventually be irrigable. But, for all this, it may still be that many small works would be preferable to a few big ones.

In the great Hirakud project, irrigation as a method of countering drought in land already cultivated is, of course, to the fore.[21] But faulty detailed planning of colonies may be seen in the field. At the oustee colony known as Sangramal B, there was no proper masonry or concrete spill to the tank on which some of the cultivation depended: the loose stone sill in the spill-way had eroded badly, so reducing the capacity of the tank. Crores had been spent on the Hirakud project: a few rupees would have sufficed to build a proper spill at Sangramal.

Hydrological Problems

No attempt will be made here to cover all colonies in which flooding occurs, for it is so strongly associated with the high intensity of monsoonal rainfall[22] and with run-off accelerated by the destruction of forest cover as to be almost universal to some degree. Rather will one or two striking examples be chosen.

One of the most interesting of these, not least because it involves the consequences of human action as well as of natural phenomena, is that of the Ghaggar in western Haryana and Rajasthan, where it affects colonization and other areas under both the Bhakra and Rajasthan Canals (the latter crosses it near Hanumangarh). Even more serious are the effects of the flooding of the Ghaggar on the Central Mechanized Farm at Suratgarh.

As was indicated in chapter 3 above, the bed of the Ghaggar used normally to be dry, except in wet years, when water might flow as far as Hanumangarh. But in recent years, since the establishment of the Suratgarh Farm, floodwaters have swept past Hanumangarh to Suratgarh and beyond. The reasons for this state of affairs, as they emerged during somewhat embarrassed discussions with irrigation officials in both Rajasthan and New Delhi, seems to be partly a consequence of the drainage to the Ghaggar of an increased area under irrigation in the Punjab and Haryana (partly in turn as a result of the Bhakra scheme), partly a consequence of a 'crash' programme undertaken in these states in an attempt to control salinity and alkalinity by applying more water to wash the land surface—again, draining to the unfortunate Ghaggar.[23] Further extensions of the Bhakra and Rajasthan Canals are likely to increase the volume of water flowing into the low-lying Ghaggar floodplain.

Flooding from the Ghaggar is liable to affect a belt a mile or so wide in colonization and other areas in the Tohana, Rori, and Sirsa

Divisions under the Bhakra Main Line and to flood wide areas of the Suratgarh Farm. This was located largely in the floodplain of the Ghaggar, the author was told, mainly because of the availability of land not otherwise occupied; the rather heavier soils in the floodplain, as compared with the high sand-dunes on either side, were an advantage rather than a reason. The annual flooding may bring welcome water and fertile silt, and wash off alkaline patches; but it delays cultivation and sowing, causes loss of crops and low yields, and has necessitated the construction of a wall round the Farm headquarters which gives it the appearance of a beleaguered fortress (as, indeed, it is in flood-time). Costs in the Farm are thus increased and benefits reduced. Moreover, roads and railways are frequently cut (the main road and railway both run along the bed of the Ghaggar).

Responsibility for the troubles that surround the behaviour of the reborn Ghaggar goes back a long way. It is not too far-fetched to say that it begins with the failure of the British irrigation engineers to provide adequate drainage in the Punjab, so that new works and the 'crash' programme have become necessary; and continues through the delay in the provision of such drainage works until *after* the Suratgarh Farm and colonies on the Bhakra Main Line had been established, to the location of the Farm in what is in effect a *wadi*, always liable to flow again. By 1971 thirteen check dams had been built on the Ghaggar to divert its floodwaters, but flooding at Suratgarh during the monsoon continued.

A further, though much less spectacular example of flooding in colonization schemes is provided by the Tarai. It will be remembered that the Tarai is a belt of flat country lying parallel to and at the foot of the Siwaliks, the outermost ranges of the Himalayan system. The local mean annual rainfall is 110–25 cm, with 33–40 cm in July. Monsoon rains, combined with run-off from the hills, the bursting forth of springs at the foot of the Bhabar, and a high local water-table produce large volumes of water on the Tarai surface. Formerly there were swampy patches in the Tarai jungles[24] and today, after reclamation, some colonies still complain of waterlogging in part of their land (for example, at Shantinagar in Pilibhit District, where *munj* grass (*Saccharum munja* Roxb.) had invaded waterlogged land, and at Gandhinagar in the same District, where some fields had produced no crop because of waterlogging). A more serious problem, however, though not by any means a universal one, is that of flooding by stream water during the southwest monsoon. This arises partly because local streams, close together, sub-parallel, tortuous, and sluggish at other seasons, tend to overflow their banks during the monsoon, partly because water also tends to sweep across the country between the streams, following depressions in the alluvium. The Sikh colonists in the Bhoodan colony at Sardapuri, in Lakhimpur-Kheri District, complained of 'flood trouble'; in Basahi, in the same District, flooding up to four feet deep during the monsoon was reported; and at Balpur, near by, it was said that a 'hydrographic survey' of the locality failed to take account of the floodwaters from Nepal that pour over the border (which here runs through the Tarai).

Not surprisingly flood protection and drainage works have been contemplated in various parts of the Tarai, notably at Gandhinagar in Pilibhit District: it was reported in October 1971 that several small detention reservoirs had been built.[25] Irrigation, both from channels and tubewells, is spreading in the Tarai,[26] and will increase the need for drainage (though it may be argued, of course, that it is the annual washing of much of the surface by floodwaters that helps to prevent alkalinity, in spite of the high water-table).

Given what has already been said about the floodplain colonies of Assam, it is not surprising that it is here that flooding, and for that matter lateral erosion by sudden changes of course on the part of rivers, is at its most spectacular and devastating. Bengali refugee colonists try to adapt themselves to deep monsoon floods by building plinths (*bastibhitha*) to keep house-sites above flood level; and by sowing *aman* rice capable of growing under deep water conditions, or *aman* mixed with *aus*, a short-season rice sown in spring with a hope to harvest before floods come. Damage and destruction attributable to flooding include loss of crops, sometimes *aman* as well as *aus*; loss of fertilizer, to such an extent that many cultivators are unwilling to use it; damage to roads and bridges; and loss of life either directly by drowning, or indirectly through the spread of cholera as a result of the pollution of wells by inflowing river water. Lateral migration of rivers locally also causes direct loss of cultivable land. It seems clear, too, that the non-adaptability of high-yielding varieties of rice to the peculiar conditions of these colonies is, quite apart from any other factor, a severe deterrent to their use.

Groundwater was being tapped for purposes of irrigation in very few of the colonization areas visited by the author in 1963. Experimental tubewells were being sunk in the Tarai colonies in Uttar Pradesh to protect crops depending primarily on rainfall, while the former State Farm in the same area used a free-flowing artesian well depending, apparently, on hydrostatic pressure built up in a water-bearing lens of sands contained by less permeable alluvium. The tubewells used thermally generated power which was, of course, expensive. Again, some of the small Madras colonies,[27] following Tamil practice, used wells for irrigation, generally to supplement tanks. The Moranam colony had no fewer than forty such wells, very successfully sited by a water diviner—though, doubtless, using empirical hydrological principles known to every Tamil villager but hidden from town-bred officials, who are all too apt to give unsound advice about these things. There were also a few deep wells (30 to 50 m) in the colonization villages on land reclaimed from the Chambal ravines; and there was some dependence on well-irrigation in certain of the colonies on the Deccan Trap (basalt), notably at Pabal in Poona District. But elsewhere irrigation, if used at all, was a matter of tanks or channels, or both (see also below, pp. 157–64).

By 1971–2, the use of tubewells for irrigation had become established practice in the Tarai colonies, and their number was still growing; in Moranam the number of wells had increased to 45, and a number of them were fitted with electric pumps. Thus did these two colonies at least reflect the facet of the so-called 'Green Revolution' which derives from the mechanized exploitation of groundwater.

In contrast to the limited, though growing, use of groundwater for irrigation was (and is) its almost universal use in the colonies as a source of water for domestic purposes—in virtually all of them, in fact, except those in the wettest and driest areas: in the wettest, like parts of Greater Malnad, because perennial streams flow past the villagers' doors; in the driest, like Punjab and Rajasthan, because channel water, where available, is less brackish than water from necessarily deep wells. This can, of course, be very unhygienic, not least when dead cattle lie in the channels. In the colonization area under the Bhakra Canal in Rajasthan, 90 per cent of borings yielded brackish water; channels are likewise used, though each village is given a tank fed by the local channel. In the Rajasthan Canal project, the provision of domestic water is seen as a first priority after irrigation, and the Master Plan envisages a network of lined channels forming 'a sort of Drinking Water "Grid" ' (though this procedure would seem open to objection on grounds of hygiene). Drinking water still has to be carted long distances by lorry to camps and colonies which channels have not yet reached: costs are, of course, high. Brackish well water is also a problem in the Raichur Doab.

Where colonists use wells, whether dug by them or for them, they were in general but reproducing local village custom concerning domestic water supply. But the wells in question vary greatly—from shallow, open pits to deep shafts (over 30 m deep in the Chambal ravine area) and to tubewells in the case of Dandakaranya and of the Tibetan colony at Bylakuppe in Mysore. In Assam 'ring-wells' with high walls seek to prevent pollution by floodwater. The wells vary, too, in terms of reliability (seasonal failure being naturally a common hazard in a monsoon-dominated country) and in terms of the chemical and biological purity of the water they provided. High iron content is a common feature in a number of areas, notably Dandakaranya, and brackishness, as already remarked, in arid and semi-arid areas; while all too commonly the author's field notes contain reference to dysentery and diarrhoea, which probably derive partly, though not wholly, from contaminated wells.

These and other features of the utilization of groundwater in Indian colonization schemes largely depend, as do associated problems, on geological conditions. These, not surprisingly, are extremely varied. The use of groundwater for irrigation in colonization schemes is confined to three types of geological environment. There is, first, the alluvium of the plains, as in the Tarai and the Chambal Valley. In strata that are probably very similar in Western Rajasthan the depth of the water-table and the brackishness of the water at present inhibit the use of underground water in the colonies; it is probable that with the spread of canal irrigation the water-table will rise and make tubewells possible—and, indeed, desirable in order to control its level and hence reduce the risk of waterlogging and alkalinity at the surface. Secondly, there are the basalts of the Deccan Trap area of Malwa and Maharashtra, which, when decayed along the joints, provide an aquifer with sufficient water, locally at any rate, for well irrigation on a small scale.[28] Thirdly, where the Archaean crystalline rocks of the plateaux (some would say 'peneplains') of peninsular India have, as in Tamil Nadu, been subjected to prolonged weathering under continental conditions, there may be a substantial aquifer in the resultant deep layer of decayed rock.[29]

But both the reliability of a well and the purity of its water (indeed often the presence in it of any water at all) depend on an appreciation of the geological and physiographic situation. As has already been remarked with reference to the wells at Moranam, in Tamil Nadu, villagers are often able to make such an appreciation, though of course without knowledge of the scientific principles involved. The author has on an earlier occasion commented on the failure of the official planners of wells in Ceylon's colonies to appreciate these principles.[30] Unfortunately much the same is true of Indian colonization schemes. Thus F. Ahmad, writing of Dandakaranya, points out that sites for villages had often been chosen without regard to water-supply conditions, and, in particular, according to 'the highly fallacious notion that tubewells, if one goes deep enough, would produce water anywhere and everywhere'.[31] Apparently the aquifer in Dandakaranya is largely confined to the zone of weathered crystalline rock which is neither very deep, nor continuous from valley to valley. By 1972 shallow wells were replacing tubewells. Again, at Srinagar, a colony for oustees from the Gandhisagar reservoir on the Upper Chambal, much money had been expended on a well which, for all its 21 m of depth, was as dry as a bone: it had been dug in the expectation that the 'Vindhyan Sandstone' in which it had been sunk would bear water, whereas in fact this 'Sandstone' is a geological formation which contains a great deal of impermeable shale—and the official well-sinkers of Srinagar had managed to dig in shale and nothing but shale.

In short, the planning of colonization schemes ought, if reliable wells are needed for domestic purposes, and *a fortiori* if they are needed for irrigation, to include a proper appreciation of the hydro-geological situation.

Soil Problems

The next chapter will show that the colonies have received more attention from the soil surveyors, in proportion to the area they cover, than India at large. But officers concerned with colonization, even agricultural officers, are often unaware of the soil surveys that have been made and are thus quite uninfluenced by them in their planning and in their policy decisions. Dandakaranya was a notable exception to this generalization. The reasons for this state of affairs, and for the neglect of soil surveys in other areas, should become clear in the course of the next chapter.

Meanwhile, attention will be focused briefly on the consequences of the lack or inadequacy of soil surveys in certain colonies, and on the general soil problems of India's colonization schemes. It was just those schemes in which no soil survey had been made before colonization or where earlier surveys had been forgotten that agricultural difficulties were most marked. It is true that such colonies were almost entirely small; but in them soils were under cultivation which would have been better left under, or replanted as, forest—or, at any rate, cultivated only after careful assessment of the consequences in terms both of the colonist's income and of the return to the state on capital invested. There were also cases in which plans for colonization schemes proved impossible of execution because of soil poverty and lack of water. One of the most glaring cases was in the High Ranges Colonization Scheme in Kerala, where, in spite of plans to settle 8,000 families, only 1,526 have actually been installed; even then some of these were forced to abandon their allotments.

There were three regions in particular in whose colonization schemes soil poverty was especially marked. The first was in the Deccan Trap (basalt) areas of Maharashtra, where, generally speaking, colonies filled gaps between existing villages, so that it is not surprising that their soils were marginal for reasons that included stoniness, shallowness, and the presence of *murram* (hardened laterite), or the gravel derived from it. Colonies on the good black cotton soils (*regur*) found in lower, flatter sites were rare; most were higher up the catena characteristic of this region, as of Malwa (where, however, fewer colonies had been forced on to the poorer soils). Secondly, there were the generally poor sandy or stony red soils in many of the small colonies of Tamil Nadu (for example, Velakapuram and Rajannagar) and of the Eastern Ghats of Andhra—soils made poorer by evident erosion, as has already been mentioned at Aminabad. Thirdly, there were the eroded lands of Jamunia in Bihar, with poorish red soils passing into ironstone gravel.

It is generally—and not surprisingly—true that in colonization areas where a prior soil survey has been utilized cultivation takes place on soils that are a great deal better than those just described; for the poorer soils, or those whose cultivation is likely to present difficulties, ought to be rejected by the surveyors. But that is not to say that these areas are without soil problems—or that soil surveys as at present conducted are a completely satisfactory guide to land potential for colonization. In the arid tracts of the Punjab coming under the command of the Bhakra Canals 39 per cent of the areas surveyed were rejected: 30 per cent because the land has so deteriorated through the spread of salinity as to need special treatment, 9 per cent as excessively sandy, so that percolation under irrigation was likely to be excessive.[32] In the area judged to be fit for irrigated cultivation if care was exercised, there was much sandy soil. There is, of course, even more in Rajasthan, where also saline and alkaline patches exist, and where expensive measures of reclamation and heavy inputs of fertilizers will be necessary if yields are to be adequate under modern conditions. Special measures may also be necessary if the spread of salinity and alkalinity is to be avoided (see below, pp. 163–4): though the fact that the canals are lined should to some extent check this.

In the Uttar Pradesh Tarai, no less than 35 per cent of the area selected for the State Farm was found on survey to consist of sandy loams, unaggregated and with poor nutrient status (except for phosphorus); it was recommended that these soils be left under pasture.[33] No less than 75 per cent of land originally selected in Pilibhit District was found to be too sandy.[34] Tarai soils actually under colonization also present difficulties: poorly drained clay loams in depressions; sandy loams on low ridges, unretentive of water and needing fertilizers. Indeed, it is a general observation in the Tarai that the soils soon lose their pristine fertility (due, as it is, largely to organic matter near the surface) and fertilizers are essential.[35]

In Dandakaranya, it was the author's observation that, although the soil survey organization was in general a most proficient one, a few areas where impeded drainage was a hazard to cultivation would have been avoided if more attention had been paid, during survey, to soil profiles. Otherwise the Dandakaranya surveyors were rejecting soils that would have been seized upon with avidity by land-hungry cultivators in other parts of India.

Finally, there are colonies with particular soil problems: a tendency to gully erosion in the Chambal Valley, particularly where soils have a high clay content and other physical characteristics tending to impede percolation and increase run-off; the stickiness when wet and the erosibility of black cotton soils in Malwa and Maharashtra (they are also difficult to irrigate); and the acidity of soils in humid parts of Kerala.

Wild Life

To the tourist, the sportsman, and the naturalist, the wild life of the Indian jungles is a matter of interest. But to the cultivator in a colonization scheme the animals and birds that emerge from the jungle are expensive nuisances which may do great damage to his crops. Not all colonization schemes are affected in this way, of course: least of all those that fill interstices between existing villages, as in much of Maharashtra and Tamil Nadu (though the colonies in the Chanda District of the former, jungle-girt as they are, complained of inroads by wild boar; and those on the borders of the Nilgiri Hills in the latter, as at Thengumarahada and Rajannagar, suffered not only from boar but also from elephants). And there were very few complaints, except about feeding by deer, in the arid zone colonies of Haryana and Rajasthan (both deer and boar affected the Chambal Canal settlements).

But colonization schemes which really represent a pioneer fringe of the jungle were very differently affected. The Malnad colonies of Mysore complained of wild boar, foxes, and wild cats (though less so than formerly, apparently) while the highly articulate colonists of Kerala added porcupine, monkeys, and even tigers (in the Attapaddy Valley) to the list. In the High Ranges colonies of Kerala, in fact, the Collector administers a discretionary fund to compensate victims of the depredations of wild animals. Bears, tigers, and wild boar are apt to cause trouble and damage in the isolated Eastern Ghat colonies of Andhra Pradesh (tigers not by damaging crops, of course, except incidentally, but by taking cattle and buffalo—and presenting the continual risk that a man-eater may carry off a colonist or his wife or child). Perhaps the worst affected colonization areas in 1963 were, not surprisingly, those on the fringes of the still-uncleared jungle in Dandakaranya and the Uttar Pradesh Tarai. Deer and boar were the worst offenders in Dandakaranya, where crops are concerned; it was estimated that 5 per cent of the cropped area in the Umarkote–Raighar Zone was devastated annually. But snakes, especially the deadly *krait*, are a hazard, particularly in the Malkangiri Zone, where bears are also apt to attack ground-nut and sugar cane. Tigers are a perpetual danger to cattle (one had carried off a bullock on the day of the author's visit to Pandripani, a tribal colony in the Orissa portion of Dandakaranya).

Much damage, too, was done at the jungle edge in the Tarai colonies of Uttar Pradesh; an argument for joint farming, seldom heard, is that it spreads the risk from incursions by wild life.

In general, however, damage from wild animals is an occupational hazard of the pioneer fringe, and planning and organization by government authorities can do little to avoid it—though it may be minimized by the planning of compact, rather than scattered, blocks of land on the jungle edge.

8

Surveying Natural Resources and Planning their Use

THE last chapter has made it clear that there are deficiencies in the assessment of natural resources and of natural hazards, and in the application of knowledge about these matters that have adversely affected colonization in India. To quote only three examples: the flooding of the Ghaggar could have been foreseen given better data and their proper application; tubewells in Dandakaranya need not have been sunk in waterless positions; and colonists in the High Ranges of Kerala need not have abandoned their allotments if these had been shown in advance to have impossibly poor soils. It is therefore useful to review the present state of surveys of natural resources and natural phenomena in India, and the suggestions and recommendations that have been, or may be, made for their improvement. These matters have a bearing not only on agricultural colonization, but also on the assessment of the cultivability of wasteland (by colonization or otherwise) and on the formulation of a general land-use policy.[1]

This task is made much easier by the production in 1963 of *A Co-ordinated Study of Organisations concerned with the Surveys of Natural Resources*[2] and, in 1971, of a revised version of this *Study*[3] issued to form the basis for discussions on 'the present status of surveys of natural resources, . . . the surveys required and further measures needed in relation to programmes of planned development'.[4]

Organizations Responsible for Mapping

The senior organization in the field, and still one of the most important, is the Survey of India, which is responsible for geodetic, trigonometric, and topographical surveys, as well as surveys for development projects and other special purposes.[5] India is indeed fortunate to possess a sound basic survey system: in this respect it resembles Pakistan and Ceylon, and has a great advantage over countries like Indonesia and Thailand in which survey and map coverage are much less complete and much less satisfactory. Most of India is in fact covered by maps on a scale either of one inch to one mile or of 1/50,000 based on surveys made since a major reorganization undertaken in 1905, and, in a great many areas, on much more recent work. All areas covered by these maps are also covered by maps on a number of smaller scales; certain areas, including some under development, are covered by maps on larger scales. The one-inch map of India is gradually being replaced by maps at 1/50,000 using the metric system, and the quarter-inch by maps at 1/250,000.

One of the problems confronting those responsible for planning or studying colonization in India is that certain of the relevant areas are covered only by one-inch maps based on pre-1905 surveys and unrevised since, with hills indicated by nothing more accurate than formlines. For example, in 1970 such maps still covered two or three of the smaller and remoter colonies in Madhya Pradesh and most of the Paralkote Zone of Dandakaranya.[6] Such are the difficulties of using these obsolete maps that it is fortunate that they apply to relatively few areas which are, in any case, diminishing in number.

It has been claimed by V. A. Janaki that the Survey of India, 'geared to the defence needs of the British . . . is still to be made aware of the need of maps for planning and national development'.[7] It is true that the Survey of India, like many ancient and honourable institutions, is a little conservative over a number of matters. But the Survey is in fact ready and able to play a far greater role in all aspects of the development process (including colonization) than might be inferred from Janaki's strictures. Indeed, resources have been diverted to surveys of development projects which were intended for, and ought to have been used for normal topographical surveys.[8] In consequence, revision cycles for the topographical map have been set back very seriously. A number of the special development-project surveys covered actual or potential colonization areas: for example, those of the Hirakud, Bhakra, and Rajasthan Canal irrigation schemes. Furthermore the Surveyor-General acts as the adviser to the Government of India on all aerial survey matters and is responsible for co-ordinating all demands for aerial survey and photography—an important function, given the vital part that air survey methods can play in development in general and in natural resource surveys in particular.

Survey of India maps at all scales are available to government officials. But unofficial workers, whether Indian or not, were for many years prevented by security regulations from obtaining maps on a scale larger than one-in-a-million (that is, about sixteen miles to the inch—useless for any sort of detailed work). This was a very grave handicap, and seriously diminished the contribution to the study of

India's problems that could be made in a number of important fields, not least in the study of colonization, by the unofficial research worker.

By March 1972 the position was easier, for maps on a scale of 1/50,000 or smaller were then available for areas away from frontiers, military installations, and coasts (unfortunately maps of the Rajasthan Canal command are still restricted).

The National Atlas Organisation, set up in 1956 under the direction of Dr S. P. Chatterjee, is producing an extremely useful series of maps for general and planning purposes: notably the *National Atlas of India*[9] with maps on a scale of 1/5,000,000, and a series of population maps on a scale of 1/1,000,000 which are invaluable in field and other studies. These productions necessarily lean heavily on the maps of the Survey of India (which also prints them) and, for data, on a wide range of other organizations from the geological and soil surveys to the Census of India. The National Atlas Organisation makes these data readily available in map form to the great benefit of researchers of many kinds. It clearly cannot be blamed for the consequences of inaccuracies, inconsistencies, and even absurdities that arise from the nature of the component data. But it *can* be blamed for such faults of compilation as affect Map 11 (Forests and Land Use) in the *National Atlas*, where a large area on the Jeypore–Bastar plateau is shown as 'rocky waste', and ends to the north along a suspiciously rectilinear boundary on the parallel of latitude 20° North, and to the south along a similar boundary drawn along the nineteenth parallel. To the north and south of these unlikely boundaries forest is indicated. Within this area of 'rocky waste' lies almost the whole of the Paralkote Zone of Dandakaranya, which is certainly not all of that nature. It has been mentioned that this zone is covered only by the old (pre-1905) survey, and this was no doubt the initial reason for the inclusion of false information about it on the *Atlas* map: but the impossibly straight boundaries should have aroused suspicion during compilation. Other and similar cases could be quoted and clearly reduce the value of the *Atlas* for research workers, and, specifically, for the study and planning of agricultural colonization.

A further series of maps on the scale of 1/1,000,000 is published by the Indian Council of Agricultural Research as part of the *International Map of Vegetation and Environmental Conditions*; compilation is the responsibility of the Scientific and Technical Section of the French Institute at Pondicherry. In addition to the basic vegetation map (which shows not only surviving natural vegetation but also main cultivated crops), there is a series of inset maps showing, *inter alia*, topography, geology and lithology, soils and bioclimates.[10] The vegetation map depends on surveys actually undertaken by the very able band of scientists based on Pondicherry, who also contribute the bioclimatic insets; both depend on the system established by the distinguished French biogeographer, Henri Gaussen, at Toulouse.[11] But other inset maps, notably those of geology and soils, depend for the most part on other surveys (although useful soil work is being done at Pondicherry).

A very different source of mapped information is provided by the Census organizations at the centre and in the states. The Census of 1961 involved a full-scale atlas project which produced a *Union Atlas* containing not only demographic maps but also maps portraying a wide range of economic and social data, and atlases for each state planned on a similarly broad scale.[12] All of these atlases cannot fail to be of interest and utility to the research worker and planner, including those concerned with colonization.

Data-providing Organizations

Geology, Water, and Forests

So far this chapter has been concerned principally with organizations responsible for making and publishing maps rather than with those whose task it is to provide data, which, by being plotted on maps or otherwise presented, can be used in the process of development. Four groups of organizations in India are concerned, from the present point of view, with data provision: the Geological Survey; the Central Water and Power Commission and Irrigation Departments in the states; the organizations for the forest surveys; and the various bodies concerned with soil, land capability, and wasteland surveys. All of these have some relevance to colonization, and to discussion of certain broader issues of land-use policy; but the fullest treatment will be given to the soil, land capability, and wasteland surveys, because of their fundamental importance to the question in hand.

The Geological Survey of India, like the Survey of India, is a body of respectable antiquity (it was founded in 1853) with a tremendous record of achievement of a high order of scientific excellence.[13] Much of its work is irrelevant to the subject of this book. Its general mapping work is, however, often necessary to an understanding of soils, even though geology and lithology alone are rarely sufficient explanations of soil characteristics. And the connection of the Geological Survey and of its Groundwater Directorates with the search for underground water resources is also of relevance to colonization: F. Ahmad, for instance, whose remarks on underground water in Dandakaranya and strictures on well-sinking without geological knowledge have already been quoted, was a member of the Geological Survey.[14] It should be made clear, too, that it is not the fault of the Geological Survey (or of the Exploratory Tubewells Organization) that so many mistakes are made in the siting of wells in colonization schemes (as in the case at Srinagar, near Gandhisagar, quoted above, neither body was consulted).

Studies of surface water resources in connection with projected irrigation works are undertaken either by the Central Water and Power Commission or by state engineers. The studies for the Chambal scheme, under which there has been a certain scope for colonization, were thus undertaken by the central body,[15] while an assessment of the water resources of both east- and west-flowing rivers rising in the hills on their common frontier was made jointly by engineers from Madras and Kerala.[16] The Planning Commission, however, in the *Third Five Year Plan*, criticized what was being done in the states: not all states had set up special investigation units, and in others progress had been inadequate. The *Draft* for the Fourth Plan (1969–74) admitted that investigations had still been inadequate; proposed to make a beginning with plans for the integrated development of land and water resources, basin by basin; and announced the setting up of a Panel on Water Resources to advise on long-term research and planning.[17]

Some work has also been done by outside agencies, for example, the US Bureau of Reclamation's study of the Beas and Rajasthan Projects.[18]

Forest surveys are not only a prerequisite for the preparation of scientific forest working plans but are also, with soil and land potential surveys, essential to rational decisions on questions of broad land-use planning (and in particular on the excision of forests from the reserves for agricultural colonization). Forest surveys, which are made by the Survey of India at the request of state governments, cover only a little over half of the total forest area.[19] There were particularly large areas of unsurveyed forests in Andhra Pradesh, Orissa, and Madhya Pradesh (particularly in Bastar)—states of obvious importance for actual or potential colonization as well as for forest development. It is officially appreciated that information on forests may best be obtained by 'a rapid aerial survey'.[20]

Soil and Land Capability Surveys

In a sense, of course, India has had a soil (indeed, a land capability) survey for a very long time, for the classification of cultivated land on which revenue is assessed goes back well before British times and involves, as well as the depth, texture, and fertility of the soils, the height of the water-table, facilities for transport, and other factors affecting productivity. Indeed, it is sometimes claimed that the Indian revenue land classification constitutes the earliest system of soil survey; and Baden-Powell talks of a 'trained establishment for soil classification' in the then United Provinces.[21]

There can be no shadow of doubt that the traditional soil classifications arise from centuries, if not millennia, of peasant experience of soils and their productivity, and that they are by no means to be despised, particularly if what is at issue is an understanding of traditional land-use technology. But, equally, these classifications are inadequate under twentieth-century conditions, in India as elsewhere. They are purely local, with no reference to general systems of classification, and thus stand aloof from the great corpus of knowledge on soils and their treatment. They are empirical and quite unscientific, with no basis in chemistry or mineralogy or any other branch of natural science. They give, in consequence, only the roughest of guides to the need for and response to fertilizers, and (very important for the present study), they provide only a very inadequate basis for a proper assessment of the potential of a given area for reclamation and colonization, or of the likely costs and benefits of the operation if undertaken.

A more scientific curiosity about Indian soil was aroused quite early in the nineteenth century, when, for example, F. Buchanan described and named the laterites of South India.[22] But organized scientific research began only in the 1890s, and received some stimulus after 1902 when various provinces of British India began to appoint agricultural chemists.[23] Already, however, two of the bugbears of soil science in India—lack of clear objectives and lack of inter-provincial co-ordination—were evident. Moreover, a mass of data was gathered, mainly about nutrient status and soil chemistry, but all rather narrowly conceived, and rarely with reference to profile development—that essential guide to an understanding of soils. There was, generally speaking, a lack of a uniform framework of reference (either in terms of theoretical basis or of sampling procedure) and a tendency for surveys to be undertaken for specific, narrow objectives. It is thus difficult, anyhow for this period, to speak of a soil survey of India in any proper sense of the term (the same might be said, of course, of many other countries too at the same period). Attempts were occasionally made, however, to see the wood in spite of the proliferation of trees, and to delimit the main groups of Indian soils, especially by applying Russian concepts of the dominance in soil formation of the action of climate and vegetation on parent material. Some went further, and drew soil maps of India; for example, the brave but premature effort of Z. J. Schokalskaya.[24] But all of these resemble the efforts of a cartographer to construct a map of a large country from a proliferation of varying local maps, but without a triangulated framework.

In the late 'thirties pleas began to be made for a soil survey of India conceived on something approaching the necessarily grand design of the Survey of India or the Geological Survey,[25] and in opposition, it should be said, to the short-sighted view of the Royal Commission on Agriculture (1928) that the advantages to be gained by such a survey would not justify the effort needed, the main classes of soils and their location being, in the Commissioners' view, already known.[26] Fortunately pressures in favour of a comprehensive soil survey mounted, and in 1940 plans were approved for 'a scheme of All-India Soil Survey' which would first assemble data already collected in the several provinces and states and later proceed to actual survey. In 1953 there appeared the misleadingly titled *Final Report of the All-India Soil Survey Scheme*;[27] misleading because the *Report* is not the definitive result of field survey, merely an assemblage of data already available from a multiplicity of scattered sources. The *Report*, it is true, contains a great deal of information on soils, their nutrient status, and agricultural response; but reveals once again a lack of clear and unified aims, and lack of co-ordination across (and sometimes even within) state boundaries. Yet most subsequent soil maps of India and its major regions are based essentially on the maps in the *Report*. The Soils Map in the *National Atlas* (1957) does, however, differ from that in the *Report* in a number of respects, and this fact is at least in part a result of work done since the *Report* appeared in 1953. But it still remains difficult to relate many of the soil types mapped to modern systems of classification; though Learmonth has recently made a bold effort to do so.[28]

Something has, however, been done to achieve closer integration of soil surveys. For instance, a *Soil Survey Manual* was issued in 1960 (with a Supplement in 1962) 'to serve as a guide to the techniques and procedural aspects of soil survey and soil mapping for the use of field workers, and to introduce uniform standards for future soil survey programmes of different States'.[29] It was strongly influenced in its concepts by a visit paid to India by C. E. Kellogg, the distinguished American pedologist, and reflected American practice of the time. It covered, in addition to soil survey *sensu stricto*, the use of field data and soil surveys for determining land capability classes and thus for the drawing up of land-use plans (based on physical, if not economic data).[30] This is clearly a matter of importance for colonization. It is understood that a revised draft of the *Manual* has been prepared.

Again, a sample survey conducted in 1951 having revealed 'a vast diversity' in methods used in India for the laboratory analysis of soils, the Indian Council for Agricultural Research approved and financed a scheme for the standardization of such methods at the Field Research Station, Bombay. The results are being published in a series of bulletins.[31] There is also a uniform system, highly relevant because of the indisputable need for the intensification in Indian agriculture, for testing soils at laboratories scattered all over the country in order to provide guidance in the proper use of fertilizers.[32] This has grown out of an Indo-US project on soil fertility and fertilizer use; and has a clear bearing on the effectiveness of extension services (see below, chapter 11).

A further measure of co-ordination was achieved in March 1958 when the All-India Soil Survey was amalgamated with the Land Utilization Survey Scheme of the Central Soil Conservation Board.[33] This Scheme was concerned with soil survey in the catchments of rivers feeding major irrigation works, and with the preparation of maps showing land in these catchments classified according to the conservation measures needed in order 'to minimize the soil erosion and to increase the life of the dams'.[34] The absorption of the Land Utilisation Survey put a great strain on the joint organization and diverted effort from reconnaissance and detailed soil survey more broadly conceived. In fact, more and more special tasks tended to be unloaded on the Survey. Its removal in December 1968 from the control of the Ministry of Agriculture to that of the Indian Council for Agricultural Research should, however, enable it more effectively to pursue long-term objectives.[35]

State soil surveys exist in a number of states, notably Andhra Pradesh and Uttar Pradesh. One of the regional soil research laboratories in the latter state, sited at Rudrapur, in the Tarai colonization area, has been functioning since 1950, and has done valuable work in both reconnaissance and detailed soil survey in the colony,[36] work now complemented by that at the Uttar Pradesh Agricultural University. But there is evidence that co-ordination between the All-India Survey and some state surveys has been far from perfect. State surveyors tend to describe soils in general and utilitarian terms, and not to categorize them in any uniform way. This, no doubt, affects the standard and the wider usefulness of soil reports on colonization schemes. Since 1966, however, a new training centre at Nagpur has attempted to give state surveyors a more uniform approach; while courses at the Indian Photo-Interpretation Institute at Dehra Dun are also available to them.

But soil and related surveys in India still suffer from fragmentation. This is not only a matter of division of responsibility between the All-India Soil and Land Utilisation Survey and the corresponding organizations in those states that possess their own soil surveys. It will be appreciated that the Survey is not alone among central and inter-state bodies in its concern with these matters: for instance, there are the Central Water and Power Commission (for irrigation areas—and, therefore, many colonization schemes), the Central Arid Zone Research Institute at Jodhpur, the Forest Department, the Dandakaranya Development Authority, and the Field Research Station at Bombay. Again, the division of responsibility between central bodies and state bodies does not follow functional lines. It may be argued, of course, with some justification, that many of the difficulties of co-ordination between all these various bodies, central and state, is a consequence of the immensity of India and of its federal political structure. But to those who know the Indian resource surveys with some degree of intimacy it seems clear that more vigour and pertinacity could have been put into the work of co-ordination, the need for which is still being stressed in official quarters.[37]

It may also be argued, again with a great deal of truth, that the amount of work in progress on soil and related surveys has increased by leaps and bounds since independence. No longer, for instance, is the All-India Soil Survey an organization concerned with no more than the collation of disparate results collected by other bodies and individuals. But, compared with the Survey of India and the Geological Survey, the All-India Soil and Land Utilisation Survey is still a Cinderella, new, small and struggling; an organization which failed to establish itself thoroughly under the British and which has been overwhelmed since independence by the consequences of federalism and of undertaking a series of short-term tasks, whose fulfilment, while greatly benefiting colonization, has done relatively little to establish a national framework of reference or to relate Indian soils and their problems to international knowledge.

Soil and land capability surveys in India have thus suffered from a number of difficulties and deficiencies, especially indifference in official quarters and insufficient co-ordination. One reason for this state of affairs has no doubt been lack of resources; for surveys, including those using aerial photography, are expensive, and it is always proper to ask whether a survey is necessary at the degree of detail proposed. But another reason lies, especially in some quarters and in some states, in the survival of older habits of thought which see the revenue-type survey as perfectly adequate for modern needs. And, at the other end of the spectrum, are those technocrats and social scientists who imagine that all that any soil needs is the right 'mix' of fertilizer to bring it up to an acceptable level of productivity: so that soil survey has no function but to indicate that 'mix' and the associated costs in relation to benefits; and no need of more than a few soil chemists armed with trowels to take samples at wide intervals. A short acquaintance with irrigation or colonization schemes, among other types of development project, will show that much more needs to be known from a soil and land capability survey before the economic justification for a project can be assessed, and, if it is judged worthwhile, its design and planning properly completed: for instance, rainfall amount and reliability, depth and physical characteristics of the soil, depth to water-table and slope as affecting drainage characteristics, and nature of conservation works required. If the soil is, for instance, an impermeable alkali clay of the sort encountered in the Anupgarh area of the Rajasthan Canal command, the cost of reclamation to be brought into a pre-scheme benefit/cost calculation may include not only the cost of conventional fertilizer but also the cost of drainage works, of applications of gypsum, of an enhanced flow of water for flushing purposes, and of soil-creating crops: indeed, all of these and more may be necessary before there is any point in applying fertilizer at all. Similar considerations apply, *mutatis mutandis,* to questions of economic marginality, and of correct soil treatment, in many other areas of the sort that tend to be taken up for colonization.

But it is time to draw out of this discussion other threads particularly relevant to the problems of agricultural colonization.

Soil and Land Capability Surveys in Colonization Areas

The Soil Survey of India, like the soil surveys of the Central Water and Power Commission and of the states, has concentrated mainly, for obvious reasons, on work in areas which were, or were to be, the scenes of major irrigation or other development projects: such areas as that in the Mahanadi valley below the Hirakud dam; the command area of the Bhakra–Nangal works; the Chambal Valley in both Rajasthan and Madhya Pradesh; the command area of the Rajasthan Canal (but see below, pp. 145–6) and of the Tungabhadra project (stretching into the Raichur Doab); and the UP Tarai.[38] Most of the areas mentioned are, of course, the scenes of colonization. The Dandakaranya Development Authority also has a good soil survey organization.[39] Again, soil surveys have been made, wisely, in connection with conservation works in the catchments above such irrigation reservoirs as Bhakra–Nangal, and Gandhisagar and Ranapratapsagar on the Chambal. These surveys are of obvious importance if the siltation of reservoirs is to be minimized and the long-term future of colonization and irrigation assured. Only the Greater Malnad area, of the four major areas of post-independence colonization, has been without a soil survey in advance of detailed planning: and even here some sort of survey seems to have been made at one colony, Thengumarahada, in 1948.

Of the smaller areas that were discussed (see pp. 59–64 above), some have had the benefit of pre-colonization soil surveys because they fall under major irrigation schemes. This applies to the upper Chambal Valley (in both Madhya Pradesh and Rajasthan),[40] though not to the ravine lands farther down the river. It also applies to that part of the Raichur Doab which is under the command of the Tungabhadra reservoir;[41] and to the land under the Hirakud reservoir.[42] Again, soil surveys for various purposes, including colonization, have been undertaken in the Andaman Islands by the Forest Department.[43] But no soil surveys appear to have preceded, accompanied, or even followed colonization in the other minor areas of colonization, with the following exceptions: a certain amount done in one or two of the small Maharashtra co-operative colonies; a post-colonization survey in the Moranam colony, in Tamil Nadu; some 'tests' said to have been made at the Jeelugumilli colony in Andhra Pradesh; and manifestly unsatisfactory work at Aminabad in the same state (which has a wide variety of soil types, including very eroded dark soils, with *kankar* at the surface) from ten samples taken outside the colony altogether.

On the face of it, then, and except in the areas noted, some attempt does appear to have been made to conduct a soil survey in advance of the planning of colonization in post-independence India. But in some areas the original survey work was sketchy in the extreme. Nowhere is this more true than in the case of the Rajasthan Canal. As a team from the US Bureau of Reclamation discovered, the soil survey of over 9 million acres was accomplished in two cool seasons in the field, with only some 500 samples.[44] A. A. Michel cogently points out that this may well represent no more than 150–300 soil profiles, 'one imperfectly analysed profile for each 30,000 to 60,000 acres [12,000 to 24,000 hectares] of the project';[45] an utterly inadequate basis on which to base the decision to launch the Canal scheme, and one that compares unfavourably with comparable operations in Pakistan.[46] Shortage of funds and of skilled workers is urged as the reason for this state of affairs. It is not surprising that a United Nations Special Fund study made in 1965 recommended detailed soil and hydrological surveys and training in survey techniques in the Rajasthan Canal area, with a new soil laboratory at Bikaner. The All-India Soil and Land Use Survey was to make 'senior soil consultants' available, and to provide base maps for aerial surveys of soils. A project following the lines set out in the study was in fact initiated in 1966, by which time water was already flowing in the upper reaches of the Canal.[47] When the project was wound up in April

1971, detailed survey had been accomplished in 4,000 hectares of Stage I, semi-detailed survey elsewhere in that Stage and in part of Stage II, and reconnaissance survey in the rest of the latter. The Survey of India supplied large-scale contoured maps on which were plotted the results of the interpretation of aerial photographs and of ground surveys (based on profile samples at one per hectare for detailed survey, one per hundred hectares for semi-detailed, and one per thousand hectares for reconnaissance). The approach was essentially that through land systems.[48] The irrigable area for Stage II was demarcated on the basis of the reconnaissance survey. The project also involved agronomic research stations, one on light-textured soils, the other on poorly permeable saline and alkaline soils, at which such problems as means of reclamation, soil and water management, and crop selection were studied. Given the problem of wind erosion, research was also undertaken on means of stabilizing sand-dunes; and, given that of water-loss from channels in desert sands, on the cheapest means of lining channels (still, nevertheless, an expensive process). And an effort has also been made, through research stations, to construct the necessary bridge between survey on the one hand, and economic assessment and successful planning on the other. As will be clear from other passages in this book, however, one still has grave doubts about the wisdom of attempting the Rajasthan Canal scheme, not least because the chosen remedy for every difficulty encountered during survey adds to cost.

Even where reasonably adequate soil surveys have been made in advance of colonization, they are not always sufficiently heeded in the planning of the schemes. Thus on the left bank of the Chambal, in Rajasthan, soil survey showed a very impermeable soil, and it was recommended that, to prevent waterlogging, drainage channels should be dug at the same time as irrigation channels. The advice was not taken, and waterlogging is already marked (though admittedly matters are made worse by lack of control over water issues, and failure to instruct the cultivator in irrigated cultivation).[49]

Surveys of Wastelands

Something must now be said of the various official surveys of wastelands[50] which have an obvious relevance to the subject of this book. These have, for the most part, proceeded without specifically commissioned soil studies by the All-India Soil and Land Utilisation Survey or by any other technically competent body. (Surveys of wastelands in Maharashtra and Mysore were an exception.)[51] These surveys have already been mentioned and were undertaken by state governments (in practice by Revenue Departments) in order to provide information in connection with the Patil Committee's proposals on the resettlement of landless labourers. A committee was set up by the Union Ministry of Food and Agriculture under the chairmanship of Dr B. N. Uppal *inter alia* to make a survey of land classified as 'other uncultivated land excluding fallow lands' (this, of course, includes the notorious category culturable waste) and 'fallow lands other than current fallows' and 'to locate areas where large blocks of land are available for reclamation and resettlement', 'to suggest suitable measures for reclamation according to conditions in different areas and estimate the cost of reclamation and colonisation' and 'to estimate the economic aspects of such reclamation in terms of the expenditure involved, the likely addition to food production and the employment and income that would become available to settlers . . . and to lay down the priorities *inter se* between different categories of reclaimable lands'.[52] The government of each state and of each Union territory was asked to provide a 'fairly senior officer' to help the Committee by collecting information for his state or territory, on the basis of a questionnaire prepared by the Uppal Committee. It was the intention to produce a report for each state or territory and a general report for the whole country. Reports have in fact appeared in respect of the following states:

Pt I	Punjab (1960)	Pt VII	Kerala (1961)
Pt II	West Bengal (1960)	Pt VIII	Madras (1961)
Pt III	Bihar (1960)	Pt IX	Jammu and Kashmir (1961)
Pt IV	Mysore (1960)	Pt X	Uttar Pradesh (1962)
Pt V	Andhra Pradesh (1961)	Pt XI	Maharashtra (1962)
Pt VI	Madhya Pradesh (1961)	Pt XII	Gujarat (1963)

Parts I–VII contain a soil map based on pre-existing information (and subject to the inadequacies discussed earlier in this chapter) but (apart from surveys in Maharashtra and Mysore) seem to represent the sum total of the contribution of the soil-surveying organizations. The pilot survey of culturable waste in Dewas District,[53] to which reference has been made and which provided a great deal of useful information (see above, pp. 78–9), also made no use of soil or land capability surveys. Officials in New Delhi in 1963 complacently thought wasteland surveying techniques adequate, and were under the mistaken impression that the organization in each state was headed by an agricultural chemist. By 1968, however, the officers of the Programme Evaluation Organization of the Planning Commission were writing:

> The existing revenue records in most of the States do furnish information regarding culturable waste lands, etc., but it is felt that for an effective programme of resettlement, it is necessary to undertake detailed soil surveys for determining the area available for settlement.[54]

They went on to show how much both the surveyors and the methods employed varied from state to state. Many inadequacies were also revealed by their inquiries.

The author's field inquiries threw up a number of unsatisfactory features of these 'surveys' of wastelands. In Madhya Pradesh, District after District on the Malwa Plateau is, on the soils map accompanying the state *Report*,[55] shown as having 'Medium Black Soil', whereas quite large areas are covered with very poor, gravelly soils derived from the weathering of indurated laterite (for example, between Biaora and Jhalrapatan, especially in the miniscular and poverty-stricken former state of Khilchipur). Yet inquiries in the state capital, Bhopal, revealed that wasteland surveys in eight Districts were being done by revenue officers with some assistance from the agricultural extension service, the Department of Agriculture being unable to lend qualified soil surveyors. The Madhya Pradesh *Report*, again, shows no blocks of reclaimable waste as existing in Dandakaranya, an obvious omission.[56] Senior officials in Bhopal in fact seemed oblivious to the scientific viewpoint in the survey of land potential. In Madras (as it then was), a senior official in the Department of Agriculture had not heard of the Uppal Committee's inquiries, even though a *Report* had been published for his state.[57] In the same state, certain agricultural officers seemed quite unaware of the technical considerations involved in surveys of wasteland; while an unpublished Report was highly critical of lands chosen for resettlement schemes, there being 'no uniform criteria and little expert inspection'.[58]

It is quite clear that for most states the Uppal Committee was supplied with data collected by Revenue officials. In some cases (as in the case of the omission of Dandakaranya from the Madhya Pradesh *Report*) the information is wrong, even if considered merely in revenue terms. It will also not have escaped the reader's notice that some of the terms of reference of the Uppal Committee cannot possibly be fulfilled without adequate technical information. This applies especially to estimates of the costs of reclamation and of the returns from it, and *a fortiori* to returns if inputs of fertilizers are contemplated, as they should be in contemporary India. The Committee was, indeed, faced with an impossible task.

It will be remembered that, in the setting and with the results already mentioned in chapters 2 and 4 above, the government of Assam decided to carry out its own 'Technical Survey' of wastelands, which was published in 1968 after some seven years of work.[59] An earlier Committee had surveyed only blocks of 100 bighas (13·4 hectares) and less; and for that reason, it is said, its results were not considered adequate (it may also be added that it found nearly 50 per cent more land within its terms of reference than did its successor). Although the 'Technical Survey' seems to have involved a certain amount of field investigation, as a result of which 'the Committee had to exclude blocks of land found to be unfit for any kind of cultivation' because they consisted of rocky hills, rivers or *bils*, or of actual or proposed reserve forests, the actual methods used remain alarmingly unclear. The survey was not detailed enough for any estimate to be made of the cost of reclaiming land selected as 'cultivable'; and there was no soil chemist or other qualified pedologist on this allegedly 'technical' survey from early in 1964 until the work of the Committee was completed two years later.

It should be said, however, that few of the criticisms just made of the Uppal and Assam surveys apply to another study of wastelands, with which the work of the Uppal Committee may be confused. This is the *Study on Wastelands including Saline, Alkali and Waterlogged Lands and their Reclamation Measures*,[60] to which reference has in fact already been made (see above, p. 113). This is a truly technical study, with which not only B. N. Uppal but also such soil scientists as Dr S. P. Raychaudhuri and Dr R. V. Tamhane were associated; and it covers the problems involved in reclaiming lands made waste through salinity, alkalinity, waterlogging and soil erosion, and through infestation with *kans* grass.

It should also be said that the Patil Committee (see above, p. 113) was by no means unaware of the need for technical soil survey before wastelands were approved for reclamation;[61] and, further, they recommended that after proper survey wastelands should be classified under four heads:

(i) the lands which could be brought under cultivation without prior reclamation;
(ii) the lands which would need reclamation before being brought under cultivation (with specification of the nature of reclamation operations that would be necessary, etc.);
(iii) the lands which could best be utilized for afforestation or plantations; and
(iv) the lands which should be used as pasture lands for the homesteads and for the common purpose of the village.

This classification in terms of land utilization brings the discussion to the subject of the final section of this chapter.

Broader Issues of Land-Use Policy

Clearly agricultural colonization, or indeed any form of cultivation, is only one broad means of land utilization, alternative in many areas to use as forest. It is one of the principal themes of this book that the mere existence of uncultivated land is an insufficient reason for its cultivation: only if it can be shown that cultivation is the best use should land be cultivated, and this can be determined only after a proper assessment of land capability and of the costs and benefits of alternative uses. In such an assessment the possibility must be borne in mind of so intensifying agriculture on some land already cultivated that other such land can be used for non-agricultural purposes, such as forest.

Under the Indian Forest Act of 1927 there are three categories of forests: Reserved Forests (the most strictly controlled), Protected Forests (less strictly controlled), and Unclassified Forests (which include 'village forests' on land classed as 'culturable waste'). The remarks that follow mainly concern the first two categories, and corresponding categories in states to which the Act does not apply.

India and its component states are often criticized, not least by foresters, for deforestation, for allegedly causing soil erosion, and for insufficiently strict control of forests. Sometimes the criticism is directed from the centre towards the states; Dr Ram Subhag Singh, Union Minister for Agriculture with responsibility for forestry, has been reported as criticizing the southern states for 'continually sacrificing forests for other purposes, "as is most glaringly happening in Kerala" '.[62] Undoubtedly there is a real need for attention to afforestation, notably in the catchments of reservoirs feeding the irrigation systems of colonization schemes. But there are also circumstances in which Forest Departments need to look again at their Reserves, with a view to excision for cultivation and the practice of more intensive forestry in surviving Reserves. True, lip service at any rate has always been paid to the possibility of sacrificing Reserves in this way. A government of India Circular of 1894, which enshrined the 'Old Forest Policy',[63] included the sentence 'Subject to certain conditions to be referred to presently, the claims of cultivation are stronger than those of forest preservation'; and went on to say that, when effective demand existed, land should be relinquished without hesitation; and that, where forests were the only grazing, village needs were paramount. The conditions referred to included the avoidance of 'honey-combing' the forest by piecemeal clearing for shifting cultivation (then as now anathema to the forester) except where forest tribes depended upon it; and of merely nominal cultivation, where the real use is for pasture. Again, the Resolution of 1952 that promulgated a 'New Forest Policy' emphasized 'the need for evolving a system of balanced and complementary land-use under which each type of land is allotted to that form of use under which it would produce most and deteriorate least'.[64] This does not resolve the possible conflict between short-term maximization of production (or of benefit/cost ratios) and avoidance of deterioration by means which may involve production (or benefit/cost ratios) short of the maximum, or benefits so long-term that conventional benefit/cost analysis is an inadequate tool. But at least the idea of a rational land-use policy is embedded in the new doctrine.

The author, in the course of his fieldwork, came across a number of examples of possible excisions from forest reserves that ought at least to have been investigated in the interests of more rational land use. Thus between Guna and the Kansal Banjara Colony, in Madhya Pradesh, much of a Reserve Forest was on steep land, where conservation was indicated and cultivation probably undesirable; but parts of the Reserve were on what appeared to be black cotton soil on flat ground. In Chanda District of Maharashtra, teak forests were growing in Reserves on flattish land with deep red loam soils; again, cultivation appeared possible. Indeed, the Uppal Committee proposed to release 7,300 hectares of forest in Chanda District under the Dina irrigation project.[65] Large areas of Forest Reserve along the Sarda River in the UP Tarai appeared to be on land basically no different from that which was the scene of successful colonization.

Of a different category are the problems presented by highly destructive charcoal-burning and shallow quarrying in the forests of the Vindhyan Range in Madhya Pradesh. Here, a more efficient system of charcoal production or even the replacement of charcoal by some other fuel, and the development of deep quarrying, would mean that a much smaller area need be kept from agriculture (if indeed areas within the forest are suitable for cultivation).

Foresters in India are no different from foresters the world over in their intense desire to conserve their forests at all costs, notwithstanding the general instructions just quoted. Sometimes their instincts are right, of course, for if any piece of land could be excised from the forest without proper consideration, the national economy might well lose, not gain, at least in the long term. And if foresters were left with nothing but steep, barren land far from communications the production and marketing of good timber would assuredly suffer. But at other times there seems no doubt that foresters' conservatism is excessive if not positively malign. Whether or not it is true, as the author was told, that in one state soil surveyors are bribed by the foresters to declare soils in Reserve Forests unsuitable for cultivation, the Tamil Nadu Forest Department does seem to be unduly restrictive in the Nilgiri Hills and elsewhere, and the Mysore Department was at one time resisting proposals for a land capability survey of some of its Reserves, though the forest area might thereby increase, owing to the exchange of a larger area of 'culturable waste' recommended for afforestation for a smaller area of Reserve Forest recommended for excision (this was, in fact, the fruits of a survey in Belgaum District). It is also, apparently, hard to persuade the UP Forest Department to excise forests.

To be set in the opposite scale, however, are efforts made by a number of Forest Departments in the interests of more rational land use. Thus in Tamil Nadu there is a programme under which poor wasteland is planted in trees useful for fuel or green manure, while the Forest Department has planted cashew nut on a Forest Reserve that naturally bore only poor scrub. Examples of planting of commercial tree crops by other Forest Departments have already been given.

Finally, it must be recognized that the commendable desire to preserve wild life may mean a departure, for the time being at any rate, from strictly economic considerations. For if forests are re-sited according to principles of optimum land use (with an eye also to the overall need for forest products) there may be no provision for forests in places where particular animals or birds need forest cover.[66] There is thus a need to preserve stretches of forest in the Bihar Tarai to provide a habitat for rhinoceros, and in the plains proper near the confluence of the Ganges and Kosi, where wild buffalo live precariously.[67] India is rightly proud of its eighty-three national parks and wildlife sanctuaries; and it is to be hoped that the intensification of production on cultivated land will come fast enough to enable essential areas to be kept as wildlife reserves.

Rational land-use planning is, then, not merely a matter of surveying natural resources and arriving at maps of land capability, basic though these matters are. It is also essential to assess the costs of and expected benefits from alternative methods of using the land so surveyed. So far as agricultural colonization is continued, costs and benefits derive not only from the land but also from the technology applied to it in order to utilize natural resources and to overcome natural difficulties. To this technology attention must now be turned.

9

Problems of Land-Use Technology

THIS chapter will be concerned with the technology by means of which the authorities and the colonist attempt to bring land in colonization schemes into productive use, and to maintain it in production. It will cover such matters as the choice and impact of techniques of clearing and reclamation, of irrigation and drainage, and of agriculture, pastoralism and forest management. Some mention will also be made of soil conservation.

Clearing and Reclamation of Land

Colonization in contemporary India is, of course, taking place in a very wide range of vegetational environments.[1] At one extreme there stand such areas as the deserts of Rajasthan, the ravines of the Chambal, and the barren, eroded areas of the Santal Parganas of Bihar, where, for natural or anthropogenic reasons, or because of some combination of the two, there is hardly any vegetation to be cleared. At the other extreme, high tropical forest presents formidable tasks of clearing, stumping, and land preparation in such areas as Dandakaranya (much of which lies naturally under moist deciduous forest), Greater Malnad (generally under moist semi-evergreen forest) and Intikheri in Madhya Pradesh (moist deciduous forest with teak). Between the two extremes fall such areas as the Tarai (with its mixture of moist forest, tall grassland, and swamp); and the Upper Chambal Valley, the small colonies of Tamil Nadu and of the Eastern Ghats in Andhra Pradesh, and areas under the Bhakra Canal in Haryana, all of which were covered before colonization with various kinds of scrub-jungle, often degraded.

But land preparation involves processes other than jungle clearing: there may also have to be earth-moving, levelling, bunding and so on, to say nothing of the reclamation of saline and alkaline lands. Here again, there is a wide range of problems, reflecting natural conditions, degree of erosion, and type of agriculture to be practised. Reclamation in this sense has not been a major problem in Dandakaranya and Greater Malnad, except for the need for paddy terraces; and it was a relatively minor problem in the Bhakra colonies and under the upper reaches of the Rajasthan Canal. But lower down the latter, near Anupgarh, levelling is costing Rs.5,000–7,500 per hectare; and, as the Master Plan recognizes, it will become a major problem if and when colonization reaches the high dune country of Jaisalmer District.[2] Patches of alkaline clay, also all too evident round Anupgarh, may demand such measures of reclamation as the application of gypsum and organic matter.[3] The need for reclamation has also been evident in the Santal Parganas and amid the Chambal ravines, both very badly eroded areas calling for heavy earthworks to create land fit for cultivation and to check further or renewed erosion.

It is not easy to generalize about methods of clearing and reclamation practised in contemporary India: here India differs markedly from Ceylon and Malaya, or for that matter from Pakistan, in each of which colonization is taking place in far more uniform environmental circumstances.[4]

Apart from tractor-ploughing of already reclaimed land, exclusively mechanical methods of clearing and reclamation were confined, among colonization schemes studied in 1963 and 1968, to Dandakaranya; to the Tarai colonization scheme[5] in Naini Tal District of Uttar Pradesh (though not to the schemes in Kheri and Pilibhit Districts in the same geographical region and state); to colonies for oustees from major irrigation works, such as Hirakud and Gandhisagar, where there were organizations commanding mechanized equipment; to Intikheri (Madhya Pradesh), a former Central Mechanized Farm cleared by the Central Tractor Organization; to major works of reclamation, as in the Santal Parganas and the Chambal ravines, and to the Kaki Project in Assam. In a number of minor colonies (for example, those run by Co-operative Societies in the Mysore Malnad and in Tamil Nadu), bulldozers or tractors were called on for certain operations only. Elsewhere, clearing and reclamation by hand methods were the rule, even in quite large colonies like those in the Tarai of Kheri and Pilibhit Districts, UP, where clearing, stumping, rooting, and burning of grass were all done by manual labour before tractors came in to plough. In many such colonies, the labour was in fact supplied by the colonists themselves, either for no reward other than the emergence of land to cultivate (as in the Chambal Canal areas of Madhya Pradesh, in the Baghbar Refugee Colony in Assam, in the Co-operative colonies of the Mysore Malnad, and at Thengumarahada under the edge of the Nilgiris); or in return for some sort of government payment or subsidy (as in the Kansal Banjara colony, in Guna District of Madhya Pradesh). Often the progress of reclamation has been slow.[6] In other cases, manual clearing was done by some government agency (as in many colonization schemes in other countries);[7] or on contract at government expense. At Bylakuppe (the colony for Tibetan refugees in Mysore) and in the High Ranges of Kerala the work was done by the Forest Department, which extracted useful timber in the process. Other government agencies involved included the Central Tractor Organization (for the Intikheri Colonies in Madhya Pradesh and in the Tarai Colony of Naini Tal District, UP) and, of course, the Dandakaranya Development Authority. What was accomplished by the manual labour, and the techniques used, varied with local needs and conditions; perhaps the most thoroughgoing job was that undertaken in the Kheri and Pilibhit Tarai, just mentioned.

The most completely mechanized operations seen by the author were those undertaken by the Dandakaranya Development Authority in 1963.[8] The work involved forest-clearing, using chain and tree-dozers, followed by the piling of trunks, branches, and stumps in 'windrows' along the contour as a soil conservation measure, and then by stumping. (Similar methods were used by the Gal Oya Development Board in its mechanized operations in Ceylon.)[9] Machines with blades were then used to sever roots in an attempt (not always completely successful) to prevent regrowth of the trees, the ground then being harrowed. Finally contour bunds for paddy cultivation, headwater tanks, and other earthworks were constructed. It was originally planned to derive a labour force largely from a specially raised Dandakaranya Development Corps; but this idea was later dropped.[10] Work could take place only from October to June, during the drier months.

It was not easy to obtain figures for the cost of clearing and reclamation, nor to know what degree of reliance to place on those figures that were obtained. In the case of mechanized operations, there is the further problem that one does not often know whether due account has been taken of maintenance costs, of depreciation, and of administrative overheads. The last item can be very considerable: one visiting expert told the author that the quoted costs of reclaiming the Chambal ravines (Rs.1,250–1,500 per hectare) would be inflated to Rs.3,700–4,200 if proper account were taken of these overheads. In any event, one would expect costs to vary enormously from scheme to scheme for reasons already made clear. Costs quoted for clearing and reclamation by manual labour included Rs.60 per hectare at Kansal Banjara Colony, Rs.50–250 per hectare in the UP Tarai, Rs.135 per hectare at Velakapuram in Tamil Nadu, and as much as Rs.990 per hectare (or so it was said) at Sindewahi in the Mysore Malnad, where, however, bunding for paddy as well as the clearing of thick jungle was involved. This last figure approximates to the total quoted by the Land Development Department in Ceylon for comparable manual operations: namely, a total of Rs.1,090 per hectare, made up of Rs.336 for felling and burning, Rs.260 for ridging, and Rs.494 for stumping.[11] Labour costs are, however, higher in Ceylon. In the High Ranges of Kerala, the value of saleable timber extracted during clearing operations outweighed total costs, with the result that jungle clearing was done at an overall profit.

It is particularly in respect of mechanical techniques, of course, that doubts on accounting procedures arise. For what they may be worth one may quote, however, Rs.300–70 per hectare for jungle clearing at Gandhisagar, Rs.445 per hectare for similar work at Kaki in Assam, Rs.860–915 per hectare for the combined operations in Dandakaranya, and Rs.800 per hectare for the very different reclamation work at Jamunia, in the Santal Parganas of Bihar.[12] Altogether, and having regard to the probable need to add elements for maintenance, depreciation, and overheads (or some of them, at least) to the figures just quoted, there is nothing in recent Indian experience to suggest a departure from the often-quoted conclusion that, in underdeveloped countries with relatively cheap and abundant labour supplies, manual labour is in general more economic than mechanized techniques in the task of jungle-clearing and reclamation.[13]

Why, then, the choice of mechanical techniques in the cases cited earlier? A general answer may well be a failure to design and to apply accounting procedures which would establish something approaching their true cost. So far as the Dandakaranya Development Authority is concerned, the argument was used that lack of labour and the need for speed made mechanization imperative.[14] Labour shortage is, of course, highly characteristic of remote areas, even in an over-populated country like India; but it should become less acute in Dandakaranya as its colonies fill with settlers. The need for speed has in part been imposed on the Authority because the state governments concerned delayed the release of blocks of land for reclamation (Madhya Pradesh being a worse culprit here than Orissa). Earlier release of land would permit better forward planning, and possibly the use of manual labour (if available) spread over a longer period.

By 1972, indeed, wisdom and altered circumstances had together promoted a shift towards manual reclamation in Dandakaranya. The labour of incoming refugees had been increasingly used from 1966 onwards, at about a third of the cost of mechanical means (which were given up altogether in 1968–9). The 1970 influx of displaced persons was put on to manual reclamation as well as minor irrigation works and well-sinking. Yet of the land released up to

June 1971, 50,820 hectares had been cleared mechanically against only 3,070 hectares cleared manually.[15]

Another problem associated with indiscriminate mechanical reclamation had, by 1971, emerged in the UP Tarai, where over-deep bulldozing had buried good surface loams and left poor sands at the surface.

Meanwhile, other states continued to be seduced by the apparent attractiveness of mechanical methods. Thus the Rangapur project, for tribal colonization in Andhra Pradesh, employed bulldozers for stumping, levelling, and works of soil conservation in 1967.

Techniques and Problems of Irrigation and Drainage[16]

It will be clear from the review of natural conditions undertaken in chapter 7 that irrigation or drainage (or both) are as much a pre-requisite of agricultural colonization in many parts of India as jungle-clearing, reclamation, and land preparation. But whereas chapter 7, in general, dealt only with irrigation and drainage in relation to the natural difficulties confronting colonization, the present discussion will look forward to, and indeed lead into, a review of agricultural production.

Table 9.I is an attempt to sum up irrigation in Indian colonization schemes initiated since independence and operating in December 1963 (December 1968 in the case of Assam). The data, both qualitative and quantitative, on which it is based were collected mainly in the course of field inquiries. The figures for the net irrigated area show the area capable of being irrigated (ground irrigated more than once a year being counted only once) and are not put forward as being in all cases reliable, partly because of problems of definition which may not always have been understood by the persons interrogated. The net irrigated area under the Rajasthan Canal is, for want of a better figure, arrived at by applying to the culturable area said to be commanded in December 1963 the percentage of that area designed to be irrigated in the project as a whole: the answer may well be an over-estimate.

It will be noted that the net irrigated area for all listed colonization schemes taken together amounted to some 120,000 hectares: that is, about half of the total area cultivated in them (as given in Table 5.I). For India as a whole in 1963–4 the net irrigated area was 25,856,000 hectares and the net sown area 136,438,000 hectares.[17] The colonization schemes tabulated thus contained under 0·5 per cent of the national net irrigated area; but, on the other hand, the proportion of the cultivated area irrigated in the colonies was about four times as high as the national proportion (12 per cent). The large colonized

TABLE 9.I

Irrigation in Colonization Schemes, 1947–63, Visited by the Author

State or Authority	*Region*	*Colonization Scheme*	*Irrigation System*	*Net Irrigated Area (hectares)*[a]	*Percentage of Cultivated Area*[a]	*Principal Crops Irrigated*	*Problems and Possible Improvements*
Andhra Pradesh	Eastern Ghats	Aminabad	3 tanks	25–40	60–100	Paddy	New tank contemplated
		Araku Valley	1 small anicut and channel	8	22	Paddy	—
		Jeelugumilli	1 small tank	20	11	Paddy	Sluice blocked; new tank contemplated
		Kannaram	None	—	—	—	—
		Piduguralla	1 well	4	2	Vegetables	—
	Coastal Deltas	Kalidindi	Tail-end of Campbell Canal (from Krishna)	310	56	Paddy	Some land too high to irrigate; other land cannot be irrigated every year
Assam (1968)	Plains	Kaki	3 tubewells	35	1	Paddy	Wells very little used, though some need for irrigation expressed. Jamuna Irrigation Scheme will eventually cover 10% of colony
		Darapathar	None	—	—	—	—
		Baghbar	None	—	—	—	Flooding the main problem; pumps might help in *rabi*
		Gobindpur & Theka	None	—	—	—	
Bihar	Rajmahal Hills	Jamunia	None apart from seepage from tanks	—	—	—	—
		Tilaiya	None except small wells and ponds	—	—	—	Lift irrigation from tank abandoned because of cost. Windmills abandoned for lack of maintenance
Dandakaranya	Dandakaranya	Malkangiri Zone	None (except headwater and village tank; see text)	—	—	—	Dam and channels planned (see text)
		Paralkote Zone	as above	—	—	—	Irrigation planned from Paralkote Dam (see text)
		Umarkote-Raighar Zone	as above	—	—	—	Irrigation planned from Umarkote Dam
Haryana	Desert	Bhakra: Tohana Divn	Canal	?485	?60	Wheat, paddy etc.	Lack of water (see text); hints of salinity; flooding

[illegible] Malnad	High Ranges	Channels feeding Maraiyoor and Kanthaloor Colonies; none elsewhere	240	37	Paddy	—
			—	—	Paddy	Possible minor works and lift irrigation
		Wynad	None	—	—	—	—
Madhya Pradesh	Chambal Valley (see also Rajasthan)	Chambal Ravines	None	—	—	—	May eventually in part be irrigated by Chambal Right Bank
		Chambal Right Bank	Canals	(in development)	—	—	—
		Gandhisagar	Virtually none	—	—	—	—
	Malwa	Gundrai	None	—	—	—	Colonists claim irrigation needed
		Intikheri (Kerala Colony)	Diesel-pump lift from river	525 (in theory)	100 (in theory)	Wheat, linseed	1 pump out of use; only 17–35% said to be irrigated
		Intikheri (others)	Tanks	1,630	100	Wheat, linseed	Reliable
		Kansal Banjara	Village well	very small	—	Paddy	Possible new tank
		Kotia Pani	None	—	—	—	—
		Mircabad	Wells mainly for supplemental irrigation; one channel (at Ratbhanpur) in disrepair	—	—	—	—
	Dandakaranya	Bunagaon	None	—	—	—	—
		Kanera & Mardel	None	—	—	—	—
		Paisra	None	—	—	—	—
Maharashtra	Dandakaranya (Chanda Dt)	Palasgaon	Tanks for protective irrigation (end of *kharif*)	27	50	Paddy	Reliable
		Sindewahi	Channel extended from old tank for same purpose	6	75	Paddy	Reliable
	Khandesh	Bhamer: Jayashree	None	—	—	—	—
		Bhamer: Mahatma Fule	Well, engine-driven pump	3	?	—	—
	—	Amalner	None	—	—	—	—
	—	Pabal	Well in hollow, oil engine	5	16	Various	—
Mysore	Greater Malnad	Arwatagi	2 old tanks	300	100	Paddy	Reliable
		Bylakuppe	New channels from 2 old tanks	65	6	Paddy, etc.	Restoration of further old tank possible
		Kambaraganavi	None	—	—	—	—
		Sorapur	2 oil engines pump from stream	15	5	Paddy	Doubtfully economic

State of Authority	*Region*	*Colonization Scheme*	*Irrigation System*	*Net Irrigated Area (hectares)*[a]	*Percentage of Cultivated Area*[a]	*Principal Crops Irrigated*	*Problems and Possible Improvements*
Orissa	Dandakaranya	Nuagam & Nuapara	None	—	—	—	—
		Pandripani	None	—	—	—	—
		Sunabeda	None	—	—	—	—
		Hirakud oustees	Not in main ayacut. New village tanks provided: one-season protective	1,820	64	Paddy, etc.	*Kharif* only; faulty works (see text)
Rajasthan	Desert	Bhakra Canal	Canal	87,600	*c.*65	Wheat, etc.	Water shortage until full supply assured
		Rajasthan Canal	Canal (future lift to Bikaner)	15,380[b]	78[b]	Wheat, etc.	Too early to judge
	Chambal Valley (see also Madhya Pradesh)	Ranapratapsagar oustees	None	—	—	—	Some colonies may eventually come under command
Tamil Nadu	Greater Malnad	Thengumarahada	Anicut and 2 channels:				
			Right Bank	145	100 (theory)	Paddy	
			Left Bank	57 light	100 (theory)	Millets, groundnuts, chillies	Irrigation not assured in dry season (Jan.–June)
	—	Moranam	40 wells	32	19	Paddy, *ragi*	Only 30–50% reliable in dry season: more wells needed
	—	Rajannagar	Individual wells	?	?	Millets, cotton	Siltation
	—	Velakapuram	Wells	?16	32	Paddy	
Uttar Pradesh	Tarai	Kheri	10 experimental tubewells (protective, esp. on sandy loam)	?1,200	?30	Sugar-cane, etc.	Some irrigation facilities unused; but also some private tubewells. Channels need remodelling. Flooding and waterlogging 'main hazard'
		Pilibhit	4 experimental tubewells	?1,150	28	Sugar-cane, etc.	Flooding and water-logging 'main hazard'
		Sardapuri	None	—	—	—	—
		Tarai (Naini Tal Dist)	Channels, tubewell	*c.* 8,500	*c.* 42	Sugar-cane, paddy	Flooding and water-logging
Total				Say 120,000	50		

areas irrigated under the Bhakra and Rajasthan Canals, together with smaller irrigated tracts elsewhere, more than outweighed the virtual lack of any irrigation at all in Dandakaranya, in Assam, and in a number of minor schemes.[18]

It is not possible, with the data available, to bring Table 9.I up to date. Developments in Dandakaranya discussed in chapter 7 had by 1972 increased the net irrigated area there to 16,550 hectares. By the same date some 167,000 hectares were being irrigated under the Rajasthan Canal, though only in *kharif* (it will be remembered that perennial irrigation has to await the completion of the Pong dam). Given that the net irrigated area in colonies outside these two areas was estimated to exceed 100,000 hectares in 1963 (Table 9.I), it may well be that the total in all colonization schemes exceeded 300,000 hectares by 1972.

The discussion of irrigation and drainage that follows refers to conditions in 1963, unless otherwise indicated.

Colonization schemes with little or no irrigation fall into a number of categories. In the first place, there are those in areas which had, or were thought to have, assured rainfall, at least during the monsoon: for example, the Wynad scheme in Kerala, together with the High Ranges colonies apart from Maraiyoor and Kanthaloor (though other colonies in the Ranges which, like these two, are towards the dry or Tamil Nadu side would benefit greatly from an assured water supply); the Assam colonies (the Kaki and Darapathar colonies lie in a rain-shadow area, and would particularly profit from irrigation; the former will gain some benefit from the Jamuna River scheme); and Dandakaranya generally (as has been seen, some irrigation has been provided since 1963, and more is planned). Secondly, there is a number of small colonies, especially those, like the schemes in the Eastern Ghats of Andhra Pradesh, or the settlements for 'ex-criminal tribes' at Mircabad in Madhya Pradesh, which exist primarily to uplift tribal peoples; they had no irrigation works or, at best, rudimentary or broken-down facilities.[19] Although it may be argued that many of these people have little knowledge of irrigation techniques, it can equally be argued that in poor or insecure rainfall areas there is but little hope of improved cultivation without assured irrigation. Thirdly, in a number of cases—and these seem to be particularly unfortunate—oustees who had been given, or who had chosen, new allotments of land had been placed outside the command of the work whose construction had displaced them: as, for example, at the Tilaiya Reservoir in Bihar, part of the Damodar Valley Project (where, as the Table shows, alternative systems of irrigation failed for economic or technical reasons: 'no one knew how to mend the windmills'); at Gandhisagar on the Chambal; and at Hirakud. The troubles of some of the Hirakud oustees have already been told; and, following reports of desertions in 1968, a panel was appointed to study rehabilitation in the area. However, some Tungabhadra oustees, given the option of land in the command, chose unirrigated land in order to be near their former village.

Colonies with irrigated land also have their problems. Thengumarahada in the Nilgiri District of Tamil Nadu made singularly good use of two channels from a simple *anicut* on a stream, one to provide irrigation to all of the colony's paddy-fields, the other for light irrigation of other crops. But it was reported in 1972 that the colony had made little progress over the previous five years because no irrigation could be provided in the dry season (January to June). Again, while traditional paddy cultivators like those in the Mysore Malnad and in Chanda District are able to use irrigation effectively and to see that the works on which they depend are kept in good repair, there were, in other areas, sad tales of works out of repair. There was also, in yet other areas, a tendency to over-extend canals, as at Kalidindi, in the delta of the Krishna (Kistna) and at the extreme tail end of the Campbell Canal; and possibly in the Bhakra command.[20] There is a fear that over-extension on a much bigger scale may ultimately affect the Rajasthan Canal command. There is no excuse for this, given India's long experience of irrigation and, indeed, of over-extension itself. Table 9.I also carries hints of a problem which will have to be more fully discussed in chapter 14, namely, that of the relation between costs of and returns from irrigation; in particular, that relation in the case of lift irrigation. It will be seen that at Tilaiya lift irrigation was abandoned on grounds of cost; thus one cannot help wondering what will be the economics of the great lift irrigation project which is to take water from the Rajasthan Canal over 160 km to Bikaner, with a lift of 60 m and at an estimated cost of Rs.7 crores.[21]

A problem frequently to be encountered in major Indian irrigation projects is under-utilization of the irrigation facilities provided: it has been stated that during the first three Plan periods 7·3 million hectares had been added to the gross irrigable area, but that only 5·6 million hectares were actually being irrigated at the end of the crop year 1965–6.[22] There is a number of reasons for this state of affairs, including failure of field-channel construction to keep pace with the completion of major canals (a universal disease in underdeveloped countries), and the unfamiliarity of the cultivators with irrigation, or, as the author saw it in the Tungabhadra Project, with light irrigation for a varied pattern of crops as distinct from heavy irrigation for paddy. In the colonization schemes, however, the complaint was rather of inadequate or unreliable irrigation facilities than of under-utilization, which was recorded as a serious problem in only a few cases: in the Kheri Tarai Colony, UP;[23] in Rajasthan, where it is claimed that difficulties are now largely overcome because of the diffusion of irrigation techniques from the Gang Canal; and in the Kaki scheme in Assam, where failure to use tubewells was due in part at least to administrative frustrations (water could be issued only on the orders of an Agricultural Engineer who lived miles away).

India and Pakistan provide some of the classic examples of the tendency for irrigation to cause a rise in the water-table—especially in arid alluvial plains—followed by waterlogging, the capillary rise of saline or alkaline waters to the surface, and their evaporation to leave substances which destroy crops and soil structure alike.[24] The only references to this complex of problems in Table 9.I concern waterlogging in the UP Tarai colonies, whose liability to flooding has already been mentioned, and 'hints of salinity' in Rajasthan under Bhakra. One explanation is that, outside the Tarai and Rajasthan, few colonies are situated in alluvial plains with high evaporation rates, initially low water-tables, and poor underground drainage: the prerequisites for the development of the rising water-table–waterlogging–salinity–alkalinity syndrome. Another reason is that the colonization schemes and their associated irrigation works have not been operating long enough, even in alluvial areas, for the syndrome to make itself evident. Warning voices are, however, raised, and rightly raised from time to time. Y. D. Pande, writing of the Naini Tal Tarai, draws attention to the dangers of waterlogging if canal irrigation is practised, and favours the use of tubewells which tend, of course, to lower the water-table.[25] The need for flood-protection and drainage works here, and in the Tarai more generally, is reinforced by this argument (see above, pp. 127–8). K. M. Mehta, in his very useful report on the Chambal Valley Project in Rajasthan, stressed the need for careful study of water-tables after irrigation has begun, and for proper drainage works, especially in low-lying lands on impermeable soils, so that water may be moved away and waterlogging prevented.[26] In 1963 drainage schemes for the area were being worked out with some hesitation because they would bring no obvious and immediate return; by 1970 waterlogging, in the absence of drainage, was all too evident.[27] The Rajasthan Canal authorities, also, will have to look to all the measures necessary to avoid the fate that overtook broad acres in the Punjab as a result of the spread of waterlogging, alkalinity, and salinity. But up to 1972 drainage was not seen as an immediate problem, comfort (or complacency) being derived from the great depth of the water-table (50 m) and the measures taken to line channels. There was, however, a suggestion abroad that a watch should be kept on the water-table to detect any dangerous rise. But, as will already be clear, the Rajasthan Canal had by 1972 run into sodium clay country whose alkalinity demanded remedial measures, including flushing with water, and whose impermeable soils would ensure that this water would not get away, however deep the water-table, unless drainage ditches were provided. Prevention being better than cure, they would do well to respect the adage attributed to the old Wiltshire water-meadowmen, 'You lets the water on at the trot and off at the gallop'[28] and to pay adequate attention to drainage from the outset;[29] but here, as in so many aspects of irrigation and colonization in Rajasthan, financial constraints may prevent an adequate solution.

A rise of the water-table with irrigation is not, however, always an undesirable phenomenon. The tanks of Tamil Nadu and of the Ceylon Dry Zone[30] are instrumental in raising the water-table and preserving it in the dry season at a depth accessible to man and to tree roots, yet, in the local geological and topographical setting, without causing waterlogging; the headwater tanks of Dandakaranya must have something of the same effect in a not dissimilar setting. Irrigation may indeed prove to be of particular importance in the lower-lying Malkangiri Zone, where the dry season lowering of the water-table is more evident than at greater elevations (presumably because of higher evaporation) but where, given suitable groundwater conditions, higher 'winter' temperatures would appear not to preclude the growing of the coconuts so much desired by the Bengali colonists. Long ago, Colonel Dixon made tanks in Ajmer-Merwara, and thereby raised the water-table and facilitated the construction of reliable wells.[31]

Agricultural Techniques: the Situation in 1963

The utilization of irrigation water is closely bound up with techniques of agriculture itself, and to these discussion must now turn. It is not intended to embark on yet another extended essay on the general state of Indian agriculture: the subject has been well treated from a number of different stand-points in recent works.[32] The state of agriculture in the post-independence colonization schemes does, however, illustrate a number of themes of wider applicability; even though to work in these schemes all over India is to have one's eyes opened anew to the tremendous variety in Indian agriculture, in terms of cropping seasons, choice of crops, and techniques. One begins to wonder, and to wish that more writers on Indian agriculture had wondered, how one can possibly generalize across such a disparate field, containing as it does variations in crops and techniques wider than those between, say, Scotland and southern Italy. What common factor is there, for example, between the agricultural systems of the cultivator of equatorial tree-crops in the Wynad colonies in Kerala and of the grower of grain and gram in unirrigated tracts of the Tarai?

However, one general theme illustrated by a study of Indian colonization schemes as they were in 1963 is the extremely wide range of responses to the possibility of modern technical innovation; and, coupled with this, the very sporadic (and sometimes unexpected) occurrence of highly positive responses.[33] At one extreme, and all too often, one's field notes read 'Slovenly cultivation in some villages' (of the Intikheri Colony for Kerala people), or 'Not a high standard of cultivation or of attack on problems' (in the Arwatagi Colony in Mysore), or 'Low yields, little use of fertilizers or irrigation' for some of the colonies, largely filled by settlers from eastern UP, in the Kheri and Pilibhit Tarai. At the other extreme (and here are the 'highly positive responses' to innovation) stood a series of widely scattered colonies the reasons for whose acceptance of improved techniques it is not always easy to discern. Among these the alert little colony at Thengumarahada, on the eastern edge of the Nilgiris, has already been singled out for special mention. It certainly seemed to practise all the then-approved innovations: for example, the entire extent of its paddy-fields was sown with improved seeds, giving high yields (average quoted as 3,362 kg per hectare, but rising to more than double that figure);[34] 10,000 plants of *Gliricidia* had been sold to members to plant on field boundaries and bunds as green manure; chemical fertilizers and pesticides were used, as were improved strains of cattle and poultry (Kangayam and Murrah cattle, Black Minorca hens). It even had its own, spontaneously organized demonstration plot for, amongst other things, improved varieties of *ragi.* All this was achieved, it should be noted, by people many of whom were 'tribal' and not amongst the ordinary cultivating castes of Tamil Nadu: the whole, in fact, standing in striking contrast to the sorry agricultural position (but one for which one must have sympathy) in many other colonies for tribal peoples. Some of the factors which made Thengumarahada shine would seem to include wise leadership and spontaneity (the group sought government permission to colonize, and were not cajoled or coerced or 'ousted' into it). It must be emphasized, too, that the dominant caste or 'tribe' in Thengumarahada is Badaga.[35] As W. A. Noble has shown, the Badagas, who seem to have come from farther north and speak, or spoke, an old Kannada dialect, have for a century shown marked enterprise and entrepreneurship in the Nilgiri Hills and in Wynad, taking rapidly to coffee- and tea-growing and even owning plantations.[36] One does not wish to detract from their achievement; but they have, of course, been in contact with improved methods in the Nilgiris and in Tamil Nadu more generally. A remark in the author's field notebook has it that 'Improvement societies really catch on in Madras', which in fact had the second highest compound growth rate in agricultural productivity of any Indian state between 1952 and 1962.[37]

There were also other encouraging spots on the colonization map, just as there were on the agricultural map of India as a whole in 1962. Thus the small colony at Moranam in North Arcot District of Tamil Nadu, designed for the resettlement of landless agricultural labourers, used green manures, compost and artificial fertilizers, together with improved varieties, iron ploughs, the practice of transplanting in the ricefield, and irrigation from no fewer than 40 wells (with further wells planned). Some of the techniques here, such as the transplanting of paddy and the use of wells, were of course part of traditional Tamil technology; but others were new. Yields of paddy[38] were said to be 1,485 kg per hectare for *samba* (the season from July–August to December–January) and 1,550 kg per hectare for *navari* (December–January to April–May): these are not very far from the state average, and are not at all bad for well irrigation on shallow sandy-loam soil; and it must be remembered that the state average is heavily weighted by the large area of good alluvial soils under canal irrigation in the Kaveri (Cauvery) delta. It was also an encouraging sign that all the 84 members of the Co-operative colonization society were working members: the situation in other colonies can be very different. Moranam also benefited, it should be said, from a high scale of aid, from belonging to a progressive state, and from the fact that its colonists were selected by Agricultural Extension Officers.

Other colonies were operating traditional techniques at a high level (as in the small paddy-growing colonies in Chanda District of Maharashtra and as also in *some* similar colonies in the Mysore Malnad); others again were introducing one or two innovations while rejecting, or remaining in ignorance of, other possibilities. Thus improved seeds were being quite widely used: they are often the first innovation to catch on, requiring no additional risk and no change in technology (though a high level of fertilizer application is necessary if they are to give maximum yields). Other colonists were using improved ploughs (iron-tipped, or fitted with a mould-board), often those issued to them by the authorities. Artificial fertilizers were beginning to come into use in some otherwise undistinguished colonies: for example, at Kalidindi in the Krishna (Kistna) delta of Andhra Pradesh, the tribal colony in the Araku Valley in the same state, and in parts of the Dandakaranya project (where free fertilizers were issued during the first year of colonization). Tractors were said to be 'coming in everywhere' in the Haryana colonies under the Bhakra Canals (not that tractors are necessarily a sign of improvement).

Yet another general theme recognizable in muted form in the colonization schemes in 1963 was the emergence of large-scale 'capitalist' agriculture. Thus several large operators had acquired land under the Chambal Right Bank Canal in Madhya Pradesh (although it was admittedly a little early to judge whether production would be traditional or 'capitalist'). Again, at Rajannager, in Coimbatore District of Tamil Nadu, where oustees from the Bhavanisagar reservoir were resettled, the Panchayat Chairman had a good house and farm buildings on 12 hectares of land irrigated from 3 wells fitted with electric pumps: he employed 10 regular labourers living in 'lines' as on a tea estate. Thirdly, a group of Sikhs, who had registered themselves as a Co-operative Farming Society and thus obtained assistance and concessions from the then Punjab government, had obtained 120 hectares of irrigable land under the Bhakra Canal system, and reclaimed it with tractors and local labour; and were in effect operating the land as an estate, for all the shareholders except the President were absentees, and the land was worked by 13 local labourers under a paid supervisor. Tractors, as well as camels and bullocks, were used for ploughing; artificial and organic fertilizers were in use, together with improved seed; and *shisham* (*Dalbergia sissoo*) and mulberry trees were planted as windbreaks. A plot of 25 hectares was set apart as an orchard and nursery. Thirty-two hectares of long-staple American cotton (yielding, it was said, 1,850 kg per hectare) and some sugar and *jowar* were grown in *kharif*; and mustard (*sarson*), wheat, and gram in *rabi*. The gross takings were said to be Rs.50,000 per annum, but it was claimed that no profits were being made as yet; nevertheless, here was budding capitalism, bristling with the spirit of improvement, sheltering behind a windbreak of collectivity.

Other similar cases within colonization schemes are hard to find. This is not surprising, given the emphasis in the schemes on 'peasant' smallholdings and given also the links between colonization and the land reform movement. But it is also true (and certainly not of necessity for the same reason) that spots of 'highly positive responses' to improvement are relatively few and far between in the colonies. This is borne out by what it is possible to say about yields in the colonization schemes, summarized in Table 9.II.

It must be strongly emphasized straight away that no great degree of reliance can be placed on the figures in this Table. In all schemes where cultivation had become established (and there were several

TABLE 9.II

Estimated Yields in Certain Colonization Schemes, 1963

State or Authority	*Crop*	*State Average Yield 1962–3 (kg/hectare)*	*Colonization Scheme Yield (kg/hectare)*	*Colonization Scheme*
Andhra Pradesh	Rice	1,202	500	Aminabad
			1,250	Araku Valley
			2,490	Jeelugumilli
			1,250	Kalidindi
	Jowar	553	750–1,120	Aminabad
			1,900	Piduguralla
	Gram	298	490	Piduguralla
	Pulses	184	375–560	Aminabad
	Ragi	905	750	Jeelugumilli
			750	Kannaram
	Small millets	397	1,460	Piduguralla
Assam (1968)	Rice	951 (1967–8)	740–930	Kaki
			1,480	Baghbar
			1,110–1,300	Gobindpur & Theka
	Pulses	425 (1967–8)	340	Baghbar
			280–560	Gobindpur & Theka
Dandakaranya	Rice	823	960–2,000	Malkangiri Zone (rainfed)
			670–740	Umarkote-Raighar Zone (rainfed)
			1,130–1,480	Umarkote-Raighar Zone, under headwater tank
		553	740–1,860	Paralkote Zone (rainfed)
	Maize	400	1,350	Umarkote-Raighar Zone
	Jowar	529	500	Umarkote-Raighar Zone
Haryana	Rice	980	820–1,520	Bhakra (Tohana)
	Wheat	1,350	1,340–1,860	Bhakra (Tohana)
			1,340–1,680	Bhakra (Sirsa)
	Gram	811	460–1,570	Bhakra (Sirsa)
	Maize	538	740–1,110	Bhakra (Tohana)
Kerala	Rice	1,403	300–370	High Ranges
			460	Wynad
Madhya Pradesh	Rice	553	300–360	Intikheri (Kerala)
	Jowar	720	740	Kotia Pani
	Wheat	668	460–550	Gundrai (unirrigated *rabi*)
			460–550	Intikheri (Kerala Colony) (unirrigated *rabi*)
			1,380–1,470	Intikheri (Kerala Colony) (irrigated *rabi*)
			645–1,380	Intikheri (Others) (irrigated *rabi*)
			460	Kotia Pani (unirrigated *rabi*)
	Gram		380–460	Kotia Pani

State or Authority	Crop	State Average Yield 1962–3 (kg/hectare)	Colonization Scheme Yield (kg/hectare)	Colonization Scheme
Maharashtra	Rice	881	1,480–1,830	Palasgaon
			980–1,220	Sindewahi
	Jowar	529	1,020	Palasgaon
	Groundnut	686	1,380	Pabal
Mysore	Rice	1,371	1,340	Bylakuppe
			740	Sorapur
			2,970	Tungabhadra oustees
	Jowar	441	220–280	Sorapur
			450–900	Tungabhadra oustees
	Groundnut	514	450–560	Tungabhadra oustees
Orissa	Rice	823	890–1,260	Hirakud oustees (irrigated)
			610–740	Hirakud oustees (unirrigated)
			300–360	Pandripani
	Ragi	465	280–370	Pandripani
Rajasthan			No data	
Tamil Nadu	Rice	1,505	2,230	Thengumarahada (irrigated *samba*)
			980	Moranam (irrigated *samba*)
			1,020	Moranam (irrigated *navari*)
			590	Velakapuram (rainfed *samba*)
	Cholam (Jowar)	792	740	Moranam (irrigated *navari*)
	Groundnut	1,207	1,160	Moranam
	Ragi	1,010	2,240	Rajannagar
Uttar Pradesh	Rice	738	910	Kheri (early June–Oct.)
			1,830	Kheri (late July–Nov.)
			610–1,220	Pilibhit
			1,540	Sardapuri
	Maize	930	1,860	Kheri
			1,860	Sardapuri

Reliability: see warnings in text.

Sources: State averages: *Estimates of Area and Production of Principal Crops in India* (*Summary Tables*) *1961–2 & 1962–3* (New Delhi, Min. Food & Agric., 1964). Assam: *Indian Agriculture in Brief*, 8th edn (1967), pp. 96–7. Colonization schemes: author's field inquiries (paddy yields converted to rice yields at 66·2 per cent extraction rate).

in which this was not so, notably those in Rajasthan) the author inquired about crops grown and about their yields. Figures so obtained are notoriously unreliable. It was clearly impossible in a reconnaissance survey to undertake crop-cutting experiments by random sample, of the sort that so revolutionized knowledge of paddy yields in Ceylon;[39] though such experiments have begun under the auspices of the Dandakaranya Development Authority. He did, however, make as many separate inquiries as possible (so that for a large colony the figure recorded is an average of, or expresses the range of, a number of answers). He also tried to cross-check the answers of officials with those of cultivators whenever possible, and to check both by field observation (where a countryman's sceptical eye was often useful). A further check is provided by consistency between nearby and similarly situated schemes (though there are few such). But, in the end, one may well have been defeated by the cultivator's tendency to under-declare, except where the spirit (if not the practice) of improvement is so much abroad that the tendency is to acquire merit by over-declaring;[40] or by official tendencies, in the same spirit, also to over-declare; or by confusion caused by declarations in such diverse units as *maunds* to the *bigha*, bags to the acre, and Madras Measures to the acre.[41] It will be noted that no attempt has been made to quote yields for cotton or sugar.

The state and national averages also shown in Table 9.II are themselves not above suspicion. A state average, too, is taken across a wide range of conditions.

Given this background, it would be building a house on shifting sand to discuss the Table in any detail. One or two points, however, should be made. The first is that, as has already been said, the Table confirms the relative scarcity of colonization schemes in which improvement had so caught on that yields high above the state average are recorded. Secondly, there is the striking—even surprising—fact that, apart from obvious black spots such as Intikheri (for rice and unirrigated crops), the small tribal colonies (Aminabad and the like), and the schemes in Kerala, and in spite of all that has been said about low technical standards, many of the schemes in the Table did record yields at least a little above the state average. There may be several reasons for this. One may be that, while the national tendency was to under-declare, colonies were so beset with official improvers and tramped over by visitors that they had by 1963 crossed the threshold to over-declaration. Another is that these were all relatively new schemes, still exploiting virgin soil, which were capable of giving higher yields than soils once more fertile but now degraded by long use. There is also the fact that irrigation was four times as widely available in colonization schemes as in the country at large; while in some colonies, at least, more effort was made than was generally the case to popularize fertilizers, new varieties, and so on.

But perhaps the most important, and at the same time most discouraging point to be made here is that in measuring yields in colonization against state or national averages one is comparing them with figures which were generally depressed by the generally very low yields prevalent in Indian agriculture in 1963 and by the particularly low yields of, for example, rice in Madhya Pradesh and Uttar Pradesh. These points are well known and need not be laboured here. Suffice it to say that rice yields were only about half those in Japan, and wheat yields only some 40 per cent those in Britain.[42]

Although so many colonization schemes appear to have had yields above their state average, and although their superiority in this respect would probably survive confrontation by accurate statistics, this does not in any sense contradict what has been said earlier about the general prevalence in colonization schemes of low technical standards. To some extent, as has been said, the colonization schemes had advantages in terms of natural fertility (though this will diminish unless fertilizers are applied) and of irrigation. There is probably only a small margin by which most colonies were technically better than the state norm; and some were manifestly inferior. Again, not many colonies show up well when measured against the best that can be done in their states (apart, that is, from the Thengumarahadas of this world). Thus a Government Farm near Gundrai Colony, Madhya Pradesh, was getting twice the colony's yield of wheat; and a similar Farm in the Umarkote Zone of Dandakaranya reaped 30 per cent more paddy than the nearby colony, under comparable conditions. Again, colony yields in Table 9.II may be compared with selected published figures for the highest yields in the crop competitions of 1962–3 (though some of these at any rate may be inflated).[43]

Rice	*Kg./hectare*	
Madras (now Tamil Nadu)	8,896	(1963–4)
Maharashtra	10,023	
Mysore	10,112	(1963–4)
Jowar		
Maharashtra	9,158	
Mysore	8,528	
Ragi		
Madras	6,499	(1963–4)

Some attention has been given to factors which may raise colony yields above the state norm. There are, it should also be stated, factors tending in the opposite direction. In the first place, colonists, faced not only with the difficulties of a pioneer existence but also with a larger holding than they have been accustomed to cultivate, may adopt an extensive rather than an intensive attitude to agriculture. It is this factor which, with the survival of patches of jungle, leads to the untidy appearance of much of the 'pioneer fringe' the world over. Extensive attitudes were particularly noted in the Wynad colonies in Kerala (where the accompanying untidiness was especially marked), to a rather less extent in the High Ranges colonies of the same state, in the Gandhisagar oustees' colony (Madhya Pradesh), and among the Hirakud oustees (Orissa).

A second factor tending in the same direction (and, again, its operation is by no means confined to India) is unfamiliarity with the environment in which the colony is set. This is not so very widespread in the Indian colonization schemes, for, as chapter 5 has made clear, there has been relatively little inter-state transfer of colonists. There have, however, been many refugee colonists, and of these it has undoubtedly been the Bengali and Santal refugees settled in Dandakaranya who have suffered the most difficult change of environment. From a semi-aquatic life in the flat deltas of the Ganges and Brahmaputra[44] they have been transferred to rolling plateau lands, generally with sandy soils unretentive of moisture, and subject to shortage of water at the beginning and end of the monsoon. From an environment in which paddy could be grown on easily inundated land during three seasons of the year (albeit of unequal importance),[45] and in which they developed the attitude known as 'paddy-fixation', they have moved to one in which paddy can be grown only with some difficulty, because of climate and soil, in *kharif*, while there is no possibility of its cultivation in *rabi* unless or until irrigation can be provided in that season. From a country in which the coconut was ubiquitous and an almost universal provider, they have moved to one in which it is only in the lower lands of the Malkangiri Zone that the coconut will grow satisfactorily, and then only if the water-table is maintained at a sufficiently high level. From terrain in which jute grows readily, they have moved to one in which there must be a substitute, *mesta* (*Hibiscus cannabinus*). The difficulties of environmental adaptation exist for all settlers in Dandakaranya except local tribal peoples (who have sufficient troubles of their own). Moreover, the relatively poor soils of Dandakaranya need careful treatment, and, in particular, fertilizers if they are to yield satisfactorily for the cultivator. But cultivation in East Bengal has long been characterized by lack of proper manuring and of rotations, with a result that yields of paddy have tended to be low and even to decline, except in areas subject to beneficial annual flooding and in those where local conditions enforce a single annual crop and thus a rest period.[46] The task of the Dandakaranya Development Authority was thus not only to encourage new crops, such as *mesta*, adapted to local conditions, but also to stimulate the sowing of crops other than paddy in *rabi* and to change the traditional technology brought by the settlers from a very different environment. H. N. C. Fonseka has shown how, even within an island as small as Ceylon, techniques learnt in source areas tend to persist in colonization schemes.[47]

The colonists from Kerala who settled, again in a very different environment, at Intikheri in Madhya Pradesh, also found it difficult to grow paddy without assured irrigation; and in any case they have had to grow alternative crops in *rabi* for reasons of temperature, and cannot grow their beloved coconut. Paddy-fixation, too, has afflicted refugees settled in the Andaman Islands, where again attempts at diversification have been made.[48]

Extreme environmental change of course also confronted the Tibetan colonists at Bylakuppe. They had exchanged the high, dry plateaux of their native country for the humid forests of the hills between Mysore and Coorg. Of the yaks, sheep, goats, and pigs that they had kept in Tibet they were able to retain only the goats and pigs. In Tibet they had grown wheat, barley, peas, and radishes, but only a little paddy. At Bylakuppe the principal crop was almost bound to be paddy, of which they were reaping 2,000 kg per hectare on land prepared for them, but nothing on land they had tried to prepare themselves. They were also growing a little *ragi*, cotton and tobacco, using fertilizer only on the last two crops mentioned.

In the case of tribal peoples settled in colonization schemes in 1963 (which will have to be explored in a rather different context in chapter 13), the problem was only occasionally and partly one of change of physical environment, for as a rule such people had not been moved over great distances. But their settlement did raise very difficult general problems of technical adaptation, if they were to increase their own incomes appreciably, and, from the point of view of the authorities, to justify the capital expended on them. Table 9.II is sufficient indication of the low yields and low levels of agricultural technology in many tribal colonies. More specifically, there was the problem of tribal peoples used to various forms of shifting cultivation, who somehow have to be induced to practise settled agriculture, with its prerequisite, the maintenance of soil fertility. This was reported to be a particularly difficult problem in tribal colonies in Orissa, where, it is said, whole colonies have been unsuccessful because of the seeming impossibility of inducing colonists to give up the practice of shifting cultivation, perhaps because they cannot without it maintain soil fertility.[49] There was no such problem, however, in the tribal colonies of Dandakaranya.

One final affliction peculiar to colonization schemes (or at least to settlers in officially organized settlements) was to suffer from faults of detailed planning by the authorities. Sometimes these stem from inadequate soil surveys of the sort described in chapter 7, with the result that colonists are expected to cultivate difficult soils. Even in

Dandakaranya, with its good soil survey organization, it sometimes happened that a colonist found part of his fields subject to waterlogging. Elsewhere, in irrigation schemes, some supposedly irrigable fields were, in whole or in part, too high for water to reach them. In the so-called 'Ex-criminal Tribes' settlements at Mircabad, in Madhya Pradesh, at least one sizeable patch of good black soil was taken out of the reach of cultivation because a village had been sited on it; whereas an attempt was being made to grow crops up-slope on very poor soils derived from *murram* (here indurated laterite). One must not leave the impression, however, that soil and land capability surveys, when made, are always systematically or perversely ignored. Under the Tungabhadra Scheme, to take one of a number of instances of which the reverse is true, soil survey was followed by land classification and the 'localization' of crops in areas where soils were suitable and other necessary conditions were satisfied in order to maximize benefits and to minimize such ill effects as waterlogging, alkalinity, and malaria.[50] Nor is India by any means the only Asian country to make difficulties for some of its colonists by faulty planning. The author some time ago drew attention to failures of this sort in Ceylon, particularly in respect of well-siting and of the layout of 'high land' (unirrigable) allotments;[51] while Kenneth R. Walker has charged the Chinese Communists with poor planning, unrelated *inter alia* to physical conditions.[52]

Agricultural Techniques: More Recent Developments

The preceding section, describing as it does the situation in colonization schemes in 1963, has in a sense become economic history: though the situation it depicts could readily be matched, with but minor variation, in many colonies (and villages) in 1972. But the author's further fieldwork in 1968 and in 1971–2, though necessarily not as comprehensive as that in 1963, enables some comments to be made on recent developments in some of the colonies, developments that reflect the momentous changes that are taking place in Indian agricultural technology as a whole, notably those associated with the introduction of new high-yielding varieties of cereal crops.

Now, the term 'improved seeds' as used so far in this chapter does not refer to the varieties that have been increasingly used in India in the last few years under the High Yielding Varieties Programme (HYVP) inaugurated in 1963.[53] Fieldwork in Assam in December 1968 came, however, after two years of the High Yielding Varieties Programme. In the Kaki colony, several cultivators interviewed had tried Taichung Native–1 (TN–1), but had given it up because, in the absence of assured supplies of irrigation water, it refused to give the expected high yields, or even gave lower yields than the traditional varieties. One colonist, however, had obtained (so he said) 5,700 kg per hectare by growing Taichung Native–1 on his better land, applying 2,800 kg of fertilizer per hectare. The same application to poorer land bearing traditional varieties yielded only 1,345 kg per hectare of paddy. This colonist was in fact a businessman who cultivated two allotments, hired labour, and, one suspected, acted not only as a merchant but also as a moneylender for less well-to-do settlers.

On the other hand in the flood-swept Baghbar, Gobindpur, and Theka colonies few of the refugee Bengali colonists had heard of the high-yielding varieties. Those who had done so found it impossible to grow them, given the need for paddy varieties adapted to the special local conditions: for example, *aman* and *aus* varieties sown mixed in order to increase the chances of getting at least some harvest come high flood, come low flood. There was also the problem of loss of fertilizer by flood action.

The Assam colonization schemes thus illustrate, in their own way, some of the circumstances surrounding attempts to introduce the new high-yielding varieties and associated practices: the need for good soils, assured but controllable water-supplies, and high inputs of fertilizers; the non-existence, so far, of high-yielding varieties adapted to special physical conditions like those of Baghbar and the other flood-prone colonies (and, for that matter, of much of the deltaic lands of Bangladesh from which the refugee colonists came); and the tendency for the wealthier cultivators to be the improvers because it is they who can command the necessary resources. This tendency confronts the authorities with the dilemma to which reference has already been made in chapter 6. Thus the colonist in Kaki colony to whose high yields reference has just been made was almost certainly not, when selected, in any of the categories for whom the colony was intended ('political sufferers', flood-affected families, and needy agriculturalists). Much more certainly he ought not to have had the two allotments which he was cultivating during the author's visit; and stood to be ejected from one or both of them as a result of the review of tenures in Kaki which was to be made because of evident irregularities in the distribution of land in the colony—irregularities, that is, given the professed aims of the scheme. On economic grounds, there is clearly a case for retaining such men in colonies, because of their own high productivity and in the hope that improvement will spread from them to others. But social and political pressures, augmented by the widespread belief that these men had used improper influence, are such that ejection, or at any rate redistribution of land, may be forced on the authorities, even though productivity may thereby suffer. The same pressures, of course, affect criteria for the initial selection of colonists.

In Dandakaranya in 1972, there was very clear evidence of the much higher degree of adaptation to a changed environment which had been attained by at least the longer-established refugee colonists: in particular, they were being weaned from paddy-fixation by the extension efforts of the Authority. *Mesta* was much more widely accepted. The cultivation of maize as a short-duration cash crop was spreading: the area under it had increased from 202 hectares in 1965 to 3,260 hectares in 1969. Most of this was hybrid maize. Millets and pulses were being accepted as minor crops, and some settlers who had the benefit of irrigation were even growing some wheat in *rabi*.

Paddy, however, remained the dominant crop, and here the impact of high-yielding varieties had obviously been felt. It was indeed claimed that as much as 80–90 per cent of the paddy land was sown in these varieties; but this may be an exaggeration. In the Paralkote Zone, local workers estimated that about 10 per cent of the area was sown in the introduced varieties TN–1 and IR–8, and about 50 per cent in newer Indian hybrids, such as Bala, Padma and Ratna, better adapted to the relatively short growing season imposed by the monsoonal rainfall régime. In some places, at least, lack of an assured water supply still appeared to be a constraint; and although many settlers were obtaining good yields, these were generally below those on research stations because insufficient fertilizer was applied.

There was still, however, very little *rabi* cropping outside irrigated areas: this is not surprising in view of the monsoonal rainfall régime and the poor water-retaining qualities of most of the Dandakaranya soils. Where irrigation was available, good crops of paddy were to be seen, and, as already indicated, some colonists were trying to grow wheat: they tended to find it difficult, however, to prepare the seed-bed after a *kharif* paddy crop; and not all were prepared to try. Some of the wheat was of the high-yielding variety Sonalika.

Altogether, it was encouraging to revisit Dandakaranya after eight years and to see so many evidences of improvement among refugee colonists; though, as will be clear from the foregoing account, new and more productive practices were by no means universally adopted, and the environmental constraints were still in evidence. But signs of technical change amongst tribal colonists in the same area were far fewer. One saw the occasional tribal cultivator taking to irrigation or to new varieties: perhaps significantly, one of these was arelatively large landholder, a 'Gond Thakur' with six hectares.

Unfortunately it was not possible in 1971–2 to revisit those areas under the Bhakra and Rajasthan Canals which have had time to overcome the first difficult years of colonization. Officials claim, however, that the high-yielding varieties and associated practices are spreading into these areas from such bases as the Gang Canal area and the Punjab; that the 'better class of cultivator' who bought land at auction has proved a faster innovator, because of his superior resources, than other categories of colonist, particularly those without experience of irrigation and of intensive cultivation more generally; that as much as half the wheat acreage is in high-yielding varieties; and that there are great possibilities for high-yielding cottons. It is admitted, however, that there has been but little progress in *bajra* cultivation.

The UP Tarai, or at least that part of it in Naini Tal District, is quite clearly an area that has taken very rapidly to high-yielding varieties, particularly the rice IR–8 (and to a lesser extent to IR–24), and to the wheats Sona 227, UP–301, and Sonalika. Improved sugar-cane has also been adopted. Tubewell construction has gone ahead rapidly, and half of the colonists are said to own tractors. The use of fertilizers is claimed to be universal. One official estimated that more than 95 per cent of the colonization area is sown in high-yielding varieties, but a rapid field reconnaissance suggested that this may be an exaggeration. It is said that the Bengali refugee colonists lag behind their fellows in accepting new practices.

Finally, the small colony at Moranam in Tamil Nadu, already progressive in 1963, had by 1972 forged ahead quite considerably (though its colonists were unwilling to admit this until confronted with the evidence in their own fields). The house lots were generally neglected, but there was a great deal of IR–8 in the paddy-fields, much of it irrigated from wells some of which had been fitted with electric pumps.

Some may believe that these sketches (they cannot be more) of recent developments in colonization schemes illustrate both the nature of the so-called 'Green Revolution' as it affects India and some of its more important implications.[54] Certainly the lack of high-yielding varieties to suit all environmental conditions, the need for an assured water-supply and for adequate inputs of fertilizer, and differential acceptance of new practices are to be met in the colonies and in India at large. But conditions in the colonies are very different from those in normal villages: there is, officially at any rate, a much higher degree of equality between landholdings and, socially, between landholders in most schemes, so that one would not expect colonies to reproduce the growing gulf between rich and poor that is said to be characteristic of many areas affected by recent agrarian change. And the colonies have no landless—in the first generation, at least. But the technical changes that have affected the colonies have implications for the prosperity of the settlers and for the economic viability of the schemes that are highly relevant to matters to be discussed later in this book; though, in the absence of detailed field research in the colonies, some of the arguments will be necessarily somewhat inconclusive.

Animal Husbandry and Pasture

Animal husbandry throughout independent India's colonization schemes is completely subsidiary to agriculture, as, indeed, it is in the Indian economy at large. But most colonists have draught-cattle (bullocks, or camels in Haryana and Rajasthan, or buffaloes in some paddy-growing schemes). Sometimes these are issued by the authorities, as in Dandakaranya, where each settler receives a pair of bullocks. In some colonies, moreover, there are goats and more rarely, sheep. Pigs are almost entirely confined to certain of the tribal colonies, for they are not kept by either Muslims or caste Hindus. Poultry are kept in a few colonies, and attempts are being made to develop poultry-keeping in Dandakaranya and in the Tibetan colony at Bylakuppe; but the birds do not seem often to thrive, and several colonies, notably those in the Mysore Malnad, reported that they had been given up for this reason. Dairying in any organized sense of the term is also rarely practised, and then gives low yields. In 1963 the Sorapur colony, in the Mysore Malnad, had a herd of 30–40 cows; Velakapuram, in Tamil Nadu, had 28, whose milk was sent to a co-operative purchasing organization; Moranam, in the same state, had a herd of 50 animals, which gave only 15 gallons daily (the herd had disappeared by 1972). Dairy cows in Wynad (Kerala) gave only 0·2 gallons daily.

There was very rarely special provision for village or colony pasture, as, indeed, is the case in the Ceylon colonization schemes.[55] In the Chambal Valley and at Intikheri, as in some other parts of Madhya Pradesh, there was supposed to be a pasture reserve equivalent to 10 per cent of the cultivated area; 6 per cent is reserved in Wynad. But these reserves tend to become encroached upon by cultivation, licit or illicit. (In the Lower Chenab Colony 20 per cent was reserved.[56]) In Dandakaranya areas handed over to the Development Authority by the state concerned, but on soil survey found unsuitable for agriculture, are used as pasture reserves, at least for the time being. Such land may amount to as much as 30 per cent of the total. In the Kaki colony in Assam there was a pasture reserve (unmanaged) of 269 hectares (compared with 3,778 hectares under cultivation), while at the Baghbar, Gobindpur, and Theka refugee colonies in the same state colonies had access to pre-existing grazing grounds near by. In one or two other colonies there was provision for pasture lots or blocks: for example, 10 hectares at Kambaraganavi (in Mysore), 60 hectares at Velakapuram, 6 hectares at Kannaram in Andhra Pradesh, and some provision for the Hirakud oustees in Orissa. The author saw little if any evidence that these blocks, large or small, were managed in any scientific way, or indeed in any way at all. There is, in fact, in India as in Ceylon,[57] virtually no tradition of pasture management.

Indeed, the state of animal husbandry in the colonization schemes of India epitomizes the national problem far more accurately and closely than is the case in agriculture itself, where, as has been seen, there is a number of features peculiar to the colonies. This is also true of the unimproved state of the animals: only rarely (Thengumarahada is an exception) did one find pure-bred animals of high quality. It is also true of the shifts that are adopted, in the absence of managed pasture. In some colonies crops like *jowar* are grown at least in part for fodder; while in Tamil Nadu there is a long tradition of stall-feeding. But generally speaking the cattle, draught and milch alike, sheep and goats too if there are any, roam over fallow fields or, more often, in whatever jungle or wasteland there may be locally. Sometimes the pasture thus found by the animals in this way is adequate: for example, in forest-girt colonies like those in Greater Malnad or the Tarai (long a famous grazing-ground for surrounding districts)[58] or like the tribal colonies of Dandakaranya, which in these respects depart from the national norm. It is often inadequate in quality; especially is this true of arid or semi-arid areas like those surrounding the irrigated colonies of the Bhakra and Rajasthan Canals.

Under the Rajasthan Canal Project, however, there are ambitious plans for the development of animal husbandry.[59] The Master Plan for the Project recognized that there are large flocks and herds in the area already and that unless animal husbandry is developed many animals will be without feed (see also below, pp. 270–2). It is proposed, in irrigated areas, to foster 'mixed farming' involving the stall-feeding of cattle; and, in unirrigated areas within the overall command of the Canal (higher sand-dunes, saline areas and so on), which are estimated to amount to 840,000 hectares, to capitalize on new-found access to drinking water, communications and markets and greatly to develop animal husbandry, starting from its traditional basis. It remains to be seen how much of this plan can be realized. Up to December 1971 the response of pastoralists had been limited: they appeared to prefer their old ways.

If earmarked pasture is rare in the colonization schemes, reserved blocks of village or colony forest, from which colonists may extract timber, firewood, leaves for green manure, and other produce are even rarer. The tribal colony of Sunabeda, in the Orissa sector of Dandakaranya, shares 48 hectares of forest with its old village, and other tribal colonies in the same state also have village forests. Rather more colonies are surrounded by forests, some of them Reserved, from which, with or without formal permission, the colonies extract forest produce; this is especially true of tribal colonies, whose occupants can only with difficulty be kept out of the forest, and who complain bitterly at any restrictions that may be imposed. One or two colonies made their own forest plantations: Moranam, in Tamil Nadu, had 500 communally owned casuarina trees in 1963, but all had gone by 1972. Otherwise colonies, especially those in more arid or more crowded areas, share the fate of village India in general, and are very short indeed of timber and firewood.

Soil Conservation

Most of the technological and related problems discussed in this chapter are primarily of significance because of their bearing on immediate or short-term problems of overcoming natural difficulties or ensuring or increasing agricultural production. The longer-term issue of maintaining such production far into the future has been mentioned only incidentally: for example, in connection with the method of arranging cleared material in windrows (above, p. 155) and with the use of drainage and other techniques in combating waterlogging, salinity, and alkalinity. Something must, however, be said about techniques of soil conservation, perhaps the most important of all in the long run.

There is a great deal of literature on soil conservation in India,[60] which has, moreover, not been without its originality and distinction. In Mysore, for example, there was developed the 'Mysore System of Soil and Water Management', involving contour-bordered strip irrigation. In certain colonization schemes, proper attention is paid to conservational measures. The Chambal Ravines project and the reclamation in Jamunia and other colonies in the Santal Parganas of Bihar are, by their very nature, works of soil conservation (though that is not to say that all is well with them: in Jamunia, for instance, sheet erosion could be seen at work, new gullies were beginning to appear in reclaimed land, and there was no planting of trees on unprotected and uncultivated upper slopes and hill-tops). Paddy cultivation, again, has its own built-in system of soil conservation, for paddy terraces and bunds, if properly constructed, hold up water and soil; and it will be appreciated how many colonization schemes do involve paddy-fields. In Dandakaranya soil conservation works are part of the initial reclamation (though there again renewed erosion could be seen on land cleared and not yet occupied); while in the Rajasthan Canal Command the Master Plan envisages measures to stabilize sand-dunes, and to plant wind-breaks and larger belts of trees and grasses in order to prevent wind-erosion and dune mobility.[61] It is also planned to induce colonists to plant castor and shrubs on their field boundaries.

In other ways and in other colonization schemes, however, the position leaves much to be desired. In paddy-growing schemes, whatever the built-in protection against erosion in the paddy lands, the unirrigable lands are often unprotected and subject to erosion, especially in hilly areas like Greater Malnad. Many smaller schemes have no soil conservation works at all: this applies, for example, to nearly all the tribal colonies in Andhra Pradesh and Madhya Pradesh (where gullies, actual or incipient, may readily be seen) in spite of schemes and subsidies for soil conservation.[62] It also applies to schemes in Orissa and to the Sardapuri Bhoodan Colony in UP Tarai.

A further problem is that in India standard methods of soil conservation tend to become all too standard, measures designed for and sensibly adapted to one area being unimaginatively transferred to another in which the needs, the problems, and the dangers are quite different. Thus in Malwa 'standard' conservation bunds, ideal for holding up water in the permeable soils on Archaean rocks in the southern Deccan, are constructed on black cotton soils, which rapidly become waterlogged, with the result that bunds burst, stored water pours forth, and the last state is worse than the first, especially because black soils tend to flow when wet.

This book, as may be imagined, has not finished with agricultural technology. The question of trying to improve technology by systems of 'agricultural extension' will be dealt with in chapter 11, where the interest of Indian society and of the government in productivity in the colonization schemes will come under review. Again the question of long-term techniques as distinct from those applicable in the short term has a bearing on issues of costs and returns to be discussed in chapter 14. But in the meantime it is relevant to take a closer look at the economy of the colonist himself.

10

Domestic Economy of the Colonist

IT IS the purpose of this chapter to ask how prosperous the post-independence Indian agricultural colonist is, given what has already been said about the resources and difficulties of the land on which he has been settled and about the technology with which he faces the task of cultivating his new holding; and then to cover other important aspects of his economic position.

Income from Agricultural Land

In the course of his fieldwork the author attempted to obtain—by inquiry of officials and colonists—data on gross and net income from the colonist's land (and, where relevant and possible, from other sources); on the percentage of the annual crop (by value) sold off the holding; and on hardship, debt, and such evidence of relative prosperity as savings and the improvement of capital assets (for example, buildings). Such data are, of course, notoriously difficult to come by, and often hard to believe when obtained. This is partly because of the world-wide tendency, reinforced in a peasant society, to avoid answering questions on income and related matters, or to under-declare; partly because those questioned, including officials, could not always be relied on to grasp the distinction between gross and net income or the meaning of percentage of crop sold; partly because, in the case of questions necessarily addressed to or through officials, one could not always decide whether there was under-estimation, through a general sympathy with the colonist or a desire to emphasize his poverty, or over-estimation intended to demonstrate the marvellous job the official had done. In some colonies, and for a variety of reasons, no figures were obtained. No attempt was made to obtain them where, as in much of Dandakaranya and the Rajasthan Canal area in 1963, colonists had arrived so recently as to make income figures meaningless or, at any rate, unrepresentative of what was to be expected once the schemes had settled down.

For what it is worth, Table 10.I records estimates for total income (value of crop sold *plus* that consumed) per colonist for a number of

TABLE 10.I

Estimated Income of Colonists from Agricultural Land in Certain Schemes, 1963

State	*Colonization Scheme*	*Colonist's Annual Income*		*Percentage (by value) of Produce Sold*[a]
		Gross (Rupees)	*Net (Rupees)*	
dhra Pradesh	Aminabad	200	190	–
	Araku Valley	–	200	5
	Kannaram	–	200	0–100
	Piduguralla	1,600[b]	900–1,000[b]	0–100
	Kalidindi	1,000–2,000	500–1,000	50
sam (1968)	Baghbar	1,000–2,000	'Almost zero'[d]	0–75
	Gobindpur & Theka	1,200	80[b]	'A little'
	Kaki	2,400–2,600[c]	2,200–2,300[c]	20–25
ar	Jamunia (Bhoodan)	–	200[c]	–
ndakaranya	Umarkote-Raighar Zone	–	500 aver.	30
ryana	Bhakra: Tohana Divn	800–2,200	600–2,000	40–60
	Sirsa Divn	300–3,050	150–2,775	0–75
rala	High Ranges	–	0–1,000 (aver. 500)	Wide range
	Wynad—Ex-servicemen	–	500–1,000	Wide range
	—Local people	–	1,000–5,000	Wide range
	—Tribals	?	?	–
dhya Pradesh	Chambal Ravines	1,500[b]	–	50
	Chambal Right Bank	?	?	30–60
	Intikheri (local people)	1,600[b]	–	–
	Bunagaon	800–1,000	400–500	20–25
	Kanera & Mardel	150–220	'Nil'[d]	'Nil'[d]
	Paisra	1,000	560–670	5
harashtra	Palasgaon	–	200	25
	Sindewahi	–	225	–
	Pabal	–	225	25–70
sore	Arwatagi	–	250	50
	Bylakuppe	–	1,000–2,000[b]	–
	Kambaraganavi	1,000–1,250[b]	–	20
	Sorapur	–	400–600	25
	Tungabhadra	–	1,000–1,500	Wide range
ssa	Sunabeda	500	400–500	30
nil Nadu	Thengumaharada	3,000–5,000	1,200	60
	Moranam	700	500	30
	Velakapuram	–	300–400	?
ar Pradesh	Kheri	800–1,500	500–1,000	50–100
	Pilibhit	800–1,500	500–1,000	?
	Sardapuri (Bhoodan)	–	750	?

e. sold off the holding or, in the case of co-operative colonies, off the scheme as whole.

articularly doubtful reliability.

robably an over-estimate; or, at any rate, a majority at the lower end of the range given.

robably an under-estimate.

urce: Author's inquiries (see text).

colonization schemes; in the case of co-operative colonies, net income from the land derived from wages paid by the society concerned *plus* dividend, if any. The estimates refer to conditions in 1963 for all colonies except those in Assam, for which the relevant year is 1968.

Not much can be obtained from published sources by way of confirmation or variation of the tabulated figures.[1] Data for a number of colonies were, however, published by the Programme Evaluation Organisation 1968,[2] and are shown in Table 10.II. In some cases, these were based on very small samples.

TABLE 10.II

Income from Agricultural Land of Sample Settlers, 1965–66

State	*Colonization Scheme*	*Income (Rupees) (presumably gross)*
Assam	Kaki	1,978·8
Bihar	Gandhidham (Bhoodan)	253·8
	Bhupnagar (Bhoodan)	310·1
Gujarat	Jethi	Not recorded
Kerala	Chittari (Cannanore Dt)	266·0
Madhya Pradesh	Six colonies, Guna Dt	530·0
Tamil Nadu	Attur	599·5
Uttar Pradesh	Pilibhit	3,141·2

Source: Resettlement Programme.

The figures for Kaki (Assam), for the Bihar Bhoodan colonies, for the small schemes in Madhya Pradesh and for Attur (Tamil Nadu) do not differ markedly from those for the same or for comparable colonies in Table 10.I. Data for Pilibhit (UP Tarai) show a greater discrepancy, and may well be nearer the mark than the author's, but were based only on a 6 per cent sample. In other cases (Jethi in Gujarat and Chittari in Kerala) no comparison is possible.

One comment that may be ventured on the two sets of dubious figures is that a very great range of incomes is recorded, from what, in terms of net income, was claimed to be 'almost zero' in the flood-swept and trouble-beset Baghbar colony in Assam, through a number of schemes in the Rs.200–300 range, to the comparative affluence of such schemes as Kaki (Assam), the UP Tarai colonies, and Haryana (at least at the upper end of the range quoted for the Bhakra scheme).

As is to be expected, there are wide variations in income between schemes. Within those colonies that have a uniform size of holding there is naturally a narrow range of incomes. Here is a marked difference from the normal village. But there are wider variations in colonies such as Bhakra, where oustees had been issued with varying amounts of land according to the size of the original holdings for whose loss they were being compensated. Variation in size of holding was also a major source of income differences *between* schemes: though Thengumarahada showed what can be done on 0·8 hectares of wet land and 0·4 hectares of dry per colonist.

The group of singularly impoverished colonies included such schemes wholly or mainly for tribal peoples as Aminabad, Araku Valley, and Kannaram; co-operative colonies for local landless labourers and 'backward classes' such as Velakapuram (where, however, there were only 40·4 hectares of land to support 72 families), Palasgaon, Sindewahi, and Pabal (of these three, only the first had ever declared a dividend; the land at the second had not been fully opened up in 1963); the Bhoodan colonies in Bihar; and the flood-prone Assam colonies with their small units of cultivation. There is sufficient of a pattern here to cast doubt on co-operative forms of tenure and on colonization as a means to tribal uplift (though some tribal colonies, such as Bunagaon, did rather better). Adverse or insufficiently appreciated natural conditions must also in part be blamed for low incomes, not only in flood-swept schemes but also in a number of tribal, co-operative, Bhoodan, and other colonies. The absence of irrigation in Andhra tribal colonies has already been noted; as have low standards of cultivation at a low-income colony, namely Arwatagi.

At the other extreme, plains colonies unaffected, or less affected by physical hazards, such as Kaki, the Haryana colonies under Bhakra (in spite of water shortage), and the UP Tarai schemes (in spite of floods) show net incomes that are a good deal higher—exceeding Rs.1,000 or even Rs.2,000 at the upper end of the income range (though it must be remembered that Kaki was recorded in 1968, after the High Yielding Varieties Programme had begun to be felt there). And the same appears to be true of certain other colonies such as Piduguralla, Kalidindi, Wynad (for local people to a greater extent than for ex-servicemen), the High Ranges colonies, Thengumarahada (with its good cultivation on small holdings), and Tungabhadra.

There is also a group of colonies falling somewhere between the extremes of the spectrum: for example, Dandakaranya, so far as figures are available; Moranam (with high standards but physical and other difficulties and small holdings—0·8 hectares wet, 1·2 hectares dry); and the Guna District colonies recorded by the Programme Evaluation Organization.

Even the prosperity of the Rs.5,000 per annum colonists in Kerala—those with the highest net income tabulated—means no more than a total net annual value of produce grown, whether consumed or sold, of under £400 sterling at rates of exchange prevailing in 1963.

Not surprisingly, hardship was recorded for colonists in a number of instances: particularly in the tribal colonies of Andhra, the flood-affected areas of the Assam plains, the Bhoodan colonies of Bihar, some parts of Wynad, and most of the co-operative colonies of Maharashtra and Mysore. And indebtedness to money-lenders was reported from much the same schemes, and also sporadically elsewhere;[3] savings, or improved or increased capital assets, were few and far between, though noted for better-off colonists in Kalidindi, Kaki, Dandakaranya (where some refugee colonists had acquired motor-lorries), Wynad (where there was a certain amount of re-investment in land), and Thengumarahada. The Programme Evaluation Organisation, in their study of the resettlement of landless labourers, tabulated for each colony or group of colonies capital assets before and after resettlement;[4] but since the assets tabulated (land, irrigation facilities, buildings, implements, and livestock) were mainly either provided free or purchased by colonists from loans or grants issued by way of initial assistance (see below, pp. 206–10), and since no effort was made to separate assets acquired as a result of the formation of capital from the income earned by colonists, they are no index whatsoever of prosperity due to production in the colonies concerned.

Generally speaking, then, the colonization schemes of post-independence India studied by the author were not the scenes of remarkable and near-universal prosperity, even by Indian standards; and it is certainly not possible to claim that each had brought to its region, as the canal colonies of British days brought to the Punjab, 'a period of prosperity without parallel in its past'.[5] Indeed, very few colonists earned a higher income in 1963 than the cultivators of average holdings in the states in which they were settled, if one accepts a comparison between Tables 10.I and 10.II on the one hand, and on the other hand data published for 1960–1 by the National Council of Applied Economic Research (NCAER).[6] The exceptions include the better-off colonists in Wynad, the High Ranges, Tungabhadra, Bhakra, and the UP Tarai. But, quite apart from the doubtfulness of the data, the concept of an average state agricultural income is not a very meaningful one, given the wide range of conditions within each state and the wide scatter of incomes even within areas of more or less uniform conditions. Comparison can also be made with the NCAER estimates in terms of net agricultural income per unit area. Here again most colonies (except Wynad, Thengumarahada, Tungabhadra, and perhaps Bhakra) made a poorer showing in 1963 than the mean for 'old' villages in 1960–1. This could have been for one or more of a number of reasons: larger holdings reducing the stimulus to intensive methods; pioneer conditions; lack of adaptation to a new environment; and marginality of land.

A more useful comparison, given the dominance of the welfare motive in the choice of colonists, where choice was possible, is that between the condition of colonists before and after their move to their new holdings. In a diversity of places colonists owned to being better off than in their old villages: for example, at Kaki; on the Chambal Right Bank in Madhya Pradesh (not tabulated), where net incomes were said to have doubled; in Velakapuram, whose colonists said that they were lucky in their old homes if they netted Rs100 a year; at Arwatagi; and under Tungabhadra. There were indeed few complaints of being worse off, except in obviously difficult colonies like those on the floodplain in Assam. The Programme Evaluation Organisation collected data on incomes before and after resettlement which show a marked improvement in income from land (presumably gross) in the case of Pilibhit (nearly fourfold); Attur (nearly threefold); Guna District (more than double) and Kaki (over sixfold): though a decline was reported in the case of Chittari. But it must be remembered that this inquiry was primarily into colonies for agricultural labourers, much of whose income before resettlement came from wages; and that the increase in *total* income was in many cases less marked. (There was a variable degree of dependence on wages after resettlement, of which more a little later on.)

Some comparisons with other recent Asian colonization schemes may here be useful. The author found in Ceylon in 1951 that 'in most established colonies the average colonist is much better off than the average villager', and even more so than the class of landless labourers from which many colonists were supposedly drawn.[7] Again, R. Ho estimated, on apparently realistic assumptions about yields and prices, that the Malaysian FLDA rubber-growing colonies would give established settlers a net income of 1,280–2,100 Malaysian dollars (about Rs.2,050–3,360) *per annum*;[8] while R. Wikkramatileke predicted that the Endau Project in Johore, which involves the cultivation of paddy and rubber, would yield gross annual incomes of 4,800 Malaysian dollars (about Rs.7,680).[9] These Malaysian figures of course apply to schemes with a high cash-crop element and can be usefully compared only with such Indian colonies as those in the High Ranges and Wynad in Kerala, and then only with some of their individual holdings. For in these Kerala schemes there is a wide variation in the balance between paddy-growing, mainly for subsistence, and the production of such cash-crops as coffee and citronella.

By 1971–2 there is evidence that well-established colonists were able, at least in some schemes, to earn net agricultural incomes higher in real terms than those prevailing in the same schemes in 1963, especially where they were able to benefit from the new high-yielding varieties and associated practices. In the UP Tarai of Naini Tal District, for instance, in the area round Kashipur, Pantnagar and Haldwani, there was an evident air of prosperity abroad. This was particularly demonstrated by the solid houses that had been built and by the type of goods displayed in *bazars*. Ashok Thapar quotes figures to suggest that some graduate colonists with 12-hectare holdings were earning Rs.1,500 net per hectare per annum.[10] Some small colonists on 2·73 hectares had net incomes of more than Rs.5,000, but others found it difficult to exploit the new technology without running heavily into debt. It has been claimed that multiple cropping will bring profits of nearly Rs.10,000 per hectare:[11] but this seems to have been under research station conditions, unhampered by the constraints that tie the small colonist.

In Dandakaranya, again, it was asserted that average net incomes had risen from Rs.500 in 1965 (the same as that shown in Table 10.I for the Umarkote–Raighar Zone in 1963) to over Rs.2,000 in 1971. This rise was associated with the technical changes discussed in the previous chapter; and with the attainment of self-sufficiency in food-grains within the project area.[12]

Unfortunately, no estimates of colonists' incomes could be obtained in the Rajasthan Canal area in 1971 or 1972.

The Cash/Subsistence Ratio

The last column in Table 10.I shows estimates of the percentage (by value) of produce grown that was sold off the holding or, in the case of co-operative colonies, off the scheme as a whole. The wide range recorded for the Kerala colonies reflects the variable paddy/cash crop ratio just mentioned. High percentages of crop sold in other schemes do not, however, necessarily mean a high incidence of what are usually considered cash crops: on the Chambal Right Bank wheat as well as sugar-cane, linseed, and groundnut is sold. Still less are they an index of prosperity: in Arwatagi, for example, the relatively high figure (50 per cent) was attributed to the need to earn money for the purchase of necessities, even at the expense of the retention of food-grain for consumption. Here one is reminded of the remark by A. M. Khusro and A. N. Agarwal that 'There are stray pieces of evidence that the degree of monetization of agricultural produce, that is the ratio of marketed produce to total produce, increases as agricultural prices decrease relative to non-agricultural prices and *vice versa*'.[13] Further, although the prevalence of ratios in excess of 20 per cent in the Table may surprise those whose stereotype of the Indian village or colony is of a closed 'subsistence' economy (whatever that may mean), the figures (Kerala apart) are not so very different from those for old villages, data from which have been used to suggest that Indian agriculture cannot be very price-responsive;[14] other work has, of course, demonstrated price-responsiveness, though with more complications than might at first sight appear.[15]

Income from Sources other than Agricultural Land

So far this chapter has been exclusively concerned with the part played in the domestic economy of colonization schemes by the agricultural land allotted to them for individual or joint cultivation. But, to an extent that varies interestingly from scheme to scheme, income may also be derived from other sources. It is even more difficult to collect data on such income than on income from cultivation, and for the most part the account must be purely qualitative; though, so far as income derived from labouring on other men's fields is concerned, data were included in the report on the Programme Evaluation Organisation's case studies,[16] and will be quoted for what they are worth.

The sources of subsidiary income that must first be mentioned are those most closely connected with the colonists' own holdings: namely, income derived from such occupations as poultry-keeping, dairying, and fishing. The first two were sources rarely exploited, and then often with difficulty and, so far as dairying is concerned, with yields that are derisory by European standards. Fishing, too, was rarely a source of subsidiary income: only, in fact, at Palasgaon, and amongst the 'ex-criminal tribes' of Mircabad; and amongst Bengali refugees, in the flood-plain colonies of Assam and in Dandakaranya, in both of which fishing was possible in small tanks like those of the colonists' semi-aquatic Bengal homeland. The Dandakaranya Development Authority issued fingerlings from fish nurseries, and to the end of June 1963 estimated net proceeds from sales of fish came to just over a lakh of rupees. Transport of surplus fish to market from remote zones of colonization was, however, a problem. It was learnt in 1972 that the fish project had not done well.

Secondly, in the tribal colonies of Andhra Pradesh, Dandakaranya, Madhya Pradesh and Kerala many colonists supplemented their meagre incomes from what was usually described as 'forest produce'.

This phrase covers a wide variety of commodities from wild honey and *mohur* flowers[17] to the products of the chase: some consumed, some sold. A number of remote non-tribal colonies (for example, Palasgaon) also took advantage of the natural products of the surrounding jungle. Forests, moreover, gave the opportunity of working for Forest Departments or for timber contractors; while in Darapathar (Assam) colonists were allowed to benefit from the sale of timber cleared by the authorities from land later to be allotted to them.

Thirdly, in a number of places colonists were apt to set up as traders. Such colonists competed with official non-agricultural colonists in Dandakaranya, where a few also operated carting businesses; and trader-colonists were also noted in Kalidindi, Kaki (where a capitalist-farmer colonist in illicit possession of two allotments was also a trader and moneylender), Baghbar, and Arwatagi. This list includes no tribal colonies, whose colonists tend to be exploited by outsiders.

Fourthly, colonists' incomes were to a rather limited extent supplemented by the practice of crafts. There were, for example, a few agricultural colonists working also as carpenters and blacksmiths in a number of schemes, including such tribal colonies as Kanera and Mardel, where two blacksmiths were able to earn Rs.250 a year (that is, more than the average gross income of colonists there from agriculture). Handlooms were only rarely in evidence: for example, at Kaki,[18] at Jamunia, in the Hirakud oustee areas, and in Thengumarahada, where women also undertook tailoring work. Some attempt was being made officially to encourage handicrafts: silk weaving was proposed for Wynad, and in Dandakaranya loans of Rs.300 could be obtained by colonists wishing to undertake a cottage industry (but there were only 26 borrowers in the Malkangiri Zone in 1963). And mention should perhaps also be made of the 'cottage industry' practised by some of the 'ex-criminal' tribal colonists at Mircabad: their illicit distillery could be smelt from afar, in spite of assurances by government officers that they had long given up 'their former evil ways'.

But by far and away the most important source of subsidiary income to the Indian agricultural colonist was in most places a wage derived from labouring. In many schemes colonists worked on other men's land to a greater or less extent: to a very considerable extent at Darapathar, where refugees not yet allotted their paddy-land went out and worked on holdings in the adjacent Kaki colony, and in Wynad, where many of the ex-servicemen hired labour from the adjacent parts of the colony; to a less extent in Intikheri and in some of the Tamil Nadu colonies (for which there were employment opportunities in adjacent old villages); and also to a less extent in the remote, jungle-set zones of Dandakaranya and in the small tribal colonies, where there was little chance of subsidiary work (apart from forestry). Some colonists in various places also sought and found work outside the agricultural sector. For example, with the Public Works Department on road construction at Bunagaon, in the Raniganj coalfield for the Jamunia Bhoodan colonists, on hydro-electric projects for colonists from the High Ranges of Kerala, on iron-ore mining and railway construction for some men from Dandakaranya.

The Programme Evaluation Organisation collected information on wages earned by colonists from agricultural and non-agricultural labour in a number of schemes, primarily those whose aim it was to resettle landless labourers. These are tabulated in Table 10.III (which should be compared with Table 10.II).

TABLE 10.III

Annual Income from Wages of Sample Settlers, 1965–66

State	*Colonization Scheme*	*Wages (Rupees)*	
		Agricultural	*Non-agricultural*
Assam	Kaki	None reporting	
Bihar	Gandhidham (Bhoodan)	191·3	310·9
	Bhupnagar (Bhoodan)	530·0[a]	None reporting
Gujarat	Jethi	199·5	215·6
Kerala	Chittari	324·0	207·0
Madhya Pradesh	Six colonies, Guna Dt	181·1[a]	126·7[a]
Madras	Attur	574·5	507·8
Uttar Pradesh	Pilibhit	183·3[a]	—

[a] Based on a very small sample.
Source: Resettlement Programme.

It would be foolish to base too many conclusions on these data. Quite apart from the general unreliability inseparable from statistics of this sort, there is the fact that in all cases they are based on averages from a number of reporting colonists smaller than the already small sample whose average income is recorded in Table 10.II, in some cases on two or three persons only (it not being clear whether or not these were the only wage-earners in the original sample). All that can sensibly be said is that the reporting colonists owned to a wage income higher in all cases than the average income from colony land, except in Pilibhit (a colony with a high income from land) and in the

Guna District colonies (presumably too remote to find labouring opportunities).

Finally, it was not only in the remoter colonization schemes that incomes from subsidiary employment were small, smaller than colonists would have wished. In several other places the complaint was made to the author that there were insufficient opportunities for earning such income. In part, of course, this is a commentary on the felt insufficiency of the income from the colonist's own holding, an insufficiency that in turn, it will now be clear, has its roots in a number of diverse factors. In part, too, it is a commentary on the unwillingness of many colonists, for reasons of caste or of dietetic prejudice, to take advantage of the possibility of earning from such activities as weaving, poultry-keeping, or pisciculture. But it is also, to a very significant extent in most colonization schemes, a commentary on under-employment and non-productivity, particularly seasonally, on the colonist's own holding.

Employment and Utilization of Agricultural Labour

It might be supposed that the agricultural colonization schemes of independent India, with their marked emphasis on the provision of land for the needy landless and their labour-intensive technology, might provide an excellent example of those labour-absorptive development projects so often enjoined on the governments of developing countries which suffer from over-population and from gross unemployment and under-employment.[19] It might also be supposed that (apart from those who, like the 'Political Sufferers' in the UP Tarai colonies, have holdings that are large by Indian standards) colonists would be able to cultivate effectively using family labour only. In point of fact, however, very few of the schemes studied provided full employment all the year round, and not very many avoided completely (so far as one could discover) the hiring of labour. One of the few colonies that did seem to succeed in preserving a nice balance at all seasons between excess and shortage of labour was that at Moranam, where in 1963 irrigation maintained cultivation through dry weather and where the colonists were kept busy, yet not too busy, on their 0·8 hectares of paddy land and 1·2 hectares of dry land. In 1972, however, there was some evidence that increased intensity of cultivation had brought in hired labour.

Elsewhere, the general rule was that India's monsoon climate and unmechanized technologies imposed a régime that swung violently from labour shortage at the peak periods of need during the wet season (normally in *kharif*, during the southwest monsoon) to labour excess, and even complete idleness, in *rabi*, during the dry northeast monsoon; though, given the wide range of climates in India and the varying provision of irrigation in the colonization schemes, there were naturally a great many local variations on the general theme, especially in Tamil Nadu (where the southwest monsoon season tends to be dry, the rainfall maximum falling during the so-called 'northeast monsoon').

Pressure on labour supplies during the busy season or seasons could not always be met by hiring workers. In some places, as at Jeelugumilli, colonists were too poor to hire; in other, remote schemes, no source of hired labour was readily available. In a few, as at Pandripani and Sunabeda (tribal colonies in the Orissa portion of Dandakaranya), families known to each other before settlement, and often related by kinship, were able to form co-operative teams to help each other through peak periods of labour demand. It tends to be a characteristic of colonization schemes, however, as the author discovered in Ceylon,[20] that such teams are harder to organize than in old villages, especially where little or no attention is paid to the grouping together of families who were kinsmen or, at least, knew each other well in the villages whence they came.

More usually, however, and to an extent that would surprise those who imagine Indian colonization schemes to be models of independent family enterprise, colonists found it necessary to hire labour at peak periods. This was done in some places, as at Piduguralla, to a limited extent. The hiring of labour was more general in *kharif* in the UP Tarai colonies (especially among 'political sufferers' and other categories with bigger holdings, some of whom had something more approaching a permanent, resident labour force); and in Intikheri, Kaki and Dandakaranya, where Bengali and Santal refugees found it impossible to cultivate their relatively large paddy holdings without help, which they obtained largely from local tribal people; even then, a seventh or more of their 2·73-hectare paddy holding tended to remain uncultivated.[21] By 1972 there was an official ban on the use of tribal labour; but since the only sanction was administrative pressure the ban tended to be honoured in the breach. A general labour shortage was still reported, however.

Tribal colonists in Dandakaranya themselves hired labour for *biasi* cultivation. This is a device to secure some of the advantages of growing transplanted paddy, such as improved tillering of the individual plant, without the heavy expenditure of labour demanded by transplanting. It involves weeding the crop when it is a few centimetres high at the onset of the southwest monsoon, incorporating the weeds in the topsoil, and replanting with due spacing any rice plants that are accidentally uprooted. Tribal colonists, members of 'ex-criminal' tribes, at Pabal near Poona also used hired labour in unusual circumstances: namely, the exodus of so many members of their co-operative to work in Poona and Bombay that not enough were left to cultivate in *kharif*. All these instances represent private labour-hiring on the part of colonists. But in the Raichur Doab, under the canals of the Tungabhadra Project, the sparsity of whose population has already been noted, the labour deficit was so enormous that the government of Mysore in 1957–8 settled 500 families of imported labourers, each on 0·8 hectares of dry land, so that they might work at peak seasons on other holdings in this region of interstitial colonization.[22] Here is an instance of the deliberate settlement of labourers as labourers, albeit with a small piece of land of their own, which runs counter to the general concern in independent India to settle labourers as independent colonists (see above, pp. 99–101).

If lack of labour at critical seasons of the year has been a marked feature of many post-independence colonization schemes in India, a surplus of labour has been an even stronger feature, particularly in *rabi* in those parts of north and central India in which cultivation at that season is ruled out, in the absence of irrigation, by lack of rainfall or lack of sufficient soil moisture retained from the southwest monsoon. Under-employment amounting to enforced idleness was particularly prominent in 1963 in Bihar colonies, in the Eastern Ghats tribal colonies of Andhra Pradesh, in Intikheri and Kotia Pani in Madhya Pradesh and in Dandakaranya, with its intensely seasonal concentration of rainfall. By 1972 there was some increase in *rabi* cropping; and the spread of *mesta* cultivation gave some employment at the same season because of the need to ret the stalks and to prepare the fibre for sale.

In the Malnad colonies of Mysore, again, colonists complained in 1963 of having no work in three or four months out of the twelve. There was also a degree of *rabi* idleness in Baghbar colony in Assam, and in the colonies of Chanda District of Maharashtra, but less in areas like the UP Tarai, where the cultivation of *rabi* crops is possible and usual.

None of this, it may be said, is news. Many observers have commented on the seasonal nature of agricultural employment in India; and on the possibility of raising living standards by employing idle hands in *rabi*, and of easing the strains associated with the peak periods of the agricultural calendar by selective mechanization.[23] Surely, however, it is of interest that these problems of ordinary Indian villages afflict so many colonization schemes, which in this respect—as in others—are far from being model settlements; indeed, such factors as remoteness may increase the difficulty of obtaining labour for colonization schemes at peak periods, and of securing alternative employment during the slack season; while alien climatic régimes, like Dandakaranya's, may exacerbate the problem of *rabi* idleness; and unusually large holdings, by Indian standards, may enhance the effect of seasonal labour shortage.

Two other points about labour conditions in Indian colonization schemes remain to be made. The first is that under-employment of colonists appeared to be more general, and less tied to seasons, in Kerala (certainly, as might be anticipated, complaint was louder there); and also in one or two colonies, such as that for oustees at Gandhisagar and the co-operative colony at Pailad (Maharashtra), where because of remoteness or the newly imposed and more uniform agrarian structure there were no large landholders for whom to work.

The second point is that, for the simple reason that in many colonies of oustees there is great variation in size of holding, there is a great deal of variation in the extent to which individual colonists have, seasonally or more generally, a surplus or a shortage of labour. This was especially true of Rajannagar, Tamil Nadu, the colonies under the Bhakra Canal (though in those in Sirsa Division colonists were more self-contained), and the colonies under the Hirakud Scheme. One colonist at Hirakud, indeed, holding 10·5 hectares of land, was able to reproduce such features of the traditional social structure as what were described as two *ghotis* ('land-servants paid in kind and almost compelled to work on the colonist's land') who each had 0·8 hectares of dry land.[24] This is indeed a far cry from 'land for the landless'. (The same colonist did no *rabi* cultivation; and was one of the very few met by the author whose attitude was, in his own words, 'If we can feed ourselves, why grow more to sell?')

Non-agricultural Colonists in the Economy of Agricultural Colonies

So far the discussion in this chapter has been virtually confined to the domestic economy of agricultural colonists. But some colonists in India's post-independence schemes are not primarily engaged in agriculture; indeed, certain of them are not cultivators at all. And, although it is agricultural colonization that forms the subject-matter of this book, a brief reference must be made to non-agricultural colonists, if only because their activities may provide alternative occupations and markets for agriculturalists.

Non-agricultural colonists were, it is true, absent or virtually absent from colonies visited by the author in a number of states: from those, in fact, in Andhra Pradesh, Bihar, Madhya Pradesh, Maharashtra, Orissa, Tamil Nadu, and Uttar Pradesh. They were also absent from most of the Mysore colonies, and from the Kerala colonies apart from Wynad (where there is a number of traders and shop-keepers: Kerala being Kerala, the reader will not be surprised to learn that some were illicit encroachers). In certain colonization schemes, non-agriculturalists are positively excluded (as at Moranam), probably from fear of the 'evil influence' of the private trader.

On the other hand, primarily non-agricultural colonists were specifically provided for in a number of colonization schemes studied in the field, though never to the extent required by V. V. Giri's neo-Gandhian self-sufficient colony-villages.[25] Amongst the smaller colonies this applied to Wynad in Kerala, as already mentioned, and to Arwatagi in Mysore, where a few labourers without land in the colony were allowed to live and to work on colonists' holdings and in adjacent forests. Much more systematic provision was, however, made in the larger schemes. In Assam, for instance, the Kaki colony contained a planned *bazar* (subject, however, to unplanned encroachment); and at nearby Darapathar, still in process of development in December 1968, there were miniature allotments of 0·27 hectares for 'small traders', refugees from East Bengal. In Haryana, under the Bhakra Canal, and in Rajasthan, under the Bhakra and Rajasthan Canals, practice has closely followed that in the old Punjab Canal Colonies in the provision of *mandis*, 'market towns deliberately spaced along the roads and railways to serve an irrigated hinterland'.[26] The role of *mandis* in marketing will have to be considered in a moment. The points to be noted here are that their establishment introduces a substantial urban population into the colonization area—as many as 386,000 according to the forecast of the Rajasthan Canal Master Plan, though it was recognized that 'predicting the exact size of Mandis to serve the commercial and industrial requirements of the area is difficult';[27] and that, if *mandis* develop successfully, they will provide employment for surplus labour from the agricultural colonies around them, and hopefully, in the fullness of time, for the descendants of colonists, not all of whom can conceivably find work on the land. This has been one of the objectives of regional settlement planned in Israel, involving agricultural villages, rural centres, and towns; not, of course, that patterns developed in the unique environment of that country can necessarily be reproduced elsewhere.[28]

In Dandakaranya, too, thought has been given to the settlement of non-agriculturalists, partly for the benefit of refugees who are not cultivators, partly to provide services for cultivator-colonists. The *Revised Project Report* envisaged that 900 families of non-agriculturalists would be settled, all but 100 of them in urban and 'semi-urban' areas because of difficulties experienced by such families in making a living in settler villages; this was partly because agricultural colonists themselves tend to set up shops and to practise as artisans, partly because the standard villages of 60 settlers are not big enough to provide sufficient custom for specialist shopkeepers or craftsmen.[29] By November 1971 there were already 830 non-agricultural settlers. Plans for craft centres for carpenters, weavers, blacksmiths, and sheet-metal workers at Jagdalpur merge with much more ambitious plans for industrialization in Dandakaranya and the belt on either side of the Godavari, plans well beyond the scope of this book.[30] One of the factories already established, a saw-mill and carpentry works at Sunabeda (Orissa), is near the tribal colony of the same name, so that it should provide a source of work for under-employed colonists;[31] while the progressive urbanization and industrialization of Jagdalpur, Koraput, Jeypore and other places in Dandakaranya provides not only employment but a number of centres able to serve the Zones of agricultural colonization, though rather remote from them (see also below, pp. 201–2, and Map 4).

Transport

Mention has already been made of the surprising extent to which cultivators in Indian post-independence colonization schemes sold produce off their holdings, whether in the form of such cash-crops as coffee or in the form of food-grains. A necessary, though not a sufficient condition for the development of an exchange economy is the existence of an adequate system of transport and marketing. Nowhere is this more true than in the remote areas which are apt to be the scenes of at least the major colonization schemes of India and other countries.[32] Many would, of course, go further, and see in the development of transport and of marketing the *sine qua non* for the improvement and intensification of agriculture: for they would argue (rightly, in the view of the author) that there cannot be sufficient incentives for improvement unless the cultivator can readily see that any increased surplus can be disposed of to his advantage.[33] Even V. V. Giri, in his neo-Gandhian scheme for self-sufficient co-operative colonies has it that no settlement should be more than four miles (6·4 km) from a metalled road or one-and-a-half miles (2·4 km) from an unmetalled road.[34]

All this may appear to be a laborious statement of the obvious; but an examination of the actual state of affairs in many Indian colonization schemes will demonstrate that the necessity of communications cannot have been obvious to all of those who planned these schemes and brought them into operation, just as it was not obvious to the British planners of the two earliest Punjab Canal Colonies (Sidhnai and Lower Chenab), which suffered terribly from lack of them.[35]

True, there are schemes in which an apparently adequate road network was specially constructed to serve the needs of the colonists. This applies especially to such large areas of colonization as Dandakaranya and the Rajasthan Canal command. In Dandakaranya all new villages of refugee colonists are on a road, usually specially constructed, though not always metalled. The Dandakaranya Development Authority, recognizing that 'the backwardness of Dandakaranya is nowhere so evident as in its lack of adequate communications', and that 'the improvement of communications is necessary not only for opening up the area and to facilitate its economic development, but also for operational reasons, to permit the movement of heavy vehicles and equipment', has also undertaken the improvement of existing tracks and the construction of roads in tribal areas.[36] This is not to say, however, that all is perfect: remoteness remains a problem of particular Zones, as will be made clear in a moment.

So far as the Rajasthan Canal area is concerned, the Master Plan had it that:

> A satisfactory standard of communications is a basic necessity for development of the Rajasthan Canal area. It is essential as amenity for its people, is even more essential for development of its economy, for movement of its vast agricultural produce as well as all the varied needs of the community . . . All the huge investment in the project will yield returns only in case the communications system is developed effectively and in time.[37]

The Plan faced realistically the special problems of the Rajasthan Canal area: for example, the lack of existing communications except through distant rail- and road-heads; the unbalanced use of the transport system that will result from the outward movement of the expected 'immense agricultural produce'; and 'the exigencies of defence' resulting from the area's position along the Pakistan border. It proposed to regard rail and road as complementary agencies, and also to use navigation on the canal system; and to ensure that *mandis* are properly linked to their several hinterlands and to their more distant markets. All this is, *mutatis mutandis*, strongly reminiscent of the co-ordinated provision of communications and marketing facilities that was so strong a feature of the Punjab Canal Colonies once the mistakes made at Sidhnai and in the Lower Chenab Colony were appreciated.[38] As in the Punjab Canal Colonies, too, road construction was to be closely dovetailed with the advancing irrigation system, so that no irrigated area might be without roads. It remains to be seen, of course, how far accomplishment will eventually match planning. Certainly the roads traversed in the Anupgarh area in 1972 were poor in the extreme.

The provision of communications has not been confined to major areas of colonization: thus a metalled road was built to Aminabad, and adequate roads to Rajannagar and Velakapuram (in the latter case under the Community Development programme); and existing roads were improved in order to benefit the tribal colony in the Attapaddy Valley, Kerala. Still other colonies have found their communications improved for fortuitous reasons: in Malnad, schemes near the former Goa border, for example, benefited from road improvements in advance of the Indian military operations in 1961.

In other cases, however, roads built to colonies were no more than *kachcha*: that is, unmetalled and therefore likely to become impassable morasses in the rains. Thus while no colony-village in the UP Tarai colonies was without a road, many were, and are, on *kachcha* roads only (in the case of the Pilibhit schemes, even these were provided only some time after colonization). Jeelugumilli's link with the main road (admittedly only two miles away) is described as 'jeepable', though this is a polite euphemism. Even such a large colony as that at Kaki, in Assam, suffered badly from roads that were mainly *kachcha*, and, moreover, in very poor condition. Small colonies in remoter parts of Madhya Pradesh were generally very poorly served: the *kachcha* road to Kotia Pani was said to be 'abandoned in the rains', while Mahodra colony, on the author's schedule in 1963, could not be visited because the road was impassable.[39] Roads in floodplain colonies in Assam, such as Baghbar, were poor and generally *kachcha*, and not surprisingly liable to floods which swept away bridges with great regularity and left whole areas cut off from their markets. The roads on *regur* in the Intikheri colony for Kerala people were appalling, and added to the difficulties of this unhappy place.

Kaki illustrates another problem of communications that frequently afflicts the larger, linear colonies: that of the remoteness and inaccessibility of the villages at the end of the line. For such villages there is no way out to the external world except through the whole length of the colony. Darapathar colony was in an even worse plight, for it lies in the forest beyond the remotest village of Kaki. What is needed in such cases in the prolongation of the main axis road beyond the end of the colony to meet some main line of communication—if such exists, as it did in the Kaki-Darapathar case. A similar problem existed in 1963 for the Paralkote Zone in Dandakaranya, which was further cut off by an unbridged river. What was needed here was a road through the end of the colony to meet the road system in the Chanda District of Maharashtra.[40] (By 1972 the river had been bridged, and a *kachcha* road had been built through to Chanda District.)

The Malkangiri Zone also lay at the end of the line in 1963. Its communications would be helped by a road through to the Godavari delta: though fears were expressed that this would serve to bring pushful Telugus into the area, to the detriment of tribal and Bengali colonists alike. By 1972 there was still no road to the delta, though there was talk of one. But a road ran eastward over the Ghats to the coastal plain.

Some of the High Ranges colonies in Kerala were also at the end of the line, though the problem here is rather the general inadequacy of the internal road network. The difficulty of communication with, and marketing from, ribbon colonies has also been noted in Ceylon, where, indeed, in one colony (Kagama New) the colonist was so far from a market that he had 'no economic incentive . . . to attend to his high land' (that is, to the unirrigable portion of his allotment).[41]

It is also unfortunately the case that where roads, *pukka* or *kachcha*, have been constructed to serve Indian colonies, they are not always subsequently maintained in good or even in passable condition. The poor maintenance of some of the roads in Kaki Colony was noticed by the Programme Evaluation Organisation;[42] although it did not mention the other difficulties already enumerated. To take another example, the author found the access road to Sindewahi 'poor, overgrown, and not maintained because it was no one's job'.

Marketing

Smaller colonization schemes, whether served by pre-existing networks or by new road construction, tended to rely on pre-existing marketing centres. But one might expect the initial planning of major colonization schemes to involve the co-ordinated layout not only of transport networks but also of a hierarchy of marketing centres, in order to ensure a high degree of efficiency in the system and hence a maximum stimulus to the development of a market economy and to productivity generally. Settlement planning in Israel has in fact proceeded rather on these lines, though the rural centres and regional towns have, of course, many other functions in addition to the provision of a market for agricultural produce. There have been similar developments in Egypt.[43] But, although new towns like Rudrapur in the UP Tarai were intended as marketing centres, the opportunity for the bold and co-ordinated advance planning of transport networks and marketing centres appears only to have been fully seized in the Rajasthan Canal area.[44] For, as has already been seen, the Plan paid attention to the careful selection of sites for *mandis* and to their transport links not only with their hinterlands but also with more distant markets. In planning the size and spacing of *mandis*, consideration was given to experience gained over some twenty-five years in the command of the Gang Canal, in the northernmost tip of Rajasthan. Here there are eleven *mandis* spaced at intervals varying from 14 to 29 km, and varying in size from the '*kachcha*' *mandis* of Ramsinghpur and Padampur (with respective populations of only 349 and 547 at the time of the 1951 Census used in the study) to Ganganagar, a flourishing town at the head of the local urban hierarchy, with a population of 36,437. *Mandis* only 14 km apart suffered from nearness to each other; others from 'want of adequate hinterland' and from deficient rail communications with the outside world. The Plan accordingly envisaged for the main Rajasthan Canal colonization area a string of *mandis* located on the railway line to be constructed near the long axis of the ribbon-like command area, and at intervals of 24 to 32 km (given the limit, about 16 km, of the present mode of transport—bullock-carts). Six of the *mandis* are planned to have a population of 20,000, and twenty-four of 6,500; thus the concept of urban hierarchy is acknowledged. Advantage will also be taken in the upper reaches of the Canal of existing *mandi* towns in the Bhakra and Gang commands. (Bhakra has its own hierarchy of *mandis*, planned and in part implemented.) The Rajasthan Canal command should thus eventually possess an efficient system of *mandis* similar to that developed in the Punjab Canal Colonies, which in so many ways have acted as a model for its Master Plan. The new *mandis* should also, of course, attract other urban functions in addition to marketing; and serve their hinterlands in a variety of ways: Darling was convinced that rural indebtedness diminished near towns because of the fairer prices that ruled where many purchasers were competing for produce, and that 'the neighbourhood of a large town, though not always good for the character, has a bracing effect on the mind'.[45]

All this is the Plan. It remains to be seen what will eventually be accomplished given amongst other things the financial constraints that so severely hem in the whole project. That all was not well in 1971-2 is suggested by the fact that the National Institute of Community Development was to study the Ganganagar area, in order to learn what should *not* be done in the Rajasthan Canal command;[46] it was hoped that the research to be done would result in a revised plan for communications, transport, and marketing.

In Dandakaranya there was, and is, no planning of *mandis*. Use is made of pre-existing, and in some cases expanded, centres on lines of communication, such as Umarkote, Narayanpur, Pharasgaon, and Malkangiri; and *hats*[47] of a more or less spontaneous nature had grown up in a number of other places, and are often the scene of trade between local tribal and immigrant Bengali people. But it is generally true to say that many new villages in the colonization Zones of Dandakaranya suffered in 1963 from inadequate access to markets. This was all the more serious because of the remoteness of the jungle areas which the state governments concerned had thought fit to make available to the Development Authority for reclamation and colonization; and was most serious of all in the Paralkote Zone, whose poor communications have already been remarked on and which lacked any focus for its economic activity. Generally, too, there was a need in Dandakaranya for more positive measures to stimulate an exchange economy. True, the Development Authority encouraged the growing of such cash-crops as ginger and turmeric, and organized the marketing of colonist-grown *mesta*; and, as has been seen, arranged for the settlement of small traders. But more attention to the provision of suitably located service centres with well-stocked bazaars would have been a bigger step in the same direction, as well as a contribution to the problem of marketing. By 1972 some progress had been made; partly as a result of the improvement of communications, partly because of more careful selection of sites for new markets. The Town and Country Planning Organization of the Government of India was, further, co-operating with the Dandakaranya Development Authority in the preparation of a plan for the Malkangiri Zone, expected to be a growth area when irrigation is fully provided.

Some other Indian colonization schemes were large enough to have warranted the provision of market centres, or have generated them more nearly spontaneously: there was a weekly market in Wynad, for example; a notable *hat* near the confluence of the Brahmaputra and Beki rivers in the Baghbar colony, using water transport to Goalpara and other towns, but inoperative in the flood season; and, in spite of the appalling roads, a weekly market for the Kerala colonists at Inṭikheri. But it was generally true that many colonies too big or too remote to use existing markets suffered from the lack of interrelated systems of transport and marketing; the Programme Evaluation Organisation emphasized this in connection with Pilibhit.[48]

The pre-independence National Planning Committee, in response to the Report of a Sub-Committee on Rural Marketing and Finance, endorsed many resolutions on credit but only a very few on marketing.[49] It may be thought that this state of affairs, like the frequent neglect of transport and marketing in colonization schemes, was the consequence of an ideological revulsion against a market economy, with its general overtone of capitalism and specific association with rapacious money-lending traders. Be that as it may, it is clear that the theoretically preferred alternative, co-operative marketing, would equally demand the proper spatial organization of transport networks and service centres. And, in any case, the author found surprisingly little co-operative marketing in his field investigations, even where colonization itself was on a co-operative basis, as in many of the Tamil Nadu, Maharashtra, and Mysore schemes. Moranam was an exception, all marketing there in 1963 being through the Co-operative Society, though this had failed by 1972; while Jeelugumilli was a partial exception, the Land Colonization Society there having been given the sole right to buy forest produce from the tribal colonists in an effort to break a private trader's monopoly. At Kalidindi, even though there was a Co-operative Colonization Society, produce formerly marketed co-operatively was now sold privately, it was said because of the incompetence of a Society official; but the Registrar of Co-operatives, as tends to be the way in India (and not only in India), insisted that colonists should sell to a Co-operative Marketing Society in Kaikalur. At Kaki there was provision for the co-operative marketing of paddy, but it was obvious in the field that many colonists preferred private traders, some of whom were themselves colonists.[50] Thengumarahada was remarkable for its co-operative marketing as in other ways: its Society was clearly very active, had its own jeep and a boat for ferrying produce across the River Moyar, and was proposing to start a rice-mill. Sindewahi also had a co-operative rice-mill, but colonists tended to use private traders. Again, as at Palasgaon, few used the co-operative for marketing their rather slender surplus. There were marketing co-operatives in each Zone of Dandakaranya in 1972; these stepped in if private traders were not forthcoming.

In some places official bodies, other than co-operatives, had undertaken marketing. The Dandakaranya Development Authority organized marketing of *mesta*, for example, while the Indian Coffee Board acted similarly for coffee in Wynad and government sugar factories bought cane from colonists (and others) in Tungabhadra and along the Chambal in Rajasthan. Elsewhere, however, the field was left to private traders, and in some places, as in the Kheri colonies in the UP Tarai, there were complaints that prices were 'unfair'.

Under the Fourth Plan (1969–74), Central assistance is available for the development of marketing complexes, link roads, and storage facilities in ten major irrigated commands, including Tungabhadra and the Rajasthan Canal.[51]

Credit and Indebtedness

The author found during his field investigations in 1963 and 1968 that it was to private individuals, rather than to co-operative institutions, that colonists often looked for credit and, accordingly, to whom they became indebted. A similar situation of course still prevails generally among small farmers in India, in spite of recent advances in the provision of co-operative credit.[52] True, the officers of the Thengumarahada Co-operative Farming Society claimed that credit to their colonists was entirely supplied by the Society; similar claims were made for other co-operative colonies in Tamil Nadu; while Pilibhiṭ apparently made some use of co-operative credit. In the case of the Pabal co-operative colony it was asserted that there was no private debt; but since the Society concerned was running at a loss and had been refused crediṭ by its co-operative central bank, it is hard to believe that the assertion was justified. Elsewhere there were few claims, and less evidence, that co-operative sources of credit were in use; though it is in the nature of things that reliable evidence on indebtedness by individuals to individuals is hard to come by.

There were, however, several instances in which credit was sought through official agencies other than co-operatives (in spite of official efforts to channel government finance through co-operatives as far as possible).[53] There were few cases (apart from the Rajasthan part of the Chambal command) in which *panchayat samitis* made loans to colonists or their co-operatives for the purchase of seeds, fertilizers, and other inputs; partly, no doubt, because the forms of initial assistance shortly to be described provided for these inputs (though in Pilibhit, as elsewhere, there was a lack of machinery for the supply of most of them),[54] partly because areas of colonization tended to be absorbed into *panchayati raj* only slowly.[55] On the other hand, considerable recourse was had to that old-fashioned form of credit, the *taccavi* loan, a direct loan from government under a succession of Acts dating from 1871.[56] *Taccavi* was cited as a principal source of credit in a number of colonies, notably Rajannagar and Hirakud (in both cases among oustees) and also at Intikheri (both colonies): the Kerala colonists at Intikheri were heavily in arrears with repayments on *taccavi*. Credit was not mentioned to the author as a facility or as a problem in any of the refugee colonies in Dandakaranya, where (as will be seen) there had been, and still is, a comprehensive programme of assistance. Under the Rajasthan Canal, however, the supply of credit facilities from official sources was recognized as a prerequisite of full land utilization and of agricultural improvement.[57]

It remains to be seen to what extent colonization schemes will come to depend on land development banks[58] and on the Agricultural

Refinance Corporation (inaugurated in July 1963), which is especially interested in long-term finance, such as that needed for land reclamation and development projects.[59] It seems likely, however, since would-be borrowers have to prepare their own schemes of development and secure state government guarantees, to be more appropriate to new large-scale plantations of commercial crops. It was learnt in December 1971, however, that the Corporation was supplying credit in connection with land-shaping in the Tungabhadra project, and was investigating the possibility of involvement in drainage on the Chambal left bank.[60]

The striking and, indeed, depressing feature in colonization schemes during the author's fieldwork was the heavy reliance for credit on traders, money-lenders, and other private sources. In one or two colonies there were claims that there was no such indebtedness: at Kalidindi and Sorapur, for example, and at Moranam in 1963 (so far as credit for productive purposes was concerned; in 1972 co-operative credit had collapsed there). Sometimes, as at Velakapuram, the initial claim that there was no borrowing from money-lenders was falsified by subsequent evidence or admissions. In other colonies (as at Kaki, Baghbar, and Gandhisagar) private borrowing was said to be slight. But there was a relatively large number of schemes in which borrowing from, and consequent indebtedness to, traders and money-lenders was admitted to be heavy: for example, in all of the Eastern Ghats colonies in Andhra Pradesh (where tribal colonists were indebted to traders from the plain); in Gobindpur and Theka; in the Rajmahal Hills colonies of Bihar; in the High Ranges of Kerala (where the problem was so serious that some holdings in the colony had been alienated for debt); in the Chambal Valley; in the tribal colonies of Dandakaranya; and in the Malnad colonies of Mysore. Most of these colonies, it will be noted, were characterized earlier in this chapter as low-income schemes. Possibly the Tribal Finance Corporation will be able to supply credit to tribal colonies in future, especially given nervousness about the vulnerability of isolated settlements to Naxalite pressure and a consequent desire to bolster their economy.[61]

Not all of this private borrowing was from 'outsiders' who were not themselves cultivating colonists. As Darling noted long ago in the Punjab, agriculturalists may be creditors as well as debtors.[62] There were notable examples in a number of colonies of Darling's 'vigorous and prosperous elements in the agricultural community', who were able to lend to their less fortunate fellows: in Kaki, where money-lending colonists were also traders and innovators using new high-yielding varieties of rice; in Gobindpur and Theka in the same state (Assam); and in Arwatagi in the Malnad of Mysore.

The pattern of credit and indebtedness thus not surprisingly shows several features similar to those of India generally: notably in the tendency of small farmers, whether colonists or not, to seek out the money-lender, or the trader, or the more substantial farmer rather than to rely on the co-operative,[63] for reasons that include their poverty and the need for loans without restriction on purpose. Many colonists, however, are more fortunate than small farmers in the villages because they benefit from various forms of special assistance, by grant or by loan. Indeed, it seems to be true that in India, as elsewhere,[64] much more careful thought has been given to the initial assistance to be given to the colonist than to the need for continuing sources of credit in the special conditions of colonization schemes. Certainly the Programme Evaluation Organisation's study of colonization schemes is much concerned with the former, but hardly mentions the latter.[65]

Assistance

As is perhaps implicit in what has been said on the subject already, 'assistance' is here taken to cover those special measures by government agencies to help the agricultural colonist to settle on his new holding—measures which are not normally available to the ordinary villager, who is not confronted with such problems as jungle clearing, land reclamation and preparation, house construction, well-sinking, the provision all at one time of such inputs as draught cattle, implements, seeds, and fertilizers, and the maintenance of himself and his family till the first crop can be harvested. Government agencies may help the colonist to overcome these problems and to become self-supporting by making grants or loans, or by remitting the whole or a part of the land revenue or water cess normally levied; and, as already hinted, the provision of special loans for colonists merges with the provision of credit by means of *taccavi* or otherwise.

The author's inquiries in the field and elsewhere reveal that assistance to Indian colonists is a matter of very great variety and complexity, which is not surprising in view of the many agencies at work (see above, pp. 107–11) and the considerable range of beneficiaries and of local conditions. It would be wearisome in the extreme to attempt a complete review of all the kinds of assistance. In fact, only a few salient points need be made.

Provision varies from the generous to the scanty.[66] At the generous end of the spectrum lie many, though by no means all, the visited colonies in which the welfare motive was dominant: for example, in the tribal colonies of Dandakaranya the Authority was, in 1972, making available to the state government a grant of Rs.2,600 in respect of each tribal family; while in other tribal colonies (as in Aminabad) jungle was cleared free, a loan was given for housing, further loans and grants covered most necessary, initial agricultural inputs from bullocks to seed and fertilizer, and there was exemption from land revenue for a number of years. Generosity also flowed towards a number of refugee colonies, notably Bylakuppe, for Tibetans, which was treated much like Aminabad except that housing was provided by means of a grant of Rs.1,610, rather than by loan; and there was an additional aid—a wage of Rs.2 a day was paid till the first harvest. Refugee colonists and ex-servicemen in the Tarai were also well treated (though they were not given a wage or subsistence allowance, and the remission of land revenue was less generous).

Scales of assistance were also generous in the case of a number of co-operative colonies, where, no doubt, inducements to co-operative cultivation were thought necessary; however, since most of the colonists involved were Harijans or members of other underprivileged groups the welfare motive was also strong.

Even these generous scales of assistance rarely included a wage or subsistence allowance to tide the colonist over till he could harvest his first crop, though this had been recommended by the Committee on the Settlement of Landless Agricultural Workers and by V. V. Giri.[67] Indeed, it was not always clear how colonists had survived during this initial period of difficulty; and the author's field notebook for one of the Tarai colonies notes that it had made a better start than some of its neighbours partly because a maintenance allowance was paid. Indian colonization schemes compare unfavourably in this respect with those in a number of other countries, for example Ceylon and Malaysia.[68]

At the other end of the spectrum lie a number of colonies in which assistance was much more exiguous. Thus the Thengumarahada Society cleared its own land and built its own houses without government help (though at the time of the author's visit it was thought that a co-operative housing society, which would rank for loan finance, might be founded). No loans had been sought. Grants had been received only for a school and drinking-water well, and for the purchase of bulls and buffaloes; and, on a recurrent basis (Rs.200 per annum), for the maintenance of a stud bull and buffalo, this cost being amply counter-balanced by the Society's allocation of Rs.6,000 per annum to maintain the road leading to the colony (properly a charge on the government). But it would be too much to expect colonies generally, whether co-operative or not, to emulate this remarkable group.

Elsewhere, oustees generally received but little aid apart from compensation for land and houses evacuated, from which they were often expected to meet the whole or a substantial part of the value and cost of reclamation of their new land. Certain other colonies, for example, those under the Bhakra Canal and Chambal Right Bank Canal in Rajasthan, were also given but little assistance (colonists there needed less because they usually came from the vicinity, and could even go on living in their existing houses).

Under the Rajasthan Canal, too, the Master Plan provided for colonization with a pattern of assistance that was somewhat ungenerous by standards prevailing at the other end of the spectrum. It will be remembered that the Rajasthan Colonization Act quite deliberately followed practice in the old Punjab Canal Colonies. Further, there was a strong emphasis on economical colonization and on a financial return to government because of shortage of resources. It is true, of course, that 'assistance' in the sense of infrastructural expenditure was here very heavy, given the desert conditions with which colonization starts and the massive and essential programme of irrigation construction, road-building, provision of *mandis*, and the like; and the cost per unit area and per colonist is bound to rise as more difficult environmental conditions are encountered. But in terms of the forms of assistance now being considered, the Master Plan has merely this to say:

> Assistance will be given to the Colonists in the form of co-operative societies where necessary . . . The colonists will have to be assisted by the [Colonisation] department in provision of facilities like drinking water, seeds, fertilisers, agricultural implements and loans for housing and for purchase of bullocks and tractors etc. Provision for all these facilities has been made under the Master Plan.[69]

It will be noticed that there is no provision for a maintenance allowance, which was thought to be unnecessary on the probably correct assumption that plenty of colonists would be available from within Rajasthan without such an additional inducement. There was still no maintenance allowance or other subsidy in December 1971.

In Dandakaranya, on the other hand, the provision for assistance has been much more generous. Given that the refugee colonists came with few, if any, personal resources, maintenance allowances were paid while they were waiting to be settled, and during the first agricultural season while they were waiting for their first harvest. A payment was also made at half-rates in the second agricultural season and at quarter-rates in the third.

Land in Dandakaranya was, of course, supplied ready-cleared to the agricultural colonist at no cost to him. Loans were made for the cost of building materials (average Rs.1,700), of Rs.1,015 for the purchase of bullocks, implements, seeds, fertilizers, and other agricultural inputs, and of Rs.150 for an irrigation well.

Attention is not being drawn to the wide variation in scales of assistance in order to permit the conclusion that uniformity is desirable. The Government of India did, in fact, in sponsoring under the Third Plan its scheme for the settlement of landless labourers in colonization schemes, lay down a flexible scale on which it was prepared to provide subsidies to state governments: Rs.500 per family (Rs.375 as grant, Rs.125 as loan) for initial expenses; a well and other amenities as necessary; and additional funds if the colony was very remote. And, as the Programme Evaluation Organisation pointed out, there was in the execution of the scheme wide variation in assistance as between the various states.[70]

What is clear, however, is that in any given set of circumstances a generous scale of assistance may be too high, and a less generous one too low. This is well illustrated by a comparison between two not dissimilar schemes in Kerala—Wynad and High Ranges. In the former, the ex-service colonists received a grant of Rs.700 towards the cost of jungle-clearing, enough to pay almost all of the cost if the land was scrub-covered and about half if it was covered with high jungle; a grant of Rs.250 towards a house in the case of early colonists and a loan not exceeding Rs.2,000 in the case of later arrivals; a subsistence grant of Rs.450 plus the possibility of an advance on account of other payments; and a generous scale of grants and loans for agricultural inputs. Even allowing for the fact that ex-servicemen may be held to need more initial assistance than those who come from nearby areas as practising cultivators, this scale was probably too high. It seems to have been instrumental in creating an ethos of continued dependence on government, of expectation that when anything goes wrong it is for government, not the individual, to set it right. Further, the fact that so much assistance was given by way of loans meant, in the Kerala context and amongst these ex-servicemen, a very poor rate of recovery.

For the landless labourers in the High Ranges colony, on the other hand, the jungle was cleared by the government, housing was subsidized, and there was an initial allowance of Rs.750; the only provision for inputs was an interest-free loan to buy implements and a cow. It may well be that the serious indebtedness and tendency to alienate land in this colony owed something to the difficulty that poor, landless colonists had in getting off the ground without more generous and grant-aided provision for initial agricultural inputs.

There have been many arguments about the optimum level of aid for colonization in any given set of circumstances.[71] Too high a scale is not only wasteful but conducive to undesirable attitudes. Too low a scale leads to indebtedness and lack of prosperity,[72] even to hopelessness and desertion, or in very difficult circumstances to real distress or even death. The correct principle is surely that the government and its agencies should, for each scheme, decide what is the minimum scale of assistance necessary to overcome initial difficulties and to ensure that the scheme achieves its objectives, these having been carefully and realistically defined. A tribal resettlement scheme designed as a rescue operation demands, other things being equal, a different scale from that designed for first-class cultivators able and willing to maximize their income, in whose case more strictly economic criteria can justifiably be applied.

11

Induced Agricultural Change in Colonization Schemes

An IMPROVEMENT in the economic status of settlers in post-independence colonization schemes and an increase in their contribution to the national economy hinge in large measure on their acceptance of changes in agricultural technology. This chapter inquires into the organization and the methods by which the authorities have sought to induce such changes; and examines some of the problems that have arisen because of the nature of contemporary Indian society.

Agricultural Extension

It is first desirable, however, to establish the context by outlining the general evolution of agricultural extension in independent India; this can be done briefly because the ground has been well trodden by a number of recent authors.[1] The First Five Year Plan (1951–6) introduced the concept of a rural extension service which would make a co-ordinated attempt to improve not only agricultural productivity but also living standards, rural amenities, health and education; and it would operate in a Block of 50–60 villages through an officer who would act as the common agent for all fields of activity. The Second Plan (1956–61) envisaged a National Extension Service to cover the whole country, not less than 40 per cent of the Blocks being designated Community Development Blocks for intensive development. By 1963, midway through the Third Plan (1961–6) and at the time of the author's original fieldwork in colonization schemes, such Blocks had (in theory at any rate) been organized to cover the entire country. In each Block there was a common pattern: work was in charge of a generalist Block Development Officer (BDO), who was to co-ordinate the work of specialist extension officers (for agriculture, animal husbandry, health, and so on) and of lower-level generalists, the Village-Level Workers (VLWs), or *Gram Sevaks*. In the Second and Third Plan periods, too, came *panchayati raj*, the attempt to develop a 'set of interconnecting popular institutions at village, block and District levels'[2] which would, amongst other things, take increasing responsibility for various aspects of the general drive for Community Development and help to build a new rural India from below. By 1963 *panchayati raj* was in operation in nine out of the fifteen states of the Union, and, in theory at any rate, extension and Community Development workers became the co-ordinators for and executive officers of popularly elected institutions.

Practice concerning Community Development has tended to diverge as between states. Thus Andhra Pradesh has reduced over-heads and staff costs by dividing its territory into fewer but larger Blocks, which have been further classified into advanced, ordinary, backward, and tribal. Madhya Pradesh abolished the post of BDO in 1965 and placed the Block Extension officers under the supervision of the district officers (Collector, Sub-Divisional Officer, and *Tehsildar*). Other states have reduced Block staff because of financial stringency. However, when a Block moves into what is described as 'Post Stage II' it is common for funds to be reduced but staff to be retained, with the result that little money is available for development activities.[3]

In terms of the institutions so far outlined, agricultural extension must be seen as no more than one of the lines of attack in a more general attempt at Community Development; though, from the Second Plan onwards, there was generally more relative emphasis on agricultural productivity and less on social amenity. But certain programmes have been exclusively concerned with agricultural improvement (see above, pp. 174–5); and all the programmes together constitute what has come to be known as 'the new strategy of agricultural development', under which (as the Draft Fourth Plan had it) 'optimum production was sought as a matter of deliberate policy in the best endowed and most promising areas'.[4] (This was watered down in the final Plan document and appeared in the form 'it was decided to direct state effort in the first instance to those areas which were best endowed for food production'.)[5] As a result of the acceptance of the recommendations of an Agricultural Production Team sponsored by the Ford Foundation (1959), the Intensive Agricultural District Programme (IADP) was taken up in 1960–1, in the first instance in that district in each state which appeared to have the greatest potentiality for agricultural improvement under the impact of an intensive 'package' of fertilizers, pesticides, new seeds, new implements, and credit facilities, all backed and propagated by a special team of extension officers.[6] From 1964–5 onwards, 'a similar approach—but with the extension staff on a reduced scale—was introduced in several other parts of the country through the Intensive Agricultural Area Programme (IAAP), which also concentrated on particular crops'.[7] Both IADP and IAAP, with their emphasis on agricultural productivity rather than on Community Development, and on areas selected for their infrastructure and potential (and therefore richer than the generality), have been seen as technocratic and anti-socialistic (or alternatively pragmatic).

From *kharif* 1966 onwards the High Yielding Varieties Programme (HYVP or HVP), designed to propagate such new crop varieties as the Mexican dwarf wheats and the exotic rices IR–8 and TN–1, was got under way, but was at first largely confined to IADP and IAAP areas.[8] Finally, a Multi-Cropping Programme was taken up in 1967–8 to take advantage of new crop rotations made possible by the development of short-duration varieties.

The author's work in colonization schemes from 1963 onwards thus began at a time when agricultural extension through Community Development and the Block organization was theoretically universal, but when HVP was as yet unknown, as was IAAP. IADP theoretically covered the small tribal colony at Jeelugumilli, in West Godavari District of Andhra Pradesh: this was one of the original IADP Districts, and all its Blocks were supposedly covered from May 1963.[9] But, although the colonists received frequent visits from an Agricultural Extension Officer, the author during his work in the colony was certainly not made aware that it was under IADP. This is, of course, not altogether surprising. West Godavari District was chosen for its rich deltaic paddy-land, not for the sandy hill soils of remote Jeelugumilli; and, given the premises of IADP, it is natural that attention was focused on the fertile plains of the District. Similarly, there was no sign during the author's visit in 1963 of IADP activity in the tribal colony in the Attapaddy Valley, Kerala, even though it is in Palghat District which, with Alleppey District, came under IADP from *kharif* 1962–3.[10]

Sambalpur District of Orissa, which contains the colonization areas in the vicinity of the Hirakud Reservoir, also came under IADP in 1962–3; but, again, there was no sign of IADP activity during the author's visit in October 1963. Indeed, the area occupied by oustee colonists had not yet been organized into either a revenue village or a Block; though there had been Camp Officers and Special Agricultural Development Officers during actual resettlement (that is, from 1955 to 1957).

So far as the later and less intensive programme, IAAP, is concerned, this of course had not been initiated in 1963; nor does it appear subsequently to have affected the colonies then studied. IAAP was, however, introduced into Kamrup District of Assam before the author's visit to the colonies in that District in December 1968; but appeared to have no impact on their agriculture. On the other hand, the Sultan's Battery[11] Block in the Wynad colony area was chosen by the Kerala government in September 1963 as one of twenty Blocks in which intensive rice cultivation was to be encouraged on lines reported as 'similar to the package programme—to concentrate in areas which provide . . . best conditions for increasing agricultural production'.[12]

Even by March 1972 there was no IADP or IAAP under the Rajasthan Canal.

The general omission of colonization schemes, whether by design or by default, from IADP and IAAP reflects the fact that the land occupied by many of them is believed to lack the desired potential for growth in productivity. As will shortly be seen, special provision has been made in major colonization areas: otherwise colonies have had to rely on such agricultural extension as is provided through the Block under Community Development or, since 1966, on such spread effects of the HVP as reach their generally remote locations (for high-yielding varieties in Assam, see above, pp. 174–6).

Community Development and Colonization

A number of official reports have been far from complimentary about the effectiveness of Community Development, working through the Block and its officers, as a stimulant to agricultural improvement in colonization schemes. For instance, the Programme Evaluation Organisation of the Planning Commission, reporting in 1968 on resettlement schemes for landless labourers, concluded that 'in most colonies the position has not been encouraging, except for adoption of one or two items in some colonies';[13] and, more specifically, found the Block 'rather ineffective' and the extension side 'altogether neglected' in the Pilibhit Colony (UP Tarai), though some colonists had taken to the iron plough and to improved sugarcane.[14] The same report criticizes the state of affairs in the small colonies in Guna District of Madhya Pradesh, where 'involvement of Block agency in the programme seems to have depended on the inclination and enthusiasm of the District Collector' and where, although special Agricultural Assistants were appointed, they were still too thin on the ground.[15] The Scheduled Areas and Scheduled Tribes Commission were even more critical, complaining that 'Block Officers seem more concerned with putting on a show than satisfying the needs of the people'.[16] It is one of the most praiseworthy features of contemporary India that critical reviews of the sort just quoted are made and published by public authorities; though it must be added that such reviews seldom if ever extend to the political dimension of development (such as the relationship of factional struggles to *panchayati raj* and thus to Community Development) unless they are made by independent, and usually foreign academics.[17]

Although by 1963 Blocks were supposed to have been organized over the whole country, they were manifestly not operative in a number of colonies studied by the author. The omission of the Hirakud oustees from both Block and revenue administration has already been commented upon. The High Ranges colonies in Kerala were designated a 'shadow Block' only in 1963 (that is, a preliminary survey was in progress); the full Block programme was to be initiated in 1964–5. There was no Block in the Paralkote Zone of Dandakaranya.

At the other end of the spectrum, there was evidence that reasonably active agricultural extension was in progress through the Blocks in a number of colonization areas. Under the Right Bank canal and in the ravined area of the Chambal Valley in Madhya Pradesh, new varieties and new crops, having been tried out in research stations, were being propagated through the Blocks. At Sindewahi, in Maharashtra, the BDO was an intelligent man, an ex-veterinary officer (perhaps specially selected because there was a *Gram Sevak* Training Centre in the vicinity) and the Agricultural Extension Officer seemed to be working well both with the local research station, which he was using as a source of seed and a place of demonstration, and with the *panchayat samiti*. In the tribal colonies of Kanera and Mardel, in the Dandakaranya area of Madhya Pradesh, the BDO was clearly dedicated to the tribal people (*si sic omnes*) and had organized a Better Farming Society which was actually selling improved seed to other cultivators: an achievement that it is a pleasure to record. In the Piduguralla colony in Andhra Pradesh, run as a land colonization society for ex-servicemen, the Block had demonstrated manures, fertilizers, and seeds, and the Extension Officer was a director of the society. Here much clearly hinged on the go-ahead spirit in the society, whose President was a Baptist pastor and whose Secretary was a Lutheran teacher: some may see *die protestantische Ethik* at work unexpectedly in this remote corner of Guntur District. In another colony already singled out for favourable comment, that at Thengumarahada in Tamil Nadu, there was a resident VLW, but it seems reasonable to assume that the spirit of improvement in that remarkable colony owed more to spontaneous generation than to Block activity.

In most colonization schemes visited by the author, whether in 1963 or more recently, the apparent impact of the Block on agricultural improvement lay somewhere between the two extremes, but, truth to tell, generally nearer to zero than to the other end. In some cases, it is only fair to stress, the Block had been but very recently organized in 1963: at Aminabad in Andhra Pradesh, for instance. But all too often the comments in the author's field notebooks are paraphrases of the 'rather ineffective' and 'altogether neglected' of the Programme Evaluation Organisation's study just cited. Thus 'no effect' is recorded for Kalidindi (Andhra Pradesh), 'practically nil' for the tribal colony at Bunagaon, in the Dandakaranya area of Madhya Pradesh; 'colonists complain nothing done' in the resettlement areas under the Bhakra Canal in Haryana; and 'no priority treatment' (admittedly a rather different comment) at Kaki in Assam (in 1968). There is, of course, nothing particularly novel about these findings, for many observers have commented on the very uneven impact of Community Development, depending as it does on many variables, not least the training, enthusiasm, dedication, and intelligence of the extension staff, and over-extended and bureaucratic as the whole programme became with the attempt to apply it to all India at once.[18] What is of more significance to the present study is implicit in the comment on Kaki: the question whether Community Development is the right approach to agricultural extension in colonization schemes, if in fact these schemes have special needs in that connection. To this point discussion must later return.

Difficulties of a special kind have arisen as a result of attempts to apply Community Development through the Block in the special circumstances of particular colonies. One set of such circumstances surrounds oustee resettlement, where colonists are highly involuntary (indeed, most reluctant) migrants, always apt to complain that their new lands are much worse than those lost for ever beneath the waters of some new reservoir, and greatly needing to be told how to cope with a new environment. Even greater was this need in the case of the Kerala colonists at Intikheri whose deep unhappiness has already drawn comment. Here, strangers in a strange land were given no special agricultural instruction, but merely picked up ideas by observing (rather inaccurately) how local farmers farmed; and were barely helped by a BDO, a local man, who did not speak their language, Malayalam.

There have, however, been cases in post-independence India in which special provision for agricultural extension in colonization schemes has been made, in replacement of or in addition to the normal Community Development through the Block. In view of the question raised at Kaki it is worth looking at these in some detail.

Special Provision for Agricultural Extension

Not surprisingly, these cases of special provision are to be found chiefly in the larger areas of colonization. Some emphasis has already been given to the great change of environment that faces refugees from East Bengal who move to Dandakaranya, and to the efforts made by the Development Authority there to encourage the necessary adaptations. That such efforts would be necessary was indeed recognized before ever the project itself was started. The preliminary Project Report cites as 'essential features of integrated development' the 'evolution of the most beneficial crop pattern appropriate to the quality of the soil, climate and irrigation facilities' together with horticulture, pisciculture, and the improvement of live stock;[19] and it recommended the establishment of five model mixed farms, one in each zone, which should, *inter alia*, 'produce improved varieties of seed locally, carry out experiments, demonstrate the proper methods of cultivation, introduce new and more paying crops, bring about improvement of local breed of livestock, and promote pisciculture on a large scale'.[20] The Revised Project Report in turn spelt out these proposals in more detail, paying due attention to the knowledge by then acquired of soil and other environmental difficulties; and to the need for a Plant Protection Scheme in an area of unknown insect and other pests, and above all for adequate technical staff to help settlers in the difficult task of adjustment to a new environment.[21] 'The enthusiasm of the settlers can only be sustained if it can be prevented from flagging by a team of informed and enthusiastic field workers, who will be at hand to resolve doubts, to dispel anxiety, and to remove misunderstandings.'[22] But the Report couples its proposals for agricultural extension with those for joint farming, of which more will have to be said in the next chapter.

In the event the Dandakaranya Development Authority was so organized as to include Departments of Agriculture (including soil survey and conservation) and of Animal Husbandry and Veterinary Services (including fisheries), of the same status as the Departments of Reclamation, Irrigation and so on; and on the whole the author was impressed in the field both in 1963 and 1972 by the energy and sense of purpose shown by the officers of these Departments both at headquarters and in the Zones. Some of the experimental mixed farms advocated in the founding documents have been established, though on a reduced scale because of shortage of funds. Ironically enough, farms established partly in the belief that the local tribal people were 'poor cultivators' from whom little could be learnt (and who would, indeed, need instruction when they became settlers in the scheme)[23] found themselves observing tribal agricultural technology and copying it in certain respects: for example, the sowing of sprouted paddy seed as an adaptation to the relative shortness of the monsoon rains; *biasi* cultivation to work weeds into the paddy-fields and so improve tillering; and the use of early-maturing varieties of paddy which leave moisture in the soil in the very dry *rabi* season.

Yet an agricultural expert team which reported to the Government of India in April 1963[24] had a poor opinion of the 'low working efficiency of the tribal people' whose 'customs, beliefs and conservative outlook have defied civilising influences through centuries'; hence, there was 'little in the agricultural situation of the . . . area from which the new settler can draw any inspiration'.[25] They recommended an accelerated programme to apply improved methods of cultivation, and, in particular, to remedy soil deficiencies (especially of organic matter and in phosphates), introduce new strains of crops, strengthen the staff at the Zonal mixed farms and in animal husbandry (research and extension), lay out demonstration plots in each village, and augment the field staff (this was coupled with the recommendation that the *Gram Sevaks* in the Project area should be placed under the Director of Agriculture).

In 1963 the *Gram Sevaks* in question were Village-Level Workers responsible to the Dandakaranya Development Authority through Zonal Resettlement Officers and the Assistant Administrative Officer of the Zone. There were also Agricultural Development Officers and Technical Officers, amongst whose duties was the maintenance of liaison with research and demonstration units (though in 1963 village demonstration plots had not yet been established). In effect, then, Dandakaranya was maintaining its own system of Community Development, with special (and proper) emphasis on agriculture. In the old, tribal villages of Dandakaranya the normal Block system prevailed; while in tribal colonies Block Development was operative (with Agricultural Extension Officers fulfilling their normal role) but the Tribal Welfare Department of the state government and special Rehabilitation Officers were also concerned.

In 1972 the Block system was universal in Dandakaranya, but the Authority retained its research and extension organization for the particular benefit of refugees. A Japanese team had begun to help in agricultural improvement in the Paralkote Zone.

Altogether, then, the special provision for agricultural extension in the area under the Dandakaranya Development Authority has been impressive, and its links with research, pedological as well as agronomic, highly commendable; though one does not doubt that the expert team's recommendations for strengthening the provision were well founded (apart from their refusal to see virtue in studying the adaptation to a difficult environment of simple people who had endured it for generations). But a number of criticisms of arrangements in Dandakaranya will emerge in the next two chapters. It is, further, quite clear that the attempts to institute a system of joint farming (a system to be reviewed critically in chapter 12) made away with time, effort, and funds that could have been better spent on agricultural research, development, and extension.

The Master Plan for colonization under the Rajasthan Canal also made special provision for linked research and extension in agriculture.[26] Agricultural research, it was asserted, 'forms the very foundation for development work to be undertaken anywhere', and 'is particularly important in the Rajasthan Canal area, where the soils and other agronomic conditions are sparingly known and the wet cultivation being started may raise many new problems requiring expeditious solutions'. Pending completion of soil survey of the whole command, it was thought expedient to intensify the research programme on an existing station at Ganganagar; but eventually to envisage new stations in areas of soils likely to produce problems for irrigated cultivation. (By December 1971 there were, in fact, such stations at Hanumangarh, in desert sands, and at Berore, in alkaline clays.) Work would also be done on mixed farming, horticulture, and plant protection. One curious omission is any reference to the Central Arid Zone Research Station at Jodhpur, much of whose work (particularly that by agronomists and veterinary scientists) is highly relevant to the problem of developing desert lands in Rajasthan.[27]

As for extension in the Rajasthan Canal command, the Master Plan appreciated that colonists would need 'guidance and technical advice in regard to laying out of farms, alignment of channels, and in adoption of improved agricultural practices so as to get maximum benefit from irrigated farming';[28] but it envisaged that Community Development Blocks would be demarcated in the normal way, though with a considerably strengthened extension staff at Division, District, and Block levels. It was, in fact, proposed to appoint a District Agricultural Officer for every 280,000 hectares of irrigated land; and in each Block—in addition to the usual Agricultural Extension Officer—two agricultural graduates, with, where necessary, an additional specialist (for example, in horticulture). At village level, this specialist staff would work through *Gram Sevaks* in the ordinary way. It was further proposed to arrange two demonstration plots in each Block; and to appoint a selected cultivator from every 800 hectares of irrigated land to 'follow the improved techniques on their own land' and to demonstrate these to their fellows. It is not clear on what basis such model cultivators were to be chosen; experience elsewhere suggests that the boldest innovators are not necessarily the best diffusers, either because they may command resources beyond those of the average cultivator, or because (in a more egalitarian situation) they may be thought eccentric individualists.

In 1971–2 the provisions of the Rajasthan Canal Master Plan for agricultural extension were, so far as one could discover, being implemented. Special Agricultural Districts, smaller than the normal Revenue Districts, had been created in the command area. Each had been placed under a District Agricultural Officer, who was given a staff of extension officers and of specialists in farm management, plant protection, and soil conservation. It remains to be seen, however, how successful these organizations will be in helping to create a prosperous agriculture amongst colonists not used to irrigation and associated practices; and also in undertaking special tasks such as the introduction of cotton cultivation (40,000 hectares was the target for 1972 under the Bhakra and Gang Canals). Government officers are apt to point to cultivation under the older Gang Canal as a success story, to claim that a 'new spirit of enterprise' has diffused thence to colonists under Bhakra, and to assert that it will spread further into the Rajasthan Canal command. It might well be a fruitful subject for future research to apply diffusion theory[29] in order to study the spread of new technology spontaneously from the Gang Canal area as against that due to deliberate effort by extension authorities in the special Districts.

The colonies in the Naini Tal District of UP Tarai have somewhat fortuitously received a great deal of special attention since the foundation of the Agricultural University at Pantnagar, on the site of the former State Farm and in the colonization area. For, whereas in other Districts of the state the extension functions of the university are exercised through the normal Block organization, in its own area it works not only through the Block but also directly with the farmers. Cultivators, including colonists, also approach the university for advice on their own initiative. In these ways the research work of the university, which includes useful experiments in wheat- and rice-breeding, is brought directly to the fields.[30]

Otherwise in India's post-independence colonization schemes resident government officers additional to those associated with Community Development have been almost entirely concerned with revenue and administration, as, indeed, were the Colonization Officers in the Punjab in British days.[31] Thus Rajasthan has its Colonization Commissioner, with responsibility essentially for the administration of the Colonization Act (though he is also Development Commissioner). Uttar Pradesh formerly had a Deputy Director of Colonization (who was, however, a remarkable person with a strong influence on agricultural development, and who later took over the management of the Tarai State Farm). Each UP Tarai colony had a resident Colonization Officer for the first few years of its existence. In undivided Punjab there was formerly a Colonization

Officer to control resettlement under the Bhakra Canals and elsewhere. The colony at Kaki in Assam also had a Colonization Officer in its early days. Madhya Pradesh has a state Colonization Officer, and in 1963 certain colonies in the state (for example, Kotia Pani and the Intikheri colonies) had a special *Naik Tehsildar*. The Wynad and High Ranges colonies in Kerala had special officers for administration, survey, and settlement. Some oustee colonies in various parts of India had Resettlement Officers for a year or two. Many of those in this long list of special local officers no doubt fulfilled developmental functions not strictly confined to administrative and revenue matters; but none, so far as the author could discover, carried quite the breadth of responsibility, and in particular the oversight of agricultural improvement, which have come to be borne by Colonization Officers in Ceylon.[32] The same may be said of the officers of Co-operative Departments who, with local managers, secretaries, and others were concerned with the generally forlorn task of establishing a co-operative system of land tenure and cultivation in such states as Andhra Pradesh, Tamil Nadu, and Maharashtra.

In fact, officers primarily concerned with improvement (and particularly agricultural improvement), yet outside or supplementary to the Block system, are, apart from Dandakaranya, Rajasthan, and Naini Tal Tarai, virtually confined to certain tribal colonies in whose operation Tribal Welfare Departments were concerned; to special cases like the colony for Tibetan refugees at Bylakuppe (Mysore) which had a Special Officer with a staff under him (it has also received aid from various foreign sources, including Switzerland); and to cases of the sparing provision of additional Agricultural Assistants or other junior staff of the sort already reported for Guna District, Madhya Pradesh.

The Social Factor in Agricultural Change

The debate continues on the role of social attitudes and behaviour in the acceptance of change in general and of new agricultural techniques in particular; and it has moved a long way since it was referred to fifteen years ago in a study of colonization in Ceylon.[33] It is not proposed here to summarize the course of this debate, nor to contribute to it at any high level of generality.[34] Indeed, it would be presumptuous for a non-sociologist to do so.

All that will be said in general terms, before moving on to certain specific issues, is this:

(1) The author is as hostile as ever to uninformed judgements on the alleged 'backwardness' and 'conservatism' (or, worse, 'laziness' and 'incorrigible ignorance') of the peasant or colonist, of the sort

that one used to hear, and still hears from the lips of visiting 'experts'; and, truth to tell, it is by no means lacking in the comments on their less fortunate brethren by town-based Indians. A recent and generally not unsympathetic report on the 'primitive tribes' of Madhya Pradesh really takes no more than a forester's view of their 'backward' shifting cultivation;[35] and that is hardly to see it through a wide-angle lens.

(2) That, at a rather higher level of sophistication, it is dangerous to generalize about alleged resistances to change springing from supposedly 'other-worldly' attitudes to living standards and to wealth;[36] or, indeed, about any all-pervasive economic influences of Hinduism.

(3) That one cannot go the whole way with T. W. Schultz in his conclusion that 'it is not necessary to appeal to differences in personality, education and social environment' to explain 'observed lags in the acceptance of particular new agricultural factors'.

(4) That, especially if unacceptable risks are recognized as a rational basis for not accepting a new technique, one is still prepared to stand by words written some time ago about Ceylon: 'Often, much more often than is generally conceded, resistance to technical change has a rational basis, as when, for example, the proposed new technique is untried, or unsuitable, or even unusable.'[37]

Problems of Tribal Peoples and Harijans

There remain, however, special problems of encouraging technical change amongst some tribal peoples on the one hand, and amongst Harijans on the other. A number of problems of tribal peoples will be taken up in chapter 13. Suffice it to say here there is tremendous variety amongst people classed as 'tribal'. After all, the Badagas of Thengumarahada are 'tribal',[38] and one has seen how enterprising they are. At the other end of the spectrum there are tribes like the so-called 'criminal tribes', whom it is extraordinarily difficult to wean from their habits of thieving, or prostitution, or illicit distilling, even when they are placed in colonies like those at Mircabad, in Madhya Pradesh: these, indeed, are no more cultivators than the occupants of Fagan's thieves kitchen.

As for Harijans, there is again great variety. But the author would not dissent from Etienne's finding that some Harijans at least display an inertia, a lack of energy and tenacity, born of long years of inferiority, poverty and malnutrition, while others show considerable enterprise.[39] After all, the Namasudras of Dandakaranya are Harijans, and sufficient evidence of their adaptability was given in the previous chapter.

Attitudes to Government

There is another kind of inertia, by no means confined to Harijans and similar to that found amongst colonists in Ceylon.[40] This is an attitude of dependence born of a tradition of autocracy, whether by raja or Raj, and nurtured by excessive scales of assistance and by the all-pervasiveness of bureaucracy, whether in the shape of revenue officers or co-operative inspectors or Block developers. This kind of inertia, the kind that expects some government agency to do everything from road construction to house repair, is of course related to the first; for great initiative is hardly to be expected amongst the poor, the downtrodden, and the ill-fed. It is also related to the caste system. But it is connected too with the Indian tendency, often noticed, for an institution—even a movement—to become a bureaucracy devoted to paperwork and to the assiduous taking-in of its own washing; devoted also to the maintenance of a sense of self-importance amongst the bureaucrats which helps to perpetuate a top-down approach and so tends to the stifling of initiative from below. Thus are attitudes *to* government and its institutions partly at least a product of attitudes *of* government and its officers.

Attitudes and Practices of Government Institutions and Officers

The point about bureaucracy that has just been made deserves, perhaps, to be taken a little further.[41] The author certainly came across a number of instances of the 'top-down' approach during his work in colonization, an approach apparently undiverted and unaffected by *panchayati raj*. Thus in one of the colonies for oustees from the Hirakud reservoir in Orissa a smallish group of clearly very poor people, Harijans and of other low castes, were persuaded, after starting with individual tenure, to form a Co-operative Joint Farming Society under the supervision of a manager. It seemed fairly clear here that poor and uninstructed people were being forced into 'Co-operation' which they did not want by minor officials whom they saw as bosses and who traded on their feeling of poverty and dependence.

Bureaucratic attitudes can also weaken, or even destroy altogether, the critically important link between the agricultural research station and its extension officers. Thus in the Wynad colonization scheme in Kerala there was a 'Government Agricultural Farm' devoted amongst other things to the breeding of rice varieties suited to the elevation, acid soils, and diseases of the locality; to research on diseases of fruit crops, and to varietal trials in an interesting range of other crops, from vanilla and ginger to camphor. Yet the local extension service, previously attached to the station, was in 1963 functioning through the Block organization, which had no official connection with the station except for the supply of seeds and plants from its multiplication plots. Liaison at the local level had clearly weakened because of the new externally imposed and thoroughly bureaucratic relationship between research and extension. When the author discovered that research and extension officers lived in adjacent bungalows and suggested to the research officer that he might take the initiative and forge informal links he was clearly taken aback and said, 'I must work through the proper channels.'

Lack of co-ordination is not only a matter of the link between agricultural research and extension. The Programme Evaluation Organisation has drawn attention, in a general way, to the multiplicity of agencies concerned with colonization in a number of states, and to the desirability of a single agency to ensure co-ordination.[42] A specific instance came to the author's notice in the Kaki scheme in Assam. Here government tubewells and diesel pumps had been installed, with a resident operator. In spite of the fact that there was a BDO and *panchayat samiti* locally, and even more locally an Agricultural Assistant, only an engineer many miles away could issue the order to man and to work the pumps, with the result that they were little used. Clearly they should have been under local control.

To revert to the essential link between research and extension, this of course should be two-way: not only should the fruits of research be made available to colonists, but the needs and problems of colonists (especially those peculiar to the pioneer fringe) need to be fed back to the research workers. But this feed-back takes place only if extension workers, and ideally cultivators, are research-minded, and if, in particular, they can formulate problems as a result of their experiences. But the formal and verbal nature of so much of Indian education stifles curiosity and problem-mindedness.[43] Another consequence of the same educational situation is that all too many research workers tend not to read widely and thus to be unaware of experience elsewhere.[44] Very few officials in the states had read anything on colonization outside India.

Educational Provision

Few colonies are without at least some provision for the primary education, in or near the colony, of colonists' children; and most have access to some sort of secondary education (though not many take advantage of it). The Dandakaranya Development Authority is concerned to provide a whole network of schools as part of its activities. But adult education (which, in most parts of India, means night schools devoted to the attainment of literacy in the vernacular) is sadly lacking in the colonies; and, where started as a result of

Community Development or otherwise, has often ground to a halt. Given the low literacy rate in most parts of India, and the particularly low rate among groups strongly represented in the colonies (such as Harijans and tribal peoples), the education of adults would surely make them more accessible to information on new agricultural methods.

The reader who believes that structural change is a prerequisite of agricultural improvement may be surprised that, apart from observations on co-operative farming, nothing has been said in this chapter on land tenure as a factor in agricultural improvement. In fact the next chapter will be largely devoted to that subject, and will include a more extended discussion of co-operative farming.

As for the particular problems associated with agricultural change among tribal peoples, again the odd remark has been made along the way; but a more connected treatment will be given to the subject in chapter 13.

Conclusion

It must be asked, in conclusion, whether there is any case for the special treatment of colonization schemes and of the colonists in them (tribal colonists apart, for the reason just stated); special treatment, that is, over and above such general provision as Community Development in its agricultural aspects.

Where colonization schemes are included in IADP or IAAP, there seems to be no case for special treatment except that implicit in the Programme. In the nature of things, remedies and inputs in such cases are prescribed after careful consideration of local circumstance, which, in the case of colonization schemes, should include their pioneer character and the nature of the colonists. But reasons have been given for the exclusion of most colonization schemes here studied from IADP or IAAP as conceived up to the moment of writing. And, if the two programmes continue, this exclusion seems likely to persist, unless in respect of such an area as the Rajasthan Canal command or parts of Dandakaranya which eventually receive adequate irrigation; but by the time that happens, if it ever does, the areas will almost by definition have lost their pioneer character.

Let it be said, too, that although the author appreciates the compassionate motives and concern for employment that animate V. V. Giri's proposals for massive land colonization, he cannot agree with his proposals for the 'training' of settlers on their admission to colonies, after which, as he puts it, they would be liable 'to be posted to other colonies' to train others and to maintain 'the expanding network of colonies'.[45] This approach neglects the consideration that even if one could 'train' a good cultivator, skills acquired in one colony would be most unlikely, given India's infinite variety, to be suitable in others.

Here, in fact, is the crux of the matter. Except where colonists move a short distance from old village to new colony, they are likely to find unfamiliar environmental conditions: the Kerala settlers on the black soils of Intikheri, the Bengali and Santal refugees in Dandakaranya, and the Rajasthani nomads or *barani* cultivators confronted with the needs of sophisticated canal irrigation. Here the need for an initial period of active extension work, effectively linked to research conducted in the local environment, is essential. And this spells provision, for a time at any rate, by resident officers over and above the normal establishment, whatever that has been or may be. This chapter has shown that certain authorities, notably those in Dandakaranya and Rajasthan, have appreciated that changed environment and an unfamiliar technology demand such measures. Other authorities have not.

12

Land Tenure in Colonization Schemes

THIS chapter will take the discussion of India's post-independence colonization schemes into the important field of land tenure, and at the same time deal with certain related structural aspects of their agrarian economy. It will begin with an attempt to classify the systems of land tenure that have been applied, or that it was intended to apply to these schemes. It will move on to discuss certain specific issues, such as sizes of holdings; charges for land and water; tenure-by-stages; certain administrative shortcomings such as uncertain tenure and delays in surveys and settlement (in the Indian sense of the term);[1] and breaches by colonists of conditions of tenure officially imposed. Considerable space will then be devoted to various forms of co-operative tenure, not because it affects large numbers of colonists but because the subject is a controversial one with wider implications.

One note of warning must be sounded: land tenure is a most complicated subject, and it is possible that the author may sometimes have misunderstood what officials told him about tenure in particular colonies.

Classes of Land Tenure

'*Reformed* Ryotwari' *Tenures with Transferable Rights*

Within a few years of independence most Indian states had enacted legislation to abolish intermediaries (for example, *zamindars*) who collected payments from cultivators and paid land revenue to the government;[2] who combined the functions of what in a European context might be seen as a tax-farmer, feudal chief, and landlord; and who, according to the Census of 1961, held sway over about 45 per cent of the area of the country.[3] The abolition of intermediaries and associated legislation generally had the effect of simplifying the tremendously varied and complex systems of tenures which had so fascinated the British rulers of India[4] and on which they, in their turn, piled further variety and complexity. According to the 1961 Census, by far the most numerous of the landholders in India were, as a result of the impact of these reforms on the pre-existing situation, those whom the Census classed as *ryotwari* holders because, like the *ryots* of the Madras Presidency and of other parts of British India,[5] they had entered into a direct engagement with the government to pay land revenue and had permanent rights in land (inscribed in a document often known as a *patta*). However, in many areas the 'reformed *ryotwari*' tenure that replaced the *zamindari* or some similar system is less absolute, more hedged about with conditions, and rather more distant from ownership as it is understood in the West than the *ryotwari* tenure of British days. According to a sample survey undertaken as part of the 1961 Census (and based, it is freely admitted, on only three villages in each *tehsil* or *taluk*, one tribal village where applicable, and one small town)[6] no less than 91·63 per cent of the land holdings in India were *ryotwari* holdings in terms of the Census definition. The names given to this tenure varied from state to state: for example, *bhumidari* in UP, *bhumiswami* in Madhya Pradesh, *khatedari* in Rajasthan. The tenure varied also from state to state in the restrictions imposed on the landholder. Outside Madhya Pradesh, Uttar Pradesh, and Himachal Pradesh most *ryotwari* holders had permanent, heritable, and transferable possession including the right to lease. In India as a whole, 71 per cent of all landholders were said to be in this position.[7] A high proportion of landholders in Himachal Pradesh and Madhya Pradesh, and a smaller proportion of those in Uttar Pradesh and Gujarat were in a second category and were subject to the condition that they could not lease their land. A third category, widely scattered in relatively small proportions but reaching 28 per cent of landholders in Bihar and nearly 60 per cent of those in UP, either lacked the right to transfer their land, or held only a limited right to do so: this category, as it affects colonies, will be separately considered later. It must be appreciated, of course; (1) that the Census figures were based on a small sample and may be otherwise subject to error; (2) that many local variations are concealed by the attempt, both of the Census authorities and of the author, to draw a bold general classification; and (3) that the state of affairs on the ground, notably in the matter of illegal leases and other irregularities, may well be very different from that inscribed in *pattas* and revenue codes or reported to Census enumerators, not least in the colonies (see pp. 247–52 below).

In a number of Indian post-independence colonization schemes the state authorities have attempted to assimilate the land tenure to their reformed agrarian structure, and, in particular, to make the colonists into *ryotwari pattedars* (or *bhumiswamis*, or whatever title is locally applicable) subject to the conditions and restrictions operative in the state in question, though sometimes to some variation of those conditions or restrictions. In a number of colonies studied by the author the tenure in operation, or that it was intended ultimately to operate when the authorities were ready, was without restriction on transfer, leasing or succession, as in the first (and largest) sub-category recognized by the Census. These included (for colonies where *pattas* had been issued and *ryotwari* tenure was operative) Rajannagar (Tamil Nadu), Tungabhadra (Mysore), Pandripani and Sunabeda (Orissa), Tilaiya (Bihar), and the Araku Valley and Kannaram (Andhra Pradesh), though in the last named it appeared that as yet unformulated restrictive conditions were to be imposed. It was the declared intention ultimately to introduce *ryotwari* tenure for the Hirakud oustees (Orissa) and for the Dandakaranya refugee colonists, and since (on the showing of the 1961 Census)[8] Orissa is one of those states in which such tenure is without restriction on inheritance, transfer or leasing, it may well be that when *pattas* are eventually issued they will be similarly unrestricted in the case of the Hirakud oustees and of those refugee colonists who are settled in Orissa. However, the Orissa Land Reforms Act, unenforced at the time the Census volume was written, bars the right of lease for all except certain 'privileged *raiyats*'; and since none of the refugees can claim privilege within the meaning of the Act they may well, in the event, find themselves subject to a bar on leasing.

Many of the colonies in Madhya Pradesh (notably Chambal Right Bank, Gandhisagar, Kotia Pani, and the Dandakaranya tribal colonies) are under the state's reformed *bhumiswami* tenure, which falls within the second of the two sub-categories recognized by the Census: that is, the colonists, as *bhumiswamis*, hold their lands on a permanent, heritable, and transferable basis. But (in theory at any rate) succession is in a prescribed order, 'to prevent fragmentation of holdings'; the right of transfer is subject to restrictions designed to prevent the creation of holdings smaller than a prescribed limit, or greater than the state ceiling; and leasing is prohibited in other than exceptional circumstances (for example, physical or mental disability or service in the armed forces).[9] Thus *bhumiswami* tenure, the nearest approach to 'ownership' in the Madhya Pradesh Land Code, is subject to restrictions that remove it far from freehold as understood in the West. Yet it appeared, during the author's field-work, to be popular, every colonist's desire being a *bhumiswami patta*. But the question of breaches of restrictive tenures must be taken up as a separate issue in a later section. It should be noted here, however, that in the Madhya Pradesh tribal colonies, tenure is subject to the further restriction, intended to protect the *adivasi* from designing plainsmen, that 'the rights of a *bhumiswami* belonging to an aboriginal tribe shall not be transferable to a person not belonging to such a tribe without the permission of the Collector'. And, finally, if and when *pattas* are issued to colonists in the Madhya Pradesh part of Dandakaranya they will presumably be subject to *bhumiswami* tenure as outlined above, with the additional restriction just mentioned in the case of tribal colonists.

About a quarter of the colonists in the schemes studied in 1963 were subject to what was recognizably 'reformed *ryotwari*' tenure, with transferable rights, or were to be so subject when the authorities were ready to proceed (some reasons for administrative delay will be given a little later). The proportion in 1972 is probably rather lower, because of increased numbers in other categories, particularly the next.

Permanent Tenure without Transferable Rights

A rather higher proportion of the colonists (about 50 per cent) were subject to permanent and heritable tenure but *without* transferable rights. Their tenure was equivalent to, or approximated to the third category of 'reformed *ryotwari*' tenure recognized by the 1961 Census and mentioned above; it was also broadly equivalent to *sirdari* tenure in Uttar Pradesh.[10] The reasons for the bar on transfer were often akin to those cited in a Report on the settlement of landless labourers in Tamil Nadu, which stressed the large financial outlay by government on the settlers and the consequential need 'to ensure that the land is not mis-used and that the interests of the Government are protected'.[11] Accordingly, it was proposed to impose not only the condition that land must be brought under cultivation within one year but also a further condition (relevant here) that, loans being recoverable over twenty-five years, there should be a ban on transfer for that period.

Established colonists in Rajasthan (and, in particular, those under the Rajasthan Canal) will ultimately be subject to *khatedari* tenure, the local equivalent of 'reformed *ryotwari*'. The rights of a *khatedar* are normally permanent, heritable, and transferable but subject to restrictions concerning minimum and maximum sizes of holdings and to special restrictions on tribal landholders similar to those already cited for Madhya Pradesh.[12] Further, simple mortgages are allowed only in favour of the state government, the Land Mortgage Bank, or a co-operative society and a holding may not be leased for more than five years at a time. All these conditions are prescribed in the Rajasthan Tenancy Act of 1955. But colonists (other than *eksali*—i.e. annual-lease—tenants) in the Rajasthan Canal, Bhakra, and Chambal colonies in Rajasthan are initially under what is known as *gair khatedari* tenure, and subject to conditions prescribed under the Rajasthan Colonization Act of 1954 and contained in the Rajasthan Colonization (General Colony) Conditions, 1955. The most important points here are (1) that land may not be transferred until *gair khatedari* tenure has been converted into *khatedari* tenure and (2) that this conversion may not take place until 'the whole amount of the purchase price and all other sums and outgoings due to Government . . . shall have been duly paid and discharged'. Here (and this is a matter to be taken up later) is the modern equivalent of the tenure-by-stages that characterized the old Punjab Canal Colonies. In 1970, however, it became possible for *gair khatedari* colonists to pledge their land in order to secure loans from recognized institutions.

In one or two small colonies elsewhere tenure was not unlike *gair khatedari* in Rajasthan, and the expectation—and certainly the hope of the colonists—was that a *patta* would be issued in due course. Thus at Kalidindi there were individual leases from the government to the ex-service colonists (individual in spite of the fact that they were grouped in a Co-operative Colonisation Society), but it was clear that no *patta* would be issued till loans were repaid. Inheritance, moreover, was limited to one nominated successor.

More important, tenure in the colonies in Kheri and Pilibhit districts of the UP Tarai approximates to *sirdari* with certain special conditions.[13] In particular, the grantee cannot sublet, transfer, or otherwise alienate his land; must use it only for agricultural purposes; and must express willingness 'to employ improved methods of cultivation' (an undertaking often honoured in the breach), to join a Co-operative Land Settlement Society (but see below), to reside on his land, and not to take up an occupation outside the colonization areas. The land is, however, heritable according to UP Law.

The two classes of tenure so far considered, taking a rather broad view and using UP terminology, represent respectively the *bhumidari* and *sirdari* variants of what has here been dubbed 'reformed *ryotwari*' tenure. They account for about three-quarters of the holdings in the author's 1963 sample. This is an index of the degree of assimilation, in theory at any rate, of colony tenure to Indian land reforms, or, rather to those limited aspects of land reform concerned with the abolition of intermediaries and associated measures. The proportion in 1972 may well be even higher, particularly because of colonization in Rajasthan.

Leases from government of more than one year, but without declared intention to introduce 'reformed ryotwari' *tenure*

Some 10 per cent of the colonists in the author's 1963 sample held their land on leases of a term longer than one year; roughly the same percentage may well apply in 1972. In spite of the evident desire of state governments to assimilate tenures to 'reformed *ryotwari*', these colonists seemed to have no expectation of a *patta*, and were in some cases subject to more onerous conditions than any in the preceding class. Clearly these methods of holding land shade into such tenures as *gair khatedari*; and it may be that, unknown to the author at the time of his fieldwork, it was the intention ultimately to work towards the issue of *pattas*, with or without an intermediate stage like *gair khatedari*.

This class need not be given much space, but includes some interesting but diverse instances. Thus at the Mukkali tribal colony in the Attapaddy Valley, Kerala, colonists held land on lease from the government subject to the conditions that they must live and work on their land, and that transfer and mortgage were forbidden. There was no condition on succession: 'tribal custom will be respected', the author was told. In the High Ranges colonies in the same state, there was 'no formal lease', but the understanding was that tenure was permanent and heritable but succession limited to one heir. In the third main colonization area in Kerala, that in Wynad, tenure was even more uncertain; indeed, discussion of it is best postponed until the section headed 'Procrastination, Confusion, and Frustration'. Not surprisingly, it is in Kerala that these wayward and anomalous tenures are to be found. As the 1961 Census report so wisely remarks:

> 'Throughout the evolution of land tenures in Kerala they consisted of a horde of rights on land varying from absolute proprietary ownership to the most transient form of tenancy devoid of all security. Having arisen time after time by causes political, sacerdotal and economic, these tenures surpass those of the rest of India in the immensity of their variety.[14]

It is, indeed, also not surprising that the Census tabulation of tenures into the broad types outlined at the beginning of the previous section does not include Kerala; or that the list of local names of tenures from government is long and complicated. Veritably land tenure in Kerala is a jungle more impenetrable than that of Wynad. But the pressure for 'land for the tiller' is strong, very strong in Kerala, and the colonists are articulate and forceful. Not unexpectedly the coalition government of November 1969 announced, as part of a programme of land for the landless, that *pattas* would be issued to peasant colonists in the High Ranges (though the conditions, if any, were unclear).[15]

Kerala people far from Kerala carry their traits with them. Those in the unhappy colony at Intikheri (Madhya Pradesh) were no exception. Because of their large debts to the government, they were not given the state's *bhumiswami* tenure, though they were said to have some form of *patta* one of whose conditions was that the land could not be sold or mortgaged. Their debts at the time of the author's visit totalled Rs.185,105 (for 200 colonists); which did not prevent their Co-operative Society asking for more: '. . . as a guilty girl crying to her father, the Intikheri Society comes with realization of great danger to request your honour for kindly granting wheat seed and fertilisers only for this year.'

Also in Madhya Pradesh, the Irrigation Department auctioned leases (with terms well short of *bhumiswami*) in certain flooded lands on the Chambal Right Bank; while Kansal Banjara colonists held on a five-year lease before winning the option of *bhumiswami*. And it was one of the complaints of the efficient Thengumarahada Society that its lease from the state government for some reason ran only for five-year stretches. It is remarkable that the Society had reached such a high level of achievement with such insecure tenure (see above, pp. 165–6).

Lastly, the colonists in the Naini Tal District of the UP Tarai were worse off than those in the Kheri and Pilibhit Districts, for they held their land under the Government Grants Act, No. 15 of 1895, and, while their rights were heritable, they were not otherwise transferable. Moreover, as the 1961 Census Report makes clear, 'all land in the Tarai (Kicha tehsil of Naini Tal district) . . . is Government Estate and the landholders . . . are merely lessees of Government, as neither the rural nor the urban Zamindari Abolition Acts has so far been made applicable to the areas'.[16] The reason for this state of affairs is not clear, but it was understood in 1971 that tenures were to be assimilated to state norms.

Annual Leases

Even more insecure were colonists (some 12 per cent of the author's 1963 sample, probably more in 1972) whose lands had been allotted to them but whose tenure was technically at any rate on a year-to-year basis; thus they were in effect no more than tenants-at-will of the state. This situation applied to all the colonies visited in Assam. There were also restrictions there on succession, and transfer or mortgage was forbidden. If complexity is the Keralian evil, the annual lease is the Assamese. The 1961 Census shows that in the state generally there is an abnormal number of tenants on annual lease: in fact, no fewer than 770,000 persons hold an annual lease compared with 1,450,000 on some more secure tenure.[17] As the 1961 Census report rightly says, 'Even Government land held on a temporary basis is inconsistent with improved agriculture and, as far as possible, settlement of all Government lands should be made on a permanent basis.'[18]

It may be remembered that the colonists in the Rajasthan Canal scheme include landless persons from Rajasthan villages, including those in the Canal area. These were originally given land on an *eksali* basis, that is, for a period of one year only. While these temporary leases could be renewed, and while it is argued by the authorities that this is a means of bringing land quickly into cultivation, there is clearly no encouragement to intensive use. Indeed, families on this basis seen in the Anupgarh area in 1972 were living in nothing more than temporary houses; and some seemed to be practising a sort of nomadic cultivation, moving to and from their old villages on camels. There was a great deal of dissatisfaction with *eksali* leases. By May 1972, however, the Revenue (Colonisation) Department was assuring the author that the land so leased would 'soon be allotted permanently'.

Assam and Rajasthan were not, however, the only culprits. Some of the land under the Chambal Right Bank canal in Madhya Pradesh was on annual lease, as was part of the reclaimed ravined area along the same river and in the same state, pending, it was said, policy decisions on the future tenure. The same applied in the Gundrai colony and among colonists, other than Bhopalis and Keralians, at Intikheri. Perhaps procrastination, or at any rate indecision, is the Madhya Pradesh evil.

Finally, the Tibetan colonists at Bylakuppe (Mysore) held on annual lease for five years before gaining the option of a *patta* if their cultivation and occupance were satisfactory.

Co-operative Forms of Tenure

Three basic types of Co-operative Society hold land in India.

(1) Co-operative Tenant Farming Societies hold land from the state (or sometimes from a private party) and lease it to cultivators for individual cultivation;

(2) Co-operative Joint Farming Societies hold land pooled by individual cultivators for joint cultivation by them, each man usually drawing wages related to the amount of work he has put in and dividend (if the Society declares one) related to the amount of land he has pooled (and over which he retains his rights);

(3) Co-operative Collective Farming Societies hold land, in which no individual retains rights, for joint cultivation, each cultivator's earnings being related only to his labour.[19]

All three types of Society have been concerned with colonization, but to a surprisingly small extent given the emphasis on co-operative tenure and operation in Indian writing, policy and planning and, in particular, the role of colonization that has from time to time been assigned to them. The only formally co-operative tenures in schemes visited by the author were as follows (and all, with the exception of Sardapuri, were small).

Co-operative Tenant Farming Societies at Arwatagi and Kambaraganavi (Mysore);[20] and at Moranam and Thengumarahada (Tamil Nadu), where the Societies were called respectively 'Co-operative Agricultural Colonization Society' and 'Co-operative Farming Society', but where both were operationally Tenant Societies.[21] The Moranam Society was dormant by 1972.

Co-operative Joint Farming Societies were operating (though not always under that title) at Velakapuram in Tamil Nadu, at Palasgaon in Maharashtra, at Piduguralla in Andhra Pradesh, and among three small groups in Pilibhit, UP Tarai, and a similar number formed from Hirakud oustees, Orissa.

Co-operative Collective Farming Societies were confined to Maharashtra (two at Bhamer, and one each at Sindewahi, Amalner, and Pabal), apart from the Bhoodan colony at Sardapuri in the UP Tarai. (By 1963 Maharashtra was registering only Collective and Joint Farming Societies, not Tenant or Better Farming Societies.)

Altogether, these accounted for only some 900 colonists (of whom 350 were at Sardapuri) and thus for under 2 per cent of those in the author's 1963 sample. The proportion today is probably no higher.

This astonishingly low figure does *not* include a number of institutions which might, at first sight, be thought to involve co-operative tenure:[22] for example, Land Colonisation Societies which were not even Tenant Farming Societies, but whose members held land individually from the state, as in a number of small colonies in Andhra Pradesh; and societies ostensibly practising co-operative tenure, but in fact existing only on paper or in shadowy form. This was the case of the Kerala colonists at Intikheri, Madhya Pradesh; or of no less than eleven societies of settlers under the Bhakra Canal, Rajasthan; or of a group of largely absent entrepreneurs who had obtained land under the same Canal in Haryana in order to grow long-staple cotton—which they were doing very well, but in fact on a private family estate masquerading as a co-operative.[23]

The following cases were also excluded. There were fifteen Joint Farming Societies in Wynad in 1963; but they had a total of only 200 members, pooled wet land only, and tenure in the colony had not been regularized. There were also in 1963 six groups amongst refugee colonists in the Paralkote Zone of Dandakaranya to practise what was described as 'group cultivation'; and 1,027 similar colonists who had been installed for a year in the Malkangiri Zone, and who had not been allotted individual holdings but had been cultivating jointly. These Dandakaranya colonists have not been included because the system was experimental and controversial, and had not been formalized (that is, the cultivating groups were not formally Joint Farming or Collective Farming Societies subject to Union and state laws on co-operatives and holding land from the state on some officially recognized tenure); and, as has been said, the long-term intention seemed to be to give the colonists a *patta* when their administration has been handed over to the state government concerned, though some officials saw group cultivation as a transition to joint farming, with regularization in terms of the issue of a *patta* to Societies, not individuals. By 1972 group cultivation had been largely abandoned, except as a temporary expedient in the first year of resettlement.

However, even if one includes the Wynad wet-land joint-farmers and the Dandakaranya group-cultivators, the total number of colonists subject to a co-operative form of tenure in 1963 would still only be some 4 per cent of the author's sample.

Size of Holdings and the 'Economic Unit'

The sizes of the holdings in the several colonies are tabulated in the Appendix.[24] Several points emerge.

First, there is the lack of very large holdings; though it is true that the word 'Variable' in the table conceals some holdings of fair size by local standards. Thus on the Chambal Right Bank in Madhya Pradesh, where the norm is a holding of not more than 8 hectares of dry land (for *jowar*) or not more than 4 hectares of irrigated land, a maharaja and an ex-army officer had each been allotted 70·8 hectares. Again, in the Rajannagar oustee colony (Tamil Nadu) where many colonists held as little as 0·8 hectares, one held 12·1 hectares (the then state maximum). (The reader will not, of course, be misled by the large totals recorded in the Appendix against the several Co-operative Joint Farming and Collective colonies; one has only to divide the total by the number of member-colonists to see that the land *per capita* is in most of these cases low—only 0·4 hectares of actually cultivated land at Sindewahi.)

Rajannagar also illustrates the second point, that the entry 'Variable' frequently occurs against oustee colonies. This is, of course, because the compensatory holding allotted in these colonies is not uniform as between individuals, but is related to the holding of each in the villages from which they have been ousted. However, 'Variable' occurs against Kaki (Assam) for quite different reasons: that there was variation in initial allotments (in spite of the statement by the Programme Evaluation Organisation that settlers were uniformly allotted 3·2 hectares, except for one who was given only 2·7 hectares);[25] and because of further irregularities that must be mentioned later. It will also be noted that in the schemes in Naini Tal District of UP Tarai there was considerable (though in this case regular) variation in the size of holding allotted not only between but also within the several categories of colonist. It was not always clear in the field why some, say, refugees got 3·0 hectares and others 6·1 hectares; though one 'political sufferer' said that most of the 'illiterate' in his category got 6·1 hectares or less, while graduates got 6·1 hectares and those with post-graduate or legal qualifications got 20·2 hectares.

Otherwise egalitarianism within any given colony was the rule, as is not surprising given the ethos of the 'socialist pattern of society'.[26] There was certainly no attempt, like that made in the Punjab Canal Colonies of British days, to put in larger landholders to provide 'leadership', an idea that was reflected in the writings of D. S. Senanayake in Ceylon and at one time influenced colonization policy there.[27] Indeed, in the Tarai colony just cited 'it was specially kept in view that settlers of one particular category are allotted land in one village to preserve homogeneity, and to avoid misunderstandings among them'.[28] The variable holdings and variable social composition of some oustee colonies did, however, provide scope for at least innovatory leadership. Thus at Rajannagar the holder of the maximum holding mentioned above was president of the *panchayat*, and lived in a good house with high-quality farm-buildings; he employed ten regular labourers, had three wells fitted with electric pumps, and used nothing but improved varieties of seeds. Here, once again, is a familiar Indian phenomenon: that the innovator is often the man who is already better off than his fellow-villagers. In this connection it is also pertinent to cite a report from Rajasthan. In spite of the fact that the state government fixed ceilings on land holdings in 1963, it announced in November 1967 that, 'to boost land development and agricultural production in the State' it was prepared to allot ravine land along the Chambal and its tributaries up to a maximum of 40·8 hectares, the ceiling not being applicable.[29]

Thirdly, it will perhaps be thought that some units of allotment are very small; no more than 2 hectares, with 0·4 hectares or a little more of wet land (not always irrigable) in several of the colonies in Andhra Pradesh, at Moranam (Tamil Nadu), and in the High Ranges colonies of Kerala (in the Deviyar colony there the figure was 0·8 hectares and there was agitation for more); 0·8 hectares of paddy-land and 0·4 hectares of dry land (with a further 0·4 hectares of orchard yet to come) at Thengumarahada; and 1·6–3·2 hectares in the Malnad colonies of Mysore. But these were all primarily paddy-growing colonies, with the possibility in most cases of double cropping; and the holdings do not compare unfavourably with those in paddy-growing colonies outside India, notably those in Ceylon (where a standard unit of 2·0 hectares of paddy-land and 1·2 hectares of high, or unirrigable land was the rule until 1953, when a 1·2 hectare/0·4- or 0·8-hectare holding was substituted),[30] or in Sabah, where there are 1·2- and 2·0-hectare paddy lots.[31] There were, however, complaints that 2·0-hectare holdings in the Araku Valley were 'too small'.

Fourthly, there is a clear difference between these apparently small paddy-based holdings and the larger holdings that obtain in the north, where, though paddy may be grown in *kharif*, wheat is the *rabi* food-crop, with *jowar* or *bajra*. Note, for example, the 4·0-hectare allotment for landless colonists in the UP Tarai; the standard unit of 6·32 hectares of irrigated land under the Bhakra Canal in Rajasthan;[32] and the 12·65 hectares advocated as the standard allotment of irrigated land under the Rajasthan Canal in the same state (but see below, pp. 239–40). There is, indeed, no case whatsoever for a uniform all-India allotment of the sort sometimes advocated in proposals for nation-wide colonization.[33]

Now, in Ceylon and elsewhere there has been much debate about the size of holding which constitutes an 'economic unit' in colonization schemes. As the author has shown, however, there has been 'little thorough investigation of the matter';[34] and much confusion about the definition to be applied: whether it should be 'the amount cultivable by means of the unaided efforts of the peasant family' or 'the area which would provide an adequate livelihood for such a family'. More recent writings have to some extent clarified the issues, while adding a third definition—the unit tending to maximize productivity.[35] It will be appreciated that an 'economic unit' based on one definition will not necessarily be identical to that based on another; thus the amount cultivable by a peasant family may or may not be more than is necessary for subsistence or for any other given standard of living (the standards of living, like standards of agricultural technology, are rarely specified in these debates); and both may differ from the amount that provides the maximum stimulus to productivity per man-hour or per hectare. Since undertaking the work on Ceylon which prompted these reflections, the author has become all the more aware that he is dealing with a fluid situation, in which one or more of such parameters as crop yields, technology, and expectations of living standards may be in process of change. For a given set of natural conditions, then, and for a given criterion, there can be no fixed and immutable 'economic unit', the same for all time. Yet there is a practical problem here for the administrator of colonization schemes, who has to fix a unit of allotment somehow; whereas his colleague working in long-established villages cannot hope to convert all the holdings to some notional and constant 'economic' size—at least, not in a South Asian context, where, quite apart from other considerations, there is just not enough land to go round. A. W. Ashby recognized that the size of a holding (and he was too pragmatic to call it an 'economic unit') depended on many factors, but that it should be large enough to provide a settler with a standard of living at least as high as that of existing farmers, but not much higher, if jealousies between established farmers and 'prosperous settlers' were to be avoided.[36] This, however, is not enough, as will shortly be suggested.

What of the discussion in India? Sir Malcolm Darling emphasized, as if to underline Ashby's point, the contrast in size of holding between a Punjab Canal Colony and an ordinary district, and the consequent greater prosperity and freedom from debt of the colonist.[37] He concluded that 'to live with his family in some measure of comfort an arable farmer in the Punjab requires from ten to fifteen acreas [4·0 to 6·1 hectares] of irrigated land'. But Darling's conclusion was based on experience a long time ago (he was writing on 'the economic holding' in 1927); and not many areas of post-independence colonization in India can compare with the Punjab Canal Colonies in terms of physical conditions.

One area that can be so compared is, of course, that under the Bhakra and Rajasthan Canals in Rajasthan. Here there has certainly been controversy about the optimum size of holdings. As indicated above, the standard irrigated holding in colonies under the Bhakra Canal was 6·32 hectares. The Central Regional and Urban Planning Organisation of the Ministry of Health, Government of India, considered that the same unit of allotment (or four times that unit on *barani* or unirrigated land) would suffice for land to be opened up under the Rajasthan Canal, on the grounds that this would yield a colonist a net income of Rs.1,200–1,300 *per annum* at the then (1962) levels of productivity and more with technical improvements in the offing.[38] This conclusion was based on data collected in the Gang Canal Colony in 1958, thirty years after irrigation reached it. The Colonisation Commissioner, Rajasthan, drew attention to the reduction in the size of holdings that had taken place in this period as a result of inheritance and other factors, and thought that a larger holding (of 12·65 hectares of irrigated land, or 39·74 hectares of *barani*) would not only allow of future subdivision but also provide a more acceptable standard of living, keep a family fully employed, and permit of mechanization. He further held that a 6·32-hectare holding would be unable to support a family during early years of non-perennial irrigation. Here, clearly, is a whole range of criteria, but no mention of stimulus to productivity, and a new source of contradiction—for a holding that keeps a family 'fully employed' with existing technology is unlikely to do so under mechanization; yet the Commissioner in another passage sets his face against the possibility of finding enough employment for those displaced from agriculture. Actually the holding was fixed at 6·32 hectares.

In Dandakaranya 2·02 hectares per family was accepted in the Preliminary Project Report as the basis of calculation—for undisclosed and perhaps undiscussed reasons.[39] The Revised Project Report, again for undisclosed reasons, used 2·83 hectares per family as a basis for calculations in the case of both refugee and tribal colonists. In the event, the standard unirrigated allotment was 2·73 hectares *plus* 0·07 hectares of homestead: 2·80 hectares *in toto*.[40]

In a later passage the Revised Project Report states that:

> The experience in the last two or three crop seasons has shown that the settler with only one pair of bullocks and a very short period during which he has to clear his land, put up rice bunds and do his sowing and ploughing, cannot really undertake intensive cultivation of the total area of 6·5 [*sic*] acres [2·63 hectares] which is given to him.[41]

In consequence the new settlers had been compelled to restrict their cultivation to two hectares of land at the most. In 1965–6 the standard unirrigated allotment was in fact reduced to 2·30 hectares, and there was a further reduction to 2·09 hectares in 1971; some settlers on poor soil agitated for a larger holding. There are also proposals to reduce existing holdings to 2·02 hectares, or to 1·62 hectares if more than 0·31 hectares were irrigable, or to 1·21 hectares if the whole holding was perennially irrigable.

Now, there has been considerable discussion in India about the definition of economic holdings in connection with land reforms and with proposals to place a ceiling on holdings.[42] Thus the Uttar Pradesh Zamindari Abolition Committee concluded that an economic holding must provide a 'fair standard of living' and a surplus to provide security in lean years, but also thought in terms of a unit which would, under given conditions of agricultural technology, make for maximum production (a classic instance of having it both ways).[43] They fixed on 4·04 hectares as the standard for their state. If there has been less argument about 'economic holdings' *for colonization schemes* in India than in Ceylon it may be partly because the subject has been considered in connection with land reform rather than with colonization; partly because in India sheer pressure of numbers has forced the authorities to crowd as many as possible into colonization schemes. It is significant that it is only in

Rajasthan and Dandakaranya, with apparently plenty of land in relation to the needs of local people, that the argument has broken out in something recognizably like that long current in Ceylon.

Sheer pressure of men on land is also unlikely, outside the same two areas, to allow for the provision of a holding large enough to be subdivided and to provide an 'economic unit', on any criterion, for the next generation. Even in these areas such a provision may be very unwise, affording insufficient stimulus to full cultivation and improvement forthwith. In Dandakaranya the next generation may benefit from land that would become available if sizes of holdings were reduced; and from the existence of uncultivated patches rejected on initial soil survey.

Similar considerations, together with the irrelevance of most forms of mechanization to a situation in which there is surplus labour, weigh against the provision of holdings large enough to enable machines to operate, as suggested by the Colonisation Commissioner, Rajasthan. But more must be said on this point in connection with joint farming.

Three other points must be made. First, it is important to reiterate the need for flexibility in the size of holdings, not only between the vastly different regions of India, but also within regions and states, because of differences of soil, crops, water supply and the like, and also because of differences in demand for land, reflecting variations in local man/land ratios.

Secondly, and whatever the man/land ratio, there is much to be said for Ashby's criterion, that the holding in a colonization scheme must be large enough to provide a settler with a standard of living no lower than that of existing farmers (if colonists are to be attracted to confront pioneer conditions) but not very much higher (lest tensions develop between existing farmers and favoured settlers).

Thirdly, and so long as it is consistent with Ashby's point, the holding should not be so large that it cannot all be properly cultivated from an early stage and that it cannot provide some incentive to improvement. As Raj Krishna and associates have sagely observed, there has been much muddled thinking about large holdings in India: they tend to be condemned as inefficient when plantations are concerned, but desirable on grounds of supposed efficiency when joint farming of previously small holdings is envisaged.[44] The real truth is that political arguments here masquerade as economic. The same authors point out with equal wisdom that economies of scale 'do not obtain to the same extent in all operations which are defined to constitute farming'.[45] Indeed, certain operations, notably those concerned with paddy cultivation, tend to become more intensive, and yields per hectare higher, as size of holding diminishes.[46] Much recent work has gone further, and shown for Indian agriculture more generally that gross output per unit area declines with increase in farm-size.[47]

Charges to Colonists for Land and Water

It will be useful at this point to look briefly at charges levied by government authorities on colonists, both because their payment is often a condition of land tenure, and because the adaptation of charges, on a sliding scale or otherwise, to the special problems of pioneer colonists is related to the tenure-by-stages to be considered in the next section.

Given the predominance of the welfare motive in Indian colonization and the large provision that has had to be made for refugees and others without resources, it is not surprising that very little has been required of Indian colonists since independence by way of purchase price for their land or other contribution towards the capital cost of colonization. In fact, the only instances brought to the author's attention were in Assam and in Rajasthan.[48] In the former state, a premium of Rs.720 for each allotment was payable in the Kaki colony. In Rajasthan the requirements were more exacting and the arrangements more complicated (thus what follows has to be a somewhat simplified account). In the Bhakra colonies there was, first, land for sale by public auction (nearly a quarter of the total acreage up to September 1966; and see also above, p. 90). Then some 50 per cent was sold at a fixed reserve price (including an element of 'betterment levy' based on the improvement of land values as a result of the coming of irrigation) payable in instalments on a sliding scale over fifteen years. It will be remembered that *gair khatedari* tenure cannot be converted to *khatedari* until this premium or purchase price has been paid in full. The categories of eligible allottee liable to pay included 'old temporary cultivation lessees'; local landless; ex-servicemen and ex-*jagirdars*. Temporary cultivation lessees who had been on their land for more than 35 years were, however, exempt from premium, though liable to betterment levy (about Rs.200 per *bigha*,[49] in twelve instalments). The premium on irrigated land varied from Rs.200 per *bigha* to Rs.400 according as the soil varied from sandy loam to silt brought down by the Ghaggar floods; but it was only Rs.50 per *bigha* on *barani* land. Under the Rajasthan Canal very similar arrangements were proposed, though with higher prices per *bigha* (Rs.300 to Rs.500 on irrigated land). The levying of these changes was held to be justified by the need of the Rajasthan state government to finance the high costs of canal construction, and, in particular, to repay loans made to it by the Centre, which urged the imposition of betterment levies and enhanced irrigation rates.[50] However, payment of premium has now, like sale by auctions, been abolished, though the betterment levy is retained.

In this, as in other respects, Rajasthan has followed the precedent set by the Punjab Canal Colonies. Under the Punjab Colonization of Government Lands Act, No. 5 of 1912, there was provision for the purchase of land, associated with tenure-by-stages. Proprietary rights could be acquired after 10 years, 5 as tenant-at-will, 5 as occupancy tenant.[51] In effect, Rajasthan practice cuts out the first stage (except for its *eksali* colonists) and lengthens the period of 'probation', with its *gair khatedari* and *khatedari* tenure. Again, the Thal Development Authority in Pakistan, another follower of Old Punjab precedents, levied a purchase price equivalent to Rs.380 for each perennially irrigated hectare, payable in instalments spread over no less than 35 years.[52] There was, again, a progression from tenancy to proprietary rights, a betterment tax (known as the Thal Increase in Value Tax) being levied on the acquisition of the latter.

Proposals for a betterment levy have not been confined to Rajasthan and the Thal. Legislation permitting it was enacted in all Indian states except Uttar Pradesh, West Bengal, and Jammu and Kashmir by the end of the Second Plan period, though enforcement lagged behind.[53] The First Plan in Pakistan recommended a betterment levy on all lands receiving irrigation from new barrages; but, again, implementation has been tardy.[54] The Ceylon Land Commission of 1955–8 thought the time opportune for the introduction of a levy there;[55] but nothing has been done. Indeed, one of the problems facing governments in South Asian countries is the increasing political difficulty of levying, not only betterment taxes, but rural taxation in general, at a time of scarce capital resources.

This is true of land revenue in India, in spite of the long-standing tradition that the government is entitled to a share of the produce of the land.[56] Indeed, by December 1971 land revenue had been abolished in West Bengal on holdings under 1·21 hectares, in Uttar Pradesh on holdings under 2·63 hectares, and in Kerala altogether. Proposals for total or partial abolition were under consideration in Mysore, Orissa, Punjab, Delhi state, Himachal Pradesh, and Tripura. The Planning Commission was examining the whole question of the taxation of agricultural incomes in terms of the substitution of a progressive scale of land revenue, or even of agricultural income tax, for the long-standing land revenue system.

But long before such radical proposals or reforms were under discussion, land in colonization schemes was receiving special treatment. Of the schemes studied in 1963 some were paying no land revenue because a survey had not yet been made, as in the Araku

Valley; or because of difficulties over title, as at Jamunia; or because of failure to complete formalities, as in the High Ranges of Kerala; or because the colony was still being administered by a Development Authority and had not yet been handed over to a state government which could levy revenue, as in the whole Dandakaranya project (this was still the position in Dandakaranya in 1972). The first three cases fall under the category of 'procrastination, confusion, and frustration' to be considered a little later on; while the situation in Dandakaranya is clearly a consequence of the colonization process when it is undertaken on such a large and inter-state scale, since the necessity for a Development Authority carries with it the necessity for a stage in which there is no settlement of either tenure or revenue with a state government.

There were other and different cases of deliberate exemption from the payment of land revenue while colonization was in an early stage, or of the institution of payment on a sliding (sometimes a gently sliding) scale. Thus Aminabad and Piduguralla, both in Andhra Pradesh, were exempt for ten and five years respectively; Sindewahi and Amalner in Maharashtra were exempt for five years; the small Mysore colonies were exempt for periods that varied, for reasons that were not very clear, from three to five years, with rent under *eksali* tenure, that is, annual lease substituted in one case; the Madhya Pradesh colonies generally operated a sliding scale whose terms varied from scheme to scheme; and the UP Tarai colonies in Kheri and Pilibhit Districts paid zero, one-third, two-thirds, and full revenue in successive years from the first onwards. Clearly exemption from land revenue forms another sort of aid to colonists for so long as land revenue is generally levied; and the considerations advanced in chapter 10 apply here too. These, it may be remembered, include the need for flexibility. But one wonders, particularly in view of the variation between apparently similar colonies, whether sufficient thought had been given to revenue exemption in relation to the level of other forms of assistance and to the criteria that should be applied to assistance as a whole.

In certain colonies it appeared that assistance by revenue exemption was to continue indefinitely, for settled revenue rates were very low: only Rs.5 per hectare in Wynad and at Moranam (all land in the latter being assessed as though dry); while at Kotia Pani in Madhya Pradesh the rate was no more than Rs.1·25 to Rs.2·50 for black soil. The rationale was not always obvious (though Kotia Pani was a tribal colony).

On the other hand there was no evident exemption from the normal level of land revenue in Assam (1968) and Haryana, nor in certain schemes such as Rajannagar and Velakapuram.

Finally, a brief word may be said about irrigation rates. Not all colonies supplied with public irrigation paid these rates; thus some colonists (as at Moranam, just cited) benefit from yet another form of special assistance. In other cases a water cess was merged with the land revenue. In those cases where a separate irrigation charge was levied, no special concession seems to have been made for the fact that it is pioneer colonists who are being charged. In Haryana and Rajasthan, colonists paid the normal rate, varying with the crop (for example, under the Bhakra Canal in Rajasthan varying from Rs.11·05 per hectare for gram and Rs.12·03 for *bajra* to Rs.24·09 for rice and Rs.40·77 for sugar-cane). There were also separate irrigation charges under the Chambal Right Bank Canal and at Intikheri in Madhya Pradesh and in such irrigated land as there was in the UP Tarai of Naini Tal District.

Tenure-by-Stages

The time has now come to draw together the threads of the argument over certain important issues. The first of these is the concept of tenure-by-stages in its special application and applicability to colonization schemes. The concept will be familiar from what has been said in the description both of tenures and of revenue charges; and there is no need to recapitulate the list of Indian colonies to which it applies.

Tenure-by-stages, especially if coupled with a sliding scale for the gradual introduction of charges, has considerable advantages: to the colonist, because it provides him with an additional form of initial assistance (though that does not prevent him from calling loudly for the best of both worlds—for a *patta* at once but full revenue charges in the distant future, or never); to the state, because it provides a period of probation, as it were, during which the colonist can prove his mettle as a cultivator and discharge his obligations (if any) by way of loans, premiums and so on. But these advantages are not infrequently somewhat theoretical—for example, when through shiftlessness, ill-fortune, or adverse natural conditions loans cannot be, or at any rate are not repaid, and (as among the Kerala colonists at Intikheri) colonists are left charged with dissatisfaction at the withholding of full tenure (in this case *bhumiswami*), while the state is left without its repayments and has little hope of recovering them.

Tenure-by-stages is familiar, too, from numerous examples outside India. In some of the Punjab Canal Colonies, for example, there was the progression from tenants-at-will to occupancy rights to proprietary rights.[57] The system in the Thal colonization scheme in

Pakistan was closely modelled on the Punjab precedent.[58] In Ceylon colonists were first given a 'permit', and gained a grant under the Land Development Ordinance only when they had fulfilled a number of conditions;[59] but it was a frequent cause of complaint that the transition from permit to grant was unduly delayed because of administrative shortcomings.

Procrastination, Confusion, and Frustration

It is, unfortunately, to a series of administrative shortcomings that attention must now be directed. Some of these have already been mentioned in this chapter: for example, the apparently unnecessary, yet strangely uninhibiting insecurity of tenure of the Co-operative Society at Thengumarahada; the procrastination and indecision about future tenure so widespread in Madhya Pradesh (though it may be said in partial extenuation that that state was formed from previously distinct political units as late as 1956 and has had a hard row to hoe); the lack of survey and consequent lack of certain tenure in the Araku Valley; and the *eksali* leases in Rajasthan. Other cases already mentioned demand a little elaboration.

The tenure in the Wynad colonies was uncertain because of a stalemate in a prolonged tussle between the colonists and the government (first of Madras, in which Wynad originally fell, then of Kerala). The order went forth from Madras as early as 1945 that the colony was to be organized on co-operative lines, and this fiat has been repeated on subsequent occasions, notably in 1948, 1954, and 1957. In 1954, in fact, the then Madras government 'ordered [*sic*] that a Land Colonisation Co-operative Society should be formed for Ex-servicemen colonists'. But the six Societies that were formed did not last and the colonists repeatedly clamoured for individual tenure. Some of them did, however, form Joint Farming Societies in 1962 to cultivate wet land, as has already been mentioned. But their real motive, the author was told on the spot, was to qualify for government subsidies, and the clamour was still for a *patta*. But stalemate, and hence uncertainty and confusion over tenure, persisted.

The irregularities in the administration of the Kaki colony in Assam, already mentioned, were of a very serious nature. Delays in gaining possession of land allotted, referred to by the Programme Evaluation Organisation, were the least of the troubles of the colony.[60] At the time of the author's fieldwork (1968) it had come to light that a number of allottees had been given more than one plot (one of them was the innovating entrepreneur mentioned on p. 175); in other cases a number of relatives had adjacent plots, only one of them being in residence and working the whole as a single small estate. The state government had had its attention drawn to the unsatisfactory state of affairs. It proposed to inquire into the whole situation in the colony, and, where irregularities were proven, to redistribute land to the needy. Meanwhile, a number of government officers and minor staff had been transferred and new staff (in particular new surveyors) brought in. In another Assam colony, that at Baghbar, such serious irregularities had not been suspected, but there had certainly been faulty demarcation of plots, with the result that some colonists received only six *bighas* instead of ten,[61] and there were constant land disputes and bickerings over boundaries.

There was also trouble, of a different nature, at Jamunia in Bihar, where, it may be remembered, colonists were settled on land that had been reclaimed from a gullied area in the Rajmahal Hills. The colony area is cheek-by-jowl with existing villages; and reclamation was (or so it was said) irrespective of previous occupance of the gullied land. A number of men in the old villages claimed land that had been cleared and allotted to colonists. Only the better land was claimed: 'the rubbish was left to the colony', the author's field notebook has it. Altogether some very ugly disputes, completely frustrating to development, had broken out.

Uncertainties of tenure and disputes or muddles over boundaries or titles are not only inhibiting to land development and to application of the inputs necessary to agricultural improvement, but make it difficult if not impossible for colonists to raise credit. This was not only the case in the glaring instances just cited, but also in colonies where the tenure had not yet been regularized for reasons that stood more serious examination: for example, in Dandakaranya.

Reference must also be made to cases unearthed by the Programme Evaluation Organisation in its study of selected colonies. Thus it reports delay in starting the selection of colonists in the Kheri and Pilibhit areas of UP Tarai because the state government could not decide whether to allot land individually or collectively.[62] Again, in surveys of culturable waste in Guna District of Madhya Pradesh, the quality of investigating staff was reported to be weak, and subject to the blandishments of influential local leaders who sought to exclude the maximum amount of culturable waste from the survey lest it be allotted to the local landless and so weaken the leaders' relative standing.[63] There were also irregularities in allotments in the same District.[64]

Colonists' Breaches of Conditions of Tenure Officially Imposed

Other problems in Indian colonization schemes arise, not from administrative shortcomings, but as a result of the reaction of colonists to certain of the provisions of the regular systems of tenure legally in force. In a very real sense, the more efficient the administration of these systems, the stronger this reaction; and certain of the problems to be mentioned are problems only if seen from the standpoint of an administration seeking fully to enforce its regulations.

It will be remembered that in a number of colonies there is an embargo on leasing. It will not surprise those familiar with the Indian (and not only the Indian) scene to learn that on several occasions during his fieldwork the author was told about evasion of this restriction;[65] though naturally enough it was not easy to establish proof. Thus in the High Ranges Colony in Kerala, there seemed to be a great amount of leasing: indeed, a Special Deputy *Tehsildar* had been appointed to try to deal with the matter. No doubt the practice was encouraged by the relatively generous size of allotment, and stimulated by the general land hunger in the state. The 'ex-criminal' tribesmen of Mircabad, Madhya Pradesh, were also alleged to be leasing their land (though here, deep in a remote area, there cannot have been so much pressure on land), probably because of their preference for pursuits more exciting than serious cultivation. At Rajannagar, again, there was said to be leasing of land, no doubt by those oustees with relatively large holdings.

Whether leasing in breach of conditions is an evil depends on one's point of view, and on the precise circumstances. To the official (when he is speaking officially, at any rate) all breaches of regulations are an evil. To some doctrinaire theoreticians, the leasing of land is tantamount to landlordism, and therefore evil. But the leasing of a morsel of land by a two-hectare holder on uncertain tenure from government in the High Ranges of Kerala is hardly landlordism, unless (and this is inherently unlikely there) the lessee is adding a parcel of leased land to his already large holding. Nor is the result necessarily the inefficient cultivation sometimes thought to stem from a system of tenancy (especially in the absence of share-cropping): two men are more likely to cultivate intensively on a two-hectare plot than one, and the overall yield per unit area may well be higher as a result. And, in the process, a little underemployment has been mopped up. Leasing of the Mircabad type is another matter, especially if one is thinking in terms of the rehabilitation of the errant tribesman through the cleansing power of agricultural labour: but that may be a forlorn hope anyway.

As for the evasion of restrictions on longer-term or permanent transfer, by sale or through a creditor foreclosing on the land, one heard few complaints from officials and few other whispers that this was taking place on a wide scale: perhaps because of the youth of so many of the colonies; perhaps also because such transfer is less often attempted than short-term leasing because it is in the long run harder to conceal (one can always pass off a lessee as one's labourer). There were, however, more generally rumours of concealed alienation in the Naini Tal Tarai colonies (UP). There were hints that free transferability would be more popular than restricted, partly because it would make it easier to raise credit on the security of the land. Thus the president of the *panchayat* at Aminabad (Andhra Pradesh) hoped that, when his people received *pattas*, they would include freedom to alienate. Asked whether he did not fear that this freedom would mean the permanent loss of land by some tribal colonists, he claimed that they would eventually redeem their land. (The cynic will deduce that he was a big man with an interest in the acquisition of his neighbour's land.) Whatever force there may be in the *panchayat* president's views, complete freedom of alienation in many parts of contemporary India would undoubtedly mean that the big men grew bigger, and the small men smaller; though to a less extent in the relatively egalitarian colonization schemes than in the country at large. Free alienation with a ceiling on holdings is theoretically possible; but ceilings are easy to evade, as recent Indian experience has shown. Another theoretical solution is to allow a free market in land, with the inevitable concentration in fewer hands that would follow, but perhaps with favourable economic results in terms of increased inputs and capital investment; and then to help the landless labourer by enforcing minimum wage laws or regulations. But it has to be admitted that the chances of effective enforcement are small in the Indian context. For the present then, and in areas where the poor are likely to suffer, a ban on transfer in colonization schemes may be easier to enforce, and necessary to the protection of the poor, whatever may be the longer-term advantages of a freer market.

There was fear of loss of land for a different reason at Moranam, where members of the Agricultural Colonization Society could, on breach of specified conditions, be deprived of their benefits 'by due process', which, though sound as a piece of reasonably benevolent bureaucracy, did not apparently include any right of appeal through the courts.

There can be no doubt at all that the most unpopular restrictions were those on succession, which (as earlier pages will have made clear) were very frequently imposed in colonization schemes and which usually involved inheritance by one nominated or specified successor, all other heirs according to traditional law or custom being barred. Thus at Kalidindi, where succession was limited to a widow or eldest son, the colonists were pressing for the right of equal division. In the High Ranges colonies in Kerala, there was supposed only to be one successor (in spite of the lack of certainty in the tenure generally) and that nominated by government, the other possible heirs having the right to object. It may be imagined that this procedure seemed calculated to maximize delay, friction, and even fracas (indeed, the example might have been quoted in the previous section). The less sophisticated colonists at Kambaraganavi (Mysore) were also subject to unitary succession, and expressed 'worry over our other sons'.

There can equally be no doubt that restrictions on succession were widely evaded (notwithstanding the youth of many colonies: as they age, succession and therefore evasion will increase). At Piduguralla, dispossessed sons cultivated by what was tactfully described as 'mutual arrangement', but which may well have included *de facto* partition. At Gobindpur and Theka colony (Assam), the eldest son succeeded, but it was admitted by officials, 'We can't stop partition.' At Mircabad *de facto* partition was again alleged. The reason why *de facto* partition is so easily concealed is, of course, that the illegal heirs can readily be passed off as relatives kindly helping with the work; though the true situation is apt, like illegal sale, to come to light in case of a dispute, when documents or *pattas* have to be produced.

Restrictions to prevent inheritance by more than one heir (or by no more heirs than will reduce the holding below the 'economic unit') have clearly become part of orthodox agrarian doctrine.[66] They are, of course, aimed to prevent what is usually described as 'fragmentation', a process which the author prefers to call 'subdivision' to avoid confusion with the separate though often related process of 'parcellization', by which the number of parcels composing each holding increases with time. This process is not dealt with here because it is so far almost inoperative in post-independence Indian colonization schemes. Restrictions on subdivision rest on three assumptions, often implicit rather than explicit: (1) that it is the laws of inheritance that 'cause' subdivision; (2) that there are economies of scale such that the continued subdivision of holdings is undesirable in the interests of productivity; and (3) that subdivided holdings yield smaller net incomes to the cultivator than undivided holdings, and in the fullness of time incomes that are unacceptably low.

The third assumption, it must be said at once, is indisputable; and low net incomes mean shortage of funds for the purchase of inputs such as fertilizers and of capital for improvements. They also spell vulnerability to exploitation or to buying-out by wealthier men.

As for the first assumption, the author has held elsewhere that:

... subdivision of holdings springs not so much from laws of inheritance associated with this or that religious or social system as from a particular economic and demographic situation. Given a static population, or given economic growth sufficient to draw a growing population from the land, subdivision is unlikely to cause much of a problem whatever the laws of inheritance.[67]

On the second assumption, enough has been said already in this chapter.

Arguments for the legislative or administrative control of subdivision tend to be accepted too uncritically. The urge to subdivide, the concern for the security that can be conceived only in terms of the possession of a plot of land, however small, is part of a rural 'culture of poverty'.[68] No conceivable intensity of cultivation, no conceivable improvement in technology, can make each of the fractions of a plot divided between four sons yield an income as high as that derived from the undivided plot. And, as Warriner observes, subdivision is still a great obstacle to the accumulation of wealth.[69] But so few authors or officials go on to ask what is to be the state of the dispossessed sons if only one can inherit. In the absence of an alternative means of livelihood (and whence is this to come in contemporary India?) the result can only be a living for some, but insecurity, cruel poverty, and unemployment for others. It is completely unrealistic for the assembled experts of the Food and Agriculture Organization to talk of compensation for the dispossessed.[70] The control of fragmentation in this situation, a situation in which to hang on to land is a desperate need, is not a recipe for putting an end to poverty or unemployment, or for diminishing inequalities of income. The only recipe is the creation of sufficient alternative means of livelihood.

If one thinks in terms of poverty and employment, if one takes a peasant's-eye view from the culture of poverty, it is indeed a godsend that evasion of rules designed to prevent subdivision remains undetected or at least unenforced (because unenforceable). Efficient enforcement could only spell growing poverty, growing inequality, family disputes, and mounting discontent, given the present demographic and economic context in India: for population presses inexorably on land, and means of livelihood become harder and harder to find (though, admittedly, these pressures are less in colonization schemes which start with an allotment of land that is larger than is usual in the locality).

Here one stands face to face with one of the many dilemmas of Indian economic and social development: that to form and apply capital in agriculture appears to demand the preservation of large holdings, if not the creation of larger; but that, to provide a living for the poor and contain discontents that may well otherwise get out of hand demands that there should be no control on subdivision. Or, as Mogens Boserup puts it, the widespread belief in a labour surplus prevents 'rationalization of the agrarian structure', for fear of aggravating unemployment; and 'the aim of protecting the economically weak tends to come into conflict with the aim of rationalizing the productive structure of agriculture'.[71]

The author sees no ready way out of this position. On balance, however, and strictly with reference to the Indian colonization schemes he has studied, he is against the general application of a bar on succession designed to prevent subdivision of holdings. There may in future, perhaps in some areas at present, be circumstances which would make such a bar desirable: for example, to give a final incentive to a peasantry underemployed on the land for whom work exists elsewhere; or to help to preserve larger parcels of land where these are indisputably desirable on all important economic and social grounds. But there is no evidence that conditions of this sort obtain in contemporary Indian colonization schemes.

Co-operative Tenures in Colonization Schemes

It is not intended here to reopen the general debate on co-operative and collective farming which caused such a flurry in India some years ago; which let loose a torrent of writing more polemic than scholarly, and, where apparently scholarly, more deductive (from premises that do not always stand up to serious scrutiny) than empirical;[72] and which seems now to have lost most of its momentum (though there have been recent re-statements of the case for co-operative farming by V. V. Giri and M. S. Swaminathan, and qualified support from the late Doreen Warriner).[73] Most of the discussion that follows will refer principally to co-operative cultivation in relation to colonization schemes; though it is of some importance to set this in a wider context.

It is well to begin with a historical excursus, since in an earlier chapter no more than passing reference could be made to the historical roots of argument and action on co-operative tenures (see above, pp. 96–7).

The history of writing and of experimentation on co-operative cultivation goes back well before independence. As early as 1907–9 Gandhi, Tagore, Ananda K. Coomaraswamy, and others were expounding the merits of what they conceived of as a return to the pristine co-operative Indian village community (though Tagore differed from Gandhi by thinking in terms of a community that would use machinery and modern agricultural methods); and studies on co-operative farming in West Bengal were launched from Shantiniketan.[74] Prescriptions for the present, based on idealizations of the past are not, of course, confined to India. In India, they owe a great deal to the writings of such authors as Sir Henry Maine on the Indian village community that had held all things in common.[75] The idea of a return to a supposed untainted pattern of communal land tenure was to be a strong thread running through the later teaching of Gandhi, and on into that of Vinoba Bhave (whose Bhoodan and Gramdan movements pressed for communal tenure of land surrendered for redistribution), and of V. V. Giri in his advocacy of 'Gardens of Eden' on wastelands which should be 'self-sufficient in all aspects of rural life and economy' and hold land communally.[76]

In Jawaharlal Nehru's thinking, however, a far stronger thread was that derived from Marx. Nehru was impressed by the Russian model, and saw co-operative cultivation as a means, not of return to an ancient rural paradise, but of the modernization of backward agriculture, with its myriad tiny patches of cultivation, in such a way as to secure at one swoop 'greater production, greater cohesion and a progressive removal of class distinction).[77] Other writers, such as H. H. Mann, also drew the attention of the Indians to Russian collective farms.[78] Mann was careful to point out that there were many difficulties in the way of reproducing the Russian pattern in India. But it has been the author's experience that it has made a deep impression there, down to relatively low levels of the official hierarchy, where (usually without appreciation of the source of the concept) 'progress' is seen as movement from individual holdings to joint cultivation and on to full collectivization. At a more sophisticated level, the source is acknowledged, but with many misapprehensions—that, for example, the October Revolution was a peasant revolt which brought in the collective system.[79]

But a far more characteristically Indian formulation is one which intertwines syncretically, and not always consistently, the Gandhian and Marxist strands, and advocates joint farming (though usually not collectivization if that would mean compulsion), *both* to stimulate productivity *and* to create ideal village societies. It seems possible to discern this syncretism in works like that of Tarlok Singh, which, in this field as in others, have had a great influence on Indian thinking and planning (compare above, p. 98).[80] India was not alone here: Robert Chambers has shown how, in the then British East African colonies, there was a post-war stream of group or co-operative schemes 'encouraged by supposed experience outside Africa, by ideology, and by what were believed to be technical considerations'.[81]

India before independence did not lack experiments in the application of these and similar ideas, on wastelands as well as in established villages. R. K. Hallikeri cites examples from as early as 1929–30 in the then Bombay Presidency, some under the sponsorship of H. H. Mann, which were in effect tenant farming societies on the model of those operated in Italy from 1886 onwards.[82] The Arya Samaj settlement at Aryanagar for 'ex-criminal' tribes, already mentioned, was, from 1939, formed into a co-operative society to reclaim land, the colonists receiving wages according to the amount of work put in by each.[83] Collective farming by tribesmen was taken up on 253 hectares of wasteland in the Araku Valley as part of the Grow More Food Campaign.[84] Of more relevance to this book was the order of the then Madras government in 1941 that government wastelands should be issued to co-operatives, and not to individuals; it was this order that was applied to the Wynad colonization scheme in 1945.

In the years before independence there was a good deal of discussion of co-operative tenure in various organs of the Congress Party. It will be remembered that a National Planning Committee was appointed in 1938. Its Sub-Committee on Land Policy, Agricultural Labour and Insurance, reporting in 1948, took up a Congress resolution of December 1936 that 'an effort should be made to introduce co-operative farming'.[85] K. T. Shah, in his introduction to the Report, fell for the myth of vast areas of culturable waste ('perhaps as much as 140 million acres' [57 million hectares]) and suggested that 'compulsory universal co-operative corporations' embracing 'the whole gamut of rural life' might be able to take up specialized farming on an intensive scale and be a more effective way of dealing with fragmentation than the enactment of radical amendments to the laws of inheritance.[86] The Report itself recommended that ownership of all forms of national wealth should be vested in the people of India, and that land should be compulsorily distributed for cultivation among collective or co-operative organizations. Here, clearly, is the hand of Nehru in the application of the Russian model. Later on, however, the Report, in a rather confused passage, seems to envisage co-operative cultivation 'without sacrificing the element of individual property',[87] cultivators sharing produce according to the labour *and capital* provided by each. Here one may see a compromise designed to meet the views of those, like Radhakamal Mukherjee, who were against collectivization and the abolition of private property;[88] Mukherjee thought, too, that India offered limited scope for large-scale mechanization.

Minds met, however, in the culturable wastes, for here there was a *tabula rasa* for the reformers, with no existing property rights to be respected.[89] All cultivation here, it was urged, should be co-operative, if not collective, individual holdings being prohibited by law. Significantly, the National Planning Council endorsed the co-operative principle (for Gandhian as well as Marxist reasons, 'so that agriculture may be conducted more scientifically and efficiently, waste avoided, and production increased, and at the same time mutual co-operation fostered');[90] but with application in the first instance to culturable waste, in which wherever feasible full collectivization should be in force.

The discussion continued after independence; for instance, in connection with the abolition of intermediaries. In UP the Committee on this matter reviewed Russian experience more critically than had some of their predecessors, voicing particular doubt about the wisdom of mechanization, but coming down in favour of voluntary co-operative cultivation (but without particular reference to wasteland).[91]

There were further inquiries and committees, too. Thus in 1956 the Programme Evaluation Organisation studied twenty-two co-operative farming societies, including the Vihad Co-operative Rehabilitation Collective Farming Colony in Chanda District of Maharashtra (which held land from the government, but for individual cultivation by refugees) and the Andhiyur Land Colonization Society in Erode District, Madras (again, for individual cultivation).[92] The aim was to collect information, not to reach conclusions. But it will be noticed that the two examples on wasteland did not involve joint farming. In 1957 an Indian delegation visited China and reported favourably if naïvely on agrarian co-operatives there.[93] The majority of the Committee reiterated support for co-operative farming in India, especially commending co-operatives of landless labourers on government land.[94]

In 1959 the Indian National Congress passed a resolution at its Nagpur meeting which has become well known rather for its political aftermath than its agrarian content. It read:

> The future agrarian pattern should be that of co-operative joint farming in which land will be pooled for joint cultivation, the farmers continuing to retain their property rights and getting a share from the net produce in proportion to their land. Further, those who actually work the land, whether they own land or not, will get a share in proportion to the work put in by them on the joint farm.[95]

The resolution was thus in favour of co-operative joint farming and not of collectivization; and Nehru was at pains to emphasize that compulsion was not contemplated. (None the less, the Swatantra Party, which was created soon after the Nagpur Congress, 'self-consciously set out to exploit the alleged menace of collectivization of agriculture' in spite of its earlier advocacy by some of the Party's leaders.)[96] Margaret Digby observes that 'The actual state of affairs

. . . as described to the Indian Working Group which reported in 1959, or the delegation of German experts who reported in 1960, does not itself give very firm grounds for a change as sweeping as that recommended in the Nagpur resolution.'[97]

The state-by-state review of the Working Group did indeed show that a number of co-operative societies had been established on wastelands (though by no means all of these necessarily involved colonization). According to their Report, in Bombay state most of the 224 Collective Farming Societies and a number of Tenant Farming Societies were operating on former waste: so were 31 Tenant Farming Societies in Madras, together with a few Joint Farming Societies; and most of the 217 Joint Farming Societies and 17 Collective Farming Societies in UP.[98] Elsewhere activity on wastelands was far more sporadic, or apparently absent altogether; and, of course, by no means all the Societies reported were genuine. The Report of the German delegation refers only briefly to societies working on wastelands, suggesting that 'the best conditions for the introduction of co-operative farming exist in new settlements', and that another reason for concentration on wasteland was to secure quick results.[99]

Reports were also produced from time to time by state governments: for instance, by Madras in 1963,[100] with some reference to land colonization co-operatives for ex-servicemen, Harijans, and others.[101] It was again clear that but little practical progress had been made.

The successive Five Year Plans also record official policy on co-operative cultivation: from the First Plan's statement that preference should be given 'to Cooperative Farming Societies in leasing culturable waste land' (this was echoed in State Land Codes, in theory if not to any considerable extent in practice: notably in the case of Madhya Pradesh);[102] through the Third Plan's stress on voluntaryism and on financial inducements to co-operation;[103] to the Fourth Plan's frank recognition of lack of substantial progress but continued commitment to co-operative farming as a means of bringing land together for purposes of cultivation.[104] There remain those who, like Tarlok Singh, have not lost faith in joint farming.[105] And in 1972, although group farming was moribund in Dandakaranya, Tamil Nadu still possessed Land Colonization Co-operatives while Andhra Pradesh was starting new Co-operative Collective Farming Societies on wasteland, some of them for tribal peoples.

What generalizations can be made about co-operative tenures in colonization schemes actually studied by the author in the field? Not much more will be said about Co-operative Tenant Farming

Societies or about Colonization Societies which are in effect Tenant Societies; for these lack the critical feature that their members cultivate jointly (except for relatively unimportant elements like the common cocoa plantation at Thengumarahada). But, because they involve or are supposed to involve joint cultivation, certain colonies excluded, or included only with reservations earlier in this chapter will be mentioned here: for instance, the Dandakaranya refugee colonies where 'group farming' was practised; and the Wynad areas of joint paddy cultivation.

There can be no doubt of the unpopularity of co-operative tenures involving joint cultivation amongst a majority of the relevant colonists studied (and it will be remembered that there were not many of them); though not all colonists found it easy, or even possible to say so in the presence of government officers. One's best opportunity to inquire into the reasons for this unpopularity came among the articulate Bengali group farmers of Dandakaranya. Various reasons were in fact given: vague utterances that 'the work is not going well'; more specific statements that incomes would be greater with individual cultivation, that the individual would then reap the benefit of his own efforts, that since under group farming workers came to the field in their own time, it was impossible properly to reflect time worked in payments made to them, that 'some work, some only quarrel about working'.[106] Again where joint farming was practised in the paddy-fields of Wynad, there was a complete lack of enthusiasm strengthened by the fact that yields had not increased with the change from individual cultivation. 'Why should I work for others?' and 'My hard work is submerged in the mass' were other reactions. There was also quite clearly resistance, for similar reasons, where official attempts were being made, as at Thengumarahada, to convert from individual to joint farming. Full collectivization also brings resistance, as is apparent from the experience of Bhupnagar and Gandhidham Bhoodan colonies in Bihar, reported by the Programme Evaluation Organisation: 'The cultivators were not willing to share the produce according to the size of households as stipulated in the bye-laws.'[107] It will be appreciated that a reason sometimes given for the failure of co-operative farming—that it meets the hostility of village landowners—cannot be sustained in the egalitarian conditions of at least these colonization schemes: indeed, the external pressures (in this case from officialdom) are in the opposite direction.

There were, however, cases of the opposite state of affairs in Dandakaranya. Three groups in village PV.17 in the Paralkote Zone had reverted to individual cultivation but wished to re-form groups in order to gain the advantage of four ploughings of their land, one with a government tractor apparently available only to groups. One group of Santals in village MV.2, Malkangiri Zone, wanted individual tenure but group cultivation (that is, 'joint' rather than collective farming). They held that it provided a form of insurance against sickness, and claimed that any lazy men were debited appropriately by what appeared to be an effective group leader. Group cultivation seemed to be working well in the Sikh Bhoodan colony of Sardapuri, in the UP Tarai. On the other hand, there have been Bhoodan colonies, such as that covering 400 hectares near Nilambur, Kerala, where despite Gandhian ideology individual tenure and cultivation have triumphed.

If co-operative tenure is unpopular, in a majority of cases, why had it arisen? It was quite clear in the field that the answer lay largely in the inducements offered by governments that were still wedded to the principle of voluntary co-operation. It will be noted that all the schemes visited in Maharashtra were either joint farming colonies or collectives. Here was a state that took its land code seriously and issued government waste only to co-operative societies: an inducement indeed. Here, and elsewhere, government contributions to the share capital of societies formed an addition to the means of assistance discussed in chapter 10 (see above, pp. 206–10) and hence a further inducement. Co-operative societies, too, were often given preferential treatment in the supply of fertilizers and other necessaries, and secured credit more easily than individual cultivators. Thus in the UP Tarai, Joint Farming Societies could obtain credit up to ten times their registered share capital, whereas Colonization Societies which were not Joint Farming Societies were not in this favourable position. As an Inspector of Co-operatives naïvely put it, 'Colonists requested joint farming after they heard of benefits from officers of the Co-operative Department.' (It was, incidentally, sometimes argued that the Department also benefited because it found loans easier to recover from societies: but this is doubtful.)

So much for the carrot. But, in spite of the principle of voluntaryism, it was clear that, in places, there was also the stick, or the threat of it. In Dandakaranya, there were fears amongst the colonists in 1963 that their allowances would be stopped if they ceased group cultivation: these fears may have been misplaced, or may have been indicative, but were in any case real. Apparently undue pressure in the Hirakud refugee colonies has already been cited.

It appears, then, that relatively rarely have co-operative colonies, whether joint-farming or collective, educed that spirit of communal enterprise and incentive which plays such a large part in the polemic of idealists and others. What, then, of economic arguments for co-operative farming, arguments that lean *inter alia* on the belief that, by achieving economies of scale, co-operation can bring higher yields and higher incomes per worker? Something has already been said in criticism of doctrines of economies of scale. It is enough to add here that it is not easy to reach any sound empirical conclusion on the basis of the co-operative colonies studied by the author. They were so few, and generally so new when visited. And while some (like many of those in Maharashtra) were on such highly marginal land that it is hard to draw general conclusions, others (as in Dandakaranya) were so favoured by preferential treatment that such conclusions elude one for the opposite reason. Where, however, comparisons can be made, as between a colony before and after joint cultivation, or in adjacent colonies (one joint, one individual) with roughly similar physical conditions, the conclusion is that there is no evidence of improvement in yields as a result of co-operative tenure or cultivation. Lack of the 'co-operative spirit' is sufficient to mask whatever scale economies there may be; and, as has already been said, it is doubtful if there are such economies, especially in the case of paddy cultivation. Here Wynad, in attempting joint cultivation of paddy and individual cultivation of other crops, seems to be wrong; and Thengumarahada right, with its individual cultivation of paddy and common ownership of a cocoa plantation and experimental plot, where specialist management is needed. In its early days the same colony demonstrated another relevant use of collectivism—in jungle clearing. Apart from the advantages of collective action at that stage, the author found little evidence of the supposed special utility of co-operative cultivation to the opening-up of wastelands.

Thengumarahada also illustrates another point of some importance: that co-operative and collective enterprises demand a high order of leadership and management. Where these are lacking, whatever advantages there may be are lost; and, indeed, the cost of maintaining a paid secretary or other Society official is a net burden on scarce funds.

Indeed, where individual skill and enterprise are lacking, as among some Harijan groups, it might be more appropriate to think in terms of State Farms under firm and skilled management rather than of colonies under either individual or co-operative tenure and cultivation:[108] not State Farms like that at Suratgarh, with its monstrous devotion to mechanization, but State Farms designed to be labour-intensive and to guarantee minimum wages to their workers. It may well be, however, that this is an unacceptable solution on political grounds, because it would not satisfy the clamour for 'land for the tiller'.

But the author, on the basis of his work here reported, would not rule out of consideration the possibility of labour-intensive State

Farms, any more than he would rule out individual tenure or, if it can be empirically demonstrated that there are real advantages, co-operative or collective tenure. As in the case of Ceylon which he studied some years ago, he favours something of an eclectic solution of the land tenure problem, in the sense that he envisages a solution that differs with land, or people, or need.[109] India has suffered from a doctrinaire attempt to apply, over far too broad a front, single but unrealistic solutions. As in the case of attempts to control sub-division, it is a mercy that these solutions are varied in practice by inefficiencies in the system.

13

Some Social Issues

CONSIDERATIONS stemming from the nature of Indian society, as reflected or varied in colonization schemes, have not been absent from the discussion in this book; but it seems well, before bringing the study as a whole to a close, to focus attention briefly on a few specific social issues as they affect the colonies or are illuminated by experience in them. These issues are:

(1) Social cohesion and community action;
(2) Religion and caste as possibly divisive forces;
(3) Relations with older settlements;
(4) Problems of tribal peoples in colonization schemes.

The author must at the outset disclaim any expertise in sociology or social anthropology: the amount of time available to him in each colonization scheme was in any case insufficient for a social study in any depth.

Social Cohesion and Community Action

The previous chapter will have made it clear that, with some exceptions, Co-operative Societies formed to organize joint tenure and cultivation were generally unpopular, and tended to break down; and that colonists generally professed strong preference for the individual holding and management of land (a preference by no means confined to colonists). In Ceylon 'most colonists were individualists' who, in spite of hopes that colonies would develop a 'community spirit', generally showed but little willingness to co-operate for economic purposes or, for that matter, for other purposes either.[1] It might be supposed that Indian colonists would demonstrate a less marked individualism than those in Ceylon, where, if Margaret Digby is right, 'the temper of village life is individualist'[2] and where a money economy, that concomitant of individualism, has generally spread further and deeper than in many parts of India. What evidence is there on this point? And what consequences are there for the quality of society in Indian colonization schemes?

In many parts of India it is the practice to form co-operative labour teams of relatives and neighbours at such critical and labour-demanding points in the agricultural calendar as ploughing-time, transplanting-time (for rice), and harvest. This practice, a sensible way of dealing with the peaks in the annual cycle of labour demand, is known as *saori* in Assam; has been described in UP by Etienne;[3] and is the Indian equivalent of *attan* in Ceylon, and *gotong royong* in Indonesia.[4] It has already been pointed out (p. 193 above) that the practice is known in one or two tribal colonies in Orissa; and asserted that it is harder to form labour teams in colonies than in established villages. Such labour teams were, however, reported in other smallish tribal colonies, such as Ramakrishnanagar in the Araku Valley, Mukkali in the Attapaddy Valley, and Kanera and Mardel in Dandakaranya; but in non-tribal colonies only in Kambaraganavi (Mysore), in Gobindpur and Theka Colony (Assam), and in the Rori and Sirsa Divisions under the Bhakra Canal in Haryana. In the case of tribal colonies, one may postulate that society is less individualistic than elsewhere, and that, to the extent that kinship matters in the formation of labour-teams, it is in small tribal colonies to which people have moved over small distances that groups of relatives are most likely to have settled together and also to have retained links with the old village. It may also be significant that the non-tribal colonies just quoted are all for refugees, who may well have moved in family groups. But further inquiry on these questions is desirable.

A second index of community spirit or social cohesion is the ability to engage spontaneously in the construction of buildings, sacred and secular, for communal use. Here a number of examples may be of interest: a community hall at Tilaiya, temples to Durga at one or two places in the Umarkote–Raighar Zone of Dandakaranya, a school-house at village MV.7 in the Malkangiri Zone, a storage shed in the Deviyar Colony in the High Ranges of Kerala, a *mandi* in Intikheri, a community centre at Arwatagi, a platform for meetings, dramas (and the reception of the author) at Moranam, a number of temples in the Hirakud oustee colonies, and (a characteristically original touch here) a public radio and a children's park at Thengumarahada. The list is, of course, short compared with that of village-size units in Indian colonies as a whole; and leaves a vast desert, a drab and discouraging monotony of colonies in which, if there were communal buildings at all, they were the insignia of dependence on an all-providing government, and correspondingly neglected.

Thirdly, one may briefly mention two other signs of group activity: the happily spontaneous singing and dancing of some of the tribal colonies; and the rather surprising claim of the Arwatagi colonists that they sometimes dined together, in spite of their mixed caste.

There is implicit in this discussion, of course, the value judgement that social cohesion, as reflected in the willingness of colonists to work together for common ends, is a good thing. The formation of co-operative work teams may, however, be seen as more objectively desirable, since, in a context in which labour-intensive methods are not only prevalent but economically valuable, they enable colonists to overcome the peaks in the annual labour cycle. One hopes that one is not following Sir Henry Maine and the Gandhians and idealizing a village community which never was perfectly co-operative.[5] There was, however, some evidence (for instance, amongst the Santals of the Malkangiri Zone of Dandakaranya) that there was a felt need for a stronger sense of community.

Given that this felt need represents a desirable goal, what evidence is there about the conditions necessary for its achievement, and how far may these be created by deliberate policy on the part of the authorities? What has already been said about the greater prevalence of work teams among small tribal colonies which have involved groups of relatives is here of some significance. So is the observation that where, as at Hirakud, former villages moved as a whole, there was stronger cohesion than at, say, Gandhisagar, where that condition was not satisfied; so also is the observation that the influence of recognized leaders had much to do with social cohesion and communal activity in such colonies as Jeelugumilli, Kansal Banjara, and Velakapuram (led by a remarkable caste Hindu).

Now it may be difficult if not impossible for official policy and practice deliberately to include leaders when colonists are being selected; for this may be thought to involve an unacceptable anachronism in the validation of, say, a tribal chieftain (this, indeed, was the status of the leader at Jeelugumilli and at Kansal Banjara colony); or of ex-*zamindars* and other landlord-like figures, and thus the furtherance of the ever-present tendency for the wealthy classes to grow wealthier and more powerful. It may not, however, be so difficult to recognize that the sort of active leadership which has colonized Thengumarahada is worthy of recognition.

Leadership apart, there is one simple measure open to the authorities in many cases: that is to adopt the principle of grouping, well known since the days of the Punjab Canal Colonies.[6] This involves the settlement in the same village (or other small unit) of people from a single source, and the adoption of nucleated rather than amorphous or scattered settlement patterns wherever this is practicable. Here the irrigation engineers, who tend to string houses out along channel-side roads, must be curbed. The principle of grouping could, indeed, be seen in operation, in whole or in part, in a number of cases. Hirakud and Gandhisagar have already been quoted. At Bylakuppe, Tibetan colonists were grouped according to region of origin and to dialect. In the Paralkote Zone of Dandakaranya, the Bengali Hindu refugees were grouped according to their wishes, which presumably reflected origins. In the Baghbar colony, and also in Gobindpur and Theka, refugee colonists were grouped according to source area and time of migration. But, obvious though the principle is, there were several cases in which it had not been applied, and some where difficulties were readily attributable to this fact. Thus in the Tarai colonies in Kheri District, 'petty quarrels' were attributed to contact between colonists with differing dialects and customs. At Jamunia no attempt was made to group people of similar origin: rather were those who had the same priority in terms of need placed together (a strange principle). There was no system of grouping in the colonies under the Bhakra Canal. And although in the Kaki colony all settlers were Assamese, they were (outside the main *bazar* area) handicapped by the very scattered distribution of their houses. India, however, is not alone in its relative neglect of grouping.[7]

Religion and Caste as Divisive Forces[8]

The discussion of social cohesion has, it will have been noticed, said nothing about religion and caste as possible divisive forces. Religion can in this context be dismissed very quickly, for colonies of mixed religious composition are very rare. Hindus and Muslims were in fact found together only in Kaki (Assam), in Jamunia (Bihar), and in the High Ranges and Wynad colonies of Kerala. In Kaki two of the Programme Evaluation Organisation's sample of 28 colonists were Muslim.[9] In Jamunia about 15 per cent of the settlers were Muslim. The size of the Muslim minority in the two Kerala colonies is not known, but appeared to be small. Muslims are, of course, absent from refugee schemes.

A number of colonies contain both Hindus and Christians: for example, Kalidindi (where Christians were in a majority and the President of the Society was a Roman Catholic); Piduguralla (where the President was a Baptist pastor and the Secretary a Lutheran); Darapathar (which held, in addition to Bengali Hindu refugees, Christian Garos who had also fled from East Bengal); and Intikheri colony for Kerala people (whose Christians were described as 'Christian caste'). Sikhs were present with Hindus in such colonies as those on the Chambal Right Bank and in the UP Tarai, though usually in large enough numbers, and with a characteristically strong enough sense of identity, to form their own villages, or even their own colony, as at Sardapuri. In no case was disharmony on religious grounds evident; though, of course, a longer stay in a colony, with field-study of an anthropological nature, might modify the picture.

Caste is a different and much more complicated issue. For a colony to be composed entirely of members of one caste is of course no guarantee that harmony, unity, and social cohesion will prevail; nor is a colony which numbers several castes amongst its people necessarily stricken with discord or riven with disunity in a way which prevents joint action—though perhaps joint action would not extend to such overt activities as the formation of work-teams across caste frontiers or the building of a single temple.

There were several colonies, or villages within colonies, composed wholly or mainly of a single caste.[10] Bengali villages in Dandakaranya consisted mainly of Namasudras. Two villages in Intikheri consisted solely of Rajputs or those who claimed to be Rajputs, in one case all refugees from Bahawalpur (now part of Pakistan); one hamlet under the Bhakra Canal only of Aroras. Pabal contained only Takaris, who were traditionally wanderers and, it is said, harvest-stealers, but who claimed to have been in old Pabal village for a hundred years. Except for one Mistri, the small Mahatma Fule co-operative colony would have consisted only of Malis, thirteen of whom, with the Mistri, split off from the neighbouring Jayashree colony: a schism that may well have arisen on caste grounds, though two Malis were left behind. Sorapur consisted of a single caste of Harijans; but Velakapuram, which also contained nothing but Harijans, illustrated the point that the term 'harijan' can cover a multitude of castes. Doreen Warriner, from surveys of joint farming societies in Maharashtra and Mysore, draws the conclusion that 'societies with a homogeneous membership, drawn from a single cultivating caste, or from the Harijans, are more stable and less corrupt'.[11] One does not dispute the findings of the surveys; but if the inference is that Harijans are a single caste, as homogeneous as 'a single cultivating caste', it is a wrong inference so far as most colonization schemes are concerned.

Other colonies consisted entirely or almost entirely of a single tribe: whether each of these is equivalent to a caste is a nice point to be taken up later in this chapter. Thus all the families in Jeelugumilli were Koyas; all those in Kansal Banjara colony by definition Banjaras, traditionally traders and carriers, especially of salt; while fourteen of the fifteen families in Bunagaon were Muria Gonds.

The author collected no evidence to suggest that single-caste colonies (or settlements within colonies) were more harmonious, or more likely to co-operate for economic purposes, than other colonies. If there was a characteristic derived from single-caste structure, it was overshadowed by other features: for example, in Pabal by absenteeism due to the call of urban opportunities, in Mahatma

Fule by small size, in Velakapuram by the dominance of the non-Harijan leader already mentioned (see above, p. 263). And in spite of the fact that Sorapur held only one caste of Harijans, there was no sign of communal activity, and, in particular, no effort to substitute Joint for Tenant Farming.

For the rest, a multi-caste structure was generally in evidence in colonies of Hindus, or of Hindus and tribals (who may, or may not be considered Hindus: see below, p. 274). The range of castes was, however, relatively small in a number of colonies: for instance, in those in the Rori and Sirsa Divisions under the Bhakra Canal, because hamlets were smaller than in older-established settlements (hence the hamlet already mentioned which consisted entirely of Aroras); in the Amalner collective colony where there were 16 'Patils' (Marathas), and one each of four other castes; and, as will already be clear, a number of colonies consisted entirely of Harijans of various castes (this applied to Sindewahi, Velakapuram, and to three-quarters of the villages in the Malkangiri Zone of Dandakaranya, the rest containing Santals). Tribal colonies with a small range of 'castes' included Ramakrishnanagar in the Araku Valley (where there were 9 Poruja, 5 Mukadora, 2 Bagata, and 2 Gondu), though it might be argued that in such small tribal colonies sheer size limited caste representation. It will be remembered that Ramakrishnanagar was one of the colonies able to form co-operative work-teams.

At the other end of the spectrum were colonization schemes with a wide range of castes. These naturally included oustee colonies, which tended to reproduce the pattern of the mixed-caste villages from which their people had been drawn. Castes were particularly mixed in the Tarai colonies in Kheri District, to whose 'petty quarrels', associated with lack of grouping, attention has already been drawn: it was said that colonization societies were trying to resolve caste and other disputes. In the colonies of Pilibhit District, however, which also contained a variety of castes, the Programme Evaluation Organisation's survey had it that there were 'no caste factions', that Harijans used wells freely, and that children of Harijans played at school with children of higher castes; but that Harijans did not 'sit on the cots of high caste people and neither do they share eatables with them'.[12] The Jayashree colony at Bhamer had a wide range of castes too, including 'non-backward' castes, Harijans, and Bhils; but the author was not told of any dissension. The small colony at Arwatagi contained an array of castes: 1 Brahmin, 10 Marathas, 10 Talawars, 4 Kuravars, 12 Lingayats, and 7 Harijans—plus 8 Muslims; yet this was the group that claimed to dine together occasionally. Amongst tribal colonies, the 28 settlers in the small colony of Gundrai, in Malwa, seemed to come from a number of tribes and castes and included Gonds and Charyas. There had been trouble here: three Belpardi (monkey-catchers) had been expelled for criminal assaults. Quite apart from that incident, this colony gave the impression of being unhappy, perhaps because it had been formed from too wide a range of social groups, including a number not associated with cultivation. Much the same applied to Aminabad, on the other side of the country in the Eastern Ghats of Andhra Pradesh, which held 14 Kammara, 1 Kondadora, 10 Kondakadu, 16 Kapu, 4 Settibalisi, 2 Velama, 2 Kamma, and 13 described as Harijans. But there were other reasons for poor performance here—notably bad soil, and a weak agricultural extension service.

A number of other points may be made before leaving the question of caste in colonization schemes. First, it was only in a few cases that government officers would own to any disunity or malfunctioning that could be attributed in whole or in part to conflict between castes. The cases of Kheri and Gundrai (very different cases) have been cited, as has the revolt of the Malis at Bhamer. At Sunabeda there were hints of 'caste rigidity' co-existing with what was declared to be harmony. This is, of course, not impossible: and one is not idealizing a supposed pristine village if one says that rigidity with harmony must have characterized, and in many places still characterizes, inter-caste relationships. Kathleen Gough puts it '. . . in all Indian villages, a unit of the whole village overrides the separateness of each caste'.[13] But, on the other hand, the author was sometimes sceptical, and wondered how far officials were deliberately playing down caste differences.

Secondly, it might be thought that friction could be avoided and desirable results achieved by forming single-caste schemes or sections of schemes; indeed, this was the policy in the old Punjab Canal Colonies.[14] But that was a long time ago. Today it would be invidious, if not politically explosive, to select colonists on the basis of caste, by the same token excluding others who also stand in need of land. The selection of Harijans is an exception to this generalization; in fact, it may be politically important to demonstrate that something is being done for the 'backward classes'. What may be more practicable is to group people within large colonies on the basis of caste (this can of course be achieved by grouping kinsfolk, thus at the same time avoiding intra-caste conflicts on a lineage basis). But even this may be difficult if, say, Harijans feel that they are being confined to a ghetto.

Thirdly, this last effect is sometimes to be observed anyway, especially in oustee colonies, which tend to reproduce the social structure and the spatial pattern of the former villages from whose destruction the need for colonies arose. In the Hirakud scheme, for instance, it was obvious that Harijans were segregated within the new villages, and had amongst other things their own well. In Gandhisagar, not all village sites were occupied as planned: in some cases, other sites were preferred, partly for reasons of caste.

Fourthly, large colonization schemes other than those for oustees may provide something like the anonymity of a large city, and enable some individuals, by changing their names, to conceal their low caste. This phenomenon is known to have occurred at Kaki, and may explain why officials in Kaki told the author that there were no Harijans (though they admitted to Boro, a Scheduled Tribe), whereas the Programme Evaluation Organisation found that 14 per cent of their sample were members of Scheduled Castes.[15] Name-changing has been one of the reactions of the lower castes to colonization in Ceylon.[16]

Fifthly, it will be appreciated that, with the principal exception of the oustee schemes, colonies in post-independence India, even where they contain a wide range of castes, do not reproduce the structure of whatever established villages it is appropriate to measure them against. The influx of refugees and a selective government policy have, with other factors, seen that this is so. The anomalous caste composition of some of the colonies would make them an interesting field for further social and political research.[17]

Finally, the Programme Evaluation Organisation was commendably frank about the caste dimension in their study of the Jethi Colonisation Project in Palampur District of Gujarat.[18] Here a Joint Farming Society originally consisted of 23 members of 'backward classes' (eight from Scheduled Castes, one from Scheduled Tribes, and fourteen others), together with 20 Rajputs, 3 Banias, and a carpenter. In the event four Harijan families left, allegedly because of maltreatment, and others (with some of higher castes) left later. At the time of the survey, only 15 Rajputs, 1 Bania and 1 Harijan were left; the Bania was the Chairman and the Harijan 'rendered menial services'. The report caustically concludes: 'It appeared that the society was formed to benefit the Rajput family mainly and some members of the other caste groups were enrolled to hide this fact.'

Relations with Older Occupants

Chapters 3 and 4 made it abundantly clear that, although independent India found itself with lands available for colonization, most of these lands already had their own population: the Rajasthan Desert its nomads and *barani* cultivators, the Tarai its Tharus and

Bhuksas, Dandakaranya its Gonds and others. And if this was true of the large areas of potential colonization, how much more was it true of colonies seeking to fill in the minute interstices of the Indian settlement pattern; as in Tamil Nadu and eastern Maharashtra, for instance. 'Relations with existing settlers have . . . caused difficulty in many different colonization schemes', the author wrote in 1957, going on to give examples from Libya, Indonesia, and the Punjab Canal Colonies, and from his own work in Ceylon.[19] What of these relations in post-independence India?

As might be expected, the least difficulty was reported from those colonies in which the settlers were themselves drawn entirely from a nearby village or from nearby villages, as in the tribal colonies of Jeelugumilli and Mukkali (Attapaddy Valley) and, for that matter, most of those of Dandakaranya; or the non-tribal colonies in the Chambal ravine lands and at Moranam. But even in such instances there might be trouble because of resentment on the part of former landlords and caste superiors (as happened at Kansal Banjara Colony).

More usually, however, disputes between colonists and occupants of older villages revolved around competition for the use of land. Sometimes the trouble was relatively trivial, as at Velakapuram, where the colony is in the catchment of the village tank, or at Gandhisagar, where there has been a small loss of forest area. One of the most frequent causes of complaint concerned trespass by cattle, both by colonists' animals into the villages and by village cattle into the colony (which may often occupy former village pasture). In some places the problem was more serious, as at Piduguralla, where the old village 'never wanted' the colony and had made this clear; or on the Chambal Right Bank, where tribal labour had been exploited by colonists (and, for that matter, by cultivators in older villages); or at Intikheri, where colonists from Kerala had been put cheek-by-jowl with old villages; or in the Sirsa and Rori Divisions under the Bhakra Canal, where officials had to contend with the sum of a number of small sources of friction, notably cattle trespass and what are described as 'difference in customs'. But at least no post-independence scheme has had to face the vigorous and militant hostility with which the Janglis reacted to colonization in the Punjab in the 1880s and 1890s, in the Sidhnai and Lower Chenab Colonies[20] (but if schemes for the settlement of the Andaman Islands are pursued, they may well encounter the Jarawas, a jungle tribe who regularly take their toll of forest labour).[21] Indeed, more often than not, the author was told that there was no trouble between colonists and villagers longer settled in the area; or even that relations were 'cordial'.

Of quite a different order are the problems of Rajasthan and of

Dandakaranya: of a different order because of the scale involved, whether in terms of area, or of potential population, or of disturbance to the pre-existing inhabitants. Some account was given in chapter 3 of the pastoral and cultivating dwellers in the Rajasthan Desert, and of the hazards that beset their attempts to derive a living from the resources of the Marusthali.[22] It is sufficient to add here that, in spite of its aridity, this region illustrates very well the thesis that agricultural colonization in India cannot fail to have an impact on pre-existing settlers. In the districts first traversed by the Rajasthan Canal the Net Sown Area was more than 40 per cent of the total area.[23] For most of its projected future course this proportion hardly ever drops below 20 per cent until Jaisalmer District is reached. There it eventually falls below 10 per cent, but the presence of a nomadic pastoral population with an extensive system of land use presents another kind of problem (not, however, that flocks and herds are absent higher up the line of the Canal: according to the Master Plan, which dates from the early 1960s, there were 850,000 head of livestock in Ganganagar District, 950,000 in Bikaner, and 1,022,000 in Jaisalmer).[24]

Already in 1963 the Rajasthan Canal was having its impact on cultivators previously established in the area, both Rajasthanis with deep roots in the area, and pioneering Sikhs, Jats, and Harijans. A number of these had already been moved, according to policy, to new *abadis* and to irrigated land. Pioneering Jats were, for instance, prominent in *Abadi* No. 14 in Naurangdesar Division some 24 km south of Hanumangarh; and had, with great energy and hard work, dug their own field channels. Always provided that those concerned take readily to irrigated farming, it does not seem likely that failure to absorb local cultivators will, in the first generation at any rate, present much of a problem given the relative abundance of land in the project and the fact that new irrigated holdings can be much smaller than old *barani*, and yet yield a better income.

Pastoralists, especially those who are nomads, are a different matter, for, as the Master Plan puts it:

> Advent of irrigation will radically transform the economy of the area. Agriculture will now receive the top priority in land use, and the area's traditional occupation, Animal Husbandry, will have to find a new balance in the changed circumstances. . . . A majority of the animal hordes now roaming free over these vast grazing grounds will in time be elbowed out of the irrigated areas.[25]

A survey by the Central Arid Zone Research Institute along the line of the Rajasthan Canal showed not only that the nomads there had flocks and herds which included some of the best breeds in the state, if not in India; but also that some of the best pasture, including that flooded by the Ghaggar, would disappear into the irrigable command.[26] The Master Plan assumed that, by bringing water, communications, markets 'and civilization generally' to its command, the Rajasthan Canal Project will permit the development of animal husbandry along less precarious and more intensive lines in the unirrigated area.[27] Plans have been made for breed improvement, veterinary services, fodder banks, livestock fairs, and grading stations for products (associated with *mandis*). It is also hoped that the effects of colonization will spread well beyond the Project area and bring 'a new stability' to pastoralism there. It remains to be seen how far the opportunities for economic advancement that come the way of pastoralists in the area will reconcile them to the loss of their traditional grazing-grounds and trading arrangements. The response up to December 1971 was rather limited; though some nomads would like land under the canal if irrigation can be assured.

A study made by S. P. Malhotra and A. B. Bose, of the Central Arid Zone Research Institute at Jodhpur, is illuminating in this connection.[28] It was concerned with the Banjaras, who have already been encountered at various points in this study as the occupants of the Kansal Banjara Colony in Madhya Pradesh. The Banjaras are among the most familiar nomads of Rajasthan and the areas to the south, and functioned, like so many nomads in other arid areas, as traders and carriers of goods. In the study area southwest of Jodhpur they were particularly concerned with the salt trade, and had been heavily hit by the opening up of formerly inaccessible areas to road transport (the Kansal Banjaras had been similarly affected by the railway). They also faced the opposition of the sedentary population, who resented the pressure put by the Banjaras on limited water and grazing resources; although the Canal will, one hopes, increase these resources, colonists will clearly not welcome a tribe of nomads drifting with their flocks and herds through unfenced fields. Most of the Banjara groups studied wished to become settled cultivators, a wish eventually shared by the originally reluctant Kansal Banjaras. Malhotra and Bose urge that their *tanda* of six to twenty related families should be the unit in resettlement (here, again, is the principle of grouping); that 'the services of anthropologists and trained social workers should be utilized' and that care should be taken 'to ensure that the benefits intended for the Banjaras are not usurped by unscrupulous groups'. One can assuredly endorse all this. A possible lesson to be learned is that the nomads and other pastoralists of Rajasthan may in due course press for irrigated land under the scheme, and may not be satisfied with the side-effects of colonization on arid and unirrigated areas; and may contrast in this respect with nomads in the Sudan who are described by H. R. J. Davies as having a 'built-in dislike' of settled agriculture for fear of losing their animals.[29]

In the old Punjab Canal Colonies, where the once-hostile Janglis were converted into 'industrious agriculturists', it was recognized that 'The indigenous population of areas affected by colonization schemes have always constituted one of the most difficult problems to be dealt with.'[30] If the Rajasthan Canal project is one of the heirs of the Punjab Canal Colonies, the Thal Scheme in Pakistan is another: here, too, land has been reserved for pastoralists, and there is a notable government livestock farm.[31]

The position in Dandakaranya is potentially much more difficult, and indeed dangerous, than that in Rajasthan. In Rajasthan the indigenous people affected by colonization, whether they be cultivators or pastoralists, may well be satisfied with land in the scheme; and, unless there is massive immigration from other parts of India to fill vacant land, they are likely to find themselves in contact with other Rajasthanis, speaking a common language (though the age-old conflict of nomad and settler has not been altogether absent from the region). In Dandakaranya colonization has meant the intrusion of an alien Bengali-speaking people into the former forest fastnesses of the Gonds, Koyas, and other tribal peoples. True, 25 per cent of the land cleared by the Authority is reserved for these peoples; and not all of it is immediately taken up. True, too, there are examples of peaceful symbiosis between Bengalis and Gonds: as has already been seen, some of the latter were in hired employment from the former; there was leasing of land by each from the other; and there was a joint weekly *hat* (market) at Silethi, in the Umarkote–Raighar Zone, started by local villagers and mainly devoted to exchange between the two groups, very few traders being present. But there was also evidence of friction: many complaints of cattle trespass, by each about the cattle of the other; and some of theft of cattle. And there were complaints of exploitation: for example, of local people working for less than the prescribed minimum wage. There has been a Press report, by a Bengali reporter it should be noted, that his fellow-countrymen have 'little respect' for the tribal people.[32] It is not surprising that the friction in 1963 was worse in the Umarkote–Raighar Zone, where colony and old village inter-digitate, than in Malkangiri, where this feature is less marked; and less again in the Paralkote Zone, which has few nearby old villages.

The problem, however, goes deeper than disputes over wages and cattle. There is no doubt that under the surface in Dandakaranya there have long smouldered the fires of resentment at the intrusion of alien immigrants from the plains. From time to time in the last century, these fires have burst into flame. The Bastar rising of 1876 and that in Kalahandi in 1882 have already been mentioned; both were brought about by the immigration of plainsmen. There was a further rebellion in Bastar in 1911. In 1963 the threat to law and order posed by the Bastar people and their peculiar relationship with their Maharaja was such that the Collector could not leave the District Headquarters at Jagdalpur; though the turbulence at this time, which culminated in the death of the Maharaja in 1966,[33] after police firing, had other causes than intrusive settlement.

By 1972 the problem in Dandakaranya had taken on a new dimension and a new urgency. As chapter 9 has made clear, many refugee colonists had by then made considerable strides in adapting themselves to the local environment and in taking to new varieties and techniques. The tribal population, on the other hand, had, with few exceptions, made but little progress. The gap between tribal and refugee incomes and living standards had thus widened. The growing disparity could be represented, rightly or wrongly, as a result of the contrast between the attention lavished on the refugees by the Authority and the relative neglect of the tribals, whether colonists or villagers, by the state governments (who, it will be remembered, are responsible for tribal settlers once the Authority has reclaimed the land). Moreover, the spread of refugee settlement had by 1962 impinged on many more old tribal villages, some of which were manifestly hemmed in by newly developed lands. There was, it is true, no conspicuous sign of serious tribal discontent: one opinion was that the tribal peoples were cowed by the events of 1966 in Bastar. But the fear was none the less expressed that time was running out, and that trouble might rise from one or more of several contingencies: for instance, Naxalite exploitation of tribal discontents of the sort that has characterized Srikakulam District of Andhra Pradesh; or similar exploitation by politicians at the opposite end of the political spectrum in the shape of the Jana Sangh, who have already been reported to be active in the region;[34] or the rise of a new generation of more educated tribal people, less content with the old ways and jealous of the relative prosperity of the refugee colonists; or even tribal separatism of the sort that has activated the Jharkand movement in Chota Nagpur. By no means all of the actual or potential sources of discontent have their origin in colonization; but it is naturally colonization and its possible effects that most worries officers of the Dandakaranya Development Authority, though others are more complacent.

One means of reducing the gap between refugees and tribals would be to make the Authority responsible for the actual resettlement of the latter, as it is for the former. This was in fact a suggestion of the

Commissioner for Scheduled Castes and Scheduled Tribes;[35] and a start has been made with implementation.

The Problems of Tribal Peoples

This leads discussion on to a review of the suitability of tribal peoples for colonization schemes, and of colonization schemes for what are conceived to be the needs or problems of tribal peoples, whether in Dandakaranya or elsewhere in India.

But what are 'tribal peoples'? F. G. Bailey has rightly said that 'The distinction between tribal people and caste people has been a problem not only . . . for sociologists, but also for administrators and politicians.'[36] The preceding pages of this book make it clear that there is indeed a problem of definition. And a particular facet of the problem presented itself during many discussions with officials in the field: namely that, whether or not the 'tribal' peoples recognized themselves as a caste, the officials, drawn from caste society, saw each tribe as a caste, with a place (usually a low one) in the hierarchy. Whatever the good intentions of national and state governments, this viewpoint affected their attitude to and treatment of 'tribal' colonists.

Bailey's convincing resolution of the problem[37] is based on his conclusions (amply illustrated in this book) that caste and tribe are not different in all respects and that not all tribes differ from caste members in being hill people, or distinctive in language, or Animists, or economically backward, or autochthonous. Thus some tribal groups originally outside Hinduism have entered the Hindu fold by the process that M. N. Srinivas has called 'sanskritization', though others may have to wait for acceptance, and others may westernize before they sanskritize (as has happened to the Khasi of Meghalaya).[38] Bailey thus postulates a continuum, a single line at whose opposite ends are placed 'caste' and 'tribe'. 'Particular societies are to be located at different points along this line. . . . Societies which fall near one pole or another, we will in a rough and ready way call either caste systems or tribal systems. For those at the centre it will be impossible to say whether they are tribes or castes, for the concrete world of social behaviour does not permit the exclusiveness and exhaustiveness which can be achieved in logic and in the framing of definitions.'[39]

Now it will be remembered that, under the Indian Constitution, the state is enjoined to promote the educational and economic interests of 'the weaker sections of the people, and in particular the Scheduled Castes and the Scheduled Tribes' (see above, p. 99). Whether or not, therefore, a 'tribal' group is Scheduled is a matter of considerable importance to it, not least in terms of preferential treatment in colonization schemes. Most of the groups which in this book have rather loosely been called 'tribal', and most who in contemporary India are called *adivasi*, are in fact Scheduled; but there are some notable exceptions—the Tharus of the Tarai and the Irula of the Nilgiris, for example.[40]

The constitutional position of the Scheduled Tribes in chapter 6 was part of a discussion of the 'welfare motive' in Indian colonization policy; and it will be appreciated that what has been said in this book about tribal colonization schemes, with their special forms of assistance, gives the lie to the statement that, whereas in British days 'the tribal peoples were administered as separate entities and isolated from the commercial life of the urban Hindu', since independence tribal peoples have been left to the state governments which 'could not have cared less'.[41] State governments *have* cared, witness tribal colonization schemes. So have individuals, official and unofficial; for instance, the author met in Sheopur (Madhya Pradesh) Shri Udaybhan Singh, who, concluding that contractors were exploiting *adivasis* (particularly Saharia), formed a co-operative to collect and sell such forest produce as gum, honey, and wax. All this is not to say that government or private motives are always idealistic. Bailey has shown that the political effectiveness developed by the Khonds of Orissa has made them a force to be reckoned with when the ballot boxes are out—and, indeed, more generally.[42] And there have also been failures of planning and execution, of which a number have been cited in the course of this book.

What, however, about the questions that were posed at the beginning of this section on the suitability of tribals for colonies and of colonies for tribals? One cannot answer these questions without defining one's criteria. Thus the colonies which, it was announced in November 1970,[43] were to be established in Srikakulam District of Andhra Pradesh in order to regroup the Girijans (that is, hill people) and to relieve them of pressure from Naxalite bands must be judged, like the emergency resettlement schemes of Malaya or the 'agrovilles' of South Vietnam,[44] according to their success in meeting their political and military objectives. Similarly, Indian tribal colonization, of a slightly older vintage than that studied by the author, and designed to wean tribal peoples away from their practice of shifting cultivation, must be judged in terms of that objective; and it may be said straight away that it was, in those terms, not very successful; thus colonists in Orissa 'found it difficult to give up habits of shifting cultivation'.[45] As for the tribal colonies studied in this book, it seems reasonable to judge them by criteria derived from the Article in the Constitution just quoted; and to ask to what extent the colonies 'promote the educational and economic interests' of the tribal people involved in them; or, more particularly, to what extent they are a means of educating the people to practise a more productive agriculture which gives them an improved standard of living. Against criteria such as these, Thengumarahada stands out as strikingly successful: though not all of the colonists were tribal by any standard, and the Badaga who provided so much of the initiative are technically non-Scheduled. Kannaram must also be judged quite successful, and its Koyas, reputedly hard-working, are members of a Scheduled Tribe (it is revealing that a Telugu official sought to explain their relative success by claiming that they were 'almost plainsmen'). At the other end of the scale, such colonies as Mircabad, Kotia Pani, Aminabad, Pandripani, Pabal, and Kambaraganavi, with their indifferent standards of cultivation, failure to 'educate' and generally low yields must be judged 'unsuccessful' (though some of them would be classed as 'fairly successful' if the criterion was the maintenance of a cohesive society). Other tribal colonies, such as Jeelugumilli, Kansal Banjara, and the tribal colonies in Wynad, come somewhere between the two extremes. One can indeed agree with the Dhebar Committee, which found that tribal colonies 'ranged from the ideal to the absurd'.[46]

Can any lessons be learned from these admittedly rough-and-ready judgements? One, it is suggested, is that tribal colonies are likely to be more successful agriculturally and economically if the people concerned are already familiar with settled cultivation; in other words, those already partly skilled are more likely to contend successfully with what are after all pioneer conditions. Another lesson is that one should not set one's sights too high and immediately expect advanced standards of cultivation from many tribal groups brought up in an easy-going economic environment. A third, and perhaps the most important is that, if one is to judge by the adoption of settled agriculture and associated living standards, the colonies for the former criminal tribes, now the denotified tribes, are generally unsuccessful. H. N. Tiwari has sought to explain that these are 'mal-adjusted tribes' who were led to steal because their wandering life on the fringes of society did not give them the means of subsistence; and that eventually crime became their life-style.[47] Early attempts to settle them had no further purpose than to control them. Later attempts, which include colonization schemes, were aimed high-mindedly at rehabilitation. But that this is not easy is demonstrated by the state of the colonies concerned. It is hard to prescribe alternative means of rehabilitation, though the Takaris of Pabal have found one by going off to work in Poona or Bombay. Perhaps, for the time-being at any rate, rehabilitation by colonization must go on, but be judged by long-term social rather than short-term economic criteria, and be considered in the nature of a continuing experiment.

Whether by colonization or otherwise, attempts should be made to induce change among India's tribal peoples, and if so, whether quickly or slowly—these are issues on which much has been written, and very little more need be said here. As André Béteille has said, 'The case for isolation seems to have been abandoned as both unrealistic and undesirable.'[48] Verrier Elwin, who wrote so much on tribes and tribal problems, was certainly not for leaving them as they are, and claimed to be in favour of road-building and development generally.[49] But he was in favour of 'hastening slowly'[50] and of what he saw as a 'middle way' between isolation and over-rapid integration.[51] Elwin's ideas appealed to Nehru: he and Nehru echoed each other's ideas and policies.[52] But Elwin admitted that he romanticized tribal people;[53] and in such areas as the North East Frontier Agency there is pressure from the tribal people themselves for more rapid change, and the feeling that Elwinism is holding them back. There has been the view, too, that swift change is the only answer to the problems of Bastar.[54] Here one is reminded of Margaret Mead's conclusions about the very rapid change that she found among the people of Manus (Great Admiralty Island) when she revisited it after 25 years: that such change is not only possible, but may be desirable, provided that the people concerned take over enough and do it quickly enough, that they take over 'whole patterns' in their entirety, and that they all change as a unit.[55] The experience of some Indian tribal peoples, notably the Khasis of Assam, endorses these conclusions. Yet, if there is one thing that work in colonization schemes among tribal peoples teaches, it is that they are almost infinitely varied in all sorts of respects, because of varying degrees of historical isolation, varying degrees of assimilation of Hindu culture (by sanskritization and otherwise) or rejection of it (for example, by conversion to Christianity), and varying degrees of acceptance by Hindu caste society around them. Margaret Mead in Manus did not face this complexity and variety. The conclusion to be drawn is surely that there is no one remedy, no one prescription of colonization or any other remedy, to be uniformly applied; and that where tribal peoples cannot just be left alone (like those at Thengumarahada) both policy and practice need to be very flexible.

14

The Future of Agricultural Colonization

THIS concluding chapter asks whether agricultural colonization should continue in the future. It will argue that the conclusion reached depends on the view that is taken of a number of issues, notably:

(1) the economic marginality of colonizing hitherto uncultivated land, as measured by the return to the cultivator for his efforts, and by the benefits to the government and to the national economy, given the costs incurred;
(2) the likely impact of agricultural colonization on food production and on the balance of payments;
(3) the potentialities of alternative means of achieving the objectives of colonization (in particular, by the intensification of production on land already in cultivation); and
(4) the contention that, even if agricultural colonization is less economic, or more uneconomic than this alternative, it should be continued because of the need to generate employment, or to redistribute wealth, or to contain potential agrarian unrest, or to deal with refugees or repatriates; or, to put the matter more compassionately, to help to alleviate the distress of the poor, the landless, and the dispossessed.

The Marginality of Land

The opening of chapter 3 drew attention to what was called 'the equilibrium assumption'—that 'rural population [in India] has everywhere settled down to a density appropriate to local land resources and that, to quote O. H. K. Spate, "with populations everywhere congested . . . and land-hungry, any land cultivable without prohibitive outlay would have been taken up long ago"'. Any inquiry into the possible future for agricultural colonization in India must ask whether the equilibrium assumption is true in strictly economic terms; that is, it must ask whether the extension of cultivation by means of colonization is at, or beyond the economic margin at which the extra cost of an advance is balanced by the return obtained from the extra output; or whether G. Kuriyan's claim that 'agriculture has been pushed to submarginal limits'[1] is true of colonization.

Michael Chisholm has shown that the application of the economic concept of marginality to the spatial limits of agriculture is more complex than might at first sight appear, for reasons that include the time taken for geographical margins to adjust themselves to economic margins; the tendency, in a real world of variable terrain and climate, for the economic margin of cultivated land to be 'normally marked by a few scattered holdings which are peculiar in their natural endowment [or in their] location with respect to communications or in the ability of the farmer'; and the acceptance of low incomes on family farms because of the value placed on independence.[2]

Labour of the Colonist

It is hard to believe, from no more than casual observation of high labour inputs in relation to abysmally low yields, that agriculture in many pockets of land scattered here and there over the face of India is not at or very near the margin, in the sense that the marginal product of labour must be very near the limit below which it ceases to overcome the cultivator's resistance to work.[3] One remembers being forcibly struck by this thought when watching a cultivator near Khilchipur, in Malwa, trying to plough a field whose unrewarding 'soil' consisted of little more than hard chunks of indurated laterite crust; and when contemplating the piecemeal encroachment of cultivation on to pocket-handkerchief-sized patches of land amid the rocks of the eastern scarp of the Mysore plateau, on the road going down from Bangalore to Madras. As for colonization schemes, it is hard to believe that similar considerations do not apply to fields in some of the poor, interstitial colonies of Tamil Nadu or Maharashtra, part of one of which, at Pabal, had 'soils' similar to those of Khilchipur; or to the rocky land on upper slopes on which some of the Gandhisagar oustees found themselves after displacement from much more fertile bottom-lands.

Estimates for net incomes from agricultural land in certain schemes have been given in Table 10.I, with a very necessary warning on the unreliability of many of the figures; and the point has been made that 'adverse or insufficiently appreciated natural conditions may . . . in part be blamed for low incomes' in a number of colonies, though other factors (such as lack of skill among cultivators, especially tribal cultivators) make it difficult to decide whether all low-income colonies are necessarily at or near the margin from the point of view of the colonist. The low-income colonies include, however, some of those just mentioned.

Cost to Government

The issue of marginality cannot, however, be settled merely by reference to the domestic economy of the colonist. Chapters 3 and 4 have shown that the areas of post-independence colonization were preserved from the earlier encroachment of massive agricultural settlement by a variety of circumstances. In a number of cases remoteness and lack of communications have been among the operative factors, so that government investment in roads has been necessary to their colonization. In other cases, such as the area under the Rajasthan Canal or in parts of Dandakaranya, expensive irrigation works have been necessary, or at any rate highly desirable, in order to create the potential for colonization. In any case, it is explicit in the definition of colonization used in this book that government organization is involved, and therefore implicit that the state will be put to expense.

Table 14.I is an attempt to set out estimated costs of colonization to the government authorities concerned. In all cases except the Rajasthan Canal Project, basic data on costs were either supplied by officers in the field, or submitted in a paper which had, in many cases, been specially prepared to meet the author's needs. It is no criticism of these officials that high reliability cannot be attributed to the Table. It must be used with caution because there can be no certainty that the figures quoted include the right items and exclude others not strictly associated with colonization.

The costs for Dandakaranya refer only to the resettlement of refugees: they exclude expenditure on tribal welfare and on general regional development.

Data for the Rajasthan Canal area present special problems. No data could be obtained on actual expenditure in relation to the number of colonists settled and the cultivated area opened up. The total cost is derived from projections published in the Master Plan[4] and includes state expenditure for the whole period of the Project as originally planned (that is, to 1981) on habitations and housing, communications, agriculture, animal husbandry, drinking water, co-operation, community development, and 'colonization' (that is the administrative and revenue aspects); but it excludes state expenditure on industries, forests, power, education and health, together with central government expenditure on railways, national highways, industries and power, on the ground that these items either do not directly contribute to agricultural colonization, or are

TABLE 14.I

Estimates of Cost to Government in Certain Colonization Schemes

Scheme	*From Inception to*	*Estimated Capital Cost, Excluding Loans (Rupees)*		
		Total	*Per Colonist*	*Per Hectare*
Andhra Pradesh				
Aminabad	1963	92,700	927	230
Jeelugumilli	1963	46,866	1,616	267
Piduguralla	1963	185,600	2,900	895
Kalidindi	1963	168,260	608	304
Assam				
Kaki	1968	2,017,048	1,422	378
Baghbar	1968	2,506,450	1,043	853
Gobindpur	1968	964,950	1,965	2,926
Dandakaranya				
Dandakaranya Project (Refugees)	1971	212,000,000	13,200	4,391
Kerala				
High Ranges	1963	3,348,076	2,194	1,085
Wynad	1963	10,591,350	3,506	1,186
Madhya Pradesh				
Kansal Banjara	1963	45,000	1,800	445
Mysore				
Bylakuppe	1963	6,000,000	12,000	5,930
Orissa				
Hirakud oustees	1963	8,670,198	3,968	3,062
Rajasthan				
Rajasthan Canal Project (Overall)	1981	659,500,000	12,000	5,930
Tamil Nadu				
Moranam	1963	33,030	393	1,942
Velakapuram	1963	64,700	899	1,599

Sources and reliability: see text.

social or infrastructural services not supplied to colonists in ampler measure than to other citizens; also excluded is that proportion of estimated administrative costs which non-colonization expenditure, as just defined, is of total expenditure. Costs per colonist are derived from total estimated colonization expenditure by dividing it by 292,200—the estimated total number of agricultural colonists when the scheme is complete: this is in turn derived from the Master Plan's assumption of 2,922 villages each of 500 people and thus of 100 colonists (taking a family to consist of five members).[5] To arrive at cost per hectare, the estimated total cultivated command of 1,883,000 hectares has been taken (though in any one year only some 1·4 million hectares would be irrigated).[6]

To take projections as a basis for the calculation on the Rajasthan Canal Project is to run the grave risk that they will be falsified by events. It is already clear that the project has run into difficulties which are adding to the real cost per irrigated hectare and per colonist, and which must add to overall costs if the project is indeed ever completed. First, there is the problem of high wind velocities producing mobility in sand-dunes so that they threaten to overwhelm cultivated land. Research on such methods of stabilization as mulching and grass-planting is proceeding. Secondly, much more lining of channels and levelling of land than was assumed in the Master Plan has been found necessary; and, although a cheap method of lining is being explored, costs are bound to be heavier than contemplated. Thirdly, there is the existence of patches of alkaline clay-flats to which attention has already been directed. Rightly or wrongly, it is not planned to dig drainage channels, though these would remove salts dissolved out of the clays by the application of irrigation water. High future costs may arise here. This has certainly been the experience in the Chambal command, where drainage works and associated levelling and bunding are estimated to cost about Rs.3,200 per hectare.[7]

In all cases included in Table 14.I funds issued as loans to colonists or their Societies have been excluded from total costs, on the undoubtedly optimistic grounds that these will in the fullness of time be recovered. Total costs include funds provided by both the centre and the states, and also by such sources as post-war ex-servicemen's resettlement funds; and the high figure for Bylakuppe represents a special vote to that very special colony for Tibetan refugees.

There are, then, many reasons for lack of comparability between the colonies tabulated. Among further reasons is the inclusion of administrative overheads in the case of relatively self-contained projects like Dandakaranya and the Rajasthan Canal (though even here the figure for overheads cannot include the cost of the time of officials in state capitals and in New Delhi who were and are in various ways involved in work on them) but their exclusion, willy-nilly, in the case of smaller schemes—figures for which include only such items as costs of, or grants for reclamation, house-construction and initial assistance to colonists, or grants towards the share-capital of Co-operatives. Again, irrigated colonies are not comparable with unirrigated colonies; and it is arguable that the cost of the large schemes, notwithstanding the items excluded from the calculation, are partly debitable to 'regional development'.

By way of comparison with Table 14.I, expenditure per colonist recorded by the Programme Evaluation Organisation of the Planning Commission is shown in Table 14.II: 'Figures indicate expenditure made per settler in respect of funds under settlement schemes and other departmental or block assistance';[8] and apparently they include loans to colonists and Societies (whereas the author's estimates do not). It will be noted that the expenditure per colonist varies almost as widely as in the author's Table 14.I; though nowhere is the figure as low as that for some of the small interstitial colonies of Andhra Pradesh and Tamil Nadu. The figure quoted by the Organisation for Assam is in respect of the Kaki colony, and is much higher than the author's figure, though all but Rs.166·7 is supposed to refer to costs of reclamation. The Organisation points out that the relatively high cost of Rs.14,798·6 per colonist in the UP Tarai colonies of Pilibhit District was inflated by the need to provide roads, bridges, houses, and tubewells. It is salutary, if one is tempted to base eventual costs on original projections, to note that the first stage of the Tarai colonization in very similar physical conditions in Naini Tal District was estimated to cost no more than Rs.4,546 per colonist, of which Rs.823 was for roads, irrigation, and related works.[9] The Organisation's high figure for the Jethi colony results from the fact that of the original 47 colonists only 17 survive to be debited with the whole cost (see also above, p. 268).

The centrally sponsored scheme for the settlement of landless labourers which was mounted under the Third Plan and which formed the subject of the Organisation's inquiry allowed Rs.5,000 for each colonist; this again may be compared with the figures given in Tables 14.I and 14.II.

TABLE 14.II

Expenditure in Selected Colonies for Landless Labourers

State	*Colony*	*Total Expenditure per Colonist (rupees)*
Assam	Kaki	2,410·5
Bihar	Bhoodan Colonies, Gaya District	1,644·5
Gujarat	Jethi	12,065·7
Kerala	Chittari	3,162·5
Madhya Pradesh	Settlements in Guna District	1,090·8
Tamil Nadu	Attur	9,416·7
Uttar Pradesh	Pilibhit District	14,798·6

Source: Resettlement Programme, p. 22, Table 3.3.

What necessarily limited conclusions can be drawn from these two Tables, having due regard to non-comparability and other difficulties inherent in the data? First, some at any rate of the small colonies in Andhra Pradesh and Tamil Nadu recorded in Table 14.I appear to be relatively inexpensive in terms both of cost per colonist and cost per hectare: this is not surprising, given their interstitial nature and the absence of costly reclamation, canal construction, and the like (it was not possible to debit Kalidindi with any part of the cost of the Campbell Canal, at whose unreliable tail-end it is situated). Secondly, there seems to be a group of schemes represented in both Tables which cost between Rs.2,000 and Rs.4,000 per settler: these include the Rajasthan Canal if overall estimates are to be believed.

Thirdly, there is a group of high-cost schemes with costs of Rs.12,000 or more per colonist. This group includes Dandakaranya and Bylakuppe (Table 14.I) and Jethi and the Tarai colonies of Pilibhit District (Table 14.II). Available information does not permit full analysis of the reasons for this state of affairs. However, it may be suggested that mechanical reclamation of high jungle, and road construction in a remote area, partly account for high costs in Dandakaranya; as does the necessity for measures of rehabilitation for refugees. The figure for the Pilibhit colonies was inflated by the need for road and bridge construction in what is also a remote area; also by the cost of tubewells.[10] An explanation has already been given for Jethi.

In the absence of firmer data, it is perhaps best to proceed by assuming, with many reservations, that the cost to government of establishing a colonist in contemporary India varies (outside small, interstitial schemes on one hand, and the high-cost group on the other) from Rs.1,500 to Rs.4,000 or Rs.5,000, to use as a convenient upper limit the allowance made in the Third Plan centrally sponsored scheme. How does this range compare with costs elsewhere? It is not easy to answer this question with any precision, as the author found in another study some years ago and as K. J. Pelzer found in Indonesia, 'because of confused or missing data and because of the changing value of money'.[11] It may not be altogether too misleading, however, to quote one or two estimates. The author found that the average cost per colonist in Ceylon Dry Zone colonies up to 1951 was Rs.12,750 of which Rs.4,600 was attributed to irrigation costs; these compare well with an estimate of Rs.14,000 per colonist from a government committee, and of Rs.8,000 for the cost of a colonist, *not* including irrigation, made by a World Bank mission.[12] In 1953 the size of allotment and expenditure on housing were cut: the total cost per colonist was thereby almost halved, to Rs.6,535. Colonization in Ceylon before 1953 appears, then, to have been much more costly than the general level in India; and still well above that general level (especially if one allows for inflation) when the 1953 cuts were made. It must be remembered, however, that all the Ceylon colonies are irrigated, and that, with the restoration of ancient works that could be relatively easily and cheaply brought back into use, there has been a tendency towards a rise in the cost per unit area. Labour and other costs are also generally higher than in India. But the more lavish scale of assistance in Ceylon must also bear some of the responsibility.

It is not possible to arrive at costs for the Thal scheme (Pakistan) based on recent data; but estimates made some years ago suggest that 'the total cost per colonist may be in the region of Rs.7,000, made up of Rs.3,400 for irrigation and Rs.3,600 for other provision'.[13] The Thal is, of course, a region not unlike the Marusthali, and the colonization project there is generally similar to the Rajasthan Canal scheme. If the Thal estimates are anything to go by, they surely again suggest that the figures for the Rajasthan Canal colonies are a very considerable under-estimate; though it must be borne in mind that in the Thal a high scale of assistance was judged desirable to hasten development, and because of the need to deal with refugees (a need that has not yet affected the Rajasthan Canal area).

Return to Government from Colonization

Whatever the intrinsic or comparative interest of estimates of the cost of colonization, they do not in isolation settle the issues of marginality raised earlier in this chapter: clearly it is necessary to relate returns from colonization to the cost of it.

Now there was a time in India when such returns were assessed in terms of direct return to the government (through increased net revenue and irrigation rates) expressed as a percentage of the capital cost in question; and there were cases in which the 'profit' thus earned would have been high enough to satisfy a private entrepreneur. Thus in 1929–30 the government earned a net profit of 32 per cent on its investment in the three major Punjab Canal Colonies, those of Lyallpur, Shahpur, and Montgomery; and 9⅓ per cent on the whole Punjab system.[14] Indeed, after the development of the Sidhnai colony in the years following 1886, no irrigation scheme was attempted in the Punjab unless it brought an easy and profitable return;[15] and the Chenab colony had by 1907 repaid the capital laid out on it and was earning the government Rs.700,000 net annually in land revenue and water charges.[16] Sales by auction helped to bring a quicker return on capital. But it must be remembered that construction in the flat lands of the Punjab was relatively easy and cheap, and production and revenue from the fertile soils were high. Few if any recent Indian colonization schemes can operate under such favourable conditions. However, large areas in the Canal Colonies have suffered grievously from waterlogging and alkalinity: 15 per cent of the Rechna Doab has gone out of production.[17] It has been estimated that it may cost Rs.5,000–6,000 million to deal with the overall problem through drainage and pumping. If one argued that the need for these costly remedial works arises from deficiencies in the original design, and added their cost to the capital invested, then profitability would be greatly reduced if it did not vanish altogether; on the other hand, there is evidence that the problem arose largely from over-watering after a relaxation of official control.

There was some mention in chapter 12 of charges to colonists for land and water, considered in relation to land tenure and related matters. In the context of the present discussion such charges constitute the direct return to government agencies on their investment in colonization since independence. The Rajasthan authorities, largely following Punjab precedent, made an effort to raise income by such measures as sales by auction (now abolished) as well as through the collection of land revenue, betterment levy, and irrigation charges. This applied to land under Bhakra as well as that under the Rajasthan Canal. Unfortunately, however, it is not possible to quote the actual return on investment in either the Bhakra[18] or Rajasthan Canal projects: nor does the Master Plan quote projected revenue from them. But, whatever may be true of the Bhakra Project (as a whole, or taking only that part of it concerned with colonization in Rajasthan), general considerations make it very doubtful whether the Rajasthan Canal Project, or, more specifically, colonization within it, will ever earn the high returns given by the profitable Punjab Canal Colonies, if indeed there is a net return at all. One has in mind here not only the high, and probably under-estimated cost—given especially the likely physical conditions—but also 'the increasing political difficulty of levying . . . rural taxation in general' in contemporary India.

For the roughly comparable Thal scheme in Pakistan, E. De Vries made some interesting projections in 1950, on stated and generally reasonable (though in some respects rather favourable) assumptions.[19] So far as return to government was concerned, he took this to include not only increased land revenue and irrigation charges, but also estimated increases in railway income, taxation of secondary incomes, and road tax which could be attributed to the scheme. His results suggested that, with the accelerated development (including organized colonization) proposed by the Thal Development Authority, annual revenue would exceed annual costs over the whole Thal area in five years; and that, over an eighteen-year period, the average return on investment would be nearly 6 per cent. If the irrigation and road programme were undertaken without accelerated development, a net profit would be earned only after sixteen years, during which a deficit of Rs.58 million would have been accumulated. There may be lessons here for the Rajasthan Canal project. One is that accelerated development may well be a way of reducing or even removing losses to government in the earlier years of a project; but there are no firm data to enable us to determine whether this would be so in the Rajasthan case, or whether in terms of return to government the project were better not undertaken at all. It is also clear that accelerated development has been, and will probably continue to be, very difficult in Rajasthan, if only for lack of further financial resources to bring nearer a return on capital already invested in such things as headworks and canals. Finally, De Vries' results were, it must be stressed, forecasts about a scheme which in British times was not pursued because of its lack of attractiveness.[20] It would be interesting to see a retrospective evaluation, like that recently undertaken for the Gal Oya Project in Ceylon (which included colonization): this showed that, in spite of a directive that the Gal Oya Development Board should earn a 'reasonable return' on capital, its expenditure in all years exceeded its income.[21]

For the rest of the colonization schemes outside Rajasthan, this book has made it clear that so much has been done to resettle refugees, or in pursuance of the 'welfare motive' examined in chapter 6, that no return on government capital has been expected, nor will it probably be obtained in a wide range of schemes;[22] and that the prevalence of arrangements for low, deferred, or unfixed and uncollected charges reinforces this conclusion.

Costs and Benefits to the National Economy

But in the context of colonization it will be appreciated that return on government capital gives no firmer an indication of the marginality or otherwise of the enterprise than does the domestic economy of the colonist. Here, where both state and individual expenditure and return are involved, there is clearly a need for social benefit/cost analysis, which might take account of the opportunity cost of dealing with refugees and the 'welfare' categories if they were not settled as colonists: and indicate whether the extension of cultivation was likely to be a net gain or a net loss to the national economy, ideally on alternative assumptions concerning irrigation (or the lack of it), scales of subsidy, and so forth. The author did explore the possibility of obtaining data which would enable such an analysis to be made, but not surprisingly his intentions were frustrated by sheer lack of information. Even where actual or forecast government expenditure was available (usually, however, omitting overheads) there was little or no information on costs to the individual colonists or on benefits beyond what could be deduced for schemes in operation by rough calculations derived from cropped areas, declared average yields, and assumed prices. Moreover, experience on the Gal Oya Project Evaluation Committee demonstrated the need not only for advanced theory and technique but also for a team of workers able to turn whatever scanty and unreliable data may exist to optimum use;[23] the individual research worker engaged in no more than a reconnaissance of colonization in India is severely limited.

Nor does there seem to be any secondary material which would enable one to answer basic questions on the marginality of Indian colonization. True, there has been a considerable volume of work which, with varying degrees of sophistication and success, applies the technique of benefit/cost analysis to Indian irrigation projects.[24] But, as the reader will appreciate, by no means all of these projects involve colonization—some, indeed, drown more cropped land than they bring newly into cultivation—and none of the studies are such that they answer the fundamental question of the marginality or otherwise of the contemporary colonization of wasteland.

However, there is one exception, though even this is indicative rather than definitive: Michel's discussion of the US Bureau of Reclamation's report on the Rajasthan Canal project—in which, of course, colonization plays a large and fundamental part.[25] The Team had no time for more than a brief inspection, and indicated that a comprehensive study would demand years of work on land classification, agricultural economics, settlement studies, and planning generally. They formed the opinion 'based upon the available data, inspection of the area, and a comparison with somewhat similar developments in the United States', that 'a cost benefit ratio for the proposed Project development would exceed 1:1': that is, costs would exceed benefits. They added that, were a formal request to be made for financial assistance, much more data would be needed. There appears never to have been a full economic feasibility study of the Project.

Michel adds that 'viewed realistically, and perhaps undiplomatically, the Rajasthan Project in its ultimate form is a dubious one', though there are obvious attractions in extending a Canal parallel to the frontier with Pakistan down to a point opposite the Sukkur barrage on the Indus.

Here again there may be a parallel with the Thal scheme. The chariness of the British about the Thal will be remembered. De Vries, in the work already mentioned, did conclude that the scheme would make an addition of about Rs.80 million annually to national income between the sixth and twelfth years, tapering off thereafter; but he appears not to have related these benefits to costs.[26]

While, therefore, one is hampered by lack of data and of relevant studies, enough is known to cast considerable doubt on the economic wisdom (in benefit/cost terms) of extending cultivation farther into the waste by means of large and expensive projects like the Rajasthan Canal; and, one might add, by small and *less* expensive projects on poor soils or otherwise subject to adverse natural conditions which increase capital costs, or increase the need for inputs like fertilizers, or reduce output. It may be that less expensive projects subject to more favourable conditions are still within the geographical limit corresponding to the economic margin of cultivation. This may apply to Greater Malnad. In spite of high costs, Dandakaranya may be within, or come within, the limit given the present higher degree of adaptation of the refugee colonists to the environment and the advent of irrigation; so may the UP Tarai, now an area of high potential.[27] Whether it will ever apply to the Rajasthan Canal Project, or to any part of it, must depend on the extent to which total production, with the introduction of new methods, crops and varieties, counterbalances total costs.[28]

Whatever the precise answer to the question of marginality, it seems possible to conclude that Indian colonization schemes, and all likely areas of colonization, are near enough to the margin for it to be highly desirable—indeed, necessary—that proposals for new colonies should be judged in the light of a proper combination of natural resource surveys and benefit/cost analysis.[29]

Colonization, Food Supply, and Foreign Exchange

It may be argued that, in a country with the acute foreign exchange crisis that has long afflicted India, an economic activity of no net benefit to the economy (as measured by benefit/cost analysis) may nevertheless be justified, at any rate in the short term, if it is a notable net earner of foreign exchange. Any claim that agricultural colonization may assert in this connection can be quickly dismissed. Production of crops that enter, or may theoretically enter into the export trade plays a very small part in the colonies: some pepper and ginger in the High Ranges of Kerala and in Wynad (which also produces citronella and coffee), cashew nuts in one or two places, oilseeds as a subsidiary crop in Dandakaranya, the Chambal Valley, and elsewhere. The limitcd production of cotton in a few colonies may, of course, be held to supply raw material for an industry which makes significant exports; there may be potential here in Rajasthan.

It is not possible to quantify the expert-oriented production of colonization schemes, but it must be very small indeed.

This book has, indeed, made it abundantly clear that the colonies devote themselves almost exclusively to the growing of foodgrains and of other foodstuffs such as pulses and sugar-cane. None of these enter into the export trade, nor can they while India's food supply is hazardous or while necessary buffer-stocks are being built up.[30] The Master Plan for the Rajasthan Canal project does, in a somewhat visionary way, contemplate the possibility of exports by rail and navigable waterways through the port of Kandla on the Gulf of Cutch;[31] but its main emphasis is naturally on production for the national market.

It is, of course, perfectly arguable that, were it not for the foodstuffs produced in the colonization schemes, India would have to import an equivalent amount, to the detriment of the foreign exchange position, unless nutritional standards were to suffer. It is well known that during the Third Plan period the slow rate of growth of agricultural production, coupled with a succession of bad harvests, 'led to an alarming increase in dependence on imports of foodgrains and other agricultural commodities'.[32] Indeed, India was on average importing annually some 5 million tonnes of foodgrains; and imports were maintained at a high level for several years thereafter. A very rough estimate (based on the yield figures given in Table 9.II, and on others not there quoted because of their unreliability) suggests that in the middle year of the Third Plan period agricultural colonization schemes were producing some 64,000 tonnes of rice and 30,000 tonnes of wheat, together with *jowar*, maize, and other foodgrains; perhaps something of the order of 120,000 tonnes of foodgrains in all—that is, a little under 2½ per cent of the average annual imports during the Plan period (or about 0·15 per cent of total national production at the time). But this, it must be remembered, was before the new varieties of the 'green revolution' had spread to the colonies, and at a time when the Rajasthan Canal had barely begun to affect its command, and then on a non-perennial basis. According to tables published with the Master Plan for the Canal,[33] production of wheat would rise from 22,400 tonnes in 1966 to 299,700 tonnes in 1971, 555,600 tonnes in 1976 and 605,000 tonnes in 1981; and of all foodgrains from 104,000 tonnes in 1966 to 531,000 tonnes in 1971, 984,000 tonnes in 1976 and 1,064,000 tonnes in 1981. By 1981 there would also be, it was said, an annual production of 83,000 tonnes of oilseeds, 1,181,000 tonnes of sugar-cane and garden produce, and 142,000 tonnes of cotton. These are, of course, but forecasts; and many reasons have been given in this book why actual production may fall far short of the projections. But it may yet be that in ten years' time colonization schemes, largely because of developments in Rajasthan, but also because of the extension of the cultivated area in Dandakaranya and elsewhere and because of improved yields per unit area in some well-placed older schemes, will be making a substantially bigger absolute and relative contribution to the national food supply, and thus to import-saving, than in the Third Plan period or at the time of writing.

But, even if it is granted that India should, because of its need to reduce food imports or even to become a food exporter, continue with colonization schemes which may be a loss to the country's internal economy, it need not do so if an economic, or less uneconomic means of achieving the same production is available. The question must now be asked whether the intensification of production on the existing cultivated land supplies just such a means, or will supply it in the foreseeable future.

Colonization *versus* Intensification

During his fieldwork in India, and in the course of discussions with officials then and subsequently, the author was struck by the frequency with which he encountered two related points of view. The first had it that the extension of the cultivated area, whether by colonization or by other means, must go on until all 'available land' had been cultivated. The idea that cultivation might stop short of totality, at some geographical limit corresponding to the economic margin, however defined, was often greeted with incredulity if not astonishment; and the notion that cultivation might eventually retreat from difficult land, as has happened in many advanced countries, notably in Provence and in Highland Britain, was considered altogether too fanciful (though the attempts in Orissa, as part of the 'Podu Prevention Campaign' to get shifting cultivators to abandon steep slopes and resettle on flatter land may be seen as a retreat of this sort). V. V. Giri's 'motto', already quoted, that 'every inch of available land everywhere' should be utilized is illustrative of this point of view.[34] Perhaps the notion of the inevitable expansion of the cultivated area is a survival from the days when the only available method of dealing with an increase in population was to take in land from the waste; and also a continuation of the long-standing Indian tradition that he who opens up and cultivates waste-land has rights in it. It is also undoubtedly bound up with misapprehensions about the nature of 'culturable waste' and imprecision in defining 'cultivability'. It is only fair to add that the notion has not been universally held by Indians or those who have worked in India. As long ago as 1912 G. Keatinge wrote, of the then Bombay Deccan,

'The fact is that cultivation has already extended to poorer land than is desirable and a diminution in the cultivated area is to be wished for rather than an increase'; and he went on to emphasize the need for improved methods on lands already cultivated.[35] There are also foresters who, ever leaping to the defence of their interests, have claimed that reclamation of land is a matter of political expediency and that there is a need to peg, or even to reverse, the present geographical limits of cultivation.[36]

The second point of view, apparently associated with the first in many minds, is that, while the intensification of agricultural production is desirable, it is necessarily complementary to, and not alternative to, the extension of the cultivated area. The detached observer of the Indian scene may perhaps be forgiven for thinking that here is another example of the characteristically Indian way of resolving a dilemma, intellectual or practical, by having it both ways. The Indian Five Year Plans, up to and including the Third at any rate, have envisaged both the extension of area and intensification. The Pakistan First Five Year Plan had it, moreover, that 'The increases in crop production under the Plan are expected to be obtained from a large number of irrigation, drainage and reclamation projects and from higher acre yields on area under crops'.[37] Ceylon, similarly, has used both methods of increasing production, though the Agricultural Plan of 1958 did say, with some acerbity:

> No attempt has however yet been made to work out comprehensively to what extent extensive cultivation—to quote a convenient term to cover schemes of land development, irrigation and colonization—can play a dynamic role in economic development or even to assess its contribution to the achievement of the oft-proclaimed target of self-sufficiency in the staple food of the country, rice. Nor has any serious attempt been made to see whether expenditure incurred on these schemes is commensurate with the returns . . .[38]

Moreover, more recent work *has* attempted to quantify the costs and benefits of colonization in Ceylon and has thrown even more serious doubts on its economics.[39]

The discussion in the present chapter (and, indeed, in this book more widely) has cast similar doubts on at least the economic arguments for extending the cultivated area by means of colonization schemes; and, at least by implication, on the extension of the cultivated area more generally. Can anything be said about the relative strength of the economic arguments for intensification as compared with those for extending the cultivated area, especially by colonization?

In theory the methods of benefit/cost analysis could be used to compare the relative performance, actual or projected, of the two methods of increasing agricultural production. Indeed, a report by the UN Economic Commission for Asia and the Far East has it that 'If the problem is to compare one project for the improvement of soils on existing cultivated lands by supplementary irrigation and drainage or fertilization, with one for reclaiming and irrigating new lands, the ratios of benefits to costs in the two ventures can provide the answer'.[40] One gathers that the method has in fact been used in the United States in order to determine the relative economic merits of the extension of the cultivated area and the improvement of water management.

But if lack of data and the 'reconnaissance' nature of the author's inquiry inhibited any attempt to assess the social benefits and costs of Indian colonization, even less is it possible to attempt a corresponding analysis of agricultural improvement. One or two considerations may, however, be urged. In the first place, agricultural improvement appears to be even more subject to hidden costs than is colonization, and a careful effort would have to be made to estimate these. One thinks in particular of the costs of the agricultural extension service. It is naïve in the extreme to assume, as a Ceylon report appears to assume, that the sole charge to be set against 'costly schemes of colonisation' is that for fertilizer (estimated at only Rs.40) which would, under conditions of good drainage and good water supply, result in improved production worth Rs.180 on an acre (0·4 hectare) of paddy.[41] Quite apart from the cost of drainage and of irrigation where the specified conditions do not obtain, and of labour, pesticides and other inputs necessary anywhere if the improvement mentioned is to be effected, there is the cost of the whole hierarchy of officials engaged in propagating improved methods, co-operative credit, and the rest. It may be argued that these constitute a social service; but the author agrees with the ECAFE Report already cited that there is a *prima facie* case for including these costs. Certainly if they are included for colonization (and it has been shown that they are there by no means negligible) they must likewise be included for agricultural improvement, where they may be very high. The author was able to obtain data in 1963 on the IADP programme in Mandya District of Mysore, where the budget provision for that year amounted to Rs.13 lakhs and covered such items as staff, transport, training, workshop, demonstration costs and soil- and seed-testing laboratories. It did not cover the costs of officials outside the District who were nevertheless concerned with the Programme. In sum, the cost to the economy of improvement, at least in its initial phases, may be much heavier than might at first sight appear. Indeed, A. A. L. Caesar has said of conditions in Yugoslavia 'intensification of agriculture . . . may involve greater costs than does extensification' (that is, the extension of the cultivated area).[42] It should not be forgotten, however, that a social benefit/cost analysis should properly attempt to assess the opportunity costs of the bureaucracy and estimate what it would cost and do for the economy if *not* organizing improvement or colonization.[43]

A second observation, arising largely from the author's experiences with the Gal Oya Project Evaluation Committee in Ceylon,[44] is that benefit/cost analysis is more likely to be a reliable guide to choice between alternatives if those alternatives fall into the same category: for example, if the choice is between two irrigation projects rather than between colonization on one hand and improvement on the other.

Thirdly, there is the important point that benefit/cost analysis as a guide to the choice between colonization and improvement (the principal concern here) needs to be disaggregated if it is to be meaningful: that is, it is not reasonable to assume that for the whole of India the choice should be either colonization (or the more general extension of cultivation) on the one hand, or improvement on the other.[45] The analysis must relate to specific projects and areas; and the upshot is likely to be a mix of extension and improvement, the best combination of economic schemes for both—unless, that is, *all* projects for colonization are even more uneconomic than this book has tentatively suggested some may be. This mix, based on careful analysis (albeit on certain assumptions which would have to be made at the outset) is not the same as uncritically having it both ways.

So far as the author is aware, no study of this sort has been made; although Michel has stated his intention 'in the next study of a twenty-year series' to investigate 'the relative advantage of expanding still further into Rajasthan rather than concentrating water on the existing canal commands'[46] and claims that the work done by the US Bureau of Reclamation already suggests that India should concentrate on the former rather than the latter. He also makes the general statement that if there is ultimately 'a shift from a policy of adding new lands of dubious productivity to one of concentrating irrigation supplies and other inputs on the best of the existing lands, then India should be far better off in the long run'.[47]

The author's guess is that the result of the comparative analysis, nation-wide but disaggregated, that has just been discussed might produce a rather different mix. It might or might not include the Rajasthan Canal Project, in whole or in part (for that Project itself is capable of disaggregation), or Dandakaranya, or UP Tarai; but it might well include areas of relatively low-cost colonization, particularly those of an interstitial character which, by the same token, do not need much by way of infrastructure (provided, of course, that they could be shown to give a sufficient return). As for other methods of extending the frontiers of cultivation, such enterprises as State farms and plantations would be susceptible to similar comparative analysis (indeed, they might be compared not only with agricultural improvement but with each other and with colonization) and the result might be yet another 'mix'. But the piecemeal encroachment, licit or illicit, of the individual cultivator on to the waste would probably defy analysis: and in any case seems bound to go on, even if the marginal return is slight, until alternative means of livelihood present themselves.

One other point must be made. Although, on the showing of Mandya District, to initiate the 'green revolution' by means of the IADP or similar programme carries expensive overheads, the hoped-for inputs of fertilizers, new varieties, pesticides, and improved methods may potentially bring with them such enormous increases in yields as to transform the benefit/cost ratio for intensification more markedly than for colonization. Or, to put the matter in plainer language, expensive methods of opening up new land may become less and less necessary as it becomes more and more possible to increase yields on existing lands. Writing on colonization in Ceylon some years ago, the author concluded that 'unless unbelievably rapid strides are made in existing paddy fields' the need for higher food production would mean 'some attention to the opening up of new lands, at least as an insurance' against the failure of a policy of giving priority to agricultural improvement.[48] And he quoted with approval a statement that none of the many authorities who have studied Ceylon 'have reached the conclusion that the agriculture of the Dry Zone (the principal area of colonization) must remain undeveloped on the ground that the gain to the national economy is incommensurate with the cost involved'.[49] He would no longer be sure, for there is mounting evidence that the cost *is* incommensurate with the return because of the impact on paddy yields of new varieties and improved practices.[50] So far as India is concerned, it may well be that, as the 'green revolution' gains momentum and as the land available grows more and more marginal, the optimum economic 'mix' of colonization and of other means of increasing agricultural production will come to include less and less of colonization.

Broader Considerations: Employment, Redistribution of Incomes, and Rehabilitation

So far, the discussion in this chapter has been conducted in purely economic terms, and, some may feel, rather narrowly at that because of its concentration on production and on benefit/cost ratios. Early in the chapter I mentioned the proclivity of individual cultivators to extend the geographical bounds of cultivation to the point of minute marginal returns, and this was taken as the starting-point for an examination of the marginality of land, especially in colonization schemes. But it might equally well have been the starting-point for an examination of the inexorable and inter-connected forces of landlessness, unemployment, and poverty that force Indians on to pathetic parcels of marginal land and make them candidates for government schemes of colonization.

The landlessness, unemployment, and poverty of the Indian village are too well known to need extended treatment here. And there is a growing realization that, although more objective and detailed research is necessary, the so-called 'green revolution' may bring benefit to the rich rather than the poor and, indeed, lead to an absolute as well as a relative deterioration in the condition of the already under-privileged tenant or agricultural labourer.[51]

Chapter 6 has shown that India has not lacked men like Tarlok Singh and V. V. Giri who have felt deep concern for the victims of rural poverty and who have believed that 'greater social and economic equality is an intrinsic good . . . possessed of an independent value'.[52] Voices like theirs are not lacking in India as the first fruits of the 'green revolution' become evident: G. Parthasarathy has, for example, recently proclaimed that 'the aim of public policy should be to ensure the benefit of the new productive forces to the weaker sections'.[53] These voices are powerfully reinforced by what appears to be a growing recognition in the world at large that economic growth as measured by rates of increase in *per capita* income must not be the sole object of policy; and that 'while there can . . . be no lasting progress without sustained high rates of growth', nevertheless 'goals must be set, and progress measured by other criteria as well—criteria which would reflect concern with the distribution as well as the growth of income'.[54]

Now it has been claimed by Pramit Chaudhuri that the reduction of unemployment has not been 'a major policy objective in the short run'—Indian planners having seen the employment objective as being in conflict with the growth objective; and that 'it has never been considered a part of planning strategy to ameliorate the condition of the poor through redistribution of income' but rather 'by chanelling the incremental benefits of economic growth to the poor'.[55] Myrdal has, on the other hand, pointed out 'a number of conditions that suggest that . . . an increase in equality would help rather than hinder development';[56] and demonstrated the importance of an egalitarian ideology in Indian thinking (while admitting that there has been 'a pattern of radicalism in talk but conservatism in action').[57]

Whatever the upshot of the conflict between economists on the influence of egalitarian policy on growth, there can be no doubt that sentiments and arguments for alleviating the condition of the rural poor have in recent years received a notable fillip from a new turn in the argument from political expediency. This is, of course, no new argument: chapter 6 has shown how the 'welfare motive' has frequently been mixed with expediency, usually to attract the support of some under-privileged group. But agrarian unrest in many parts of India, some of it connected with the unequal division of the spoils of the 'green revolution',[58] some of it more deeply seated, has led to renewed pressure for reform before it is too late and, more specifically, for greater attention to landlessness, unemployment, maldistribution of incomes, and poverty generally. Gross inequalities of economic opportunities and of incomes are seen as threats to economic and social stability, and therefore to economic development.[59]

Chapter 6 has also shown that, whatever the concentration on growth during the successive Five Year Plan periods, one of the concessions to the needs of the poor and unemployed was a programme of settlement on wasteland, by means which included agricultural colonization. Given the renewed interest in a more egalitarian distribution of income, it seems likely, then, that such programmes will continue, especially if in the Fifth and later Plans rather more financial resources are available. In March 1973 the President of India, V. V. Giri, whose views on colonization have frequently been quoted in this book, was able to announce that the government had decided 'to set up pilot land colonisation projects in some States to promote gainful employment in the rural areas' and to be the centre of 'a vast network of cottage and small-scale industries'.[60] The colonization schemes of the future will probably, then, continue to cater not only for oustees and other dispossessed cultivators but also for the needy, particularly Harijans and landless labourers (who may, or may not be Harijans). In the author's view, this is right, on grounds of equity and of concern for the poor, whatever the argument in terms of political expediency or of the effect on growth of a higher degree of equality.

But it does not mean that the findings of this book, and particularly those reached earlier in the present chapter, are irrelevant and that there is a case for settling the maximum number of the rural poor in colonies irrespective of other considerations and criteria. Colonization is likely to move as time goes on to more and more marginal land, at ever-increasing real cost: and perhaps, in spite of the 'green revolution', with gradually diminishing real returns. Therefore, on this ground alone, there is an overwhelmingly strong case for reviewing colonization policy nationally, regionally, and locally in the light of the costs and returns of alternative means of conferring equal benefits on those whom it is designed to help: for example, by the intensification of cultivation coupled with land reform. Reviews of this sort must, on the showing of this book, be based on a proper appraisal of natural resources and difficulties; and because the general context in India is changing so rapidly, there must be careful reconsideration from time to time.

Again, concern for the rural poor does not mean that no attention need be paid to cultivating ability when individual colonists are selected. The number of rural poor is so vast, the effect that can be made on their number by colonization so small, that no harm would be done if the best cultivators were chosen. Nor does concern for tribal peoples mean that colonization schemes must, of necessity, be created for them: on social grounds as well as economic, such schemes may not be a solution to the problem.

For the rest, this book has tried to bring out points about many different facets of colonization—from agricultural extension and the organization of land tenure to social conditions—which, the author believes, ought to be carefully considered by those responsible for the planning and administration of present and future colonization schemes in India, and, for that matter, elsewhere.

APPENDIX — COLONIES VISITED BY THE AUTHOR

State or Authority	Region (see p. 36)	Year of Visit	No. on Map 1	Colonization Scheme	Beneficiaries (type)	Number of Colonists* (to Dec. 1963)	Size of Holdings (hectares)
ANDHRA PRADESH	Eastern Ghats	1963	1A	Aminabad	Tribal (Land Col. Soc., Individual cultivation)	62	4
		1963	1B	Araku Valley (Ramakrishnanagar)	Tribal	18	2 (0·4 wet)
		1963	1C	Jeelugumilli	Tribal (Land Col. Soc., Individual cultivation)	29	6 (0·5 irrigated)
		1963	1D	Kannaram	Tribal	30	2 (0·4 wet)
		1963	1E	Piduguralla	Ex-servicemen's Co-op. Col. Soc. (Individual cultivation)	64	3·2
	Coastal deltas	1963	1F	Kalidindi	Ex-servicemen's Co-op. Col. Soc. (Individual cultivation)	273	2
ASSAM	Dry plains	1968	2A	Kaki	Landless	1,419 (1968)	Mostly 3·2
		1968	2B	Darapathar	Refugees	1,400 (1968)	0·87 paddy, 0·13 homestead
	Flooded plains	1968	2C	Baghbar	Refugees	2,400 (1968)	1,900 × 1·3; 500 × 0·8
		1968	2D	Gobindpur & Theka	Refugees	118 (1968)	0·67
BIHAR	Rajmahal Hills	1963	3A	Jamunia	Local Landless (Bhoodan, Individual cultivation)	112	2, 0·8 homestead
		1963	3B	Tilaiya	Oustees	1,001	Various
DANDAKARANYA	Dandakaranya	1963, 1972	4A	Malkangiri Zone	Refugees (some 'Group Farming')	1,027	2·71, 0·12 homestead
		1963, 1972	4B	Paralkote Zone		2,262	2·73, 0·07 homestead
		1963	4C	Pharasgaon Zone		251	2·73, 0·07 homestead
		1963	4D	Umarkote–Raighar Zone		2,839	2·71, 0·12 homestead
HARYANA	Desert	1963	5A,B	Bhakra	Local Landless, Oustees	199	Various
KERALA	Greater Malnad	1963	6A	Attapaddy Valley (Mukkali)	Tribal	25	2
		1963	6B	High Ranges	Landless, Oustees	1,526	2 (Oustees, 6·8–1·6)
		1963	6C	Wynad	Ex-service, Tribal, Local Landless	3,021	2 + 0·8 wet, or 4 dry

State or Authority	Region (see p. 36)	Year of Visit	No. on Map 1	Colonization Scheme	Beneficiaries (type)	Number of Colonists* (to Dec. 1963)	Size of Holdings (hectares)
MADHYA PRADESH	Chambal Valley (see also Rajasthan)	1963	7A	Chambal Ravines	Local Landless and Ex-servicemen	64	4 mainly
		1963	7B	Chambal Right Bank	Local Landless and Others	500	Various
		1963	7C	Gandhisagar	Oustees	1,400	Various (up to 40)
	Malwa	1963	7D	Gundrai	Local Landless	28	5·3–6·1
		1963	7E	Intikheri (Kerala)	Kerala people	128	4·8
		1963	7F	Intikheri (others)	Local Landless and Refugees	320	3·6, 4·0, 6·1
		1963	7G	Kansal Banjara	Tribal	25	4
		1963	7H	Kotia Pani	Tribal	25	4
		1963	7I	Mircabad	Tribal	55	2, 4
	Dandakaranya	1963	7J	Bunagaon	Tribal	16	4 paddy (*less* old holding), 0·4 garden
		1963	7K	Kanera & Mardel	Tribal	20	4
		1963	7L	Paisra	Tribal	20	4
MAHARASHTRA	Dandakaranya (Chanda Dist)	1963	8A	Palasgaon	Local Landless (Co-op. Joint Farming Soc.)	29	63 *total*
		1963	8B	Sindewahi	Local Landless (Co-op. Joint Farming Soc.)	20	8 *total* (to 1963)
	Khandesh	1963	8C	Bhamer: Jayashree	Local Landless (Co-op. Joint Farming Soc.)	16	61 *total*
		1963	8D	Bhamer: Mahatma Fule	Local Landless (Co-op. Joint Farming Soc.)	24	123 *total*
	—	1963	8E	Amalner (Pailad)	Local Landless (Co-op. Collective Farming Soc.)	20	40 *total*
	—	1963	8F	Pabal	Local Landless, Backward Classes (Co-op. Joint Farming Soc.)	12	29 *total*
MYSORE	Greater Malnad	1963	9A	Arwatagi	Local Landless (Tenant Farming Soc.)	50	1·6–3·2
		1963	9B	Bylakuppe	Tibetan Refugees	500	2
		1963	9C	Kambaraganavi	Local Harijans	33	2·4 wet, 1·6 dry
		1963	9D	Sorapur	Local Landless (Tenant Farming Soc.)	39	1·6–6·1
	Raichur Doab	1963	9E	Tungabhadra	Oustees	2,277	0·8–4·0

State or Authority	*Region* (see p. 36)	*Year of Visit*	*No. on Map 1*	*Colonization Scheme*	*Beneficiaries (type)*	*Number of Colonists** (*to Dec. 1963*)	*Size of Holdings* (*hectares*)
ORISSA	Dandakaranya	1963	10A	Nuagam & Nuapara	Tribal	28	2·8
		1963	10B	Pandripani	Tribal Oustees	40	2·8
		1963	10C	Sunabeda	Tribal	62	2·8 dry + 0·3 garden
	—	1963	10D	Hirakud Oustees	Oustees	610	Various
RAJASTHAN	Desert	1963	11A	Bhakra Canal	Local Landless, Ex-service, Various	15,802	Standard 6·32
		1963, 1972	11B	Rajasthan Canal	Local Landless, Various	1,578	Standard 12·65
	Chambal Valley (see also Madhya Pradesh)	1963	11C	Chambal Valley Project	Oustees	N/A	Various
		1963	11D	Ranapratapsagar	Oustees	1,926	Various
TAMIL NADU	Greater Malnad	1963	12A	Thengumarahada	Local Landless (Some Tribal) (Co-op. Col. Soc., Individual cultivation)	141	0·8 wet, 0·4 dry
	—	1963, 1972	12B	Moranam	Local Landless (Co-op. Col. Soc., Individual cultivation)	84	0·8 wet, 1·2 dry
	—	1963	12C	Rajannagar	Oustees	138	Various (0·8–12·1)
	—	1963	12D	Velakapuram	Local Landless (Co-op. Joint Farming Soc.)	72	40 *total*
UTTAR PRADESH	Tarai	1963	13A	Kheri	Landless, Educated unemployed	688	4, 8
		1963	13B	Pilibhit	Landless, Educated unemployed	457	4, 8
		1963	13C	Sardapuri	Sikh Refugees (Bhoodan Joint Farming)	350	1,821 *total*
		1963, 1972	13D	Tarai (Naini Tal Dist)	Refugees, Ex-service, Political Sufferers, Landless, etc.	4,599	2·0–20·2

* For later figures (when available) see text.

GLOSSARY

(Geographical names more familiar in an alternative version are included.)

abadi site of a village and its houses
adivasi member of an 'aboriginal' tribe (see p. 275)
aman rice crop in Bengal and Assam grown under deep-water conditions; transplanted in May–June, harvested Nov.–Jan.
anicut weir to divert water from a stream or river into an irrigation channel
aus rice crop in Bengal and Assam grown under not more than 0·75 m of water; sown in April, harvested July–Sept.
ayacut area commanded by an irrigation work
bajra the millet *Pennisetum typhoideum*
bar the higher and drier part of a *doab*, away from the rivers in the Punjab
barani rain-fed, i.e. unirrigated, land or cultivation
bazar permanent market or street of shops
BDO Block Development Officer
bhadralok the urban élite in Bengal
bhil or *bil* marsh or lagoon in Bengal and Assam
Bhil tribe whose members are found over wide areas of western India
Bhoodan movement originating with Vinoba Bhave, involving the gift of land to the poor and landless (lit. 'land-gift')
bhumidar see ch. 12, p. 228
bhumiswami see ch. 12, p. 228
bigha Indian measure of area varying from region to region
bund artificial embankment, especially of an irrigation tank or of a paddy-field
chowkidar watchman
crore ten million or one hundred *lakhs*
dacoit robber belonging to an armed gang
doab land between two rivers
Duars Tarai-like tracts at the foot of the outermost Himalayan range in Bengal and Assam
eksali tenure for one year
gair khatedari see ch. 12, pp. 230–1
Ganga (river) Ganges (and the word 'Gangetic' is still used)
Gramdan movement originating with Vinoba Bhave, later than Bhoodan, involving the communalizing of entire villages (lit. 'village-gift')
Harijan 'man of god', name given by Gandhi to 'untouchable' castes
Haryana the Indian state created on 1 Nov. 1966 from the Hindi-speaking parts of Punjab state
hat a market-place (Bengali equivalent of *mandi*)

HYVP or HVP High Yielding Varieties Programme
IAAP Intensive Agricultural Area Programme
IADP Intensive Agricultural District Programme
jamindar see *zamindar*
jowar the millet *Sorgham vulgare*
kachcha Hindi for raw, crude, unripe, uncooked; but used metaphorically to convey inferiority or temporary nature, e.g. a *kachcha* road is unmetalled, a *kachcha* house is built of mud. Opposite of *pukka*
kankar layer of limestone concretions found in the soil profile in dry areas of India
Kanyakumari town in southernmost Tamil Nadu whose anglicized form gave the name to Cape Comorin
Kaveri (river) Cauvery
kharif the southwest monsoon cropping season
khatedari see ch. 12, pp. 230–1
Krishna (river) Kistna
lakh one hundred thousand
mandi market-place
mesta *Hibiscus cannabinus*, a jute substitute
maund Indian measure, generally 82·28 lb (37·32 kg)
mirasi tenure by large landowners cultivating with hired labour or share-croppers
Naik Tehsildar revenue official
Namasudra name acquired by caste of 'untouchables' in Bengal
Narmada (river) Narbada
oustee person ejected from his land because it is required for a public purpose, e.g. an irrigation reservoir
panchayat local or village council
panchayat samiti committee at Block level of heads of *panchayats*
patta a written document settling title and/or land revenue
pattedar holder of a *patta*
patwari village accountant and record-keeper
podu patch under shifting cultivation (Orissa)
pukka Hindi for ripe, cooked, mature; used metaphorically to convey superiority or permanence, e.g. a *pukka* road is metalled, a *pukka* house is built of stone or burnt brick. Opposite of *kachcha*
rabi 'winter' or northeast monsoon cropping season
ragi the millet *Eleusine coracana*
raiyat see *ryot*
Ramanathapuram Ramnad
regur black cotton soil
ryot peasant or cultivator
ryotwari tenure by cultivators who have permanent rights in land and who pay revenue direct to government
sal the timber tree *Shorea robusta*
sarpanch president of a *panchayat*
Srirangapatnam Seringapatam
Sudra fourth rank of castes, usually cultivators

taccavi direct loan from the government
taluk, taluka administrative subdivision of a District
Tarai flat belt of country along the foot of the southernmost range of the Himalayan system
tehsil administrative subdivision of a District
Tehsildar revenue official in charge of a *tehsil*
Varanasi Benares or Banaras
Vishakhapatnam Vizagapatam
VLW Villege-Level Worker
Yamuna (river) Jumna
zamindar generally an intermediary between the cultivators and the state; *zamindars* were often recognized by the British as landlords

ABBREVIATIONS FOR STANDARD REFERENCES

Baden-Powell	B. H. Baden-Powell. *The Land Systems of British India: Being a Manual of the Land-Tenures and of the Systems of Land-Revenue Administration Prevalent in the Several Provinces.* 3 vols. Oxford, Clarendon Press, 1892.
Baden-Powell (Holderness)	B. H. Baden-Powell. *A Short Account of the Land Revenue and its Administration in British India: with a Sketch of the Land Tenures.* 2nd edn, rev. T. W. Holderness. Oxford, Clarendon Press, 1907.
Census 19—	*Census of India, 19—.* New Delhi, Registrar-General, year of publication indicated.
Chambers	R. J. H. Chambers. *Settlement Schemes in Tropical Africa: a Study of Organizations and Development.* London, Routledge & Kegan Paul, 1969.
Champion and Osmaston	E. P. Stebbing. *The Forests of India*, vol. 4: *History from 1925 to 1947 of the Forests now in Burma, India, and Pakistan*, ed. Sir Harry Champion and F. C. Osmaston. London, OUP, 1962.
Dandakaranya Project Report	*The Dandakaranya Project: Revised Project Report*, duplicated. Koraput, Dept of Rehabilitation, n.d.
Darling	Sir Malcolm Darling. *The Punjab Peasant in Prosperity and Debt.* 4th edn. Bombay, OUP, 1947.
Etienne	Gilbert Etienne. *Studies of Indian Agriculture*, M. Mothersole, trans. Berkeley, Calif., Univ. of California Press, 1968.
Farmer (1957)	B. H. Farmer. *Pioneer Peasant Colonization in Ceylon: a Study in Asian Agrarian Problems.* London, OUP for RIIA, 1957.
Farmer (1969)	B. H. Farmer. *Agricultural Colonization in South and South-East Asia.* The St John's College, Cambridge, Lecture 1968–9. Hull, Univ. of Hull, 1969.
First Plan	*The First Five Year Plan.* New Delhi, Planning Commission, 1951.
First Plan (Draft Outline)	*The First Five Year Plan: a Draft Outline.* New Delhi, Planning Commission, 1951.
Fourth Plan (Draft Outline)	*Fourth Five Year Plan: a Draft Outline.* New Delhi, Planning Commission, n.d. [1966].
Fourth Plan 1969–74 (Draft)	*Fourth Five Year Plan 1969–74, Draft.* New Delhi, Planning Commission, 1969.
Fourth Plan	*Fourth Five Year Plan, 1969–74.* New Delhi, Planning Commission, n.d. [1970].

Giri	V. V. Giri. *Jobs for Our Millions*. Madras, Vyasa Publications, 1970.
Irrigation Commission	*Report of the Irrigation Commission, 1972*. 3 vols, vol. III in 2 pts. New Delhi, Ministry of Irrigation and Power, 1972.
Legris	P. Legris. 'La Végétation de l'Inde', *Travaux de la Section Scientifique et Technique de l'Institut Français de Pondichéry*, vol. 6 (1963).
Michel	A. A. Michel. *The Indus Rivers: a Study of the Effects of Partition*. London, Yale UP, 1967.
Punjab Colony Manual	J. G. Beazley and F. H. Puckle. *The Punjab Colony Manual*, vol. 1. Lahore, Supt of Govt Printing, 1922.
Rajasthan Canal Master Plan	*Rajasthan Canal Project: Master Plan of Development*, duplicated. Jaipur, Rajasthan Canal Board, n.d., quoted by kind permission of the Chief Secretary, Rajasthan.
Rajasthan Canal Soil Survey	UN Development Programme and Food and Agriculture Organization of the UN. *Soil Survey and Soil and Water Management Research and Demonstration in the Rajasthan Canal Area, India, Technical Report 1* (Rome, 1971), *Soil Survey and Land Classification:* 1.1 Reconnaissance Survey of the Phase II Area 1.2 Semidetailed Soil Survey of the Anupgarh Shakha Area 1.5 Semidetailed Soil Survey of the South Phase II Area (Other parts of the *Report* had not been released at the time of writing.)
Rajputana Desert Symposium	'Proceedings of the Symposium on the Rajputana Desert', *Bull. National Inst. Sciences, India*, no. 1 (1952).
Resettlement Programme	*Resettlement Programme for Landless Agricultural Labourers: Case Studies of Selected Colonies*, duplicated. New Delhi, Programme Evaluation Organisation, Planning Commission, 1968.
Second Plan	*The Second Five Year Plan*. New Delhi, Planning Commission, 1956.
Soil Survey	*Final Report of the All-India Soil Survey Scheme*. Delhi, Manager of Publications, 1953.
Spate	O. H. K. Spate. *India and Pakistan*, 2nd edn. London, Methuen, 1957.
Spate and Learmonth	O. H. K. Spate and A. T. A. Learmonth. *India and Pakistan*. 3rd rev. edn of the above. London, Methuen, 1967.
Study on Wastelands	*Study on Wastelands including Saline, Alkali and Waterlogged Lands and Their Reclamation Measures*. New Delhi, Planning Commission, 1963.

Surveys of Natural Resources 1963	*A Co-ordinated Study of Organisations concerned with the Surveys of Natural Resources*, duplicated. New Delhi, Planning Commission, 1963.
Surveys of Natural Resources 1971	*A Co-ordinated Study of Organisations concerned with the Surveys of Natural Resources*, duplicated. New Delhi, Planning Commission, 1971.
Survey of Wastelands (followed by name of state)	Wastelands Survey and Reclamation Committee (the Uppal Committee). *Report on Location and Utilisation of Wastelands in India.* New Delhi, Ministry of Food and Agriculture: Pt I Punjab (1960) Pt II West Bengal (1960) Pt III Bihar (1960) Pt IV Mysore (1960) Pt V Andhra Pradesh (1961) Pt VI Madhya Pradesh (1961) Pt VII Kerala (1961) Pt VIII Madras (1961) Pt IX Jammu and Kashmir (1961) Pt X Uttar Pradesh (1962) Pt XI Maharashtra (1962) Pt XII Gujarat (1963)
Tarai Report	*Report of the Tarai and Bhabar Development Committee: Appointed by the United Provinces Government for the Investigation of Land Development and Colonization Schemes for Ex-servicemen.* Allahabad, Supt of Govt Printing, 1947.
Third Plan	*The Third Five Year Plan.* New Delhi, Planning Commission, 1961.

Notes

Chapter 1: Introduction

1 See Farmer (1957).
2 Chambers, p. xii.
3 Ibid. p. 10.
4 *Resettlement Programme.*
5 Giri.

Chapter 2: Historical Background

1 See B. C. Law, *Historical Geography of Ancient India* (Paris, Société Asiatique de Paris, n.d. [?1954]), pp. 40–2.

2 See *The Travels of Fa-hsien (399–414 A.D.), or Record of the Buddhistic Kingdoms*, re-trans. H. A. Giles (Cambridge, CUP, 1932), pp. 36 and 38; also p. 41 for mention of the large forest north of Pataliputra (near modern Patna).

3 W. H. Moreland, *India at the Death of Akbar* (London, Macmillan, 1920), pp. 7–22.

4 Ibid. p. 126.

5 cf. Spate, pp. 148–9.

6 Ashin Das Gupta, *Some Characteristics of Medieval Asian Trade* (cyclostyled, paper read at a seminar under the auspices of the South Asia Inst., Univ. of Heidelberg, at Herrenalb, West Germany, 1966).

7 cf. Morris D. Morris, 'Towards a Reinterpretation of Nineteenth-Century Indian Economic History', *J. Econ. Hist.*, vol. 23 (1963), pp. 606–18, at p. 607.

8 Irfan Habib, *The Agrarian System of Mughal India, 1556–1707* (London, Asia Publishing House for Dept of History, Aligarh Muslim Univ., 1963), p. 1.

9 R. C. Majumdar and others, *An Advanced History of India*, 2nd edn (London, Macmillan, 1950), p. 197 (where the form Hiuen Tsang is used).

10 *Imperial Gazetteer of India, The Indian Empire*, vol. 2 (Historical), (Oxford, Clarendon Press, 1909), p. 300.

11 Ibid. p. 304.

12 W. H. Moreland, *The Agrarian System of Muslim India* (Cambridge, Heffer, 1920), pp. 50–1.

13 Ibid. p. 132 and Moreland's *From Akbar to Aurangzeb* (London, Macmillan, 1923), p. 202.

14 S. C. Gupta, *Agrarian Relations and Early British Rule in India: a Case Study of Ceded and Conquered Provinces* (*Uttar Pradesh*) (*1801–1833*) (London, Asia Publishing House, 1963), p. 29.

15 T. H. Beaglehole, *Thomas Munro and the Development of Administrative Policy in Madras, 1792–1818* (Cambridge, CUP, 1966), p. 47.

16 H. K. Trevaskis, *The Land of the Five Rivers* (London, OUP, 1928), p. 187.

17 Moreland, *From Akbar to Aurangzeb*, ch. 7.

18 See, for one region, S. S. Padhye, 'Desertion of Villages in the Deccan Trap Region of Vidarbha', *Bombay Geogr. Rev.*, vol. 13 (1965), pp. 137–48.

19 See Romila Thapar, *Aśoka and the Decline of the Mauryas* (London, OUP, 1961), p. 62.

20 See R. S. Sharma, *Light on Early Indian Society and Economy* (Bombay, Manaktalas, 1966), p. 66. See also D. D. Kosambi, *Introduction to the Study of Indian History* (Bombay, Popular Book Depot, 1956), p. 218.

21 Moreland, *The Agrarian System of Muslim India*, pp. 50–1.

22 Vincent Smith, *The Oxford History of India*, 3rd edn revd, ed. T. G. P. Spear (London, OUP, 1958), p. 304.

23 Beaglehole, p. 47.

24 Irfan Habib, p. 252.

25 Moreland, *The Agrarian System of Muslim India*, pp. 101–23.

26 Trevaskis, *The Land of the Five Rivers*, pp. 130–1.

27 Irfan Habib, pp. 207, 214, 264, and 275–82.

28 Spate and Learmonth, p. 522.

29 Walter C. Neale, *Economic Change in Rural India: Land Tenure and Reform in Uttar Pradesh, 1800–1955* (London, Yale UP, 1962), p. 19.

30 Baden-Powell, vol. 1, pp. 177–8.

31 Ibid. p. 230.

32 Ibid. pp. 106–8. Cf. Ainslie T. Embree, 'Landholding in British India and British Institutions' in R. E. Frykenberg, ed., *Land Control and Social Structure in India* (Madison, Univ. of Wisconsin Press, 1969), pp. 33–52.

33 See Irfan Habib, p. 111.

34 U. N. Ghoshal, *The Agrarian System of Ancient India* (Calcutta, Univ. of Calcutta, 1930), p. 40.

35 See Farmer (1957), pp. 66 and 109 and works there quoted.

36 Baden-Powell, vol. 1, pp. 128–9.

37 Quoted by Ghoshal, p. 93.

38 See e.g. *The Laws of Manu*, G. Bühler, trans. (Oxford, Clarendon Press, 1886), ch. ix, v. 44 (Sacred Books of the East, vol. 25).

39 Quoted by the *Report of the Uttar Pradesh Zamindari Abolition Committee*, 2 vols (Allahabad, Govt Central Press, 1948), vol. 1, pp. 70–1 (which is, however, a somewhat eclectic and undiscriminating document, to be used with care).

40 Baden-Powell (Holderness), p. 56; and R. C. Dutt, *The Economic History of India under Early British Rule*, 2nd edn (London, Kegan Paul, 1906), pp. 67 and 90. For the south, see Dharma Kumar, *Land and Caste in South India* (Cambridge, CUP, 1965), pp. 107–8.

41 Baden-Powell (Holderness), p. 201,

42 Ibid. p. 357.

43 See H. H. Mann, 'The Early History of the Tea Industry in North-east India', *Bengal Econ. J.*, vol. 2 (1918), pp. 44–59 (reprinted in H. H. Mann, *The Social Framework of Agriculture*, ed. D. Thorner (Bombay, Vora, 1967, and London, Cass, 1968), pp. 402–36: see esp. p. 424).

44 E. T. Atkinson, ed., *Statistical, Descriptive and Historical Account of the North-Western Provinces of India*, vol. 6 (Allahabad, Govt Press, 1881), p. 286.

45 Sir W. W. Hunter, *Annals of Rural Bengal*, 7th edn (London, Smith, Elder, 1897), p. 61.

46 Ibid. p. 64.

47 H. K. Trevaskis, *The Punjab of Today: an Economic Survey of the Punjab in Recent Years, 1890–1925*, 2 vols (Lahore, Civil & Military Gazette, 1931–2) vol. 2, p. 196.

48 See Eric Stokes, *The English Utilitarians in India* (Oxford, Clarendon Press, 1959), p. 134.

49 *Bombay Geogr. Rev.*, vol. 13 (1965).

50 The author is indebted to Professor E. T. Stokes for pointing out the importance of the revenue systems in this context, especially in UP.

51 Dharma Kumar, *Land and Caste in South India*, pp. 114–15; see also p. 111.

52 George Blyn, *Agricultural Trends in India, 1891–1947: Output, Availability and Productivity* (Philadelphia, Univ. of Pennsylvania Press, 1966), p. 231.

53 Neale, p. 69; Smith (ed. Spear), p. 641; and W. H. Moreland and Sir Atul Chatterjee, *A Short History of India*, 4th edn (London, Longmans, 1957), p. 382. The author is also indebted to Dr S. C. Gupta for a discussion on this topic.

54 *Report of the Uttar Pradesh Zamindari Abolition Committee*, vol. 1, p. 139.

55 Neale, p. 143.

56 G. Keatinge, *Rural Economy in the Bombay Deccan* (London, Longmans, 1912), pp. 48–9.

57 See V. R. Pillai and P. G. K. Panikar, *Land Reclamation in Kerala*, Kerala Univ. Econ. Ser., No. 1 (London, Asia Publishing House, 1966), esp. pp. 14–22. It is now hoped to raise two or three crops a year from *kayal* land: *Statesman Weekly*, 7 Oct. 1967, p. 6.

58 These hopes had long been expressed. As early as 1776 Sir Philip Francis, though hostile to 'colonies of settlement', admitted the need for European plantations, but insisted that they must be on wasteland: R. Guha, *A Rule of Property for Bengal*, Le Monde d'Outre-Mer, 1ère Série, Etudes, 19 (Paris, Mouton, 1963), p. 156.

59 W. Nassau Lees, *The Land and Labour of India: a Review* (London, Williams & Norgate, 1867), pp. 56–97; see also pp. 98–128.

60 Atkinson, ed., vol. 6, pp. 286–8, 390, and 474; see p. 537 for jungle grants in the Tarai of Basti District.

61 Moreland and Chatterjee, p. 385.

62 Lees, pp. 59–60 and 63.

63 Ibid. p. 66.

64 Ibid. pp. 67–9: see also T. F. Rasmussen, 'Population and Land Utilization in the Assam Valley', *J. Tropical Geogr.*, vol. 14 (1960), pp. 51–76, esp. pp. 55–6 on the empty Districts of 1835 and subsequent immigration and colonization.

65 Lees, pp. 67–9; P. P. Courtenay, *Plantation Agriculture* (New York, Praeger, 1965), pp. 193–202; Sir E. A. Gait, *A History of Assam* (Calcutta, Supt Govt Printing, 1906), pp. 346–56; Mann; and a very important and definitive work, Sir Percival Griffiths, *The History of the Indian Tea Industry* (London, Weidenfeld & Nicolson, 1967), esp. pp. 36–75, 88–92 and 96–155.

66 Griffiths, p. 129 (and p. 144 for area under tea in 1913); and Gait, pp. 346–356.

67 The Duars are Tarai-like tracts at the foot of the outermost Himalayan range. See Spate (1957), p. 533, and Griffiths, p. 114.

68 Griffiths, pp. 85–8 and 102.

69 Ibid. pp. 83–5.

70 Ibid. pp. 76–83, 114 and 121.

71 J. McSwiney, *Census, 1911*, vol. 3, pt 1, p. 3.

72 C. S. Mullen, *Census, 1931*, vol. 3, pt 1, p. 8.

73 Rasmussen, p. 57.

74 Steen Folke, 'Evolution of Plantations, Migration, and Population Growth in Nilgiris and Coorg', *Geogr. Tidsskrift*, vol. 65 (1966), pp. 198–239 at p. 201. See also Baden-Powell, vol. 3, pp. 181–4 and 469–77; and Griffiths, pp. 157–60.

75 Griffiths, p. 204.

76 D. Williams, 'Clements Robert Markham and the Introduction of the Cinchona Tree into British India', *Geogr. J.*, vol. 129 (1963), pp. 431–42. See also Folke, pp. 205–7.

77 Folke, p. 209.

78 Griffiths, pp. 157–9 and 161–2.

79 C. von Fürer-Haimendorf, 'The Position of the Tribal Populations in Modern India', in P. Mason, ed., *India and Ceylon: Unity and Diversity* (London, OUP for Inst. Race Relations, 1967), p. 182.

80 Jacques Dupuis, 'L'Économie des Plantations dans l'Inde du Sud', *Travaux de la Section Scientifique et Technique de l'Institut Français de Pondichéry*, vol. 1 (1957), pp. 6–47 at pp. 10–13.

81 Mann, ed. Thorner, p. 412.

82 Compare S. Thirumalai, *Post-war Agricultural Problems and Policies in India* (Bombay, Indian Soc. Agric. Econ. and New York, Inst. Pacific Relations, 1954), p. 116 and *The Food Situation in India*, Cmd 6479 (London, 1943), p. 794. See also the series of reports 'Grow More Food Policy in India', *Ind. J. Agric. Econ.*, vol. 4 (1949), pp. 239–327; and *Report of the Grow More Food Enquiry Committee* (New Delhi, Min. of Food and Agric., 1952).

83 Lakshman Prasad Sinha, 'Growing More Food in Bihar', *Ind. J. Agric. Econ.*, vol. 4 (1949), p. 324.

84 T. C. Goswami, extract from Budget Speech, *Indian Farming*, vol. 6 (1945), p. 183.

85 Editorial Note, *Indian Farming*, vol. 7 (1946), p. 273. Compare M. D. Chaturvedi, *Land Management in the United Provinces* (Allahabad, Supt Govt Printing, UP, 1946), p. 34.

86 Editorial Note, *Indian Farming*, vol. 7 (1946), p. 273.

87 R. P. Padhi's contribution on Orissa in the article 'Grow More Food Policy in India', *Indian J. Agric. Econ.*, vol. 4 (1949), pp. 242–4.

88 B. Natarajan, on Madras, ibid. p. 264. For the Wynad Colonization Scheme of 1945 see also A. Aiyappan, *Report on the Socio-Economic Conditions of the Aboriginal Tribes of the Province of Madras* (Madras, Govt Press, 1948), p. 34 and p. 186, App. V.

89 V. Ramantha Ayyar, 'Grow More Food Campaign in Madras', *Indian Farming*, vol. 6 (1945), p. 33.

90 *Report of the Foodgrains Policy Committee, 1943* (Delhi, Manager of Publications, 1943), pp. 25–6.

91 D. V. G. Krishnamurty, 'Food Position in Hyderabad State', *Indian Farming*, vol. 6 (1945), pp. 309–18.

92 C. S. Venkattasuban, 'Cochin', *Indian Farming*, vol. 6 (1945), p. 37.

93 *Grow More Food Enquiry Committee*, pp. 17–18.

94 Champion and F. C. Osmaston, p. 158. See also E. K. Janaki Ammal, '*Report on the Humid Regions of South Asia*', in *Problems of Humid Tropical Regions* (Paris, UNESCO, 1958), pp. 43–53, esp. p. 43.

95 See P. C. Goswami, *The Economic Development of Assam* (London, Asia Publishing House, 1963), p. 287.

96 *Resettlement Programme*, pp. 74–5.

97 I am greatly indebted to Shri H. N. Tiwari, District Organizer of Tribal Welfare, Guna, for much useful information and for a copy of the privately published *Illustrated Report of the Reclamation Work among the Criminal Tribes in Gwalior State* (n.d., ?1933).

98 Champion and Osmaston, p. 423.

99 A society founded by Swami Dayananda in 1875 which attacked many orthodox Hindu institutions, particularly caste, and promoted social uplift. See Percival Spear, *India: a Modern History* (Ann Arbor, Univ. of Michigan Press, 1961), pp. 293–4. See also C. H. Heimsath, *Indian Nationalism and Hindu Social Reform* (Princeton, NJ, Princeton UP, 1964), pp. 292–308.

100 C. S. Krishnaswami, 'The Annamalai University Colonisation Scheme', *Madras Agric. J.*, vol. 28 (1940), pp. 420–5.

101 Ujagir Singh, 'Gosaba—a Study in Land Reclamation in Sunderbans', *Indian Geogr. J.*, vol. 23 (1948), pp. 16–21.

102 See e.g. R. Maclagan Gorrie, 'Establishment of Demobilized Soldiers on the Land', *Indian Farming*, vol. 5 (1944), p. 300; Radha Kant, *Meerut Ganges Khadir Colonization Scheme for Ex-Servicemen* (Allahabad, Supt Govt Printing, 1947); and *Tarai Report*—the subtitle of this work is *Appointed by the United Provinces Government for the Investigation of Land Development and Colonization Schemes for Ex-servicemen.*

103 Darling, p. 114.

104 *Rajasthan Canal Project* (Jaipur, Rajasthan Canal Board, 1961), p. 11.

105 A *doab* is the land between two rivers. For a description of the *doabs* before irrigation see Darling, pp. 111–12.

106 See *A Handbook of the Thal Development Authority* (Jauharabad, Thal Development Authority, 1954).

107 See the map in Darling, facing p. 113.

108 *Rajasthan Colonization Act*, No. 27 of 1954.

109 *Colonization of Government Lands Act*, 1912, as amended 1920.

110 cf. Baden-Powell (Holderness), p. 58.

111 See H. Calvert, *Wealth and Welfare of the Punjab* (Lahore, Civil & Military Gaz., 1922), pp. 55–6, 67–9 (a 2nd edn was published in 1936); Darling, esp. pp. 111–37; P. W. Paustian, *Canal Irrigation in the Punjab* (New York, Columbia UP, 1930), esp. pp. 26–63 and 48–70; Trevaskis, *The Punjab of Today*, vol. 1, pp. 273–90; Kazi Ahmed, 'Settlements in the Irrigated Area of Recent Colonization in the Indo-Gangetic Plain', *Indian Geogr. J.*, vol. 17 (1942), pp. 183–99; and Michel (which is, however, concerned with water use rather than colonization), pp. 58–98. See also *Punjab Colony Manual* and Rashid A. Malik, 'Irrigation Development and Land Occupance in the Upper Indus Basin' (unpub. Ph.D. thesis, Indiana Univ., 1963).

112 Darling, pp. 112–13; Paustian, pp. 50–4; and Trevaskis, *The Punjab of Today*, vol. 1, pp. 250, 281. See also *Punjab Colony Manual*, pp. 2–5. There had been an unsuccessful British attempt to found a colony for disbanded cavalry in the eastern Punjab in 1818, but this was unirrigated: Michel, p. 66, n. 20.

113 Darling, pp. 112–13; see also Paustian, pp. 54–7 and Michel, pp. 77–9; and *Punjab Colony Manual*, pp. 5–10.

114 cf. the description in Darling, pp. 111–12.

115 Paustian, pp. 58–9 and Darling, p. 113, n. 3; and *Punjab Colony Manual*, pp. 11–12.

116 Paustian, p. 60 and Michel, pp. 79–80; *Punjab Colony Manual*, pp. 13–14.

117 Darling, p. 113 and Michel, pp. 85–93; *Punjab Colony Manual*, pp. 15–19.

118 Darling, p. 113.

119 Spate (1957), p. 471.

120 Darling, pp. 116–18. See also *Punjab Colony Manual*, pp. 1 and 20.

121 N. Gerald Barrier, 'The Punjab Disturbances of 1907; the Response of the British Government in India to Agrarian Unrest', *Modern Asian Studies*, vol. 1 (1967), pp. 353–83, at p. 356.

122 Michel, pp. 65–6 and 74–6.

123 Darling, pp. 118–21; see also Trevaskis, *The Punjab of Today*, vol. 1, pp. 277–8; and Barrier, pp. 359–60.

124 See Farmer (1957), pp. 158 and 305–7.

125 Quoted in *Punjab Colony Manual*, p. 298.

126 Darling, pp. 123–4.

127 Ibid. p. 126.

128 Ibid. pp. 116–17 and Paustian, pp. 60–1 and 70–2.

129 Darling, pp. 116–17.

130 Trevaskis, *The Punjab of Today*, vol. 1, p. 279.

131 See Farmer (1957), pp. 65 and 81–2.

132 Baden-Powell (Holderness), p. 57.

133 Ibid. p. 59.

134 Ibid. p. 58.

135 For a recent account see Barrier, esp. pp. 357–60, on which the following paragraphs are largely based. The author is also indebted to discussions in West Pakistan in 1956, particularly of a memorandum by Khan Niaz Muhammad Khan Tarin, 'A Note on the Land Revenue System of Former Punjab Province'.

136 Farmer (1957), pp. 289–92.

137 Ibid. See also the *Report of the Land Commission*, (Ceylon) Sessional Paper No. 10 of 1958 (Colombo, Govt Press, 1958), p. 86, and B. H. Farmer's Memorandum of Dissent, pp. 175–9; and B. H. Farmer, 'On Not Controlling Subdivision in Paddy-Lands', *Trans. Inst. Br. Geogr.*, vol. 28 (1950), pp. 225–235.

138 See *Report of the Colonies Committee* (Lahore, Supt Govt Printing, 1908).

139 *Report of the Land Commission*, pp. 82–94.

140 See E. H. Aitken, *Gazetteer of the Province of Sind* (Karachi, Govt Press, 1907), pp. 322, 415–16, and 501.

141 Trevaskis, *The Land of the Five Rivers*, p. 144. It some areas (e.g. the *mirasi* areas of the south) there was uncertainty about government rights to waste: see Dharma Kumar, p. 111.

142 I am indebted to Professor Morris D. Morris for this point.

143 Trevaskis, *The Land of the Five Rivers*, pp. 239–42.

144 Stokes, esp. ch. 2, 'Political Economy and the Land Revenue'.

145 Lees, pp. 129–36. See also Neale, pp. 29–30.

146 Baden-Powell, vol. 1, pp. 479–80 and *Bengal Waste Lands Manual* (Alipore, Bengal Govt Press, 1936), pp. 1–10.

147 See P. C. Goswami, pp. 285–6; Gait, pp. 353–4; and Griffiths, pp. 92–5, 99–101. See also Baden-Powell, vol. 1, pp. 479–88. For 'jungle grants' in Gorakhpur District (UP) see above, p. 12.

148 Lees, pp. 67–84. W. Nassau Lees (1825–89) was a major-general in the Indian army and an oriental scholar as well as a prolific writer on issues of public policy.

149 See above, pp. 13–14; also Griffiths, pp. 99–101.

150 See M. D. Chaturvedi, *Land Management in the United Provinces* (Allahabad, Supt Govt Printing, 1946), p. 65.

151 See *Indian Agricultural Statistics*, vol. 1, *Summary Tables* [India and States], and vol. 2, *Detailed Tables* (New Delhi, Ministry of Food and Agric., annually). See also Table 5.III above.

152 *Indian Agriculture in Brief*, 11th edn (New Delhi, Min. of Food, Agric. and Community Development, 1971), pp. 24–5.

153 *Report of the Royal Commission on Agriculture in India*, Cmd 3132 (London, HMSO, 1928), pp. 604–5.

154 Spate, pp. 201–3, and pp. 249–50.

155 Chaturvedi, pp. 94–5.

156 Editorial, 'Food Shortage', *Indian Farming*, vol. 7 (1946), pp. 273–4.

157 N. K. Das, 'Assam', ibid. vol. 6 (1945), p. 33.

158 See e.g. R. M. Mathur, 'Food Resources and Population Growth', in *Proceedings of the International Geography Seminar, Aligarh Muslim University, 1956* (Aligarh, Dept of Geogr., Aligarh Muslim Univ., 1959), pp. 228–41, at p. 235.

159 Moonis Raza, 'Is India Over-populated?', *The Geographer* (Aligarh), vol. 3 (1950), pp. 36–40, at p. 39.

160 For an explanation of the terms see *Guide to Current Agricultural Statistics*, rev. edn (New Delhi, Min. of Food and Agric., 1962), pp. 3–4.

161 *Population* [Report of Population Sub-Committee of National Planning Committee] (Bombay, Vora, 1947), pp. 9–10, 40–4, and 144.

162 See e.g. Vijaya Ram Singh, 'Study of Cultivable Waste in the Neighbourhood of Mirzapur', *Indian Geographer*, vol. 6 (1961), pp. 81–9; and V. V. Giri, *Jobs for our Millions* (Madras, Vyasa Publications, 1970), p. 41.

163 Kingsley Davis, *Population of India and Pakistan* (Princeton, NJ, Princeton UP, 1951), pp. 207–8.

164 Theodor Bergmann, 'Co-operation in India' in A. M. Khusro, ed., *Readings in Agricultural Development* (Bombay, Allied Publishers, 1968), p. 441; P. T. Bauer, *Indian Economic Policy and Development* (London, Allen & Unwin, 1961), p. 63.

165 B. R. Davidson, *The Northern Myth: a Study of the Physical and Economic Limits to Agricultural and Pastoral Development in Northern Australia* (Melbourne, Melbourne UP, 1965), pp. 5–17.

166 Quoted by S. Clarkson, 'L'Analyse Soviétique des Problèmes Indiennes du Sous-développement 1955–63' (unpublished doctoral thesis, Fondation Nationale des Sciences Politiques, Paris, 1964), kindly drawn to the author's attention by Dr Daniel Thorner.

167 See Baden-Powell (Holderness), pp. 148–9.

168 J. N. H. Maclean, *Report of the Land Revenue Settlement of the Saugor District, Jubbulpore Division, Central Provinces* (Calcutta, Supt Govt Printing, 1868), p. 38.

169 F. W. Porter, *Final Report on the Survey and Revision of Records recently completed for the Benares District* (Allahabad, NW Prov. and Oudh Govt Press, 1887), p. 17.

170 Chaturvedi, p. 43.

171 See *Guide to Current Agricultural Statistics,* pp, 3–4; where 'culturable waste' is defined as 'all lands available for cultivation whether not taken up for cultivation or taken up for cultivation once but not cultivated during the current year and last five years or more in succession. Such lands may be either fallow or covered with shrubs and jungles which are not put to any use. They may be assessed or not assessed and may lie in isolated blocks or within cultivated holdings.'

172 See *Pilot Survey of Culturable Waste Land in Dewas District, 1958–59* (Gwalior, Govt Regional Press, 1961), p. 7. See also R. Giri, 'Pilot Survey of Culturable Wasteland', *Agric. Situation in India*, vol. 15 (1960), pp. 983–8. (Readers are reminded that the author cited simply as Giri is V. V. Giri: see Abbreviations for Standard References.)

173 Baljit Singh and Shridhar Misra, *A Study of Land Reforms in Uttar Pradesh* (Calcutta, Oxford Book Co., 1964, and Honolulu, East-West Center Press, 1965), p. 59.

174 S. Thirumalai, *Post-war Agricultural Problems and Policies in India* (Bombay, Indian Soc. Agric. Econ. and New York, Inst. Pacific Relations, 1854), pp. 81–2 and 163.

175 Sir T. Vijayaraghavacharya, *The Land and its Problems*, Oxford Pamphlets on Indian Affairs, No. 9 (London, OUP, 1943), pp. 4–5.

176 *Fourth Plan, 1969–74, Draft*, p. 125.

177 *Report of the Waste Land Survey (Technical) Committee* (Shillong, Govt Press, 1968).

178 Ibid. p. 12. See also *Land Settlement Policy (1968) of the Government of Assam* (Shillong, Directorate of Information, 1968), pp. 2–6.

179 Giri, p. 92.

Chapter 3: Areas of Colonization: 1

1 Spate, p. 202; see also S. P. Chatterjee, 'Regional Patterns of the Density and Distribution of Population in India', *Geogr. Rev. India*, vol. 24 (1962), pp. 1–28; and the notes printed on the back of the excellent population maps of the *National Atlas of India*, scale 1:M.

2 cf. J. Dresch, 'Le "désert" de Thar', *Bull. Assoc. Géogr. Français*, Nos 332–3 (1965), pp. 36–47.

3 *Report of the Indian Irrigation Commission, 1901–1903*, pt 2, Cd 1852 (London, HMSO, 1904), p. 212. See also *Proceedings of the Symposium on the Rajputana Desert, Bull. Nat. Inst. Sci. India*. No. 1 (1952); see also V. C. Misra, 'Geographical Regions of Rajasthan', *Indian J. Geogr.*, vol. 1 (1966), pp. 37–48; V. C. Mishra, 'The Marusthali', in R. L. Singh, ed., *India: Regional Studies* (Calcutta, National Committee for Geogr., 1968), pp. 245–65; and *Rajasthan Canal Soil Survey*.

4 See e.g. C. T. Oldham, 'The Sarasvati and the Lost River of the Indian Desert', *J. R. Asiatic Soc.*, vol. 25 (1893), pp. 49–76; and Sir Aurel Stein, 'A Survey of Ancient Sites along the "Lost" Sarasvati River', *Geogr. J.*, vol. 99 (1942), pp. 173–82.

5 See *Rajasthan Canal Soil Survey*.

6 K. D. Erskine, *The Western Rajputana States Residency and Bikaner Agency, Rajputana District Gazetteers*, vol. 3A (Allahabad, Pioneer Press, 1909), p. 345. See also C. S. Chandrasekhara and K. V. Sundaram, 'A Note on Anticipated Land Use Changes in the Rajasthan Canal Area', *Bombay Geogr. Mag.*, vol. 10 (1962), pp. 61–9, esp. pp. 61–2; and B. B. Roy and A. K. Sen, 'Soil Map of Rajasthan', *Ann. Arid Zone*, vol. 7 (1968), pp. 1–14.

7 Erskine, p. 342.

8 See also W. Burns, 'The Desert Edge of Indian Agriculture', *J. Roy. Soc. Arts*, vol. 89 (1941), pp. 689–97 at p. 690.

9 K. C. Zachariah, *A Historical Study of Internal Migration in the Indian Subcontinent, 1901–1931* (London, Asia Publishing House, 1964), p. 215; see also A. Geddes, 'Half a Century of Population Trends in India', *Geogr. J.*, vol. 98 (1941), pp. 228–53, esp. p. 237, for a study of the longer period 1881–1931.

10 *Report of the Indian Irrigation Commission, 1901–3*, pt 2, p. 217.

11 Ibid. pp. 19–20, 23.

12 Ibid. pp. 217–20. See also Michel, p. 58.

13 W. Burns, *J. Roy. Soc. Arts*, vol. 89 (1941), pp. 689–90.

14 See Michel, esp. chs 6 and 7. For a simple and brief exposition see Anne Prentice, 'The Indus Basin Settlement Plan', *Geogr.*, vol. 49 (1964), pp. 128–31. See also 'Indus Waters Treaty', *World Affairs*, vol. 123 (1960), pp. 99–101; and, for earlier conditions, F. J. Fowler, 'Some Problems of Water Distribution between East and West Punjab', *Geogr. Rev.*, vol. 40 (1950), pp. 583–99.

15 *Rajasthan Canal Project* (Jaipur, Rajasthan Canal Board, 1961), p. 11. See also Michel, pp. 205–8, 286, and 316–40, esp. p. 320; and Map 2 on p. 39.

16 Spate, pp. 497–501; and L. R. Singh, 'The Tarai Region of Uttar Pradesh', in R. L. Singh, ed., *India: Regional Studies*, pp. 106–36.

17 Spate, p. 533. For the nineteenth-century spread of tea plantations into the eastern Tarai and Duars, see p. 14 above.

18 Where the Nepal government's first colonization scheme was launched at Nawalpur in 1963 (*Times of India*, 21 Dec. 1963).

19 Legris, p. 25.

20 H. Brammer, the distinguished soil scientist, doubts if the Tarai was a swamp under natural conditions (personal communication); but compare the

many references to swamps in nineteenth-century literature, e.g. E. T. Atkinson, ed., *Statistical, Descriptive and Historical Account of the North-Western Provinces of India*, vol. 12 (Allahabad, Govt Press, 1886), pp. 697–712, esp. p. 699.

21 Legris, p. 236.

22 Y. D. Pande, 'Agriculture in Naini Tal Tarai and Bhabar', *Geogr. Rev. India*, vol. 23 (1961), pp. 19–39 at pp. 21–2; and *Multiple Cropping in Tarai*, Research Bull. No. 5, U.P. Agric. Univ. (Pantnagar, U.P. Agric. Univ., 1969), pp. 19–21.

23 M. H. Rahman, *L'Oudh: Etude de Géographie Economique sur les Plaines de l'Oudh du Nord* (Paris, Muller, 1940), pp. 18–21.

24 S. R. Christophers and J. A. Sinton, 'A Malaria Map of India', *Indian J. Medical Research*, vol. 14 (1926–7), pp. 173–8. See also A. T. A. Learmonth, 'Some Contrasts in the Regional Geography of Malaria in India and Pakistan', *Trans. Inst. Br. Geogr.*, no. 23 (1957), pp. 37–59.

25 S. R. Christophers and C. A. Bentley, *Blackwater Fever*, Sci. Memoirs by Officers of the Medical and Sanitary Depts, no. 35 (Calcutta, Supt Govt Printing, 1909).

26 R. S. Srivastava and A. K. Chakrabarti, 'Malaria Control Measures in the Terai Area under the Terai Colonization Scheme, Kichha, District Naini Tal, 1949–1951: Second Report', *Indian J. Malariology*, vol. 6 (1952), pp. 281–94.

27 D. Clyde, 'Report on the Control of Malaria during the Sarda Canal Construction', *Records Malaria Surv. India*, vol. 2 (1931), p. 56.

28 W. Crooke, *The North Western Provinces of India* (London, Methuen, 1897), pp. 14–15.

29 e.g. ibid.; *Imperial Gazetteer of India*, vol. 2 (Oxford, Clarendon Press, 1909), p. 293; and H. R. Nevill, *Naini Tal, District Gazetteers of the United Provinces*, vol. 34 (Allahabad, Supt Govt Printing, 1904), pp. 194–203.

30 J. Sion, 'La Population de l'Inde d'après les Derniers Recensements', *Ann. de Géogr.*, vol. 35 (1926), p. 335.

31 Clyde, p. 55.

32 See e.g. R. Burn, *Census, 1901*, vol. 16, North-West Provinces and Oudh, pt 1 (Allahabad, Supt Govt Printing, 1902), p. 32.

33 Clyde, *Records Malaria Surv. India*, vol. 2 (1931), pp. 53–4; and R. Burn, cited in n. 32, pp. 9–10. See also *Tarai Report*, pp. 55–6; R. S. Srivastava and A. K. Chakrabarti, 'Malaria Control Measures under the Terai Colonization Scheme, Kichha, District Naini Tal, Sept. 1947–Dec. 1948: First Report', *Indian J. Malariology*, vol. 4 (1950), pp. 151–65; and D. N. Majumdar, 'The Tharus and their Blood Groups', *J. R. Asiatic Soc. Bengal* (*Science*), 3rd Ser., vol. 8 (1942), pp. 25–37.

34 M. D. Chaturvedi, *Land Management in the United Provinces* (Allahabad, Supt Printing and Stationery, 1946), p. 87.

35 R. S. Srivastava and Diwan Chand, 'Control of Malaria in Sarda Hydel Power-House Construction', *Indian J. Malariology*, vol. 5 (1951), p. 584.

36 Chaturvedi, p. 35.

37 See e.g. Srivastava and Chakrabarti, *Indian J. Malariology*, vol. 4 (1950) and ibid. vol. 6 (1952); Srivastava and Diwan Chand, *Indian J. Malariology*, vol. 5 (1951); J. Rahman, M. Singh and M. Pakrasi, 'Malaria Control in the Colonization Scheme, Kashipur, District Naini Tal, U.P. (1949–54)', *Indian J. Malariology*, vol. 10 (1956), pp. 155–63; and A. T. A. Learmonth, *Health in the Indian Sub-Continent*, Occasional Paper No. 2, School of General Studies, Australian Nat. Univ. (Canberra, 1965), p. 6. See also Ritchie Calder, *Men Against the Jungle* (London, Allen & Unwin, 1954), pp. 139–54.

38 See Lekh Raj Singh, *The Tarai Region of U.P.* (Allahabad, Ram Narain Lal Beni Prasad, 1965); and *Resettlement Programme*, p. 35.

39 See e.g. A. T. A. Learmonth and L. S. Bhat, *Mysore State*, vol. 2: *A Regional Synthesis* (Calcutta, Indian Statistical Inst., 1962), pp. 72–142; and A. T. A. Learmonth, *Sample Villages of Mysore State*, mimeograph (Dept of Geogr., Univ. of Liverpool, 1963), ch. 3.

40 A good description of Wynad is given by G. Covell and J. Harbhagwan, 'Malaria in the Wynaad, South India', *J. Malaria Inst. India*, vol. 2 (1939), p. 342: 'It consists for the most part of a succession of low rounded laterite [*sic*] hills, some forest or jungle-clad, some overgrown with grass or *Lantana*, some cleared and planted with tea, which here and there rise into bare rugged peaks ranging up to 7,000 feet in height. This mountainous character is most marked in in the south and west; south-east, or Nilgiris–Wynaad, is on the contrary considerably flatter and more open.

'In the dips between and among these low hills runs a network of swamp, mostly covered with tall, rank jungle. As the swamp descends, a streamlet generally forms, here and there losing itself and spreading out amid grass, *Lantana* or hill-rush, but eventually emerging in a more defined and strong-flowing stream.'

41 See Spate, pp. 645–6 and Fig. 121, p. 630.

42 See *International Map of Vegetation*, 1/M., Mysore and Cape Comorin Sheets; H. Gaussen, P. Legris, and M. Viart, 'Notes on the Sheet Cape Comorin', *Trav. Sec. Sci. Tech., Inst. Français, Pondichéry*, Hors Série, No. 1 (1961), pp. 31–82; and H. Gaussen, L. Labroue, and others, 'Notice de la Feuille Mysore', ibid. no. 7 (1966).

43 Gaussen, Labroue, and others, 'Notice . . . Mysore', pp. 10–11 and Legris, pp. 39–42. See also A. T. A. Learmonth and L. S. Bhat, *Mysore State*, vol. 1: *An Atlas of Resources* (Calcutta, Indian Statistical Inst., 1960), pp. 53–5; and J. Dupuis, 'L'Economie des Plantations dans l'Inde du Sud', *Trav. Sec. Sci. Tech., Inst. Français, Pondichéry*, vol. 1 (1957) pp. 8–9.

44 Compare *Mysore Agricultural Calendar and Year Book, 1959* (Bangalore, Director of Agriculture, 1959), p. 15: 'Northern Malnad:—The mixed soils derived from trap rock, sandstone, shales, granites and gneisses. They vary in colour from dark-brown to medium black and are loamy to clayey in texture. The p^H varies from 5·3 to 6·9 and these soils are fair in bases and are well supplied with phosphate and potash but nitrogen is rather low.'

45 See Learmonth and Bhat, vol. 2, p. 59.

46 See e.g. *National Atlas*, Map 21 and *National Atlas (Population)*, Plates 121 and 122; and Learmonth and Bhat, vol. 2, pp. 194–9.

47 *Tribal Map of India* (Dept of Anthropology, Govt of India, 1956).

48 Ibid. and L. A. Krishna Iyer, 'Coorg Ethnology', *Indian Geogr. J.*, vol. 22 (1947), pp. 157–225.

49 A. Aiyappan, *Report on the Socio-Economic Conditions of the Aboriginal Tribes of the Province of Madras* (Madras, Govt Press, 1948), pp. 95, 101–5, 125–8, 135–7; also E. Thurston, *Castes and Tribes of Southern India*, 7 vols (Madras, Govt Press, 1909); W. Francis, *The Nilgiris*, vol. 1, pp. 129 and 151–2 and C. A. Innes, *Malabar and Anjengo*, vol. 1, Madras Dist. Gazetteers (Madras, Govt Press, 1908), p. 467.

50 Aiyappan, pp. 135–7, 141–2 (who draws attention to the high degree of confusion in tribal nomenclature: 'Muthuvan' is the Tamil form of 'Mudugar').

51 See Aiyappan, *passim*, and Baden-Powell, vol. 3, p. 476.

52 Francis, pp. 129, 151–2, and Marguerite Milward, *Artist in Unknown India* (London, Werner Laurie, 1948), who describes the Irula (pp. 119–21), Kurumba (p. 212), Mannan, and Muthuvan (pp. 127–33) as she found them in 1935–6.

53 See Learmonth, *Sample Villages of Mysore State*, pp. 30–4, and L. S. Bhat, 'Some Aspects of Regional Planning in India' (unpublished Ph.D. thesis, Indian

Statistical Inst., 1963). The author is greatly indebted to Dr Bhat for the opportunity to read his thesis.

54 Sion, *Ann. de Géogr.* vol. 35 (1926), pp. 330–51 and 427–48; at p. 348, n. 3, Sion notes the 'constant movement of migration' from the plains to the plantations and the 99·2 per cent increase in the population of the hills of Travancore between 1872 and 1921 (cf. 62·6 per cent in the plains). The population of Devikulam District doubled between 1901 and 1911.

55 Innes, p. 467. See also Baden-Powell, vol. 3, p. 153. The author is greatly indebted to Shri Babu Shetty for information in the field.

56 *Statesman Weekly*, 15 May 1971.

57 See Steen Folke, 'Evolution of Plantations, Migration and Population Growth in Nilgiris and Coorg', *Geogr. Tideskrift*, vol. 65 (1966), pp. 198–239.

58 V. L. S. Prakasa Rao, *Towns of Mysore State* (Calcutta, Indian Statistical Inst., 1964), 1964), p. 20 and Fig. 8.

59 Dupuis, *Trav. Sec. Sci. Tech., Inst. Français, Pondichéry*, vol. 1 (1957), p. 10; cf. P. Vidal de la Blache, 'Le Peuple de l'Inde', *Ann. de Géogr.*, vol. 15 (1906), pp. 367–9.

60 C. D. Deshpande, *Western India: a Regional Geography* (Dharwar, Students' Own Book Depot, 1948), p. 99, n. 18. (All of these talukas registered an increase in the period 1941–51.)

61 L. S. Bhat, 'Some Aspects of Regional Planning in India', pt 4; S. Silva, *Malnad or Male Nadu: its History and Antiquities* (Sirsi, Mysore, All-India Malnad Third Conference, 1957), pp. 4–23.

62 See also F. Buchanan, *A Journey from Madras through the Countries of Mysore, Canara and Malabar*, 3 vols (London, Cadell & Davies, 1807), vol. 3, p. 393 for an account of a decayed dam in Malnad.

63 N. Subramhanya Aiyar, *Census of India, 1911*, vol. 23, pt 1, Travancore, p. 22.

64 See e.g. for Malnad, L. Rice, *Mysore and Coorg*, vol. 2 (Bangalore, Mysore Govt Press, 1878), p. 298; B. Ananthaswami Rao, 'A Short Account of the Malaria Problem in Mysore State', *Indian J. Malariology*, vol. 2 (1948), pp. 285–300; and D. K. Viswanathan, 'A Study of the Effects of Malaria and of Malaria Control Measures on Population and Vital Statistics in Kanara and Dharwar Districts as Compared with the Rest of the Province of Bombay', ibid. vol. 3 (1949), pp. 69–107: for Coorg, Jaswant Singh and C. D. Kariapa, 'Malaria Control in Coorg', ibid. vol. 3 (1949), pp. 191–8: for Wynad and the lower Nilgiris, G. Covell and J. Harbhagwan, *J. Malaria Inst. India*, vol. 2 (1939), pp. 341–76; and P. F. Russell and V. P. Jacob, 'On the Epidemiology of Malaria in the Nilgiris District, Madras Presidency', ibid. vol. 4 (1941–2), pp. 349–92: for the lower slopes of the High Ranges, H. A. Stuart, *Census, 1891*, vol. 13, Madras, p. 191. See also Christophers and Sinton, *Indian J. Medical Research*, vol. 14 (1926–7).

65 See e.g. J. C. Vedamanikkam, 'Seasonal Variation in the Breeding Places of *Anopheles fluviatilis* (James) in Wynaad and its Relationship to Eradication of the Species', *Indian J. Malariology*, vol. 6 (1952), pp. 367–79; and A. T. A. Learmonth, 'Some Contrasts in the Regional Geography of Malaria in India and Pakistan', *Trans. Inst. Br. Geogr.*, no. 23 (1957), pp. 37–59, esp. pp. 39–40; and Learmonth and Bhat, vol. 2, pp. 252–7.

66 Jaswant Singh and C. D. Kariapa, *Indian J. Malariology*, vol. 3 (1949), p. 193. See also D. K. Viswanathan, ibid. p. 70 (for northern Malnad and adjacent areas).

67 J. M. Campbell, *Kanara, Gazetteers of the Bombay Presidency*, vol. 15, pt 2 (Bombay, Govt Central Press, 1883), p. 146 (see also pp. 149, 151). See also Buchanan, vol. 3, p. 288.

68 Buchanan, vol. 3, p. 14.
69 Ibid. p. 115.
70 Buchanan, vol. 2, pp. 96–7, 116–18, 121.
71 W. Logan, *Malabar* (Madras, Govt Press, 1887), esp. pp. 453, 518–19, 528, 531, 544, 546–7, 555; and Buchanan, vol. 3, pp. 484–5.
72 See Silva, p. 24.
73 See e.g. Silva, pp. 23–4; Campbell, vol. 15, pt 2, p. 143; and T. H. Beaglehole, *Thomas Munro and the Development of Administrative Policy in Madras, 1792–1818* (Cambridge, CUP, 1966), pp. 46–8.
74 Campbell, vol. 15, pt 1, p. 19.
75 Innes, vol. 1, p. 475. For abandoned coffee in Wynad see also Logan, vol. 1, p. 145.
76 Logan, vol. 1, p. 713.
77 Deshpande, pp. 99–100.
78 See e.g. D. K. Viswanathan and T. Ramachandra Rao, 'Control of Rural Malaria with D.D.T. Indoor Residual Spraying in Kanara and Dharwar Districts, Bombay Province: First Year's Results', *Indian J. Malariology*, vol. 1 (1947), pp. 503–42.
79 Learmonth and Bhat, vol. 2, pp. 42–7. An earlier, wartime proposal for such a Board had not been proceeded with for financial reasons: *Report of the Grow More Food Enquiry Committee* (New Delhi, Min. of Food and Agric., 1952), p. 40.
80 *Ceylon News*, 30 Dec. 1965; *The Hindu*, 28 Jan. 1972.

Chapter 4: Areas of Colonization: 2

1 For an expanded version of this section see B. H. Farmer, 'The Neglected Plateaus of Dandakaranya', *Bombay Geogr. Mag.*, Principal C. B. Joshi Memorial Volume, vol. 13 (1965) [1967], pp. 21–39. See also M. M. Joshi, *Bastar, India's Sleeping Giant* (New Delhi, People's Publishing House, 1967) and (a more reliable source), P. C. Agarwal, *Human Geography of Bastar District* (Allahabad, Garga, 1968); also S. C. Bose, 'Dandakaranya—a Developing Hinterland of Vishakapatnami Port', *Deccan Geographer*, vol. 7 (1964), pp. 48–55.
2 But compare the discussion of the former extent of this forest, and its probable erosion at the hand of man, in C. D. Deshpande, *Western India* (Dharwar, Students' Own Book Depot, 1948), p. 99 and R. G. Bhandarkar, *Early History of the Deccan*, 4th edn (Calcutta, Susil Gupta, 1957), pp. 11–12. See also F. E. Pargiter, 'The Geography of Rama's Exile', *J. Roy. Asiatic Soc.*, vol. 26 (1894), pp. 231–64; B. C. Law, *Historical Geography of Ancient India* (Paris, Soc. Asiatique, n.d.), pp. 41 and 280; and Baden-Powell, vol. 3, p. 112.
3 For the Chanda District see N. G. Jain, 'The Emergence of Urban Centres in the Eastern District of Vidarbha (Maharashtra)', *National Geogr. J. India*, vol. 10 (1964), pp. 146–63, esp. pp. 149, 153, 162–3.
4 W. V. Grigson, *Maria Gonds of Bastar* (London, OUP, 1938), pp. 21–5.
5 *Development of Dandakaranya* (New Delhi, National Council of Applied Economic Research, 1963).
6 'Report of the Agricultural Expert Team on Dandakaranya Project' (unpublished, 1963), pp. 6–7. See also Agarwal, pp. 80–2.
7 E.g. C. L. R. Glasford, *Report on the Dependency of Bastar, 1862*, from the Records of the Govt of India, Foreign Dept, No. 39 (Calcutta, Foreign Dept Press, 1863), p. 63; and Baden-Powell, vol. 2, pp. 402–3, on Chanda District, half of whose area was forest in 1887.

8 R. V. Russell and Rai Bahadur Hiralal, *Tribes and Castes of the Central Province of India*, 4 vols (London, Macmillan, 1916), esp. vol. 2, pp. 41, 120; Grigson; and Verrier Elwin, *The Muria and their Ghotul* (Bombay, OUP, 1947) and *The Tribal World of Verrier Elwin* (Bombay, OUP, 1964), esp. pp. 102–3. See also the *Reports on the Administration of Bastar State* (Jagdalpur, State Press).

9 Agarwal, p. 15.

10 V. P. Menon, *The Story of the Integration of the Indian States* (London, Longmans, 1956), p. 152.

11 The deposed ex-ruler, Pravir Chandra Bhanj Deo (revered by his tribal people, and the chief priest of the titular deity of Bastar, Danteswari Devi), was found dead in his palace at Jagdalpur in Mar. 1966, after police firing which followed disturbances. See also below, p. 273.

12 Grigson, p. 4.

13 Menon, p. 152.

14 Spate, pp. 146–9.

15 Bhandarkar, p. 18; and P. Gourou, 'Quelques Observations de Géographie Tropicale dans l'Inde', *Rév. Univ. Bruxelles*, vol. 3 (1950–1), pp. 268–9.

16 C. B. Lucie-Smith, *Final Report on the Land Settlement of Chanda District 1897–1906* (Nagpur, Govt Press, 1910), p. 13.

17 F. G. Bailey, *Caste and the Economic Frontier* (Manchester, Manchester UP, 1957), p. 7.

18 E. L. Perry, 'Endemic Malaria of the Jeypore Hill Tracts of the Madras Presidency', *Indian J. Medical Research*, vol. 2 (1914–15), pp. 456–91 at 461.

19 Grigson, p. 25.

20 Ibid. p. 14.

21 E. Reclus, *Universal Geography*, ed. A. H. Keane, vol. 8 (London, Virtue, n.d.), p. 261.

22 See B. H. Farmer, *Bombay Geogr. Mag.*, vol. 13 (1965) [1967], pp. 21–39 and N. G. Jain, *National Geogr. J. India*, vol. 10 (1964).

23 See S. R. Christophers and J. A. Sinton, 'A Malaria Map of India', *Indian J. Medical Research*, vol. 14 (1926–7), pp. 173–8 (which shows most of Dandakaranya in the same category as Tarai and Malnad). See also Perry, *Indian J. Medical Research*, vol. 2 (1914–15), p. 456 and M. F. Boyd, ed., *Malariology* (London, Saunders, 1949), vol. 1, pp. 569 and 698–9; and vol. 2, p. 810.

24 *Survey of Wastelands: Maharashtra*, pp. 9–10.

25 Farmer (1957), pp. 3–18.

26 Spate, p. 553. See also T. F. Rasmussen, 'Population & Land Utilization in the Assam Valley', *J. Tropical Geogr.*, vol. 14 (1960), pp. 51–76.

27 The author is deeply grateful to Shri A. N. Kidwai, then Chief Secretary to the government of Assam, for much help in preparation for field work, and to Shri P. C. Saikia and Shri T. C. Dutta for their company and assistance in the field itself. None of these gentlemen is in any way responsible for opinions on Assam expressed by the author.

28 *Survey of India One-Inch Map*, Sheets 83 B/16, 83 C/13, 83 F/4, 83 G/1 (1923).

29 Ibid. Sheet 78 J/11 and 15 (1907, but largely based on surveys made in 1876).

30 Ibid. Sheet 78 J/15 and 16 (1923).

31 See Sir Edward Gait, *History of Assam*, 3rd edn, revd B. K. Barua and H. V. S. Murthy (Calcutta, Thacker Spink, 1963), p. 403.

32 See Nafis Ahmad, *An Economic Geography of East Pakistan*, 2nd edn (London, OUP, 1968).

33 Rasmussen, p. 65.

34 Ibid. p. 66.

35 Quoted in *Land Settlement Policy (1968) of the Government of Assam* (Shillong, Dir. of Information and Public Relations, 1968), p. 4. For reasons why culturable waste statistics are even more unreliable in Assam than elsewhere in India, see above, p. 34.

36 *Report of the Waste Land Survey (Technical) Committee* (Shillong, Assam Govt Press, 1968), p. 9.

37 *Land Settlement Policy (1968) ... Assam*, pp. 6–8.

38 Rasmussen, p. 71.

39 *Statesman Weekly*, 18 Oct. 1969.

40 *Statistical Handbook, Assam 1967* (Shillong, Dept of Economics and Statistics, 1968), p. 31.

41 B. H. Farmer, 'The Social Basis of Nationalism in Ceylon', *J. Asian Studies*, vol. 24 (1965), pp. 431–9 at p. 433.

42 Spate, pp. 576–80. See also S. P. Chatterjee, 'Geographic Regions of East Rajasthan Pathar', *Geogr. Rev. India*, vol. 19 (1954), pp. 42–7.

43 Sir W. H. Sleeman, *Rambles and Recollections of an Indian Official* (London, Constable, 1893), p. 366.

44 W. Crooke, *The North Western Provinces of India* (London, Methuen, 1897), p. 26. See also L. R. Singh and R. P. Singh, 'The Ravines of the Lower Chambal Valley', *Nat. Geogr. J. India*, vol. 7 (1961), pp. 150–64.

45 Irfan Habib, *The Agrarian System of Mughal India, 1556–1707* (London, Asia Publishing House for Dept of History, Aligarh Muslim Univ., 1963), p. 14.

46 Ibid. See also *Continuous Village Surveys, 1956–57*, No. 23, Agric. Econ. Research Sec., Delhi Sch. of Econ., Univ. of Delhi (1958) for such spontaneous reclamation in a village in Agra District.

47 D. L. Shah, *A Note on the Prevention of the Extension of Erosion in Ravine Lands and Improvement of Fodder and Grazing Grounds in Waste and Ravine Lands*, Leaflet no. 10 of UP Forest Dept, reprinted in *Agric. and Livestock in India*, vol. 9 (1939), pp. 575–83 (see esp. p. 578). See also H. L. Chhibber, 'The Reclamation of the Ravine Lands of the Yamuna (Jumna), Uttar Pradesh', *Bull. Nat. Geogr. Soc. India*, 2 (1946); W. T. Hall, 'Erosion in the Jumna and Chambal Ravines', *Indian Forester*, vol. 73 (1947), pp. 195–8; and A. P. F. Hamilton, 'Chambal Ravines Reclamation Scheme', ibid. pp. 99–101.

48 By the Committee on Natural Resources of the Planning Commission: see *Statesman Weekly*, 2 Apr. 1966.

49 *Statesman Weekly*, 29 May 1971.

50 *Chambal Valley Development* (Delhi, Min. of Irrigation and Power, 1960) and *The Chambal Multi-purpose Project* (Bhopal, Director of Information, 1960).

51 See the excellent report, K. M. Mehta, *Report of Soil and Crop Investigation Survey, Chambal Commanded Area, Rajasthan* (Udaipur, Agric. Chem. Sec., Dept of Agric., Rajasthan, 1958), esp. pp. i–ii.

52 The author is grateful to Shri K. M. Mehta, Joint Director of Agriculture, Kota, for data and for an instructive period in the field.

53 See Y. Bhargave, 'New Life for the Displaced' in *All About Chambal Development* (New Delhi, Min. of Information and Broadcasting, 1960), pp. 67–71.

54 R. Lal, *Census, 1931*, vol. 22, pt 1, p. 4.

55 J. N. Datta, *Census, 1921*, vol. 20, p. 8.

56 A. W. T. Webb, *Census, 1941*, vol. 24, pt 1, p. 61.

57 A. D. Bannerman, *Census, 1901*, vol. 25, pt 1, pp. 21–5.

58 R. Lal, *Census, 1931*, vol. 15, p. 4.

59 J. W. D. Johnstone, *Census, 1901*, vol. 21, p. 14.

60 See e.g. C. E. Luard, *Census, 1911*, vol. 17, p. 14.

61 *The Chambal Multi-purpose Project*, pp. 8–9.

62 Spate, pp. 576–80.

63 See R. L. Pendleton, 'Soils of India: Four Soil Surveys in Gwalior State', *Soil Sci.*, vol. 62–3 (1946–7), pp. 421–35, esp. pp. 426–7.

64 C. E. Luard, *Gwalior State Gazetteer* (*Central India State Gazetteers*, vol. 1), pt 1 (Calcutta, Supt Govt Printing, 1908), p. 3; and *Indore State Gazetteer*, ibid. vol. 2 (Calcutta, Supt Govt Printing, 1908), p. 61.

65 Luard, *Gwalior State Gazetteer*, pt 1, p. 57.

66 C. E. Luard, *Census, 1901*, vol. 19, p. 20.

67 Luard, *Indore State Gazetteer*, p. 224.

68 Irfan Habib (p. 21) speaks of its 'established reputation for fertility and unfailing abundance' in Mughal times.

69 C. E. Luard, *Bhopal State Gazetteer* (*Central India State Gazetteers*, vol. 3) (Calcutta, Supt Govt Printing, 1908), p. 35.

70 Luard, *Gwalior State Gazetteer*, pt 1, p. 43.

71 J. Sion, *Asie des Moussons*, Géographie Universelle, tome IX, 2ème partie (Paris, Armand Colin, 1929), p. 249.

72 Sleeman, p. 314.

73 *Central Agency Admin. Report, 1889–90* (Calcutta, Supt Govt Printing, 1890), p. 9.

74 *Report of the Grow More Food Enquiry Committee* (New Delhi, Min. of Food and Agric., 1952), p. 40.

75 W. Kirk, 'The Damodar Valley—"Valles Optima"', *Geogr. Rev.*, 40 (1950), pp. 415–53.

76 P. C. Tallents, *Census, 1921*, vol. 7, pt 1, p. 60. For the Parganas generally see L. S. S. O'Malley, *Santal Parganas*, Bihar District Gazetteers, vol. 18 (Patna, Supt Govt Printing, 1938). See also Sir J. Houlton, *Bihar: the Heart of India* (Bombay, Orient Longmans, 1949), pp. 73–87.

77 Houlton, pp. 75, 87.

78 See the *Administration Reports of the Western Bhil Agency* (Bombay, Govt Central Press, 1884–1906), which, however, cover a rather larger area. See also J. Campbell, ed., *Khandesh District Gazetteer*, Bombay Series, vol. 12 (Bombay, Central Govt Press, 1880), pp. 81–3.

79 J. Campbell, ed., vol. 12, p. 82.

80 E.g. *Administration Report of the Western Bhil Agency* (Bombay, Govt Central Press, 1893), p. 3, which also speaks of the 'excellent' soil going begging, and of Bhil colonies.

81 J. Campbell, ed., vol. 12B, p. 111.

82 G. V. Chalem, 'Land Reclamation Work in Orissa', *Indian Farming*, vol. 11, (1950), pp. 289–91.

83 *Hirakud Dam Project (1950)* (New Delhi, Central Waterpower, Irrigation and Navigation Commission, 1950).

84 See e.g. P. K. Sen, 'Some Aspects of the Recent Colonization in the Andamans', *Geogr. Rev. India*, vol. 16 (1954), pp. 33–41 and *Statesman Weekly*, 14 May 1966 and 11 Jan. 1969; for the Laccadives see *Statesman Weekly*, 1 Feb. 1964.

85 See e.g. S. R. Christophers, 'Malaria in the Andamans', *Sci. Mems. Medical & Sanitary Depts*, no. 56 (Calcutta, Supt Govt Printing, 1912).

86 See *Tungabhadra Project* (Delhi, Min. of Information and Broadcasting, 1956); *Tungabhadra Project, Hyderabad, July 1956* (Raichur, Office of the Collector-Director, 1956); *Tungabhadra Project, Resumé of Work, 1954–58* (Tungabhadra Dam, Tungabhadra Board, 1959); and *Development Activities under Tungabhadra Project in Raichur District* (Munirabad, Dep. Administrator, 1961). See also *Varuna* (Munirabad), Journal of the Tungabhadra Advisory Board, and *Evaluation of Major Irrigation Projects: Some Case Studies* (New

Delhi, Programme Evaluation Organisation, Planning Commission, 1965), pp. 78–125.

87 Spate, p. 657.

88 W. Francis, *Bellary*, Madras District Gazetteers (Madras, Supt Govt Press, 1904), vol. 1, p. 7.

89 R. Sewell, *A Forgotten Empire* (London, Swan Sonnenschein, 1900), p. 162.

90 A. Butterworth, *The Southlands of Siva* (London, Bodley Head, 1923), p. 210.

91 See e.g. G. T. Boag, *Census, 1921*, vol. 13, pt 1, *Madras* (Madras, Supt Govt Press, 1922), p. 7; M. Rahnatulla, *Census, 1921*, vol. 21, pt 1, *Hyderabad State* (Hyderabad, Govt Central Press, 1923), pp. 17 & 30; G. A. Khan, *Census, 1931*, vol. 23, pt 1, *H.E.H. The Nizam's Dominions* (Hyderabad, Govt Central Press, 1933), p. 21; and C. K. Murthy, *Census, 1951*, vol. 9, pt 1A (Hyderabad, Govt Press, 1953), pp. 17–18. See also A. T. A. Learmonth, *Sample Villages in Mysore State*, mimeograph (Dept of Geogr., Univ. of Liverpool, 1963), p. 86.

92 *Tungabhadra Project, Resumé of Work, 1954–58*, pp. 47–8, 121–3.

93 Ibid.; and *Development Activities under Tungabhadra Project*, p. 29.

94 See *A Handbook of the Thal Development Authority, 1949–54* (Jauharabad, Thal Development Authority, 1954), pp. 55–6; J. D. Shaw, 'Recent Developments in the Gezira Scheme', *Information on Land Reform*, no. 2 (1964), pp. 8–22; R. A. Smith and B. P. Birch, 'The East Ghar Irrigation Project in the Jordan Valley', *Geogr.* vol. 4 (1963), pp. 406–9; and J. Naylon, 'The Badajoz Plain, *Erakunde*, vol. 20 (1966), pp. 50–60, at p. 51.

95 Sion, *Asie des Moussons*, p. 300.

96 The author is indebted to Shri S. N. Misra, IAS, for information on this area.

Chapter 5: Nature and Scale of Colonization

1 Two small colonies were started later: *Resettlement Programme*, pp. 159 & 161.

2 Some of the data on which these estimates are based are given in *Tungabhadra Project: Résumé of Work, 1945–1958* (Tungabhadra Dam, Tungabhadra Board, 1959), pp. 65–79; and *Development Activities under Tungabhadra Project in Raichur District* (Munirabad, Deputy Administrator, 1961), pp. 2–11.

3 Rashid A. Malik, 'Irrigation Development and Land Occupance in the Upper Indus Basin' (unpublished Ph.D. dissertation, Indiana Univ., 1963), pp. 225–6.

4 See *Rajasthan Canal Master Plan*, chap. 3, p. 6 (consulted by kind permission of the Chief Secretary, Rajasthan).

5 In this connection see Farmer (1969).

6 *Report of the Land Utilization Committee—Aug. 1967*, Ceylon Sessional Paper No. 11 of 1968 (Colombo, Govt Press, 1968), p. 34. These figures cover all types of peasant colonization. For dry-zone colonization (which began well before independence) see Farmer (1957).

7 *A Brief Report on the Thal Development Authority, 1949–55* (Jauharabad, Thal Development Authority, n.d. [1955]), pp. 7–8.

8 W. A. Withington, 'The Distribution of Population in Sumatra, Indonesia, 1961', *J. Tropical Geogr.*, vol. 17 (1963), pp. 203–12.

9 Tunku Shamsul Bahrin, 'Policies on Land-Settlement in Insular South-East Asia', *Modern Asian Studies*, vol. 5 (1971), pp. 21–34.

10 C. A. Fisher, *South-east Asia* (London, Methuen, 1964), p. 609; K. J.

Pelzer, 'Resettlement in Malaya', *Yale Rev.*, 41 (1952), pp. 391–404, and 'Mass Migrations and Resettlement Projects in Southeast Asia since 1945', *Proc. 9th Pacific Sci. Congr., 1957*, vol. 3 (1963), pp. 189–94 at pp. 189–92; E. H. G. Dobby, 'Resettlement Transforms Malaya', *J. Econ. Development and Cultural Change*, vol. 1 (1952), pp. 163–89 and 'Recent Settlement Changes in South Malaya', *Malayan J. Tropical Geogr.*, vol. 1 (1953), pp. 1–8 (which points out that one-third of the rural population of Johore was resettled); and Hamzah Sendut, 'The Resettlement Villages in Malaya', *Geogr.*, vol. 18 (1962), pp. 41–6 (whose figures have been used here: see his p. 46, note 3).

11 See, *inter alia*, R. Wikkramatileke, 'A Study of Planned Land Settlement in the Eastern Marchlands of Malaya', *Econ. Geogr.*, vol. 38 (1962), pp. 330–46; 'State Aided Rural Colonization in Malaya: an Appraisal of the F.L.D.A. Programme', *Ann. Ass. Am. Geogr.*, vol. 55 (1965), pp. 365–403; and 'Federal Land Development in West Malaysia', *Pacific Viewpoint*, vol. 13 (1972), pp. 62–86; and Tunku Shamsul Bahrin, *Modern Asian Studies*, vol. 5 (1971), pp. 21–34.

12 K. J. Pelzer, *Proc. 9th Pacific Sci. Congr., 1957*, vol. 3, pp. 192–4. See also R. Teulières, 'Les Paysans Vietnamiens au Sud Viet-Nam et la Réforme Rurale', *Cahiers d'Outre-Mer* (Bordeaux), vol. 15 (1962), pp. 47–84, pp. 73–82.

13 J. J. Zasloff, 'Rural Resettlement in South Vietnam: The Agroville Problem', *Pacific Affairs*, vol. 35 (1962–3), pp. 327–40.

14 See C. von Fürer-Haimendorf, 'The Position of the Tribal Populations in Modern India', in Philip Mason, ed., *India and Ceylon: Unity and Diversity* (London, OUP for Inst. Race Relations, 1967), p. 199.

15 Information from Shri C. H. Damodaran Nambiar, Administrative Officer, Wynad Colonization Scheme, to whom the author is further indebted for much help in the field.

16 See T. F. Rasmussen, 'Population and Land Utilization in the Assam Valley', *J. Tropical Geogr.*, vol. 14 (1960), pp. 51–76, esp. p. 71.

17 See e.g. Suresh Ramabhai, *Vinoba and his Mission*, 2nd edn (Sevagram (Wardha), Akhil Bharat Sarva Seva Sangh, 1958).

18 See 'The Bihar Bhoodan Yagna Act, 1954' (Bihar Act XXII of 1954).

19 The author is very grateful to Shri M. Janardhanan Nair, Director of Agriculture, Kerala, for the benefit of a most interesting discussion.

20 According to M. Krishnan, 'The Animals of the Dwindling Forest', *S. Asian Rev.*, vol. 4 (1970), p. 54, such plantations are still 'reckoned as part of the forest land'.

21 *Statesman Weekly*, 5 Sept. 1970; *The Statesman*, 4 Dec. 1968.

22 The Uttar Pradesh Agricultural University, Pantnagar.

23 The author is indebted to Shri I. P. Mathur, formerly of the Min. of Food and Agric., Govt of India, for information on Central Mechanized Farms. The use of the adjective 'Central' signifies that the project concerned is run by the central government and not the government of the state in which it falls.

24 *Making the Desert Bloom* (Delhi, Min. of Food and Agric., 1959), p. 4; and *The Desert Blooms* (Delhi, Min. of Food and Agric., 1961). See also H. H. Mann, 'The Central Mechanized Farm at Suratgarh', *Econ. Weekly*, vol. 12 (1960), pp. 1827–8, reprinted as ch. 26 in H. H. Mann (ed. D. Thorner), *The Social Framework of Agriculture* (Bombay, Vora, 1967); and 'Large-Scale Mechanized Farming', *Agric. Situation in India*, 15 (1961), pp. 1392–5.

25 *First Report of the Committee on Large-sized Mechanized Farms* (New Delhi, Min. of Food and Agric., n.d. [1961]).

26 *Pilot Survey of Culturable Waste Land in Dewas District, 1958–59*, Govt of Madhya Pradesh, Directorate of Land Records (Gwalior, Govt Regional Press, 1961), esp. p. 7.

27 Communication from Govt of Madhya Pradesh to Planning Commission, passed on to the author.

28 *Indian Agricultural Statistics* (New Delhi, Directorate of Economics and Statistics, Min. of Food and Agric., annually): Vol. I, All-India and States; Vol. II, detailed statistics with breakdown to Districts. More up-to-date figures are often to be found in *Indian Agriculture in Brief*, published annually by the same Directorate.

29 *Guide to Current Agricultural Statistics* (New Delhi, Directorate of Economics and Statistics, Min. of Food and Agriculture, 1962), p. 4.

30 For another study based on estimates adjusted for changes in the reporting area see J. W. Mellor and U. J. Lele, 'Alternative Estimates of the Trend in Indian Foodgrains Production during the First Two Plans', *Econ. Development and Cultural Change*, vol. 13 (1965), pp. 217–32.

31 Rasmussen, *J. Tropical Geogr.*, vol. 14 (1960), p. 66.

32 See e.g. *Growth Rates in Agriculture* (New Delhi, Min. of Food and Agric., 1964), p. 11, and, for the use of the 'chain-base method' to cover changes in the reporting area, ibid. pp. 5–6. See also George Blyn, *Agricultural Trends in India, 1891–1947: Output, Availability and Productivity* (Philadelphia, Univ. of Pennsylvania Press, 1966); and A. Heston, 'Variations in Agricultural Growth and Output between and within Regions of India', *Asian Survey*, vol. 8 (1968), pp. 174–87.

Chapter 6: The Beneficiaries

1 The author is indebted to Shri Prem Krishen, ICS, for the benefit of a general discussion of refugee settlement problems.

2 See S. M. Haider, 'Social Organization of Refugees in Bhopal State', *Sociol. Bull.*, vol. 6 (1957), pp. 61–71.

3 *Statesman Weekly*, 20 June 1970.

4 *Statesman Weekly*, 29 May 1971.

5 The author is grateful to Shri Iqbal Singh, Deputy Commissioner, Resettlement, Hissar, for interesting information on compensation procedure under the Bhakra scheme.

6 Farmer (1957), p. 208, Table 19.

7 See T. E. Hilton, 'The Volta Resettlement Project', *J. Tropical Geogr.*, vol. 24 (1967), pp. 12–21; and 'World Food Program Resettlement Projects', *Information on Land Reform*, no. 2 (1964), pp. 61–3.

8 *Resettlement Programme*, p. 9; and *Land Settlement Policy (1968) of the Government of Assam* (Shillong, Directorate of Information, 1968), p. 10.

9 *Resettlement Programme*, pp. 161–2.

10 Quoted by G. Kotovsky, *Agrarian Reform in India* (New Delhi, People's Publishing House, 1964), p. 14; also p. 48. See also *Land Tenures in India, Census of India 1961*, vol. I, pt XI–A(11), pp. liv–vi.

11 See e.g. H. K. Trevaskis, *The Punjab of Today*, vol. 1 (Lahore, Civil & Military Gaz., 1931), pp. 276–8. Trevaskis says of 'yeomen' and 'landed gentry' that 'when they cultivate the land themselves there is no better medium for the spread of agricultural progress'.

12 See *Punjab Colony Manual*, pp. 37–9, where sales by auction are justified in terms of speedier return on capital, the provision of openings for non-agriculturalists, and the need for the government to obtain an indication of market values.

13 *Statesman Weekly*, 25 Nov. 1967.

14 *A Brief Report on the Thal Development Authority, 1949–55* (Jauharabad, Thal Development Authority, 1955), p. 18.

15 S. Z. Ahsan, 'Gudu Barrage Project: a Geographical Analysis', *Geografia* (Karachi), vol. 4 (1965 [1967]), pp. 47–60 at p. 53.

16 Farmer (1957), pp. 218, 296–7.

17 *A Brief Report on the Thal Development Authority, 1949–55*, p. 17.

18 See e.g. *Ceylon News*, 11 Nov. 1965, 13 Jan. 1966, and 26 Aug. 1966.

19 See also *Resettlement Programme*, esp. pp. 15–16. For a discussion of definitions within the 'Backward Classes' see A. Béteille, 'The Future of the Backward Classes' in P. Mason (ed.), *India and Ceylon: Unity and Diversity* (London, OUP for Inst. Race Relations, 1967), pp. 83–93.

20 Farmer (1957), pp. 204–20.

21 Farmer (1969).

22 *Resettlement Programme*, p. 1.

23 Ibid. p. 9.

24 Migration in India from one rural area to another is in fact relatively slight: see e.g. Gurdev Singh Gosal, 'Internal Migration in India—a Regional Analysis', *Indian Geogr. J.*, vol. 36 (1961), pp. 106–21.

25 Giri, p. 43. Cf. D. S. Senanayake's views on the creation of Ceylonese nationality: Farmer (1957), p. 299.

26 The author is grateful to Professor A. N. Pandeva for the benefit of a discussion on the standards of cultivation attained by political sufferers in the Tarai.

27 See P. W. Paustian, *Canal Irrigation in Punjab* (New York, Columbia UP, 1930), pp. 60–1.

28 C. H. Heimsath, *Indian Nationalism and Hindu Social Reform* (Princeton, NJ, Princeton UP, 1964), esp. p. 6.

29 Ibid. p. 245.

30 Ibid. p. 342.

31 See e.g. D. Dalton, 'The Gandhian View of Caste, and Caste after Gandhi' in P. Mason, ed., *India and Ceylon: Unity and Diversity* (London, OUP for Inst. Race Relations, 1967), pp. 159-81.

32 See 'Gandhiji as a Farmer', *The Sunday Standard*, 29 Sept. 1963.

33 See e.g. Dhanajay Keer, *Dr. Ambedkar: Life and Mission*, 2nd edn (Bombay, Popular Prakashan, 1962), esp. ch. 10.

34 'Gandhiji as a Farmer', *Sunday Standard*, 29 Sept. 1963.

35 Judith M. Brown, 'Gandhi in India, 1915–20' (unpublished Ph.D. dissertation, Univ. of Cambridge, 1968), p. 96. See also her *Gandhi's Rise to Power: Indian Politics, 1915–22* (Cambridge, CUP, 1972), pp. 45–6.

36 G. Myrdal, *Asian Drama*, 3 vols (Harmondsworth, Penguin Books, 1968), vol. 2, p. 753.

37 Ibid. vol. 1, p. 261.

38 *Report of a Sub-Committee of the National Planning Committee on Land Policy, Agricultural Labour and Insurance* (Bombay, Vora, 1948).

39 Ibid. pp. 34, and 60–1. See also K. T. Shah, 'The Problem of Waste Land', ibid. Appx I, pp. 63–83.

40 *Report*, as cited in n. 38, pp. 55–6.

41 See H. L. Erdman, *The Swatantra Party and Indian Conservatism* (Cambridge, CUP, 1967), esp. pp. 69–70, 72–3 and 80.

42 *Report*, as cited in n. 38, pp. 125–31.

43 Ibid. p. 55.

44 J. Nehru, 'Le Premier Principe', *Nouvelle Revue Internationale*, no. 4 (Dec. 1958), p. 94.

45 *Report of the Population Sub-Committee of the National Planning Committee* (Bombay, Vora, 1947), pp. 9–10 and 40.

46 Ibid. pp. 41–4.

47 Ibid. p. 144.

48 Tarlok Singh, *Poverty and Social Change: a Study in Economic Reorganisation of Indian Rural Society* (London, Longmans, 1945): 2nd edn, Bombay, Orient Longmans, 1969).

49 Myrdal, *Asian Drama*, vol. 3, pp. 1005–6.

50 Tarlok Singh, *Poverty and Social Change* (1945), pp. 29–32.

51 Myrdal, *Asian Drama*, vol. 2, pp. 745–53.

52 Giri, *passim.*

53 cf. Béteille in Mason, ed., *India and Ceylon*, pp. 83–93.

54 *Report of the Backward Classes Commission*, 3 vols (New Delhi, Manager of Publications, 1956).

55 Ibid. vol. 1, p. 36.

56 Daniel and Alice Thorner, 'The Agricultural Labour Enquiry: Reflections on Concepts and Methods' in their *Land and Labour in India* (London, Asia Publishing House, 1962), pp. 173–88, at p. 173. See also Tarlok Singh, *Towards an Integrated Society* (Bombay, Orient Longmans, 1969), ch. 10, 'The Landless Labourer'.

57 *Report on Intensive Survey of Agricultural Labour*, 7 vols (Delhi, Manager of Publications, 1955).

58 *Report on the Second Agricultural Labour Enquiry*, vol. 1, *All-India* (Delhi, Manager of Publications, 1960).

59 See V. K. R. V. Rao, ed., *Agricultural Labour in India* (London, Asia Publishing House, 1962); and D. and A. Thorner (as n. 56 above).

60 J. E. Schwartzberg, 'Agricultural Labour in India: a Regional Analysis', *Econ. Development & Cultural Change*, vol. 11 (1963), pp. 337–53. See also H. Laxminarayan, 'Regional Variations in Conditions of Agricultural Labourers', in V. K. R. V. Rao, ed., *Agricultural Labour in India*, pp. 135–51.

61 *Report of the Committee on Settlement of Landless Agricultural Workers*, duplicated (New Delhi, Planning Commission, 1961).

62 *Report of the Commissioner for Scheduled Castes and Scheduled Tribes, 1963–64*, 2 parts (Delhi, Manager of Publications, 1965), pt I, pp. 74–5.

63 e.g. Giri, p. 31. Land colonization is included in the list of measures for the economic uplift of 'backward classes' in the *Fourth Five Year Plan, 1969–74*: see *Fourth Plan*, p. 419.

64 *Survey of Wastelands: Madras*, p. iii.

65 *Punjab Colony Manual*, pp. 29–30.

66 Trevaskis, *The Punjab of Today*, vol. I, pp. 276–7.

67 Darling, pp. 115–16.

68 Farmer (1957), pp. 200–20.

69 cf. Chambers, pp. 150–4.

70 G. D. Agrawal, *The Story of the Hirakud Dam Project* (New Delhi, Min. of Irrigation and Power, n.d.), p. 75.

71 For contradictory reports, compare *Statesman Weekly*, 1 Dec. 1966 and 1 Feb. 1964.

72 cf. *Statesman Weekly*, 23 Dec. 1967, for encroachment in Lakhimpur District of Assam, and ibid., 24 Jan. 1970, for encroachment of grazing grounds at Barpeta in the same state.

73 Encroachment is, of course, a widespread problem in many other countries: for Ceylon, see e.g. *Report of the Land Commission*, Sessional Paper No. 10 of 1958 (Colombo, Govt Press, 1958), pp. 31–4.

74 *Resettlement Programme*, p. 103.

75 Ibid. p. 113.

76 Ibid. pp. 8–9.

77 Giri, p. 43, is insistent that only those 'willing to make agriculture their mode of life' should be admitted for training in his neo-Gandhian co-operative colonies but yet has it that 'no serious employment-seeker should be denied a place'.

78 The author is grateful to Professor A. N. Pandeva for observations on this point.

79 Darling, p. 115.

80 *Resettlement Programme*, p. 77.

81 Ibid. p. 35.

82 Ibid. p. 58.

83 *Report of the Committee on Settlement of Landless Agricultural Workers*, (1961), pp. 9–10.

84 For *panchayati raj* see e.g. *Third Plan*, pp. 337–41; and Myrdal, *Asian Drama*, vol. 1, p. 299.

85 Farmer (1957), pp. 204–7.

86 *Report of the Special Officer on the Scheme of the Resettlement of Landless Agricultural Labourers*, typescript (Madras, 1964).

87 Farmer (1957), pp. 219–20.

88 The author is grateful to Mr Tissa Devendra, then Assistant Land Commissioner, Ceylon, for this information.

89 D. Christodoulou, *Report to the Government of the United Arab Republic on Land Settlement and Related Rural Institutional Problems of the General Desert Development Organization* (Rome, FAO, 1964), p. 8.

90 R. Ho, 'Land Settlement Projects in Malaya', *J. Tropical Geogr.*, vol. 20 (1965), p. 9.

91 Farmer (1957), pp. 168–74.

92 See the annual *Report of the Min. of Rehabilitation* and (beginning with 1961–2) the *Report of the Dept of Rehabilitation, Min. of Works, Housing and Supply* (later *Min. of Labour, Housing and Rehabilitation* and later still *Min. of Labour, Employment and Rehabilitation*). In the pages that follow 'Ministry' should be taken to mean the Min. (or later the Dept) of Rehabilitation. The number of refugees mentioned of course excludes those who fled in 1971.

93 *The Dandakaranya Project: Report (Preliminary)* (New Delhi, Ministry of Rehabilitation, n.d. [1959]).

94 Farmer (1957), pp. 171–4.

95 Ibid. pp. 173–4.

96 *Report of the Gal Oya Project Evaluation Committee*, Sessional Paper no 1 of 1970 (Colombo, Govt Publications Bureau, 1970).

97 For more general proposals for the development of Dandakaranya see *Development of Dandakaranya* (New Delhi, National Council of Applied Economic Research, 1963), a 'techno-economic' survey.

98 Dilip Mukerjee, 'Taking the D.V.C. to Pieces', *Statesman Overseas Weekly*, 25 July 1964, p. 5.

99 *Third Plan*, pp. 310 and 232, resp.

100 *Tarai Report*, pp. 1–2, and Appendix II.

101 S. Thirumalai, *Post-war Agricultural Problems and Policies in India* (Bombay, Indian Soc. Agric. Econ. and New York, Inst. Pacific Relations, 1954), pp. 117–20; and *Final Report of the Foodgrains Policy Committee* (Delhi, Govt of India Press, 1948), pp. 10 and 18 (but cf. V. K. R. V. Rao's dissent, pp. 47–56).

102 *Report of the Grow More Food Campaign Enquiry Committee* (New Delhi, Min. of Food and Agric., 1952), pp. 20–33.

103 *Report of the Scheduled Areas and Scheduled Tribes Commission, 1960–61*, vol. 1 (Delhi, Manager of Publications, 1961), p. 149.

104 *First Plan* (*Draft Outline*), p. 107.

105 G. Kuriyan, 'Agricultural Planning in India' in *Proc. of the International Geography Seminar, Aligarh Muslim Unlv., 1956* (Aligarh, Dept of Geogr., Muslim Univ., 1959), pp. 405–18 at p. 406.

106 *Second Plan*, pp. 313–20.

107 See the *Surveys of Wastelands* (published 1960–3) listed on p. 147 below.

108 See *Study on Wastelands.*

109 *Report of the Scheduled Areas and Scheduled Tribes Commission, 1960–61*, vol. 1, p. 149.

110 *Third Plan*, p. 310.

111 Subsequently reduced to Rs.7 crores: *The Third Plan Mid-term Appraisal* (New Delhi, Planning Commission, 1963), p. 96.

112 Ibid. pp. 377–8.

113 *Third Five Year Plan* (*1961–1966*) (Bhopal, Govt of Madhya Pradesh, Planning and Development Dept, n.d. [1961]), pp. 70–1.

114 *Third Five Year Plan* (Jaipur, Govt of Rajasthan Planning Department, n.d. [1961]).

115 *Fourth Plan* (*Draft Outline*).

116 Ibid. p. 132.

117 Ibid. pp. 193–4.

118 The author is indebted to Shri Saran Singh, Joint Secretary, Dept of Agric., Govt of India, for the benefit of a discussion on these matters in Dec. 1968.

119 *Fourth Plan 1969–74: Draft; Fourth Plan.*

120 *Fourth Plan*, p. 138.

121 Ibid. p. 17.

122 Ibid. p. 180.

123 Ibid. p. 151.

Chapter 7: Natural Difficulties Confronting Colonization

1 Farmer (1957), p. 39 and ch. 11.

2 cf. K. N. Raj, *Some Economic Aspects of Bhakra-Nangal Project* (Bombay, Asia Publishing House, 1960), p. 95.

3 *The Desert Blooms* (Delhi, Min. of Information and Broadcasting, 1961), p. 4.

4 See, *inter alia*, *Annals of the Arid Zone* (Jodhpur). For recommendations on the reclamation, irrigation, and treatment of the Rajasthan Canal command, see *Rajasthan Canal Soil Survey.*

5 Pierre Gourou, 'Quelques Observations de Géographie Tropicale dans l'Inde', *Rev. Univ. Bruxelles*, vol. 3 (1950–1), pp. 254–69, esp. pp. 268–9.

6 See the map accompanying H. G. Champion, 'A Preliminary Survey of the Forest Types of India and Burma', *Indian Forest Rec.* (N.S.), *Silviculture*, vol. 1 (1936), pp. 1–287.

7 See in this connection H. C. Hart, *New India's Rivers* (Bombay, Orient Longmans, 1956), pp. 43–4.

8 K. A. Walvekar, 'Development and Planning', *Varuna* (Munirabad, Journal of the Tungabhadra Advisory Board), vol. 11 (1958), p. 7.

9 For waterlogging and salinity problems in similar terrain a little farther north along the axis of aridity, see R. P. Talati, 'Damaged Lands in the Deccan and their Classification', *Indian J. Agric. Sci.*, vol. 11 (1941), pp. 959–77.

10 Spate, pp. 57–9.

11 Farmer (1957), esp. pp. 22–8; also B. H. Farmer, 'Rainfall and Water-supply in the Dry Zone of Ceylon' in R. W. Steel and C. A. Fisher, eds, *Geographical Essays on British Tropical Lands* (London, Philip, 1956), pp. 227–68.

12 See *East Africa Royal Commission, 1953–1955, Report*, Cmd 9475 (London, HMSO, 1955), esp. pp. 6–10 and Maps 2–4.

13 The author is greatly indebted to Shri C. C. Patro and Shri G. K. Nair of the Dandakaranya Development Authority for supplying rainfall and agronomic data, and for many useful discussions in the field and by correspondence.

14 Only 2·5% of total cropped area of Bastar District is said to be irrigated: *Report of the Scheduled Areas and Scheduled Tribes Commission, 1960–61*, vol. 1 (Delhi, Manager of Publications, 1961), pp. 152–3.

15 S. P. Chatterjee and Bikash Basu, 'The Physiographic and Economic Basis of Urbanization in the Gond and Adjoining Lands of the Central Provinces', *Calcutta Geogr. Rev.*, vol. 6 (1944), p. 19. For an account of tank construction in Chanda District by immigrants from UP, see J. H. Rivett-Carnac, *Many Memories of Life in India* (Edinburgh and London, Blackwood, 1910), pp. 147–50. Rivett-Carnac was Settlement Officer in the District in 1865–6.

16 Personal communication from Shri C. C. Patro.

17 Farmer (1957), pp. 45–56; and E. R. Leach, *Pul Eliya* (Cambridge, CUP 1966), esp. chs 1–3.

18 Farmer (1957), ch. 12.

19 Spate, p. 667.

20 See *Dandakaranya: a Symbol and a Hope*, duplicated (Koraput, Dandakaranya Development Authority, 1971), p. 15.

21 See *Hirakud Dam Project* (New Delhi, Central Waterpower, Irrigation and Navigation Commission, 1950), pp. 4–5; and G. D. Agrawal, *The Story of the Hirakud Dam Project* (New Delhi, Min. of Irrigation and Power, n.d.). See also N. V. Sovani and N. Rath, *Economics of a Multi-purpose River Dam* (Poona, Gokhale Inst. and Bombay, Asia Publishing House, 1960),

22 See M. F. Blanford, *A Practical Guide to the Climates and Weather of India, Ceylon and Burmah* (London, Macmillan, 1889), esp. pp. 76–80, and Spate, pp. 57–9.

23 cf. Michel, pp. 27 and 512–13, where the emphasis is placed on a rising water-table and canal seepage; it is claimed that no serious attempt is being made to provide a drainage system in East Punjab and Rajasthan.

24 See *Tarai Report*, pp. 15–16. But cf. H. Brammer's views, above p. 42, n. 20.

25 *Statesman Weekly*, 2 Oct. 1971.

26 See Y. D. Pande, 'Agriculture in Nainital Tarai and Bhabar', *Geogr. Rev. India*, vol. 23 (1961), pp. 19–39, esp. pp. 37–8 and *Multiple Cropping in Tarai* (Pantnagar, U.P. Agric. Univ., 1969), p. 1.

27 See also *Resettlement Programme* (1968), pp. 19 and 62.

28 See the map in Spate, p. 205.

29 See B. H. Farmer, 'Land Use Lessons Learnt in Madras and Applicable to the Dry Zone of Ceylon', *Bull. Ceylon Geogr. Soc.*, vol. 10 (1956), pp. 9–19, esp. pp. 14–17.

30 Farmer (1957), pp. 227–32, esp. pp. 228–9.

31 F. Ahmad, *Preliminary Report on the Possibilities of Domestic Water Supply in the Proposed Colonies in the Dandakaranya Project Area*, duplicated paper (Calcutta, Geol. Survey of India, 1960).

32 C. L. Dhawan and others, 'Pre-irrigation Soil Survey of Some Districts of the Punjab', *Indian J. Agric. Sci.*, vol. 27 (1957), pp. 375–94.

33 R. R. Agarwal and others, 'Soil Classification and Soil Mapping, in Naini Tal Tarai', *Proc. Nat. Acad. Sci. India*, Sec. A, vol. 24 (1955), pp. 46–60.

34 *Resettlement Programme*, p. 33.

35 Compare the observation in E. T. Atkinson, ed., *Statistical, Descriptive and Historical Account of the North-Western Provinces of India*, vol. 12 (Allahabad, Govt Press, 1886), p. 703, that Tarai soil is 'good' and 'seldom requires manure'.

Chapter 8: Surveying Natural Resources and Planning Their Use

1 On the general subject matter of this chapter, though primarily in a Latin American context, see O. C. Herfindahl, *Natural Resource Information for Economic Development* (Baltimore, John Hopkins Press for Resources for the Future 1969). See also B. H. Farmer, 'The Environmental Sciences and Economic Development', *J. Development Studies*, vol. 7 (1971), pp. 257–69.

2 Hereafter referred to as *Surveys of Natural Resources 1963*. See also *Soil and Water Research in India in Retrospect and Prospect* (New Delhi, Indian Agric. Research Inst., 1971), which has a good bibliography.

3 *A Co-ordinated Study of Organisations concerned with the Surveys of Natural Resources*, hereafter referred to as *Surveys of Natural Resources 1971*.

4 Ibid. p. ii.

5 *Surveys of Natural Resources 1963*, pp. 1–21 and 56–69; *Surveys of Natural Resources 1971*, pp. 1–25 and 67–82.

6 *Survey of India Map Catalogue* (Dehra Dun, Survey of India, 1970).

7 V. A. Janaki, 'Maps and National Development', *Indian J. of Geogr.* (Jodhpur), vol. 1 (1966), pp. 11–19, at p. 14.

8 *Surveys of Natural Resources 1963*, pp. 22–4 and 70.

9 *National Atlas of India*, Preliminary (Hindi) edn (Calcutta and Dehra Dun, Min. of Education and Scientific Res., 1957).

10 Each sheet is accompanied by a descriptive memoir published Hors Série, *Travaux de la Section Scientifique et Technique de l'Institut Français de Pondichéry*.

11 See e.g. H. Gaussen, *The Vegetation Maps, Trav. Sec. Sci. Tech., Inst. Français, Pondichéry*, vol. 1 (1959), pp. 155–79.

12 See *Census of India, 1961: Union and States Atlases* (New Delhi, Office of the Registrar General, n.d. [1964]).

13 See *Surveys of Natural Resources 1963*, pp. 39–46 and *1971*, pp. 44–51; and the various Memoirs, Records, and Reports of the Geological Survey of India. The transfer of groundwater surveys from the Geological Survey of India to the Central Ground Water Board was criticized by the recent Irrigation Commission: see *Irrigation Commission*, vol. I, pp. 49–56 and 285–287.

14 F. Ahmad, *Preliminary Report on the Possibilities of Domestic Water Supply in the Proposed Colonies in the Dandakaranya Project Area*, duplicated (Calcutta, Geol. Surv. of India, 1960).

15. *The Chambal Multi-purpose Project* (Bhopal, Director of Information, 1960), p. 10.

16 *Hindustan Times*, 13 Aug. 1963.

17 *Fourth Plan 1969–74* (*Draft*), pp. 191–2. See also *Statesman Weekly*, 3 May 1969.

18 US Dept of Interior, Bureau of Reclamation, *Evaluation of Engineering and Economic Feasibility, Beas and Rajasthan Projects* (Washington DC, Dept of State, 1963).

19 *Surveys of Natural Resources 1963*, p. 72 and *1971*, pp. 41 and 87.

20 See also *The Statesman*, 9 Dec. 1968.

21 Baden-Powell, vol. 2, p. 78.

22 F. Buchanan, *A Journey from Madras through the Countries of Mysore, Canara and Malabar*, 3 vols (London, Cadell & Davies, 1807), vol. 2, pp. 436–7, 440–1, 460, 559 and vol. 3, pp. 60, 89, 251, and 258.

23 *Surveys of Natural Resources 1963*, pp. 25–36 for this and subsequent developments.

24 Z. J. Schokalskaya, 'The Natural Conditions of Soil Formation in India',

in B. B. Polynov, ed., *Contributions to the Knowledge of Soils of Asia*, no. 2 (Leningrad, Acad. of Sci., Dokuchaiev Inst., 1932).

25 See e.g. *The Need for a Soil Survey of India, a symposium: Proc. Indian Sci. Congr., Hyderabad, 1937*, pp. 482–92. See also the plea for 'a real soil survey' by the distinguished Scottish geographer, A. G. Ogilvie, in 'The Technique of Regional Geography—with Special Reference to India', *J. Madras Geogr. Assoc.*, vol. 13 (1938), pp. 109–24, at p. 114.

26 *Report of the Royal Commission on Agriculture in India*, Cmd 3132 (London, HMSO, 1928), pp. 70–9.

27 This is the work whose title is hereafter abbreviated as *Soil Survey*.

28 A. T. A. Learmonth, 'Soils' in Spate and Learmonth, pp. 95–118. See also S. P. Raychaudhuri, *Soils of India*, Indian Council of Agric. Research Review Series no. 25 (New Delhi, Indian Council of Agric. Research, 1958), and Legris, ch. 2.

29 *Soil Survey Manual* (mimeograph, New Delhi, Indian Agric. Research Inst., 1960); and *Suppl.* no. 1 (1962).

30 *Soil Survey Manual*, ch. 9, pp. 33–8; *Suppl.* no. 1.

31 See e.g. A. N. Puri, *Standardization of Methods of Soil Analysis, Pt 1—Introductory and Physico-Chemical Constants of Indian Soils*, Field Research Station Bull., Ser. A, no. 2 (Bombay, Field Research Station, 1963).

32 S. P. Raychaudhuri, *Soil Survey and Soil Tests in relation to Soil Fertility and Agricultural Production* (mimeograph, paper read at UN Conference on the Application of Science and Technology for the Benefit of Less Developed Areas, n.d.).

33 *Surveys of Natural Resources 1963*, pp. 32–3.

34 Ibid. p. 33.

35 The author is indebted to Dr S. V. Govinda Rajan for the benefit of discussions on this and related points. For a rather different opinion, though one that still insists on a strengthened organization, see B. B. Vohra, 'The Human Environment in India', paper for first meeting of Indian Committee on Human Environment (New Delhi, Min. of Food, 1972), p. 18.

36 The author is indebted to Dr A. N. Misra, for a brief note on the work of the Rudrapur Laboratory. See also R. R. Agarwal, R. L. Mehrotra, and R. N. Gupta, 'Soil Classification and Soil Mapping in Naini Tal Tarai', *Proc. Nat. Acad. Sci. India*, Sec. A, vol. 24 (1944), pp. 46–60; and *Resettlement Programme*, p. 31.

37 *Surveys of Natural Resources 1971*, p. 40.

38 *Surveys of Natural Resources 1963*, pp. 30–2 and *1971*, pp. 34–5. See also R. C. Hoon, 'Agri-irrigational Potential of Land Commanded by Some of the Proposed Multi-purpose Projects in India', *Bull. Nat. Inst. Sci. India*, vol. 3 (1954,) pp. 185–92, esp. pp. 191–2; R. R. Agarwal and others, *Proc. Nat. Acad. Sci. India*, Sec. A, vol. 24 (1955), pp. 46–60 (which deals, however, only with the area of the former State Farm); C. L. Dhawan and others, 'Pre-irrigation Soil Survey of Some Districts of the Punjab', *Indian J. Agric. Sci.*, vol. 27 (1957), pp. 375–94; K. M. Mehta, *Report of Soil and Crop Investigation Survey, Chambal Commanded Areas, Rajasthan* (Udaipur, Dept Agric., 1958); K. M. Mehta, C. M. Mathur, and H. S. Shankara Narayana, 'Classification of Land under Chambal Commanded Area according to Capability', *J. Soil & Water Conservation, India*, vol. 7 (1958), pp. 27–34; and R. S. Gupta, 'Investigations on the Desert Soils of Rajasthan', *J. Indian Soc. Soil Sci.*, vol. 6 (1958), pp. 113–20. See also K. N. Raj, *Some Economic Aspects of Bhakra-Nangal Project* (London, Asia Publishing House, 1960), p. 96.

39 Few results appear to have been published; but see *Report of the Agricultural Expert Team on the Dandakaranya Project*, duplicated (New Delhi, Min. of Food and Agric., 1963), pp. 6–7.

40 K. M. Mehta, *Report of Soil and Crop Investigation Survey, Chambal Commanded Areas, Rajasthan*, and K. M. Mehta and others, *J. Soil & Water Conservation, India*, vol. 7 (1958).

41 Some soil survey work was done here before independence and, indeed, before World War II; see P. V. Ramiah, *A Report on the Soil Survey of the Tungabhadra Project Area* (Madras, Supt Govt Press, 1937). See also K. V. Joshi, 'Agricultural Planning under Tungabhadra Project for Soil and Water Conservation', *J. Soil & Water Conservation, India*, vol. 5 (1957), pp. 128–33.

42 Hoon, *Bull. Nat. Inst. Sci. India*, vol. 3 (1954).

43 C. J. Thampi, 'Survey and Land Classification in the Andaman Islands', *J. Soil & Water Conservation, India*, vol. 9 (1961), pp. 170–9.

44 US Dept of Interior, Bureau of Reclamation, *Evaluation of Engineering and Economic Feasibility, Beas and Rajasthan Projects.*

45 Michel, pp. 333–4.

46 Ibid. p. 464. (The Master Plan did however envisage a survey of 5·8 million acres [2·3 million hectares] in 1960–8, with profile pits every mile [1·6 km], except in very uniform terrain: *Rajasthan Canal Master Plan*, ch. 5, p. 5).

47 The author is indebted to Shri C. M. Mathur, formerly Project Director of the Rajasthan Canal Soil and Water Study Project, for the benefit of discussion at Bikaner in Mar. 1972. Unfortunately many of the publications on the Project had not been released for publication at the time of writing; for those released see Abbreviations for Standard References, *Rajasthan Canal Soil Survey*, p. 308 below.

48 For a critical discussion of the land systems approach, see Farmer, *J. Development Studies*, vol. 7 (1971), esp. pp. 259–64.

49 Personal communication from Prof. Sir Joseph Hutchinson, to whom the author is greatly indebted for a discussion on these matters.

50 *Survey of Wastelands* (published 1960–3), listed on p. 147 below.

51 *Surveys of Natural Resources 1971*, p. 35.

52 *Survey of Wastelands*, pt I: *Punjab*, pp. i–ii. There is also a centrally sponsored scheme, less relevant to this book, to survey small blocks of waste.

53 *Pilot Survey of Culturable Waste Land in Dewas District 1958–59*, Govt of Madhya Pradesh, Directorate of Land Records (Gwalior, Govt Regional Press, 1961).

54 *Resettlement Programme*, pp. 6–7 and 12–13; see also pp. 55 and 57–8, 73, 114, and 160–1.

55 *Survey of Wastelands*, pt VI: *Madhya Pradesh*, map I, facing p. 2.

56 Ibid. map facing p. 11.

57 Ibid. pt VIII: *Madras.*

58 *Report of the Special Officer on the Scheme for the Resettlement of Landless Agricultural Labourers*, typewritten (Madras, 1964).

59 *Report of the Waste Land Survey* (*Technical*) *Committee* (Shillong, Assam Govt Press, 1968).

60 *Study on Wastelands* (for details, see Abbreviations for Standard References, p. 308 below).

61 *Report of the Committee on Resettlement of Landless Agricultural Workers*, duplicated (New Delhi, Planning Commission, 1961), esp. p. 4.

62 As quoted in *The Statesman*, 1 Nov. 1963.

63 Government of India Circular no. 22-F, 19 Oct. 1894.

64 Govt of India, Min. of Food and Agric. Resolution no. 13–1/52F of 12 May 1952. The author is indebted to Shri A. Oswald, then Assistant Inspector-General of Forests, for the benefit of a discussion of forest policy. The author, however, takes responsibility for the views expressed.

65 *Survey of Wastelands: Maharashtra*, pp. 9–10 (where an accompanying soil map shows almost all of Chanda District as having 'skeletal soils').

66 Champion and F. C. Osmaston, contains a section on wild life in almost all its chapters.

67 See *The Statesman*, 8 Oct. 1963.

Chapter 9: Problems of Land-Use Technology

1 For recent accounts of these environments see G. S. Puri, *Indian Forest Ecology*, 2 vols (New Delhi, Oxford Book Co. and London, Allen & Unwin, 1960), and Legris. See also Spate and Learmonth, ch. 3, for a succinct account.

2 *Rajasthan Canal Master Plan*, ch. 5, p. 7.

3 Dalip Singh and S. D. Nijhawan, 'A Study of the Physico-Chemical Changes Accompanying the Process of Reclamation in Alkali Soils', *Indian J. Agric. Sci.*, vol. 2 (1932), pp. 1–18; and *Study on Wastelands*, pp. 13–14.

4 Farmer (1957), esp. pp. 194–9 for Ceylon; R. Ho, 'Land Settlement Projects in Malaya', *J. Tropical Geogr.*, vol. 20 (1965), pp. 1–15; R. Wikkramatileke, 'State Aided Land Colonization in Malaya', *Ann. Assoc. Amer. Geogr.*, vol. 55 (1965), pp. 377–403, for Malaya; and *A Handbook of Thal Development Authority* (Jauharabad, Thal Development Authority, 1954), for West Pakistan.

5 Ritchie Calder, *Men Against the Jungle* (London, Allen & Unwin, 1954), pp. 139–44, esp. pp. 147–8.

6 *Resettlement Programme*, p. 17.

7 See e.g. Farmer (1957), pp. 148 and 194–9, for Ceylon; R. Ho, *J. Tropical Geogr.*, vol. 20 (1965), and R. Wikkramatileke, *Ann. Assoc. Amer. Geogr.* vol. 55 (1965).

8 *Dandakaranya Project Report*, pp. 55–61.

9 Farmer (1957), pp. 197–9.

10 cf. the special labour organizations raised in Ceylon: Farmer (1957), pp. 195–6.

11 Ibid. p. 198.

12 cf. *Consolidated Report on the Land Revenue Administration of the State of Bihar, 1957–58—1959–60* (Patna, Secretariat Press, 1962), pp. 18–19, which quotes Rs.400 per acre (Rs.160 per hectare) for tractor reclamation and Rs.100 per acre (Rs.40 per hectare) for manual reclamation 'in the lateritic areas' (i.e. the plateau), and Rs.170 per acre (Rs.68 per hectare) quoted for reclamation under the Gudu Barrage in Sind by S. Z. Ahsan, 'Gudu Barrage Project', *Geografia* (Karachi), vol. 4 (1965 [1967]), pp. 47–60.

13 See e.g. Farmer (1957), pp. 197–9; K. D. S. Baldwin, *The Niger Agricultural Project* (London, OUP, 1957), p. 169; and *Report on the Center on Land Settlement for Asia and the Far East, Inginiyagala, Ceylon, 14 November–15 December 1958*, FAO/59/8/6194 (Rome, FAO, 1959), pp. 69–70.

14 cf. the arguments used by the Gal Oya Development Board in Ceylon: Farmer (1957), p. 197.

15 *Dandakaranya: a Symbol and a Hope*, duplicated (Koraput, Dandakaranya Development Authority, 1971), p. 2.

16 On the subject of this section see *Evaluation of Major Irrigation Projects: Some Case Studies* (New Delhi, Programme Evaluation Organisation, Planning Commission, 1965), esp. pp. 6–14.

17 *Indian Agriculture in Brief*, 8th edn (New Delhi, Min. of Food and Agric., Community Development and Co-operation, 1967), pp. 37–8.

18 cf. Giri, p. 42.

19 cf. *Resettlement Programme*, pp. 82 and 88.

20 Nasim Ansari, 'Some Economic Aspects of Irrigation Development in Northern India', in A. M. Khusro, ed., *Readings in Agricultural Development* (Bombay, Allied Publishers, 1968), p. 210.

21 *Statesman Weekly*, 13 July 1968.

22 *Fourth Plan* (*Draft Outline*), pp. 216–17.

23 cf. *Resettlement Programme*, pp. 19 and 40 for a similar problem at Pilibhit, where defective channels were blamed.

24 See e.g. H. K. Trevaskis, *The Punjab of Today*, vol. 1 (Lahore, Civil & Military Gazette, 1931), p. 229; S. P. Raychaudhuri and N. R. Datta Biswas, 'Saline and Alkaline Soils of India', *Proc. Nat. Acad. Sci. India*, Ser. A, vol. 24 (1955), pp. 611–20; R. R. Agarwal, C. L. Mehrotra and C. P. Gupta, 'Speed and Intensity of Soil Alkalinity with Canal Irrigation in Gangetic Alluvium of Uttar Pradesh', *Indian J. Agric. Sci.*, vol. 27 (1957), pp. 363–73; *Study on Wastelands*; P. C. Raheja, *Soil Productivity and Crop Growth* (London, Asia Publishing House, 1966), ch. 7, and Michel, pp. 509–14 (for India) and pp. 455–508 (for Pakistan).

25 Y. D. Pande, 'Agriculture in Nainital Tarai and Bhabar', *Geogr. Rev. India*, vol. 23 (1961), pp. 19–39, esp. p. 37.

26 K. M. Mehta, *Report of Soil and Crop Investigation Survey, Chambal Commanded Area, Rajasthan* (Udaipur, Dept of Agric., 1958), pp. iii–iv. See also *Irrigation Commission*, vol. I, p. 312 and vol. II, pp. 204–6, 211–12, and 352–3.

27 Personal communication from Professor Sir Joseph Hutchinson; see also p. 146 above.

28 George Attwood, 'A Study of the Wiltshire Water Meadows', *Wilts. Archaeol. Nat. Hist. Mag.*, vol. 58 (1963), p. 404.

29 The US Bureau of Reclamation advised the appointment of foreign consultants to investigate and design drainage systems: Michel, p. 383.

30 Farmer (1957), pp. 46–7.

31 J. D. La Touche, *Ajmer-Merwara Settlement Report* (Calcutta, Foreign Dept Press, 1875), pp. 4–5.

32 See e.g. M. Lipton, 'Strategy for Agriculture: Urban Bias and Rural Planning', in P. Streeten and M. Lipton, eds, *The Crisis of Indian Planning* (London, OUP for RIIA, 1968), pp. 83–147; Etienne; Khusro, ed., *Readings in Agricultural Development*; and Pramit Chaudhuri, ed., *Readings in Indian Agricultural Development* (London, Allen & Unwin, 1972) and works quoted therein.

33 cf. *Resettlement Programme*, pp. 44–5, 63–4, 68, and 127–8.

34 cf. the Tamil Nadu state average (1964–5) of 1,535 kg per hectare (*Indian Agriculture in Brief*, 8th edn, p. 98).

35 For the difficulty of separating 'caste' and 'tribe' see below, p. 274.

36 W. A. Noble, 'The Badagas, Entrepreneurs of South India', *Abstr. of Papers, 21st International Geogr. Congr., India, 1968* (Calcutta, National Committee for Geogr., 1968), pp. 323–4. See also A. Aiyappan, *Report on the Socio-Economic Conditions of the Aboriginal Tribes of the Province of Madras* (Madras, Govt Press, 1948), pp. 117–20; the entry 'Badega' in H. Yule and A. C. Burnell, ed. W. Crooke, *Hobson-Jobson*, reprint edn (London, Routledge & Kegan Paul, 1968), p. 46.

37 *Growth Rates in Agriculture* (New Delhi, Min. of Food and Agric., 1964), p. 34. See also V. Nath, 'The Growth of Indian Agriculture: a Regional Analysis', *Geogr. Rev.*, vol. 59 (1969), pp. 348–72.

38 Note that these are *paddy* yields; those in Table 9.II are *rice* yields at 66·2 % extraction rate.

39 See R. S. Koshal, *Report to the Government of Ceylon on the Development of Sample Surveys for the Estimation of Agricultural Production*, Ceylon Sessional

Paper no. 19 of 1954 (Colombo, Govt Printer, 1954); and B. H. Farmer, 'Available Food Supplies', in Sir J. B. Hutchinson, ed., *Population and Food Supply* (Cambridge, CUP, 1969), pp. 78–9.

40 Farmer, in Hutchinson, ed., p. 80.

41 One ('government') maund = 82·28 lb. (37·33 kg), but the Madras maund is 25 lb. (11·34 kg) and the Bombay, 28 lb. (12·71 kg). A bigha is quoted by *The Economist Guide to Weights and Measures* (London, *The Economist* [n.d.]), p. 46, as 0·625 acres (0·253 hectares) but actually it varies over the country, as did the acre in medieval England. A Madras Measures is 2½ lb. (1·13 kg), and a bag (of rice) is, or may be 1½ cwt. (76·20 kg).

42 Spate and Learmonth, p. 264.

43 *Indian Agriculture in Brief*, 8th edn, pp. 114–15.

44 See e.g. Nafis Ahmad, *An Economic Geography of East Pakistan*, 2nd edn (London, OUP), pp. 117–98; and B. L. C. Johnson, 'Crop-Association Regions in East Pakistan', *Geogr.*, vol. 43 (1958), pp. 86–103; 'Dry Season Agriculture in East Pakistan', *Geogr. Studies*, vol. 5 (1958), pp. 61–71; and *Agricultural Geography of East Pakistan* (unpublished Ph.D. thesis, Univ. of London, 1960).

45 Nafis Ahmad, pp. 123–31.

46 Ibid. pp. 190–1.

47 H. N. C. Fonseka, 'Parakrama Samudra Colony: an Example of Peasant Colonisation in the Dry Zone of Ceylon', *J. Tropical Geogr.*, vol. 22 (1966), pp. 10–22, esp. p. 13.

48 C. J. Thampi, 'Survey and Land Classification in the Andaman Islands', *J. Soil & Water Conservation in India*, vol. 9 (1961), pp. 170–9, at pp. 177–8; but the suggestions for diversification do not appear particularly realistic.

49 The author is indebted to Shri G. C. Dash, Secretary to Government, Agriculture and Animal Husbandry Dept, Govt of Orissa, for information on this point. See also *Report of the Scheduled Areas and Scheduled Tribes Commission, 1960–61*, 2 vols (Delhi, Manager of Publications, 1961), vol. 1, p. 149, which advocates the development of shifting cultivation 'on scientific lines' since it did not appear possible to resettle all tribal peoples practising shifting cultivation. The same *Report* tabulates land under shifting cultivation by tribes and estimates the area annually so cultivated over 545,000 hectares (p. 145).

50 K. V. Joshi, 'Agricultural Planning under Tungabhadra Project for Soil and Water Conservation', *J. Soil & Water Conservation in India*', vol. 5 (1957), pp. 128–33.

51 Farmer (1957), pp. 227–32 and 249–55.

52 Kenneth R. Walker, *Planning in Chinese Agriculture: Socialization and the Private Sector* (London, Cass, 1965), p. 64.

53 See Etienne, pp. 150, 184–5, and 229; B. Sivaraman, 'The Strategy of Food Production', *Ind. J. Public Admin.*, vol. 13 (1967), pp. 433–47, and *Evaluation of the High Yielding Varieties Programme, Kharif 1967* (New Delhi, Programme Evaluation Organisation, Planning Commn, 1968). It may be of interest that Pantnagar Agricultural Univ., on the site of the former Tarai State Farm, is to multiply and provide 'wonder seeds': *Statesman Weekly*, 12 Oct. 1968.

54 See e.g. Francine R. Frankel, *India's Green Revolution: Economic Gains and Political Costs* (Princeton, NJ, Princeton UP, 1971).

55 See Farmer (1957), pp. 255–8.

56 H. K. Trevaskis, *The Land of the Five Rivers*, vol. 1 (London, OUP, 1928), p. 284.

57 Farmer (1957), p. 257.

58 M. D. Chaturvedi, *Land Management in the United Provinces* (Allahabad, Supt Govt Printing, 1946), p. 87.

59 *Rajasthan Canal Master Plan*, ch. 7.

60 See e.g. Sir H. Glover, *Soil Erosion*, Oxford Pamph. Indian Affairs, no. 23 (Bombay, OUP, 1944); R. Maclagan Gorrie, *Report to the Government of India on Soil Conservation* (Rome, FAO, 1957); 'Soil Conservation in India', *Farm Bull.* no. 58 (New Delhi, Min. of Food and Agric., 1960); and M. S. V. Rama Rao, *Soil Conservation in India* (New Delhi, Indian Council Agric. Research, 1962). See also *Journal of Soil & Water Conservation in India.*

61 *Rajasthan Canal Master Plan*, ch. 5, section 3.

62 cf. *Resettlement Programme*, p. 81.

Chapter 10: Domestic Economy of the Colonist

1 cf. official data for colonists' incomes in Ceylon cited in Farmer (1957,) pp. 260–1.

2 *Resettlement Programme*, pp. 47–8, 70, 91, 110, 133, 155, and 170.

3 Also ibid. for tables of colonists' indebtedness (see also below, pp. 204–6).

4 *Resettlement Programme.*

5 Darling, p. 114; see also pp. 132–44.

6 *Agricultural Income by States, 1960–61*, Occasional Paper no. 7, National Council of Applied Econ. Research (New Delhi, National Council of Applied Econ. Research, 1963), p. 31.

7 Farmer (1957), pp. 261–2.

8 R. Ho, 'Land Settlement Projects in Malaya', *J. Tropical Geogr.*, vol. 20 (1965), pp. 1–15 at p. 11.

9 R. Wikkramatileke, 'A Study of Planned Land Settlement in the Eastern Marchlands of Malaya', *Econ. Geogr.*, vol. 38 (1962), pp. 330–46.

10 Ashok Thapar, 'Changing Face of the Terai', *Times of India*, 14 Dec. 1971.

11 *Multiple Cropping in Tarai*, Research Bull. no. 6, UP Agric. Univ. (Pantnagar, UP Agricultural Univ., 1969), pp. 22–5.

12 *Dandakaranya: a Symbol and a Hope*, duplicated (Koraput, Dandakaranya Develt Auth., 1971), pp. 12–13, where average incomes 1965–9 are also cited.

13 A. M. Khusro and A. N. Agrawal, *The Problem of Co-operative Farming in India* (Bombay, Asia Publishing House, 1961), p. 4, n. 2.

14 W. C. Neale, *Economic Change in Rural India* (London, Yale UP, 1962), p. 180, note a, and works there cited.

15 See e.g. M. Lipton, 'Should Reasonable Farmers Respond to Price Change?', *Modern Asian Studies*, vol. 1 (1967), pp. 95–9, a review of Dharm Narain, *The Impact of Price Movements on Areas under Selected Crops in India, 1900–39* (Cambridge, CUP, 1965). See also Raj Krishna, 'Farm Supply Response in India–Pakistan: a Case-Study of the Punjab Region', *Econ. J.*, vol. 73 (1963), pp. 477–87; and T. N. Krishnan, 'The Marketed Surplus of Foodgrains', in Pramit Chaudhuri, ed., *Readings in Indian Agricultural Development* (London, Allen & Unwin, 1972), pp. 99–109.

16 *Resettlement Programme.*

17 The flowers of the *mohur* tree, *Bassia latifolia*, from which liquor can be made by fermentation.

18 See *Resettlement Programme*, p. 111.

19 cf. Giri.

20 Farmer (1957), pp. 295–6.

21 cf. Farmer (1957), p. 276.

22 *Development Activities under Tungabhadra Project in Raichur District* (Munirabad, Deputy Administrator, 1961), pp. 20–2.

23 See e.g. Neale, pp. 166–9; J. P. Bhattacharjee, 'Underemployment among

Indian Farmers: an Analysis of its Nature and Extent based on Date for Bihar' in A. M. Khusro, ed., *Readings in Agricultural Development* (Bombay, Allied Publishers, 1968), pp. 488–526. See also such studies as B. V. S. Baliga and S. B. Tambad, 'Labour Utilisation in Paddy, Bangalore District', *Farm Management Studies in Mysore State*, vol. 3, duplicated (Bangalore [1965]).

24 cf. Dharma Kumar, *Land and Caste in South India* (Cambridge, CUP, 1965), pp. 45–7.

25 Giri, pp. 47–9, 56, and 60–6.

26 Michel, p. 13. See also *Punjab Colony Manual*, vol. 1, p. 25.

27 *Rajasthan Canal Master Plan*, ch. 3, pp. 12–21.

28 See e.g. *The Composite Rural Structure: a Settlement Pattern in Israel* (Rehovot, Agric. Settlement Dept, 1960); R. Weitz, ed., *Rural Planning in Developing Countries* (London, Routledge & Kegan Paul, 1965), pp. 92–5; R. Weitz and A. Rokach, *Agricultural Development: Planning and Implementation* (Dordrecht, Reidel, 1968), pp. 24–8 and 278–304, and A. Berler and others, *Urban-Rural Relations in Israel*, Publications on Problems of Regional Development, Settlement Study Centre, Rehovot, no. 8 (1969). See also R. F. Kinloch, *Agricultural Settlement in Southern Israel* (unpublished Ph.D. dissertation, Univ. of Cambridge, 1963).

29 *Dandakaranya Project Report*, pp. 31 and 80–1.

30 See *Development of Dandakaranya: a Techno-economic Survey* (New Delhi, National Council of Applied Econ. Research, 1963).

31 *Amrita Bazar Patrika*, 26 Oct. 1963.

32 See e.g. B. W. Hodder, *Economic Development in the Tropics* (London, Methuen, 1968), pp. 192–3. See also, for an area that includes Dandakaranya, W. H. Wake, 'Causal Role of Transportation Improvement in Agricultural Changes in Madhya Pradesh, 1834–1954: A Type Study', *Indian Geogr. J.*, vol. 37 (1962), pp. 133–52.

33 In this connection, see J. P. Lewis, *Quiet Crisis in India* (Washington, DC, Brookings Instn, 1962), pp. 152–5.

34 Giri, pp. 28–80.

35 Rashid A. Malik, *Irrigation Development and Land Occupance in the Upper Indus Basin* (Ph.D. dissertation, Univ. of Indiana, 1963), p. 88.

36 *Dandakaranya Project Report*, p. 172.

37 *Rajasthan Canal Master Plan*, ch. 4, p. 1.

38 Rashid A. Malik, pp. 88 and 168–9. See also Trevaskis, *The Punjab of Today*, vol. 2 (Lahore, Civil & Military Gazette, 1932), p. 99.

39 cf. *Resettlement Programme*, p. 76.

40 cf. *Report of the Scheduled Areas and Scheduled Tribes Commission, 1960–61*, vol. 1 (Delhi, Manager of Publications, 1961), pp. 260–1.

41 Farmer (1957), pp. 237 and 255.

42 *Resettlement Programme*, p. 167.

43 D. Christodoulou, *Report to the Government of the UAR on Land Settlement and Related Rural Institutional Problems of the General Desert Development Organization*, duplicated (Rome, FAO, 1964).

44 *Rajasthan Canal Master Plan*, ch. 3, pp. 12–21. The author is grateful to Shri H. K. Mawada, Chief Town Planner, Rajasthan, for the benefit of discussions on the planning of service centres; for which see also K. V. Sundaram, 'Settlement Pattern for an Irrigated Colony—an Application of the Central Place Theory', in R. P. Misra, ed., *Regional Planning: Concepts, Techniques, Policies and Case Studies* (Mysore, Univ. of Mysore, 1969).

45 Darling, p. 104.

46 The author is grateful to the then Dean of the Institute, Dr R. N. Haldipur, for this information.

47 A *hat* is a market, the Bengali equivalent of a *mandi*.

48 *Resettlement Programme*, p. 53.

49 *Rural Marketing and Finance*, Report of a Sub-Committee of the National Planning Committee (Bombay, Vora, 1947), pp. 159–60.

50 cf. the situation in Ceylon described in Farmer (1957), pp. 274–5.

51 *Fourth Plan*, p. 156. In this connection see also *Market Towns and Spatial Development in India* (New Delhi, National Council of Applied Econ. Research, 1965), and E. A. J. Johnson, *The Organization of Space in Developing Countries* (Cambridge, Mass., Harvard UP, 1970), esp. pp. 191–8.

52 See, *inter alia*, H. B. Shivamaggi, 'Provision of Credit for Small Cultivators: Reconsideration of the Problem', in Khusro, ed., *Readings in Agricultural Development*, pp. 240–61, esp. pp. 243–5. See also *Rural Credit Follow-up Survey, General Review Reports* (Bombay, Reserve Bank of India, from 1960).

53 See, *inter alia*, Shivamaggi, in Khusro, ed., p. 241.

54 *Resettlement Programme*, p. 53.

55 See, *inter alia*, G. Myrdal, *Asian Drama*, 3 vols (Harmondsworth, Penguin Books, 1968), vol. 2, p. 872.

56 Etienne, p. 37.

57 *Rajasthan Canal Master Plan*, ch. 5, p. 16.

58 *Fourth Plan 1969–74* (*Draft*), p. 130.

59 Ibid. See also *The Statesman*, 2 July 1963, and *The Times of India*, 10 July 1963.

60 The author is grateful to the Managing Director of the Corporation, Shri K. Madhava Das for the benefit of a discussion on these matters.

61 *The Statesman Weekly*, 5 Dec. 1970.

62 Darling, pp. 17–18.

63 For credit to small farmers in India generally see D. Thorner, 'Context for Co-operatives in Rural India', *Econ. Weekly*, Annual Number 1962, pp. 251–7; Shivamaggi, in Khusro, ed.; Etienne, *passim*; and Myrdal, *Asian Drama*, vol. 2, pp. 871–2 and 1334–9. Cf. for Ceylon, Farmer (1957), pp. 274–5.

64 As e.g. in Egypt: Christodoulou, *Report to the Government of UAR on Land Settlement . . .*, p. 9.

65 *Resettlement Programme, passim.*

66 cf. *Resettlement Programme*, pp. 5–6, 11, 17–18, 84–6, and 96–7.

67 *Report of the Committee on the Settlement of Landless Agricultural Workers* [the Patil Committee], duplicated (New Delhi, Planning Commission, 1961), p. 17; and Giri, pp. 43–4.

68 Farmer (1957), pp. 279–80, and R. Wikkramatileke, 'A Study of Planned Land Settlement in the Eastern Marchlands of Malaya', *Econ. Geogr.*, vol. 38 (1962), pp. 30–46.

69 *Rajasthan Canal Master Plan*, ch. 15, p. 2.

70 *Resettlement Programme*, pp. 5–6.

71 See e.g. Farmer (1957), pp. 279–80; *Report of the Land Commission*, Ceylon Sessional Paper no. 10 of 1958 (Colombo, Govt Press, 1958), pp. 96–107; and Farmer (1969), pp. 18–19.

72 See e.g. the case of virtually unassisted colonization in Mindanao, Philippine Islands, reported in P. R. Sandoval, 'Socio-economic Conditions of Settlers in Kidapawan, Mindanao', *Philippine Agriculturist*, vol. 40 (1956–7), pp. 498–518.

Chapter 11: Induced Agricultural Change in Colonization Schemes

1 See e.g. Etienne, pp. 30–9; G. Myrdal, *Asian Drama*, 3 vols (Harmondsworth, Penguin Books, 1968), esp. vol. 2, pp. 870–81 and 1339–45; and D.

Warriner, *Land Reform in Principle and Practice* (Oxford, Clarendon Press, 1969), pp. 197–8.

2 *Third Plan*, p. 332.

3 *Study of Development Staff at the District and Lower Levels*, P.E.O. Publication no. 66 (New Delhi, Programme Evaluation Organization, Planning Commission, 1968), pp. 7–9.

4 *Fourth Plan 1969–74* (*Draft*), p. 106.

5 *Fourth Plan*, p. 113.

6 *Third Plan*, p. 316. See also Etienne, p. 39; D. K. Desai, 'Intensive Agricultural District Programme: Analysis of Results', in Pramit Chaudhuri, ed., *Readings in Indian Agricultural Development* (London, Allen & Unwin, 1972), pp. 140–54; and V. Shanmugasundaram, ed., *Agricultural Development of India: a Study of Intensive Agricultural District Programme* (Univ. of Madras, 1972).

7 *Fourth Plan 1969–74* (*Draft*), p. 107. On IADP and IAAP see M. Lipton, 'Strategy for Agriculture: Urban Bias and Rural Planning', in P. Streeten and M. Lipton, eds, *The Crisis of Indian Planning* (London, OUP for RIIA, 1968), pp. 83–146 at pp. 109–20.

8 *Evaluation of the High Yielding Varieties Programme, Kharif 1967* (New Delhi, Programme Evaluation Orgn, Planning Commn, 1968), pp. 4 and 29.

9 *Intensive Agricultural District Programme: Report 1961–63* (New Delhi, Min. of Food and Agric., n.d. [1963]), pp. 94–114.

10 Ibid. p. 12.

11 In wars with the British, Tipu Sultan allegedly had a battery here.

12 *Indian Express*, 6 Sept. 1963.

13 *Resettlement Programme*, p. 19.

14 Ibid. pp. 44–5, 49, and 51.

15 Ibid. pp. 72–3.

16 *Report of the Scheduled Areas and Scheduled Tribes Commission 1960–61*, vol. 1 (Delhi, Manager of Publications, 1961), p. 265.

17 In this connection see M. C. Carras, *The Dynamics of Indian Political Factions* (Cambridge, CUP, 1972).

18 See e.g. Myrdal, *Asian Drama*, vol. 1, pp. 870–4 and 1339–46, and Lipton in Streeten and Lipton, eds, pp. 121–2.

19 *Dandakaranya Project Report* (*Preliminary*) (New Delhi, Min. of Rehabilitation, n.d. [1959]), p. 7.

20 Ibid. pp. 19–20 and 45.

21 *Dandakaranya Project Report*, pp. 112–35.

22 Ibid. p. 133.

23 *Dandakaranya Project Report* (*Preliminary*), p. 19.

24 *Report of the Agricultural Expert Team on Dandakaranya Project* (New Delhi, Min. of Food and Agric., 1963).

25 Ibid. p. 7.

26 *Rajasthan Canal Master Plan*, sections 7–10.

27 See P. C. Raheja, 'Research for Rural Development in the Arid Zone', *Science and Society* (Calcutta), vol. 1 (1962), pp. 89–97; and, for a specific example of agronomic research at the Institute, D. K. Misra, 'Role of Legumes in Crop Husbandry in Western Rajasthan', *J. Soil & Water Conservation in India*, vol. 9 (1961), pp. 124–39.

28 *Rajasthan Canal Master Plan*, section 7, p. 1.

29 D. W. Harvey, 'Theoretical Concepts and the spread of Agricultural Land-Use Patterns in Geography', *Ann. Assoc. Am. Geogr.*, vol. 56 (1966), pp. 361–74. See also the review in Janet D. Henshall, 'Models of Agricultural Activity', in R. J. Chorley and P. Haggett, eds, *Models in Geography* (London, Methuen, 1967), pp. 425–58 at pp. 446–8.

30 See e.g. *Progress Report for 1970–71, UP Agricultural University, Pantnagar* (Pantnagar, UP Agric. Univ., 1970), pp. 7–10 (plant-breeding) and pp. 28–31 (extension).

31 Farmer (1957), pp. 166–9; though see also the critical comments on pp. 303–6. For agricultural extension in a particular Ceylon colonization scheme see S. J. Tambiah, 'Agricultural Extension and Obstacles to Improved Agriculture in Gal Oya Peasant Colonization Scheme', *Second International Conference of Econ. Hist., 1962, Aix-en-Provence* (Paris, Mouton, 1965), pp. 323–42.

32 Farmer (1957), pp. 166–9.

33 Ibid. ch. 14.

34 See e.g. T. W. Schultz, *Transforming Traditional Agriculture* (New Haven, Conn., Yale UP, 1964), which discounts social and cultural factors and envisages an economically rational and profit-maximizing peasant, and which had a great influence on IADP and IAAP, as is shown by Lipton, 'Strategy for Agriculture', in Streeten and Lipton, eds, pp. 112–18; Lipton on the risk-minimizing cultivator, ibid., and 'The Theory of the Optimising Peasant', *J. Development Studies*, vol. 4 (1967–8), pp. 327–51; Myrdal, Asian Drama, vol. 1, ch. 3, as a far-ranging summary; and Everett M. Rogers, *Modernization among Peasants: the Impact of Communication* (New York, Holt, Rinehart & Winston, 1969), a cross-cultural sociological study drawing on Indian evidence, and provided with a full bibliography. See also (because of its Indian interest) P. Roy, F. B. Waisanen and Everett M. Rogers, *The Impact of Communication on Rural Development* (Paris, UNESCO, and Hyderabad, National Inst. of Community Development, 1969).

35 *Socio-Economic Survey of Primitive Tribes in Madhya Pradesh* (New Delhi, Nat. Council Applied Econ. Research, 1963), pp. 102–8.

36 cf. for Ceylon, Farmer (1957), p. 283; and see Myrdal, *Asian Drama*, vol. 1, p. 112.

37 Farmer (1957), p. 284.

38 W. A. Noble, 'The Badagas, Entrepreneurs of South India', *Abstr. of Papers, 21st International Geogr. Congr., India, 1968* (Calcutta, Natl Cttee for Geogr., 1968), pp. 323–4.

39 Etienne, pp. 96–8, 156–7 and 248.

40 Farmer (1957), p. 288.

41 In this connection see H. C. Rieger, 'Bureaucracy and the Implementation of Economic Plans in India', *Indian J. Public Admin.*, vol. 13 (1967), pp. 23–42; and, in a very different setting, Chambers, esp. pp. 140–201.

42 *Resettlement Programme*, p. 27.

43 The author is indebted to the late Shri D. R. Gadgil, then Director, Gokhale Institute, Poona, for the benefit of a discussion on these matters.

44 cf. T. H. Shen, *Agricultural Development in Taiwan since World War II* (Ithaca, NY, Comstock Publishing Associates, 1964), p. 102.

45 Giri, p. 43.

Chapter 12: Land Tenure in Colonization Schemes

1 'Settlement' here is used to mean the settlement of land revenue (and associated inquiries into tenure), not colonization as understood in this book.

2 See e.g. D. Warriner, *Land Reform in Principle and Practice* (Oxford, Clarendon Press, 1969), pp. 156–65; G. Myrdal, *Asian Drama*, 3 vols (Harmondsworth, Penguin Books, 1968), vol. 2, pp. 1305–11, and *Census 1961*, vol. I, pt XI-A (i), pp. xvi–xvii. (The whole of this part, together with part XI-A (ii) is concerned with land tenure.)

3 Ibid.

4 See e.g. Baden-Powell and Baden-Powell (Holderness).

5 Baden-Powell (Holderness), pp. 199–213.

6 *Census 1961*, vol. I, pt XI-A, p. v. This is the source for the rest of the paragraph.

7 Ibid. p. xii.

8 Ibid. p. lii. For complications introduced by 'group farming' in Dandakaranya see below, pp. 235–6.

9 *Census 1961*, vol. I, pt XI-A, p. xlv, and Madhya Pradesh Land Revenue Code 1959, no. 20 of 1959, in *The Madhya Pradesh Revenue Manual*, vol. 1 (Bhopal, Govt Central Press, 1962), ch. 12.

10 *Census 1961*, vol. I, pt XI-A, pp. lvii–lviii; see also W. C. Neale, *Economic Change in Rural India* (London, Yale UP, 1962), pp. 226–7.

11 *Report of the Special Officer on the Scheme of Resettlement of Landless Agricultural Labourers*, unpublished typescript (Madras, 1964), p. 20.

12 *Census 1961*, vol. I, pt XI-A, pp. lv and lvi.

13 The Programme Evaluation Organisation referred to colonists under this tenure as 'Pattedars of the Government' without any proprietary rights, as enjoyed by 'Bhumidars' and 'Sirdars': *Resettlement Programme*, p. 37. But the author's usage appears to conform more closely with that of the Census, which classifies 'Pattadars' as 'Sirdars': *Census 1961*, vol. I, pt XI-A (i), p. 168.

14 Ibid. p. xxxvii.

15 *Statesman Weekly*, 8 Nov. 1969.

16 *Census 1961*, vol. I, pt XI-A, p. lviii.

17 Ibid. pp. xvii and xxviii.

18 Ibid. p. xvii.

19 See, *inter alia*, *Report of the Working Group on Co-operative Farming* (New Delhi, Min. of Community Development and Co-operation, 1959), vol. 1, pp. 22–4. The Report also recognizes Better Farming Societies, but these do not involve co-operation in the tenure or cultivation of the land.

20 See R. K. Hallikeri, *Co-operative Farming in Dharwar District* (unpublished M.Sc. thesis, Univ. of Karnatak, 1952), pp. 97–154. The Arwatagi Society was cultivating 2·8–3·3 hectares of paddy jointly, and was to plant 16 hectares of sugar-cane for joint cultivation.

21 See M. Srinivasan, 'Experience of Co-operative Farming and Other Systems of Mutal Aid in the Madras State', *Indian J. Agric. Econ.*, vol. 13 (1958), pp. 162–73 (who, however, wrongly cites Thengumarahada as being run by a Joint Farming Society; see below, pp. 256–7).

22 cf. the categories excluded by A. M. Khusro, 'Co-operative Farming: Fundamental Considerations', in A. M. Khusro, ed., *Readings in Agricultural Development* (Bombay, Allied Publishers, 1968), pp. 424–5.

23 For the extent of such practices in Punjab and Western Punjab see H. Laxminarayan and Kissen Kanungo, *Glimpses of Co-operative Farming in India* (Bombay, Asia Publishing House, 1967).

24 cf. *Resettlement Programme*, pp. 10–11.

25 Ibid. p. 109.

26 Chambers suggests (pp. 155–6) that uniformity in size of allotment in British colonial schemes in Africa was due rather to an official 'preoccupation with orderliness'.

27 *Punjab Colony Manual*, pp. 114–15; D. S. Senanayake, *Agriculture and Patriotism* (Colombo, Lake House Press, 1935), p. 23. See also Farmer (1957), pp. 303–8.

28 From a typescript note on the scheme kindly supplied to the author.

29 *Statesman Weekly*, 25 Nov. 1967.

30 Farmer (1957), pp. 276–9.

31 See Y. L. Lee, 'Land Settlement for Agriculture in North Borneo', *Tijdschrift voor Econ. en Soc. Geogr.*, vol. 52 (1961), pp. 184–90.

32 Some allotments under Bhakra were larger: e.g. 25·3 hectares for 'temporary tenants' who had held land before 31 Dec. 1947.

33 See e.g. Giri, p. 44.

34 Farmer '1957', pp. 276–9; for a recent praiseworthy investigation see S. Selvanayagam, *The Problem of Economic Holdings in the Peasant Agriculture of the Dry Zone of Ceylon* (unpublished Ph.D. thesis, Univ. of London, 1971).

35 See e.g. L. C. Arulpragasam, 'A Consideration of the Problems arising from the Size and Subdivision of Paddy Holdings in Ceylon', *Ceylon J. Hist. & Soc. Studies*, vol. 4 (1961), pp. 58–70; and A. B. Andarawewa, 'Some Thoughts on the Economic Size of Production Holdings in Tropical Agriculture', ibid. vol. 8 (1965), pp. 38–46.

36 A. W. Ashby, 'Land Settlement; The Making of New Farms', *International J. Agrarian Affairs*, vol. 1 (1953), pp. 2–6.

37 Darling, p. 127; cf. H. Calvert, *Wealth and Welfare of the Punjab* (Lahore, Civil & Military Gaz., 1922), pp. 81–3.

38 From a note kindly supplied by the Colonization Commissioner, Rajasthan.

39 *The Dandakaranya Project Report* (Preliminary) (1959), p. 6.

40 *Dandakaranya Project Report*, pp. 25–7.

41 Ibid. p. 125.

42 Warriner, *Land Reform in Principle and Practice*, pp. 145–6 and 154.

43 *Report of the Uttar Pradesh Zamindari Abolition Committee*, 2 vols (Allahabad, Govt Central Press, 1948), vol. 1, pp. 19–23.

44 Raj Krishna and others, 'Economic Policy for Agricultural Development' in Khusro, ed., *Readings in Agricultural Development*, pp. 585–607 at p. 600.

45 Ibid. pp. 600–1. See also B. Mukhoti, 'Agrarian Structure in Relation to Farm Investment', *J. Farm Econ.*, vol. 48 (1966), pp. 1210–15; and D. Kanel, 'Size of Farm and Economic Development', *Indian J. Agric. Econ.*, vol. 22 (1967), pp. 26–44.

46 B. H. Farmer, 'On Not Controlling Subdivision in Paddy-Lands', *Trans. Inst. Br. Geographers*, no. 28 (1960), pp. 225–35, esp. pp. 229–33.

47 Khusro, 'Returns to Scale in Indian Agriculture' in Khusro, ed., pp. 123–59, at p. 132. See also Warriner, pp. 188–91; Dipak Mazumdar, 'Size of Farm and Productivity in Indian Peasant Agriculture', *Economica*, vol. 22 (1965), pp. 161–173; D. Kanel, 'Size of Farm and Economic Development', *Indian J. Agric. Econ.*, vol. 22 (1967), pp. 26–44; and Lipton, in Streeten and Lipton, eds, p. 106. But see, in a wider context, U. Patnaik, 'Economics of Farm Size and Farm Scale: Some Assumptions Re-examined', *Econ. and Pol. Weekly*, vol. 7 (1972), pp. 1613–24.

48 *Resettlement Programme*, p. 103.

49 A *bigha* is here 0·253 hectares.

50 Michel, pp. 373 and 433.

51 The author is indebted to the late Sir Malcolm Darling for a lucid exposition, many years ago, of the procedure in the Canal Colonies.

52 *A Handbook of the Thal Development Authority 1949–54* (Jauharabad, Thal Development Authority, 1954), pp. 88–9.

53 *Third Plan*, p. 388.

54 Michel, p. 392.

55 *Report of the (Ceylon) Land Commission* (Sessional Paper no. 10 of 1958, Colombo, Govt Press, 1958), pp. 116–17.

56 Baden-Powell (Holderness), esp. pp. 33–55.

57 See e.g. P. W. Paustian, *Canal Irrigation in Punjab* (New York, Columbia UP, 1930), p. 67, and pp. 24–6 above.

58 Statement of Conditions issued under Thal Development Act, 1949 as amended by Thal Development (Amendment) Act 1955.

59 Farmer (1957), esp. pp. 271–2, 287 and 289–92; and *Report of the (Ceylon) Land Commission* (1958), pp. 82–96.

60 *Resettlement Programme*, p. 109.

61 An Assam *bigha* is equivalent to 0·134 hectares.

62 *Resettlement Programme*, p. 35.

63 Ibid. p. 74.

64 Ibid. pp. 94–5.

65 cf. e.g. M. R. Haswell, *Economics of Development in Village India* (London, Routledge & Kegan Paul, 1967), pp. 89–90, and, for Ceylon, Farmer (1957), p. 289.

66 See e.g. *Report on the Center on Land Settlement for Asia and the Far East, Inginiyagala, Ceylon, 1958*, FAO/59/8/6194 (Rome, FAO, 1959), pp. 15 and 79–80.

67 Farmer, *Trans. Inst. Br. Geographers*, no. 28 (1960), p. 234.

68 The term is Oscar Lewis's and is admittedly used in a different context: see e.g. his 'The Culture of Poverty', *Scientific American*, vol. 215 (1966), pp. 19–25. See also C. A. Valentine, *Culture and Poverty* (London, Univ. of Chicago Press, 1968).

69 Warriner, p. 149.

70 *Report on the Center on Land Settlement* (cited fully in n. 66 above), pp. 79–80.

71 Mogens Boserup, 'Agrarian Structure and Take-Off' in W. W. Rostow, ed., *The Economics of Take-Off into Sustained Growth* (London, Macmillan, 1963), pp. 221–2 (with specific reference to 'the South Asian contrast' to Western conditions).

72 For the protagonists see, amongst others, N. S. Randhawa, 'Returns to Scale and Co-operative Farming', *Indian J. Agric. Econ.*, vol. 15 (1960), pp. 22–33; A. M. Khusro and A. N. Agarwal, *The Problem of Co-operative Farming in India* (London, Asia Publishing House, 1961), and A. K. Goyal, *Some Aspects of Co-operative Farming in India* (Bombay, Asia Publishing House, 1966). For the antagonists, see e.g. Charan Singh, *Joint Farming X-Rayed* (Bombay, Bharatiya Vidya Bhavan, 1959) and what is virtually a second edn, *India's Poverty and its Solution* (New York, Asia Publishing House, 1964); Raj Krishna, 'Agrarian Reform in India: the Debate on Ceilings', *Econ. Development and Cultural Change*, vol. 7 (1958), pp. 302–17; and Baljit Singh, *Next Step in Village India* (New York, Asia Publishing House, 1961). See also S. Thirumalai, *Post-war Agricultural Problems and Policies in India* (Bombay, Indian Soc. Agric. Econ. and New York, Inst. Pacific Relations, 1954), pp. 156–9; and a series of papers in *Indian J. Agric. Econ.*, vol. 13 (1958), pp. 58–183; and, for non-Indian authors, O. Schiller, *The Reorganisation of Individual Farming on Co-operative Lines* (Chandigarh, Punjab Co-op. Union, 1955); Margaret Digby, *Co-operative Land Use* (Oxford, Blackwell, 1963), pp. 47–53; Warriner, *Land Reform in Principle and Practice*, pp. 174–8; Myrdal, *Asian Drama*, vol. 2, pp. 1346–56; and P. Worsley, ed., *Two Blades of Grass* (Manchester, Manchester UP, 1971), pp. 16 and 38.

73 Giri, esp. pp. 36–40, 43, 51, and 54–5; M. S. Swaminathan as reported in *Statesman Weekly*, 18 Nov. 1972; Warriner, p. 178.

74 The author is indebted to Dr E. N. Komarov for a translation of his writings on the development of socio-political thought in India, and to Dr J. P.

Bhattacharjee for discussions on Tagore. For Gandhi's ideas see M. K. Gandhi, compiled H. M. Vyas, *Co-operation* (Ahmedabad, Navajivan, 1963).

75 Sir Henry S. Maine, *Village Communities in East and West* (London, Murray, 1871). See also C. Dewey, 'Images of the Village Community: a Study in Anglo-Indian Ideology', *Modern Asian Studies*, vol. 6 (1972), pp. 291–328.

76 Giri, pp. 47–9.

77 Ibid. pp. 37–40.

78 H. H. Mann, ed. D. Thorner, *The Social Framework of Agriculture* (Bombay, Vora, 1967), pp. 338–47 (originally written in 1938).

79 Hallikeri, *Co-operative Farming in Dharwar District*, pp. 49–55.

80 Tarlok Singh, *Poverty and Social Change* (London, Longmans, 1945).

81 Chambers, pp. 25–7; for African post-independence co-operative colonization, see pp. 34–7, and for Tanzanian *Ujamaa* (co-operative) villages see *The Guardian*, 13 Oct. 1971.

82 Hallikeri, pp. 19–20.

83 C. Maya Das, 'Commercial Farming for Ex-Criminals', *Indian Farming*, vol. 3 (1942), pp. 126–8.

84 B. Natarajan, 'Madras' in reports on Grow More Food Campaign, *Indian J. Agric. Econ.*, vol. 4 (1949), p. 264.

85 *Report of a Sub-Committee of the National Planning Committee on Land Policy, Agricultural Labour and Insurance* (Bombay, Vora, 1948), pp. 19–21.

86 Ibid. p. 35.

87 Ibid. pp. 68–70.

88 Ibid. pp. 61 and 84.

89 Ibid. pp. 60–1.

90 Ibid. pp. 160–2.

91 *Report of the Uttar Pradesh Zamindari Abolition Committee*, vol. 1, pp. 311–35, 475–6, 488–92, and 505–18.

92 *Studies in Co-operative Farming* (New Delhi, Programme Evaluation Organisation, Planning Commission, 1956), pp. 59–85.

93 *Report of the Indian Delegation to China on Agrarian Co-operatives* (New Delhi, Planning Commission, 1957).

94 Ibid. p. 187.

95 As quoted in Digby, *Co-operative Land Use*, pp. 47–9.

96 H. L. Erdman, *The Swatantra Party and Indian Conservatism* (Cambridge, CUP, 1967), p. 62 (see also pp. 65, 68–70, 72–5, and 79); for earlier advocacy of collectives see M. Masani, *Our India* (Bombay, OUP, 1940), pp. 93–5.

97 Digby, *Co-operative Land Use*, p. 49.

98 *Report of the Working Group on Co-operative Farming*, 2 vols (New Delhi, Min. of Community Development and Co-operation, 1959), vol. 1, pp. 27–42.

99 *Report of the German Agricultural Delegation to India on Co-operative Farming, Farm Machinery, Fertilizer, Land Consolidation and Dairy Processing* (New Delhi, Ministries of Food & Agric. and Community Development and Co-operation, 1960), pp. 4–5.

100 *Report of the Committee on Co-operative Farming* (Madras, Govt of Madras, 1963).

101 Ibid. pp. 9–10.

102 *First Plan (Draft Outline)*, p. 104.

103 *Third Plan*, pp. 210–11.

104 *Fourth Plan 1969–74 (Draft)*, p. 22.

105 Tarlok Singh, *Towards an Integrated Society* (Bombay, Orient Longmans, 1969), pp. 141–56, also pp. 28–30, 92–5, and 129–40.

106 cf. Everett Rogers, *Modernization among Peasants* (New York, Holt Rinehart & Winston, 1969), p. 27.

107 *Resettlement Programme*, p. 122.
108 cf. Worsley, ed., *Two Blades of Grass*, p. 38.
109 Farmer (1957), pp. 371–4.

Chapter 13: Some Social Issues

1 Farmer (1957), pp. 295–9.
2 Margaret Digby, *Agricultural Progress through Co-operation* (Oxford, Blackwell, 1951), p. 93.
3 Etienne, pp. 73 & 90.
4 See C. A. Fisher, *South-east Asia* (London, Methuen, 1964), pp. 77, 296, 313, and 381.
5 In this connection see Louis Dumont, 'The "Village Community" from Munro to Maine', in his *Religion/Politics and History in India* (Paris, Mouton, 1970), pp. 112–32, and, for the view that 'peasant communities are characterized by a mentality of mutual distrust' and a lack of co-operation, see Everett M. Rogers, *Modernization among Peasants* (New York, Holt, Rinehart & Winston, 1969), pp. 26–8. See also G. Myrdal, *Asian Drama*, vol. 2 (Harmondsworth, Penguin Books, 1968) pp. 1052–64.
6 See e.g. H. K. Trevaskis, *The Punjab of Today*, vol. 1 (Lahore, Civil & Military Gazette, 1931), pp. 276–7, and Darling, pp. 115–16.
7 See, for Ceylon, Farmer (1957), pp. 297–8.
8 On the subject of this section see, for Ceylon, ibid. pp. 299–302.
9 *Resettlement Programme*, p. 108.
10 cf. David Pocock, 'Social Anthropology: Its Contribution to Planning', in P. Streeten and M. Lipton, eds, *The Crisis of Indian Planning* (London, OUP for RIIA, 1968), pp. 271–89 at p. 277.
11 D. Warriner, *Land Reform in Principle and Practice* (Oxford, Clarendon Press, 1969), p. 178.
12 *Resettlement Programme*, pp. 36–7.
13 Kathleen Gough, 'A Tanjore Village' in M. N. Srinivas, ed., *India's Villages*, 2nd edn (Bombay, Asia Publishing House, 1960), p. 97.
14 *Punjab Colony Manual*, vol. 1, p. 201.
15 *Resettlement Programme*, p. 108.
16 Farmer (1957), p. 302.
17 cf. Pocock, in Streeten and Lipton, eds, p. 281.
18 *Resettlement Programme*, p. 162.
19 Farmer (1957), p. 308.
20 See e.g. P. W. Paustian, *Canal Irrigation in the Punjab* (New York, Columbia UP, 1930), pp. 52–3 and 56.
21 Champion and Osmaston, p. 436.
22 See also V. C. Mishra, 'The Marusthali', in R. L. Singh, ed., *India: Regional Studies* (Calcutta, National Committee for Geography, 1968), pp. 245–65.
23 Spate and Learmonth, p. 234, Fig. 8.2.
24 *Rajasthan Canal Master Plan*, ch. 7, p. 1.
25 Ibid.
26 Information gathered at a conference in the Institute kindly called by the Director, Dr P. C. Raheja, during the author's visit.
27 *Rajasthan Canal Master Plan*, ch. 7.
28 S. P. Malhotra and A. B. Bose, 'Problems of Rehabilitation of Nomadic Banjaras in Western Rajasthan', *Annals of the Arid Zone*, vol. 2 (1963), pp. 69–81. See also Mishra, in R. L. Singh, ed., pp. 262–4.

29 H. R. J. Davies, 'Nomadism in the Sudan', *Tijdschrift voor Econ. Soc. Geogr.*, vol. 57 (1966), pp. 193–202 at p. 202. For other African examples of conflict between nomad and new settlers see R. J. Harrison Church, 'Observations on Large-scale Irrigation Development in Africa', *FAO Agric. Econ. Bulletin for Africa*, no. 4 (1963).

30 *Punjab Colony Manual*, vol. 1, pp. 22–3.

31 *A Handbook of the Thal Development Authority 1949–54* (Jauharabad, Thal Development Authority, 1954), pp. 57 and 122–4.

32 Niranjan Majumder, 'Dilemmas of Dandakaranya are Built In', *Statesman Weekly*, 24 Dec. 1966, p. 5.

33 See *The Observer*, 27 Mar. 1966.

34 *Indian Express*, 10 Mar. 1972.

35 *Report of the Commissioner for Scheduled Castes and Scheduled Tribes for 1967–68* (Delhi, Manager of Publications, 1969), vol. 1, p. 7. Cf. K. V. Sundaram, R. P. Misra, and V. L. S. Prakasa Rao, *Spatial Planning for a Tribal Region; a Case Study of Bastar District, Madhya Pradesh*, Development Studies no. 4 (Mysore, Inst. of Development Studies, Univ. of Mysore, 1972), esp. pp. 23–6.

36 F. G. Bailey, '"Tribe" and "Caste" in India', *Contributions to Indian Sociol.*, vol. 5 (1961), pp. 7–19 at p. 7.

37 F. G. Bailey, ibid.; and *Tribe, Caste and Nation* (Manchester, MUP, 1960), pp. 263–6; cf. G. S. Ghurye, *The Aborigines—'So-called' and Their Future* (Poona, Gokhale Inst., 1943), of which the 3rd edn was retitled *The Scheduled Tribes* (Bombay, Popular Prakashan, 1963).

38 See e.g. M. N. Srinivas, 'A Note on Sanskritization and Westernization', *Far Eastern Quarterly*, vol. 15 (1955–6), pp. 481–96; *Social Change in Modern India* (Berkeley, Univ. of California Press, 1966) and 'The Cohesive Role of Sanskritization' in Philip Mason, ed., *India and Ceylon: Unity and Diversity* (London, OUP for Inst. Race Relations, 1967), pp. 67–82. See also Philip Mason, ibid. pp. 19–22 and C. von Fürer-Haimendorf, 'The Position of the Tribal Populations of Modern India', ibid. pp. 182–222 (with full bibliography).

39 Bailey, *Contributions to Indian Sociology*, vol. 5 (1961), p. 14.

40 In this connection see the *Tribal Map of India* compiled by the Dept of Anthropology, Govt of India (1956). I am indebted to Mr T. N. Pandey for the information that the Tharus were Scheduled in 1970.

41 See Rawle Knox, 'India's Problem Sons', *Daily Telegraph*, 29 Mar. 1966 (an article occasioned by the shooting of the Maharaja of Bastar).

42 Bailey, *Tribe, Caste and Nation*, pp. 185–93.

43 *Statesman Weekly*, 5 Dec. 1970.

44 See Kernial Singh Sandhu, 'Emergency Resettlement in Malaya', *J. Tropical Geogr.*, vol. 18 (1964), pp. 157–83; and J. J. Zasloff, 'Rural Resettlement in South Vietnam: the Agroville Problem', *Pacific Affairs*, vol. 35 (1962–3), pp. 327–40.

45 Personal communication from Shri G. C. Dash, Secretary to Government, Agric. and Animal Husbandry Dept, Govt of Orissa. In this connection see also *Report of the Scheduled Areas and Scheduled Tribes Commission 1960–61*, vol. 2 (Delhi, Manager of Publications, 1961), pp. 119–20, and *Socio-Economic Survey of Primitive Tribes in Madhya Pradesh* (New Delhi, Indian National Council for Applied Econ. Research, 1963), pp. 107–8.

46 *Socio-Economic Survey . . . Madhya Pradesh*, p. 150.

47 The author is indebted to Shri H. N. Tiwari for a thoughtful note on tribal welfare colonies in Guna District of Madhya Pradesh.

48 André Béteille, 'The Future of the Backward Classes' in Mason, ed., *India and Ceylon*, pp. 83–120 at p. 115.

49 V. Elwin, *The Tribal World of Verrier Elwin* (Bombay, OUP, 1964), p. 294.
50 Ibid. p. 245.
51 V. Elwin, *A Policy for NEFA*, 2nd edn (Shillong, Sachin Roy for NEFA, 1959), p. 54.
52 Ibid. Nehru's Foreword and Elwin's quotations from Nehru, pp. 54, 147, 223. The author is indebted to Shri N. K. Rustomjee for the benefit of a discussion on these matters.
53 Elwin, *The Tribal World of Verrier Elwin*, p. 286.
54 See e.g. *Hindustan Times*, 7 Dec. 1968.
55 Margaret Mead, *New Lives for Old: Cultural Transformation in Manus, 1928–1953* (London, Gollancz, 1956), pp. 445–52. See also B. K. Roy Burman, 'Meaning and Process of Tribal Integration in a Democratic Society', *Sociol. Bull.*, vol. 10 (1961), pp. 27–40.

Chapter 14: The Future of Agricultural Colonization

1 G. Kuriyan, 'Agricultural Planning in India', *Proc. of the International Geography Seminar, Aligarh Muslim Univ., 1956* (Aligarh, Dept of Geogr., Aligarh Muslim Univ., 1959), p. 405.
2 M. Chisholm, *Geography and Economics* (London, Bell, 1966), pp. 47–56, esp. pp. 47–8.
3 I prefer this view of the marginal productivity of labour to the commonly held view that this quantity is in India at or near zero, for reasons set out in M. Lipton, 'Population, Land and Diminishing Returns to Agricultural Labour', *Bull. Oxford Inst. Econ. & Statistics*, vol. 26 (1964), pp. 123–57, esp. p. 126. See also G. Myrdal, *Asian Drama*, vol. 3 (Harmondsworth, Penguin Books, 1968), pp. 2050–55.
4 *Rajasthan Canal Master Plan*, Foreword, p. 7.
5 Ibid. ch. 3, p. 11.
6 Ibid. ch. 1, appendix A; see also Michel, pp. 311–12.
7 B. B. Vohra, *Development of the Command Area of the Chambal Project*, duplicated (New Delhi, Dept of Agric., 1972), pp. 3–4.
8 *Resettlement Programme*, pp. 22–3.
9 *Tarai Report*, pp. 333–4.
10 *Resettlement Programme*, p. 22.
11 Farmer (1957), pp. 320–1 and K. J. Pelzer, *Pioneer Settlement in the Asiatic Tropics* (New York, Amer. Geogr. Soc., Special Publ. no. 29, 1945), pp. 199 and 214.
12 Farmer (1957), p. 319; *Report of the Committee on the Utilization of Crown Lands*, Ceylon Sessional Paper no. 3 of 1953 (Colombo, Govt Press, 1953), p. 26; and International Bank of Reconstruction and Development, *The Economic Development of Ceylon* (Baltimore, Johns Hopkins Press, 1953), p. 425.
13 Farmer (1957), p. 321.
14 Darling, pp. 113–14.
15 P. W. Paustian, *Canal Irrigation in Punjab* (New York, Columbia UP, 1930), p. 54.
16 N. G. Barrier, 'The Punjab Disturbances of 1907', *Modern Asian Studies*, vol. 1 (1967), p. 356.
17 Spate and Learmonth, pp. 231–2. I am greatly indebted to Dr Clive Dewey for information on the history of British irrigation policy and practice in the Punjab Canal Colonies.
18 See, however, for 'a preliminary analysis in terms of selected investment

criteria' K. N. Raj, *Some Economic Aspects of the Bhakra–Nangal Project* (New York, Asia Publishing House, 1960).

19 Quoted in *A Handbook of the Thal Development Authority, 1949–54* (Jauharabad, Thal Development Authority, 1954), pp. 31–4.

20 Michel, p. 216.

21 *Report of the Gal Oya Project Evaluation Committee*, Sessional Paper no. 1 of 1970 (Colombo, Govt Publications Bureau, 1970), pp. 121–2.

22 cf. Giri, p. 50.

23 See *Report of the Gal Oya Project Evaluation Committee*, esp. ch. 4 on the nature and reliability of the data used.

24 See e.g. K. W. Kapp, 'River Valley Projects in India; their Direct Effects', *Econ. Development and Cultural Change*, vol. 8 (1958–60), pp. 24–47; N. V. Sovani and N. Rath, *Economics of a Multipurpose Dam: Report of an Enquiry into the Economic Benefits of the Hirakud Dam* (Poona, Gokhale Inst. and Bombay, Asia Publishing House, 1960); K. N. Raj, *Some Economic Aspects of Bhakra–Nangal Project* (London, Asia Publishing House, 1960); S. K. Basu and S. B. Mukherjee, *Evaluation of Damodar Canals 1959–60* (London, Asia Publishing House, 1963); K. S. Sonachalam, *Benefit-Cost Evaluation of Cauvery–Mettur Project* (New Delhi, Planning Commission Research Programmes Cttee, n.d. [1963]); *Evaluation of Major Irrigation Projects* (New Delhi, Programme Evaluation Organisation, Planning Commission, 1965); Divakar Jha, *Evaluation of Benefits of Irrigation—Tribeni Canal Report* (Bombay, Orient Longmans, 1967); and N. Ansari, 'Some Economic Aspects of Irrigation Development in Northern India' in A. M. Khusro, ed., *Readings in Agricultural Development* (Bombay, Allied Publishers, 1968), pp. 186–239.

25 Michel, pp. 329–30.

26 *A Handbook of the Thal Development Authority*, p. 31.

27 *Progress Report, UP Agricultural University, 1970–71*, p. 36.

28 Compare Ansari, in Khusro, ed., p. 239, n. 27.

29 On this theme more generally, see Farmer (1969). For all its advocacy of benefit/cost analysis and of a proper rate of financial return, the Irrigation Commission which reported in 1972 does not appear to have been particularly cost-conscious: see *Irrigation Commission*, vol. I, pp. viii–ix and 252.

30 *Fourth Plan 1969–74 (Draft)*, p. 172.

31 *Rajasthan Canal Master Plan*, ch. 4, p. 3.

32 *Fourth Plan 1969–74 (Draft)*, p. 6.

33 *Rajasthan Canal Master Plan*, ch. I, Appendix C. The data there given have been subjected to a certain amount of correction and interpretation by the author, and have also been converted from 'long tons' to tonnes to make them comparable with figures quoted from the *Fourth Plan 1969–74 (Draft)*.

34 Giri; and cf. V. R. Pillai and P. G. K. Panikar, *Land Reclamation in Kerala*, Kerala Univ., Econ. Ser. no. 1 (London, Asia Publishing House, 1966), p. 173, 'land reclamation has become an unavoidable necessity'.

35 G. Keatinge, *Rural Economy in the Bombay Deccan* (London, Longmans, 1912), pp. 48–9.

36 See e.g. S. B. Palit, 'Forests and Land Use in India', *Indian Forester*, vol. 96 (1970), pp. 339–46.

37 *The First Five Year Plan* [*Pakistan*] (Karachi, National Planning Board, 1957), p. 220.

38 *Agricultural Plan: First Report of the Ministry Planning Committee* (Colombo, Min. of Agric. and Food, 1958), p. 33.

39 See *The Short-Term Implementation Programme* (Colombo, Dept of National Planning, 1962), pp. 122 and *Report of the Gal Oya Project Evaluation Committee*, pp. 31–42 and 140.

40 'Economic Development and Planning in Countries of Asia and the Far East', *Econ. Bull. for Asia & The Far East*, vol. 8 (1957), p. 53.

41 *Agricultural Plan*, 1958 (as cited in n. 38 above), p. 35.

42 A. A. L. Caesar, 'Yugo-slavia: Geography and Post-war Planning', *Trans. Inst. Br. Geographers*, no. 30 (1962), pp. 33–43 at p. 36.

43 I am indebted to Prof. Edith Penrose for making this and other points in discussion.

44 *Report of the Gal Oya Project Evaluation Committee.*

45 The author is indebted to Mrs E. A. Porter for the benefit of a discussion on this matter.

46 Michel, p. xii.

47 Ibid. p. 524.

48 Farmer (1957), p. 362.

49 Ibid. quoting *Report of the Joint United Kingdom and Australian Mission on Rice-Production in Ceylon, 1954* (Ceylon) Sessional Paper no. 2 of 1955 (Colombo, Govt Printer, 1955), p. 24.

50 The 'green revolution' in Ceylon is insufficiently documented as yet. See however, D. V. W. Abeygunawardena, ed., *Research and Production of Rice in Ceylon* (Colombo, Ceylon Assoc. for the Advancement of Sci., 1966).

51 See e.g. W. Ladejinsky, 'Ironies of India's Green Revolution', *Foreign Affairs*, vol. 48 (1969–70), pp. 758–68, esp. pp. 764–5; Uma Lele and J. W. Mellor, 'Jobs, Poverty and the "Green Revolution" ', International Affairs, vol. 48 (1972), pp. 20–32; and G. Parthasarathy, *Green Revolution and the Weaker Section* (Bombay, Thacker, 1971).

52 Myrdal, vol. 2, p. 745.

53 Parthasarathy, p. 43.

54 D. A. Morse, 'The Employment Problem in the Developing Countries', in R. Robinson and P. Johnston, eds, *Prospects for Employment Opportunities in the Nineteen Seventies*, Papers for the Seventh Cambridge Conference on Development (London, HMSO, 1971), pp. 5–13 at p. 8.

55 Pramit Chaudhuri, 'India: Objectives, Achievements and Constraints' in Pramit Chaudhuri, ed., *Aspects of Indian Economic Development* (London, Allen & Unwin, 1971), pp. 42–4.

56 Myrdal, *Asian Drama*, vol. 2, p. 747.

57 Ibid. pp. 749–56.

58 See Francine Frankel, *India's Green Revolution: Economic Gains and Political Costs* (Princeton, NJ, Princeton UP, 1971).

59 See e.g. Parthasarathy, p. 43 and Pramit Chaudhuri, p. 46.

60 *The Hindu*, 26 Mar. 1973; see also Giri's *Jobs for Our Millions.*

Index of Authors and Authorities

Abeygunawardena, D. V. W., 295 n.50
Agarwal, A. N., 188, 252 n.72
Agarwal, P. C., 52 n.1, 55 n.9
Agarwal, R. R., 132 n.33, 142 n.36, 144 n.38, 163 n.24
Agrawal, G. D., 102 n.70, 126 n.21
Agricultural Expert Team on the Dandakaranya Project, 144 n.39, 218 n.24
Agricultural Labour Enquiry, Second, 100 n.58
Agricultural Labour, Intensive Survey on, 100 n.57
Agriculture in India, Royal Commission on (1928), 29 n.153, 141 n.26
Ahmad, F., 130, 138
Ahsan, S. Z., 90 n.15, 156 n.12
Aitken, E. H., 26 n.140
Aiyappan, A., 16 n.88, 47 nn.49–51, 166 n.36
Ananthaswami Rao, B., 49 n.64
Andarawewa, A. B., 238 n.35
Ansari, N., 288 n.24, 289 n.28
Arulpragasam, L. C., 238 n.35
Ashby, A. W., 239, 241
Atkinson, E. T., 10 n.44, 12 n.60, 42 n.20, 132 n.35

Babu Shetty, 47 n.55
Backward Classes Commission, 99 nn.54–5
Baden-Powell, B. H., 8 n.30, 9 nn.31–2 & 36, 10 nn.40–2, 14 n.74, 20 n.110, 24 nn.132–4, 28 nn.146–7, 31 n.167, 47 nn.51 & 55, 52 n.2, 54 n.7, 140, 227 n.4, 228 n.5, 243 n.56, 307
Bailey, F. G., 56 n.17, 274–5
Baldwin, K. D. S., 156 n.13
Baliga, B. V. S., 194 n.23
Baljit Singh, 33, 232 n.72
Bannerman, A. D., 62 n.57
Barrier, N. Gerald, 22, 26, 285 n.16
Barua, B. K., 58 n.31
Basu, B., 123 n.15
Basu, S. K., 288 n.24
Batalov, A. L., 31
Bauer, P. T., 31
Beaglehole, T. H., 8 n.23, 50 n.73
Beazley, J. G., 90 n.12, 308
Bentley, C. A., 44 n.25
Bergmann, Theodor, 31
Berler, A., 196 n.28
Béteille, A., 91 n.19, 99 n.53, 277
Bhandarkar, R. G., 52 n.2, 55 n.15
Bhargave, Y., 61 n.53
Bhat, L. S., 46 nn.39 & 43, 47 nn.45–6 & 53, 48, 49 n.65, 50 n.79
Bhattacharjee, J. P., 194 n.23
Birch, B. P., 66 n.94
Blanford, M. F., 126 n.22
Blyn, G., 11
Boag, G. T., 65 n.91
Bose, A. B., 271
Bose, S. C., 52 n.1
Boserup, M., 252
Boyd, M. F., 56 n.23
Brammer, H., 42 n.20, 127 n.24
Brown, Judith M., 96 n.35
Buchanan, F., 48 n.62, 49 nn.67–71, 140
Burn, R., 44 nn.32, 45 n.33
Burnell, A. C., 166 n.36
Burns, W., 40 n.8, 41
Butterworth, A., 65

Caesar, A. A. L., 293
Calder, Ritchie, 9 n.5, 45 n.37
Calvert, H., 20, 239 n.37
Campbell, J., 64 nn.78–9, 81
Campbell, J. M., 49, 50 nn.73–4
Carras, M. C., 215 n.17
Chakrabarti, A. K., 44, 45 nn.33 & 37
Chalem, G. V., 64 n.82
Chambers, R. J. H., 102 n.69, 223 n.41, 237 n.26, 253, 307
Champion, Sir H. G., 17 n.94, 18 n.98, 121 n.6, 152 n.66, 307
Chandrasekhara, C. S., 40 n.6
Charan Singh, 252 n.72
Chatterjee, Sir Atul, 11 n.53, 12 n.61

Chatterjee, S. P., 36 n.1, 60 n.42, 123 n.15, 137
Chaturvedi, M. D., 16 n.85, 29, 32 n.170, 45 nn.34 & 36, 179 n.58
Chaudhuri, Pramit, 164 n.32, 212 n.6. 296 n.55, 297 n.59
Chhibber, H. L., 60 n.47
Chisholm, M. I. C., 279
Chorley, R. J., 220 n.29
Christodoulou, D., 106, 107 n.89, 200 n.43, 206 n.64
Christophers, S. R., 44, 49 n.64, 56 n.23, 64 n.85
Clarkson, S., 31 n.166
Clyde, D., 44 nn.27 & 31, 45
Colonies Committee (Punjab), 25 n.138
Co-operative Farming, Working Group on, 234 n.19, 256 n.98
Courtenay, P. P., 13 n.65
Covell, G., 46 n.40, 49 n.64
Crooke, W., 44 nn.28–9, 60, 166 n.36

Dalip Singh, 154 n.3
Dalton, D., 96 n.31
Damodaran Nambiar, C. H., 76 n.15
Darling, Sir Malcolm, 19 nn.103, 105 & 107, 20, 21 nn.113–15 & 117, 22–3, 101, 105 n.79, 186 n.5, 200, 205, 239, 243 n.51, 263 n.6, 285 n.14
Das, N. K., 30 n.157
Das Gupta, Ashin, 6
Dash, G. C., 173 n.49
Datta, J. N., 62 n.55
Datta, K., 7 n.9
Datta Biswas, N. R., 163 n.24
Davidson, B. R., 31
Davies, H. R. J., 272
Davis, Kingsley, 31
Desai, D. K., 212 n.6
Deshpande, C. D., 48, 50 n.77, 52 n.2
Devendra, T., 106 n.88
De Vries, E., 286–9
Dewey, C., 253 n.75, 286 n.17
Dhanajay Keer, 96 n.33
Dharm Narain, 189 n.15
Dharma Kumar, 10 n.40, 11 n.51, 27 n.141, 195 n.24
Dhawan, C. L., 132 n.32, 144 n.38
Digby, Margaret, 252 n.72, 255 n.95, 256, 261
Diwan Chand, 45 nn.35 & 37
Dobby, E. H. G., 74 n.10
Dresch, J., 38 n.2
Dumont, Louis, 263 n.5
Dupuis, Jacques, 15 n.80, 46 n.43, 48
Dutt, R. C., 10 n.40

East Africa Royal Commission, 122 n.12
Elwin, Verrier, 55 n.8, 277
Embree, Ainslie T., 9 n.32
Erdman, H., 97 n.41, 255 n.96
Erskine, K. D., 40
Etienne, G., 164 n.32, 174 n.53, 204 nn.56 & 63, 211 n.1, 212 n.6, 222, 262, 307

Farmer, B. H., 9 n.35, 21 nn.136–7, 23 nn.124 & 131, 52 n.1, 53 n.22, 54 n.25, 59 n.41, 73 n.5, 89 n.6, 91 n.16, 92 nn.20–1, 93 n.25, 101 n.68, 106 nn.85 & 87, 107 n.91, 108 n.94, 109 n.95, 118 n.1, 122 n.11, 124 nn.17–18, 130 nn.29–30, 135 n.1, 146 n.48, 153 nn.13–14, 154 n.4, 155 nn.7 & 9–10, 164 n.30, 169 n.39, 170 n.40, 174 n.51, 178 n.55, 179 n.57, 184 n.1, 187 n.7, 193 nn.20–1, 200 n.41, 203 n.50, 206 n.63, 207 n.68, 209 n.71, 220 n.31, 221, 222 nn.36–7, 223 n.40, 237 n.27, 238 nn.30 & 34, 241 n.46, 246 n.59, 248 n.65, 251 n.67, 260 n.109, 261 n.1, 264 nn.7–8, 284 n.11, 289 n.29, 295 nn.48–9, 307
Fisher, C. A., 74, 122 n.11, 262 n.4
Folke, Steen, 14 nn.74 & 76, 15 n.77, 48 n.57
Fonseka, H. N. C., 172
Foodgrains Policy Committee, 16 n.90
Fowler, F. J., 41 n.14
Francis, Sir Philip, 12 n.58
Francis, W., 47 nn.49 & 52
Frankel, Francine R., 177 n.54, 297 n.58
Frykenberg, R. E., 9 n.32
Fürer-Haimendorf, C. von, 15 n.79, 75 n.14

Gadgil, D. R., 224 n.43
Gait, Sir E. A., 13 n.65, 14 n.66, 58 n.31
Gal Oya Project Evaluation Committee (Ceylon), 109 n.96, 287 n.21, 288, 292 n.39, 294
Gaussen, H., 46 n.42, 138
Geddes, A., 40 n.9
Ghoshal, U. N., 9
Giles, H. A., 6 n.2

Giri, R., 33 n.172
Giri, V. V., 35, 93, 98, 101 n.63, 105 n.77, 161 n.18, 192 n.19, 196–7, 207, 225, 238 n.33, 252–3, 287 n.22, 291, 296–7, 307
Glasford, C. L. R., 54 n.7
Glover, Sir H., 180 n.60
Gorrie, R. Maclagan, 180 n.60
Goswami, P. C., 17 n.95
Goswami, T. C., 16 n.84
Gough, Kathleen, 267
Goyal, A. K., 252 n.72
Griffiths, Sir Percival, 13 n.65, 14 nn.66–70, 74–5 & 78, 29 n.149
Gourou, P., 55 n.15, 121–2
Govinda Rajan, S. V., 142 n.35
Grigson, W. V., 52, 55 nn.8 & 12, 56 nn.19–20
Grow More Food Enquiry Committee, 15 n.82, 17 n.93, 50 n.79, 112 n.102
Guha, R., 12 n.58
Gupta, C. P., 163 n.24
Gupta, R. N., 144 n.36
Gupta, R. S., 144 n.38
Gupta, S. C., 7 n.14, 11 n.53
Gurdev Singh Gosal, 93 n.24
Gurvic, R. P., 31

Haggett, P., 220 n.29
Haldipur, R. N., 201 n.46
Hall, W. T., 60 n.47
Hallikeri, R. K., 235 n.20, 253 n.79, 254
Hamilton, A. P. F., 60 n.47
Hamzah Sendut, 74 n.10
Harbhagwan, J., 46 n.40, 49 n.64
Hart, H. C., 121 n.7
Harvey, D. W., 220 n.29
Haswell, M. R., 248 n.65
Heimsath, C. H., 18 n.99, 95 n.28
Henshall, Janet D., 220 n.29
Herfindahl, O. C., 135 n.1
Hilton, T. E., 89 n.7
Hiralal, Rai Bahadur, 213 n.8
Ho, R., 107 n.90, 154 n.4, 155 n.7, 187
Hodder, B. W., 197 n.32
Holderness, T. W., 10 nn.40–2, 20 n.110, 24 nn.132–4, 31 n.167, 227 n.4, 228 n.5, 243 n.56, 307
Hoon, R. C., 144 n.38, 144 n.42
Houlton, Sir J., 63, 64 n.77
Hunter, W. W., 10 nn.45–6
Hutchinson, Sir J. B., 146 n.49, 163 n.27, 169 n.39

Indian Irrigation Commission (1901–1903), 38 n.3, 40 nn.10–12
Innes, C. A., 47 nn.49 & 55, 50 n.75
International Map of Vegetation, 46 n.42
Iqbal Singh, 89 n.5
Irfan Habib, 6 n.8, 8 n.27, 9 n.33, 60, 63 n.63
Irrigation Commission (1972), 138 n.13, 163 n.26, 289 n.29

Jacob, V. P., 49 n.64
Jain, N. G., 52 n.3, 56 n.22
Janaki Ammal, E. K., 17 n.94
Janaki, V. A., 136
Janardhanan Nair, M., 76 n.19
Jaswant Singh, 49
Jha, Divakar, 288 n.24
Johnson, B. L. C., 172 n.44
Johnson, E. A. J., 203 n.51
Johnston, P., 296 n.54
Johnstone, J. W. D., 62
Joshi, K. V., 145 n.41, 174 n.50
Joshi, M. M., 52 n.1

Kanel, D., 241 n.45, 242 n.47
Kapp, K. W., 288 n.24
Kariapa, C. D., 49 nn.64 & 66
Kazi Ahmed, 20
Keane, A. H., 8 n.21
Keatinge, G., 11 n.56, 291
Kellogg, C. E., 144
Khan, G. A., 65 n.91
Khan Niaz Muhammad Khan Tarin, 24 n.135
Khusro, A. M., 162 n.20, 164 n.32, 188, 189 n.13, 194 n.23, 204 n.52, 235 n.22, 241 nn.44–5, 242 n.47, 252 n.72, 288 n.24, 289 n.28
Kinloch, R. F., 196 n.28
Kirk, W., 63 n.75
Kissen Kanungo, 235 n.23
Komarov, E. N., 253 n.74
Kosambi, D. D., 8 n.20
Koshal, R. S., 169 n.39
Kotovsky, G., 89 n.10
Krishan, Prem, 87 n.1
Krishna Iyer, L. A., 47 n.48
Krishnamurty, D. V. G., 17 n.91
Krishnan, M., 76 n.20
Krishnan, T. N., 189 n.15
Krishnaswami, C. S., 18 n.100
Kuriyan, G., 113 n.105, 279

Labroue, L., 46 n.42
Ladejinsky, W., 296 n.51
Lal, R., 61 n.54, 62 n.58
Land Commission (Ceylon), 25 n.137, 26 n.139, 103 n.73, 209 n.71, 243 n.55, 246 n.59
Land Policy, Agricultural Labour and Insurance, Sub-Committee of the National Planning Committee on, 96–7 nn.38–40, 97 nn.42–3, 254–5 nn.85–90
Land Utilization Committee (Ceylon), 73 n.6
Large-sized Mechanized Farms, Committee on, 78 n.25
La Touche, J. D., 164 n.31
Law, B. C., 4 n.2, 6 n.1
Laxminarayan, H., 100 n.60, 235 n.23
Leach, E. R., 124 n.17
Learmonth, A. T. A., 8 n.28, 44 n.24, 45 n.37, 46 nn.39 & 43, 47 nn.45–6 & 53, 49 n.65, 50 n.79, 65 n.91, 141, 153 n.1, 286 n.17, 308
Lee, Y. L., 240 n.31
Lees, W. Nassau, 12 n.62, 13 nn.63–5, 27–8
Legris, P., 19, 46 nn.42–3, 141 n.28, 153 n.1, 308
Lele, Uma, 296 n.51
Lewis, J. P., 197 n.33
Lewis, O., 251 n.68
Lipton, M., 164 n.32, 189 n.15, 213 n.7, 216 n.18, 221 n.34, 242 n.47, 265 n.10, 279 n.3
Logan, W., 49 n.71, 50
Luard, C. E., 62, 63 nn.69–70
Lucie-Smith, C. B., 55 n.16

Maclean, J. N. H., 32 n.168
McSwiney, J., 14 n.71
Madhava Das, K., 205 n.60
Maine, Sir Henry, 8, 253, 263
Majumdar, D. N., 45 n.33
Majumdar, R. C., 7 n.9
Malhotra, S. P., 271
Malik, Rashid, A., 20 n.111, 73 n.3, 198 nn.35 & 38
Mann, H. H., 10 n.43, 13 n.65, 15 n.81, 77 n.24, 253–4
Masani, M., 255 n.96
Mason, P., 15 n.79, 75 n.14, 91 n.19, 96 n.31
Mathur, C. M., 144 n.38, 145 nn.40 & 47
Mathur, I. P., 77 n.23
Mathur, R. M., 30 n.158
Mawada, H. K., 201 n.44
Maya Das, C., 254 n.83
Mazumdar, D., 242 n.47
Mead, Margaret, 277
Mehrotra, C. L., 142 n.36, 164 n.24
Mehta, K. M., 61 n.51, 144 nn.38 & 40, 163
Mellor, J. W., 296 n.51
Menon, V. P., 55 nn.10 & 13
Michel, A. A., 20, 21 nn.113 & 116–17, 22 n.122, 40 n.12, 41 nn.14–15, 126 n.23, 145, 163 n.24, 164 n.29, 196 n.26, 243 nn.50 & 54, 282 n.6, 287 n.20, 288, 294 nn.46–7, 308
Milward, Marguerite, 47 n.52
Mishra, V. G., 38 n.3
Misra, A. N., 142 n.36
Misra, D. K., 219 n.27
Misra, R. P., 201 n.44
Misra, Shridhar, 33
Misra, V. C., 38 n.3
Moonis Raza, 30
Moreland, W. H., 6 n.3, 7 nn.12–13 & 17, 8 n.25, 11 n.53, 12 n.61
Morris, Morris D., 6 n.7, 27 n.142
Morse, D. A., 296 n.24
Mukerjee, D., 109 n.98
Mukherjee, Radhakamal, 97, 254
Mukherjee, S. B., 288 n.24
Mukhoti, B., 241 n.45
Mullen, C. S., 14 n.72
Murthy, C. K., 65 n.91
Murthy, H. V. S., 58 n.31
Myrdal, G., 96 nn.36–7, 98, 106 n.84, 204 n.55, 206 n.63, 211 n.1, 216 n.18, 221 n.34, 222 n.36, 227 n.2, 252 n.72, 263 n.5, 279 n.3, 296

Nafis Ahmad, 58 n.32, 172 nn.44–6
Nair, G. K., 123 n.13
Nasim Ansari, 162 n.20
Natarajan, B., 16 n.88, 254 n.84
Nath, V., 166 n.37
Natural Resources, Committee on (Planning Commission), 61 n.48
Naylon, J., 66 n.94
Neale, Walter C., 8 n.29, 11 nn.53 & 55, 27 n.145, 189 n.14, 194 n.23, 230 n.10
Nevill, H. R., 44 n.29
Nijhawan, S. D., 154 n.3
Noble, W. A., 165, 166 n.36, 222 n.38

Ogilvie, A. G., 141 n.25
Oldham, C. T., 38 n.4
O'Malley, L. S. S., 63 n.76
Osmaston, F. C., 17 n.94, 18 n.98, 152 n.66, 307
Oswald, O., 150 n.64

Padhi, R. P., 16 n.87
Padhye, S. S., 7 n.18, 10 n.49
Pakrasi, M., 45 n.37
Palit, S. B., 292 n.36
Pande, Y. D., 44 n.22, 128 n.26, 163
Pandeva, A. N., 95 n.26, 105 n.78
Panikar, P. G. K., 12 n.57, 291 n.34
Pargiter, F. E., 52 n.2
Parthasarathy, G., 296 n.51, 297 n.59
Patnaik, U., 242 n.47
Patro, C. C., 123 n.13, 124 n.16
Paustian, P. W., 20 nn.111–12, 21 nn.113 & 115–16, 23 n.128, 95 n.27, 245 n.57, 285 n.15
Pelzer, K. J., 74 nn.10 & 12, 284
Pendleton, R. L., 62 n.63
Penrose, Edith, 294 n.43
Perry, E. L., 56 nn.18 & 23
Pillai, V. R., 12 n.57, 291 n.34
Pocock, David, 265 n.10
Polynov, B. B., 140 n.24
Population Sub-Committee of the National Planning Committee, 98 nn.45–7
Porter, Elizabeth A., 294 n.45
Porter, F. W., 32 n.169
Prakasa Rao, V. L. S., 48 n.58
Prentice, Anne, 41 n.14
Puckle, F. H., 90 n.12, 308
Puri, A. N., 142 n.31
Puri, G. S., 153 n.1

Raheja, P. C., 163 n.24, 219 n.27
Rahman, J., 45 n.37
Rahman, M. H., 44
Rahnatulla, M., 65 n.91
Raj, K. N., 119 n.2, 144 n.38, 286 n.18, 288 n.24
Raj Krishna, 189 n.15, 241, 252 n.72
Ramachandra Rao, T., 50 n.78
Ramantha Ayyar, V., 16 n.89
Rama Rao, M. S. V., 180 n.60
Ramiah, P. V., 145 n.41
Ram Subhag Singh, 150
Randhawa, N. S., 252 n.72
Rao, V. K. R. V., 100 nn.59–60, 112 n.101
Rasmussen, T. F., 13 n.64, 14 n.73, 57 n.26, 58, 59 n.38, 75 n.16, 82
Rath, N., 126 n.21, 288 n.24
Raychaudhuri, H. C., 7 n.9
Raychaudhuri, S. P., 141 nn.28 & 32, 149, 163 n.24
Reclamation, Bureau of, US Dept of Interior, 139 n.18, 145 n.44, 164 n.29, 288
Reclus, E., 56 n.21
Resettlement Programme for Landless Agricultural Labourers: Case Studies of Selected Colonies, 2, 18 n.96, 45 n.38, 71 n.1, 89 nn.8–9, 91 n.19, 93 n.22, 104–5 nn.74–6, 105 nn.80–2, 128 n.27, 132 n.34, 142 n.36, 147 n.54, 154 n.6, 161 n.19, 163 n.23, 165 n.33, 181 n.62, 184 n.2, 186 n.4, 189 n.16, 190 n.18, 191, 199 n.39, 200 n.42, 202 n.48, 204 n.54, 206 nn.65–6, 209 n.70, 223 n.42, 231 n.13, 236 n.24, 242 n.48, 246 n.60, 247 nn.62–4, 257 n.107, 264 n.107, 266 n.12, 268 nn.15 & 18, 283 n.8, 284 n.10, 308
Rice, L., 49 n.64
Rieger, H. C., 223 n.41
Rivett-Carnac, J. H., 123 n.15
Robinson, R., 296 n.54
Rogers, E. M., 221 n.34, 257 n.106, 263 n.5
Rokach, A., 196 n.28
Rostow, W. W., 252 n.71
Roy, B. B., 40 n.6
Roy, P., 221 n.34
Russell, P. F., 49 n.64
Russell, R. V., 55 n.8

Sandoval, P. R., 210 n.72
Saran Singh, 116 n.118
Scheduled Areas and Scheduled Tribes, Commission, 1960–61, 112 n.103, 114 n.109, 123 n.14, 173 n.49, 200 n.40, 214 n.16,
Scheduled Castes and Scheduled Tribes, Commissioner for, 101 n.62, 274 n.35
Schiller, O., 252 n.72
Schokalskaya, Z. J., 140
Schultz, T. W., 221 n.34, 222
Schwartzberg, J. E., 100
Selvanayagam, S., 238 n.34
Sen. A. K., 40 n.6
Sen, P. K., 64 n.84

Senanayake, D. S., 92 n.25, 237
Settlement of Landless Agricultural Workers, Committee on, 100 n.61, 106 n.83, 207 n.67
Sewell, R., 65 n.89
Shah, D. L., 60 n.47
Shah, K. T., 97 n.39, 254
Shamsul Bahrin, Tunku, 74 nn.9 & 11
Shankara Narayana, H. S., 144 n.38, 145 n.40
Shanmugasundaram, V., 212 n.6
Sharma, R. S., 8 n.20
Shaw, J. D., 66 n.94
Shen, T. H., 224 n.44
Shivamaggi, H. B., 204 nn.52–3, 206 n.63
Silva, S., 48, 49 n.72, 50 n.73
Singh, L. R., 42 n.16, 45 n.38, 46 n.44
Singh, M., 45 n.37
Singh, R. L., 38 n.3, 42 n.16
Singh, R. P., 60 n.44
Sinha, Lakshman Prasad, 16 n.83
Sinton, J. A., 44, 49 n.64, 56 n.23
Sion, Jules, 44, 47 n.54, 63 n.71, 66 n.95
Sivaraman, B., 174 n.53
Sleeman, Sir W. H., 60 n.43, 63 n.72
Smith, Vincent, 8 n.22, 11 n.53
Sonachalam, K. S., 288 n.24
Sovani, N. V., 126 n.21, 288 n.24
Spate, O. H. K., 6 n.5, 8 n.28, 14 n.67, 22 n.119, 24, 36, 42 nn.16–17, 46 n.41, 55 n.14, 57 n.26, 58, 60 n.42, 62 n.62, 65, 122 n.10, 125 n.19, 130 n.28, 141 n.28, 153 n.1, 278, 286 n.17, 308
Spear, T. G. P., 8 n.22, 11 n.53, 18 n.99
Srinivas, M. N., 274
Srinivasan, M., 235 n.21
Srivastava, R. S., 44, 45 nn.33, 35 & 37
Stebbing, E. R., 17 n.94, 152 n.66, 307
Steel, R. W., 122 n.11
Stein, Sir Aurel, 38 n.4
Stokes, E. T., 10 n.48, 11 n.50, 27
Streeten, P., 164 n.32, 213 n.7, 265 n.10
Stuart, H. A., 49 n.64
Subramhanya Aiyar, N., 48 n.63
Sundaram, K. V., 40 n.6, 201 n.44
Suresh Ramabhai, 75 n.17
Swaminathan, M. S., 252

Talati, R. P., 121 n.9
Tallents, P. C., 63 n.76
Tambad, S. B., 194, n.23
Tambiah, S. J., 220 n.31
Tamhane, R. V., 149
Tarai and Bhabar Development Committee, 19 n.102, 45 n.33, 112 n.100, 283 n.9, 309
Tarlok Singh, 98, 99 n.56, 253, 256, 296
Teulières, R., 74 n.12
Thal Development Authority, 19 n.106, 66 n.94, 73 n.7, 90 n.14, 91 n.17, 154 n.4, 243 n.52, 286 n.19, 289 n.26
Thampi, C. J., 145 n.43, 173 n.48
Thapar, Ashok, 188
Thapar, Romila, 7 n.19
Thirumalai, S., 15, 33, 112 n.101, 252 n.72
Thorner, Alice, 99 n.56, 100 n.59
Thorner, D., 10 n.43, 15 n.81, 31 n.166, 77 n.24, 99, 100 n.59, 206 n.63, 253 n.78
Thurston, E., 10 n.49
Tiwari, H. N., 18 n.97, 276
Trevaskis, H. K., 7 n.16, 10 n.47, 20 nn.111–12, 22 n.123, 23, 27, 90 n.11, 101, 163 n.24, 178 n.56, 198 n.38, 263 n.6

Ujagir Singh, 18 n.101
Uppal, B. N., 147, 149
Uttar Pradesh Zamindari Abolition Committee, 9 n.39, 11 n.54, 240 n.43, 255 n.91

Valentine, C. A., 251 n.68
Vedamanikkam, J. C., 49 n.65
Venkattasuban, C. S., 17 n.92
Viart, M., 46 n.42
Vidal de la Blache, P., 48
Vijayaraghavacharya, Sir T., 33
Vijaya Ram Singh, 31 n.162
Viswanathan, D. K., 49 nn.64 & 66, 50 n.78
Vohra, B. B., 142 n.35, 282 n.7
Vyas, H. M., 253 n.74

Waisanen, F. B., 221 n.34
Wake, W. H., 197 n.32
Walker, K. R., 174
Walvekar, K. A., 121 n.8
Warriner, Doreen, 211 n.1, 227 n.2, 240 n.42, 242 n.47, 251–2, 265 n.11
Waste Land Survey (Technical) Committee (Assam), 34 n.177, 58 n.36

Wastelands Survey & Reclamation Committee (the Uppal Committee), 56 n.24, 101 n.64, 113 n.107, 163 n.24
Webb, A. W. T., 62 n.56
Weitz, R., 196 n.28
Wikkramatileke, R., 74 n.11, 154 nn.4 & 7, 187, 207
Williams, D., 14 n.76
Withington, W. A., 74 n.8
Worsley, P., 252 n.72, 259 n.108

Yule, H., 166 n.36

Zachariah, K. C., 40 n.9
Zasloff, J. J., 75 n.13

Subject Index

No attempt has been made to include in this Index, under the name of any given state or region, reference to all pages on which a colonization scheme in that state or region is mentioned in the text. The reader interested in any one state or region should first refer to the Appendix, and then turn to Index references to relevant schemes.

Abujhmar Hills, 52, 55
Adilabad District, 52–8, 88
Adivasis, see Tribal peoples
Aerial survey, 136, 138, 143
Agrarian unrest, 117, 297
Agricultural colonization: agricultural change in colonies, 104, 129, 164–81, 188, 211–26, 237, 276; agricultural research and extension, 4, 105, 148, 175, 211–21, 223–6, 298; agriculture generally, 4, 22–3, 58, 94–5, 104, 133–4, 153–88, 192–5, 211–26, 279–280; area colonized, 4, 45, 56–7, 61, 67–73; areas of, 4, 36–66; beneficiaries, 87–94, 299–301; British period, 1, 17–27, 90, 94–5, 101–10 (*see also* Punjab Canal Colonies); by Europeans, 12–13; by intensification of existing cultivation, 65–6; conflicts of aims, 94–8, 111, 175; cost of, 147–8, 206–10, 280-5; definition of, 1–2, 68–9; domestic economy, 182–210; food supply, contribution to, 22, 289–91; foreign exchange implications, 289–91; future of, 4, 278–98; government role, 107–11; inter-state migration, 93, 97–8, 172; labour in, 167, 192–7, 279–80; land tenure in, 4, 175, 225, 227–60, 286; leaders in, 23, 165–6, 263; motives for, 22, 90–101; natural difficulties of, 4, 88–90, 118–34, 225–6; number of settlers, 56, 67–73, 299-301; phases of, 111–17; pre-British, 5–9; return from, 42, 90, 131, 208, 242–5, 285–9; spontaneous, 47, 50, 65, 75, 93, 121; types of settler, *see above* beneficiaries; versus intensification, 291–5; 'welfare motive', 94–107, 111, 187, 192, 206–7; *see also* Colonists; Land Colonization Societies
Agricultural Labour Enquiries, 100, 113
Agricultural labourers, *see* Landless labourers
Agricultural Refinance Corporation, 204–5
Agricultural research and extension, 105, 148, 175, 211–21, 223–6, 298
Agricultural universities, 77, 142, 174 n.53, 220
'Agriculturally utilized area', 79–86
Agriculture in British period, 11, 22–3
— in colonization schemes, *see* Agricultural colonization
— elsewhere in India, 38–40, 45, 47, 65, 75–9, 164–5
— Royal Commission on, 29 n.153, 141
— statistics on, 32–3, 79–86
Alkaline soils, alkalinity, 38, 113, 119–20, 127–8, 130, 146, 149, 153–4, 163–4, 174, 219, 282, 286
All-India Soil and Land Utilization Survey, 141–6
Amalner (Pailad) Colony, 104, 159, 195, 235, 244, 266–7, 300

Aminabad Colony, 64, 102, 104, 132, 145, 158, 161, 183, 185, 199, 207, 216, 244, 249, 267, 276, 281, 299
Andaman Islands, 64, 68, 70–1, 77, 145, 173, 269
Andhiyar Colony, 255
Andhra Pradesh, 1, 16, 52, 56, 64, 66, 68–71, 76, 78, 83, 85, 88, 93, 108, 111–12, 114, 125, 132–3, 139, 142, 147, 153, 157–8, 161, 168, 181, 188, 194–5, 205, 212, 221, 235, 237, 256, 283–4, 299
Animal husbandry, 124, 133, 165, 173, 178–80, 206–10, 217, 219–20, 270–2
Annamalai University Colony, 18, 20
Anopheles fluviatilis, 44, 49
Anupgarh, 38, 144, 153–4, 199, 234
Araku Valley, 16; Ramakrishnanagar Colony, 102, 104, 158, 166, 168, 183, 185, 229, 238, 243–4, 246, 254, 262, 266, 299
Aridity, 36-41, 103, 119–22, 179
Aroras, 265–6
Arwatagi Colony, 122, 159, 165, 183, 185, 187, 190, 235, 262, 266, 300
Aryanagar Colony, 18, 254
Arya Samaj, 18, 95, 254
Ashoka, 7, 48
Assam, 2, 10, 13–17, 24, 28–31, 33–4, 42, 56–9, 66, 68–73, 75, 82–3, 88–9, 102, 117, 128–9, 148–9, 158, 161, 183–4, 186–7, 189, 199, 214, 233, 244, 299
Attapaddy Valley (Mukkali Colony), 50, 110, 133, 199, 213, 232, 262, 269, 299
Attur Colony, 105, 184, 187, 191, 283
Auctions, 1, 25, 70, 90, 100, 243, 285–6
Australia, 31

Badagas, 50, 165, 222, 276
Baghbar Colony, 57, 154, 158, 168, 175, 178–9, 183–4, 190, 194, 199, 202, 205, 247, 264, 281, 299
Bahawalpuris, 88, 265
Bajra, 238, 303
Banana, *see* Plantain
Banaras, *see* Varanasi town and District
Bangladesh, 58–9, 88–9, 92, 172, 175; *see also* Bengal; East Bengal; and East Pakistan (former)
Banjaras, 265, 271; *see also* Kansal Banjara Colony
Bari Doab, 20–2
Barpeta Sub-division, 57, 87 n.72
Basalt, *see* Deccan Trap
Bastar District, 33, 52–6, 108, 139, 272–3, 277
Bastar State (former), 52–3, 272–3
Beas River and Project, 19, 41, 139
Belgaum District, 152
Bellary District, 72
Benares, *see* Varanasi town and District
Bengal, 8, 10–11, 13, 15, 24, 28–9, 42, 54, 124–5, 172; *see also* Bangladesh; East Bengal; West Bengal
Bengalis, 17, 56–9, 87–8, 109, 124–5, 128, 172, 175, 189, 193, 200, 202, 226, 257, 264, 272–4
Betterment levy, 242–3, 286
Bhabar, 42, 127
Bhadralok, 28, 303
Bhakra Canal and Colonies, 41, 68, 70, 73, 89–90, 104–5, 113, 119–20, 126–7, 129, 132, 153, 160–3, 167–8, 177, 179, 183–7, 196, 201, 208, 216, 220–1, 230–1, 235, 238–9, 242, 245, 262, 264–6, 286, 299, 301
Bhakra–Nangal Dams, 41, 89, 119, 144
Bhamer Colonies, 102, 122, 159, 235, 265–7, 300
Bhaskal Dam, 125
Bhils, 10, 62, 64, 266
Bhonslas, 55
Bhoodan movement and colonies, 75–6, 114, 183–6, 191, 235, 253, 258, 283, 299–301, 303; *see also* Jamunia Colony; Sardapuri Bhoodan Colony
Bhopal (town and former State), 63, 77, 121, 148
Bhuksas, 45, 268–9
Bhumidari, bhumiswami, 228–33, 245
Bhupnagar Colony, 184, 191, 257
Biasi cultivation, 193, 217
Bihar, 6, 14, 16, 45, 68, 70–1, 76, 83, 85–6, 88, 105, 110–12, 147, 152, 183–5, 191, 194–5, 205, 257, 299
Bikaner District and town, 38–41, 145, 162, 270
Bikaner Canal, *see* Gang Canal
Birbhum District, 10
Blackwater fever, 14, 44, 56
Block Development Officer (BDO), *see* Community Development
Bombay, 194, 276
Bombay Deccan, 11, 121, 291
Bombay Presidency and State, 10, 12, 16, 24, 83, 254, 256

Brahmaputra River, 13, 57–8, 172, 202
British, The, 10–32, 49, 58, 90, 127, 136, 143, 229, 237, 275
Buffaloes, *see* Animal husbandry
Bunagaon Colony, 159, 183, 185, 191, 265, 300
Bureaucracy, 109, 223–4, 293–4; shortcomings of, 246–7
Burma, 18, 30, 51, 88
Bylakuppe Colony, 50, 80, 102–3, 115, 122, 129, 155, 159, 169, 173, 178, 183, 207, 234, 281–2, 284, 300

Cachar District, 13, 57
Calicut, *see* Kozhikode
Camels, 23, 178
Cape Comorin, *see* Kanyakumari
Capitalists, 23, 25–6, 45, 95, 167, 190
Cardamon, 47, 76
Cash/subsistence ratio, 183, 188–9, 195, 197
Cashew-nut, 76, 152
Caste, 192, 223, 262, 265–8, 274–7
Cattle, 23, 120, 124, 133, 165, 178–80, 186, 206–9, 268–72
Cauvery, *see* Kaveri River
Central Arid Zone Research Institute, 120, 143, 219, 270–1
Central Ground Water Board, 138 n.13
Central Mechanized Farms, *see* State Farms
Central Provinces, 14, 24, 30–1, 55
Central Regional and Urban Planning Organisation, 239
Central Tractor Organization (CTO), 112, 154–5
Central Water and Power Commission, 138
Ceylon, 1, 9, 23, 25, 44–5, 51, 57, 59, 73, 75, 77, 88, 91–2, 94, 106–8, 111, 122, 124–5, 130, 154–6, 164, 169, 172–4, 178–9, 187, 193, 200, 207, 221–3, 238, 240–1, 243, 246, 260–2, 268–9, 284–5, 287, 292–3, 295
Chambal Ravines and Colonies, 60–1, 88, 90, 93, 113, 129, 145, 153–5, 159, 180, 183, 215, 234, 269, 300
Chambal Right Bank Colony (Madhya Pradesh), 61–2, 121, 130–1, 139, 144, 153–4, 159, 167, 178, 183, 187–8, 215, 229, 233–4, 236, 245, 264, 269, 289, 300
Chambal River, 60–2, 113, 121, 300–1
Chambal Valley Project and Colonies (Rajasthan), 1, 60–2, 68, 121, 130, 133, 139, 144–5, 153, 159, 163–4, 203, 230–1, 282, 289, 301
Chanda District, 24, 52–6, 88, 108, 123, 125, 151, 162, 166, 194, 200, 255, 300
Chenab River, 19, 21, 73
Chhattisgarh Plateau, 52–6
China, 115, 174, 255
Chittagong, 13–14
Chittari Colony, 184, 187, 191, 283
Cholera, 21, 128
Chota Nagpur, 14, 55, 272
Christians, 264, 277
Chunian Colony, 21–2
Clearing of land, *see* Reclamation of land
Cochin, 17, 75
Cocoa, 51, 257, 259
Coconut, 124, 164, 173
Coffee, 13–14, 47–50, 76, 95, 165, 188, 197, 203, 289
Collective farming societies, *see* Cooperative tenure and cultivation
Colonies Committee (Punjab), 23, 25
Colonists: assistance to, 8, 76, 115, 154–5, 167, 178, 186, 190, 204, 206–10, 223, 243–4, 282–5; capital assets, 186–8; charges to, 242–5, 286; desertion by, 20, 102–3, 210, 265; holding size, 236–42, 299–300; houses, 206–10, 234, 281–3; income of, 182–92, 205, 239–40, 279–80; indebtedness, 186, 188, 201, 204–6; middle-class, 18; non-agricultural, 195–7; numbers of, 67–73, 299–301; percentage of produce sold, 183, 188–9; relations with other occupants, 268–74; selection of, 101–7, 175–6, 267, 298; types of, 4, 87–94
Colonization, *see* Agricultural Colonization
Colonization Commissioners and Officers, 8, 25, 28, 220–1
Colonization of Government Lands (Punjab) Act (1912), 20 n.109, 26, 243
Communications, *see* Railways; Roads
Community development, 199, 211–16, 218–21, 223–5
'Compensation' colonists, *see* Oustees
Congress Party, 3, 115, 254–5; ideology, 3, 96–9, 115, 202–3
Constitution of India, 99, 274–5
Coomaraswamy, Ananda K., 252

Co-operative colonization, 56, 64, 75–6, 96–7, 102, 104, 111–17, 134, 145, 154, 166, 182–6, 188, 193, 195, 197, 203, 207, 217, 221, 223, 234–6, 241, 246, 252–60, 268, 299–301

Co-operative credit, 204, 206, 230, 233

Co-operative labour teams, 193, 261–2, 266

Co-operative marketing, 203

Co-operative tenure and cultivation, 18, 96–7, 102, 104, 221, 225, 234–6, 241, 252–60, 265; *see also* Co-operative colonization

Coorg, 14, 46–7, 49–50, 88, 173

Cornwallis, Lord, 10

Cotton, 22, 160, 167, 170, 173, 177, 220, 235, 289–90

Crafts, craftsmen, 105, 190, 192, 197

Credit, 25, 203–6, 212, 230, 232–3, 247, 249, 258; *see also* Co-operative credit

'Criminal' and 'Ex-criminal' Tribes and Castes, 18, 23, 95, 99, 161, 174, 189–90, 193–4, 222, 248, 254, 276

Cultivability, concept of, 34–5, 135

Cultivated area, 10–11, 79–86

Culturable waste, 4–5, 12, 16, 29–31, 32 n.171, 33–5, 57–9, 63, 78–86, 97–100, 115, 147–8, 150–2, 247, 254–5, 291

Dacoits, 10, 60, 303

Dairying, 178, 189

Damodar River and Valley, 63, 102, 109, 113, 161

Dandakaranya, 2, 52–6, 59, 75, 122–4, 148, 153, 269–70, 272–4, 299–301; Colonies, 2, 17, 19, 56, 68–73, 86–8, 92–3, 102, 114–15, 123–5, 129–30, 132–5, 154, 156–9, 161, 166, 168, 172–4, 176, 178–9, 182–3, 185–6, 188–91, 193–206, 208–9, 216–19, 221–2, 225–6, 229–30, 240–1, 244, 256–9, 280–2, 289, 291, 294, 299, 307; Development Authority, 52, 54, 56, 68–71, 108–9, 124–5, 143–4, 155–7, 169, 172, 198, 202–3, 216–18, 224, 244, 272–4; Malkangiri Zone, 54, 124–5, 134, 158, 164, 168, 172, 190, 200, 202, 235–6, 258, 262–3, 266, 272, 299; Paralkote Zone, 54, 125, 137, 158, 168, 176, 199–200, 202, 215, 218, 235–6, 257–8, 264, 272, 299; Pharasgaon Zone, 114, 299; Umarkote–Raighar Zone, 54, 125, 134, 158, 168, 171, 183, 262, 272, 299

Darapathar Colony, 57, 158, 161, 190, 196, 199, 264, 299

DDT spraying, 45, 50

Death rates, 44–5, 49, 64

Debt, *see* Indebtedness

Deccan, 18, 55, 65, 124; *see also* Bombay Deccan

Deccan Trap, 62, 64, 121, 129–31

Dehra Dun, 13–14, 142

Deltas, 1, 7, 13, 64, 172, 175, 299

Depopulation, 6–7, 10, 44, 48–9, 57–8, 61–3

Depressed classes, *see* Harijans

Desert, 38–42, 285, 299, 301

Desertion, 20, 102–3, 210, 265

Dewas District, 33, 78–9, 82, 147

Dhebar Committee, 276

Dina Irrigation Project, 56, 151

Disease, 129–30, 211

Displaced persons, *see* Refugees.

Disturbances, agrarian, 25, 297

Domestic water supply, 129–30

Drainage, 61, 121, 126, 128, 132–3, 144, 146, 157–64, 205, 282, 286

Drought, *see* Rainfall variability.

Duars, 14 n.67, 42–5, 303

East Africa, 122, 253

East Bengal, 8, 13, 34, 87–8, 93, 172, 196, 217; *see also* East Pakistan (former); Bangladesh

Eastern Ghats, 16, 52–6, 64, 132–3, 153, 161, 194, 205, 299

East Pakistan (former), 56, 61, 87

Economic unit of land, 194–5, 236–42

Educated unemployed colonists, 70, 76, 91, 94

Education, 224–5

Egypt, 106, 200

Eksali tenure, *see* Leases

Employment, 78, 101, 103, 116, 192–7, 225, 239, 295–8; *see also* Under-employment and unemployment

Encroachment, 1, 28, 33, 58, 75, 78, 103, 178, 196, 295

Ex-*jagirdars*, 70, 89–90, 242

Ex-servicemen, 16, 19, 23, 64, 70, 91, 94, 101–2, 109, 111, 113, 115, 183, 185, 190, 207, 209, 215, 242, 246, 256, 282, 299–301

Fallow, 16, 30, 32, 80, 113, 147, 179
Famine, 7, 10, 15, 22, 38, 62–5, 121
Fauna, *see* Wild life
Federal Land Development Authority (FLDA), Malaysia, 74, 107, 187
Fertilizer, 128, 132, 140, 142–4, 148, 165–7, 170–3, 175–7, 206–10, 212, 215, 258, 289
Fishing, 124, 189, 192, 217
Five Year Plans, 79, 111–17, 256, 292, 307–9; First, 112–13, 211, 256; Second, 113–14, 211–12; Third, 114–115, 139, 211–12, 256, 284; Fourth (1966–71, abortive), 116; Fourth (1969–74), 116–17, 139, 203, 212, 256; Fifth, 86, 117, 212, 297
Floods, 10, 57–8, 89, 126–9, 135, 158–160, 163, 172, 175, 185, 199, 202, 233, 242
Food and Agriculture, etc., Ministry of, 110, 113–14, 142, 147
Foodgrains Policy Committee, 16 n.90, 112
Food production, 95–8, 101, 111–12, 212–14
Ford Foundation, 212
Forest, 5–6, 10, 13–15, 17, 24, 29–30, 32, 42, 46, 48, 54–6, 58–9, 64, 76, 80–1, 126, 133–4, 137, 149–53, 173, 179–80, 189–90, 196, 199
— Act (1865), 24
— Act (1927), 150
— Departments, 18, 76, 108, 143, 145, 152, 155, 189–90
— policy, 58–9, 150–2
— produce, 189–90, 275
— reserved, 15, 24, 29, 32, 50, 59, 117, 139, 149–52, 180
— survey, 138–9
— village, 24, 150, 180
Fragmentation, *see* Subdivision of holdings
Fruit, 17, 23, 77, 167, 223

Gair khatedari, see Khatedari, gair
Gal Oya Development Board, 108–9, 156 n.14
Gandhi, M. K. (Mahatma Gandhi), Gandhian, 96–7, 105, 252–3, 255, 258, 263
Gandhidham Colony, 184, 191, 257
Gandhisagar Project and Colonies, 61, 113, 130, 139, 144, 154, 156, 159, 161, 195, 205, 229, 263–4, 268–9, 279, 300
Gang Canal and Colony, 40, 163, 201, 220, 239
Ganga River, 13, 42, 152, 172
Ganganagar District and town, 41, 201, 219, 270
Ganges, *see* Ganga River
Gangetic Plain, 6, 11–12, 152
Gaya District, 283
Geological conditions, 62–4, 121, 129–31, 137
— survey, 138–9, 142
Germans, 255–6
Ghaggar River, 38–40, 126–8, 135, 158, 242, 270–1
Goalpara District and town, 58, 202
Goats, 173, 178–9
Gobindpur and Theka Colony, 57, 86, 158, 168, 175, 179, 183, 205, 250, 262, 264, 281, 299
Godavari River, 1, 52, 197, 200
Gogra River, 44
Goldsmiths, 92, 101
Gonds, 55, 265, 267–9, 272–4
Gorakhpur District, 10, 12–13, 42, 44
Government of India (British period), 12, 15, 18, 22–3, 25–9
— (Independent), 4, 29, 59, 63, 107–17, 136, 203, 209, 242–3
Graduate colonists, 18, 188, 237
Gramdan movement, 253, 303
Gram Sevak, *see* Community development
Grazing reserves, 16, 24, 57, 59, 86, 103 n.72, 178; *see also* Pasture
Greater Malnad, *see* Malnad, Greater
Groundnuts, 134, 160, 188
Groundwater, 40, 42, 113, 127–31, 138–9, 144, 163–4, 172
Group cultivation and farming, *see* Co-operative tenure and cultivation
Grow More Food Campaign, 15–17, 29–30, 112, 254
Gudu Barrage, 90, 156 n.12
Gujarat, 7, 18, 68, 70–1, 83, 89, 93, 105, 147, 184, 191, 228
Guna District, 18, 63, 105, 151, 184–5, 187, 191–2, 214, 221, 283
Gundrai Colony, 159, 168, 171, 234, 267, 300
Guntur District, 64, 215
Gwalior State, 17–18, 61–3, 95, 99

Haidar Ali, 7, 48
Hanumangarh, 38, 120, 126, 270
Harijans, 18, 23, 70, 87, 91–2, 96, 99–100, 104, 109, 117, 207, 222–3, 225, 256, 259, 265–8, 270, 297, 303
Harike Barrage, 41
Haryana, 38–42, 68, 70–1, 83, 86, 104, 119–20, 126–7, 133, 158, 168, 178, 235, 244, 299, 303
Health, *see* Disease
High Ranges (Kerala), 14, 17, 45–51
High Ranges Colonies, 50, 74, 102, 104, 110, 113, 131, 133, 135, 155–6, 158, 161, 168, 170, 183, 185–6, 191, 200, 205, 209, 215, 221, 232, 237, 244, 248–50, 262, 264, 281, 289, 299
High-yielding varieties, 174–8, 188, 205, 213–14
High Yielding Varieties Programme (HYV or HYVP), 174–8, 185, 213–214, 304
Himachal Pradesh, 228, 243
Himalayas, 13-14, 42, 127
Hindus, Hinduism, 9, 69, 93, 178, 222, 264, 266, 274–5, 277
Hirakud Project and Colonies, 64, 66, 72, 77–9, 93, 102, 126, 136, 144–5, 154, 158, 161, 168, 172, 179, 190, 195, 204, 213, 215, 223, 229, 235, 258, 262, 268, 281, 301
Hissar District, 40–1, 119–20
Horse-breeding grants, 23, 26
Hyderabad State, 16, 55, 72
Hydrological problems, 126–31; *see also* Water resources survey

Income of colonists, 182–92; redistribution of, 295–8
Indebtedness, 186, 188, 201, 204–6, 209
Indian Agricultural Statistics, 79–86
Indian Council for Agricultural Research, 137, 142
Indian National Congress, *see* Congress Party
India Office (London), 25, 27
Indonesia, 74, 135, 262, 269, 284
Indore (town and former State), 60, 62
Indus River, 19, 73, 90, 288
Indus Waters Agreement, 21, 41
Industries, 196–7; cottage, 18, 297
Intensification of agriculture, 65–6, 149–50, 192–5, 211–26, 291–5
Intensive Agricultural Area Programme (IAAP) and District Programme (IADP), 212–14, 221 n.34, 225, 293, 295
Intikheri Colonies, 63, 77–8, 88, 93, 102–3, 112–13, 121, 153–5, 159, 165, 168, 170, 173, 178, 183, 190–1, 193–4, 199, 202, 204, 216, 221, 226, 232–5, 245, 262, 264–5, 269, 300
Iron, iron ore, 54, 191,
Irrigation, 6, 10, 15–17, 19–22, 40–4, 56, 60–2, 65–6, 78, 119–21, 123–9, 132, 142–6, 150, 157–64, 166, 168–77, 179–80, 186, 192–4, 198, 203, 217, 219–20, 225–6, 236, 239–40, 242–5, 263, 270, 280–96
— Commission (1901–3), 38 n.3, 40
— Commission (1972), 138
Irula, 47, 275
Israel, 196, 200
Italy, 254

Jabalpur town and District, 13
Jagdalpur, 197, 273
Jagirs, Jagirdars, 41, 89
Jaisalmer District, 38–41, 154, 270
Jammu and Kashmir, 68, 70–1, 77, 83, 88, 147
Jamunia Colony, 132, 156, 158, 180, 183, 190–1, 205, 243–4, 247, 264–5, 299
Jana Sangh, 273
Janglis, 23, 269, 272
Japan, Japanese, 77, 171, 218
Jats, 270
Jayashree Colony (Bhamer), *see* Bhamer Colonies
Jeelugumilli Colony, 64, 102, 145, 158, 168, 193, 199, 203, 213, 263, 265, 269, 276, 281, 299
Jethi Colony, 184, 191, 268, 283–4
Jeypore–Bastar Plateau, 52–8, 137
Jeypore (Orissa), town and Zamindari, 52, 56, 197
Jhelum River, 19, 21
Jodhpur, 120–1, 143, 219, 271
Joint Farming Societies, *see* Cooperative tenure and cultivation
Jordan, 66
Jowar, 167–8, 171, 179, 236, 238
Jumna, *see* Yamuna River
Jungle, *see* Forest; Wasteland
Jute, 124, 172

Kaki Colony, 57, 103–4, 122, 154, 156,

158, 161, 163, 168, 174–5, 178, 183–7, 190–1, 193, 196, 199–200, 203, 205, 216, 221, 224, 236–7, 246–7, 264, 268, 281, 283, 299
Kalahandi District (former State), 33, 52, 56, 108, 273
Kalidindi Colony, 64, 91, 112, 158, 162, 166, 168, 183, 185–6, 190, 203, 205, 231, 249, 264, 281, 284, 299
Kambaraganavi Colony, 159, 179, 183, 235, 249, 262, 276, 300
Kamrup District, 16, 57, 213
Kandla, 290
Kanera and Mardel Colonies, 159, 183, 190, 215, 262, 300
Kankar, 60, 145, 304
Kannaram Colony, 104, 111, 158, 168, 179, 183, 185, 229, 276, 299
Kansal Banjara Colony, 102, 151, 154–155, 159, 233, 263, 265, 269, 271, 276, 281, 300
Kanyakumari, 51
Kashmir, *see* Jammu and Kashmir
Kaveri River, 16, 45, 166
Kerala, 12, 14–15, 45–51, 68, 70–1, 74–6, 78, 83, 86, 91, 93–4, 102, 104, 110, 113, 122, 131, 133, 135, 139, 147, 150, 168–70, 183–5, 189, 195–6, 232–3, 243, 246, 299
Kerala, people and colonists from, 63, 77, 93–4, 102–4, 121, 173, 199, 204, 216, 226, 232–3, 235, 243, 262, 269, 300
Khandesh, 10, 64, 300
Khasi Hills, 13
Khasis, 274, 277
Khatedari tenure, 228, 230–1, 242–3
—, *gair*, 230–2, 242–3
Kheri Colony, 42–5, 69, 75, 102, 104, 110, 113–15, 128, 154–5, 160, 163, 165, 169, 183, 185–6, 194, 199, 203, 220, 231, 244, 247, 264, 266–7, 289, 294, 310
Khonds, 56, 275
Kistna, *see* Krishna River
Koraput District and town, 52, 108, 197
Kota (town and former State), 60–2, 88
Kotia Pani Colony, 102, 159, 168, 194, 199, 221, 229, 244, 276, 300
Koyas, 265, 272, 276
Kozhikode (Calicut) town and District, 46, 50, 75–6
Krishna River, 1, 7, 45, 64–5, 204
Labour, 14, 18, 47, 49–50, 79, 100–1, 156, 263, 279–80; *see also* Agricultural Colonization: Labour in
Labourers, 14–15, 47, 65, 97, 167, 237
— landless, *see* Landless labourers
— repatriated, *see* Repatriates
Laccadive Islands, 64
Lakhimpur District (Assam), 103 n.72
Lakhimpur–Kheri District (UP), 42, 128
Land capability survey, 139–49, 151–2, 174
Land Colonization Societies, 203, 215, 246, 299–301
Land Commission (Ceylon), 25 n.137, 26, 103 n.73, 243
Land Development Ordinance (Ceylon), 25–6, 246
Land reform, 98, 100–1, 111, 113–16, 167, 231, 237, 240
Land revenue, 8, 11, 22, 27–8, 44, 63, 99, 139–40, 148, 206, 227–8, 243–4, 286
Land Settlement Policy (1968) of the Government of Assam, 34 n.178
Land tenure, 4, 8, 10–12, 24–7, 29, 227–60; breaches of conditions, 247–52; by stages, 230–1, 242–3, 245–6; co-operative, *see* Co-operative tenure and cultivation; difficulties, 246–7
Land-use policy, 17, 135, 139, 149–52
Land-use survey, 142
Landless labourers, 2, 34, 47, 70, 76–9, 89, 91–2, 95–102, 104–5, 110, 112–17, 147, 166, 178, 185–7, 192, 195–6, 209, 214, 230, 234, 238, 242, 247, 249, 255, 283, 296–301
Laterite, 22, 131, 148, 174
Leaders, leadership, 22–3, 263
Leases, 12, 17, 28, 231–4, 248
Linlithgow Commission, *see* Agriculture, Royal Commission on
Lower Bari Doab Canal and Colony, 21, 101
Lower Chenab Canal and Colony, 21–2, 25, 178, 198, 285
Lower Jhelum Canal and Colony, 21–3, 26
Lucknow, 18, 95
Lyallpur town and District, 20–2, 76, 285
Lyallpur Colony, *see* Lower Chenab Canal and Colony

Madhya Pradesh, 52, 56, 61, 66, 68–71, 78–9, 83, 86, 88, 92–3, 101–2, 105, 108, 110, 112–13, 117, 136, 139, 147–8, 151, 153, 156, 168, 171, 178, 181, 183–4, 189, 191–2, 195, 199, 212, 221–2, 228–30, 233–4, 244, 246, 256, 300

Madras Presidency and State, 11–12, 14–16, 24, 30, 72, 83, 101, 106, 113, 147–8, 166, 246, 254–6; *see also* Tamil Nadu

Madurai District, 46

Mahanadi River, 52, 56, 93, 144

Maharashtra, 10, 52, 55–6, 66, 68, 70, 72, 83, 88, 102, 104, 108, 111–13, 115, 121–2, 125, 130–1, 133, 145–7, 151, 166, 169, 171, 186, 194–5, 203, 221, 235, 258–9, 265, 269, 279, 300

Mahatma Fule Colony (Bhamer), *see* Bhamer Colonies

Mahodra Colony, 199

Maize, 76, 168–9, 176

Malaria, 10, 13–14, 18, 44–5, 49–50, 56, 62, 64–5, 174

Malaya, *see* Malaysia

Malayalam, 15, 216

Malaysia, 74–5, 107, 111, 154, 187, 207, 275

Malkangiri Plateau, 54–6

Malnad, Greater, 14, 45–51, 75, 122, 129, 144, 153, 179, 181, 289, 299–301

Malnad (Mysore), 45–51, 102, 133, 154, 162, 166, 178, 194, 199, 205, 237–8

Malwa, 7, 11–12, 60, 62–3, 78, 121, 130, 132–3, 148, 181, 279, 300; Development Board, 63

Mandis, 196, 198, 200–1, 262, 271, 304

Mandya District, 293–5

Marathas, Marathis, 18, 49, 55, 266

Marginality of land, 2, 19, 144, 187, 278–89, 291, 295, 297

Marketing, 200–3; *see also Mandis*

Marusthali, 38–42, 285, 299, 301

Marx, Karl and Marxism, 96, 253–5

Mechanization, 45, 63, 77–8, 112, 154–57, 194, 240–1, 252, 254–5, 259, 284

Mechanized Farms, Central, 77–8

Meghalaya, 274

Mesta, 124, 172, 176, 194, 202, 304

Mircabad Colonies, 18, 159, 161, 174, 189–90, 222, 248, 250, 276, 300

Moneylenders, 104, 175, 186, 190, 203–6

Montgomery District, 21, 285

Moranam Colony, 104, 112, 128, 130, 145, 160, 166, 169, 177, 180, 183, 185, 192, 196, 203, 205, 235, 237, 244, 249, 262, 269, 281, 301

Mortgages, 25, 230

Moyar River, 50–1, 112, 203

Mughals, 8–9, 20, 55, 60

Mukkali Colony, *see* Attapaddy Valley

Multan District, 21

Muslim Law, 9

Muslims, 17, 55, 58, 64–5, 69, 88, 111, 178, 264, 266

Mysore State, 45, 47, 50, 68, 70, 72, 78, 83, 86, 88, 102–3, 111, 113, 115, 117, 121–2, 133, 146–7, 151, 155, 166, 169, 171, 173, 178, 180, 186, 194–6, 203, 205, 237–8, 244, 265, 279, 300

Nagpur, 55, 142; Resolution, 255

Naini Tal District, 42, 45, 77, 177; *see also* Tarai Colony (Naini Tal District)

Namasudras, 87, 222, 265, 303

Narbada, *see* Narmada River

Narmada River, 55, 62, 304

National Atlas Organisation, 137, 141

National Council of Applied Economic Research, 186

National Institute of Community Development, 201

National parks, 152

National Planning Committee, 30, 33, 96, 202, 254

Native States, *see* Princely States

Natural resources, survey and planning of, 135–52

Naxalites, 205, 273, 275

Nehru, Jawaharlal, 96–7, 253–5, 277

Nepal, 42, 128

Nicobar Islands, 64

Nilambur Colony, 258

Nilgiri Hills, 14, 17, 45–51, 76, 112, 133, 151, 165–6

Nilgiris District, 15

Nili Bar Colony, 21

Nomads, 10, 19–21, 23, 38, 95, 179, 226, 234, 268–72

North East Frontier Agency (NEFA), 59, 277

Nowgong District, 57

Nuagam and Nuapara Colonies, 160, 301

Orissa, 16, 52, 56, 64, 66, 68, 70–2, 76, 82–3, 86, 88, 92, 102, 108, 112, 125, 134, 139, 160, 169, 173, 181, 229, 243, 262, 291, 300
Oriyas, 56, 109
Oustees, 61, 63, 66, 70, 72, 89, 93, 100, 102, 110, 113–14, 119–20, 154, 161, 184–5, 195, 207–8, 213, 216, 221, 229, 235–6, 248, 266, 279, 297, 299–301, 302

Pabal Colony, 102, 112, 121, 129, 159, 169, 183, 185, 193–4, 204, 265, 276, 279, 300
Paddy, 47–8, 50, 65, 76–7, 123–5, 128, 153, 155–6, 158–60, 162, 165–78, 180–1, 187–8, 190, 192–4, 203, 205, 213–14, 220, 223–4, 235–8, 241, 257, 259, 261–2, 290, 295
Pailad Colony, *see* Amalner (Pailad) Colony
Paisra Colony, 159, 183, 300
Pakistan, 19, 41, 66, 73, 75, 88, 90–1, 108, 135, 145, 154, 163, 198, 243, 245–6, 272, 285–7, 292; *see also* East Pakistan (former)
Palasgaon Colony, 159, 169, 183, 185, 189–90, 203, 300
Palghat District and town, 46–7, 213
Panchayat, Panchayati raj, 106, 204, 211–12, 214–15, 223–4, 237, 304
Pandripani Colony, 134, 160, 169, 193, 229, 276, 301
Paralkote Dam, 125, 158
Pasture, 12, 23, 40, 45, 80, 132, 150, 178–81, 270–2; *see also* Grazing reserves
Patil Committee on Settlement of Landless Agricultural Labourers, 100–1, 105, 113, 147, 159, 207
Patta, 79, 108, 228–34, 245, 249–50, 304
Pattedar, 231 n.13, 304
Patwari, 32, 78–9, 82, 304
Periyar River and Reservoir, 46–7, 75
Permanent tenure without transferable rights, 230–1
Pesticides, 212, 217
Philippines, 210 n.72
Piduguralla Colony, 64, 91, 112, 158, 168, 183, 185, 193, 215, 244, 264, 269, 281, 299
Pigs, 173, 178
Pilibhit Colonies, 42–5, 69, 75, 102, 104–5, 110, 113, 115, 127–8, 155–6, 160, 163, 165, 169, 183, 185, 187, 191–2, 194, 199, 202, 204, 214, 220, 231, 235, 244, 247, 266, 283–4, 289, 294, 301
Pilibhit District, 42, 76, 132, 155
Planning Commission, 2, 71, 98, 108, 110, 112–17, 139, 147, 243
Plans, Five Year, *see* Five Year Plans
Plantations, 1, 12–15, 76, 89, 165, 205, 241, 295
Plateaux, *see* Chhattisgarh; Jeypore–Bastar; Kalahandi District (former State); *Kankar*; Malkangiri; Malwa
Podu, *see* Shifting cultivation
Political issues and factors, 59, 89–90, 95–101, 109–10, 116–17, 214–15, 237, 241, 275, 297–8
'Political sufferers', 70, 91, 93–5, 104, 113, 192–3, 237, 301
Pondicherry, French Institute, 137
Pong Dam, 41–2, 161
Poona, 193–4, 276
Population, 31, 44, 98; change, 10–11, 15, 22, 30, 44, 48–9, 62–4; distribution of, 6, 10–11, 14, 44, 47, 55, 57–8, 61–3, 65, 278; pressure, 22, 29, 31, 36, 102–3, 251, 278
Population Sub-Committee of National Planning Committee, 31, 33
Poultry, 165, 178, 189, 192
Princely States, 12, 16–17, 19, 29, 32–3, 41, 55, 62, 82, 89
Programme Evaluation Organisation of Planning Commission 2, 147, 184–7, 189, 191, 200, 202, 206, 209, 214, 216, 224, 231 n.13, 236–7, 246–7, 255, 257, 266, 268, 283
Proprietary rights, 24–5
Provence, 291
Punjab: British period, 7, 13, 19–26, 40, 90, 98, 127, 163, 186, 205, 220, 272; independent India, 68, 70–1, 83, 86, 110, 112, 126, 129, 147, 167, 177, 220–1, 243; *see also* Haryana
— Canal Colonies, 1, 13, 19–27, 90–1, 94, 101, 110, 186, 196–8, 201, 208, 220, 231, 237, 239, 243, 245, 263, 267, 269, 272, 285–6, 308
— Plains, 3, 24
Punjabis, 26, 61, 63, 87–8

Quarrying, 151

Raichur Doab, 64–6, 72, 78–9, 88, 93, 121, 129, 144, 194, 300
Railways, 127, 191, 198, 201, 271, 286
Rainfall, 38, 42, 46, 54–5, 60–1, 63–4, 119–22, 126–7, 144, 158–60, 176, 194
Rainfall variability, 7, 54, 61–2, 64, 118–26, 144
Ragi, 47, 165, 169, 171, 173, 304
Rajannagar Colony, 132–3, 160, 167, 169, 195, 199, 204, 229, 236–7, 244, 248, 301
Rajasthan, 1–2, 6–7, 36–42, 61–2, 68–73, 75, 80, 83, 86–95, 113, 115, 117, 119–21, 126–7, 133, 153, 169, 178, 208, 226, 228, 230–1, 237, 242–5, 268, 300; *see also* Rajputana
Rajasthan Canal Project, 2, 19–21, 36–42, 78, 86, 89–90, 93, 104, 113–15, 117, 119–21, 126–7, 133, 136–7, 139, 145–6, 161–3, 286, 288–9, 308; Colonies, 2, 17, 19, 68, 70, 72–3, 89–90, 92–3, 110, 119–22, 129, 132, 136, 144, 153, 157–8, 160, 162–4, 177, 179–80, 182, 188, 196, 198–201, 203–4, 214, 219–21, 225–6, 230–1, 234, 238–43, 269–72, 280–2, 286–91, 294, 301, 308
Rajasthan Colonization Act, 1, 20, 208, 220, 231
Rajasthan Tenancy Act, 231
Rajmahal Hills, 63, 205, 299
Rajputana, 19, 26, 30
Rajputs, 55, 62, 64, 265, 268
Ramakrishnanagar Colony, *see* Araku Valley
Ramanathapuram District, 76, 121
Ramnad, *see* Ramanathapuram
Ranapratapsagar Colony and Dam, 61, 144, 160, 301
Rangapur Colony, 157
Ravi River, 19, 21, 41
Rechna Doab, 286
Reclamation of land, 2, 60–1, 118–21
Refugees, 19, 50, 56–9, 63, 70, 74, 76, 87–8, 93, 102, 104, 108–9, 111, 113, 125, 128, 155–6, 172–3, 175–6, 186, 189–90, 196–7, 204, 207–9, 216–19, 221, 229, 235–6, 242, 255, 262, 264, 268, 272–4, 282, 284, 287, 299–301
Rehabilitation, Ministry (later Department) of, 59, 107–8
Religion, 264–5
Repatriates, 77, 88–9
Revenue, land *see* Land revenue
Revenue settlement, *see* Settlement (of revenue)
Rice, *see* Paddy
Roads, 48, 56, 62, 65, 128, 191, 197–203, 207, 271, 277, 280, 283–4, 286–7
Rubber, 15, 47, 74, 76, 187
Rudrapur, 142, 200
Run-off, surface, 126–8, 133
Russia, Russians, 77, 96, 253–5
Ryotwari tenure, 11, 24, 27–8, 31, 58, 227–31, 304

Sabah, 238
Saithsila Colony (Assam), 57
Sal tree (*Shorea robusta*), 42, 54, 304
Saline soils, salinity, 38, 113, 120–1, 126, 130, 132, 146, 149, 153, 158, 163–4, 179–80
Sand dunes, 38–9, 41, 119–20, 127, 146, 153, 179, 219, 281
Sanskritization, 274
Santal Parganas, 63, 76, 110, 153–4, 172, 180
Santals, 56, 63, 87–8, 124, 193, 226, 258, 263, 266
Sardapuri Bhoodan Colony, 76, 104, 112, 128, 169, 181, 183, 258, 264, 301
Sarda River, 45, 151
Savings, 186
Scheduled Castes, *see* Harijans
Scheduled Tribes, 99–100, 117, 274–6
Service centres, *see* Mandis; Urban hierarchy
Settlement of Landless Agricultural Labourers, Committee on, *see* Patil Committee
Settlement (of revenue), 2, 10, 24, 31–2, 227 n.1
Settlement projects, schemes, *see* Agricultural Colonization
Shahpur District, 285
Sheep, 173, 178–9
Sheopur District and town, 61–2, 275
Shifting cultivation, 16, 47, 55 n.64, 112, 150, 173, 222, 275, 291
Sidhnai Colony, 20–2, 197–8, 269, 285
Sikander Colony, 111
Sikhs, 18, 69, 76, 127, 167, 264, 270, 301
Sind, 13, 19, 26
Sindewahi Colony, 155, 159, 169, 183, 185, 200, 203, 215, 235, 244, 266, 300
Sindis, 63, 87–8
Sind Sagar Doab, 19
Sirdari tenure, 230–1

Sirhind Canal, 40
Social attitudes and behaviour: in agricultural change, 221–2; of government institutions and officers, 223–4; to government, 223
Social cohesion, 261–4, 276
Sohag-Para Colony, 20–2
Soil, 38, 44, 46, 54–5, 60–3, 65, 76, 121, 131–3, 135, 137–47, 153–4, 157, 163, 166, 170, 172–6, 178, 180–1, 213, 217, 219, 223, 244, 279, 282, 285, 289
— conservation, 17, 120, 144, 151, 155, 180–1
— erosion, 60, 63, 76, 131–3, 149–50, 154, 180–1
— survey, 54, 138–46, 151–2, 219, 308
Sorapur Colony, 159, 169, 178, 183, 205, 265–6, 300
Spices, 47, 49
Squatting, *see* Encroachment
Srikakulam District, 273, 275
Sri Lanka, *see* Ceylon
State farms, 1, 8, 77–8, 110–11, 119, 126–8, 132, 154, 174, 220, 259, 295
Subdivision of holdings, 25–6, 229, 249–52, 254
Sudan, 89, 271–2
Sugar-cane, 22, 134, 160, 167, 170, 177, 188, 203, 214, 290
Sukinda Project, 64
Sukkur Barrage, 288
Sunabeda Colony, 160, 180, 183, 193, 197, 229, 301
Sundarbans, 13, 18, 24, 28
Suratgarh, 78, 119–20, 126–7, 259
Survey of India, 135–9, 143–4
Sutlej River, 19–21, 40–1
Swamps, 42–4, 46, 127
Swatantra Party, 255
Switzerland, 221

Taccavi loans, 204, 206, 305
Tagore, Rabindranath, 252
Tamil Nadu, 51, 68, 70, 72, 77, 83, 86, 93, 105, 111–13, 115, 124–5, 128–30, 132–3, 139, 145, 147, 151–3, 165–6, 169, 171, 183–4, 190–3, 195, 203–4, 221, 230, 256, 269, 279, 283–4, 300; *see also* Madras Presidency and State
Tamils, 15, 129
Tanks, 123–5, 128–9, 155, 158–9, 164, 189
Tapti River, 55, 64
Tarai, 2–3, 12, 14, 17, 24, 42–5, 77, 87–8, 127–8, 130, 134, 144, 151–3, 163, 165, 177, 179, 301, 305
Tarai and Bhabar Development Committee, Report of, 19 n.102, 309
Tarai Colony (Naini Tal District), 2, 42–5, 69, 75, 87–8, 91, 94, 102, 110–113, 128–9, 142, 154–5, 160, 163, 177, 185–6, 188, 192, 194, 199–200, 207, 220–1, 233, 237–8, 245, 249, 258, 264, 283, 289, 294, 301
Tea, 13–15, 28, 47, 57, 165
Teak, 54, 76, 151, 153
Telugus, 65–6, 79, 93, 121, 200, 276
Temporary cultivation leases, old, 70, 78, 87, 91–2, 242
Tenant Farming Societies, *see* Co-operative Cultivation
Tenure-by-stages, 243, 245
Thailand, 135
Thal Colonies (Pakistan), 66, 73–5, 90–1, 243, 245–6, 272, 285–8
Tharus, 45, 268–9, 275
Thengumarahada Colony, 50, 104, 112, 133, 145, 154, 160, 162, 165, 169, 171, 179, 183, 185–6, 190, 203–4, 207, 215, 222, 233, 235, 237, 246, 257, 259, 262, 276–7, 301
Tibetans, 50, 88, 103, 115, 155, 173, 207, 221, 282, 300
Tilaiya Colony and Reservoir, 63, 158, 161–2, 229, 262, 299
Tipu Sahib or Sultan, 7, 10, 49, 214 n.11
Tobacco, 122, 173
Town and Country Planning Organization, 202
Tractors, 17, 154, 156, 167, 257–8
Traders, 104, 175, 190, 195–7, 202–3, 205–6, 265, 271
Transport, 140, 189, 197–200
Travancore, 12, 15, 75
Tribal colonies and colonists, 70, 91–3, 102, 110–13, 117, 125, 157, 170, 172–3, 176, 178, 180–1, 183, 185–6, 189–91, 193–4, 200, 203, 205–7, 213, 215, 221–2, 225, 229, 240, 248, 262, 265–6, 274–7, 279–80, 299–301
Tribal peoples, 10, 16, 18, 23, 45, 47–8, 50, 55–6, 62–4, 75, 95–6, 98–9, 101, 123–5, 150, 165–6, 173, 201–2, 205, 212, 217–18, 222, 225, 228, 269, 274–7, 303
Triple Canal Project, 21, 23, 95

Tripura, 14, 243
Tubewells, *see* Wells
Tungabhadra River, Project and Colonies, 65, 72, 144–5, 162, 169, 174, 183, 185–7, 194, 203, 205, 229, 300

Under-employment and unemployment, 2, 192–5, 197, 248, 251–2, 296–8; *see also* Educated unemployed colonists
United Provinces, *see* Uttar Pradesh
United States of America, 293
Uppal Committee on Location and Utilisation of Wastelands in India, 33, 101, 113, 146–9, 151
Upper Bari Doab Canal, 20–1
Upper Chenab Canal and Colony, 21–2, 285
Upper Jhelum Canal and Colony, 21–2
Urban hierarchy, 200–1
US Bureau of Reclamation, 139, 145, 164, 294
Utilitarianism, 27
Uttar Pradesh (UP), 2, 6–7, 11–12, 16, 18, 24, 29, 32–3, 42–5, 68–70, 72, 76, 83, 86, 91, 93–4, 102, 104–5, 110–13, 128, 132, 142, 147, 152, 154, 165, 169, 171, 228, 240, 243, 255–6, 262, 300
— Zamindari Abolition Committee, 9, 11, 240

Varanasi town and District, 13, 32, 76
Vegetables, 17, 158
Velakapuram Colony, 104, 132, 160, 169, 178–9, 183, 185, 187, 199, 205, 235, 244, 263, 265–5, 269, 281, 301
Vietnam, South, 74–5, 275
Vihad Colony, 255
Vijayanagar, 8, 48, 65
Village expansion, 1, 24, 78–9, 110, 114
Village Level Worker (VLW), *see* Community Development
Vinoba Bhave, 75, 253
Vishakhapatnam, 16, 76
Vizagapatam, *see* Vishakhapatnam

Wainganga River, 123
Waste, culturable, *see* Culturable waste
Wasteland, 2, 6–7, 57–8, 61, 63–4, 179; amount of, 10, 12–13, 66, 116; assault on, 1, 4, 6–8, 10–12, 14–16, 23–4, 41–2, 47–51, 55–8, 60–1, 63, 66, 75–86, 110, 112–15; clearing and reclamation of, 15–17, 19, 64, 110, 204–9, 282–4; government control of, 23–4, 66; marginality of, 2, 19, 144, 187, 278–89, 291, 295, 297; re-advance of, 6–7, 10, 44–5, 48–50, 57; surveys of, 16, 31–2, 58–9, 105, 112–16, 146–9, 247, 308; tenure of, 8–11, 23–9, 97, 100–1, 252–6; *see also* Culturable waste; Forest
Waste Land Rules, 12, 27–8, 79
Waste Land Survey (Technical) Committee (Assam), 34 n.177
Waterlogging, 127, 163–4, 174, 286
Water resources survey, 130, 138 n.13, 139, 145
Water-table, *see* Groundwater
'Welfare motive' in land policy, 90–101, 111, 187, 192, 206–7, 242, 287, 297
Wells, 40, 65, 121, 124, 128–31, 135, 138–9, 158–60, 163, 166, 174, 177, 206–10, 224, 237, 283–4
West Bengal, 68, 70–1, 83, 87, 147, 243, 252–3
West Godavari District, 64, 213
Western Ghats, 46, 75
Wheat, 76, 158–60, 167, 171, 173, 177, 188, 220, 238, 290
Wild life, 10, 45, 55, 133–4, 152
World Food Program, 89
Wynad, 8, 14, 45–51, 165, 232
— Colony, 16–17, 19, 50, 74, 91, 103–4, 110, 112–13, 115, 122, 159, 161, 165, 168, 172, 178, 183, 185–8, 190, 195–6, 202–3, 209, 213–14, 221, 223–4, 232, 235, 244, 254, 257, 259, 264, 276, 281, 289, 299

Yamuna River, 10, 60
— (Jumna) Canals, 40
'Yeomen', 22–3, 25–6, 28
Yerava, 47
Yields (of crops), 165–78
Yugoslavia, 293–4

Zamindars, zamindari, 9, 11 n.54, 28, 31, 47, 58, 76, 227–8, 233, 263, 305